About the Author

Sherry Kinkoph has authored more than 25 computer books for Macmillan Publishing over the past five years, including books for both adults and children. Her recent publications include *Easy Word 97*, *Office 97 Small Business Edition 6-in-1*, *The 10 Minute Guide to Lotus Organizer 97*, and *The Big Basics Book of Microsoft Office 97*.

Sherry started exploring computers back in college, and claims that many a term paper was whipped out using a trusty 128K Macintosh. Today, Sherry's still churning out words, but now they're in the form of books, and instead of using a Mac, she's moved on to a trusty PC. A native of the Midwest, Sherry currently resides in Fishers, IN and continues in her quest to help users of all levels master the ever-changing computer technologies. You can email Sherry at **skinkoph@inetdirect.net**.

Acknowledgements

Special thanks to Jill Byus and Jamie Milazzo for their excellent acquisitions work; to Rick Kughen and Noelle Gasco for their fine development work; to Barb Hacha for dotting the Is and crossing the Ts; to Karen Walsh for shepherding this book every step of the way until its final form; and to Jon Brimacomb for checking the technical accuracy of the book. Finally, extra special thanks to the production team for assembling this visual masterpiece.

Dedication

To all my old camping buddies of yesteryear: the Sechrests, the Farmers, the Lovings, the Howells, the Tolivers, the Janeses, the Crossons, and the Willards. Happy 20th reunion!

Tell Us What You Think!

As the reader of this book, you are our most important critic and commentator. We value your opinion and want to know what we're doing right, what we could do better, what areas you'd like to see us publish in, and any other words of wisdom you're willing to pass our way.

As the Executive Editor for the General Desktop Applications team at Macmillan Computer Publishing, I welcome your comments. You can fax, email, or write me directly to let me know what you did or didn't like about this book—as well as what we can do to make our books stronger.

Please note that I cannot help you with technical problems related to the topic of this book, and that due to the high volume of mail I receive, I might not be able to reply to every message.

When you write, please be sure to include this book's title and author as well as your name and phone or fax number. I will carefully review your comments and share them with the author and editors who worked on the book.

Fax: 317-817-7448

Email: **office@mcp.com**

Mail: Executive Editor
General Desktop Applications
Macmillan Computer Publishing
201 West 103rd Street
Indianapolis, IN 46290 USA

Contents

How to Use This Book

The Complete Visual Reference

Each chapter of this book is made up of a series of short, instructional tasks, designed to help you understand all the information that you need to get the most out of your computer hardware and software.

Each task includes a series of easy-to-understand steps designed to guide you through the procedure.

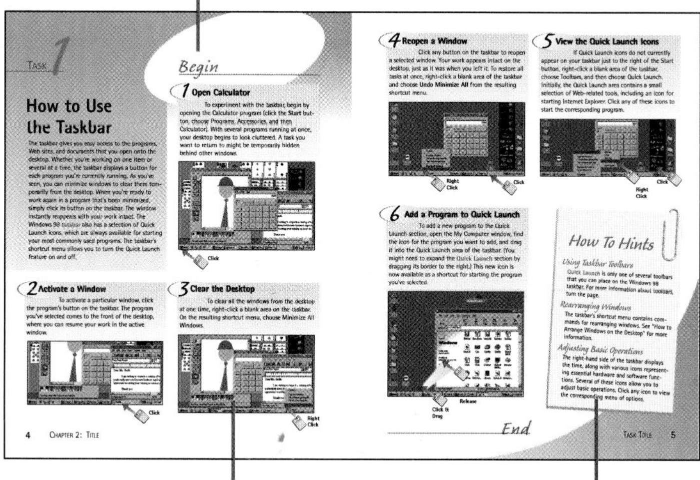

Each step is fully illustrated to show you how it looks onscreen.

Extra hints that tell you how to accomplish a goal are provided in most tasks.

Click: Click the left mouse button once.

Double-click: Click the left mouse button twice in rapid succession.

Right-click: Click the right mouse button once.

Pointer Arrow: Highlights an item on the screen you need to point to or focus on in the step or task.

Selection: Highlights the area onscreen discussed in the step or task.

Click and Type: Click once where indicated and begin typing to enter your text or data.

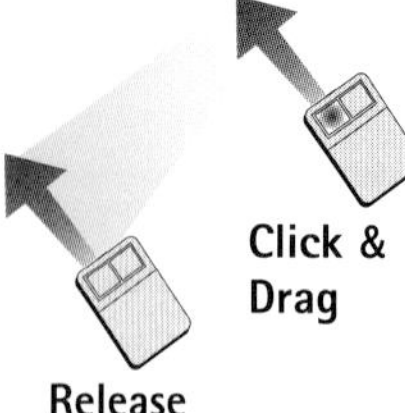

How to Drag: Point to the starting place or object. Hold down the mouse button (right or left per instructions), move the mouse to the new location, and then release the button.

Key icons: Clearly indicate which key combinations to use.

Menus and items you choose or click are shown in **bold**. Words in *italic* are defined in more detail in the glossary. Information you type is in a **`special font`**.

Continues →

If you see this symbol, it means the task you're in continues on the next page.

Introduction

Are you a visual learner—like to see how to do things rather than read about them? Need to learn how to use Microsoft Office 97, but don't have time to wade through an exhaustive tome to find out what you need to know? If you answered yes to one or both of these questions, *How to Use Microsoft Office 97, Second Edition* is the book for you.

This book is written and assembled especially for visual learners and users who want to get up and running fast with new software. In the pages to follow, you will learn how to use the basic features and functions of the Office 97 suite of programs in an easy-to-understand, straightforward manner. You will learn

- ✓ How to create and format Word documents
- ✓ How to work with Excel formulas and functions
- ✓ How to create slide show presentations with PowerPoint
- ✓ How to use Access to organize your data
- ✓ How to send and receive email with Outlook 98
- ✓ How to use Internet Explorer 4.0 to download files
- ✓ How to use the Office 97 graphics tools to add pictures and shapes to your files
- ✓ How to integrate the Office programs to work together

Each topic is presented visually, step by step, so you can clearly see how to apply each feature and function to your own computer tasks. The illustrations show exactly what you will see on your own computer screen, making it easy to follow along.

You can choose to use this book as a tutorial, progressing through each section one task at a time, or as a reference, looking up specific features you want to learn about. There's no right or wrong way—use the method that best suits your own learning style.

In no time at all, you will have mastered all the basic tools needed to use the software for your own office or home needs. In addition, you will have gained the fundamental skills for working more productively on your computer. You can't find a more powerful set of computer applications than Microsoft Office 97, and you can't learn them more easily than with *How to Use Microsoft Office 97, Second Edition.*

Task

CHAPTER 1

How to Get Started with Office 97

Microsoft Office 97 is a powerful suite of productivity tools that includes Word, Excel, PowerPoint, Access, and Outlook. Depending on which package you purchased—Standard or Professional—the programs may vary; Access only comes with the Professional edition. Although Access is a full-blown database program, you can also use Excel to create simple databases. There's also a Microsoft Office 97 Small Business Edition, which includes Publisher 98 (a desktop publishing program), but not PowerPoint or Access. Regardless of which package you bought, you will find each program in the suite incredibly useful, whether you're working with text, crunching numbers, creating presentations, building a database, or scheduling appointments and exchanging email. (If you're working with Office 97 Small Business Edition, check out the *How to Use Microsoft Office 97 Small Business Edition* book.)

Before you begin using all the great features Office 97 offers, you first have to install the programs. Because Office has many installation options, your first job will be to choose the parts you want to install. Don't worry about installing everything right away; you can easily add and remove items later. In addition to installing Office 97, be sure to see the add-in items found on the Office 97 Valupack CD.

TASK 1

How to Install Office 97

You will need to answer a few simple questions during the installation process for the Office 97 programs. You can choose to install the entire suite of programs or only the programs you plan to use the most. If you're running short of disk space on your computer, you can also choose to run the programs from the Office 97 CD-ROM.

Start by inserting the Office 97 CD into your CD-ROM drive. The Microsoft Office 97 startup screen appears automatically (wait a few seconds). If the startup screen doesn't appear, you can also open My Computer and double-click the CD-ROM drive, then locate and double-click the **Setup.exe** file. After the Office 97 startup dialog box appears, click the **Install Microsoft Office** button to begin the Setup program.

Begin

1 Start Setup

The first dialog box to greet you is a Welcome box. If you haven't already done so, use Alt+Tab or the taskbar to close any other Windows applications that are running. Then click **Continue** to start the installation.

2 Fill In Your Name

In the Name and Organization Information dialog box, Windows automatically enters the name and organization information from your Windows 95 setup. You can change it if you want or accept it as it is. Click **OK** to proceed to the Confirm Name and Organization Information dialog box. If the information is correct, click **OK**.

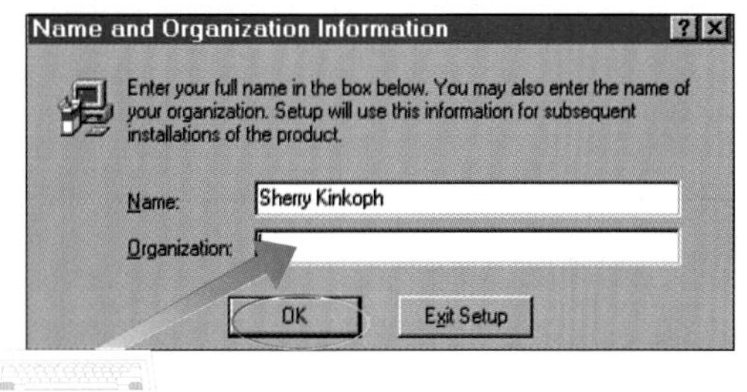

3 Enter Your CD Key

On the back of the jewel case containing your Office 97 CD is an 11-digit CD key code. Enter it in the **CD Key** box. You don't need to enter the hyphen—just type the 11 digits. Double-check to be sure you entered the correct number and click **OK**.

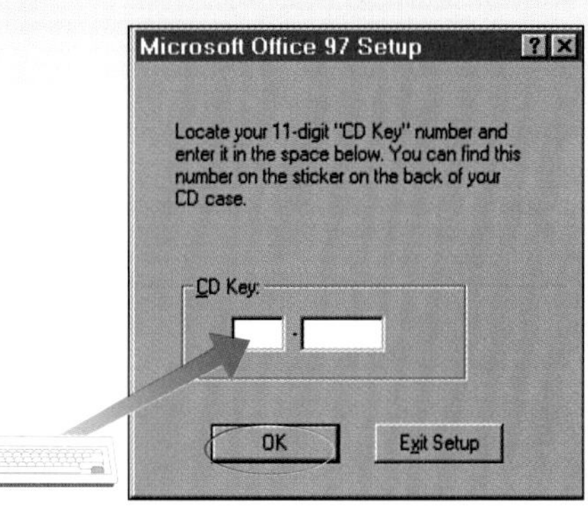

4 Designate a Folder

By default, Setup automatically installs Office 97 in the C:\Program Files\Microsoft Office folder unless you instruct it otherwise. If you prefer another location for the installation, click **Change Folder** and indicate the new folder; otherwise, click **OK** to continue.

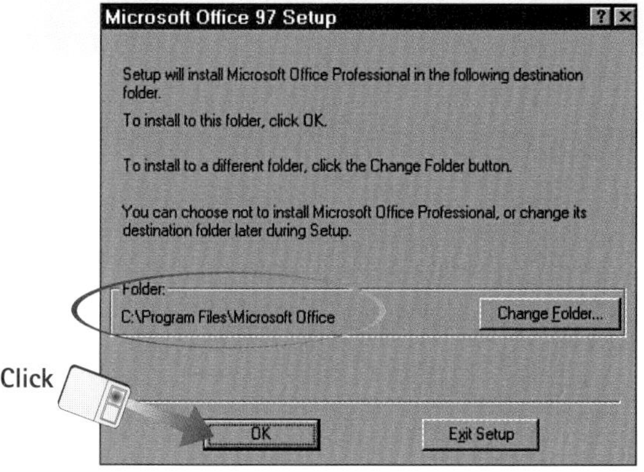

5 Choose an Installation

The next dialog box offers you three installation choices. If you're familiar with previous Office versions and know exactly which elements you want to install, choose **Custom**. If you are short on disk space, choose the CD-ROM installation to run the software from the Office CD-ROM. Otherwise, select the **Typical** installation option.

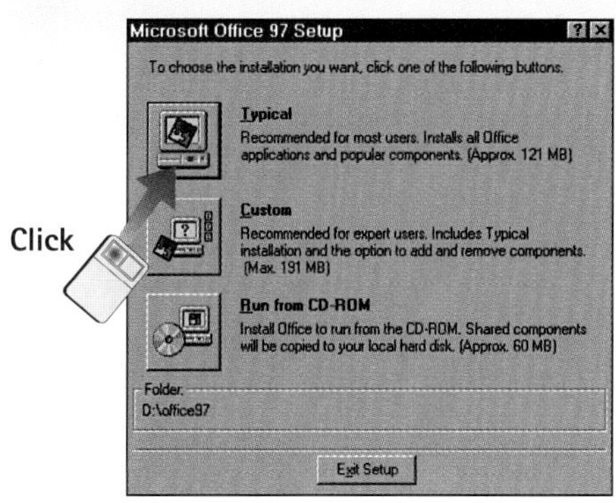

6 Choose Components

Depending on which installation choice you made in the previous step, review and confirm (or change) your choices when they're displayed in the Options list. A check mark next to the option indicates the option will be installed. Click a check box to add or remove a check mark. Click **Continue** to begin the actual installation of the Microsoft Office 97 software.

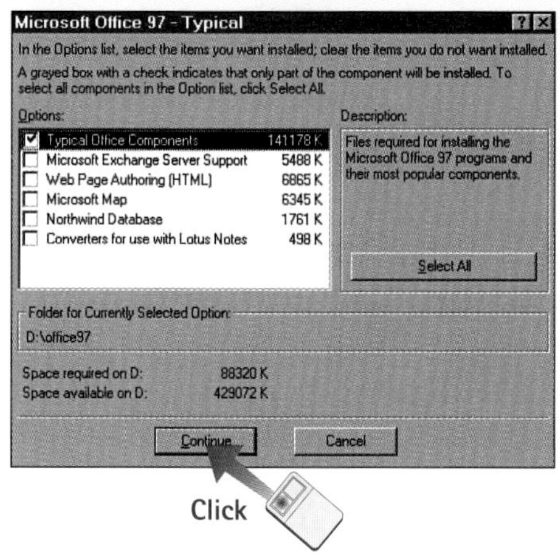

7 Close Setup

When the installation is complete, a prompt box notifies you; click **OK** to return to the Windows desktop. Click the **Close** button (**X**) on the startup box to exit the startup screen.

End

How-To Hints

Turn On Auto Insert Notification

Click **Start** on the Windows taskbar and choose **Settings, Control Panel**. Double-click the **System** icon to open the System Properties dialog box. Click the **Device Manager** tab, double-click **CD-ROM**, and then double-click the icon for your specific CD-ROM drive. Click the **Settings** tab and place a check (click) in the **Auto Insert Notification** option box. Click **OK** until you return to Windows.

TASK 2

How to Add and Remove Office Components

If you chose to install only certain Office 97 components and decide later to add more, you can easily open the Setup program again and make the necessary changes. You can also return to the Setup program and remove any components you no longer need to free up some disk space.

To add or remove components, you will need to insert the Office 97 CD-ROM into your CD-ROM drive. Be sure to close any open programs before installing or removing Office components.

Begin

1 Start the Setup Program

After you insert the Office 97 CD, a window opens displaying the contents of the CD. Scroll through the list of folders and double-click the **Setup.exe** file.

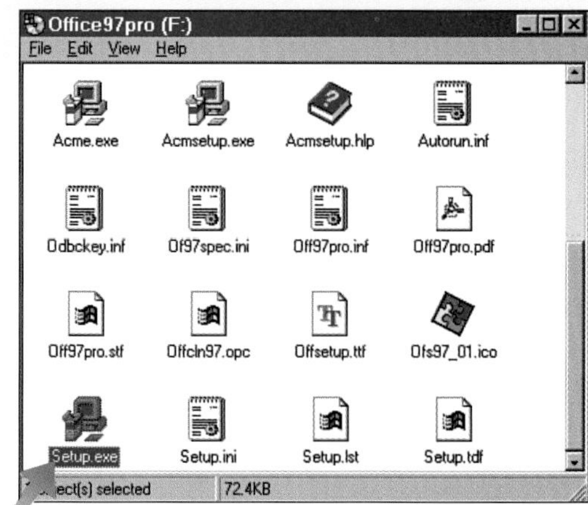

2 Choose Add/Remove

The maintenance portion of the Setup program opens with several options to choose from. Click the **Add/Remove** button.

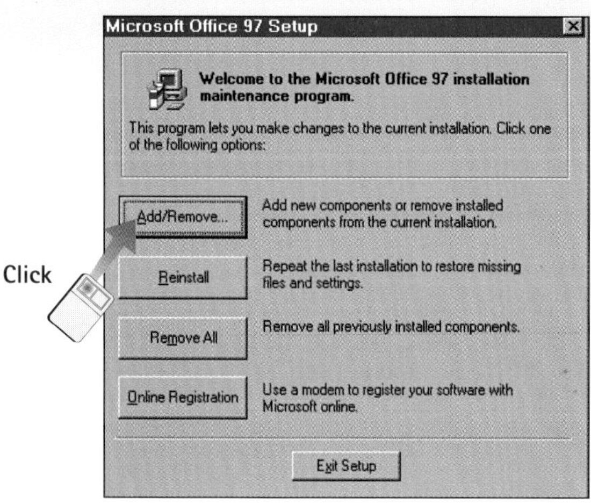

3 Select Components

In the Maintenance dialog box list of options, select or deselect the necessary components. A check mark next to the option indicates the component is already installed. To install an additional component, click the options you want, and then click the **Continue** button.

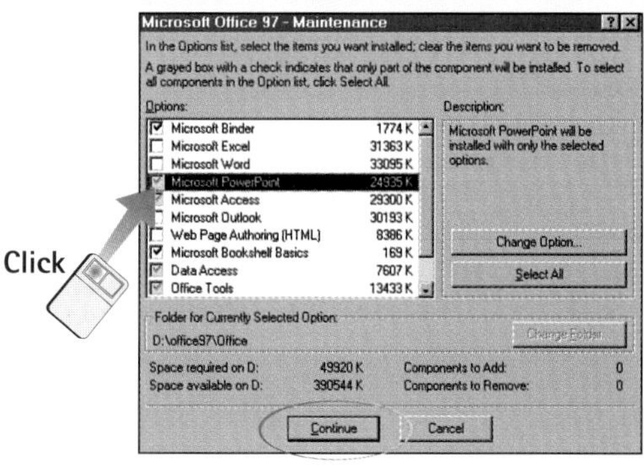

4 Install New Components

Setup begins installing the selection(s). When the installation is complete, a prompt box notifies you; click **OK** to exit the Setup program and return to the Windows 95 desktop and the Office 97 CD-ROM window (click the window's **Close** button to close the startup window).

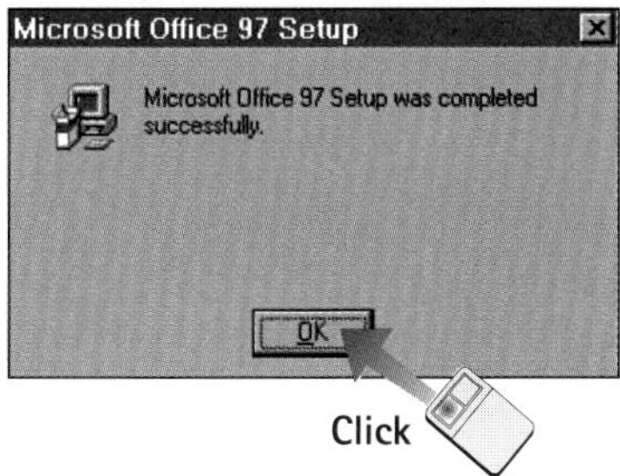

5 Select Components to Remove

To uninstall a component, deselect it from the list of options in the Maintenance dialog box, and then click **Continue**.

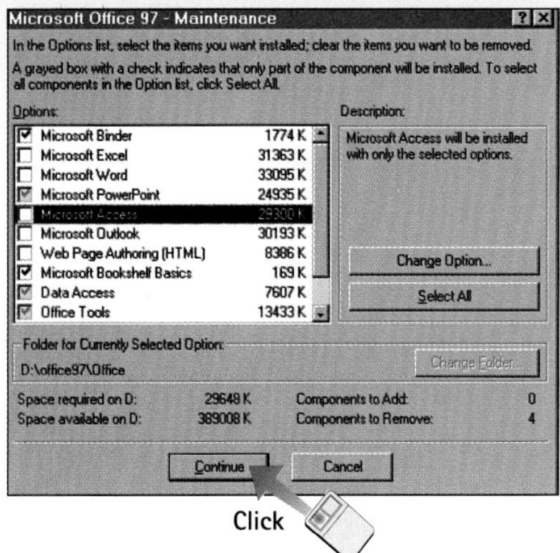

6 Confirm the Removal

A confirm box appears, asking you if you're sure you want to remove the component. Click **Yes** and Setup begins removing the item.

7 Uninstall Components

When the uninstallation is complete, a prompt box notifies you; click **OK** to return to the Windows desktop and the Office 97 CD-ROM window (click the window's **Close** button to close the window).

End

How-To Hints

Other Options

In addition to adding and removing components with the Maintenance portion of Setup, you can also reinstall or completely remove all the Office programs. Use the **Reinstall** option to repeat the installation process to restore any missing files. Use the **Remove All** option to uninstall all the Office 97 programs from your computer.

TASK 3

How to Use the Office 97 Valupack

Your Office 97 CD-ROM comes with a collection of extra features, add-ins, and files, called the Office 97 Valupack. The collection includes extra templates you can use in Word, Excel, Outlook, and PowerPoint; RealAudio and ActiveMovie add-ins you can use to play audio and video clips; additional clip art files; and more.

To view what's in the Valupack, run the Overview presentation, a PowerPoint interactive presentation that lets you click items you want to know more about.

Begin

1 Open the Valupack Folder

Insert the Office 97 CD. A window opens displaying the contents of the CD. Scroll through the list of folders and double-click the **Valupack** folder.

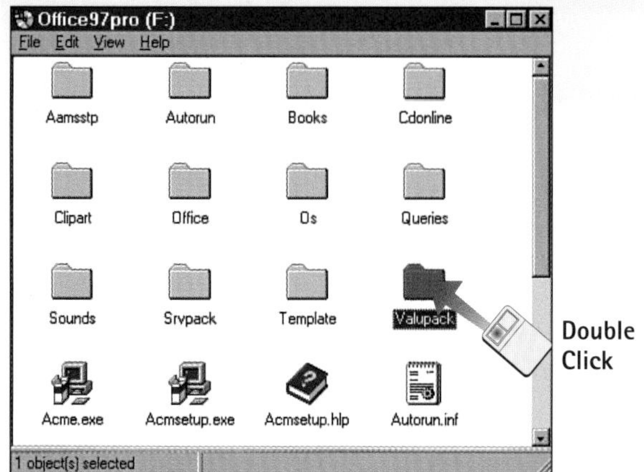

2 Start the Presentation

Scroll through the contents of the Valupack folder and double-click the **Overview.pps** file.

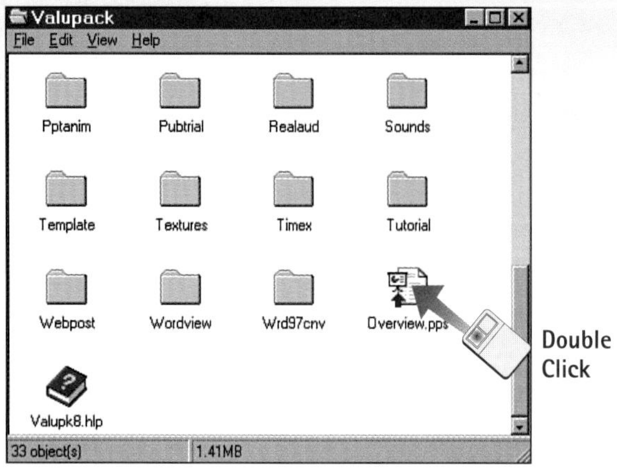

3 The Macros Warning Box

A warning prompt box appears, informing you that the presentation you're about to open contains macros. In recent years, computer viruses have been known to be hidden in macros, but if you purchased a licensed Microsoft product, you don't need to worry about viruses on the CD. Click the **Enable Macros** button to continue. It's a good idea to leave the **Always ask before opening documents with macros** check box selected so you will always see this prompt box before opening files with macros, just as a reminder.

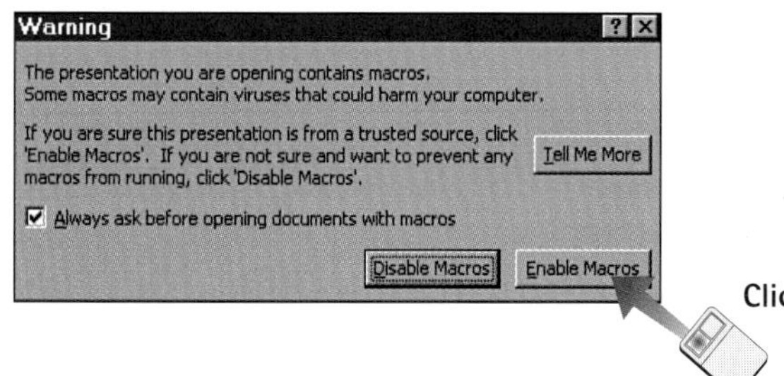

4 View the Presentation

PowerPoint opens and displays the first slide in the presentation. The presentation is interactive; you can use your mouse pointer to click buttons in the slide, view additional slides, or start an installation program. When you hover your pointer over an interactive element onscreen, the pointer takes the shape of a pointing hand icon. Click the item to select it and move to another slide. For example, click the **Audio** button.

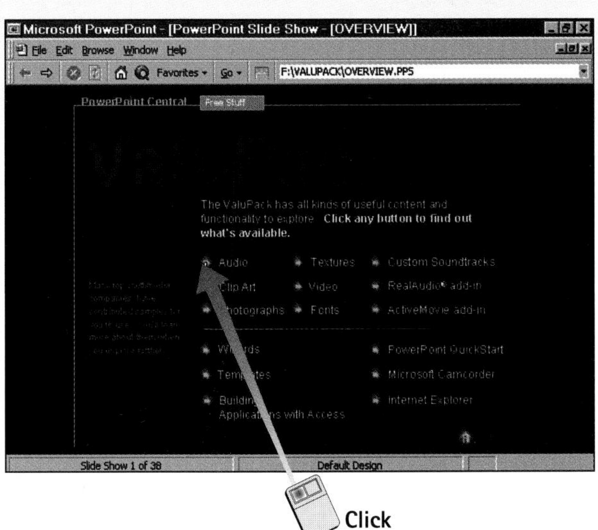

5 Read More About It

Depending on which Valupack item you select, additional slides appear that enable you to read more information, start a download procedure, or—in the case of Audio—sample sounds and copy them to the Windows Clipboard to insert into your Office files. Click the appropriate buttons as directed by the presentation text.

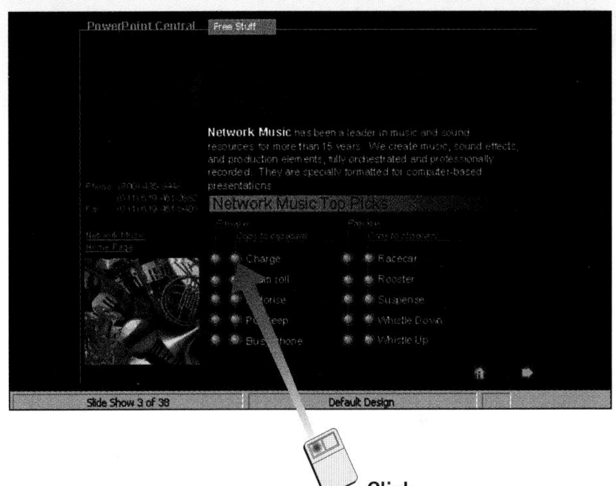

6 Exit the Presentation

To close the presentation, click the program window's **Close (X)** button in the upper-right corner. Then close the windows from the Valupack folder and the Office CD.

End

How-To Hints

Navigate the Presentation

Use the Back and Forward arrow buttons on the PowerPoint toolbar to move back and forth between the overview slides.

Task

CHAPTER 2

How to Use Common Office Features

Each program in the Office 97 suite has a common look and feel, with plenty of shared features and procedures, such as saving and opening files.

In this chapter, you will learn to use many of the shared features of Office 97. Each program, for example, is opened and closed in the same way. As you use the programs, you will notice similar dialog boxes for common tasks, enabling you to apply the skills you learn in one program to another.

The Office programs also share help features, including Office Assistant. Within Office, you will also encounter smaller applications that are shared across the programs, such as WordArt—a program for creating text-based graphics effects. (You will learn more about the drawing and graphics tools in Chapter 16, "How to Work with Office Graphics Tools.")

TASK 1

How to Start and Exit Office Applications

You can start each Office 97 program in the same way, via the Windows Start menu. When you install the programs, each application's name is added to the Programs menu list. With Outlook, a shortcut icon is added to the Windows desktop for quick access to your daily schedule and email. You can easily add shortcut icons for the other Office programs, but you can also access them quickly using the Start menu.

After you finish using an application, use one of several methods for closing the program window. Don't forget to save your work before exiting.

Begin

1 Open the Start Menu

Click the **Start** button on the Windows taskbar.

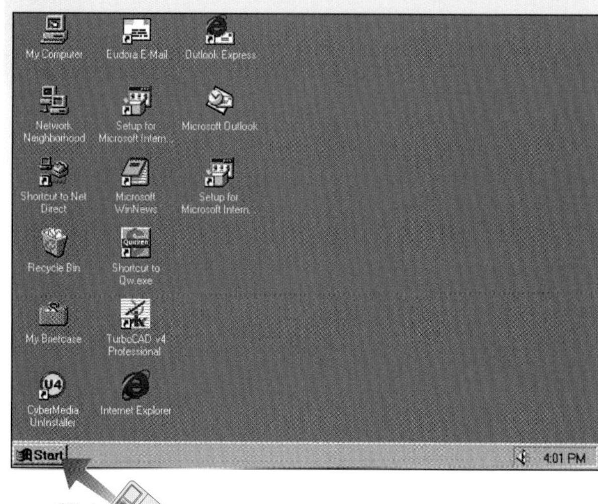

2 Choose Programs

Click **Programs** to display the menu list.

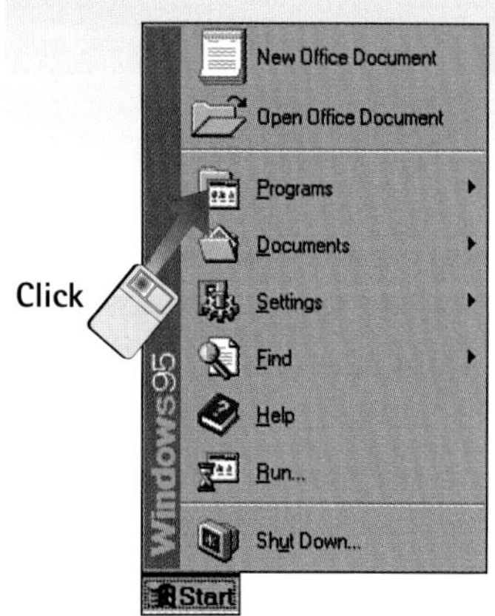

3 Choose an Application

Click the name of the Microsoft Office program you want to open. To open Word, for example, select **Microsoft Word**.

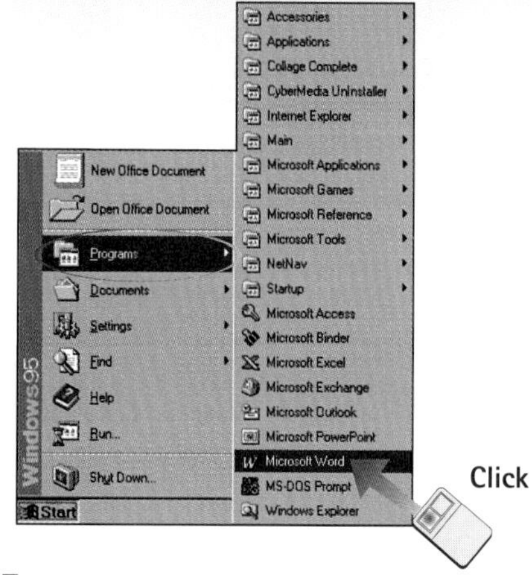

4 The Program Window Opens

Immediately, the program opens into its own window, with its name in the title bar. Depending on which program you open, you can begin working on a blank Word document, an Excel worksheet, a new PowerPoint presentation, an Access database, or start using Outlook.

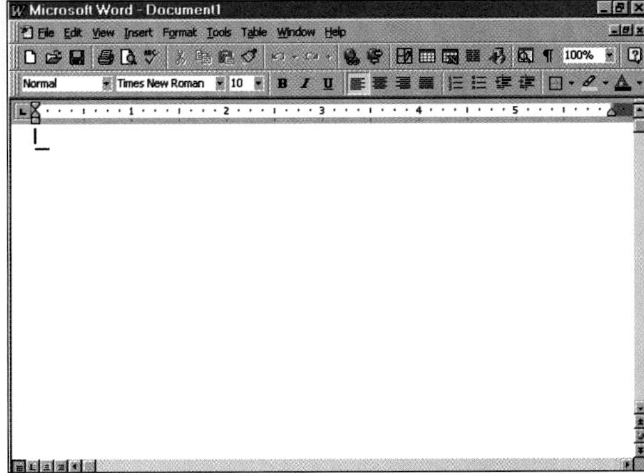

5 Quick Exit

The quickest way to close an Office program is to click the window's **Close** button, the button with an X in the upper-right corner of the window, or press Alt+F4 on the keyboard.

Click

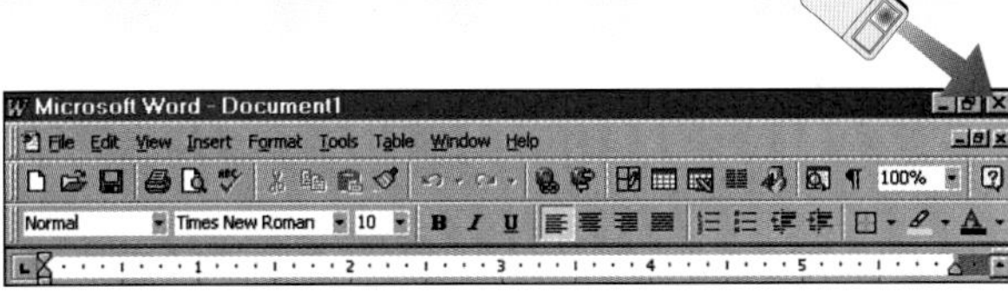

6 Save It

If you haven't saved your work yet, the program prompts you to do so before exiting. Click **Yes** to save, **No** to exit without saving, or **Cancel** to cancel the exit procedure. (Outlook doesn't work with files like the other programs, so you won't see this prompt box when exiting.) To learn more about saving files, turn to Task 3 in this chapter.

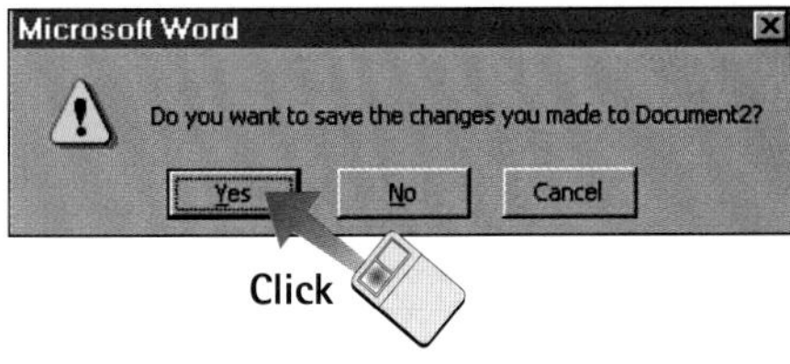

Click

End

How-To Hints

Other Exit Routes

You can also close the program window by displaying the **File** menu and selecting **Exit**. Yet another way to exit is to click the **Control menu** icon (the icon that looks like a tiny document at the far left end of the Menu bar), and then select **Close**, or just double-click the icon itself.

Switch Between Open Programs

To switch between open program windows, use the Windows taskbar. Each open program is represented as an icon on the taskbar. Press Ctrl+Esc to display the taskbar, then click the program you want to see onscreen.

Create a Shortcut Icon

You can easily create a shortcut icon for any Office program you want to access from the Windows desktop. Right-click a blank area of the desktop and select **New**, **Shortcut**. Use the Browse button to locate and double-click the executable file for the program, such as **WINWORD.EXE** or **EXCEL.EXE**. Then click **Next** and give the shortcut a name you will easily recognize. Click **Finish** and the icon is added to the desktop. Next time you want to open the program, just double-click its shortcut icon.

TASK 2

How to Create a New File

As with many tasks in Office 97, you can create a new file several ways; the file may be a Word document, an Excel spreadsheet, a PowerPoint slide, or an Access database. When you installed Office 97, two new items were added to the top of the Start menu. One is the New Office Document command. This feature, when selected, opens the New Office Document dialog box, which enables you to select the type of file you want to create.

You can also open new files within each Office program (with the exception of Outlook). Use the program window's File menu to start a new file based on a template, or use the New button on the Standard toolbar.

Begin

1 New Office Document

One way to start a new file is with the New Office Document command. Click the **Start** menu and choose **New Office Document**.

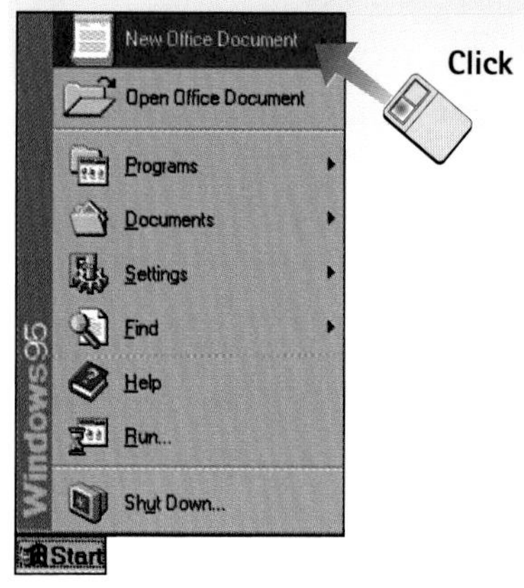

2 Select a File Type

From the New Office Document dialog box, use the tabs to locate the type of template you want to base the new file on, then double-click to open both the program window and the new file. To start a new Word file based on the Normal default template, for example, double-click the **Blank Document** icon on the **General** tab.

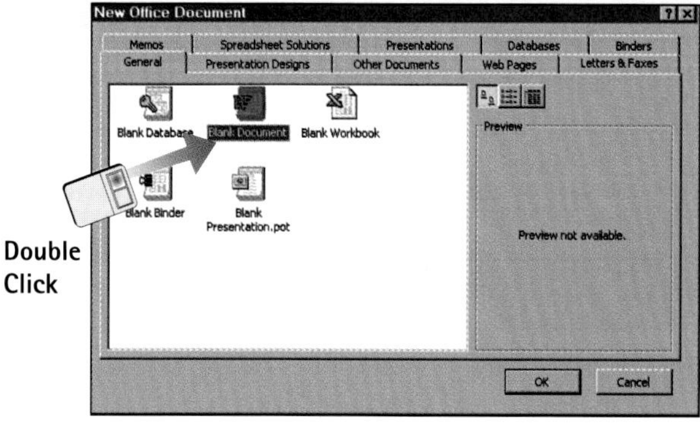

3 A New File Opens

The file type you selected opens into the appropriate program window.

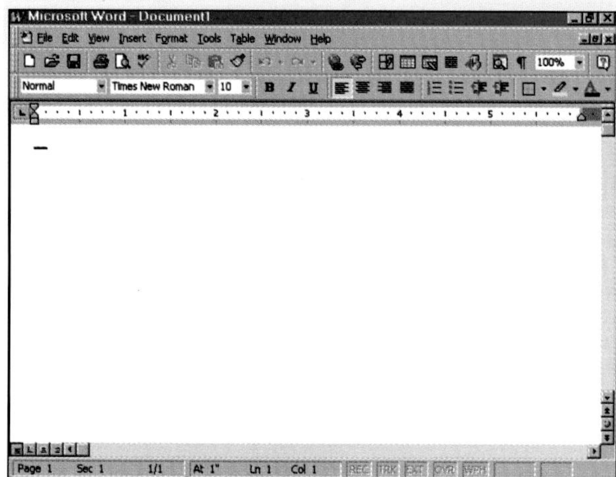

4 Open New Files Within Programs

You can also open new files within a program window. To open a file based on another template, display the **File** menu and select the **New** command.

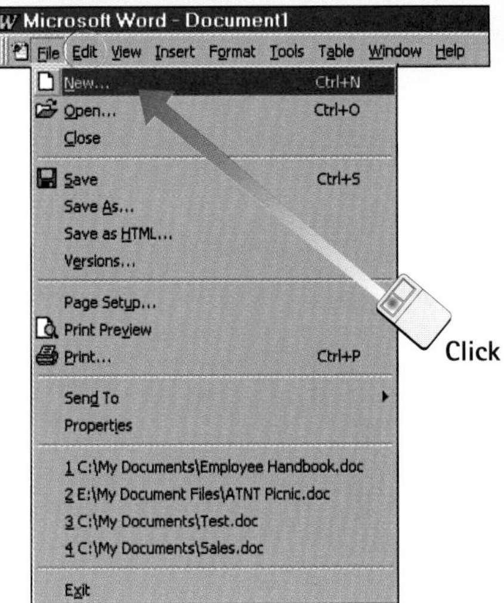

5 Use the New Dialog Box

When the New dialog box appears, double-click the template on which you want to base a new file.

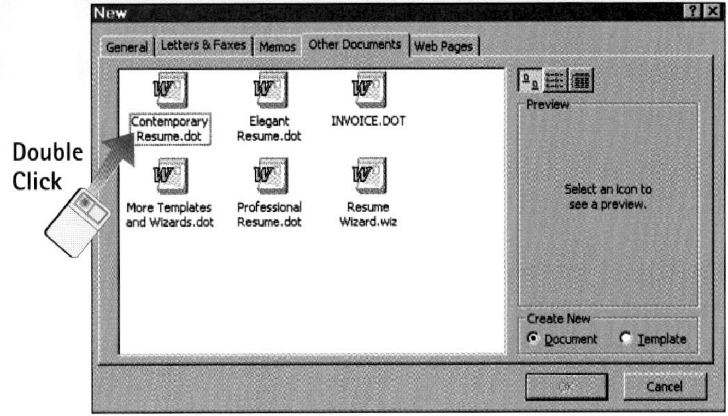

6 Use the New Button

You can also click the **New** button on the Standard toolbar to open a new file. In the case of Word and Excel, a new file immediately opens based on the default template. In PowerPoint, a dialog box appears for you to select a slide layout; choose a layout and click **OK**. In Access, the New dialog box opens (same as selecting **File**, **New**).

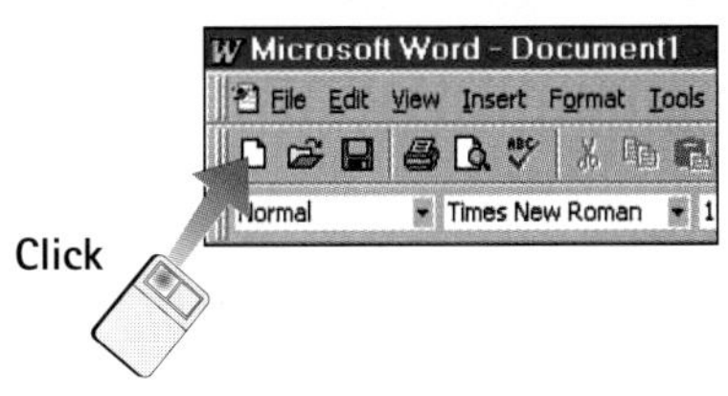

End

How-To Hints

All Files Are Templates

Every file you open in Office starts from a *template*, a bare-bones, ready-made document, worksheet, presentation, or database. When you first open Word, for example, a blank document awaits you. The document, although blank, is actually based on the Normal template—a no-frills template.

What's a Wizard?

Some of the file types listed in the New Office Document dialog box are wizards. Use wizards to help you create a new document, step by step, based on choices you make in the Wizard dialog boxes. You can start a wizard the same as any other file by double-clicking the icon.

What About Outlook?

The Outlook program doesn't work with files in the same way as the other Office programs. Outlook keeps track of all the items you enter or change, such as email or appointments, and saves them as you exit.

TASK 3

How to Save Your Work

After you start working in an Office file, you will want to save it so you can open it again later. It's a good idea to save your work often in case of power failures or other unpredictable computer glitches. When you save a file the first time, you must give the file a name. Technically, it already has a name, but the default name assigned by the Office programs are not very descriptive or useful.

You can use up to 256 characters, upper- or lowercase letters, in a filename. You can also choose a specific folder or disk to save the file to, and choose to save the file under a specific file format.

Begin

1 Save a New File

To save a file for the first time, open the **File** menu and select **Save** or **Save As** to display the Save As dialog box.

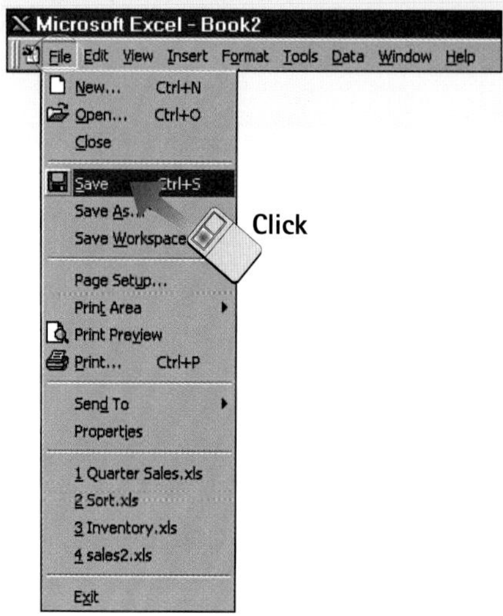

2 Designate a Folder

In the Save As dialog box, choose a folder in which to save the file. Use the **Save in** drop-down list, if necessary. To open a folder, double-click the folder icon.

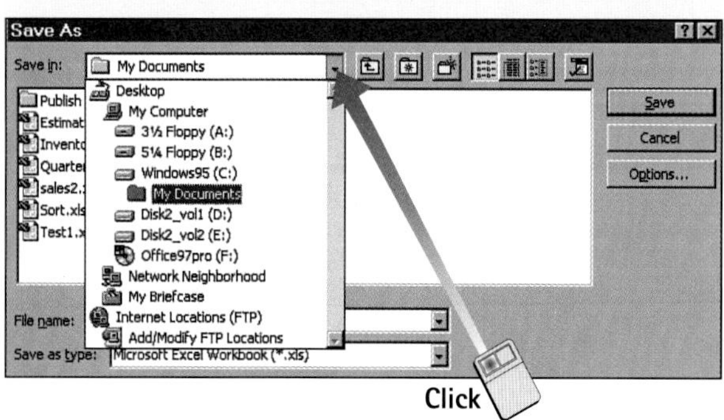

3 Enter a Filename

Type a name for the file in the **File name** box.

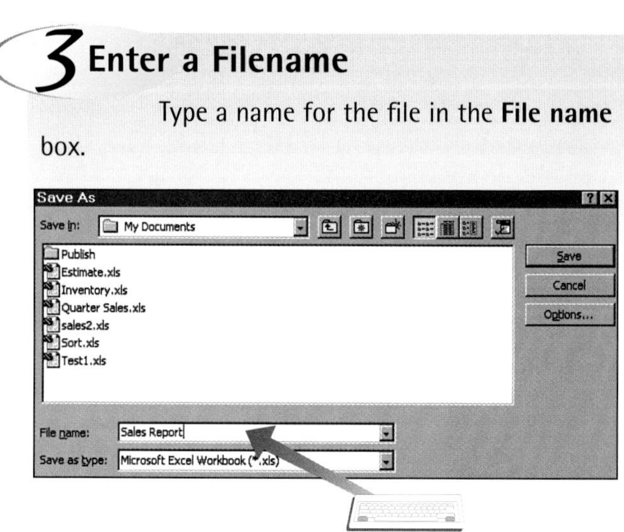

4 Click Save

Click the **Save** button and the file is saved.

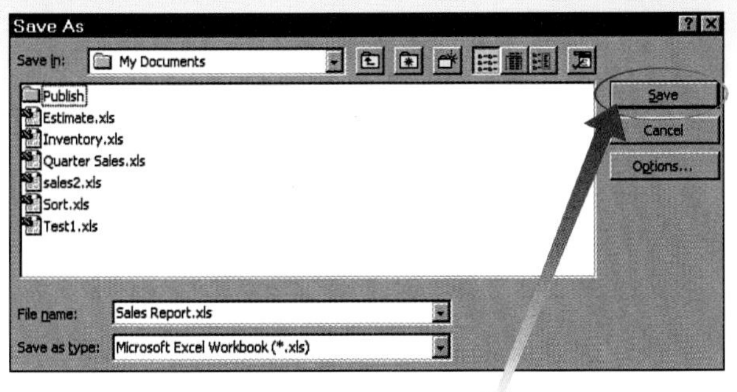

Click

5 Title Bar Name

Notice the program's title bar now reflects the name you assigned in the Save As dialog box.

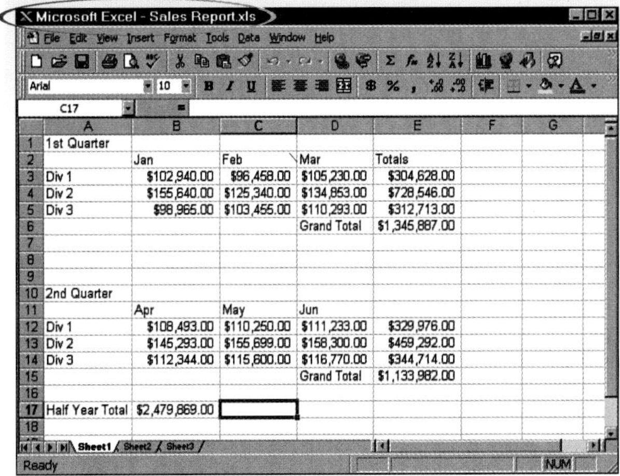

	A	B	C	D	E
1	1st Quarter				
2		Jan	Feb	Mar	Totals
3	Div 1	$102,940.00	$96,458.00	$105,230.00	$304,628.00
4	Div 2	$155,840.00	$125,340.00	$134,853.00	$728,546.00
5	Div 3	$98,965.00	$103,455.00	$110,293.00	$312,713.00
6				Grand Total	$1,345,887.00
10	2nd Quarter				
11		Apr	May	Jun	
12	Div 1	$108,493.00	$110,250.00	$111,233.00	$329,976.00
13	Div 2	$145,293.00	$155,699.00	$158,300.00	$459,292.00
14	Div 3	$112,344.00	$115,600.00	$116,770.00	$344,714.00
15				Grand Total	$1,133,982.00
17	Half Year Total	$2,479,869.00			

6 Use the Save Button

For subsequent saves of the same file, click the **Save** button on the Standard toolbar.

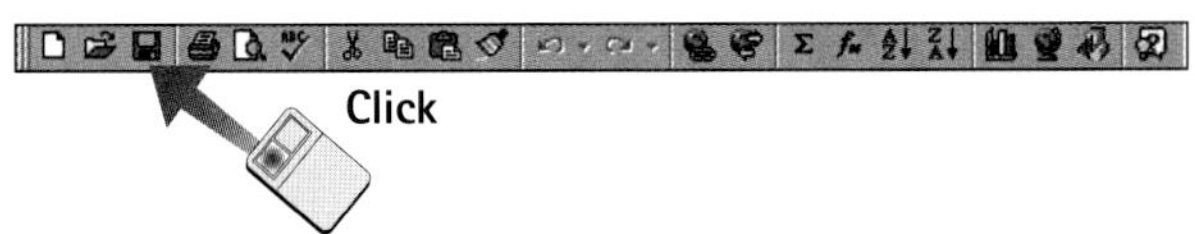

Click

End

How-To Hints

Change the Format

To save a file in another format, such as saving an Excel file as a Lotus 1-2-3 file to share with someone else, select the Save As dialog box. Then click **Save as type** and choose a file type from the drop-down list.

Saving as a New File

To save an existing file under a new name, use the same steps shown in this task, but enter a different filename. A duplicate of the original file is saved under the new filename and the original file remains intact.

Saving Again

After you have saved a file for the first time, subsequent saves don't require renaming (unless you're saving a duplicate of the file under a different name). Just click the **Save** button on the toolbar.

TASK 4

How to Open and Close Files

If the program window is already open, you can quickly open existing files you have previously saved using the Open dialog box. If you haven't started the program yet, you can use the **Open Office Document** command on the Start menu to open both the file you want and the program it was created in. (The only exception to this is Outlook, which doesn't work with individual files.)

When you're done working with a file but want to keep the program window open, select the **Close** command. This closes only the file, leaving the program window open to work on other files or start new ones. If you haven't saved your work, you will be prompted to do so before closing the file.

Begin

1 Use the Open Dialog Box

To open a file from within a program window, display the **File** menu and select **Open**, or click the **Open** button on the Standard toolbar.

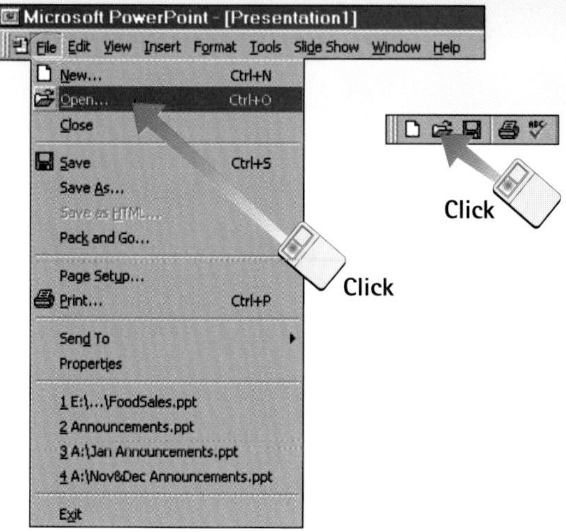

2 Locate the File

Next, you must locate the file you want to open. The list box displays the files stored in the default folder. To open a different folder in the list box, double-click the folder icon to display the folder contents. You may need to use the **Look in** drop-down list to find the folder.

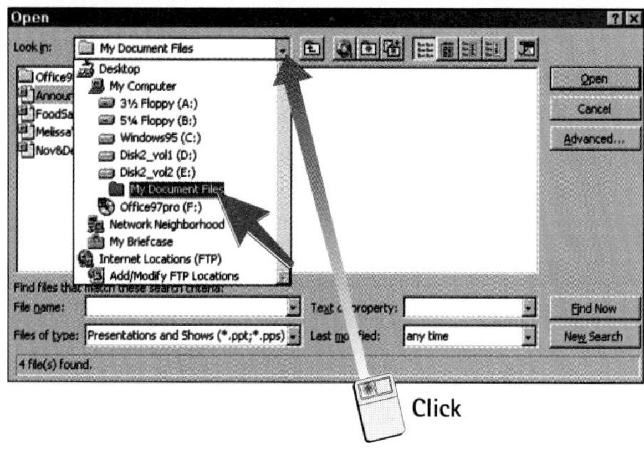

3 Select the File

When you find the file you want to open, double-click the desired filename, or select it and choose **Open**.

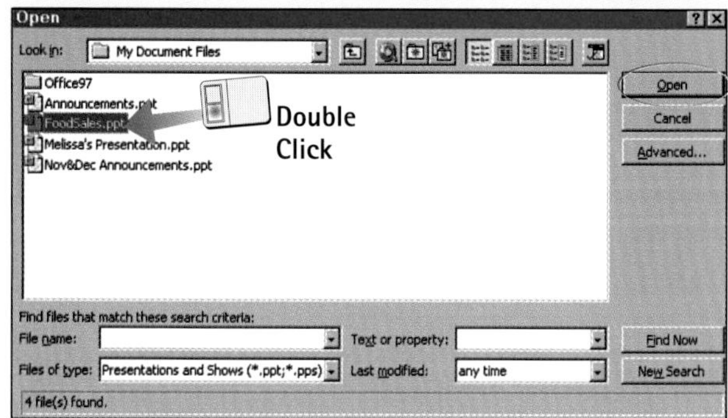

4 Open Office Document

Another way to open files is with the Open Office Document command. This is a quick way to open both the file and the program window (if it's not already open). Click the **Start** button on the Windows taskbar and choose **Open Office Document** at the top of the menu.

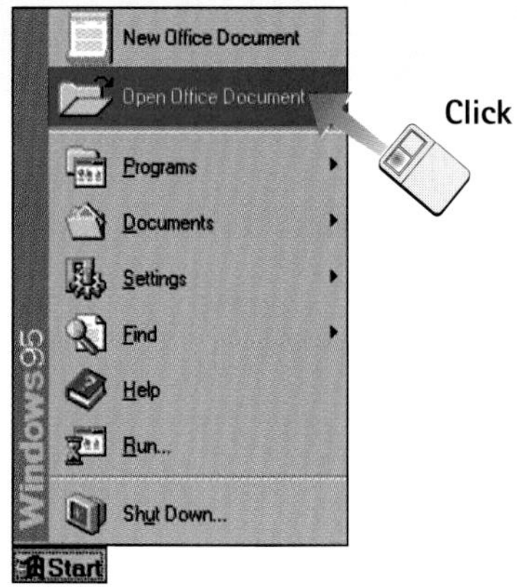

5 Choose a File

From the Open Office Document dialog box, locate the file you want to open. Double-click the filename to open both the file and the program, or select the file and click **Open**.

6 Close a File

To close a file, but not the program window, open the **File** menu and choose **Close**.

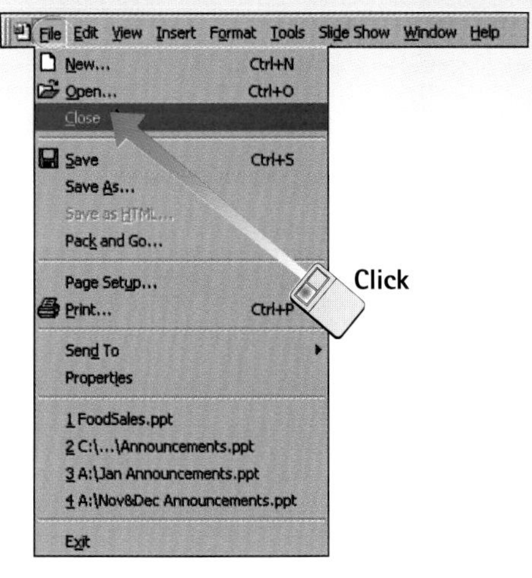

End

How-To Hints

Preview the File

If you're not sure about a file's contents, use the **Preview** button on the Open dialog box's toolbar to peek at the file before opening.

TASK 5

How to Preview a File

Before you print out a file, whether it's a Word document or a note you've created in Outlook, it's a good idea to preview how it looks using the Preview window. Print Preview lets you examine exactly how your file will print and make any last minute changes before printing. When working on the file, for example, you can't always see how all the page elements look, such as page numbers or graphics, or tell whether the page layout is pleasing to the eye. With the Preview feature, you can get an overall look at your file, page by page.

The Preview window has a toolbar you can use to adjust your preview. Depending on the program, the Preview window may offer various tools for working with the file.

Begin

1 Open Print Preview

Open the **File** menu and select **Print Preview**, or click the **Print Preview** button on the Standard toolbar.

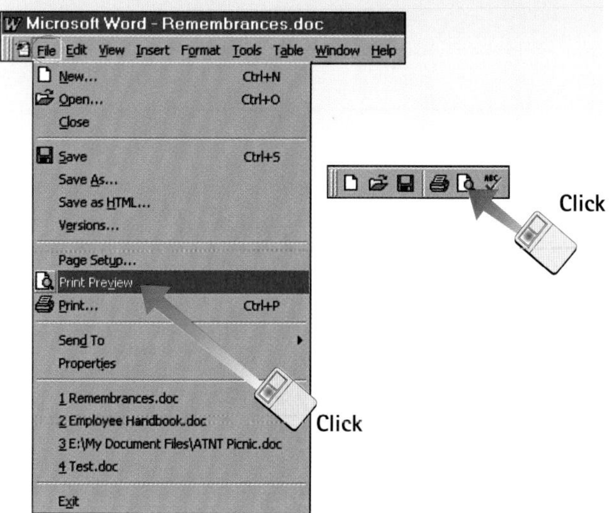

2 The Preview Window

The file opens in a full-page preview. Use the toolbar buttons on the Preview toolbar to adjust your view of the page or pages. Click the **Magnifier** tool, for example, then click anywhere on a page to zoom in for a closer look.

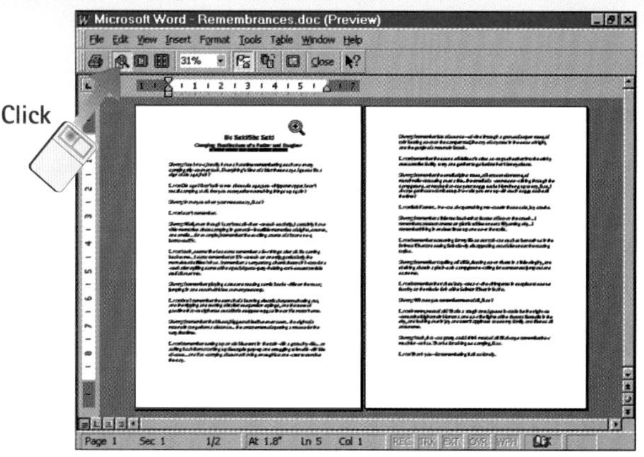

3 Zoom In

Preview zooms in on the area you clicked. To return to Full Page view, click again.

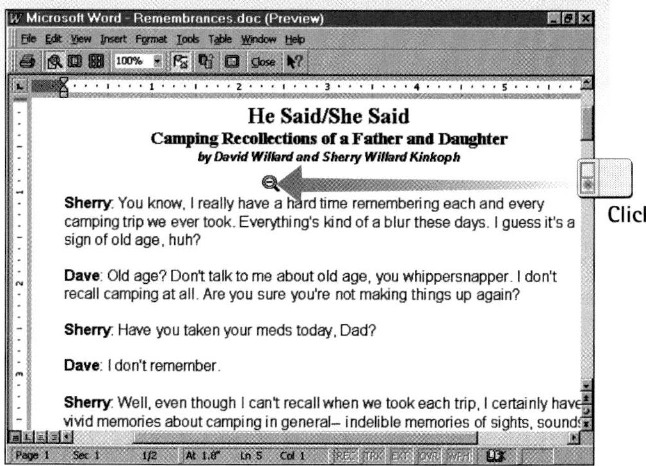

4 Make Changes

To edit while in the Preview window, use the Magnifier tool to zoom in on the area you want to edit, then deselect the **Magnifier** button on the toolbar by clicking it a second time. The mouse pointer becomes a cursor you can click in the text and make changes to the data.

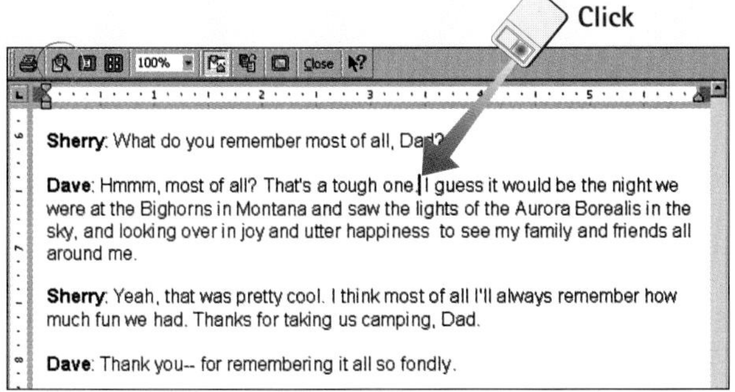

Click
Sherry: What do you remember most of all, Dad?
Dave: Hmmm, most of all? That's a tough one. I guess it would be the night we were at the Bighorns in Montana and saw the lights of the Aurora Borealis in the sky, and looking over in joy and utter happiness to see my family and friends all around me.
Sherry: Yeah, that was pretty cool. I think most of all I'll always remember how much fun we had. Thanks for taking us camping, Dad.
Dave: Thank you-- for remembering it all so fondly.

5 Print the File

If your file is exactly as you want it to print, click the **Print** button on the toolbar to send it immediately to your printer.

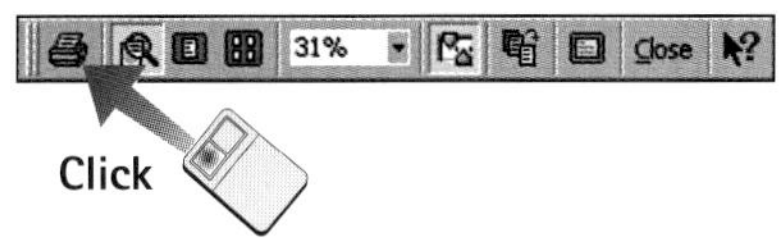

6 Close the Preview Window

To exit the Preview window, click the **Close** button.

End

How-To Hints

Page or Pages?

Use the **One Page** button on the Preview toolbar to view a single page. Use the **Multiple Pages** button to view several pages at once; click the button and drag over the number of pages you want onscreen.

TASK 6

How to Print a File

Printing an Office file requires that you have a printer connected to your computer, the appropriate printer driver (printer software) installed, and the printer turned on and online (ready to print). When you're ready to print, you can send the file immediately to the printer using the default printer settings, or set specific printing options first by using the Print dialog box.

Depending on the program and your setup, the printer options you see may vary slightly. Despite subtle differences, the Print dialog box works the same way for every Office file or Outlook item you print.

Begin

1 Open the Print Dialog Box

To set printing options, open the **File** menu and select **Print**.

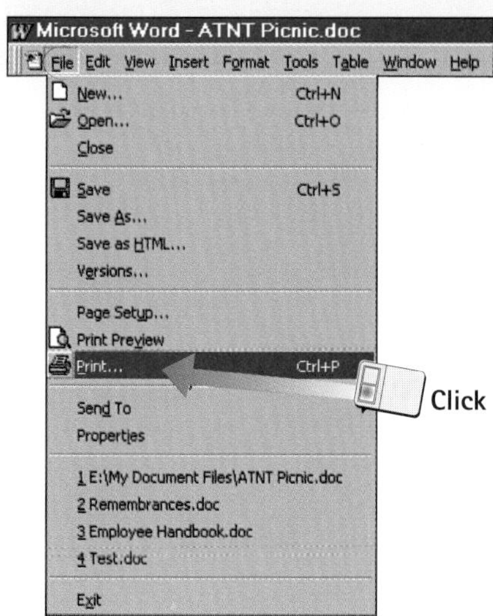

2 Choose a Printer

The Print dialog box reveals several options you can choose. If you have access to more than one printer, use the **Printer Name** drop-down list to choose another printer.

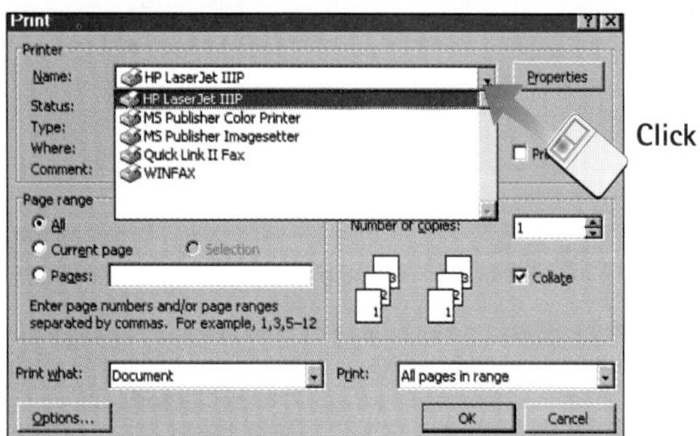

3 Choose a Page Range

To print every page, select the **All** option. To print only the current page (the page you're currently viewing), click the **Current page** option. Use the **Selection** option to print only the selected text or range. Use the **Pages** text box to indicate exactly which pages to print. You can type a single page number or a range, such as 2-3.

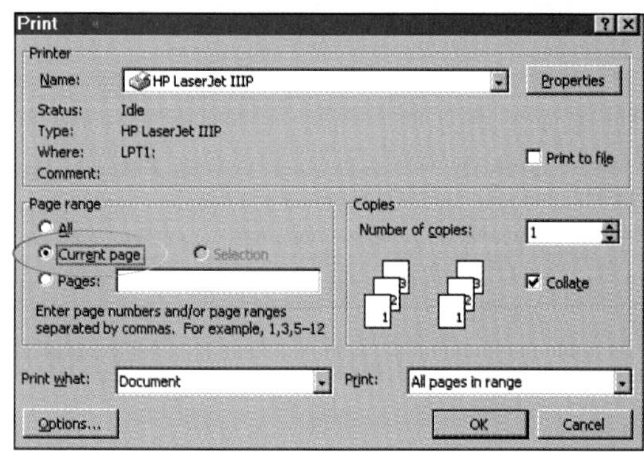

4 Number of Copies

To print multiple copies of the file, indicate a number in the **Number of copies** box.

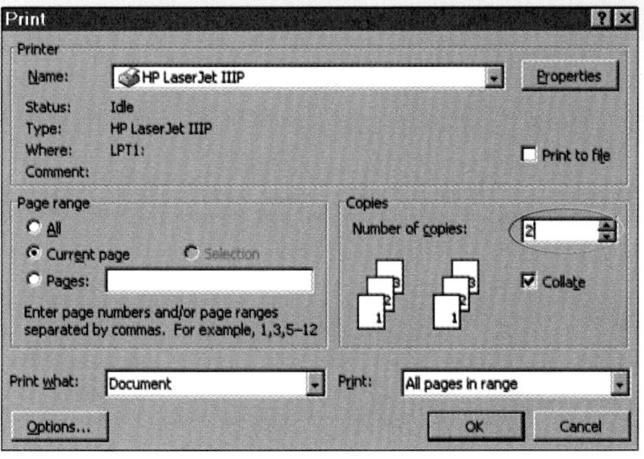

5 Print

Click **OK** to print the file.

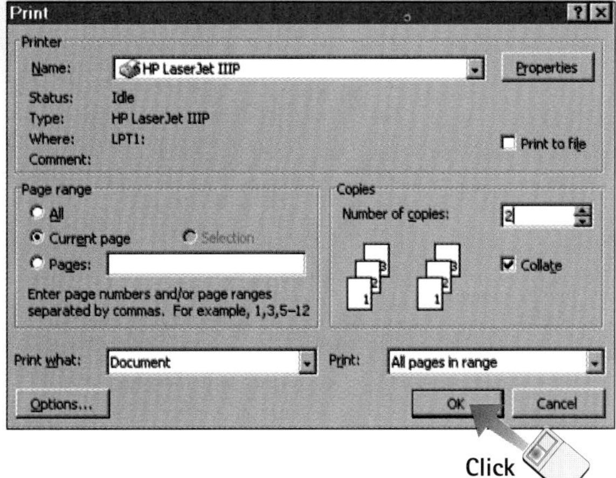

6 Use the Print Toolbar Button

To print the file without selecting any new options, click the **Print** button on the Standard toolbar.

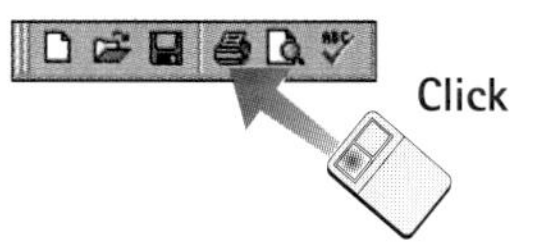

End

How-To Hints

Print in Outlook

Use the Print Style area in the Print dialog box to choose a print style for the Outlook item you're printing. You can also edit the style using the **Define Styles** button, or change the Page Setup settings with the **Page Setup** button.

What to Print

Printer options vary from program to program. In Outlook, for example, you can choose a print style based on the type of item you want to print. Items from Outlook's Calendar folder print differently than items from the Contacts folder. In Excel, you can choose to print a range from a worksheet, or the entire workbook.

TASK 7

How to Work with Multiple Files

You can have several files open at the same time while working with Word, Excel, Access, or PowerPoint. You can easily switch between them using the **Window** menu, or you can choose to view multiple files onscreen at the same time. With multiple files open, you can copy and move data from one file to another.

Begin

1 Open the Files

Open two or more files. Use the Open dialog box to locate the files, if needed (click the **Open** button on the toolbar or select **File, Open**).

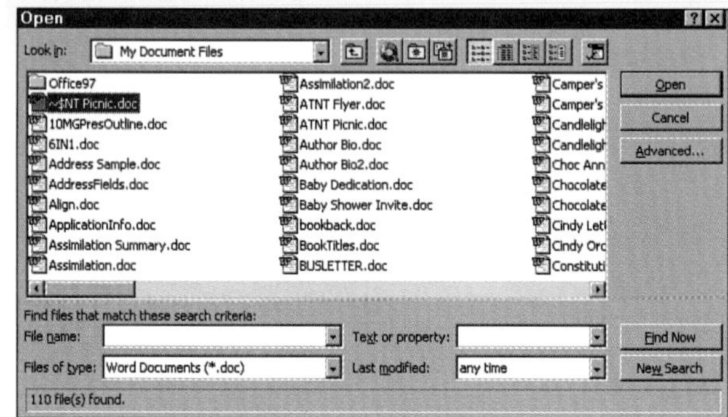

2 Display the Window Menu

To switch between open files, display the **Window** menu. The bottom of the menu lists the names of the open files. The currently active file has a check mark next to its name. Click the file you want to view.

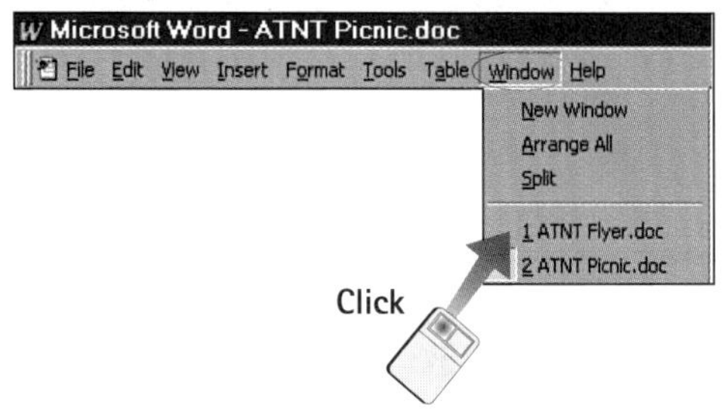

3 The Active File

The program window now displays the file you selected.

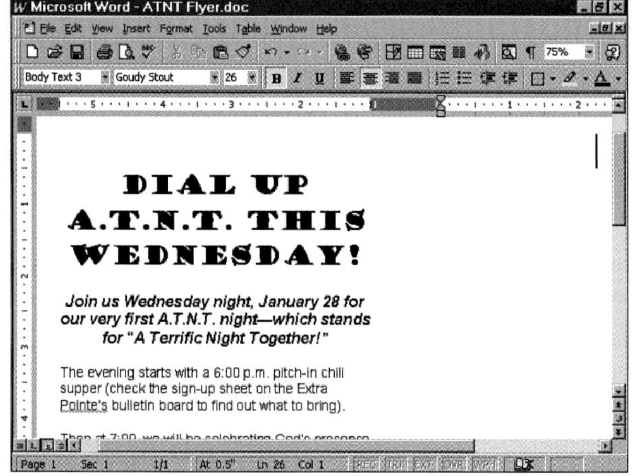

4 View Multiple Files

To see all the open files onscreen at the same time, open the **Window** menu and select **Arrange All**.

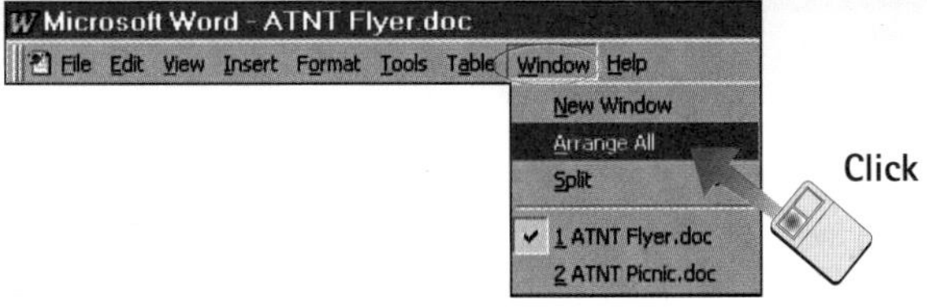

5 Two Open Files

Each file window appears in the program window. Depending on how many files you arrange, you probably won't see much of each file's contents. To make a file active, click its title bar.

6 Maximize the File Window

To return the file window to its full size, click the **Maximize** button on the file's title bar.

End

How-To Hints

Copy and Move Data

With two or more files open and viewable at the same time, you can drag data from one file to place in another using the drag-and-drop method. Select the data, click and hold the left mouse button, and drag the data to a new location in the other file. To copy the data, hold down the Shift key while dragging.

TASK 8

How to Find Files

Use the Open dialog box in Word, Excel, PowerPoint, or Access to find Office files. When you install Office 97, the Find Fast feature is installed. Find Fast indexes all the Office documents you create so you can quickly find them when you need them. It also updates the index automatically. This task will show you how to locate files using the Find features in the Open dialog box.

Begin

1 Open the Open Dialog Box

Start by opening the Open dialog box. From any Office program window, click the **Open** button on the toolbar. If you've not yet opened an Office program, click the **Start** button on the taskbar and choose **Open Office Document**, as shown in this figure.

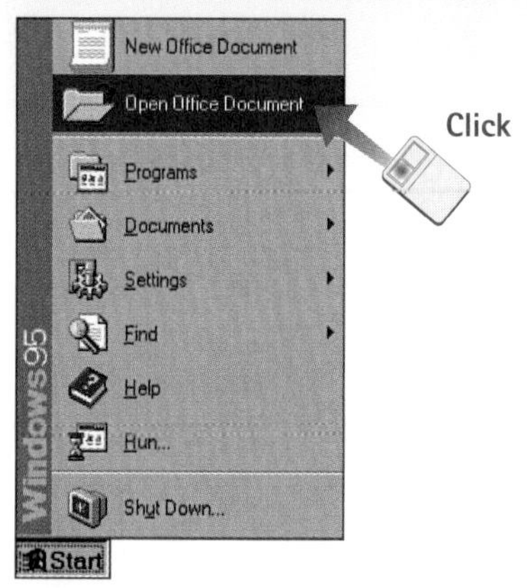

2 Conduct a Simple Search

From the **Look in** drop-down list, select the drive you want to search, then type the name of the file you're looking for in the **File name** text box; then choose the type of file you're looking for with the **Files of type** drop-down list. Click **Find Now** to conduct the search.

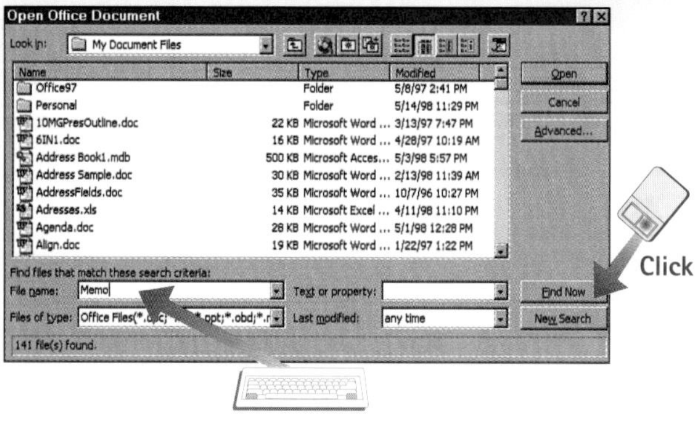

3 Search for Specific Text

If you remember where you saved the file but don't remember what you named it, use the **Text or property** text box. Click inside the **Text or property** text box and type some text that you know is in the file, such as a name or a category. Click **Find Now** to conduct a search.

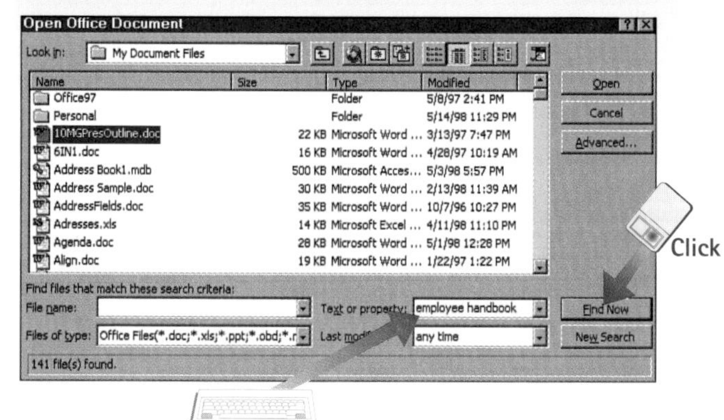

4 Find a File by Date

If you don't remember the filename you're looking for, but you do remember the date you last worked on the file, use the **Last modified** option. Click the **Last modified** drop-down arrow and choose a day, then click **Find Now** to conduct the search.

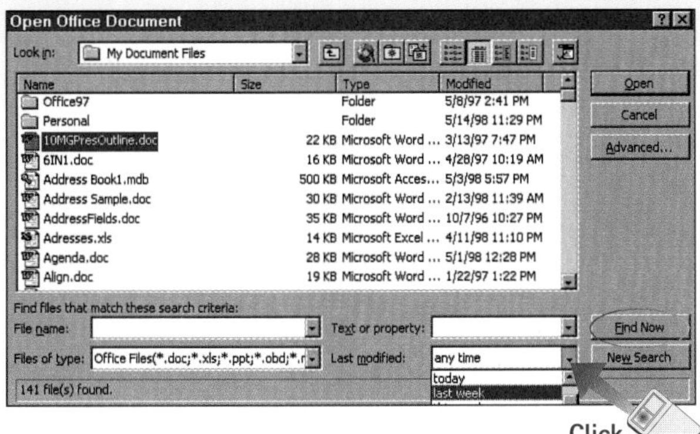

5 Use Advanced Search Options

If the previous steps didn't produce the file you're looking for, click the **Advanced** button. This opens the Advanced Find dialog box where you can enter search criteria.

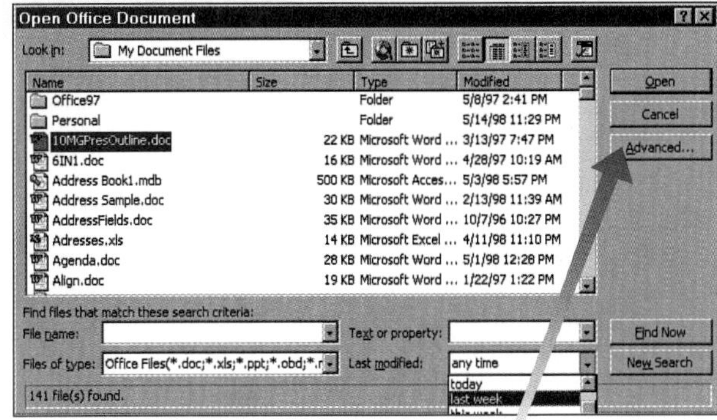

Click

6 Specify Search Criteria

Use the **Define more criteria** area to select options in addition to those you tried in the previous steps. Use the **Property** drop-down list to choose the property you want to search for; use the **Value** text box to enter specific text you're looking for; click **Add to List** to add the criteria to the search list. Then choose **Find Now** to conduct the search and return to the Open dialog box.

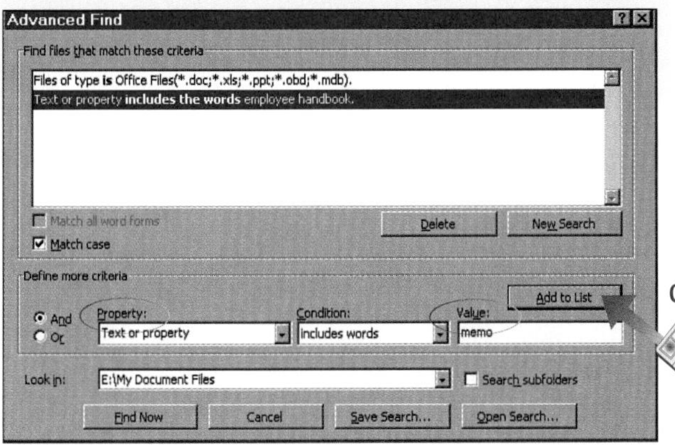

Click

End

How-To Hints

Start a New Search

Each time you finish conducting a search and you want to search again, you must click the **New Search** button to start another search. This clears the previous search criteria.

TASK 9

How to Use the Office Assistant

Regardless of your level of computer experience, you may need help from time to time, especially when you're learning a new software program. By default, Microsoft's Office Assistant appears ready to help you as soon as you start a program.

The Office Assistant is an animated help feature you can use to help you navigate new tasks or find additional information about a feature. Use Office Assistant to look up specific instructions or topics you want help with.

Begin

1 Open Office Assistant

By default, Office Assistant appears when you first use a program or tackle a new feature. To summon the Assistant at any time, simply press F1 or click the **Office Assistant** button on the toolbar.

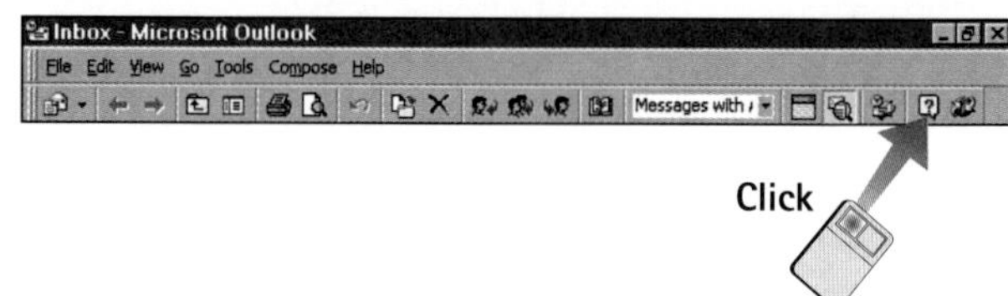

2 Ask a Question

From the Office Assistant balloon, you can type a question or select from options the Assistant lists. To type a question, click inside the text box and enter the question text. Click **Search** or press Enter.

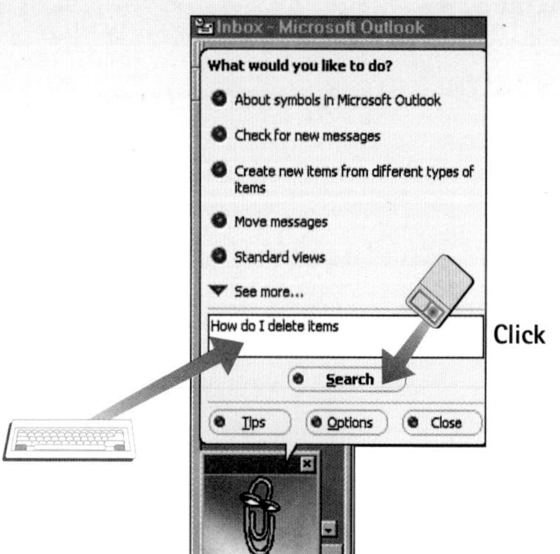

3 Choose a Topic

Office Assistant produces a list of possible topics for you to choose from. Click a topic that most closely matches the information you desire. (If the question you typed didn't produce the results you expected, try entering a new question.)

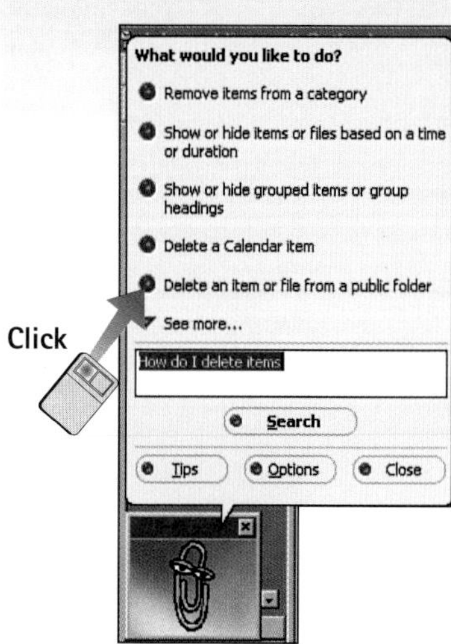

4 Read the Help Window

A Help window appears with more information detailing the topic, or shows additional topics you can choose.

5 Close the Help Window

To close the Help window when you're finished reading, click the window's **Close** (**X**) button.

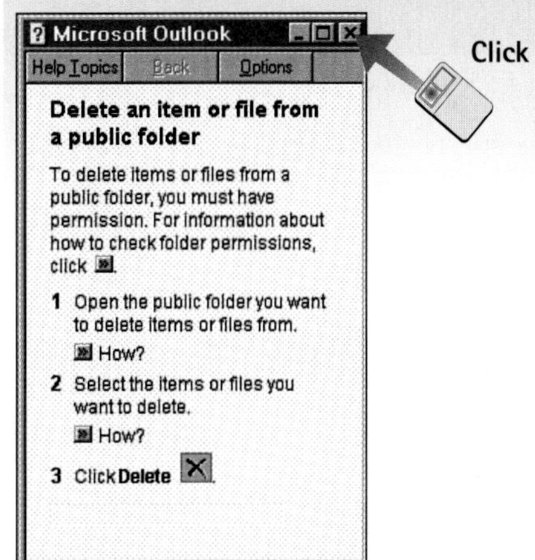

6 Close the Office Assistant

To close the Office Assistant completely, click its **Close** button (**X**) or **Close** option. You can also choose to leave the Office Assistant open onscreen in case you need more help. As you work with the file, the Office Assistant will move out of your way as needed.

End

How-To Hints

Check Out the Tips

Click the **Tips** option in the Office Assistant balloon to read tips about using the program you're working in.

Customize the Office Assistant

If you don't like the default Clippit character (the animated paper clip), you can change it. Click the **Options** button in the Office Assistant balloon, click the **Gallery** tab and choose another character. Make sure your Office 97 CD is loaded; additional characters are not copied onto your hard disk during installation, so you will need the CD to copy them when changing the character. Other Office Assistants are available from Microsoft's Web site at **http://www.microsoft.com/office/**.

Change the Office Assistant Settings

Use the **Options** tab in the Office Assistant dialog box to change which options are turned on or off.

TASK 10

How to Use the Office Help System

Microsoft Office 97 help comes in three basic flavors: the Office Assistant, the online Help system, and the What's This? help feature. For friendly and, at times, entertaining help, try the Office Assistant (refer to Task 9, "How to Use the Office Assistant"). If you're not too keen on asking an animated character for help, try using the online Help system.

Use the Help Topics window to look up specific help on Office features and terms. Use the What's This? feature for help with onscreen elements.

Begin

1 Open Contents and Index

Open the **Help** menu and select **Contents and Index** to display the Help Topics dialog box.

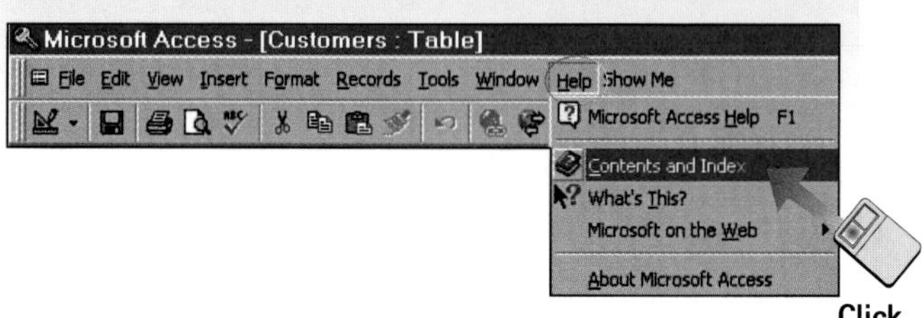

2 The Contents Tab

Use the **Contents** tab like a book's table of contents. Double-click a topic to open a list of subtopics. From the list of subtopics, double-click a topic to open a Help window with more information about the topic. The following example shows **Working with Data** with a subtopic of **Ways to work with data in a form**.

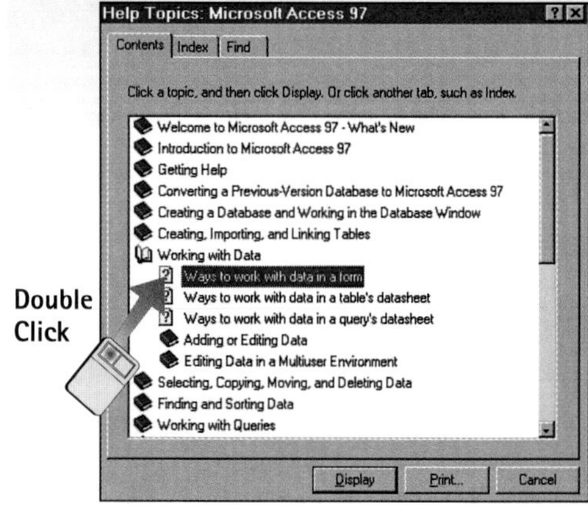

3 The Index Tab

The **Index** tab is an alphabetized list of help topics, much like a book's index. You can type the term you want to look up (for example, `fields`) and the list box scrolls alphabetically to the term or related terms. Double-click an entry in the list to open a Help window containing detailed information.

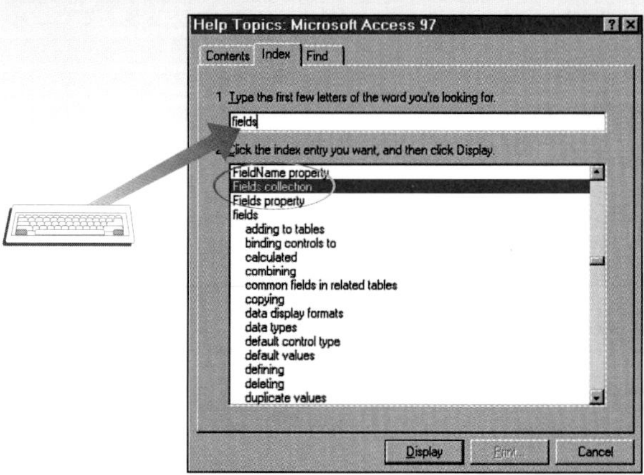

4 The Find Tab

To look up a word or phrase in the Help system rather than searching for a topic by category, use the **Find** tab. Enter the word or phrase (for example, **query**), and then double-click an entry in the list to open a Help window containing detailed information.

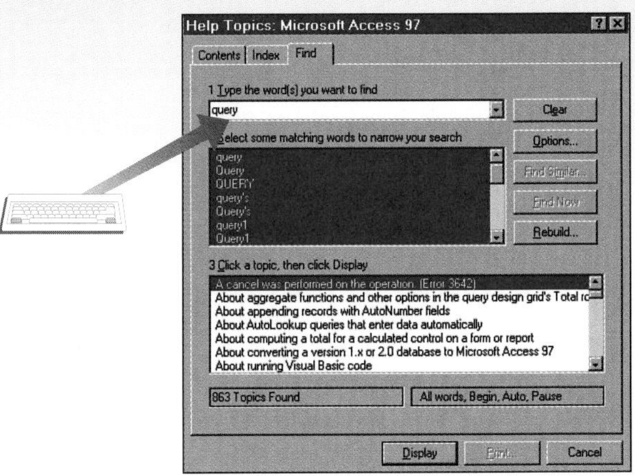

5 Close the Help Window

To close the Help window when you're finished reading, click the window's **Close** (**X**) button.

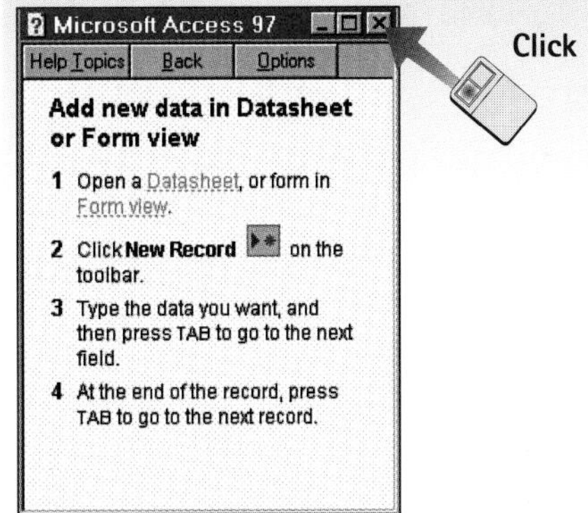

6 Use the What's This Feature

To find quick information about an onscreen element, use the What's This tool. Open the **Help** menu and choose **What's This?**. The mouse pointer takes the shape of a question mark. Click the onscreen element you want to know more about, such as a toolbar button or dialog box option. (Click anywhere onscreen or press Esc to close the help information.)

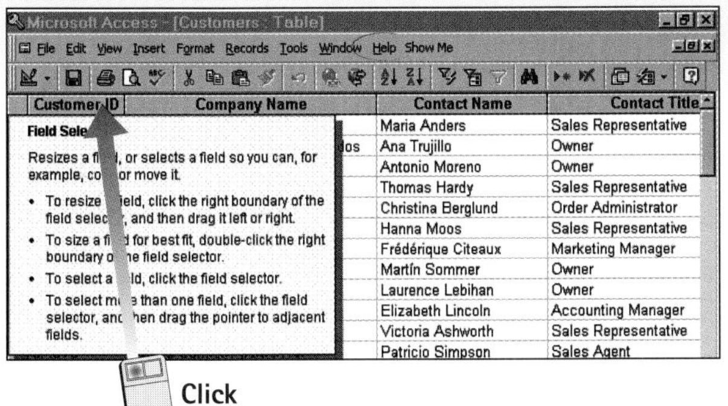

End

How-To Hints

Print Help Topics

From the Help window, click the **Options** button and click **Print Topic**.

Find Setup Wizard

The first time you use the **Find** tab, the Find Setup Wizard appears to help set up the database of Help topics. Click **Next** to continue and **Finish** to create the word list.

Task

CHAPTER 3

How to Use Word 97

Microsoft *Word* is one of the most popular, best-selling word processing programs ever created. With it, you can create all manner of *documents*, including letters, memos, reports, manuscripts, newsletters, and more. When it comes to working with text, there's no match for Microsoft Word. Of all the programs that make up Office 97, Word will probably become your most-used application; it's so versatile, you will use it for just about anything involving text.

In this part of the book, you will learn how to get up and running fast with Word—acclimate yourself with the various elements in the program window, learn how to begin working with text, and how to assign templates to help you build better documents. The fundamental skills covered in this chapter will prepare you for working with Word's numerous formatting tools in the chapter that follows.

TASK 1

How to Get Around the Word Window

When you first open Word 97, a blank document opens onscreen. The document is surrounded by tools you can use to help you enter and work with text and other items you place in the document. Many of the elements can be hidden, if you prefer, to free up window workspace. Use the View menu to turn the display of certain onscreen items on or off (such as *toolbars* or the ruler).

Each Office program uses similar onscreen elements, so if you learn how to use them in one program, you will be able to use these same elements in another. If you're new to Word, take a few moments and familiarize yourself with the window elements in this task.

Begin

1 The Blank Document Window

The program window opens along with a blank document window. Usually, both windows are maximized. (When both are maximized, two Restore buttons—one for each window—are displayed in the set of buttons in the upper-right corner of the window's screen.)

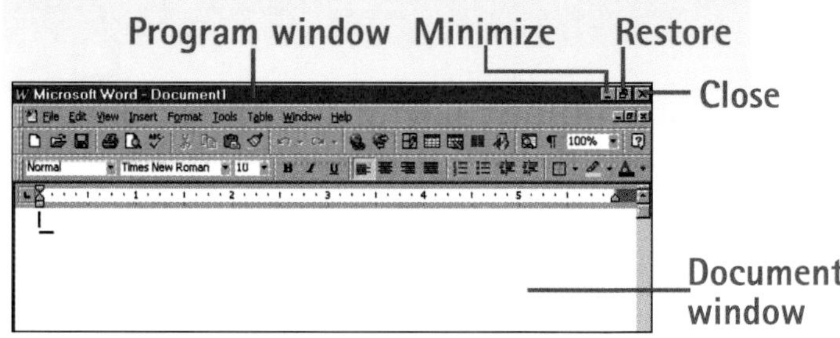

2 Viewing the Title Bar

The title bar tells you what is in the window. When the document window is maximized, it has to share the title bar with the program window, so the title bar contains the names of both the program (Microsoft Word) and the file. (Document1 is a temporary name; when you save the file for the first time, you can replace the default name.)

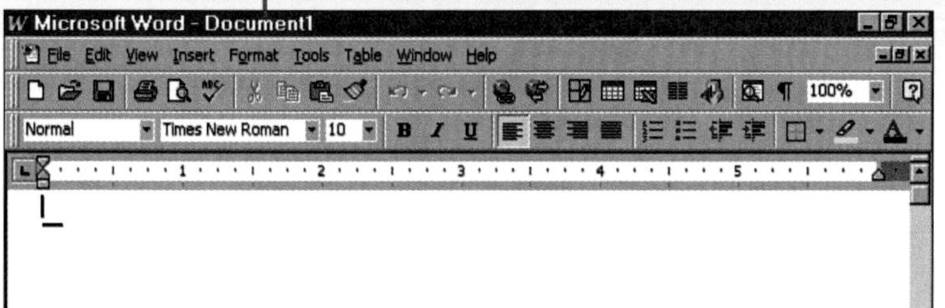

3 Use the Menu Bar

The Word menu bar contains menus, which in turn contain all the available Word commands. All the tasks you need to perform are available through menu commands. To use the menu commands, click the menu name to display the menu, and then click the command you want.

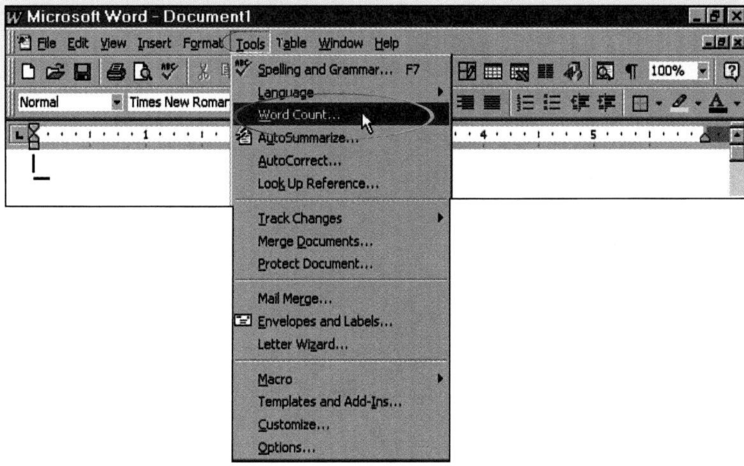

4 Use the Toolbars

The Standard toolbar contains shortcuts for frequently used commands such as those to open, save, and print documents, and to undo mistakes. The Formatting toolbar (below the Standard toolbar) contains shortcuts for commands that change the appearance of the document. To activate a toolbar button, click it. To see a button name, hover the mouse pointer over the button for a moment; a *ScreenTip* appears with the button name.

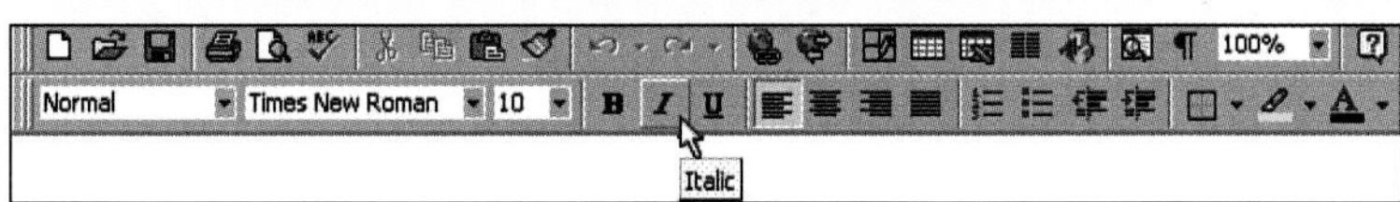

Continues

5 Use the Ruler

The ruler (located below the two toolbars) shows you where your margins are, and it lets you set tabs and indents. If you don't see the ruler, you can display it by choosing **View**, **Ruler**.

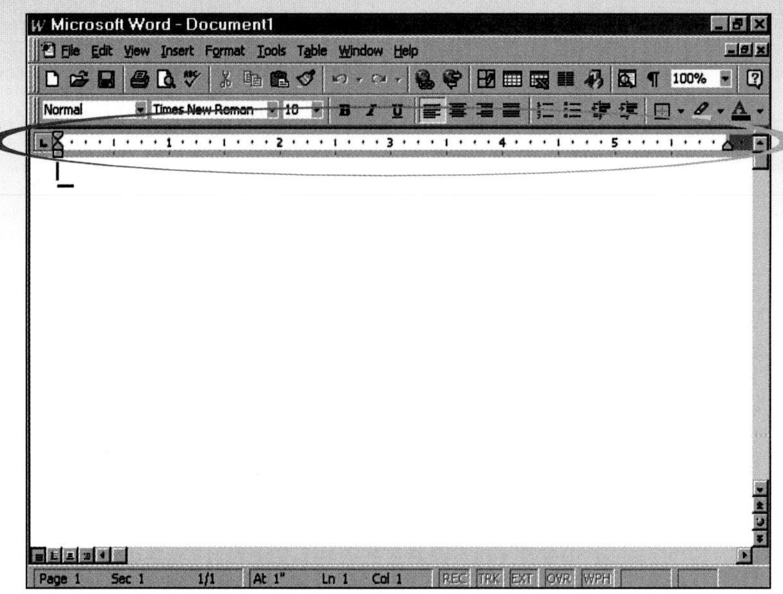

6 Use the Work Area

The typing area in a new document is the large blank space bordered by vertical and horizontal scrollbars. The *insertion point* (a vertical, blinking line, also known as the *cursor*) shows you where the next character you type will appear. The end-of-document marker (a horizontal line) shows you where the document ends. When the mouse pointer is placed over the typing area, it resembles an I-beam.

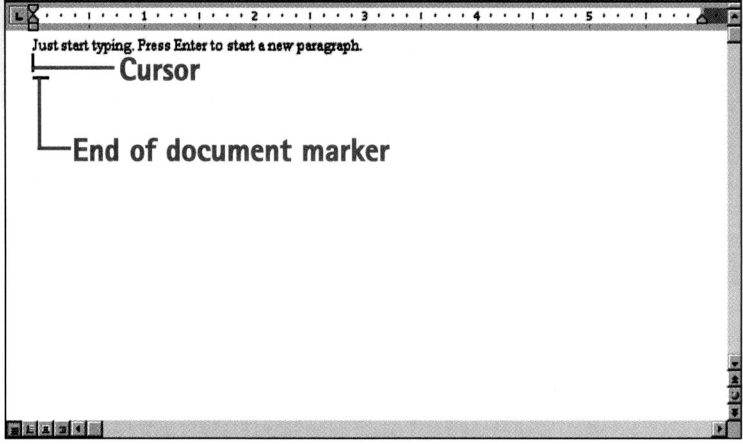

7 Use the Scrollbars

The vertical and horizontal scrollbars allow you to view different portions of your document. Use the arrows on the scrollbars to scroll in the appropriate direction or drag the scrollbox. Use the **Previous Page** and **Next Page** buttons (at the bottom of the vertical scrollbar) to quickly jump from one part of your document to the next.

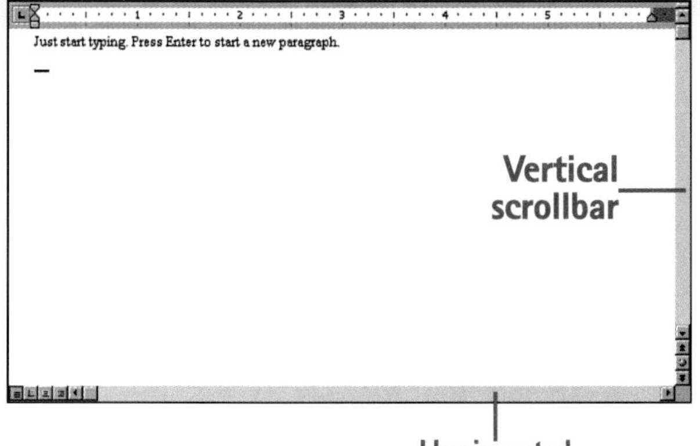

8 View the Status Bar

The status bar indicates the current page, the total number of pages, and the location of your insertion point on the page. As you use Word, the status bar sometimes displays other information as well.

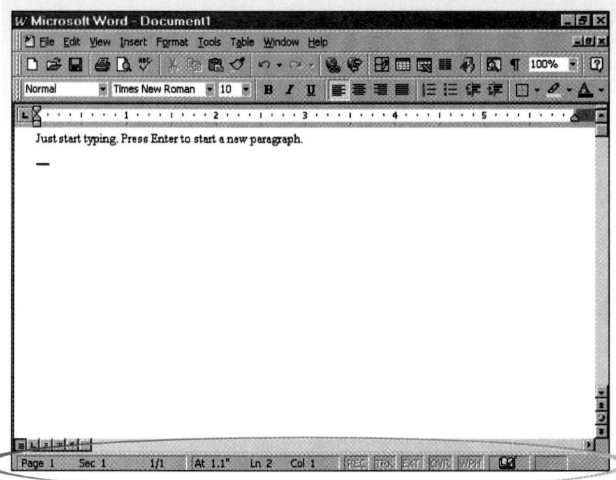

End

How-To Hints

What Toolbars?

If you don't see the Standard or Formatting toolbar, or if you see other toolbars you would like to hide, choose **View**, **Toolbars**. Select the **Standard** or **Formatting** toolbar. A check mark next to the toolbar name means the toolbar is displayed.

No Scrollbars?

If either of your scrollbars or your status bar isn't showing, choose **Tools**, **Options**. Click the **View** tab; then, under the Window heading, click any check box that isn't already marked—**Status Bar**, **Horizontal Scroll Bar**, or **Vertical Scroll Bar**—and click **OK**.

Use the Shortcut Menu

To open a shortcut menu that contains often-used commands, click an object with the right mouse button (called a right-click); then use the left mouse button to click the command you want. Almost everything in the Word window has its own shortcut menu.

Keyboard Shortcuts

To choose menu commands with the keyboard: Press the Alt key, and then press the underlined letter in the desired menu; then press the underlined letter in the desired command. To display the Format menu, for example, press Alt+O; when the Format menu is displayed, press P to choose the Paragraph command.

TASK 2

How to Enter and Edit Text

Microsoft Word opens with a blank document window ready for you to begin typing text, whether it's in the form of a bestseller novel, a personal letter, or an interoffice memo. The flashing insertion point indicates where the next character you type will appear. Simply start typing to enter text. If you make mistakes, use the Backspace key to delete unwanted characters.

Begin

1 Start a New Paragraph

Each time you press Enter, you start a new paragraph. Press Enter to end short lines of text, to create blank lines, and to end paragraphs. Don't press Enter to start new lines within a paragraph; Word wraps the lines for you.

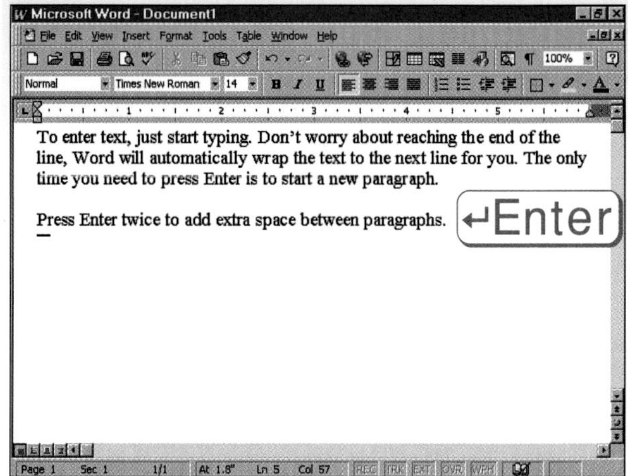

2 Indent with the Tab Key

Press the Tab key to quickly indent the first line of a paragraph. If you keep pressing Tab, you increase the indent one-half inch at a time. (To indent all the lines in the paragraph instead of just the first one, right-click in the paragraph, and then click **Paragraph** on the shortcut menu; click the **Indents and Spacing** tab, reset the indentation settings, and click **OK** to apply them.)

To enter text, just start typing. Don't worry about reaching the end of the line, Word will automatically wrap the text to the next line for you. The only time you need to press Enter is to start a new paragraph.

Press Enter twice to add extra space between paragraphs.

Press Tab to create an indent like this. The Tab key is handy for quick indents. If you prefer to use specific types of indents, open the Paragraph dialog box.

3 Type Repeating Characters

To type the same character repeatedly, hold the key down. Word automatically converts some repeated characters into different types of lines, as shown here. If you type three or more asterisks (*) and press Enter, for example, Word replaces them with a dotted line. Do the same with the equal sign (=) for a double line, the tilde (~) for a wavy line, the pound (#) symbol for a thick decorative line, or the underscore (_) for a thick single line.

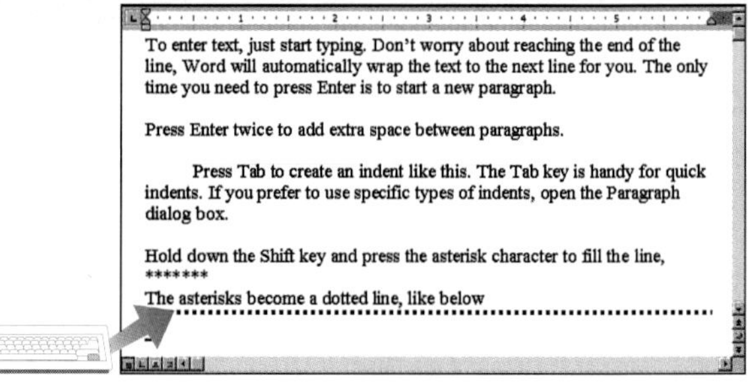

4 Type Uppercase Letters

To produce all uppercase letters without having to hold down the Shift key, press the Caps Lock key once before you begin typing. Press the Caps Lock key again when you're ready to switch caps off. Caps Lock affects only the letter keys, not the number and punctuation keys. So you always have to press Shift to type a character on the upper half of a number or punctuation key, such as @ or %.

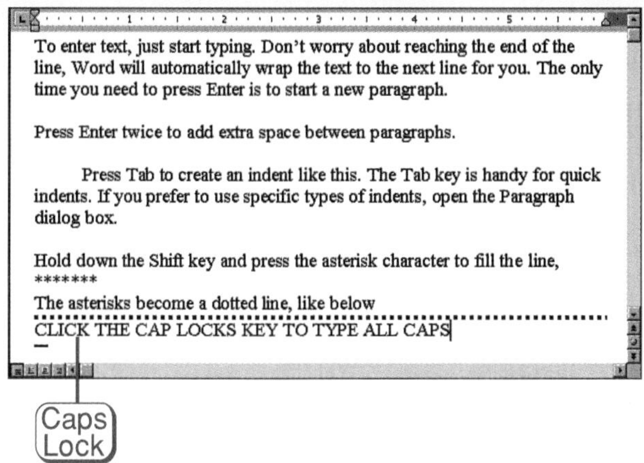

5 View NonPrinting Characters

Every time you press Enter, the spacebar, or the Tab key, Word marks the spot in your document with a nonprinting character. You can't see these characters unless you click the **Show/Hide** button in the Standard toolbar. You can use the Show/Hide button to check whether you accidentally typed an extra space between two words or to see how many blank lines you have between paragraphs. To turn off **Show/Hide**, click the button again.

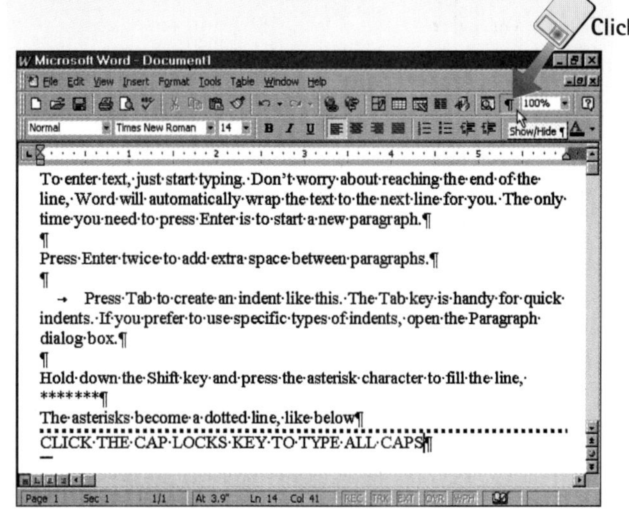

6 Fix Mistakes

Press the Backspace key to delete characters to the left of the cursor. You can also click inside a word and press the Delete key to remove characters to the right of the cursor.

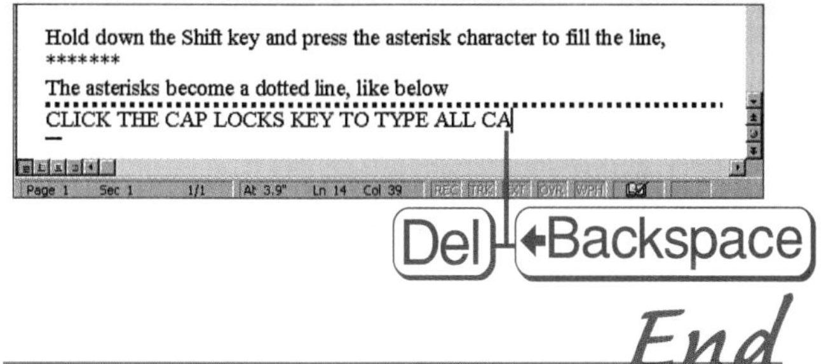

End

How-To Hints

Overtype and Insert Modes

By default, Word starts you in Insert mode, which means any time you click the cursor in the document and start typing, any existing text moves to the right to make room for new text you type. If you prefer to replace the existing text entirely, use the Overtype mode. Press the Insert key to toggle Overtype mode on or off or double-click the letters **OVR** on the status bar.

Need a New Page?

By default, Word starts a new page when the current page is filled with text. At times, you may want to start a new page without filling the current page. Press Ctrl+Enter to insert a manual page break.

TASK 3

How to Navigate a Document

As you begin filling a document with text, the view area will move down to show your current cursor location as you type. When your document becomes longer or wider than a full screen of text, use Word's navigation tools to view different parts of the document.

Begin

1 Use the Scrollbars

Depending on your document's size, use the vertical or horizontal scrollbars to view different portions of the document. Click the scrollbar's arrow buttons to scroll in the appropriate direction.

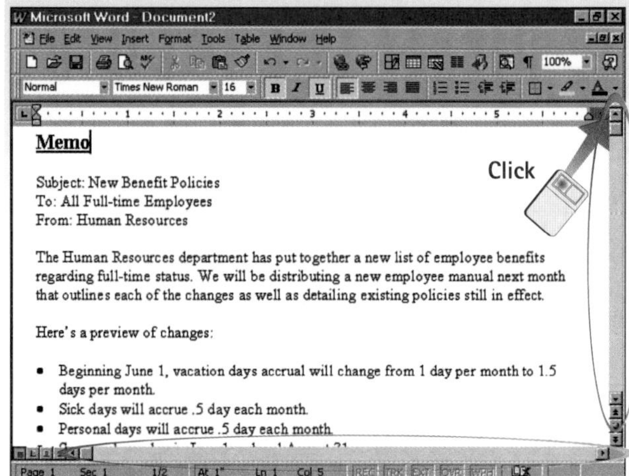

2 Drag the Scrollbox

You can also drag the scrollbox to move your view. Drag the vertical scrollbox up or down or drag the horizontal scrollbox to the left or right to move your view of the document page.

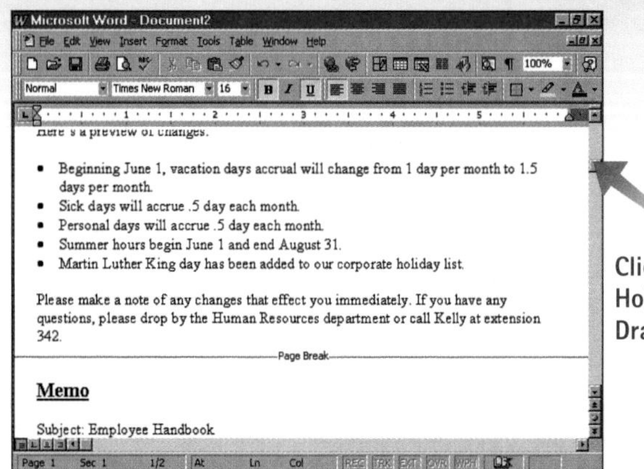

3 Use the Page Buttons

If your document is longer than a page, click the **Next Page** button to immediately scroll to the next page. Click the **Previous Page** button to scroll back a page.

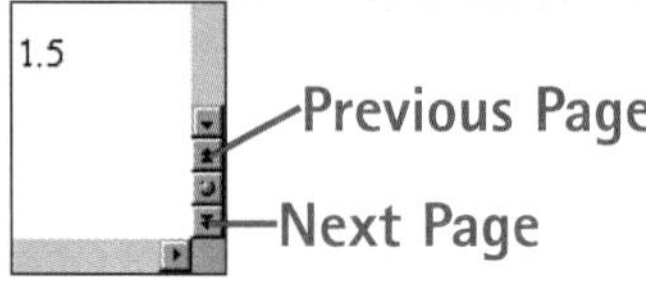

4 Use the Mouse

Click the mouse anywhere in your document to move the insertion point to that spot.

Click

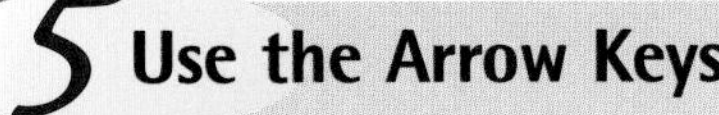

5 Use the Arrow Keys

Use the arrow keys on the keyboard to move up, down, right, or left in the document. Press the right arrow key, for example, to move right one character; hold the right arrow key down to quickly move across many characters.

6 Use Keyboard Shortcuts

In addition to the navigational arrow keys, you can use numerous other keyboard shortcuts to navigate documents. For example, press Ctrl+→ to move right one word; press Ctrl+← to move left one word.

Control + → Control + ←

End

How-To Hints

Go To

If you know the page you want to view onscreen, use the Go To command to get there. Select **Edit**, **Go To**, or click the **Select Browse Object** button on the vertical scrollbar, and then click the **Go To** icon. In the **Go To** tab, enter the page number, and then click the **Go To** button. (You can also locate specific document elements, such as footnotes or headings.)

More Keyboard Shortcuts

To learn more about Word's many shortcut keys, use the Help system. Open the **Help** menu and select **Contents and Index**. Click the **Index** tab and type **shortcut keys** to look up the subject matter.

TASK 4

How to Select Text

After entering text, you can do a variety of things with it, such as applying formatting, or moving and copying the text. But before you can do any of these things, you must first learn to select text. Selecting text means to highlight the specific text you want to change or apply commands to. Selected text, whether it's a single character, a word, a paragraph, or an entire document, always appears highlighted onscreen with a black bar.

Begin

1 Select Text with the Mouse

To select a character, word, or phrase, click at the beginning of the text you want to select, and then hold down the left mouse button and drag to the end of the selection. Release the mouse button and the text is selected.

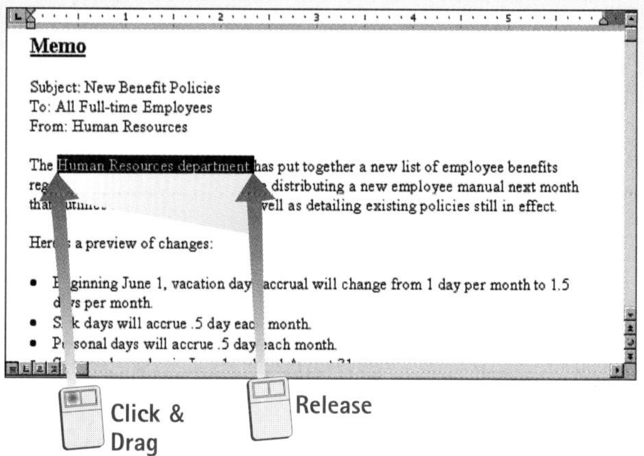

2 Select Text with the Keyboard

To select text using the keyboard, press the arrow keys to move the cursor to the beginning of the word or phrase you want to select. Hold down the Shift key and move the appropriate arrow key to select the desired text. To select a word, for example, move the cursor to the beginning of the word, hold down the Shift key, and press the right arrow key until the text is selected.

The Human Resources department has put together a new list of employee benefits regarding full-time status. We will be distributing a new employee manual next month that outlines each of the changes as well as detailing existing policies still in effect.

Here's a preview of changes:

- Beginning June 1, vacation days accrual will change from 1 day per month to 1.5 days per month.
- Sick days will accrue .5 day each month.
- Personal days will accrue .5 day each month.

3 Mouse Shortcuts

To quickly select a single word, double-click inside the word. To select a paragraph, triple-click inside the paragraph.

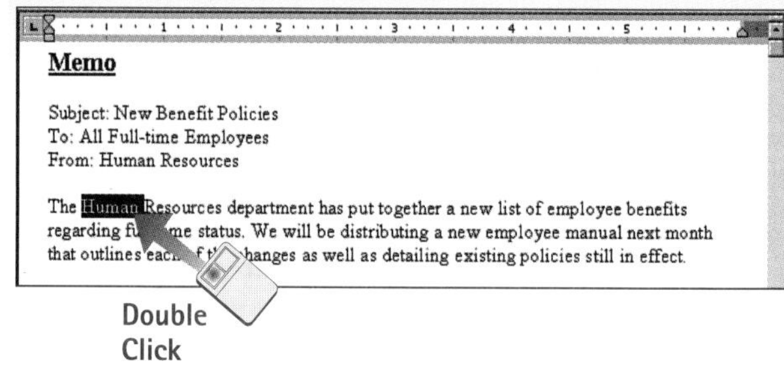

4 Click Inside the Left Margin

You can also click inside the left margin to select paragraphs and lines of text. Hover your mouse pointer to the left of the line you want to highlight until the mouse pointer takes the shape of a northeast pointing arrow; click once to select the line, double-click to select the paragraph, or triple-click to select the entire document.

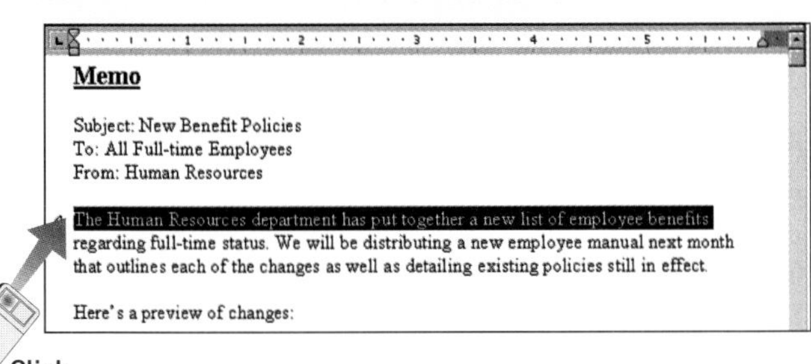
Memo
Subject: New Benefit Policies
To: All Full-time Employees
From: Human Resources
The Human Resources department has put together a new list of employee benefits regarding full-time status. We will be distributing a new employee manual next month that outlines each of the changes as well as detailing existing policies still in effect.
Here's a preview of changes:
Click

5 Unselect Text

To quickly unselect text, click anywhere outside the text or press any arrow key.

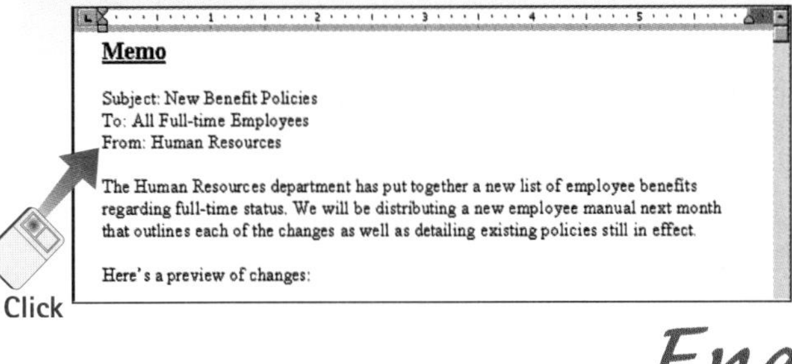
Memo
Subject: New Benefit Policies
To: All Full-time Employees
From: Human Resources
The Human Resources department has put together a new list of employee benefits regarding full-time status. We will be distributing a new employee manual next month that outlines each of the changes as well as detailing existing policies still in effect.
Here's a preview of changes:
Click

End

How-To Hints

Edit Selected Text

You can easily replace selected text with new text. Just start typing, and the selected text is deleted and replaced with any new text you type. To delete selected text without typing new text, press the Delete key.

Keyboard Shortcuts

To quickly select one word at a time using the keyboard keys, press Ctrl+Shift+right arrow or Ctrl+Shift+left arrow. To select one paragraph at a time, press Ctrl+Shift+up arrow or Ctrl+Shift+down arrow. To select all the text from the insertion point onward, press Ctrl+Shift+End. To select all text above the insertion point, press Ctrl+Shift+Home.

TASK 5

How to Move and Copy Text

Use Word's Cut, Copy, and Paste functions to move and copy text from one location to another. Word makes it easy to pick up characters, words, sentences, paragraphs and more, and move or copy them to a new location. You can even move and copy them between files.

You can apply a variety of methods to move and copy text. You can use menu commands, shortcut menu commands, toolbar buttons, keyboard shortcuts, and *drag-and-drop* techniques; everyone finds his favorite method. To move text, you cut it from its position and paste it somewhere else; to copy text, you make a copy of the text and paste it elsewhere.

Begin

1 Select the Text

Select the text you want to cut or copy.

2 Use Cut and Copy

An easy way to cut and copy is to use the toolbar buttons. To move the text, click the **Cut** button in the Standard toolbar. The text is deleted from your document, but it remains in a special Windows storage area called the *Clipboard*. To copy the text, click the **Copy** button in the Standard toolbar. When you copy text, nothing appears to happen because the text remains in its original location, but a copy of the selected text is sent to the Clipboard.

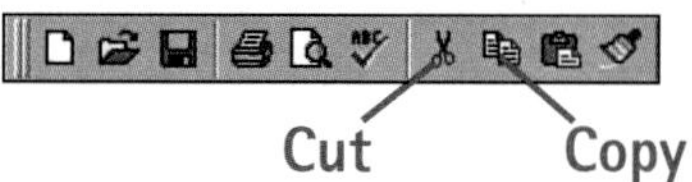

3 Relocate the Cursor

Click to place the cursor in the document where you want to paste the cut or copied text. If necessary, you can open another document or switch to another already open document to paste text there.

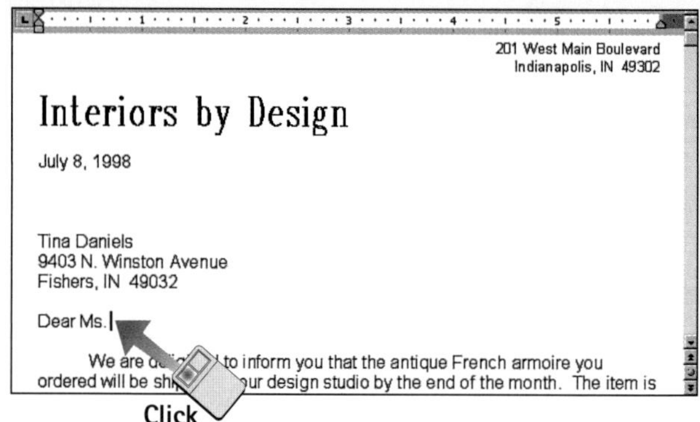

4 Use Paste

Click the **Paste** button in the Standard toolbar to paste the text. The text is pasted into the document beginning at the position of the insertion point.

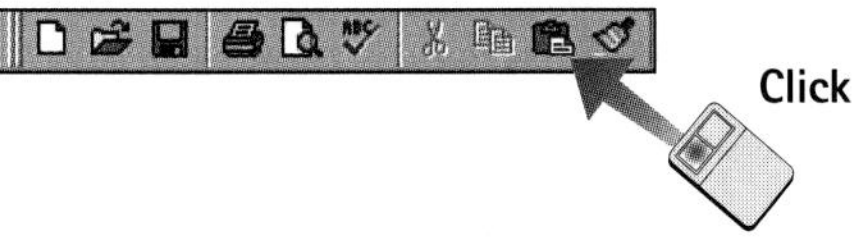

5 Drag and Drop to Move Text

Another easy method to move or copy text is to drag and drop it. To move text, click in the selected text and hold the mouse button down, then drag the mouse where you want to paste the text. Release the mouse button to drop, or paste, the cut text.

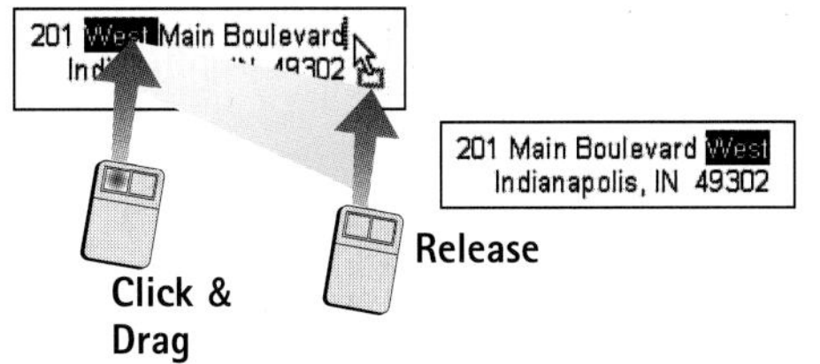

6 Drag and Drop to Copy Text

To copy text by dragging and dropping it, select the text you want to copy. Click in the selected text and hold down the mouse button, hold down the Ctrl key, then drag the mouse to the new location. Release the mouse button to drop, or paste, the copied text.

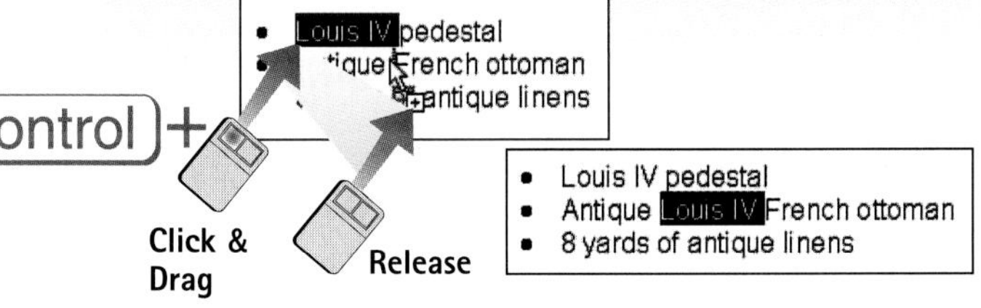

End

How-To Hints

Keyboard Shortcuts

If you prefer using the keyboard, try these shortcut commands: Ctrl+X for Cut, Ctrl+C for Copy, and Ctrl+V for Paste. These keyboard shortcuts are standard for all Windows-based programs.

Keep Pasting

After you cut or copy text, a copy of it remains in the Clipboard, so you can repeatedly paste more copies of the text without cutting or copying it again. The Clipboard contents are replaced only when you use the Cut or Copy command again. The Clipboard empties when you exit Windows.

Paste to Other Programs

You can also cut or copy text to a document in another program that supports OLE (object linking and embedding). Cut or copy the desired text, and then switch to the other program and open the document in which you want to paste the text; position the insertion point, and then use the Paste command provided in that program.

TASK 6

How to Use Word's Views

Word offers you several ways to view your document. For starters, you can use the Zoom tool to zoom in to view your document in detail, or zoom out to view your document from a "bird's-eye view." You can also change the way you view a document page using four main view options: Normal, Online Layout, Page Layout, and Outline.

By default, Word opens in Normal view, and you see only the text area of the page; no graphics or special elements appear. Switch to Page Layout view to see graphics, page margins, and elements such as headers and footers. Use Outline view to help you build and maintain outline levels in your document. Online Layout view takes its cue from Web pages, splitting your document into two panes—one for viewing the overall organization of the document, and the other for viewing specific sections.

Begin

1 Use the Zoom Tools

The quickest way to zoom your view of the document is to use the **Zoom** control on the Standard toolbar. Click the drop-down arrow to display the list of zoom percentages, and then click a percentage (such as **75%**) to zoom your view.

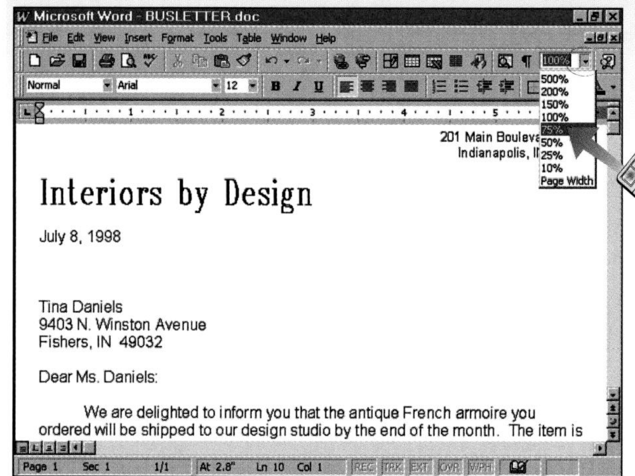

Click

2 Your View Is Zoomed

Word zooms (for example, 75% from previous step) your view of the document based on the selection you made in step 1.

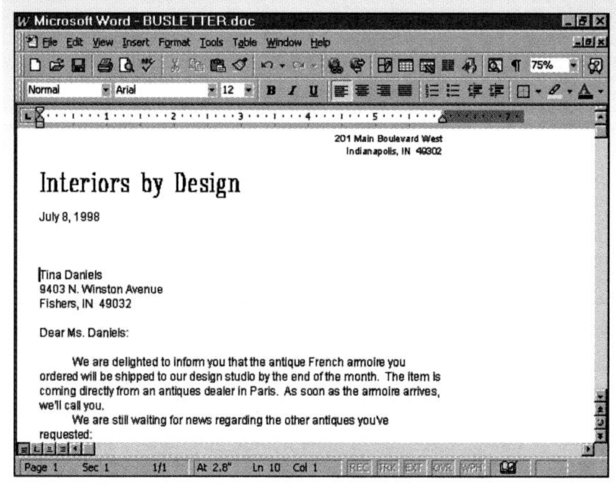

3 Open the Zoom Dialog Box

To specify an exact zoom percentage, open the **View** menu and select **Zoom**.

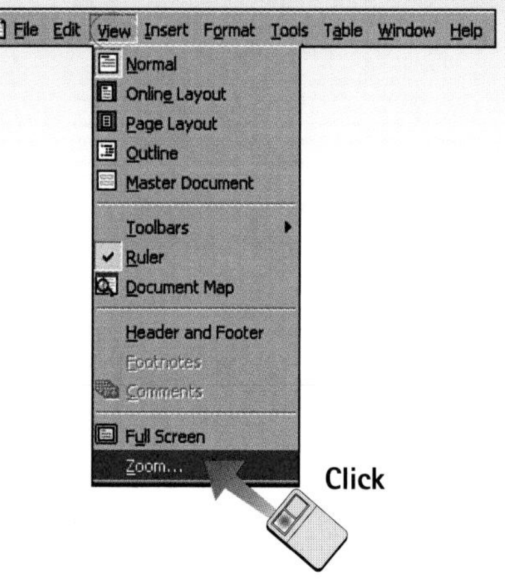

4 Specify a Zoom Percentage

In the Zoom dialog box, you can enter an exact zoom percentage in the **Percent** box (such as **50%**). The **Preview** area gives you an idea of how the zoomed text will look. Click **OK** to apply the new view.

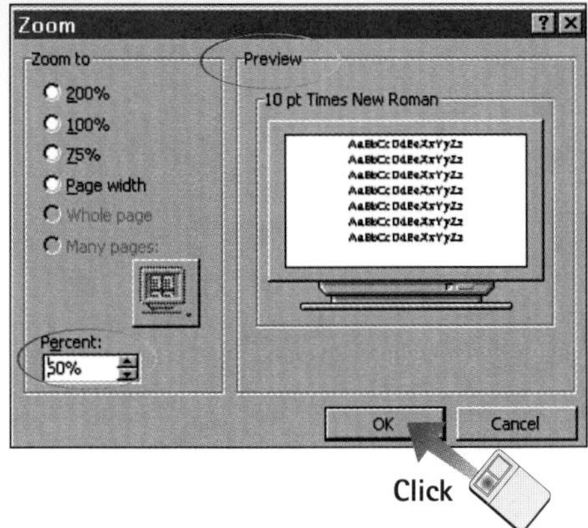

5 Use the View Buttons

Use the View buttons in the lower-left corner of the Word window to switch between Normal, Online Layout, Page Layout, and Outline views. Click the view button you want to switch to; for example, click **Page Layout view**.

6 Change the View

Word displays the document just as it will print. Most users stick with Normal and Page Layout views to work with and view document pages. To change your view again, click the View button you want to use.

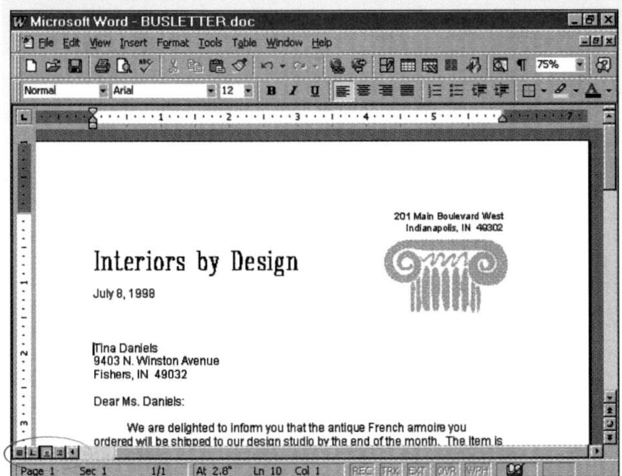

End

How-To Hints

Use the View Menu

You can also switch your document page views using the **View** menu.

Use the Outline View

Outline view is intended to help you modify the structure of your outline. In Outline view, you can move headings—and any body text or subheadings they contain—by dragging and dropping them; you can hide and display heading levels by clicking toolbar buttons. You can also apply heading styles or outline levels to your headings while you're using Outline view.

What About Document Map?

Document Map view works a lot like Online Layout view, using the two panes. The left pane lets you view the document's outline; the right pane lets you view the contents.

What About Master Document?

Word's Master Document feature lets you break down large documents into smaller documents and is particularly useful in a network workgroup setting. Several people can work on subdocuments within the master document simultaneously. To learn more about this feature, check out Word's online Help system. Also, see *Special Edition Using Word 97, Bestseller Edition* published by Que, for help with master documents.

TASK 7

How to Use Templates

Use Word's *templates* to create documents quickly when you don't have time to format and design them yourself. A template is a ready-made document. All you have to do is fill in your own text. Word comes with numerous templates you can use, and additional templates are available on the Office 97 CD (see Chapter 1, "How to Get Started with Office 97," to learn more about installing Office components from the CD).

If you don't see a template that meets your specific needs, you can choose a template that is close, add your own design and formatting elements, and save the document as a new template. The next time you need the template, it's ready to go.

Begin

1 Open the New Dialog Box

Open the **File** menu and select **New** to display the New dialog box. (You can't use the New button on the Standard toolbar as a shortcut. If you click the **New** button, Word assumes you want to start a new document based on the Normal template.)

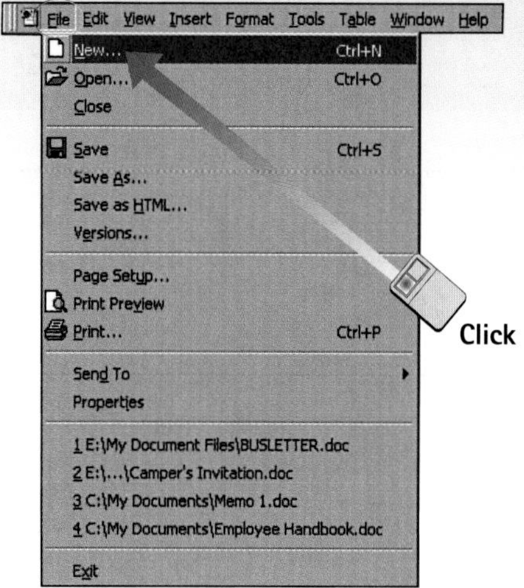

2 Choose a Tab Category

The New dialog box has several tab categories. Depending on the type of document you want to create, click each tab and see what is available. (Your tabs and templates may vary.)

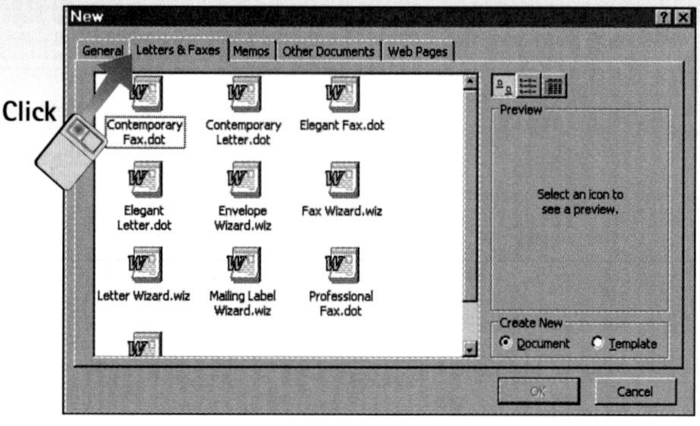

3 Preview a Template

When you locate a template you want to use, select it (by clicking just once on the icon), and the **Preview** area lets you see what the design looks like.

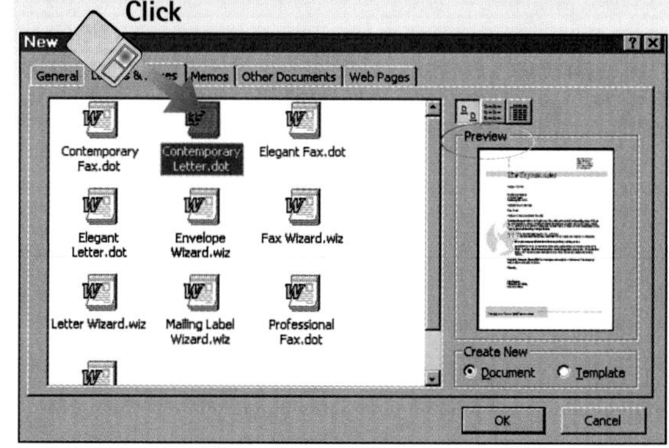

4 Open the Template

If you decide you like the template, double-click its name or select it and choose **OK**.

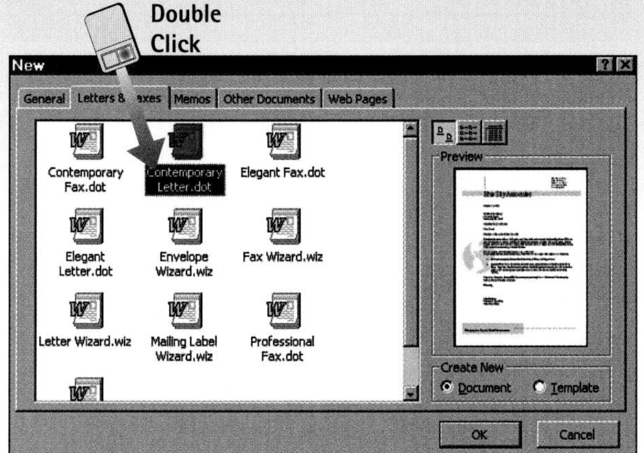

5 Fill It In

Word creates a new document based on the template you chose. Many templates, such as the one shown here, include placeholder text with instructions to "Click here and type" to help you fill in your text. Click the placeholder text and type your own text.

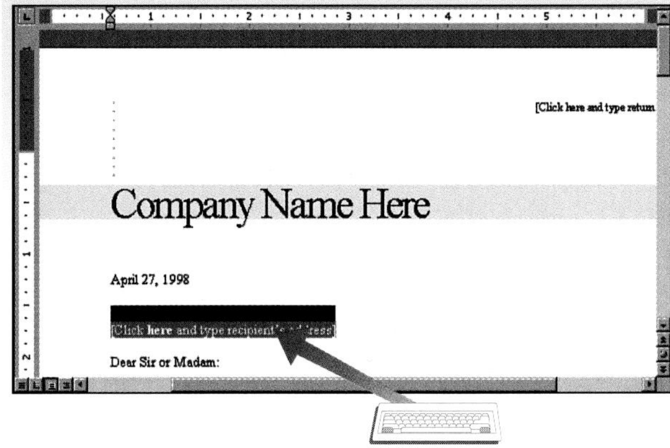

6 Save, Print, and Close

The text you typed replaces the "click here" text. Continue replacing all the "click here" instructions with the text you want in the document. When you have completed the document, use the regular methods to save, print, and close it.

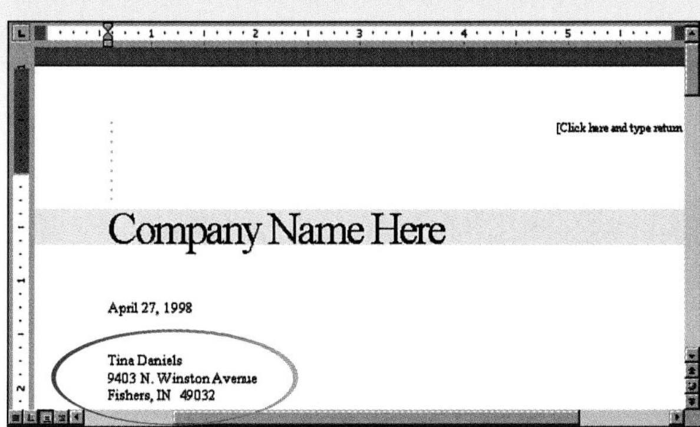

End

How-To Hints

Use Wizards

You may notice some templates in the New dialog box are called wizards. *Wizards* are specialized templates that let you customize the document you create by walking you through each step necessary to build the document. To start a wizard, double-click its name.

Create a Custom Template

You can save a Word template as your own personalized template without changing the built-in template. In the New dialog box, click the **Template** option in the lower-right corner before you open the template. This opens a copy of the built-in template that you can save as your own template with a different name; you can personalize the text and formatting in this template. After you save this template, its icon appears on the **General** tab the next time you choose **File, New**.

TASK 8

How to Work with AutoText

AutoText is a great tool for saving you time entering text. If you find yourself typing the same company name, phrase, or address over and over again, make the text an AutoText entry. Assign the entry a brief abbreviation, and the next time you enter the abbreviation, AutoText inserts the entire text entry for you. AutoText entries can be of any length, from a short sentence to an entire letter, and they are easy to save and use.

Begin

1 Select the Text

Type the text you want to include in your AutoText entry (for example, **Human Resources Department**) and apply any formatting you want.

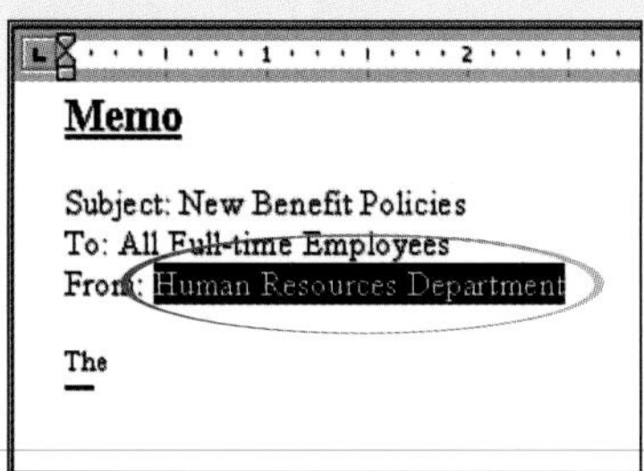

2 Choose the AutoText Command

Open the **Insert** menu and select **AutoText, New**.

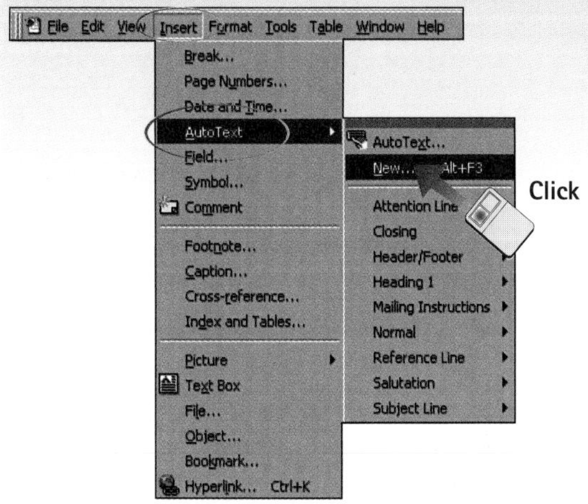

3 Enter a Name

In the Create AutoText dialog box, type a name for the entry in the **Please name your AutoText entry** box, such as **Human Resources**, or use the default suggestion, and choose **OK**. Although you can have AutoText names that are more than one word long, it's best to use a name or abbreviation that's short and memorable.

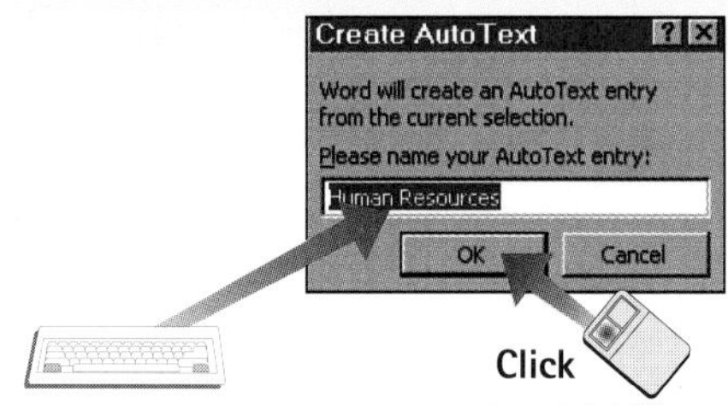

4 Insert AutoText

The next time you're ready to use the entry, click your document where you want the entry inserted and type the first few letters of an AutoText entry's name. As you type, an AutoComplete tip containing the name may appear next to the characters you typed; if you press Enter, the AutoText entry is inserted at the location.

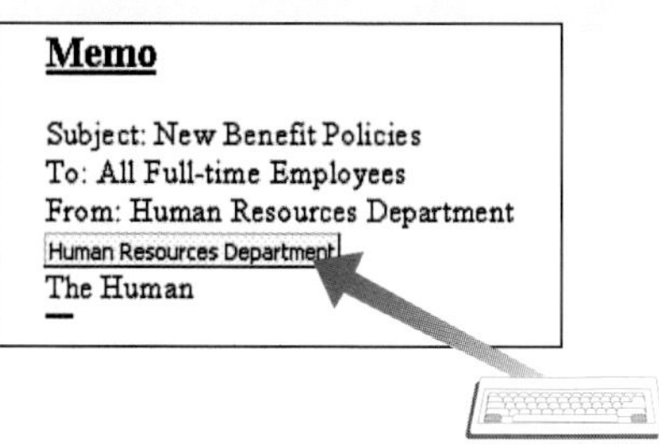

5 Open the AutoText Tab

You can also choose which AutoText entry to use by opening the **Insert** menu and selecting **AutoText**, **AutoText**. This opens the AutoCorrect dialog box with the AutoText tab displayed.

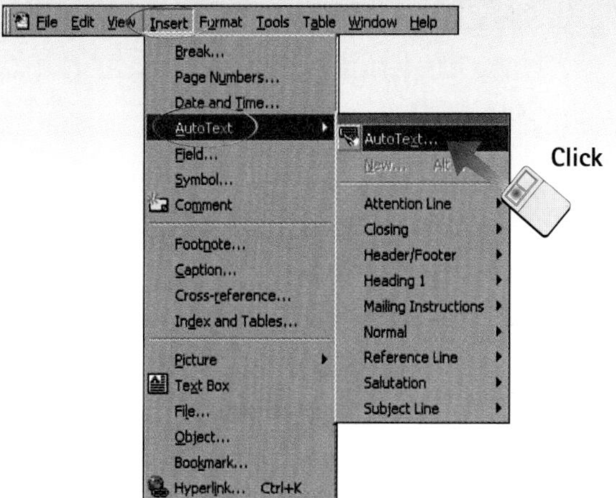

6 Choose an Entry

On the list of AutoText categories, point to the category where your entry is stored and click the name of the entry (such as **ATTN:**). Click the **Insert** button and the entry is pasted into your document.

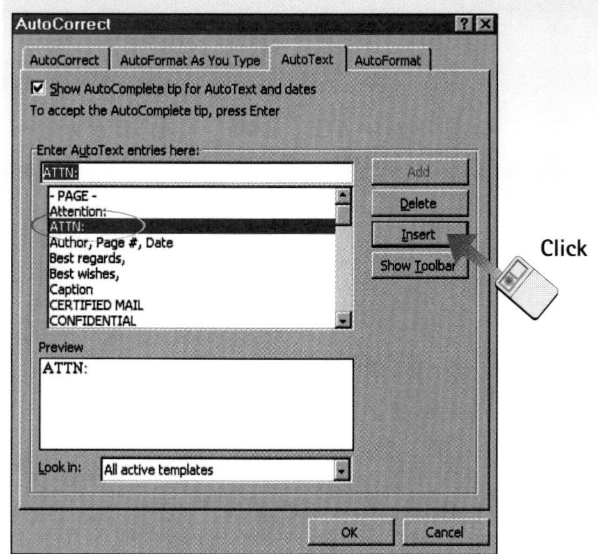

End

How-To Hints

Delete Entries

To delete an AutoText entry, open the **Insert** menu and select **AutoText**, **AutoText** to display the AutoText tab of the AutoCorrect dialog box. Click the entry you want to delete from the list, click the **Delete** button, and then click **OK**.

Use the AutoText Toolbar

Another way to create and insert AutoText entries is with the AutoText toolbar. Display the toolbar on your screen (select **View**, **Toolbars**, **AutoText**), and then use the **New** button to add new entries as you encounter them. To insert an entry, click the AutoText button and choose the entry from the list, and then click **Insert**.

Turn AutoComplete On or Off

To turn automatic AutoText entries on/off, choose **Tools**, **AutoCorrect**; at the top of the AutoText tab, mark or clear the **Show AutoComplete tip for AutoText and dates** check box.

Task

CHAPTER 4

How to Use Word's Formatting Tools

The term *formatting* refers to all the techniques that enhance the appearance of your document, including character, paragraph, and page formatting. Character formatting refers to all the features that can affect individual text characters, such as fonts, sizes, bold, or italic. Paragraph formatting includes line spacing, indents, alignment, tabs, paragraph spacing, and so on. Page formatting includes page orientation, margins, and page breaks.

Word's numerous formatting tools are what makes the program such a valuable part of the Office 97 suite. In this chapter, you'll learn about many of these formatting features and how they can help make your own documents more professional-looking and polished.

TASK 1

How to Format Text

By far the easiest formatting to apply is Bold, Italic, and Underline. These three formatting commands are the most commonly used formatting commands. They are so frequently used, in fact, they have their own buttons on the Formatting toolbar. You can easily turn these three formatting options on or off as needed using the toolbar buttons.

In addition, you can also find them in the Font dialog box, a comprehensive dialog box for applying formatting options in one fell swoop.

Begin

1 Click the Appropriate Button

Select the text you want to format, or choose the formatting commands before typing the text. To boldface text, click the **Bold** button on the Formatting toolbar. To italicize text, click the **Italic** button. To underline text, click the **Underline** button.

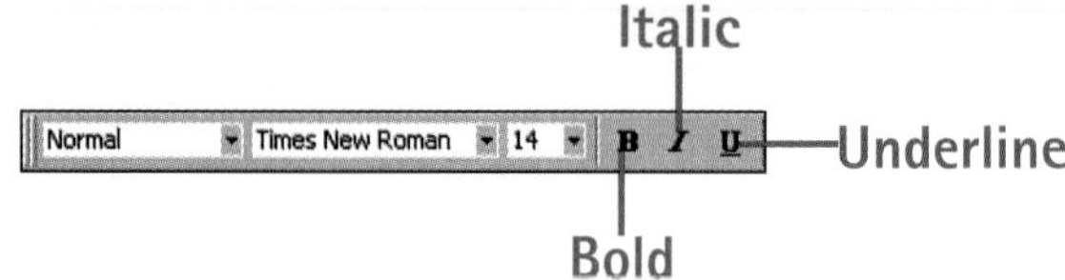

2 Formatting Applied

Depending on which buttons you select, the formatting is immediately applied to your selected text.

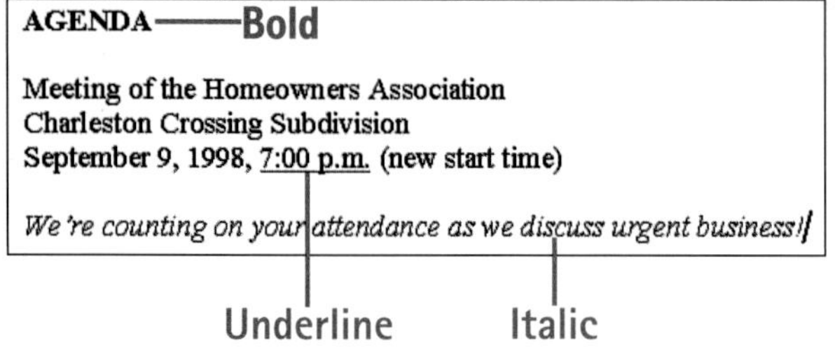

3 Open the Font Dialog Box

If you want to see what the formatting will look like before you apply it, open the **Format** menu and choose **Font**. This opens the Font dialog box with the Font tab displayed.

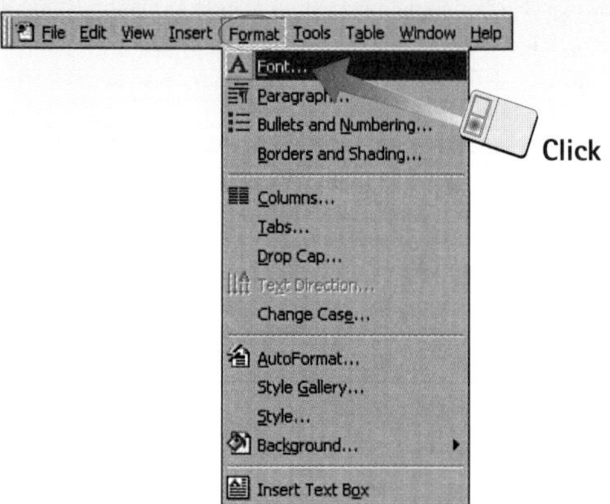

4 Use the Font Dialog Box

In the **Font style** list, choose **Bold**, **Italic**, or **Bold Italic** to boldface or italicize your text. To underline text, click the down arrow on the **Underline** list box to display the list of choices, and then click the desired underline style.

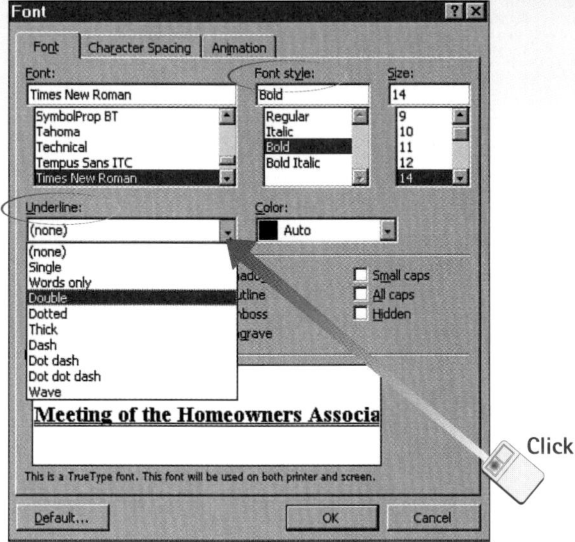

5 Preview Your Selections

In the **Preview** area at the bottom of the dialog box, you can preview how your choices will affect the text.

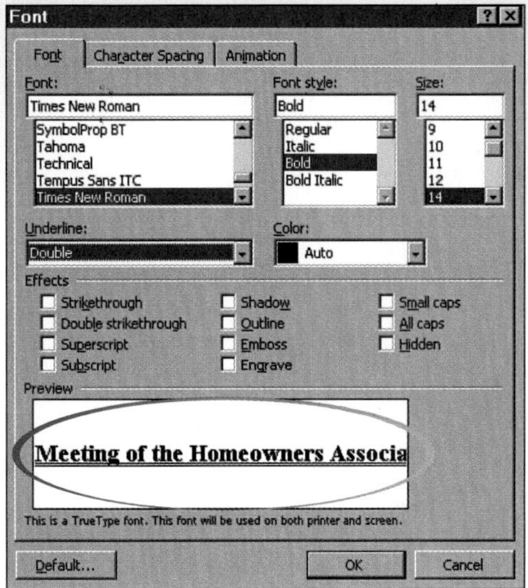

6 Exit the Dialog Box

When you've made your selections, choose **OK** to close the dialog box and apply the changes to the selected text.

End

How-To Hints

Toggle On or Off

The Bold, Italic, and Underline buttons on the Formatting toolbar toggle on or off. To remove the formatting, click the appropriate toolbar button again.

Keyboard Shortcuts

To format text from the keyboard, select the text, and then use these keyboard shortcuts: Ctrl+B for boldface, Ctrl+I for italic, Ctrl+U for underline, or Ctrl+Shift+D for double underline.

Add Color

To color text, click the down arrow on the **Color** list box in the Font dialog box to display the list of choices, and then click the color you want to use. You can also use the **Font Color** button on the Formatting toolbar; click the button's arrow and choose a color from the palette that appears.

TASK 2

How to Change the Font and Size

Changing fonts and sizes is an easy way to alter the appearance of words to change the appearance of the document. By default, Word assigns Times New Roman, 10 point every time you open a new document. But you can easily apply another font or size any time you want. You can change the font or size for one word, a paragraph, or the entire document.

Don't go overboard and use so many fonts and sizes that the document becomes excessively busy and difficult to read. Two or three fonts per document is usually enough.

Begin

1 Select the Text

Select the text whose font you want to change.

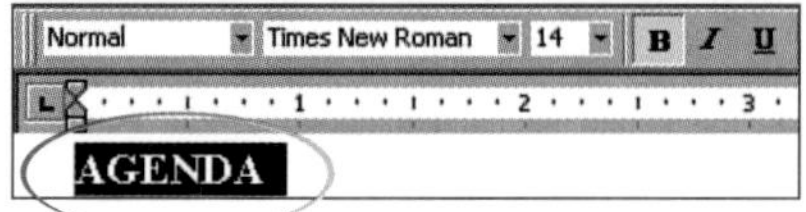

2 Choose a Font

On the Formatting toolbar, click the down arrow on the **Font** box to display a list of your installed fonts. Scroll through the list to find the font you want, and then click it to apply it to the selected text. (Word places the fonts you've used recently above a double line at the top of the list; below the double line is an alphabetical list of all the fonts.)

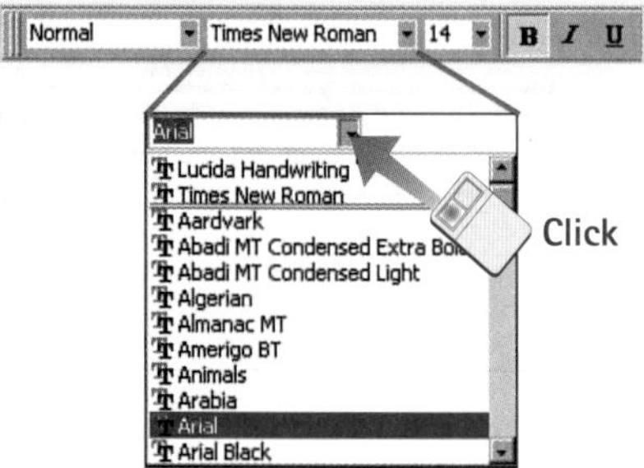

3 Choose a Size

After you have chosen a font, you can make it larger or smaller by changing the font size. On the Formatting toolbar, click the down arrow on the **Font Size** box to display the list of font sizes. Scroll, if necessary, to find the size you want, and then click it to apply it to the selected text. (You can also click in the **Font Size** box and type a point size that's not on the list.)

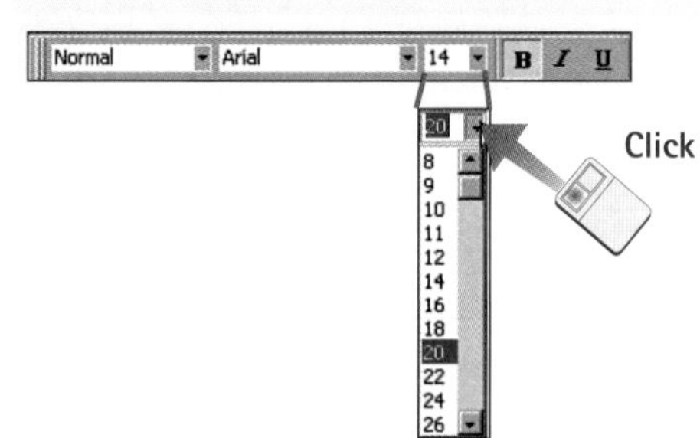

4 Open the Font Dialog Box

The quickest way to experiment with fonts, sizes, and other characteristics is to use the Font dialog box. Select the text you want to format, and then choose **Format, Font**.

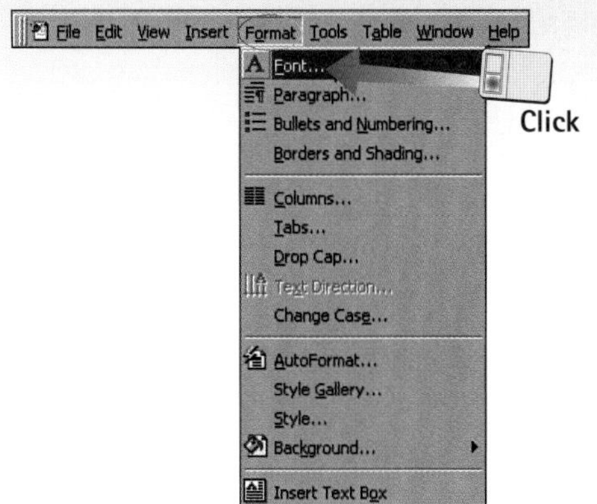

5 Choose a Font

Use the **Font** tab to change the font and size, and then check the results in the **Preview** area. Choose a font from the **Font** list, for example, to see what it looks like in the **Preview** area. Click **OK** to exit and apply the settings.

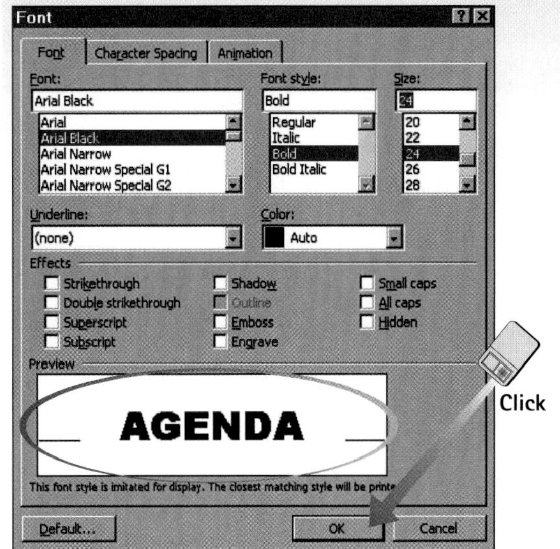

End

How-To Hints

Don't Like It?

If, after applying a new font or size, you decide you don't like it, click the **Undo** button on the Standard toolbar; the text will revert back to the previous font or size.

Different Fonts

The number and type of available fonts depend on what has been installed on your computer, but most computers have a wide selection of TrueType fonts. They're displayed in font lists with a TT symbol next to their names. The advantage of TrueType fonts is that they look the same onscreen as they do when printed.

What's Assigned?

The buttons and list boxes on the Formatting toolbar—for font, font size, style, and so on—always reflect the formatting at the current location of the insertion point. This comes in handy when you aren't sure which font is applied to a particular block of text. Just click in the text, and then look at the Formatting toolbar to see what characteristics are in effect.

TASK 3

How to Copy Text Formatting

If you have applied several character formats—such as a font, a font size, and a format (bold, italic, underline)—to a block of text in your document, and then later decide you would like to apply the same formatting to another block of text, you don't have to apply those formats one by one to the new location. Instead, you can use the Format Painter button to take all the formats from the original block of text and "paint" them across the new text.

Begin

1 Select the Text

Select the text that has the formatting you want to copy (characters, words, whole paragraphs, headings, and so on).

How to Change Fonts and Sizes

Changing fonts and sizes is a easy way to alter the appearance of words to change the look and feel of the document. By default, Word assigns Times New Roman, 10 point every time you open a new document. But you can easily apply another font or size any time you want. You can change the font or size for one word, a paragraph, or the entire document.

Don't go overboard and use too many fonts and sizes to the point that the document becomes excessively busy and difficult to read. Two, or at most three, fonts per document is usually enough.

How to Copy Text Formatting

If you've applied several different character formats—such as a font, a font size, and a format (bold, italic, underline)—to a block of text in your document, and then later decide you'd like to apply the same formatting to another block of text, you don't have to

2 Choose Format Painter

Click the **Format Painter** button in the Standard toolbar.

3 Mouse Pointer Changes

Your mouse pointer changes to a paintbrush pointer.

How to Change Fonts and Sizes

Changing fonts and sizes is a easy way to alter the appearance of words to change the look and feel of the document. By default, Word assigns Times New Roman, 10 point every time you open a new document. But you can easily apply another font or size any time you want. You can change the font or size for one word, a paragraph, or the entire document.

Don't go overboard and use too many fonts and sizes to the point that the document becomes excessively busy and difficult to read. Two, or at most three, fonts per document is usually enough.

How to Copy Text Formatting

If you've applied several different character formats—such as a font, a font size, and a format (bold, italic, underline)—to a block of text in your document, and then later decide you'd like to apply the same formatting to another block of text, you don't have to

4 Drag to Copy Formatting

Drag the paintbrush pointer across the text where you want to paint the format.

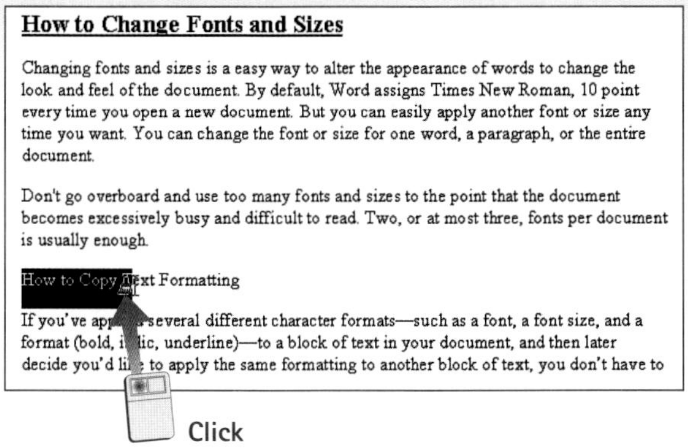

How to Change Fonts and Sizes

Changing fonts and sizes is a easy way to alter the appearance of words to change the look and feel of the document. By default, Word assigns Times New Roman, 10 point every time you open a new document. But you can easily apply another font or size any time you want. You can change the font or size for one word, a paragraph, or the entire document.

Don't go overboard and use too many fonts and sizes to the point that the document becomes excessively busy and difficult to read. Two, or at most three, fonts per document is usually enough.

How to Copy Text Formatting

If you've applied several different character formats—such as a font, a font size, and a format (bold, italic, underline)—to a block of text in your document, and then later decide you'd like to apply the same formatting to another block of text, you don't have to

Click Hold & Drag

5 Formatting Is Applied

Release the mouse. The formatting is painted to the block of text (click anywhere to deselect the text).

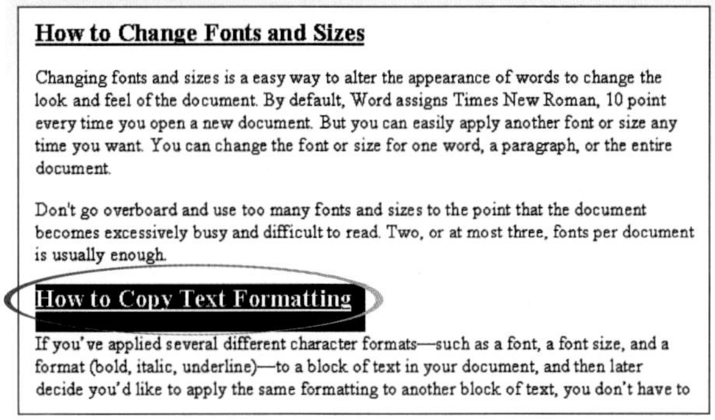

How to Change Fonts and Sizes

Changing fonts and sizes is a easy way to alter the appearance of words to change the look and feel of the document. By default, Word assigns Times New Roman, 10 point every time you open a new document. But you can easily apply another font or size any time you want. You can change the font or size for one word, a paragraph, or the entire document.

Don't go overboard and use too many fonts and sizes to the point that the document becomes excessively busy and difficult to read. Two, or at most three, fonts per document is usually enough.

How to Copy Text Formatting

If you've applied several different character formats—such as a font, a font size, and a format (bold, italic, underline)—to a block of text in your document, and then later decide you'd like to apply the same formatting to another block of text, you don't have to

End

How-To Hints

Keep Painting

To paint the same formatting to several blocks of text more quickly, double-click the **Format Painter** button. Format Painter remains turned on so you can paint the formatting repeatedly. For example, you could paint across all the headings in the document shown here. When you're finished painting the formatting, click the **Format Painter** button again to turn it off.

Another Route

Another way to copy formatting is to apply formatting to a selection with the Font dialog box (by using the Font dialog box, you can apply several formatting characteristics at once); then select a block of text where you want to copy the formatting, and choose **Edit**, **Repeat Font Formatting**. You can also press F4 or press Ctrl+Y to repeat an action.

Use AutoFormat

Don't like the pressures of coming up with formatting yourself? Use Word's AutoFormat feature to automatically format your documents. Open the **Format** menu and select **AutoFormat**. In the AutoFormat dialog box, select the type of document you're creating and click **OK**.

TASK 4

How to Use Styles

A *style* is a collection of formatting specifications that has been assigned a name and saved. You might have a report, for example, that uses specific formatting for every heading. Rather than reapply the formatting for every heading, assign the formatting to a style. You can then quickly apply the style whenever you need it. Word comes with a few pre-made styles, but you can easily create your own and use them over and over.

Begin

1 Format the Text

Format the text as desired. You can apply any of Word's formatting commands, including character, paragraph, and page formatting. Then select the text or click anywhere in the formatted text.

How to Change Fonts and Sizes

Changing fonts and sizes is a easy way to alter the appearance of words to change the look and feel of the document. By default, Word assigns Times New Roman, 10 point every time you open a new document. But you can easily apply another font or size any time you want. You can change the font or size for one word, a paragraph, or the entire document.
Don't go overboard and use too many fonts and sizes to the point that the document becomes excessively busy and difficult to read. Two, or at most three, fonts per document is usually enough.

How to Copy Text Formatting

If you've applied several different character formats—such as a font, a font size, and a format (bold, italic, underline)—to a block of text in your document, and then later decide you'd like to apply the same formatting to another block of text, you don't have to

2 Use the Style List Box

Click inside the **Style** list box on the Formatting toolbar.

3 Enter a Name

Type a name for the new style. Be careful not to use any of the existing style names. Press Enter when finished. The style is added to the list and ready to assign. For example, I assigned a new style called Paragraph Title.

4 Assign a Style

To assign a style to text, select the text first.

How to Change Fonts and Sizes

Changing fonts and sizes is a easy way to alter the appearance of words to change the look and feel of the document. By default, Word assigns Times New Roman, 10 point every time you open a new document. But you can easily apply another font or size any time you want. You can change the font or size for one word, a paragraph, or the entire document.
Don't go overboard and use too many fonts and sizes to the point that the document becomes excessively busy and difficult to read. Two, or at most three, fonts per document is usually enough.

How to Copy Text Formatting

If you've applied several different character formats—such as a font, a font size, and a format (bold, italic, underline)—to a block of text in your document, and then later decide you'd like to apply the same formatting to another block of text, you don't have to

5 Open the Style List

Click the **Style** drop-down arrow and select the style you want to apply.

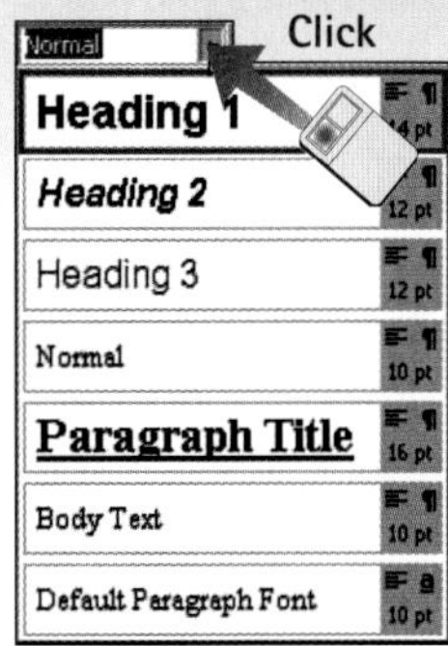

6 Formatting Is Applied

The style is immediately applied to the selected text. Continue applying the style to other text in your document as needed.

How to Change Fonts and Sizes

Changing fonts and sizes is a easy way to alter the appearance of words to change the look and feel of the document. By default, Word assigns Times New Roman, 10 point every time you open a new document. But you can easily apply another font or size any time you want. You can change the font or size for one word, a paragraph, or the entire document.
Don't go overboard and use too many fonts and sizes to the point that the document becomes excessively busy and difficult to read. Two, or at most three, fonts per document is usually enough.

How to Copy Text Formatting

If you've applied several different character formats—such as a font, a font size, and a format (bold, italic, underline)—to a block of text in your document, and then later decide you'd like to apply the same formatting to another block of text, you don't have to

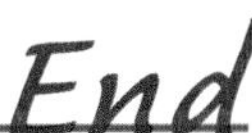

How-To Hints

Use the Style Dialog Box

Another way to assign styles is with the **Format**, **Style** command. Open the **Format** menu and select **Style** to display the Style dialog box where you can select, modify, add, or delete styles.

Add Style Shortcuts

You can assign keystroke combinations to styles to help speed up style assignment. Open the **Format** menu and select **Style**. Select the style you want to add a keyboard shortcut to, and then click the **Modify** button. Click the **Shortcut Key** button and assign a keystroke combination to the style in the **Press new shortcut key** text box. If the keystroke combination is already in use by another feature, the dialog box will tell you and you can try another. When you find one that's available, click **Assign** and exit the dialog boxes. Of course, now you have to remember what the shortcut key is to use the style.

TASK 5

How to Insert Symbols

Need to insert a special character or symbol not found on the keyboard? Tap into Word's collection of characters and symbols to find exactly what you're looking for. You can insert a copyright or trademark symbol, for example, into your text for products you mention. Depending on the fonts you have installed, you may have access to additional symbols, such as mathematical or Greek symbols, architectural symbols, and more.

Begin

1 Open the Symbol Dialog Box

Click the insertion point where you want the symbol inserted, and then open the **Insert** menu and select **Symbol**.

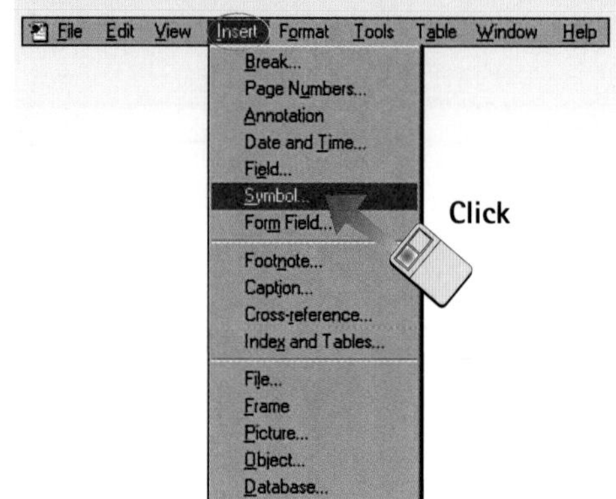

2 Choose a Symbol

From the **Symbols** tab, click a symbol to magnify it. Each symbol you click is magnified so you can see clearly what it looks like (for example, click the ® symbol).

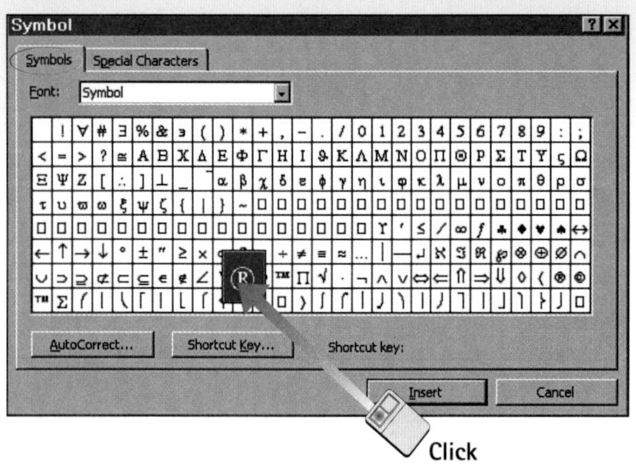

3 Insert the Symbol

After selecting the symbol you want to use, click the **Insert** button and the symbol is placed in your text.

4 Choose a Special Character

If you want a special character inserted, click the **Special Character** tab to view what's available.

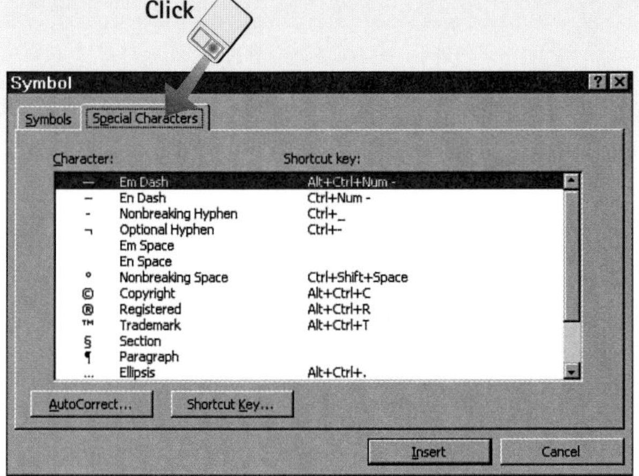

5 Insert the Special Character

Select the special character you want to insert, and then click the **Insert** button. The character is added to your text.

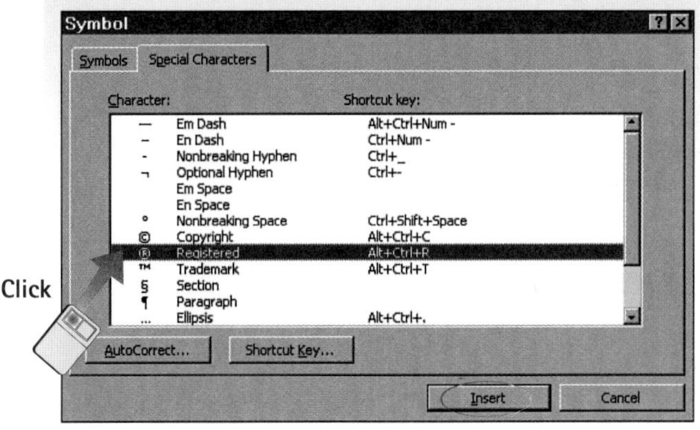

6 Close the Dialog Box

The Symbol dialog box remains open in case you want to add another symbol. Click the **Close** button to exit the dialog box.

Click

End

How-To Hints

Customize the Symbols

Use the **Font** drop-down list in the Symbol dialog box to change the font used. Use WingDings, for example, to insert character icons such as clocks and telephones. Be sure to check out the symbols available for the fonts you have installed on your computer.

TASK 6

How to Set Margins

The default margins in Word are 1 inch on the top and bottom of the page and 1.25 inches on the left and right. These margins are fine for most documents, but like all features in Word, they can be changed. Wider margins can give the page a more spacious appearance, for example. Or you may find you have just a line or two more than will fit on a page, but if you adjust the margins slightly, everything fits.

Begin

1 Open the Page Setup Dialog Box

Open the **File** menu and select **Page Setup**.

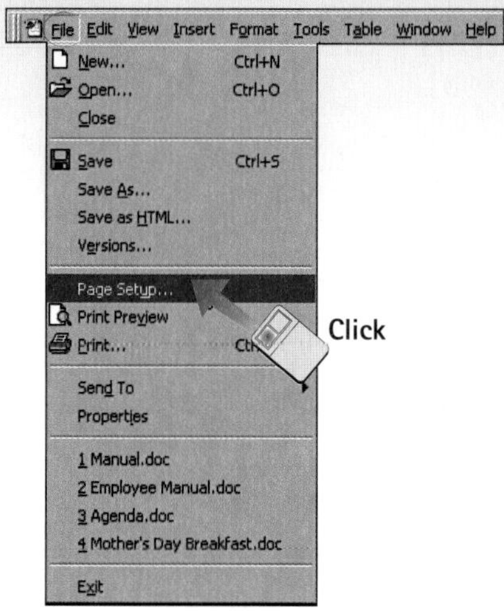

2 View the Margins Tab

In the Page Setup dialog box, click the **Margins** tab if it's not already displayed.

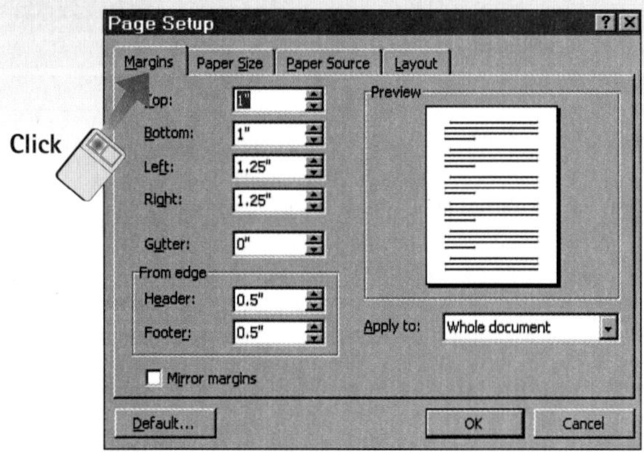

3 Change the Margins

Type new margin settings in **Top**, **Bottom**, **Left** and **Right** boxes; the settings are measured in inches. You can also use the spin arrows to set new measurements; click the up arrow to increase the measurement, click the down arrow to decrease the measurement.

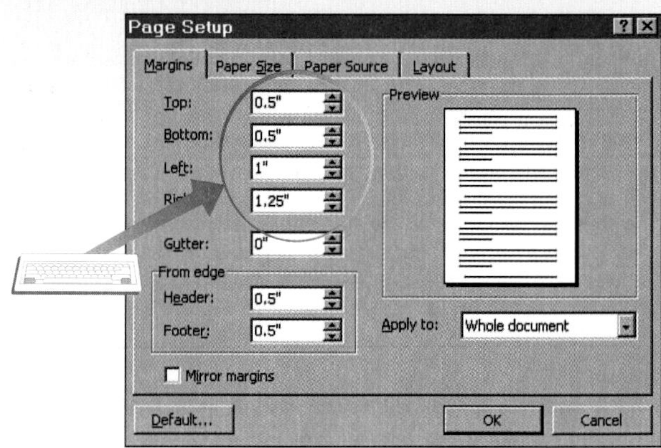

4 Apply the New Settings

Click **OK** to apply the new margins to your document.

5 View the New Margin Settings

On the Standard toolbar, click the **Print Preview** button to switch the document to print preview. In Print Preview you get a whole-page view of your document, and it's easier to check margin settings for a good visual appearance.

6 Change Margins Manually

Instead of setting inch measurements, you can change margins manually in either Print Preview or Page Layout view. The margins are displayed as gray bars at each end of the horizontal and vertical rulers; you can drag a margin to reset it.

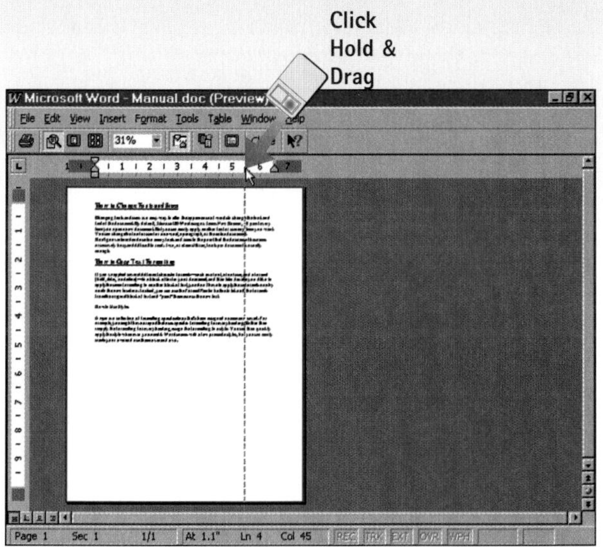

End

How-To Hints

Use Caution

Be careful about setting margins too narrow or wide—most printers have a minimum margin that's not printable (commonly, less than .25 inches is outside the printable area).

Change the Default Margins

If your company wants margin settings on all its documents that differ from Word's default margins, you can set the default margins to match those used in your company (then you won't have to change the margins each time you start a new document). To set new default margins, follow steps 1 through 3, but before you choose OK in step 4, click the **Default** button. When Word asks if you want to change the default settings for page setup, click **Yes**, and then choose **OK**. You can change the default margins as often as you like.

TASK 7

How to Set the Line Spacing

Line spacing is the amount of space between lines within a paragraph. By default, Word starts each new document with single spacing, which provides just enough space between lines so that letters don't overlap. You might want to switch to double-spacing for rough drafts of documents because it gives you extra room to add edits by hand. Or try one-and-a-half spacing, which makes text easier to read by separating lines with an extra half-line of blank space.

You can also control the amount of space between paragraphs. For example, documents with an extra half-line of space between paragraphs are easier to read, and you don't need to type an extra blank line between paragraphs.

Begin

1 Select the Paragraph

To change the line spacing of only one paragraph, click in the paragraph. To change the line spacing of several paragraphs, select them first. To change the line spacing for the entire document, press Ctrl+A to select the entire document.

How to Change Fonts and Sizes

Changing fonts and sizes is a easy way to alter the appearance of words to change the look a
feel of the document. By default, Microsoft® Word assigns Times New Roman, 10 point eve
time you open a new document. But you can easily apply another font or size any time you w
You can change the font or size for one word, a paragraph, or the entire document.
Don't go overboard and use too many fonts and sizes to the point that the document becomes
excessively busy and difficult to read. Two, or at most three, fonts per document is usually
enough.

How to Copy Text Formatting

2 Open the Paragraph Dialog Box

Open the **Format** menu and select **Paragraph** to display the Paragraph dialog box.

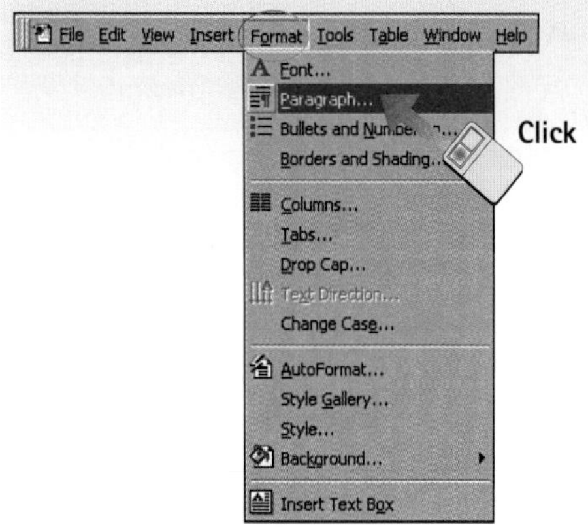

3 Choose a Line Spacing

At the top of the Paragraph dialog box, click the **Indents and Spacing** tab if it's not already in front. Then click the down arrow on the **Line spacing** list box. Select a line spacing: **Single**, **1.5 lines**, or **Double**.

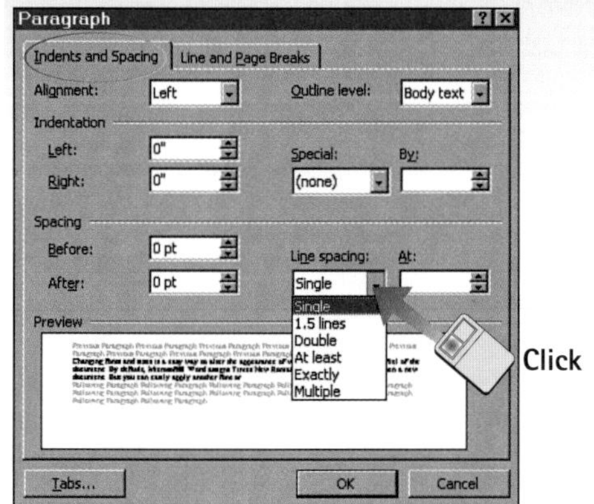

4 Change Paragraph Spacing

To change paragraph spacing for the selected text, designate a new setting in the **Before** and **After** boxes under **Spacing**. Use the spin arrows to set paragraph spacing in points, or type a setting. The **Before** box sets spacing at the top of the paragraph(s); the **After** box sets spacing at the bottom of the paragraph(s).

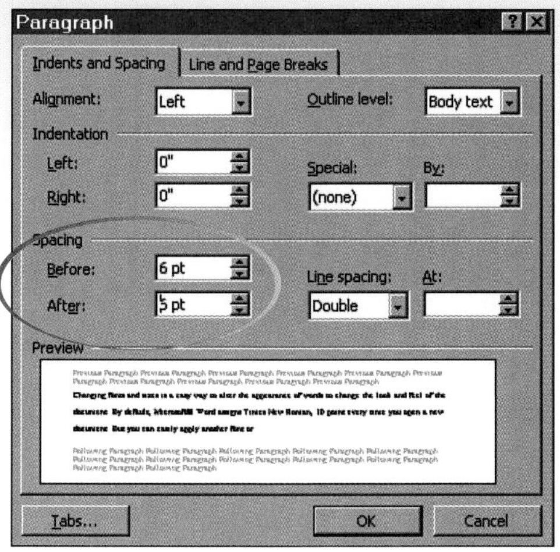

5 Exit the Dialog Box

Choose **OK** to close the dialog box.

Click

6 Apply Line Spacing

Any changes you made in the Paragraph dialog box are applied to the selected text.

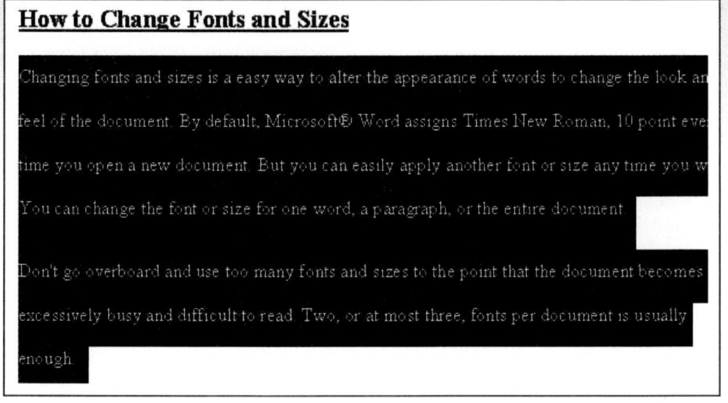

How to Change Fonts and Sizes

Changing fonts and sizes is a easy way to alter the appearance of words to change the look an feel of the document. By default, Microsoft® Word assigns Times New Roman, 10 point eve time you open a new document. But you can easily apply another font or size any time you w You can change the font or size for one word, a paragraph, or the entire document.

Don't go overboard and use too many fonts and sizes to the point that the document becomes excessively busy and difficult to read. Two, or at most three, fonts per document is usually enough.

End

How-To Hints

Preview First

When changing the settings in the Paragraph dialog box, check out the effects in the Preview area to see how similar effects will appear in your own text.

TASK 8

How to Align Text

Use Word's alignment commands to change the way your text is positioned horizontally on the document page. By default, Word automatically aligns your text with the left margin as you type. You can choose to align text to the right margin, center text between the left and right margins, or justify text so it aligns at both the left and right margins.

For example, if you're creating a title page for a report, you might want to center the title text. If you're creating a newsletter or columns of text, justify the text to create even alignments on both sides.

Begin

1 Select the Text

Select the text or paragraphs you want to align.

Centered Text
aligns in the center of the document

Right-aligned text
lines up at the right margin

Left-aligned text
lines up at the left margin

Justified text lines up at both the left and right margins. You can't justify a single word or sentence; justification works best with paragraphs. Use justified text when creating newsletters and brochures.

2 Use the Alignment Buttons

The alignment buttons on the Formatting toolbar will quickly align the text for you. Click **Align Left** to left-align text. Click **Center** to center text, click **Align Right** to right-align text. Click **Justify** to justify text between the left and right margins.

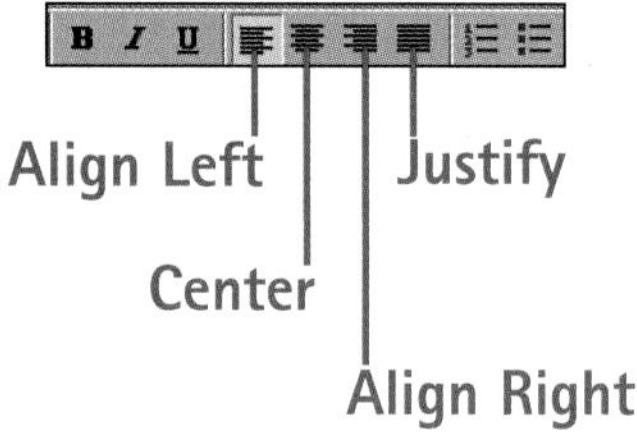

3 Word Aligns Your Text

Depending on what alignment button you chose, Word aligns your text accordingly. The figure below shows several alignment examples in effect.

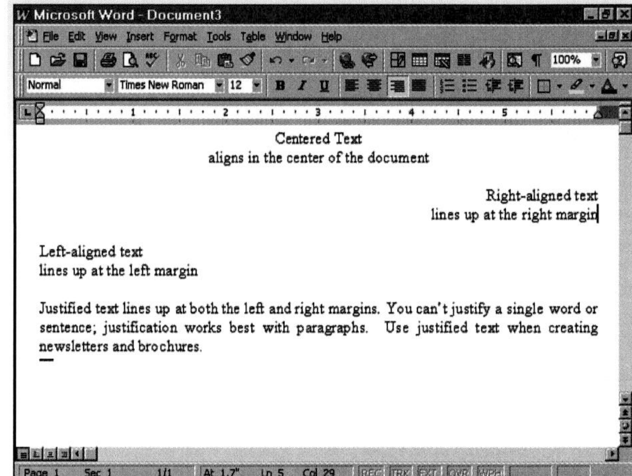

4 Use the Paragraph Dialog Box

Another way to apply alignment is with the Paragraph dialog box—one-stop shopping for Paragraph formatting commands. Open the **Format** menu and choose **Paragraph**.

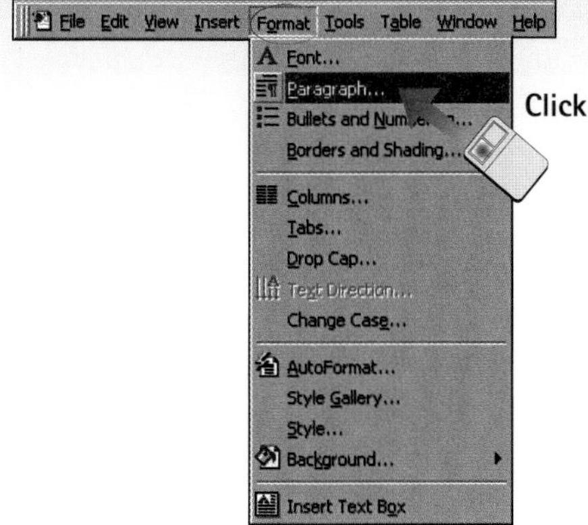

5 Choose an Alignment

In the **Indents and Spacing** tab, click the **Alignment** drop-down list and choose an alignment. Notice the **Preview** area gives you a glimpse at what the alignment will do to your text.

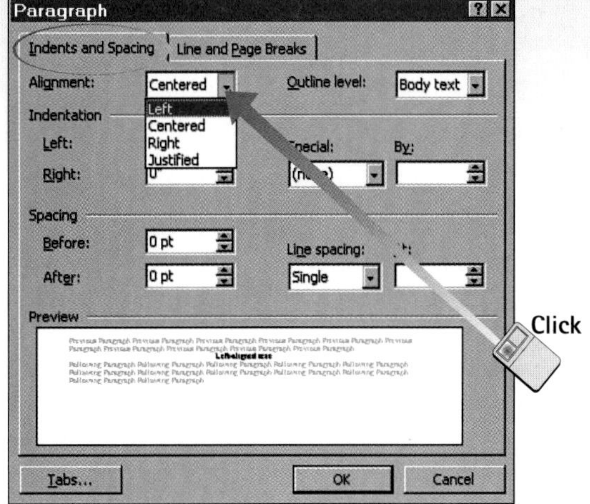

6 Exit the Dialog Box

Click **OK** to exit the dialog box and apply the settings to your document.

End

How-To Hints

Undo Alignment

To undo any alignment you assign, select the text again and choose a new alignment. Unlike Bold or Italic, the alignment buttons don't toggle on or off.

Keyboard Shortcuts

To center text using only the keyboard, press Ctrl+E. Press Ctrl+L for left alignment, Ctrl+R for right alignment, and Ctrl+J for justified alignment.

TASK 9

How to Indent Text

Indents are simply margins that affect individual paragraphs or lines. Indents can help make paragraphs easier to distinguish. The quickest way to indent a line of text is with the Tab key. However, other ways will indent text more precisely. You can set exact measurements for left and right indents, choose to indent only the first line of text, or create a hanging indent that leaves the first line intact, but indents the rest of the paragraph.

Begin

1 Use the Indent Buttons

For quick indents, use the Indent buttons on the Formatting toolbar. To increase the indent, click in front of the paragraph or sentence you want to indent, and then click the **Increase Indent** button. To decrease the indent, click **Decrease Indent**.

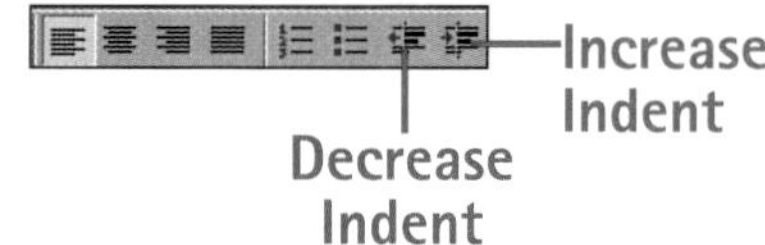

2 Use the Paragraph Dialog Box

For specific kinds of indents or to set an exact indent, open the Paragraph dialog box. Click in front of the paragraph or text you want to indent, and then display the **Format** menu and select **Paragraph**.

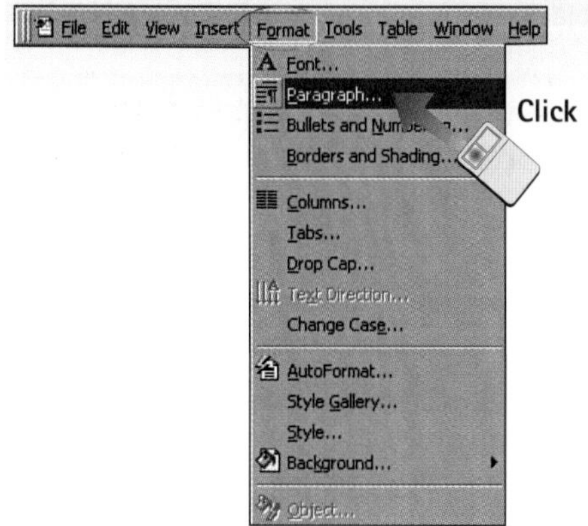

3 Set an Indent Measurement

From the **Indents and Spacing** tab, use the **Left** or **Right** indent boxes to set a specific measurement for the indent. You can type directly into the boxes, or use the spin arrows to increase the settings.

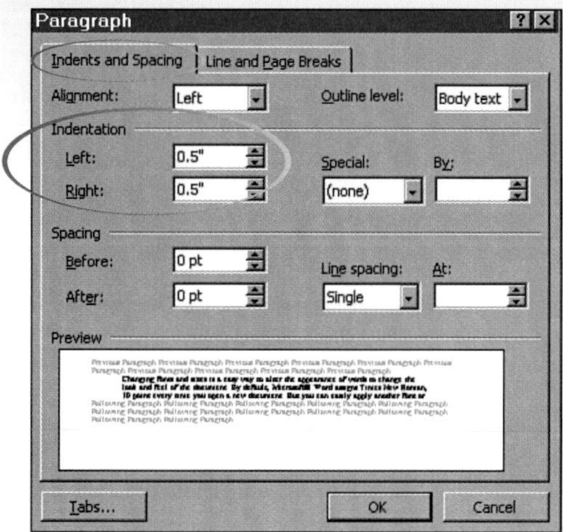

4 Set a Special Indent

To set a first line indent or a hanging indent, click the **Special** drop-down list and make a selection.

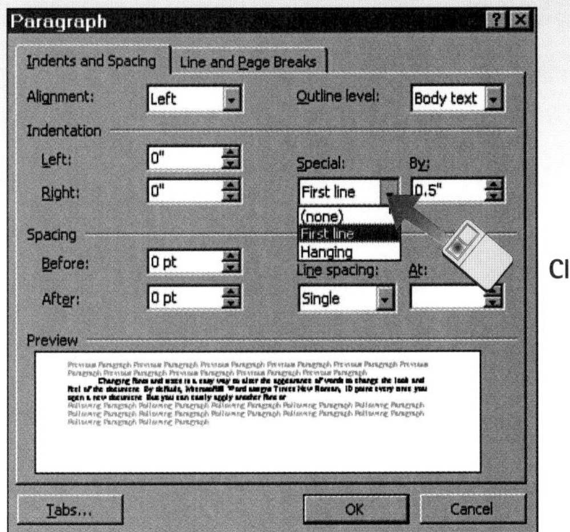

Click

5 Exit the Dialog Box

After setting the indent, check the **Preview** area to see how it will look. Click **OK** to exit the dialog box.

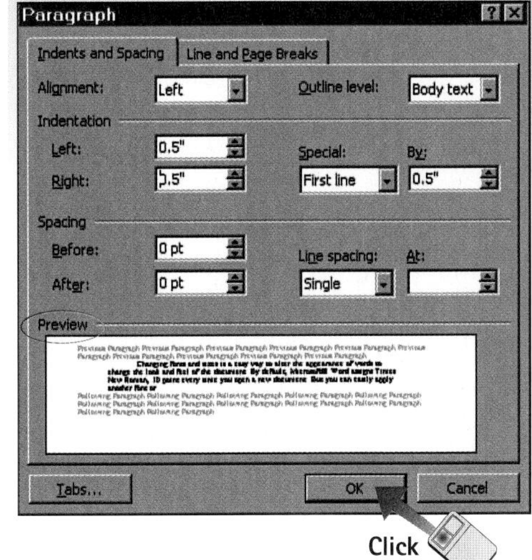

Click

6 Indents Applied

Word applies your indent specifications to the selected text. The figure below shows an example of a first-line indent and a hanging indent.

How to Change Fonts and Sizes

Changing fonts and sizes is a easy way to alter the appearance of words to change the look and feel of the document. By default, Microsoft® Word assigns Times New Roman, 10 point every time you open a new document. But you can easily apply another font or size any time you want. You can change the font or size for one word, a paragraph, or the entire document.

Don't go overboard and use too many fonts and sizes to the point that the document becomes excessively busy and difficult to read. Two, or at most three, fonts per document is usually enough.

How to Copy Text Formatting

If you've applied several different character formats—such as a font, a font size, and a format (bold, italic, underline)—to a block of text in your document, and then later decide you'd like apply the same formatting to another block of text, you don't have to apply those formats one one to the new location. Instead, you can use the Format Painter button to take all the formats

First Line Indent

Hanging Indent

End

How-To Hints

Another Quick Indent

For a quick indent while you're typing, press the Tab key. This indents your text line by 1/2", which is perfect for most paragraphs.

Other Indent Ideas

Use both a left and right indent to indent quotes or special text you want to set off in a document.

TASK 10

How to Work with Numbered and Bulleted Lists

Use Word's Bulleted and Numbered list features to set off lists of information in your documents. For example, a bulleted list can make a list of related information easy to spot on a page, and a numbered list organizes items that must be listed in a certain order.

You can start a bulleted or numbered list before typing in text, or you can turn existing text into an organized list.

Begin

1 Select Text

To turn existing text into a list, first select the text.

2 Use the Formatting Buttons

To add bullets, click the **Bullets** button on the Formatting toolbar. To turn the text into a numbered list, click the **Numbering** button.

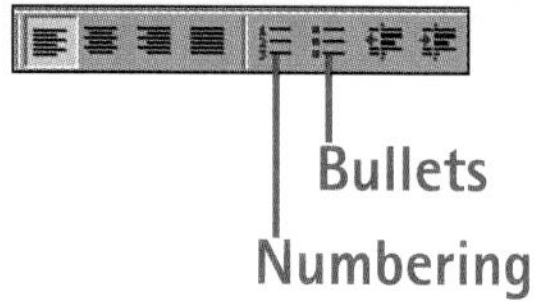

3 Bullets or Numbers Are Applied

If you selected Bullets, the text is immediately indented with bullet points in front of each line. If you selected Numbering, the list is numbered sequentially, as shown in the figure below.

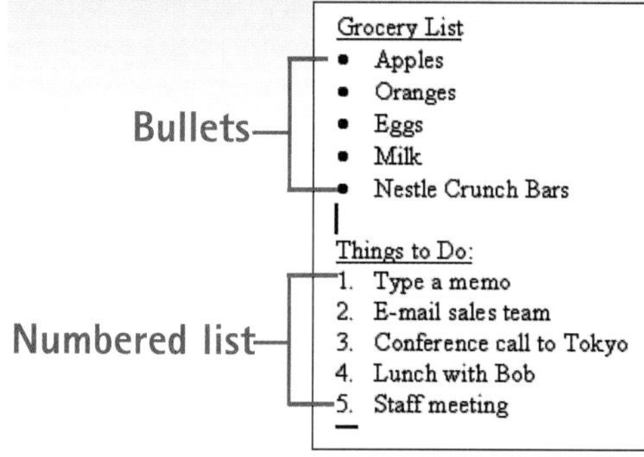

4 Add to the List

To add items to the list, click at the end of the last line and press Enter. Word inserts a new bullet or numbered step for you; just type the new text. After you type the last item, press Enter twice to turn the numbered or bulleted list off; or click the **Numbering** or **Bullets** button on the toolbar to turn the feature off.

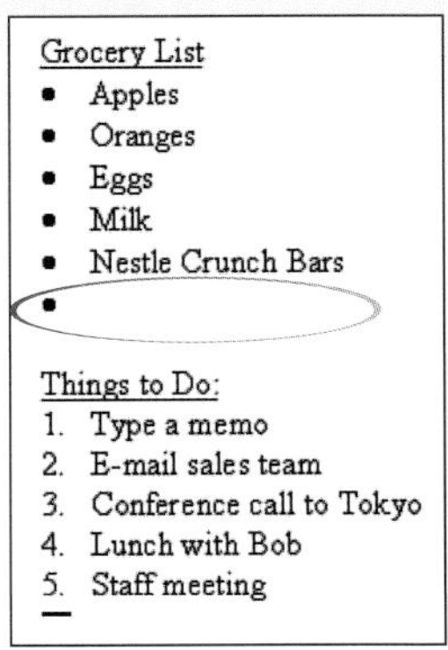

5 Change the Style

If you prefer to use a different bullet or numbering style in your list, open the Bullets and Numbering dialog box. Select the list text, and then open the **Format** menu and choose **Bullets and Numbering**.

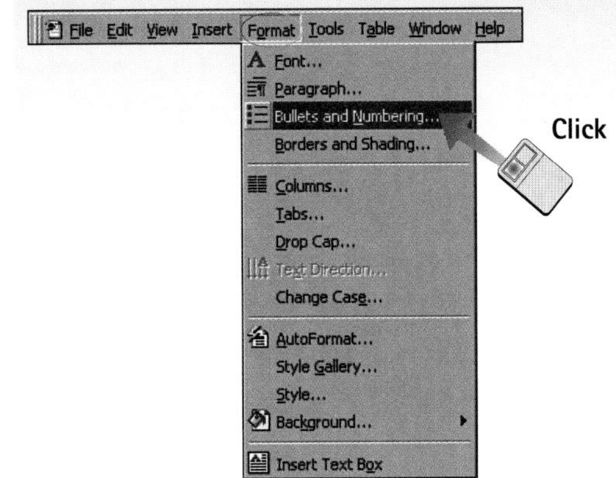

6 Bullets and Numbering Dialog

To change the bullet style, click the **Bulleted** tab and choose another style. To change the number style, click the **Numbered** tab and select another style. Click **OK** to exit the dialog box and apply the new style.

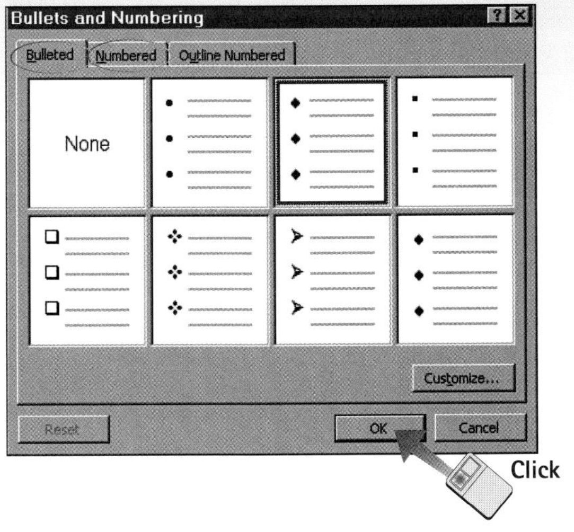

End

How-To Hints

Create the List from Scratch

You can also create a bulleted or numbered list as you type. For a numbered list, type **1.** followed by a space, and then type the text for the first item and press Enter. To create a bulleted list, type an asterisk (*) followed by a space, and then type the text for the first item and press Enter. Continue entering list items as needed. Press Enter twice after the last item to turn off the list feature.

Customize Bullets or Numbers

Use the **Customize** button in the Bullets and Numbering dialog box to set another font for the bullets or numbers you use, or customize the way in which they are positioned in the document.

TASK 11

How to Set Tabs

Tabs are used to indent and create vertically aligned columns of text. By default, Word has tab stops set at every .5-inch interval in your document; the tab text is always aligned at the left. You can create your own tab stops and change how the tab text is aligned at a tab stop. You can, for example, align tab text to the right, center, or to the decimal point. You can use the ruler to set tabs, or open the Tabs dialog box.

Begin

1 Set a Tab Stop on the Ruler

To set a tab stop on the ruler, first select the type of tab alignment. By default, the Left Tab alignment is selected. To select another, you must cycle through the selections. Each click on the alignment button displays a different tab alignment symbol (hover your mouse pointer over the button to display the tab alignment name).

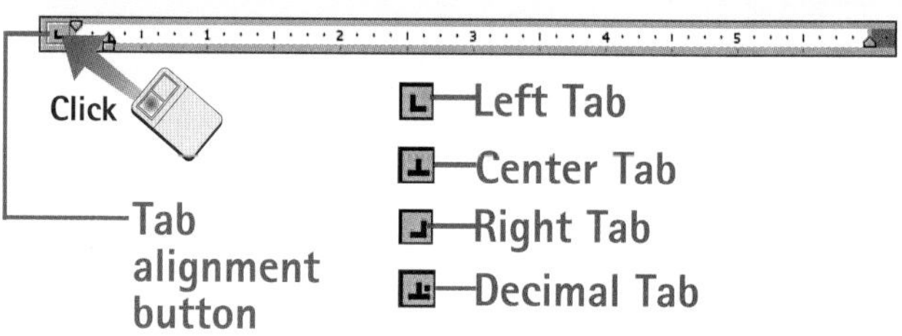

2 Click in Place

On the ruler, click where you want the tab inserted; the tab symbol is added to the ruler.

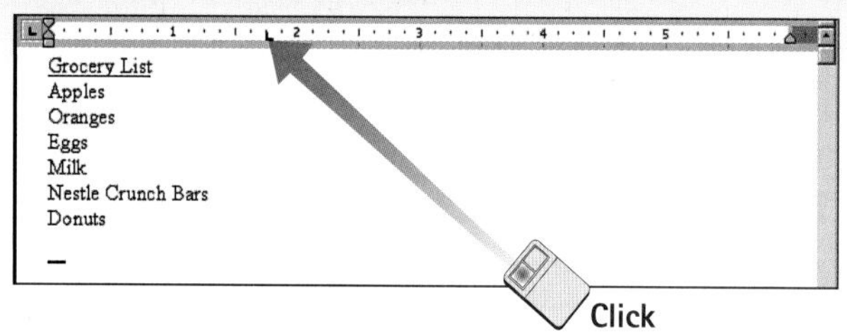

3 Apply a Tab

To use the new tab stop, place the cursor at the beginning of the line and press Tab, or place your cursor in front of the text you want to reposition and then press Tab. The tab is in effect until you change it to another setting.

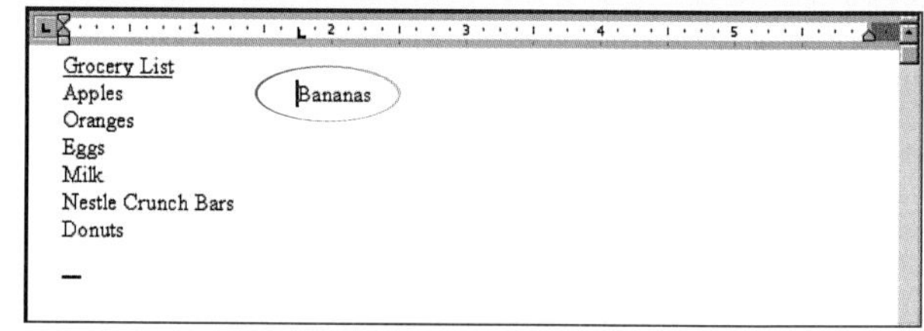

4 Open the Tabs Dialog Box

Another way to set tabs is to use the Tabs dialog box. Open the **Format** menu and choose **Tabs**.

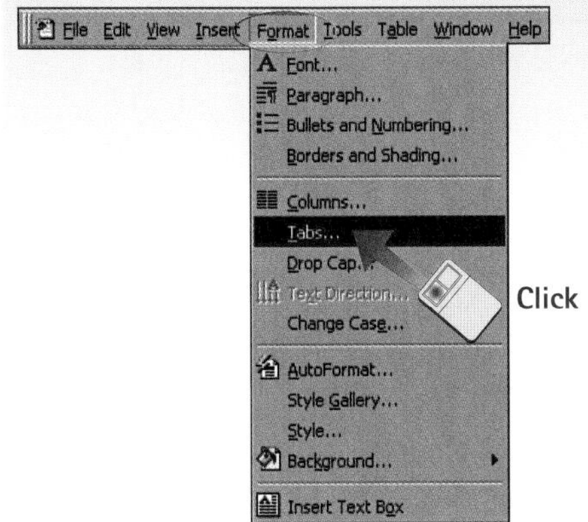

5 Enter a Tab Stop

In the **Tab stop position** text box, enter a new tab stop measurement. Use the **Alignment** options to change the tab stop alignment.

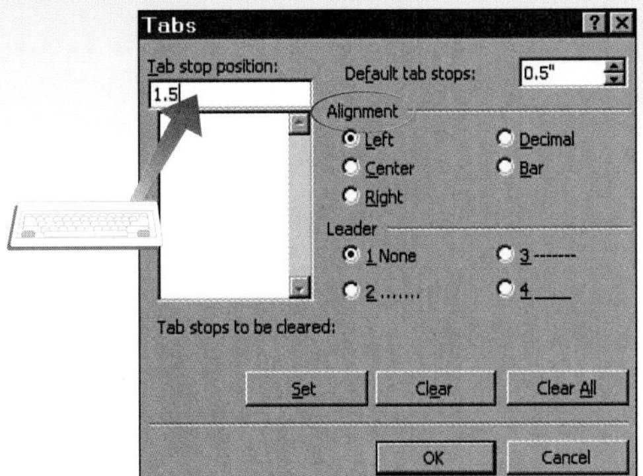

6 Exit the Dialog Box

Click **OK** to exit the dialog box. The new tab stop is ready to go.

End

How-To Hints

Delete Tabs

To delete a tab, drag it off the ruler, release the mouse button, and it's gone. To delete tabs from the Tabs dialog box, select the tab from the list box and click **Clear**.

Leader Tabs

Use the Tabs dialog box to set leader tabs (tabs are separated by dots or dashes) or bar tabs (vertical lines at tab stops).

TASK 12

How to Create Columns

If you're creating a newsletter or brochure with Word, consider formatting the text into columns, much like a newspaper or magazine. Word's columns are newspaper-style columns, which means the text flows to the bottom of a column and then continues at the top of the next column.

Begin

1 Select Text

Select the text you want to format into columns, then open the **Format** menu and choose **Columns**.

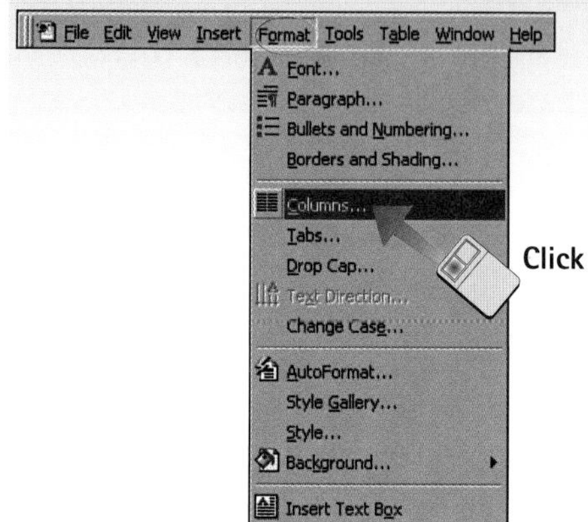

2 Select a Column Type

Under the **Presets** area, click the type of column style you want to use, such as **Two** or **Three**. Use the **Width and spacing** options to set an exact measurement for the columns and the space between them (or go with the default settings). The **Preview** area lets you see what the columns will look like.

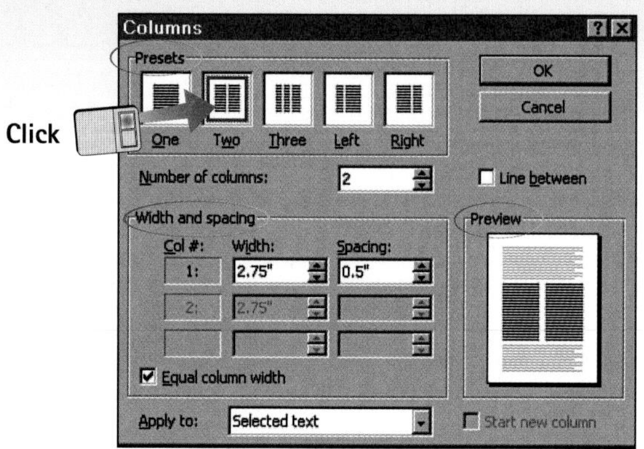

3 Apply To Area

To apply the column format to a specific area, click the **Apply to** drop-down arrow and choose the extent to which the columns apply in the document. For example, choose **Whole document** if you want the entire document to use columns.

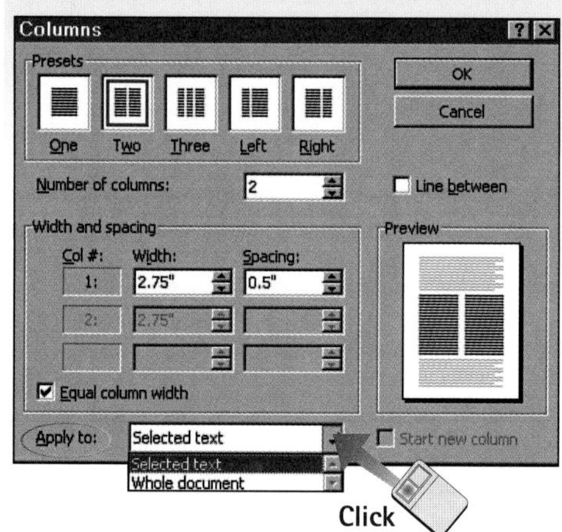

4 Exit the Dialog Box

Click **OK** to exit the dialog box and apply the column format to your text.

5 Quick Columns

Another way to set columns is with the Columns button on the Standard toolbar. Select the text you want to apply columns to, and then click the **Columns** button and drag the number of columns you want to use.

6 Column Format Applied

Release the mouse button and the columns are assigned.

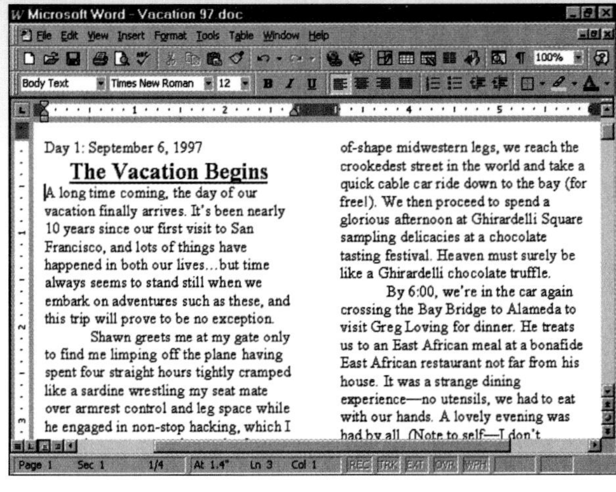

End

How-To Hints

Can't See Them?

You can only see columns in Page Layout view or in the Print Preview window. Click the **Page Layout View** button to switch views as needed.

Set Column Breaks

To make a break within a column and cause the text to flow to the next column, click where you want the break to occur, then press Ctrl+Shift+Enter. To remove a column break, select it and press Delete.

Turn Columns Off

To turn your column text back into normal text (which is really just one column anyway), select the text, click the **Columns** button on the Standard toolbar, and drag to select a single column.

TASK 13

How to Insert a Table

If you want to create a complex list or chart, the best option is to use a Word table. A *table* is a grid of rows and columns; each box in a table is called a *cell*. You can use tables to create anything from simple charts to invoices and employee lists. Tables are useful for any kind of information that needs to be organized in a row-and-column format. Tables are flexible; you can specify exactly the number of rows or columns, control the size and formatting of each cell, and include anything from text to graphics.

Begin

1 Create a Quick Table

To create a table the quick way, click in the document where you want to place the table, then click the **Insert Table** button on the Standard toolbar. A grid appears where you can tell Word how many columns and rows you want in the initial table; drag to select squares that represent cells in the table (for example, drag to select 3 columns by 4 rows).

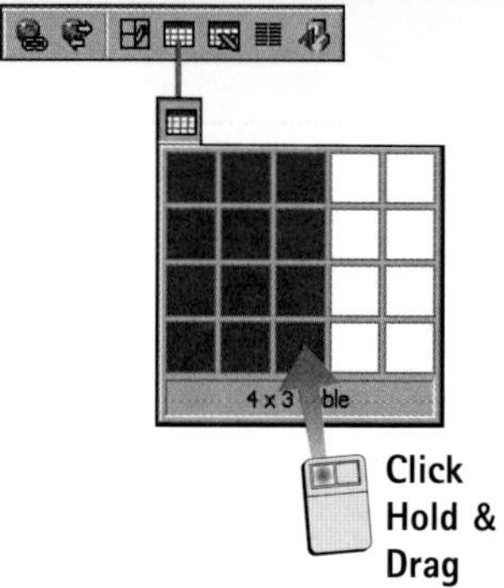

2 Instant Table

Release the mouse button, and a table with the number of rows and columns you selected appears on the page. The table stretches across the width of the page; to make a column narrower, point to a vertical border and drag it to a new position (drag the right table border to narrow the entire table).

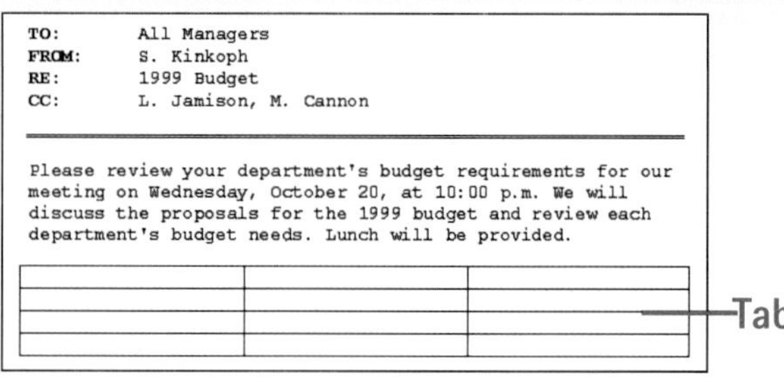

TO: All Managers
FROM: S. Kinkoph
RE: 1999 Budget
CC: L. Jamison, M. Cannon

Please review your department's budget requirements for our meeting on Wednesday, October 20, at 10:00 p.m. We will discuss the proposals for the 1999 budget and review each department's budget needs. Lunch will be provided.

3 Enter Table Text

Click in a cell and begin typing. The text in each cell behaves like a paragraph; if you press Enter, a new paragraph is started in the same cell. You can format the text in each cell the same way you format text in a normal paragraph.

TO: All Managers
FROM: S. Kinkoph
RE: 1999 Budget
CC: L. Jamison, M. Cannon

Please review your department's budget requirements for our meeting on Wednesday, October 20, at 10:00 p.m. We will discuss the proposals for the 1999 budget and review each department's budget needs. Lunch will be provided.

10:00	Department A	Tina Daniels
10:30	Department B	

4 Draw Your Own Table

To draw an asymmetrical table, cell by cell, click the **Tables and Borders** button on the Standard toolbar. The Tables and Borders toolbar appears, and the mouse pointer becomes a pencil.

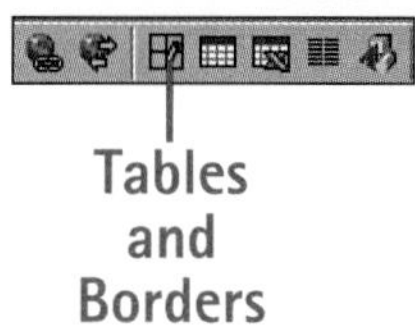

5 Choose Table Options

Click the **Draw Table** button if it isn't already selected, and then use the **Line Style**, **Line Weight**, and **Border Color** buttons to choose the type and color of line you want for the outside border of your table. Drag the mouse to draw a rectangle for the outside border of the table.

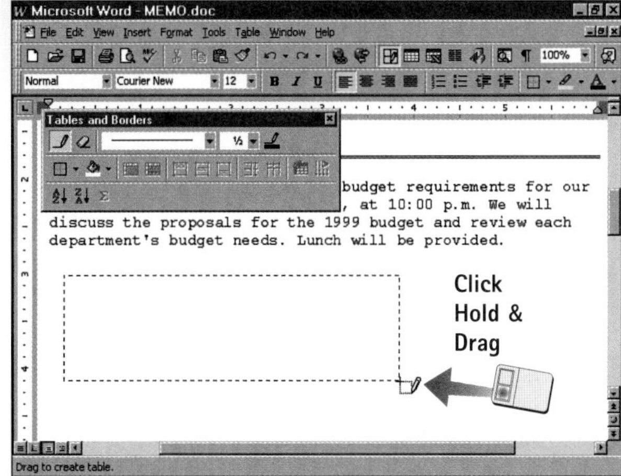

6 Draw the Table Lines

Select a different line type or color for the inside borders, if you want; then draw internal lines to delineate rows and columns. As you drag, a dashed line shows you where the line will be inserted. Release the mouse as the line extends across the entire width or height of the table. You can draw a table as complex as you want with this method.

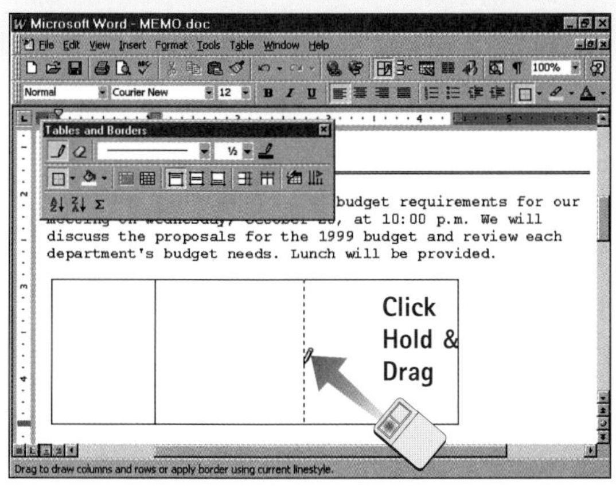

End

How-To Hints

Navigate a Table

Press Tab to move cell by cell to the right, and Shift+Tab to move cell by cell to the left. (To insert a tab character in a cell, press Ctrl+Tab.)

Add and Delete Rows

To insert a new row within a table, click in the row below where you want the new row inserted, then click the **Insert Rows** button on the Standard toolbar; or choose **Table**, **Insert Rows**. To delete a row, click in the row, then choose **Table**, **Select Row**; then choose **Table**, **Delete Rows**.

Format Gridlines

You can show your table's gridlines and format them with the Borders formats (see Task 15), or hide them. To hide gridlines, click in the table, then choose **Table**, **Hide Gridlines**; to show them again, click in the table and choose **Table**, **Show Gridlines**.

TASK 14

How to Add Borders and Shading

You don't have to know anything about graphics to add attractive borders and shading to headings, paragraphs of text, and tables. You can even create a decorative border around the entire page. This task shows you how to work with the options available in the Borders and Shading dialog box, but you can also issue most of the commands with the Tables and Borders toolbar (click the **Tables and Borders** button on the Standard toolbar).

Begin

1 Open Borders and Shading Dialog

Click anywhere within the paragraph (or table cell) to which you want to add borders and shading, or select adjacent paragraphs (or table cells) if you want to add borders and shading around the group of them. Choose **Format**, **Borders and Shading** to display the Borders and Shading dialog box.

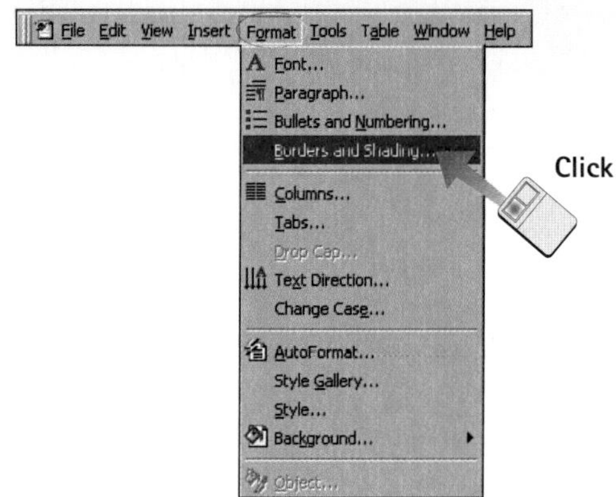

2 Apply a Border

Click the **Borders** tab if it isn't already in front. If you see an option under **Setting** that closely matches the type of border you want to add, click it.

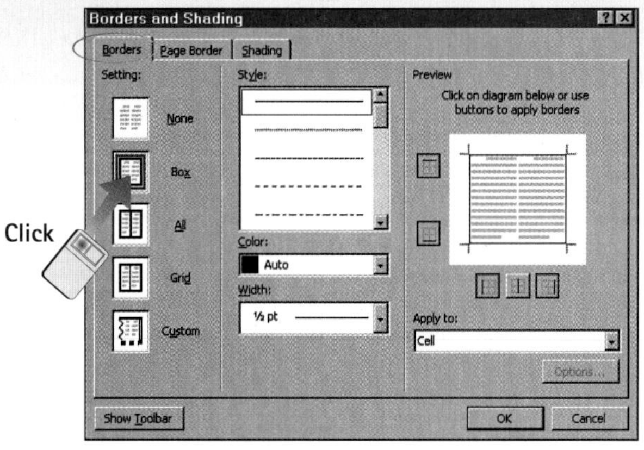

3 Select a Line Style

To customize the style of the lines in your border, scroll through the **Style** list, and click the desired style. You can also use the **Color** and **Width** drop-down lists to change the color and width of the lines.

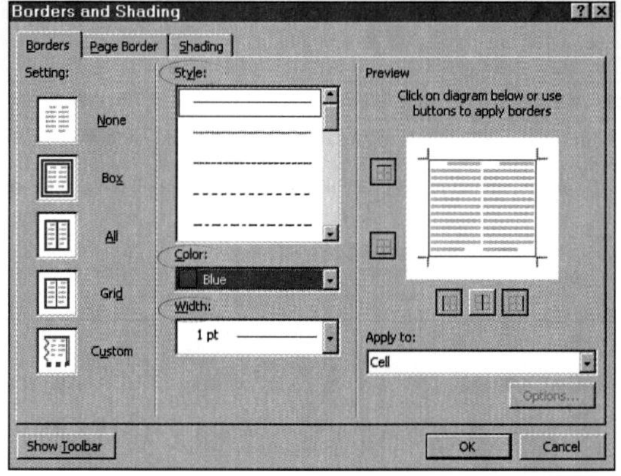

4 Add Shading

To add shading, click the **Shading** tab, and then click the color you want under **Fill**. When you have made all your selections in the Borders and Shading dialog box, choose **OK**.

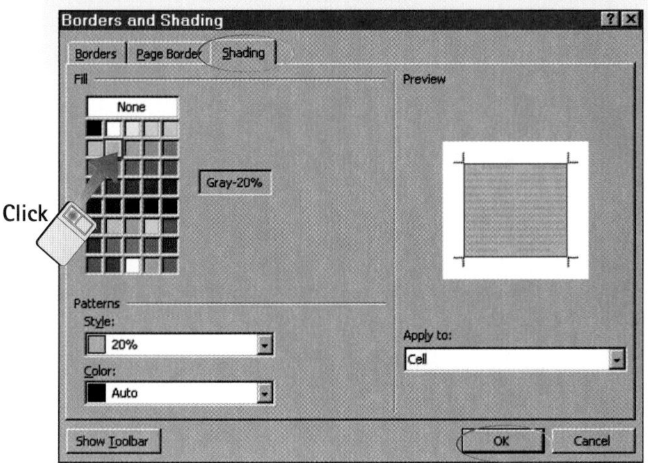

5 Resize the Border

To change the distance between the top and bottom borders and the text, point to the border you want to adjust, drag it up or down, and then release the mouse.

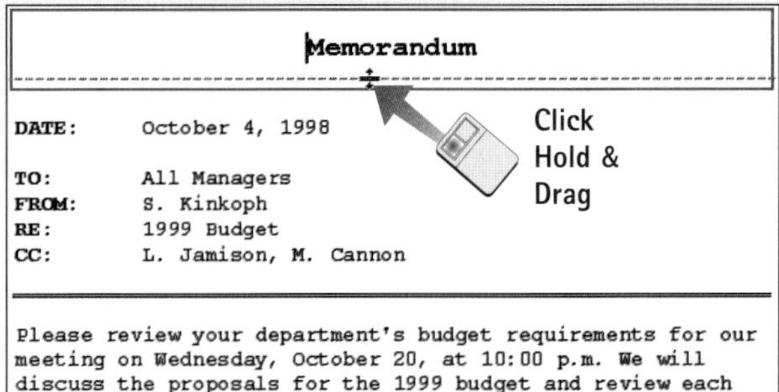

Memorandum

DATE: October 4, 1998

TO: All Managers
FROM: S. Kinkoph
RE: 1999 Budget
CC: L. Jamison, M. Cannon

Please review your department's budget requirements for our meeting on Wednesday, October 20, at 10:00 p.m. We will discuss the proposals for the 1999 budget and review each department's budget needs. Lunch will be provided.

6 Create a Page Border

To create a border around your page, click the **Page Border** tab in the Borders and Shading dialog box, specify the type of border you want, and choose **OK**. Word creates the border around every page in your document.

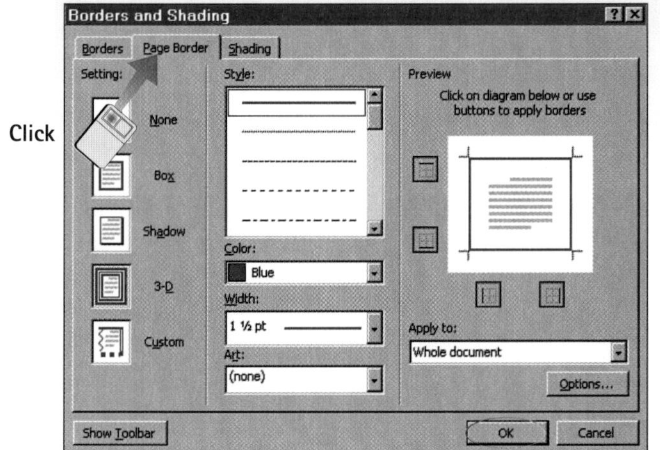

End

How-To Hints

Custom Borders

If you want to design a border from scratch, choose **Setting, Custom** in the Borders and Shading dialog box (on the **Borders** tab), select the desired style, color, and width options for one of the lines, and then click the line in the sample box under **Preview**. Repeat this process to create the remaining three lines.

Quick Borders

To quickly add a single-line horizontal border, click the line where you want the border to go, type - - - (three hyphens, no spaces) and press Enter. To create a double-line border, type === (three equal signs) and press Enter. To enable/disable this feature (it's turned on by default), choose **Tools, AutoCorrect**, click the **AutoFormat As You Type** tab, mark or clear the **Borders** check box, and choose **OK**.

TASK 15

How to Use Headers and Footers

A *header* is text that appears at the top of every page, and a *footer* is text that appears at the bottom of every page. You might want to use headers and footers to display the document title, your name, the name of your organization, and so on. You can also insert *fields* in headers and footers—a field is a holding place for information that Word updates automatically, such as the current date.

Begin

1 Open the Header and Footer

To add a header and/or a footer to a document, choose **View, Header and Footer**.

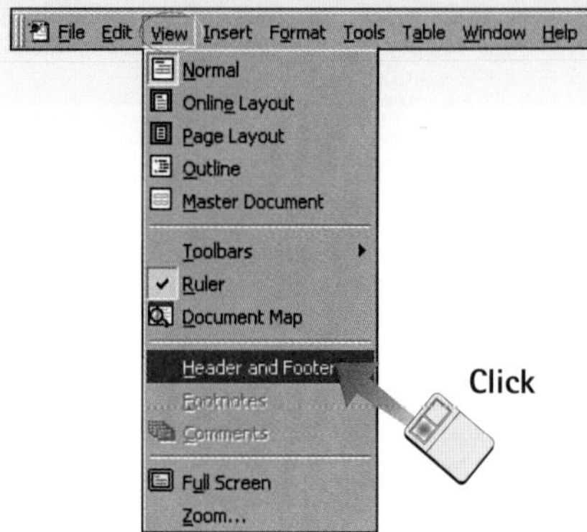

2 Enter Header Text

Word switches to Page Layout view, places the insertion point in the header area, and displays the Header and Footer toolbar. You type and format text in a header or footer just like normal text. By default, Word places the cursor in the header section. Type any header text.

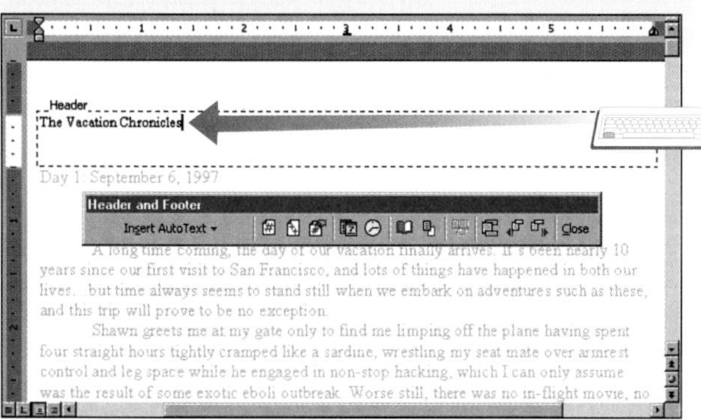

3 Enter Footer Text

To create a footer, click the **Switch Between Header and Footer** button on the Header and Footer toolbar to place the insertion point in the footer area. You can switch between the header and footer by clicking this button.

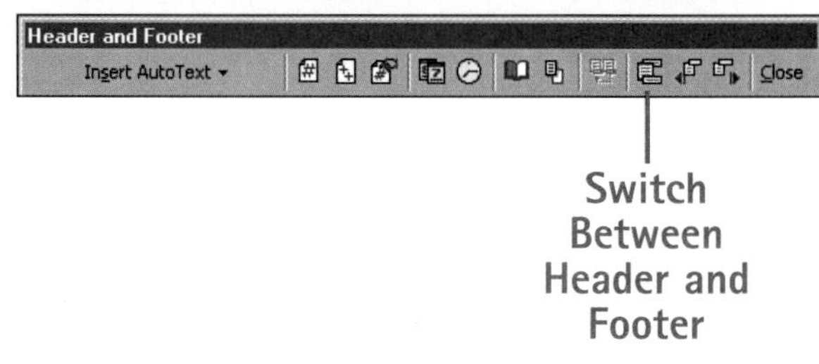

4 Insert Fields

You can select built-in header and footer entries from the AutoText button on the Header and Footer toolbar. For example, click the **Date** button to insert a field for the current date. Click the **Time** button to insert the current time.

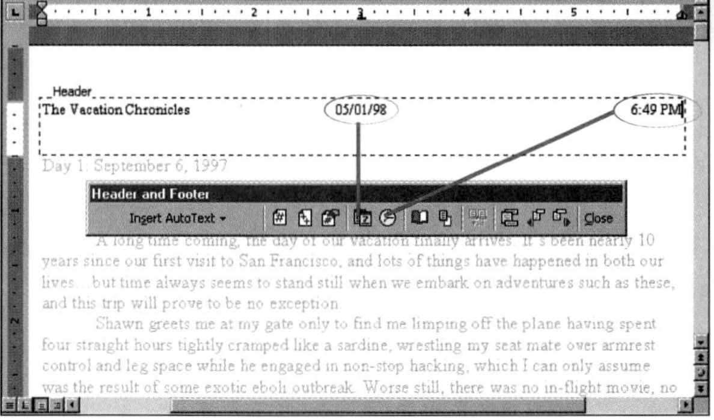

5 Close Header and Footer

Click the **Close** button in the Header and Footer toolbar to return to the body of the document.

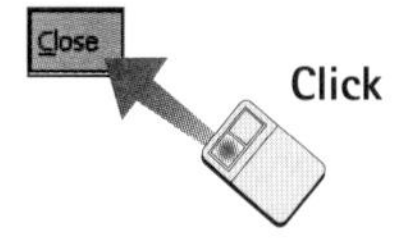

6 View Headers and Footers

Headers and footers aren't visible in Normal view, but you can see them in both Page Layout view and in Print Preview.

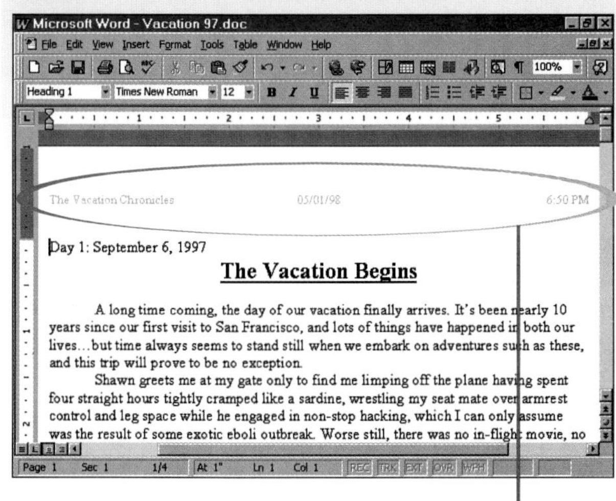

End

How-To Hints

How Do I Switch?

After you've created a header or footer, you can switch to the header or footer area from within Page Layout view by double-clicking the pale-gray header or footer text. Switch back to the body text by double-clicking the pale-gray body text.

Odd or Even Pages?

If you want different headers or footers on odd and even pages of your document (which is common for documents that are bound), choose **File**, **Page Setup**, and click the **Layout** tab; mark the **Different Odd and Even** check box, and choose **OK**. You can use the **Show Next** and **Show Previous** buttons in the Header and Footer toolbar to switch between the headers and footers for odd and even pages.

TASK 16

How to Work with Drop Caps and Text Case

In some documents you create, you may want the first letter of the first word in a paragraph to stand out—perhaps larger than the rest or in a different font. Use Word's Drop Cap command to format the letter.

In other documents, you may decide you need to use all capital letters, or turn an all-caps title into upper- and lowercase letters. Use Word's Change Case command to change the text case exactly as you want it.

Begin

1 Select the Text

Select the letter you want to change to a drop cap character.

The Vacation Begins

A long time coming, the day of our vacation finally arrives. It's been nearly 10 years since our first visit to San Francisco, and lots of things have happened in both our lives...but time always seems to stand still when we embark on adventures such as these, and this trip will prove to be no exception.

Shawn greets me at my gate only to find me limping off the plane having spent four straight hours tightly cramped like a sardine, wrestling my seat mate over armrest control and leg space while he engaged in non-stop hacking, which I can only assume was the result of some exotic eboli outbreak. Worse still, there was no in-flight movie, no

2 Open the Drop Cap Dialog Box

Open the **Format** menu and select **Drop Cap** to display the Drop Cap dialog box.

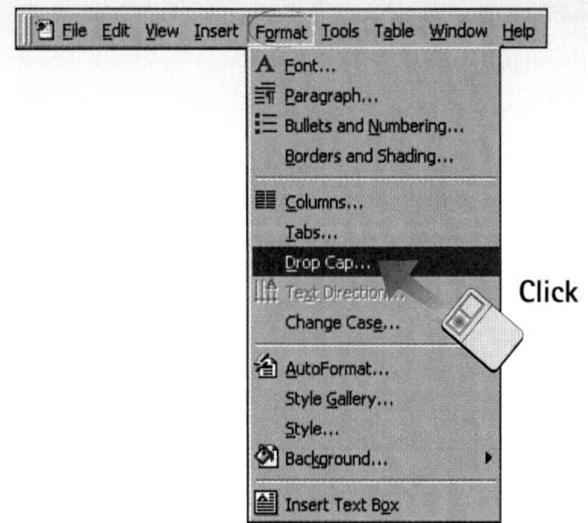

3 Choose a Drop Cap

Choose a position for the drop cap: **Dropped** or **In Margin**. Then assign any formatting, such as a new font or size.

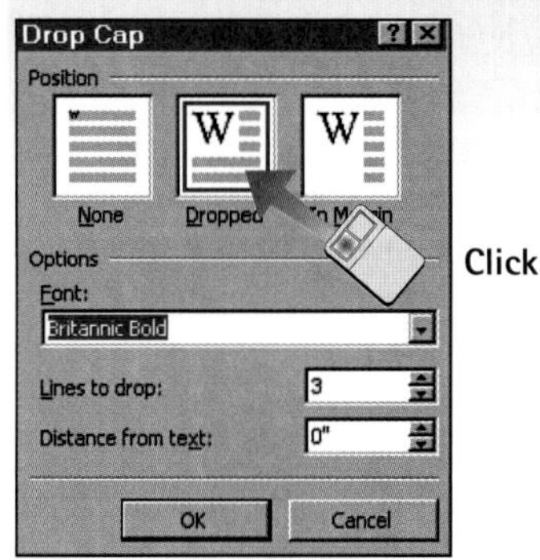

4 Apply the Settings

Click **OK** to exit the dialog box and apply the new settings.

The Vacation Begins

A long time coming, the day of our vacation finally arrives. It's been nearly 10 years since our first visit to San Francisco, and lots of things have happened in both our lives...but time always seems to stand still when we embark on adventures such as these, and this trip will prove to be no exception.

Shawn greets me at my gate only to find me limping off the plane having spent four straight hours tightly cramped like a sardine, wrestling my seat mate over armrest control and leg space while he engaged in non-stop hacking, which I can only assume was the result of some exotic eboli outbreak. Worse still, there was no in-flight movie, no

5 Change Text Case

Select the text whose case you want to change, and then open the **Format** menu and choose **Change Case** to display the Change Case dialog box.

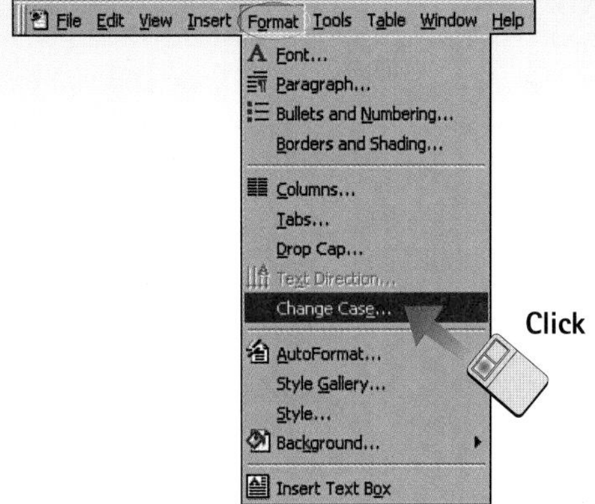

6 Select a Case Option

Choose a case option from those available. To make lowercase letters all caps, for example, click the **UPPERCASE** option. To make capital letters all lowercase, choose **lowercase**. Click **OK** to exit and apply the new case.

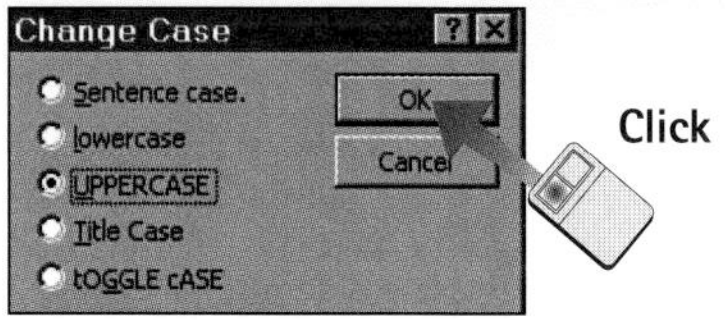

End

How-To Hints

Which Is Which?

The way the options are written in the Change Case dialog box shows how the text case will appear. For example, the Sentence case option capitalizes the S in sentence and ends the phrase with a period. The lowercase option is written in all lowercase letters.

Task

CHAPTER 5

How to Use Word's Proofing and Printing Tools

After you have created and formatted a Word document, you're ready to print it out or distribute it to others. Before you do, you need to proof it and make sure everything is in order. Word has several proofing tools you can use to make sure your documents are accurate and readable.

You can use the Spelling and Grammar check to go over your document and locate any spelling and grammar problems. Word's AutoCorrect feature helps you proof your document as you type. Use the Find and Replace tools to quickly locate text in your document and correct it as needed. When you finally have the document the way you want it, use the Print command to create a hard copy of the file. Printing is a common feature for all the Office programs, so you will find specific instructions for printing in Chapter 2, "How to Use Common Office Features." But some of your documents may require different printing needs. In this chapter, you will learn how to change the paper size and print envelopes and labels.

TASK 1

How to Find and Replace Text

When you need to search your document for a particular word or phrase, don't bother scrolling and reading; use Word's Find command. If you need to locate and replace every occurrence of a word, use the Replace command. If you misspelled a client's name throughout a report, for example, you can quickly fix the mistake using Find and Replace.

Begin

1 Find a Word or Phrase

To perform a quick search of your document for a particular word or phrase, open the **Edit** menu and select **Find**. This opens the Find and Replace dialog box with the **Find** tab displayed.

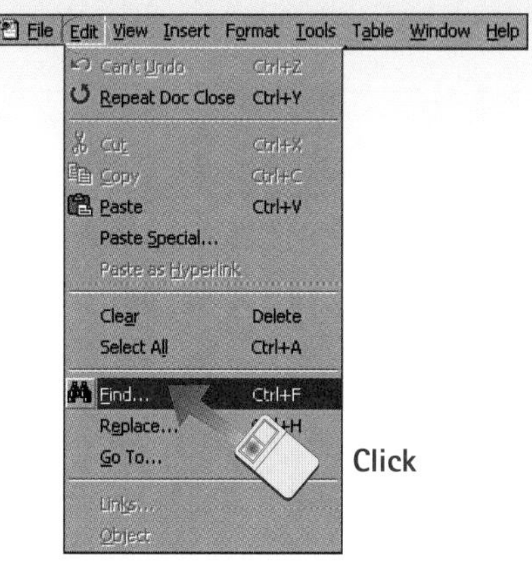

2 Enter the Text

Enter the text you want to search for in the **Find what** text box (for example, type **`Palace`**). If you want to specify search criteria, such as matching case or finding whole words only, click the **More** button to reveal search options you can choose.

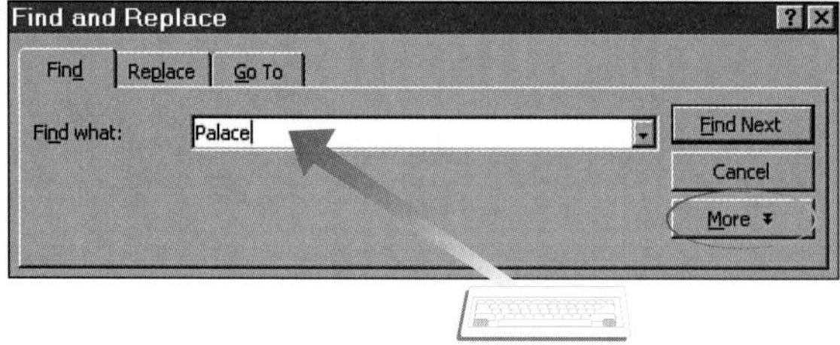

3 Conduct the Search

Click the **Find Next** button to locate the first occurrence of the word or phrase. Word highlights the text in your document, and the Find and Replace dialog box remains open on your screen. To search for the next occurrence, click **Find Next** again, or click **Cancel** to close the dialog box.

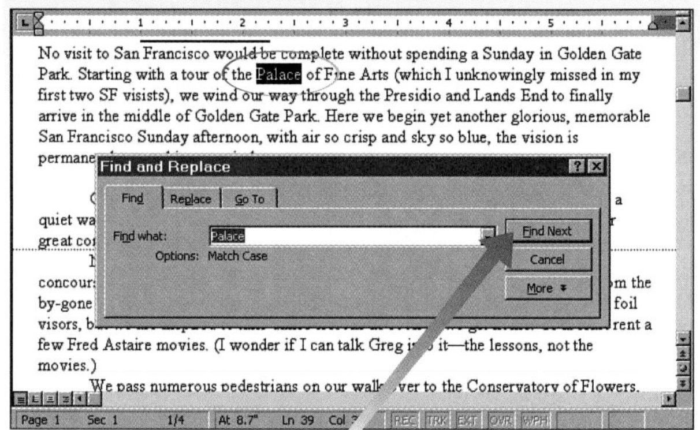

4 Find and Replace Text

To find the text and replace it with new text, use the Replace command. Open the **Edit** menu and select **Replace**. This opens the Find and Replace dialog box with the **Replace** tab up front.

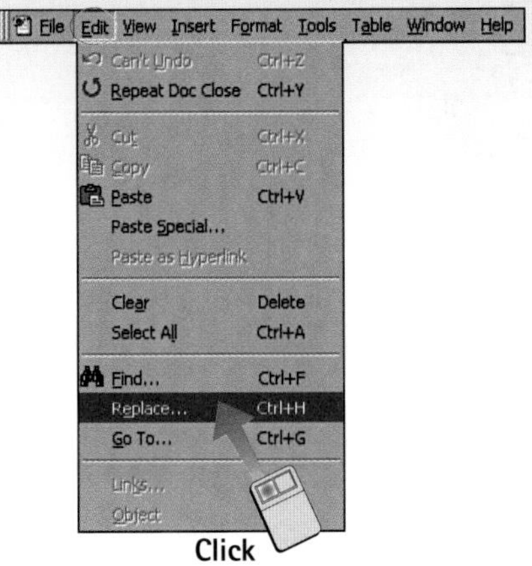

5 Enter the Text

Type the word or words you're looking for in the **Find what** text box (such as **`trip`**). Type the replacement text in the **Replace with** text box (such as **`journey`**). (If you want to specify any search criteria, click the **More** button and select from the available options.)

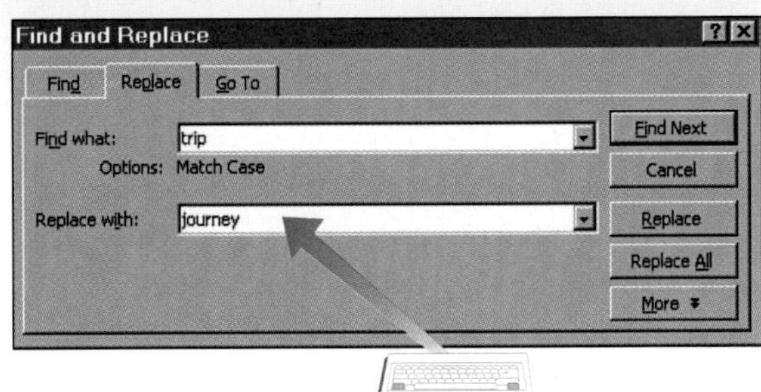

6 Search and Replace

Click the **Find Next** button to locate the first occurrence. Word highlights the text in the document. Click the **Replace** button to replace the text with the new text. Click **Replace All** to replace every occurrence in the document. Click **Find Next** to ignore the first occurrence and move on to the next.

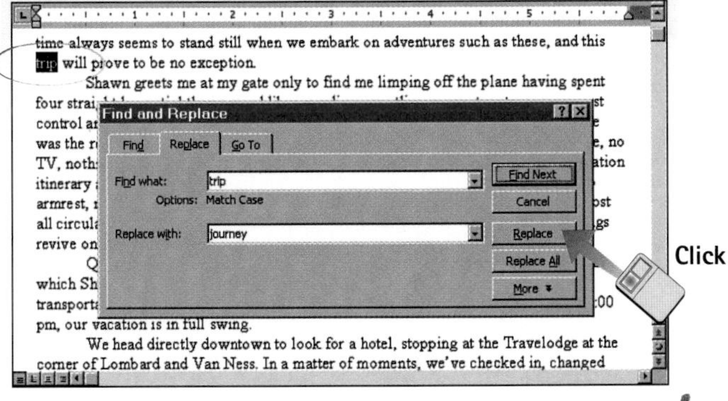

End

How-To Hints

Search Complete

When Word completes a search, it displays a prompt box telling you the search is complete. Click **OK**. If the search didn't reveal any occurrences of the text, a prompt box alerts you; click **OK** and try another search.

Search and Delete

Use the Find and Replace tools to delete text from your document. Open the Find and Replace dialog box, enter the word you're looking for in the **Find what** text box, but leave the **Replace with** box empty. Word will search and delete the text from your document without replacing it with new text. Don't forget to delete the extra space in front of the word, or you will end up with double spaces!

TASK 2

How to Check Your Spelling and Grammar

The Spelling and Grammar Checker enables you to check the spelling and grammar of an entire document as you type, or all at once. Because most of us tend to forget about running the Spelling Checker when we finish typing, the Automatic Spelling Checker can save errors by pointing them out (with red wavy underlines) as we type and making them difficult to ignore.

If Automatic Spelling Checker isn't on, choose **Tools, Options**, and click the **Spelling and Grammar** tab. Click the **Check spelling as you type** check box to turn it on (click the **Check grammar as you type** check box if you want to turn on Automatic Grammar Checking).

Begin

1 A Red Wavy Line

When you type, any word that Word can't find in its dictionary gets a red wavy line under it to tell you it may be misspelled (in this figure, for example, Word points out "**eboli**" as a possible misspelling).

A long time coming, the day of our vacation finally arrives. It's been nearly 10 years since our first visit to San Francisco, and lots of things have happened in both our lives…but time always seems to stand still when we embark on adventures such as these, and this trip will prove to be no exception.

Shawn greets me at my gate only to find me limping off the plane having spent four straight hours tightly cramped like a sardine, wrestling my seat mate over armrest control and leg space while he engaged in non-stop hacking, which I can only assume was the result of some exotic eboli outbreak. Worse still, there was no in-flight movie, no TV, nothing. Wisely, I spent the time studying my travel books planning out our vacation itinerary and making sure my seat mate couldn't get a clear look out my window. No armrest, no view out the window—that's the rule. The downside, however, is that I lost all circulation in my limbs and posterior during the agonizing flight. Thankfully, things revive on their own without any ugly side-effects.

Quickly, we make our way to a shuttle and eventually to our generic rental car,

2 Display the Shortcut Menu

Right-click the word to open a shortcut menu displaying possible alternative spellings. To choose an alternative, click it. If your spelling is correct (for example, someone's last name), click **Add**; the word is added to Word's dictionary and won't be picked up by the Spelling Checker again.

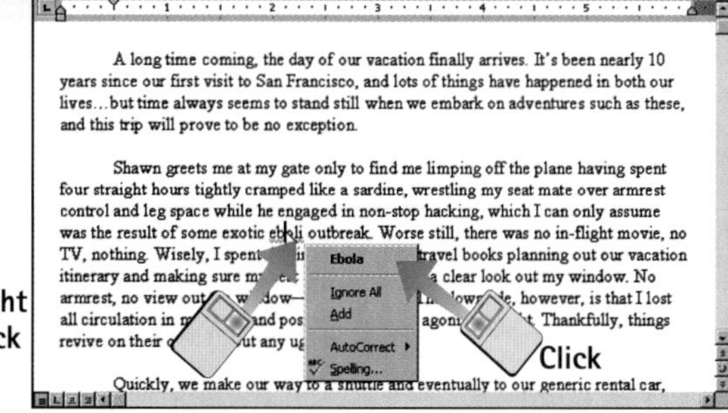

3 Ignore the Spelling

To leave the word spelled as is in the current document, click **Ignore All** from the shortcut menu. To add the correct spelling to your AutoCorrect list, click **AutoCorrect** (see Task 3, "How to Work with AutoCorrect," to learn about AutoCorrect).

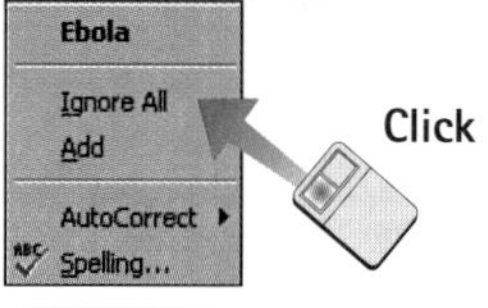

4 A Green Wavy Line

If the wavy underline is green, Word detects a possible grammatical error. Follow steps 2 and 3 to fix the error.

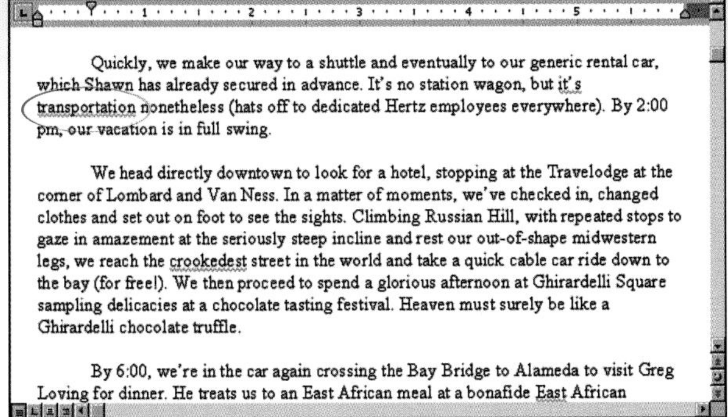

5 Spell Check Your Document

To run the Spelling and Grammar Checker for the whole document at one time, click the **Spelling and Grammar** button on the Standard toolbar, or select **Tools, Spelling and Grammar**.

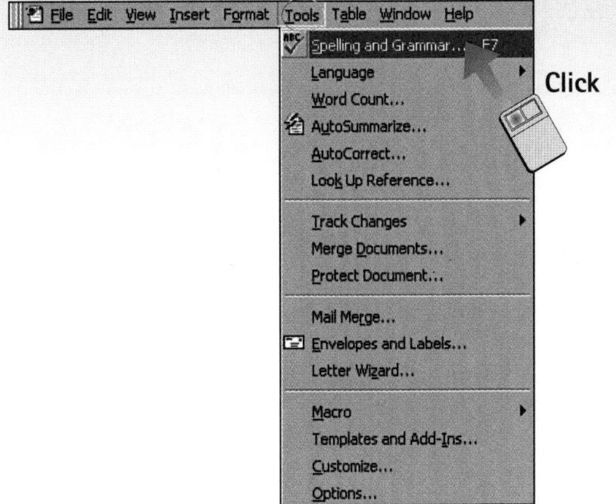

6 The Spelling and Grammar Box

Word checks every word in your document against its dictionary and list of grammatical rules, and presents the Spelling and Grammar dialog box when it encounters a word that is not in its dictionary or does not conform to a grammatical rule. The buttons in the dialog box work like the commands on the shortcut menu.

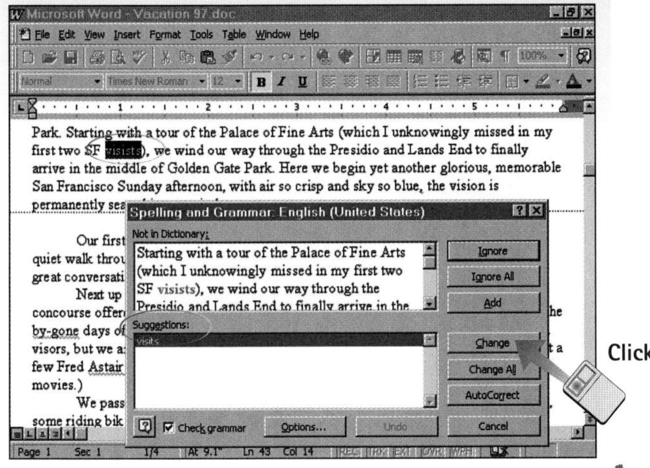

End

How-To Hints

Turn It Off

To turn the Automatic Spelling Checker off, choose **Tools, Options**; on the **Spelling and Grammar** tab, clear the **Check spelling as you type** check box. Click **OK** to exit.

Check a Section

To check the spelling and grammar of only a portion of the document, select that portion before starting the check. When Word finishes checking the selection, it asks if you want to check the rest of the document. Click **No** to end the check.

Check the Writing Style

To modify what Word looks for in a grammar check, choose **Tools, Options**, and click the **Spelling and Grammar** tab. In the **Writing Style** drop-down list, select a style that best describes your document. You can choose which items Word checks by clicking the **Settings** button. Choose **OK**.

TASK 3

How to Work with AutoCorrect

Word's *AutoCorrect* feature can save you time by automatically correcting misspelled words as you type—no need to run a spelling checker. AutoCorrect comes with a list of common misspellings, but the list isn't comprehensive; you can add your own common misspellings to the list to personalize it to your work habits.

What makes AutoCorrect even more useful is that you can use it to do your typing for you. If you often type a particular word or long phrase, you can create an AutoCorrect entry that types the word for you when you type a short acronym.

Begin

1 Try It Out

Test AutoCorrect to see how it performs—type **teh**, then press the spacebar or type a punctuation mark such as a comma or a period. Because "teh" is a common misspelling, AutoCorrect corrects it to "the" before you realize you mistyped it.

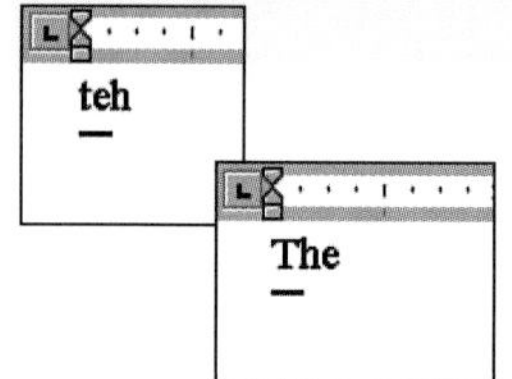

2 Undo AutoCorrect

If you type something you don't want corrected (for example, **Mr. Edmund Teh**), press Ctrl+Z to undo the correction before you type any other characters. The AutoCorrection is undone, and you can continue typing.

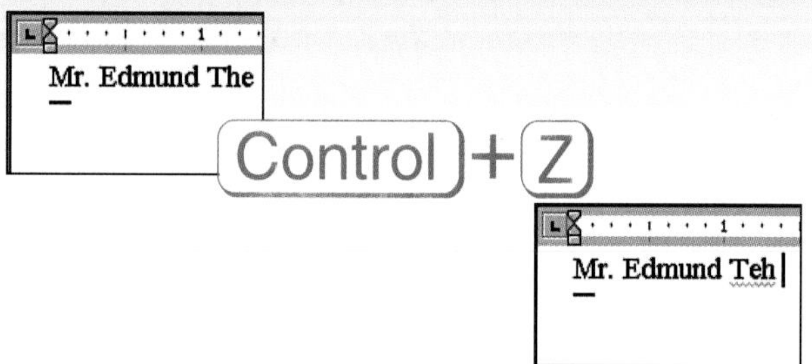

3 Remove a Word from AutoCorrect

To remove a word from the AutoCorrect list, choose **Tools, AutoCorrect**.

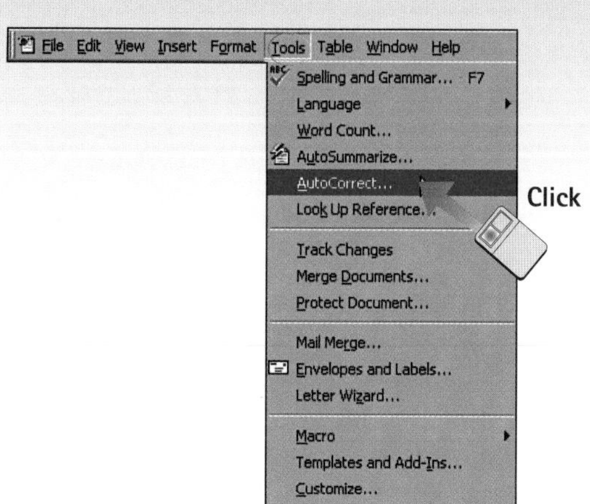

4 Delete the Word

Click the **AutoCorrect** tab. In the **Replace** box, type the first few letters of the word you want to delete from AutoCorrect; the list of words and replacements scrolls to the point in the list where you can find your word. Click your word in the list, then click **Delete**. Click **OK** to exit the dialog box.

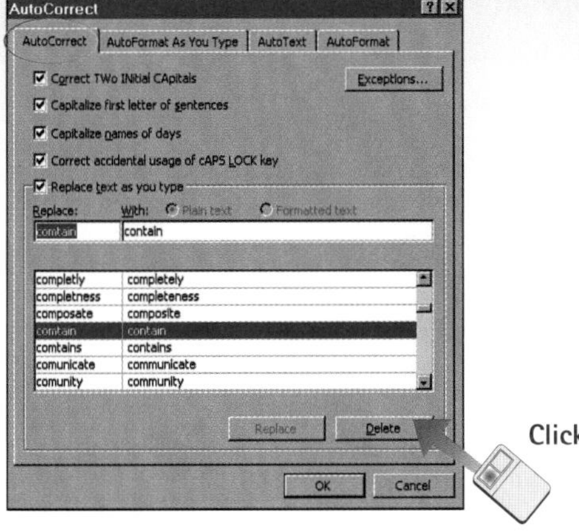

5 Add a Misspelling

To add a word you frequently misspell to the AutoCorrect list, open a document and type the correct spelling. (You can also add a long phrase you want to create a shortcut to; type in the phrase, including any special capitalization.) Select the word, then choose **Tools**, **AutoCorrect**.

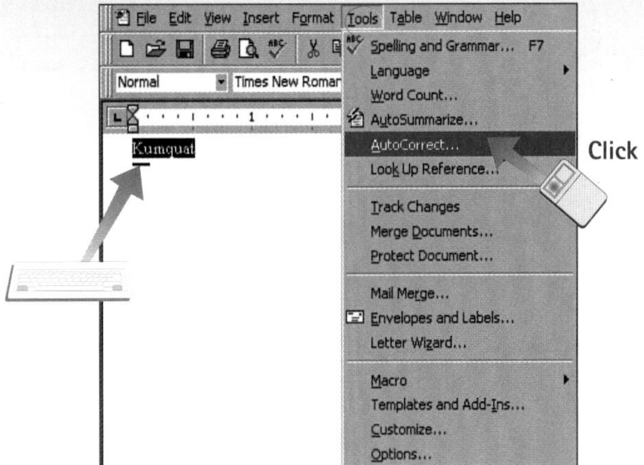

6 Click Add

Click the **AutoCorrect** tab. Your word or phrase appears in the **With** box. In the **Replace** box, type the incorrect word (for example, `Kumqat`) or acronym you want to replace (this text is what you will mistype in your document). If you only want to add a single word, choose **OK** to close the dialog box; if you want to add more words to the AutoCorrect list, click **Add** to add each word, and choose **OK** when you're finished.

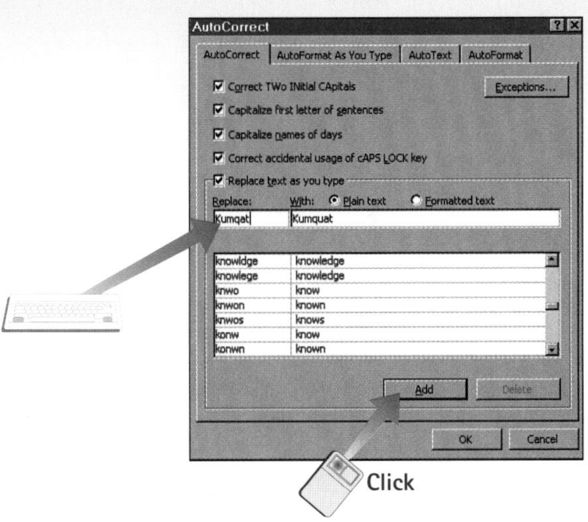

How-To Hints

Turn It Off

Turn AutoCorrect off or on by clearing or marking the **Replace text as you type** check box on the **AutoCorrect** tab.

Other Options

As you can see in the AutoCorrect tab, Word automatically corrects other items. Set or turn off other convenient automated options, such as capitalization of weekday names and the first word in sentences, by marking or clearing those check boxes in the AutoCorrect dialog box.

AutoCorrect Long Phrases

To add a long word or phrase to the AutoCorrect list, enter the phrase in the **With** box. Enter an abbreviation or acronym you want to substitute for the phrase in the **Replace** box.

End

TASK 4

How to Change Paper Size

By default, Word assumes your document is a standard 8 1/2" by 11" page. If you need to create a document that uses a different paper size, open the Page Setup dialog box and change the settings. From the **Paper Size** tab, you can change the paper size, page orientation, or enter the measurements for a custom paper size.

Begin

1 Open Page Setup

Open the **File** menu and select **Page Setup**. This opens the Page Setup dialog box.

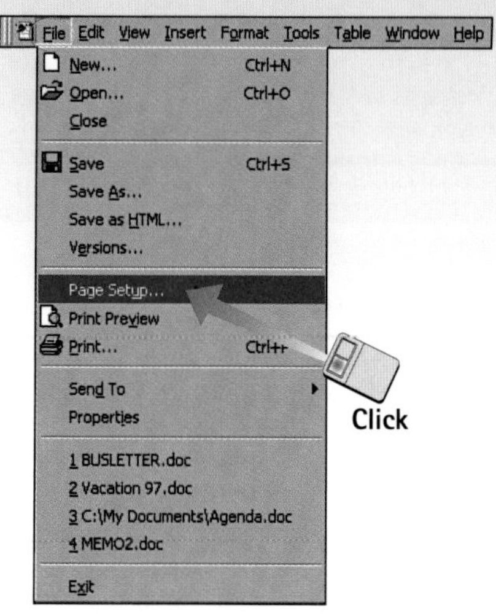

2 Select the Paper Size Tab

Click the **Paper Size** tab to view the options associated with paper sizes and orientation.

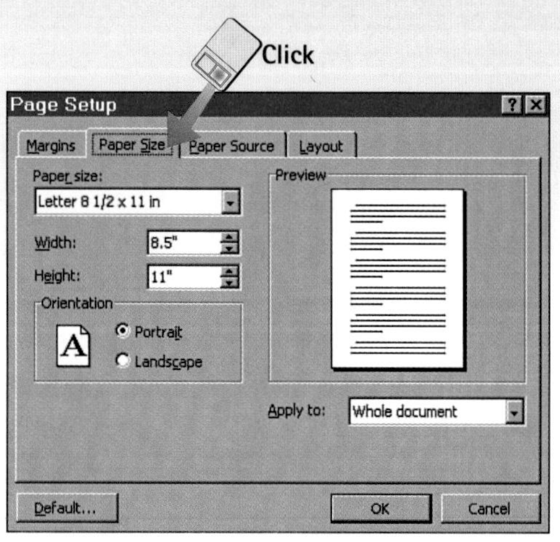

3 Change the Paper Size

Use the **Paper size** drop-down list to select another paper size. As you scroll through the list, you may notice Word is ready to handle legal-size paper and a variety of envelope sizes. To create a custom size, select **Custom** and enter the parameters of the paper.

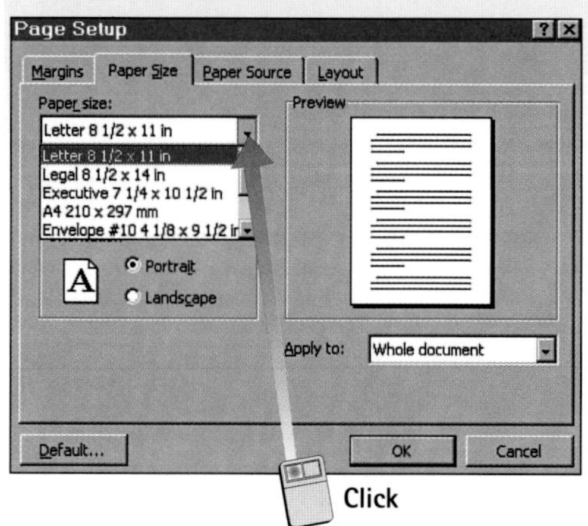

4 Change the Page Orientation

With some documents, you may need to change the way the text is printed on the page—the Orientation settings. By default, Word prints the document "shortways" (across the width of the 8 1/2" page). This is called *Portrait*. You can switch to *Landscape* to print across the length of the page (longways across the width of the 11" page).

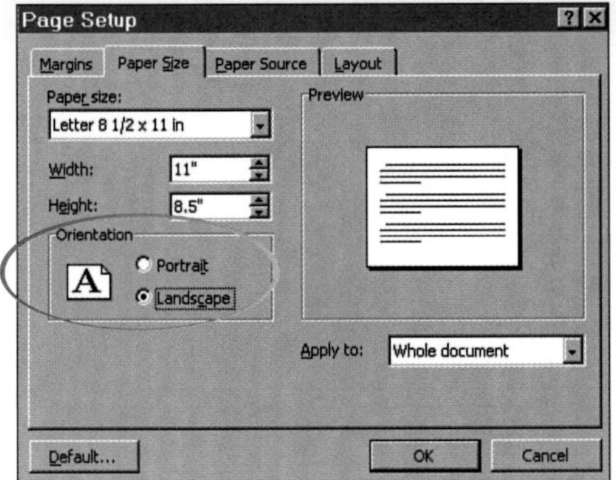

5 Exit the Dialog Box

After you have set your paper size options, click **OK** to exit the Page Setup dialog box and start creating the document.

End

How-To Hints

Need Help Printing?

To find out more about printing files, see Task 6, "How to Print a File," in Chapter 2 of this book.

Caution!

If you choose to set a new paper size after you have already designed and created the document, you may need to make a few adjustments to the document. Be sure to check the document in Print Preview (click the **Print Preview** button on the Standard toolbar) to see if everything still fits properly or needs adjusting.

TASK 5

How to Print an Envelope

Task 6 in Chapter 2 covers the basics of printing your Office files. However, some Word projects you tackle may involve some special printing needs, such as envelopes. When you create letters in Word, you can create envelopes to go along with them. Use Word's Envelopes and Labels dialog box to enter addresses and select from a variety of envelope sizes.

Begin

1 Use the Envelopes Feature

If you have created a letter with an address you want to print on an envelope, open the letter document. If not, you can open the Envelopes feature from any document and create a quick envelope. Open the **Tools** menu and select **Envelopes and Labels**.

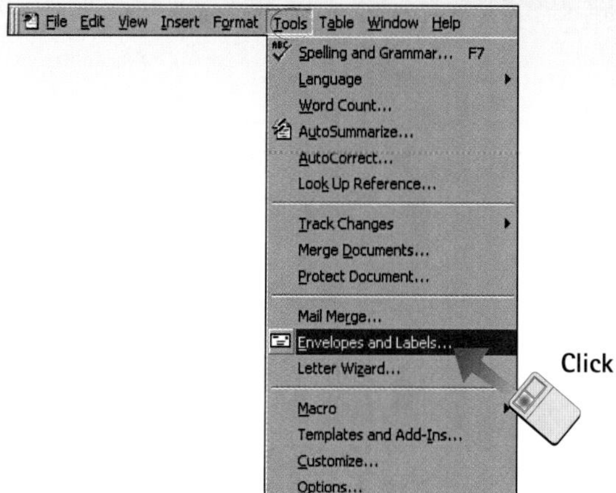

2 Use the Envelopes Tab

Click the **Envelopes** tab. If needed, type in the delivery address and the return address in the appropriate text boxes. If you're using this feature with a letter file, Word borrows the addresses you entered in the letter document.

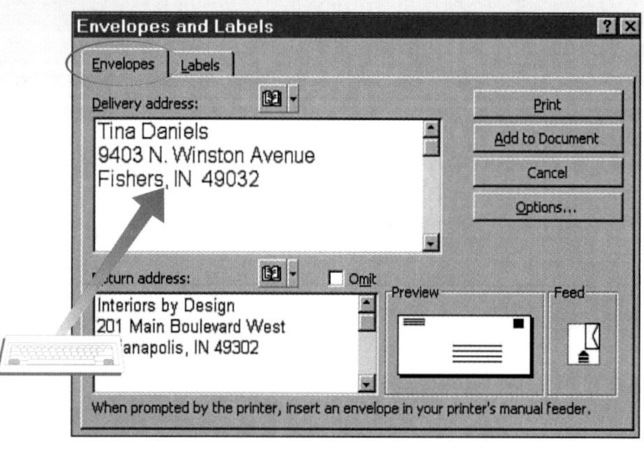

3 Open the Envelope Options

To choose an envelope size other than the default size, click the **Options** button to open the Envelope Options dialog box.

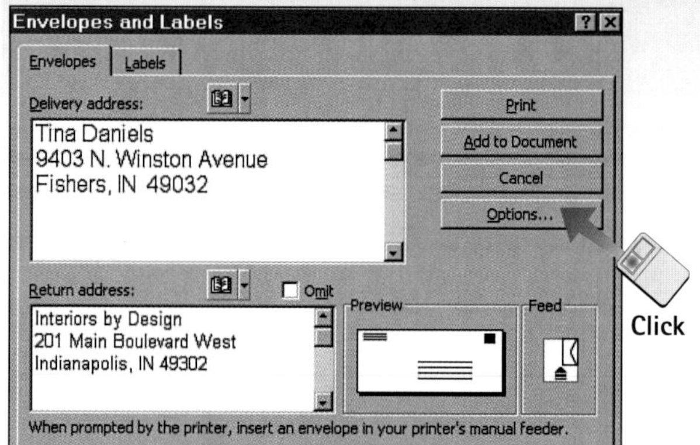

4 Choose an Envelope Size

Select another size from the **Envelope size** drop-down list.

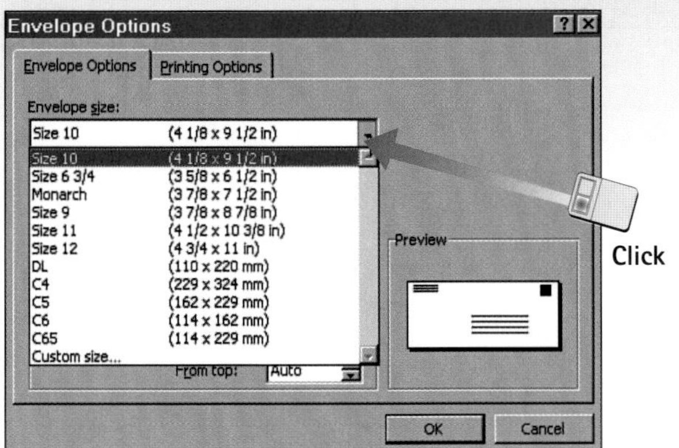

5 Exit Envelope Options

You can also change the font used for the addresses and control the spacing between the addresses and the edges of the envelope. Click **OK** to return to the Envelopes and Labels dialog box after you're finished setting envelope options.

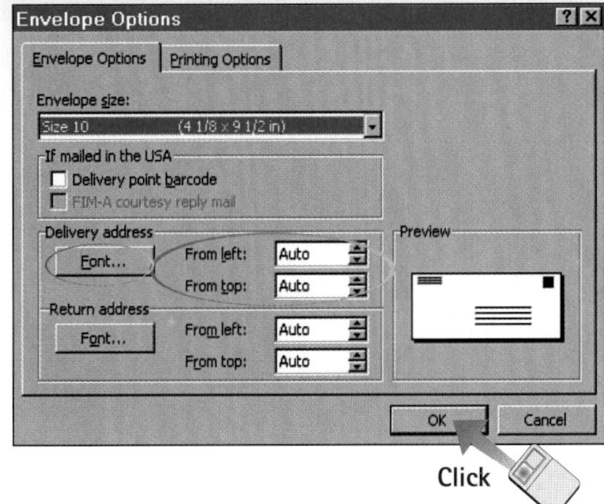

6 Print

To print the envelope, click the **Print** button. Be sure to feed the envelope into your printer correctly. Depending on your printer setup, the Feed area in the dialog box gives you a clue as to how to feed the envelope.

End

How-To Hints

Omit

Select the **Omit** check box in the Envelopes and Labels dialog box if you have pre-printed envelopes that already have a return address or company logo.

Add to Document

Select the **Add to Document** button in the Envelopes and Labels dialog box to add the envelope style and contents to the document to save it for later use.

TASK 6

How to Print a Label

Word makes it easy to print labels as well as envelopes. You can choose to print a single label or a full page of labels. Word supports a variety of Avery sizes (a popular label brand). You can even import addresses from your Outlook Address Book or another address database to use as labels.

Be sure to set up your printer to handle the labels first, then follow the steps in this task to create and print the labels.

Begin

1 Select Envelopes and Labels

Open the **Tools** menu and select **Envelopes and Labels**.

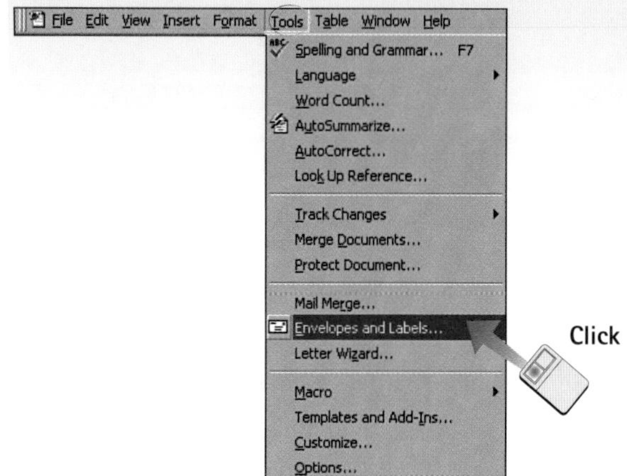

2 Click the Labels Tab

Click the **Labels** tab. If needed, type the address in the **Address** text box. To import an address, click the **Address Book** icon and open the address database you want to use, such as Outlook's Personal Address Book, and select the address to use as label.

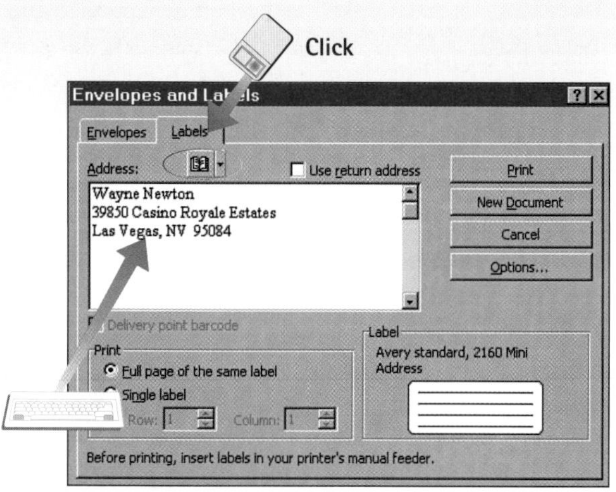

3 Choose a Print Option

Under **Print** options, select to print a single label or a page of labels. To print a return address label, select the **Use return address** check box.

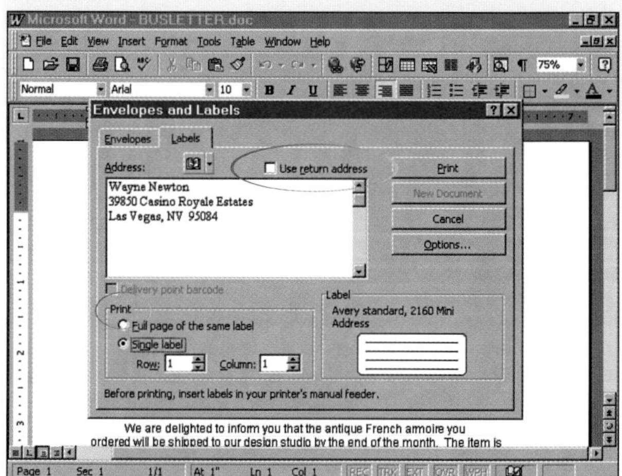

4 Choose Label Options

Click the **Options** button to open the Label Options dialog box where you can select a label product and size.

5 Choose a Label Size

Use the **Label products** drop-down list to choose a product, then select the product number from the **Product number** list box. The **Label information** area displays the dimensions of the label and label page. Click **OK** to return to the Envelopes and Labels dialog box.

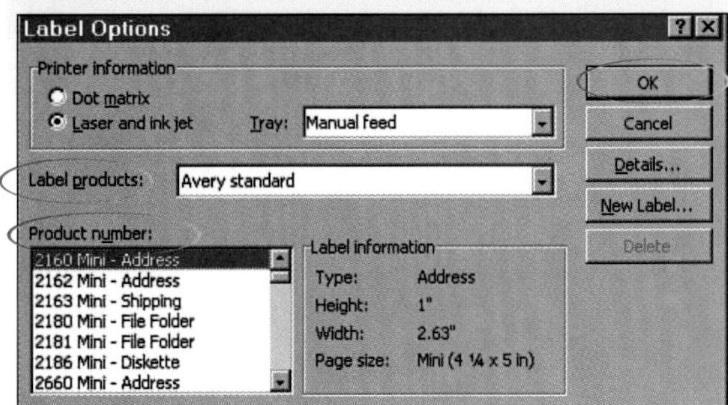

6 Print

To print the label, click the **Print** button.

End

How-To Hints

Print a Particular Label

To print a specific label on your label sheet, select the **Single label** option in the **Labels** tab and use the **Row** and **Column** settings to specify the label's location on the sheet.

Task

Chapter 6

How to Use Excel 97

The second most popular program included in Office 97 is Excel. Excel 97 is an excellent tool for keeping track of data and crunching numbers. With Excel, you can create worksheets to total sales for your department or to track your personal expenses. You can use Excel to set up a budget or to create an invoice. You can even use Excel as a simple database program. With Excel, you can perform any kind of mathematical calculation, from the simplest to the most complex, and organize data so that it becomes meaningful and useful.

Although, at first, it resembles an accounting spreadsheet, Excel is much easier to use because you're not always erasing data and rewriting it somewhere else; to reorganize data on a worksheet, you can either drag it around or tell Excel to sort it or filter it for you. In this chapter, you will learn how to use Excel's basic features, such as entering data, adding and deleting rows and columns, and working with worksheets.

TASK 1

How to Use the Excel Window

When Excel starts, a blank workbook opens. A *workbook* is an Excel file, just as a document is a Word file. A workbook is a container for at least one *worksheet*, which looks like an accountant's spreadsheet divided into a grid of columns and rows. Each little rectangle in the worksheet grid is a *cell*, which holds its own parcel of data that you enter.

Above the worksheet grid is the *Formula bar*, where the value or formula in a specific cell is displayed with the cell's address. Above the Formula bar are two toolbars and the menu bar. As with all Microsoft programs, the menu bar contains menus of commands you use to direct Excel's activities, and the toolbars contain buttons that help you carry out commands faster.

Begin

1 At the Top of the Screen

The title bar (at the very top of the Excel window) shows the program name (Microsoft Excel) and the filename of the active workbook, which is the workbook displayed on the screen. A new workbook will be named Book1 until you save it with a permanent filename.

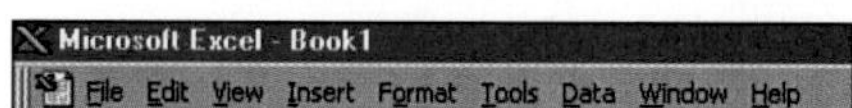

2 Choose a Menu Command

Below the title bar is the menu bar. Click a menu name to drop the menu list, then click the name of the command you want. If you change your mind about clicking a command, click anywhere in the Excel window to close the menu.

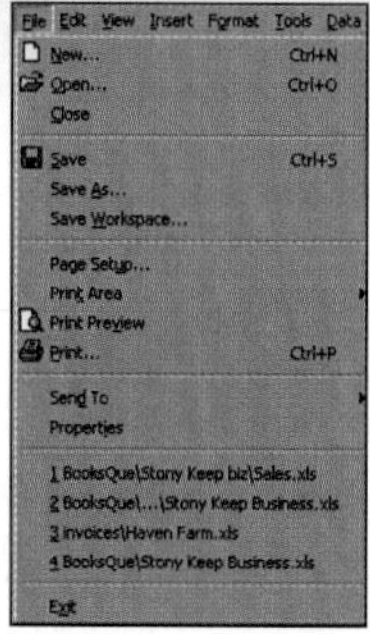

3 Below the Menu Bar

The Standard toolbar (the upper toolbar) and the Formatting toolbar (the lower toolbar) contain buttons for quicker access to many of the commands on the menu bar. If you're not sure about what a button's icon represents, hover your mouse pointer over the button for a moment until a ScreenTip appears with the button's name.

4 The Big Picture

This figure shows the entire Excel screen and the names of its important parts.

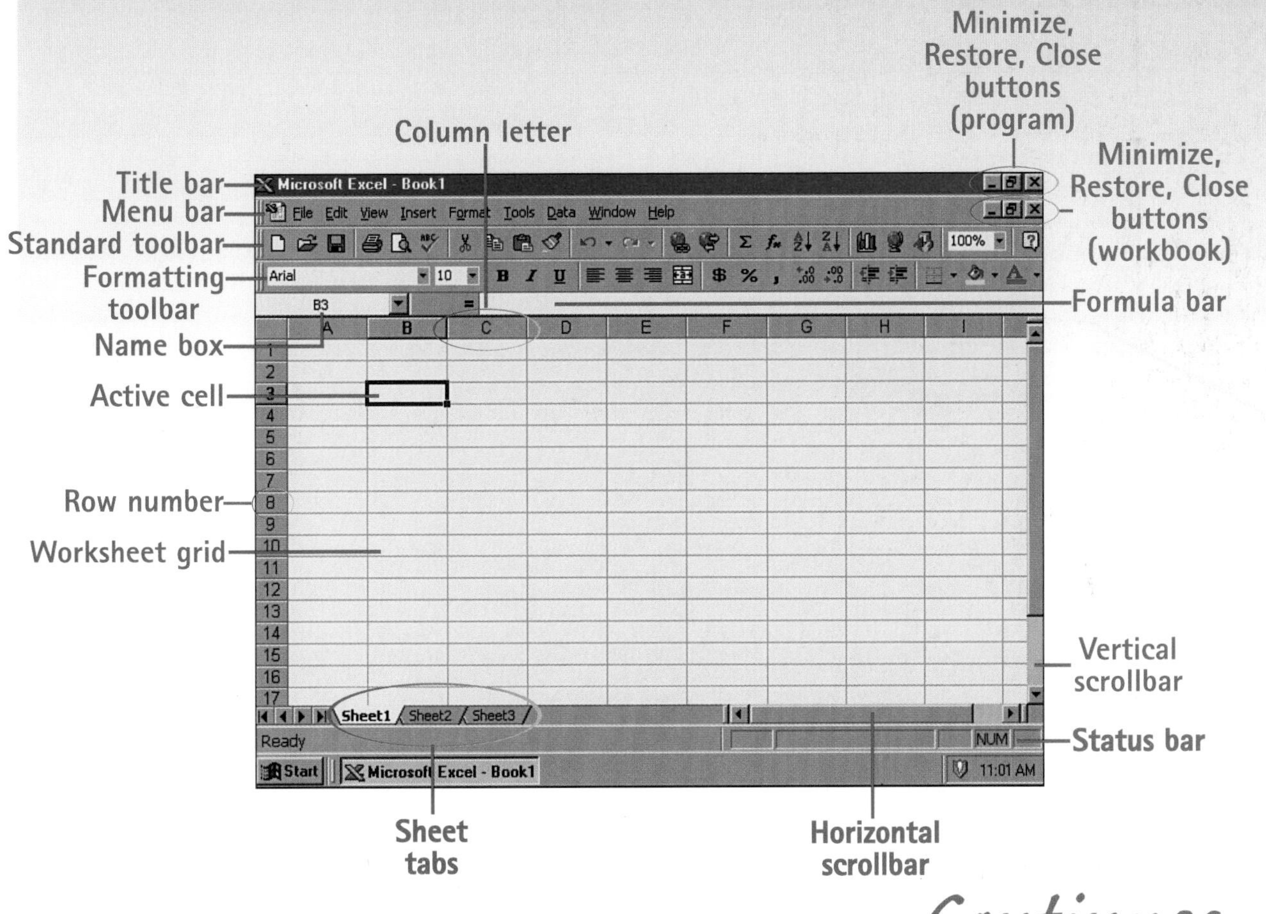

Continues

5 Button Explanations

If seeing the button name doesn't help, choose **Help**, **What's This?**, and click the toolbar button. A bigger *ScreenTip* appears with an explanation of the button's function.

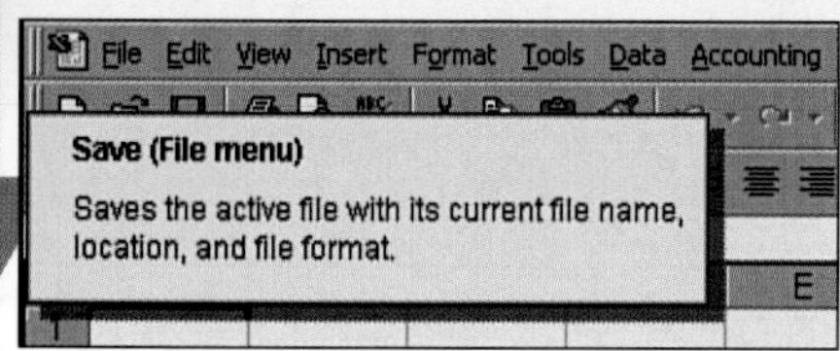

6 Below the Screen

At the bottom of the window, *sheet tabs* tell you the name of the worksheet in which you are working (a workbook contains several worksheets unless you delete them). To select another worksheet, click its sheet tab.

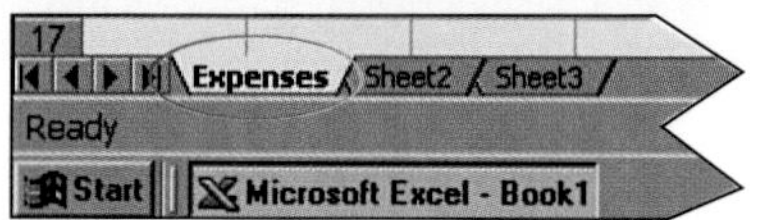

7 Below the Toolbars

The Formula bar, above the worksheet grid, has two main sections. On the left is the Name box, where you will see the active cell's address; on the right is the formula area, where the content of the active cell is displayed.

8 Rename Sheet Tabs

To rename a worksheet for easier identification, double-click the sheet tab, type a new name, and press Enter.

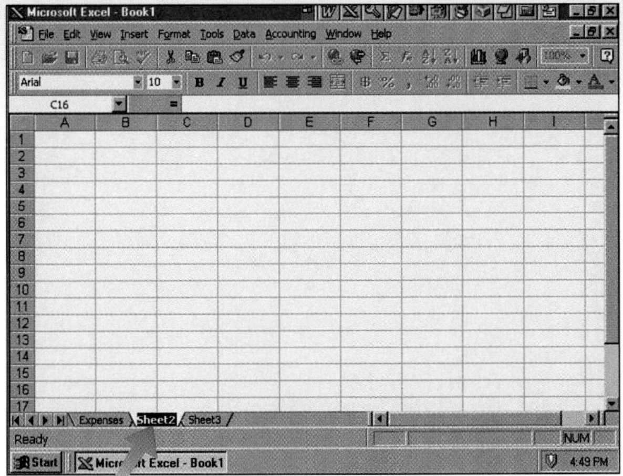

9 A Single Cell, Close Up

The *active cell*, also called the selected cell, is the cell in which data is entered when you type. This cell has a dark border, and its location, or *cell address*, is the intersection of its column letter and row number. On the worksheet, the mouse pointer appears as a white plus symbol.

10 The Pointer Changes

When you move the mouse pointer over a border of the selected cell, the pointer becomes an arrow symbol.

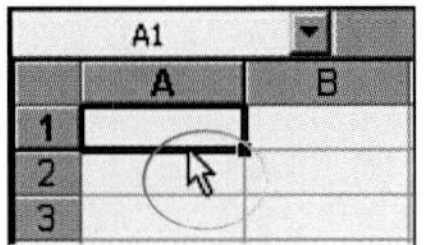

End

How-To Hints

Customize Your Environment

You can customize your Excel environment to suit your preferences. If toolbars are missing, or if unwanted toolbars are displayed, right-click any toolbar. A shortcut menu appears with multiple toolbar names—the toolbars that are currently displayed have check marks next to their names. Click a toolbar name to show or hide that toolbar.

The Worksheet Is Bigger Than You Think

The worksheet grid you see is only a small part of the whole worksheet—a worksheet is actually 256 columns wide and 65,536 rows long. You can scroll to the hinterlands of a worksheet with the vertical and horizontal scrollbars. When you scroll past column Z, the columns are labeled AA, AB, and so on; the last column in any worksheet is labeled IV.

TASK 2

How to Enter and Edit Cell Data

Data in a worksheet is always entered in cells. To enter data, click a cell, type the data, and press Enter (or press Tab, or click another cell in the worksheet). You can use a number of tricks for making data entry more efficient, such as entering the same word or number in several cells at the same time, or copying an entry from another cell in the same column.

In Task 5, "How to Use the Fill Handle to Enter Data Automatically," you will learn to use *AutoFill* to enter lists of data automatically.

Begin

1 Select a Cell

Click the cell in which you want to enter data. The cell you click becomes the active cell and displays a dark border.

2 Enter Data in the Selected Cell

Type your entry (numbers and/or letters) and press Enter. The active cell border moves down one cell, and your characters are entered in the cell in which you typed them. If you press Tab after you type, the active cell shifts to the right (which is convenient for typing multicolumn lists).

	A	B	C	D
1				
2				
3				
4			100	
5			200	
6				
7				
8				

3 Enter a Multicolumn List

To enter a list, begin at the upper-left corner of the list. As you type the entries, press Tab to move to the right to enter the data for each cell in the row. After you type the last entry in the row, press Enter instead of Tab; the active cell moves to the beginning of the next row—this function is called AutoReturn.

	Jan	Feb	Mar
Mugs	452	521	352
Dipping Bowls	225	264	241
Mixing Bowls	385	334	341

4 Copy the Cell Above

To copy the entry from the cell above the active cell, press Ctrl+' (press Ctrl and the apostrophe key simultaneously).

	A	B	C
45	7/22/98	Post Office	P.O. box rental (1 yr)
46	7/24/98	US West	business phone
47	8/8/98	Business VISA	interest
48	8/11/98	Northland Times	newspaper - 3rd qtr
49	8/14/98	Office Depot	boxes to move office
50	8/15/98	Mudville Clays	clay
51	8/15/98	Restaurant Supplies. Inc	bulk oils
52	8/16/98	Sprint	long distance charges
53	8/23/98	Sprint	long distance charges
54	8/24/98	US West	business phone
55	8/26/98	Custom Printing	print booklets
56	8/27/98	Custom Printing	copies
57	9/1/98	Custom Printing	
58			
59			

5 AutoComplete an Entry

If you want to repeat an entry from anywhere in the same column (which not only saves time, but also prevents typing mistakes), type the first few letters of the entry. A possible match appears in the cell—this function is called AutoComplete. If the entry is correct, press Enter. If you don't want that entry, just continue typing.

	A	B	C
45	7/22/98	Post Office	P.O. box rental (1 yr)
46	7/24/98	US West	business phone
47	8/8/98	Business VISA	interest
48	8/11/98	Northland Times	newspaper - 3rd qtr
49	8/14/98	Office Depot	boxes to move office
50	8/15/98	Mudville Clays	clay
51	8/15/98	Restaurant Supplies. Inc	bulk oils
52	8/16/98	Sprint	long distance charges
53	8/23/98	Sprint	long distance charges
54	8/24/98	US West	business phone
55	8/26/98	Custom Printing	print booklets
56	8/27/98	Custom Printing	copies
57	9/1/98	mudville Clays	
58			
59			
60			

6 Pick a Repeated Entry

If you want to repeat an entry that already exists in the column somewhere, you can select it from a list instead of retyping it. Right-click the active cell, and choose **Pick From List**. A list of all the entries in the column appears; click the entry you want.

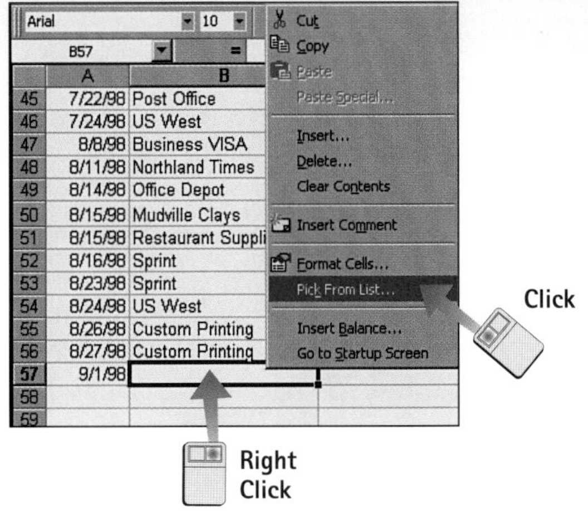

End

How-To Hints

Ways to Move

You can move the active cell using the Arrow, Page Up, Page Down, Home, and End keys. You can jump to the end of a row or column of filled cells or blank cells by pointing to the border of the active cell and double-clicking when the mouse pointer becomes an arrow. (The border you double-click should be the direction in which the active cell jumps; that is, double-click the top border to jump upward, double-click the right border to jump right, and so on.)

TASK 3

How to Navigate Worksheets

Because worksheets are huge (256 columns by 65,536 rows), you need some techniques for moving around efficiently in them. The examples in this book are necessarily small so that I can show you what I'm talking about with minimal confusion. At times, however, you might have a table or list of data that's several screens wide or long, and you might not have the time to spend scrolling back and forth.

Begin

1 Double-click a Cell Border

To jump to the bottom of a list, click a cell in the list to select it. Point to the bottom border of the cell so that your mouse pointer becomes an arrow. Double-click the bottom border of the cell.

	A	B	
1	Date	Vendor	
2	1/5/98	Papers'n'Stuff	ta
3	1/15/98	Mudville Clays	cl
4	1/15/98	Restaurant Supplies, Inc	bu
5	1/15/98	Sprint	lo
6	1/15/98	US West	bu
7	2/3/98	Radio Shack	
8	2/8/98	Papers'n'Stuff	
9	2/9/98	Business VISA	in
10	2/10/98	Northland Times	ne
11	2/15/98	Mudville Clays	cl
12	2/15/98	Restaurant Supplies, Inc	bu
13	2/15/98	Sprint	lo
14	2/15/98	US West	bu
15	3/7/98	Papers'n'Stuff	co
16	3/11/98	Business VISA	in
17	3/12/98	Papers'n'Stuff	co
18	3/15/98	Mudville Clays	to

Expenses / Contacts / Sales / Pr

Ready

Double Click

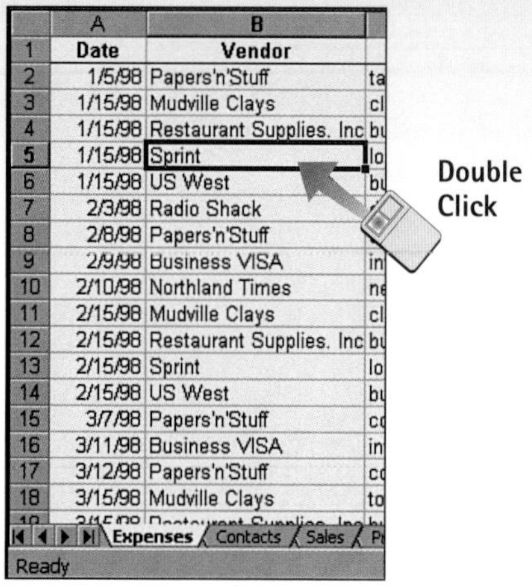

2 The Active Cell Jumps

The active cell jumps to the last cell in the column that contains data, which takes you to the bottom of the list. Move back to the top, or from side to side, by double-clicking the top or side borders.

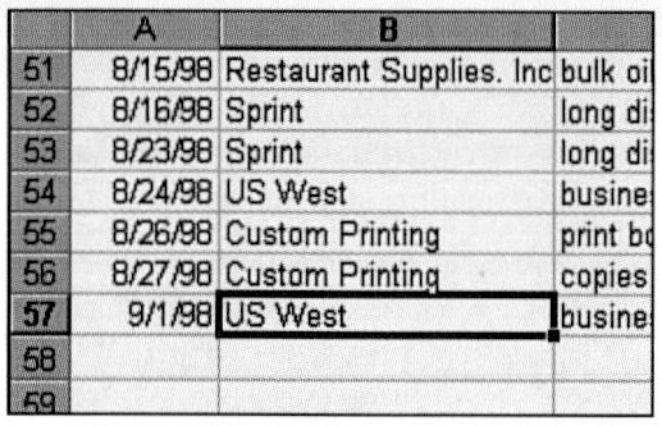

	A	B	
51	8/15/98	Restaurant Supplies, Inc	bulk oi
52	8/16/98	Sprint	long di
53	8/23/98	Sprint	long di
54	8/24/98	US West	busine
55	8/26/98	Custom Printing	print bo
56	8/27/98	Custom Printing	copies
57	9/1/98	US West	busine
58			
59			

3 Jump Home, or Jump to the End

To jump back to the first cell in the worksheet, A1, press Ctrl+Home. To jump to the lower-right corner of the working area of the worksheet (the area you've been working in, not cell IV65536), press Ctrl+End.

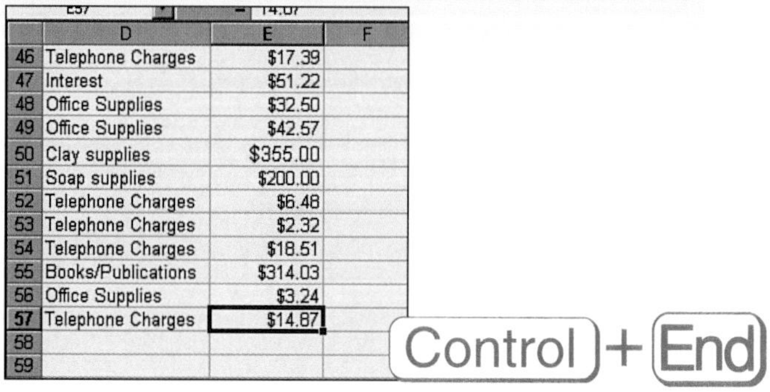

	D	E	F
46	Telephone Charges	$17.39	
47	Interest	$51.22	
48	Office Supplies	$32.50	
49	Office Supplies	$42.57	
50	Clay supplies	$355.00	
51	Soap supplies	$200.00	
52	Telephone Charges	$6.48	
53	Telephone Charges	$2.32	
54	Telephone Charges	$18.51	
55	Books/Publications	$314.03	
56	Office Supplies	$3.24	
57	Telephone Charges	$14.87	
58			
59			

Control + End

4 Jump from Beginning to End

To jump to the beginning of the row (column A), press Home. To jump to the right-most cell in the row (within the working area of the worksheet), press End, and then press Enter (this instruction is often written as "press End, Enter").

18	Mudville Clays	tools	Clay supplies	$83.14
19	Restaurant Supplies, Inc	bulk oils	Soap supplies	$250.00
20	Sprint	long distance charges	Telephone Charges	$18.90
21	US West	business phone	Telephone Charges	$14.87
22	Business VISA	interest	Interest	$58.59
23	Toshiba	laptop carrying case	Office Equipment	$49.95
24	Mudville Clays	clay	Clay supplies	$125.00

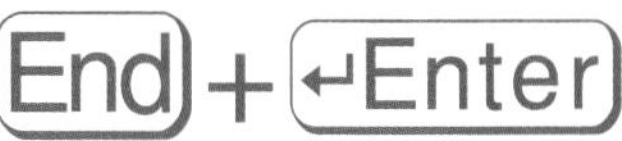

5 Select an Entire Table or List

To select an entire contiguous table or list, click any cell in the list, and then click **Edit**, **Go To**. In the Go To dialog box, click **Special**. In the Go To Special dialog box, click the **Current region** option, and choose **OK**. When you need to select a really big list for some operation, this is a fast way to do it.

Click

6 Scroll Around and Return Quickly

As you drag a scrollbar, a ScreenTip tells you which row is at the top of the window, or which column is on the left side of the window (it's a fast way to get to a specific row or column). Scrolling doesn't move the active cell, so you can return your view to the active cell quickly by pressing Ctrl+Backspace.

E
$215.00
$27.62
$16.01
$2.61
$63.07
$32.50
$250.00
$175.00
$3.39
$1.56
$60.63
Row: 25
$180.00
$26.10
$16.47
$53.71
$245.00
$1.26

End

How-To Hints

Jump to the End of the Data

When you double-click a cell border to jump, the active cell jumps to the end of a contiguous block of data, so it jumps to the end of the list and stops short of the first empty cell. If you double-click again, the active cell jumps to the end of the block of empty cells and stops short of the next block of data.

Other Ways to Use Go To

Open the Go To dialog box by pressing F5 or Ctrl+G.

A Useful Custom Toolbar Button

The Customize toolbar button can select the current region for you without using dialog boxes. Right-click any toolbar and choose **Customize**. In the **Edit** category, on the **Commands** tab, drag the **Select Current Region** command onto a toolbar. Click **Close** to close the dialog box. Now you can click any cell in a table, and then click the **Select Current Region** button to select the entire table.

TASK 4

How to Select a Range of Cells

If cells are the building blocks of worksheets, then ranges are the mortar for holding them together. A *range* is a rectangular group of related cells that you can connect in a column, a row, or a combination of columns and rows. After you select a range of cells, you can perform a variety of tasks upon them in one simple step.

You can format a group of cells all at once, for example, rather than one cell at a time. You can use a range to print a specific group of cells from your worksheet. You can also use ranges in *formulas*, which can really save you time. (Learn how to name ranges in Task 12, "How to Define a Range Name.")

Begin

1 Click the First Cell

To select a range, start by clicking the first cell in the range.

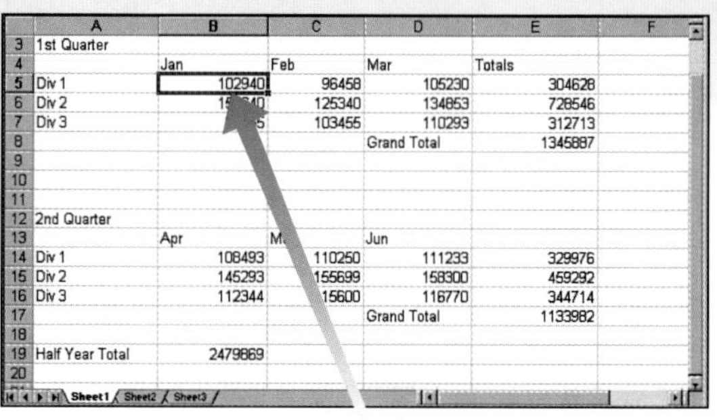

2 Drag to Select

Hold down the mouse button and drag across the cells you want to include in the range.

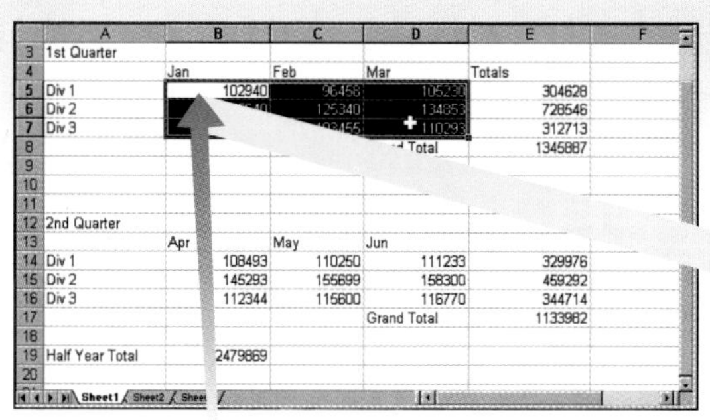

3 Release the Mouse Button

When you release the mouse button, the range is selected. Ranges are referred to by their anchor points, the upper-left corner and the lower-right corner. After selecting a range, you can format the cells using Excel's formatting features (see Chapter 8, "How to Use Excel's Formatting Tools"), or use the range in a formula (see Chapter 7, "How to Use Formulas and Functions").

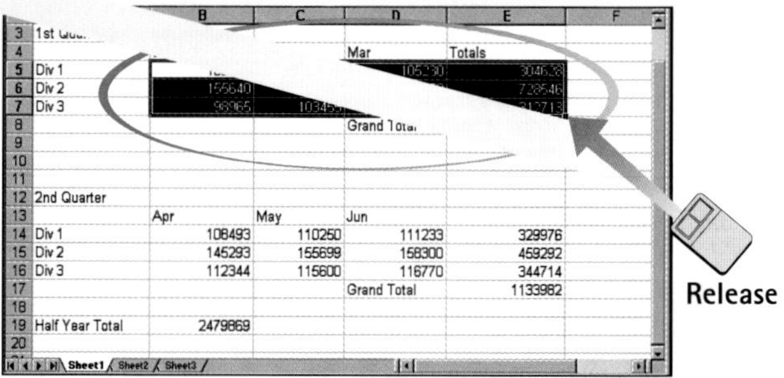

4 Select a Range with the Keyboard

To select a range using the keyboard, use the arrow keys to move to the first cell in the range.

	A	B	C	D	E	F
3	1st Quarter					
4		Jan	Feb	Mar	Totals	
5	Div 1	102940	96458	105230	304628	
6	Div 2	155640	125340	134853	728546	
7	Div 3	98965	103455	110293	312713	
8				Grand Total	1345887	
9						
10						
11						
12	2nd Quarter					
13		Apr	May	Jun		
14	Div 1	108493	110250	111233	329976	
15	Div 2	145293	155699	158300	459292	
16	Div 3	112344	115600	116770	344714	
17				Grand Total	1133982	
18						
19	Half Year Total	2479869				
20						

5 Use the Shift Key

Press and hold the Shift key, and then use the arrow keys to select the range.

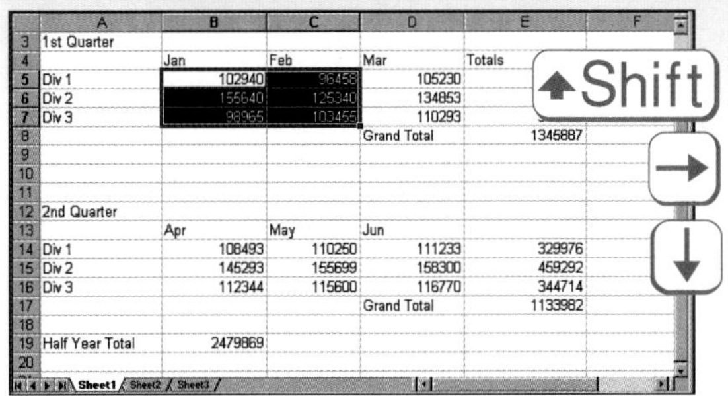

	A	B	C	D	E	F
3	1st Quarter					
4		Jan	Feb	Mar	Totals	
5	Div 1	102940	96458	105230		
6	Div 2	155640	125340	134853		
7	Div 3	98965	103455	110293		
8				Grand Total	1345887	
9						
10						
11						
12	2nd Quarter					
13		Apr	May	Jun		
14	Div 1	108493	110250	111233	329976	
15	Div 2	145293	155699	158300	459292	
16	Div 3	112344	115600	116770	344714	
17				Grand Total	1133982	
18						
19	Half Year Total	2479869				
20						

End

How-To Hints

Selecting Cells

Remember, to select a cell, click the cell. A selector, a black outline around the cell, surrounds it. When you select a cell, its reference or address appears in the Name box in the Formula bar.

To deselect a range, click outside the range or press any arrow key.

TASK 5

How to Use the Fill Handle to Enter Data Automatically

A feature called *AutoFill* can speed up data entry dramatically by filling in series or duplicate entries for you. By dragging the mouse across the worksheet, you can use AutoFill to fill in lists of day or month names, a series of numbers, or a list of identical text entries.

Day and month names, and their standard three-letter abbreviations, are built-in lists in Excel; that's how AutoFill knows what to enter. You can create custom lists—of people or product names, for example—and AutoFill will fill them, as well.

Begin

1 Start a Month List with One

To AutoFill a list of month names, enter a single month name in a cell, and then select that cell.

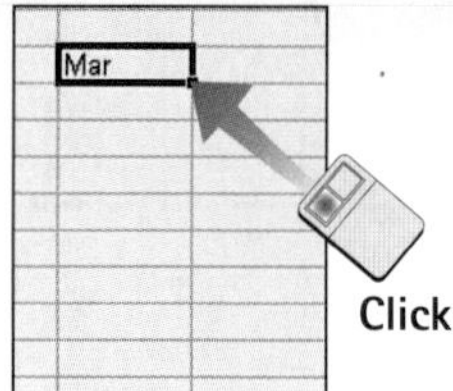

2 Drag the Fill Handle

Move the mouse pointer over the *fill handle* (the small black square in the lower-right corner of the cell), and click and hold down the left mouse button while you drag across a row or column of cells (you can fill cells in any direction). A ScreenTip shows what's being filled into each cell you drag (so you can tell when you've dragged far enough).

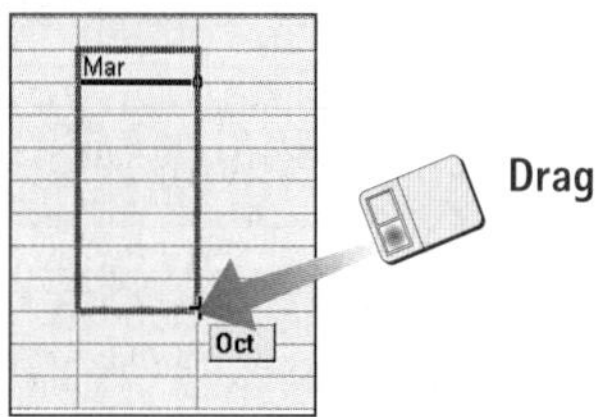

3 Release the Fill Handle

Release the mouse button at the end of the row or column of cells you want to fill. The series is entered in the cells, in the proper order.

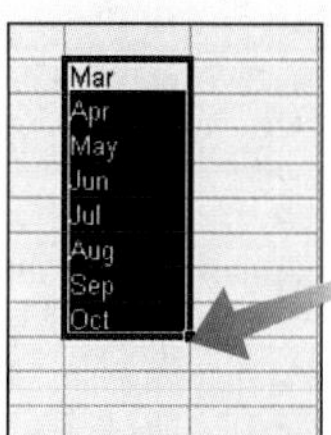

4 Start a Number Series

To fill a number series that increases by 1, start the series by entering **1** and **2**, then select the two cells and drag the fill handle to fill the series.

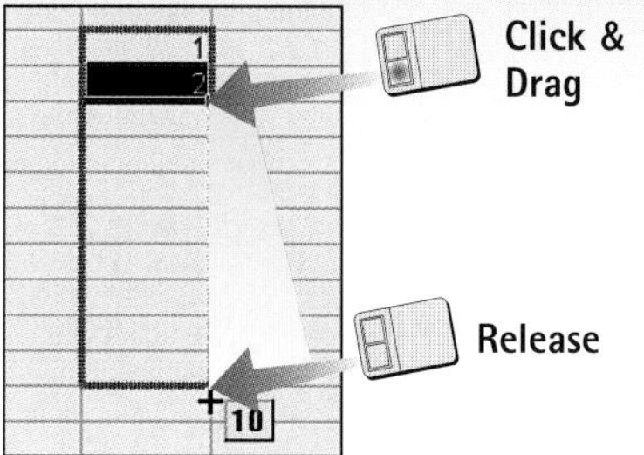

5 Fill a List with a Repeated Entry

To fill a list with a repeated text entry, type the entry, then select it and drag the fill handle to copy the entry repeatedly.

3/15/98	US West	business phone	Telephone Charges
4/15/98	US West	business phone	Telephone Charges
6/24/98	US West	business phone	Telephone Charges
7/24/98	US West	business phone	Telephone Charges
8/24/98	US West	business phone	Telephone Charges
9/1/98	US West		
10/1/98	US West		
11/1/98	US West		
12/1/98	US West		

business phone

Click & Drag

Release

End

How-To Hints

Copy a Formula with AutoFill

You can use AutoFill to copy a formula down the side or across the bottom of a table; the cell references in the formula adjust so the formula calculates the correct cells (see Chapter 7, Task 3, "How to Work with Cell Addresses," to learn how to use cell references).

Create a Custom List

To create a custom list, enter the whole list in any worksheet. Select the list, and then choose **Tools**, **Options**. On the **Custom Lists** tab, click **Import**, and choose **OK**. The list is saved in the Custom Lists window. You can fill the list in any workbook by typing any entry in the list, and then dragging with the fill handle.

TASK 6

How to Move and Copy Data with Drag and Drop

If you need to move or copy data to another location on a worksheet, and the new location is only a short distance from the original location, the easiest way is to drag the data and drop it with the mouse.

Begin

1 Select Cells to Move

To move cells, select the range of cells you want to move, and point to any border of the selected range so that the mouse pointer becomes an arrow. Drag the range to a new location.

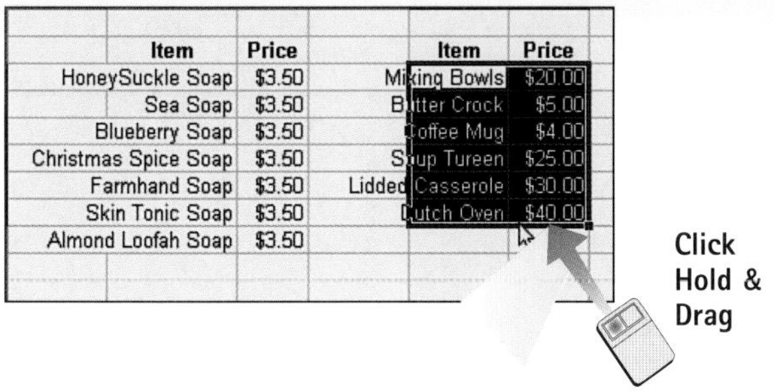

Click Hold & Drag

2 Drop the Cells

While you drag, an outline of the range moves across the worksheet, and a ScreenTip tells you the reference of the range location. When the range border is where you want it, drop the data by releasing the mouse button.

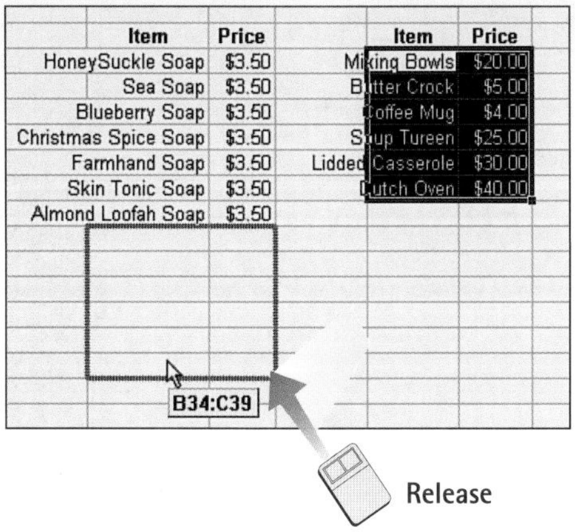

B34:C39

Release

3 The Range Moves

The range moves to its new location.

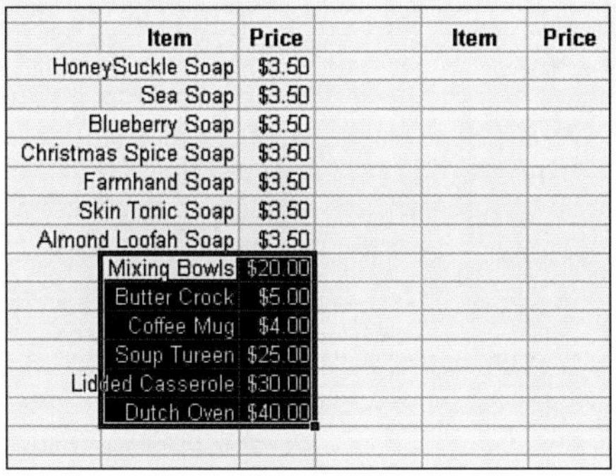

4 Select Cells to Copy

To copy cells, select the range of cells you want to copy, and point to any border of the selected range so that the mouse pointer becomes an arrow. Drag the range to a new location.

Item	Price		Item	Price
HoneySuckle Soap	$3.50			
Sea Soap	$3.50			
Blueberry Soap	$3.50			
Christmas Spice Soap	$3.50			
Farmhand Soap	$3.50			
Skin Tonic Soap	$3.50			
Almond Loofah Soap	$3.50			
Mixing Bowls	$20.00			
Butter Crock	$5.00			
Coffee Mug	$4.00			
Soup Tureen	$25.00			
Lidded Casserole	$30.00			
Dutch Oven	$40.00			

Click & Drag

5 Drag the Cells

While you drag, an outline of the range moves across the worksheet, and a ScreenTip tells you the reference of the range location.

Item	Price		Item	Price
HoneySuckle Soap	$3.50			
Sea Soap	$3.50			
Blueberry Soap	$3.50			
Christmas Spice Soap	$3.50			
Farmhand Soap	$3.50			
Skin Tonic Soap	$3.50			
Almond Loofah Soap	$3.50			
Mixing Bowls	$20.00			
Butter Crock	$5.00			
Coffee Mug	$4.00			
Soup Tureen	$25.00			
Lidded Casserole	$30.00			
Dutch Oven	$40.00			

E27:F32

6 Press Ctrl and Drop the Cells

When the range border is where you want it, press and hold Ctrl, and then drop the data by releasing the mouse button. When you press Ctrl, the mouse pointer acquires a small plus symbol that tells you it's copying. A copy of the data is dropped in the new location.

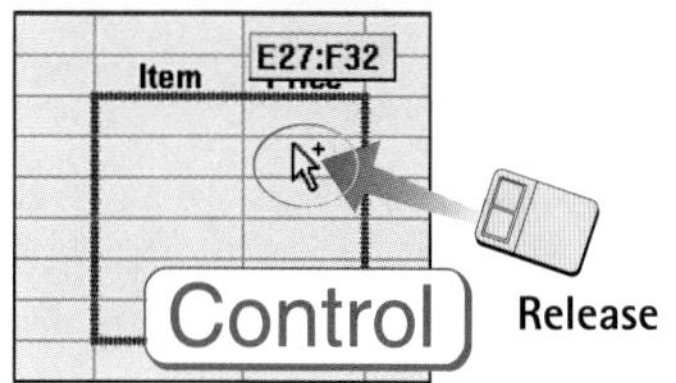

Release

End

How-To Hints

Press Ctrl Only When You Drop

Many books will tell you that you must hold down Ctrl while you drag a range you want to copy—not so. You must press and hold down Ctrl *while you release the mouse button*; it doesn't matter whether you press Ctrl while you drag. This is true of any drag-and-drop copy operation in any Microsoft software.

Drag with the Right Mouse Button

You can drag data with the right mouse button, and then choose a command—choose from several Move and Copy commands—on the shortcut menu that appears when you drop the data in its new location.

TASK 7

How to Move and Copy Data with the Clipboard

If you need to move or copy data over a long distance or to another worksheet or workbook (or even to another Office program, such as Word), it's easier to cut or copy the text to the Windows Clipboard, and then paste it where you want it.

The *Windows Clipboard* is a temporary holding area in Windows for data you have cut or copied in any of the Office programs; data on the Clipboard can be pasted repeatedly, and it is kept on the Clipboard until you cut or copy another chunk of data, or until you close Windows.

Begin

1 Select the Data to Move

To move data, you will use the Cut and Paste commands. Select the data you want to move. Right-click the selected cells.

2 Cut the Selected Data

Choose the **Cut** command on the shortcut menu. The selected data will have a moving border around it that disappears when you paste it somewhere else.

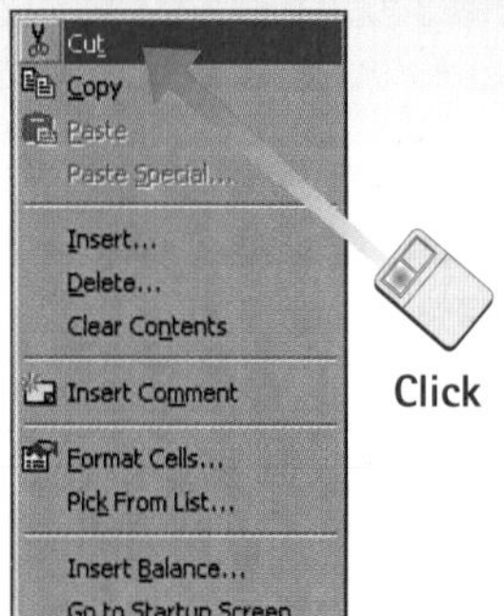

3 Paste the Cut Data

Right-click the upper-left cell of the range where you want to paste the data, and choose **Paste** on the shortcut menu. The data is pasted into its new location and disappears from its original location.

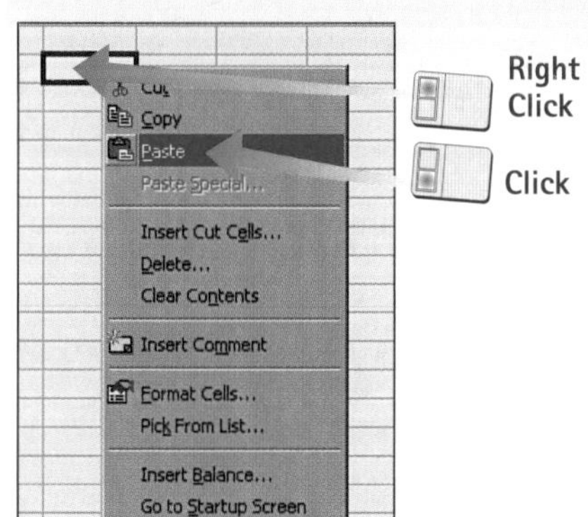

4 Select the Data to Copy

To copy data, you will use the Copy and Paste commands. Select the data you want to copy. Right-click the selected cells.

5 Copy the Selected Data

Choose the **Copy** command on the shortcut menu. The selected data will have a moving border around it.

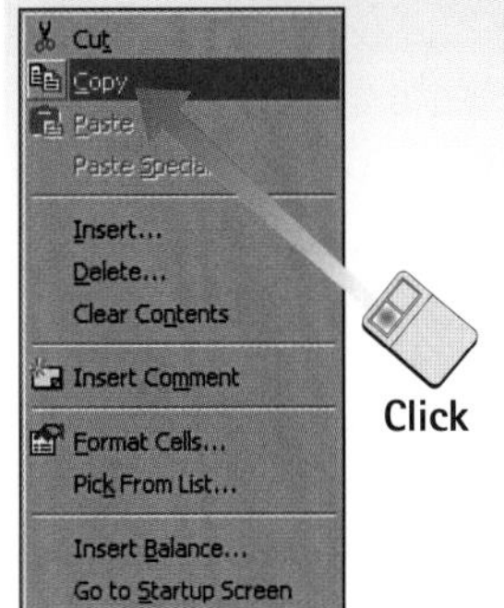

6 Paste the Copied Data

Right-click the upper-left cell of the range where you want to paste the copied data, and choose **Paste** on the shortcut menu. The data is pasted into its new location (the moving border remains around the copied data until you begin typing in another cell, or until you press Enter or Esc).

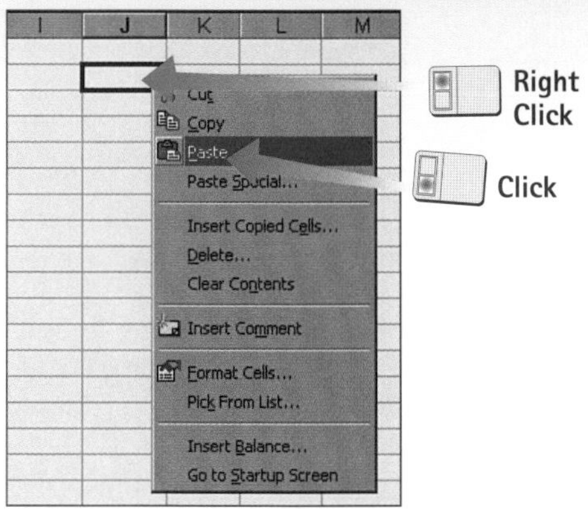

End

How-To Hints

Icons Are the Same Everywhere

The icons next to the commands on the shortcut menu and Edit menu are the same icons as on the toolbar buttons; between the command icons and the button ScreenTips, you should be able to figure out which toolbar buttons are Cut, Copy, and Paste.

Keystrokes

You can also cut data with the keystroke Ctrl+X; copy with the keystroke Ctrl+C; and paste with the keystroke Ctrl+V.

Paste with Enter

You can also paste cut or copied data by pressing Enter. If you press Enter to paste data, the data is removed from the Clipboard and is not available for more pasting.

Undo a Mistake

If you make a mistake, click the **Undo** button on the Standard toolbar; choose **Edit**, **Undo**; or press Ctrl+Z to undo the mistake.

Task 8

How to Insert Columns and Rows

If you need to add a row or column of data in the middle of a table, you could move the existing data by dragging and dropping it to make room for the new row or column. But it's faster to insert a new row or column.

If you're adding an item to an alphabetical list, you don't need to insert it yourself; you can type it at the end of the list and tell Excel to sort the list alphabetically (see Task 14, "How to Sort Data," to learn how to sort data). But if you need to add a new row of data above existing subtotal formulas, then you must insert rows and columns.

Begin

1 Select the Row

To insert a row in a list, select the row you want to place below the inserted row (click the row number to select it). Right-click the selected row.

	A	B	C	D	E
1	Sales				
2					
3		Mugs			
4			Jan	$521	
5			Feb	$352	
6			subtotal	$873	
		Dipping Bowls			
8			Jan	$225	
9			Feb	$264	
10			subtotal	$489	
11		Mixing Bowls			
12			Jan	$385	
13			Feb	$334	
14			subtotal	$719	
15					

2 Choose Insert

Choose **Insert** on the shortcut menu.

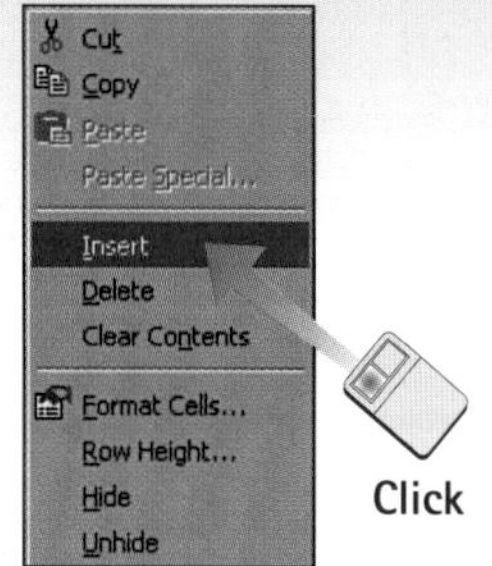

3 A New Row Is Inserted

A new row is inserted above the row you selected.

	A	B	C	D	E
1	Sales				
2					
3		Mugs			
4			Jan	$521	
5			Feb	$352	
6					
7			subtotal	$873	
8		Dipping Bowls			
9			Jan	$225	
10			Feb	$264	
11			subtotal	$489	
12		Mixing Bowls			
13			Jan	$385	
14			Feb	$334	
15			subtotal	$719	
16					

4 Select the Column

To insert a column in a list, select the column you want to place on the right of the new column (click the column letter to select it). Right-click the selected column.

C	D	E	F
Street	City	State	Zip
5850 W. Mallory Road	Westwood	[illegible]	83899
17200 N. Trails End Road	Westwood	ID	[illegible]
5755 W. Kruger Road	Westwood	ID	[illegible]
PO Box 184	Westwood	ID	[illegible]
5775 W. Mallory Road	Westwood	ID	83899
5980 E. Mallory Road	Westwood	ID	83899
PO Box 150	Lodi	ID	83462
5650 W. Kruger Road	Westwood	ID	83899
5730 W. Mallory Road	Westwood	ID	83899
5775 W. Mallory Road	Westwood	ID	83899
16750 N. Trails End Road	Westwood	ID	83899
16980 N. Trails End Road	Westwood	ID	83899
6195 W. Mallory Road	Westwood	ID	83899
255 N. Trails End Road	Westwood	ID	83899
16105 N. Trails End Road	Westwood	ID	83899
5755 W. Kruger Road	Westwood	ID	83899

5 Insert a New Column

Click **Insert** on the shortcut menu. A new column is inserted to the left of the column you selected.

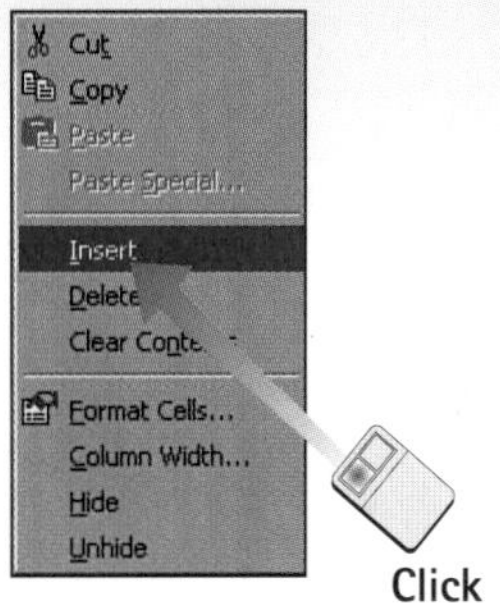

6 Insert Several Rows or Columns

To insert several adjacent rows or columns at one time, select that many rows or columns in the table, right-click the selection, and choose **Insert**. An equal number of rows or columns is inserted.

2					
3		Mugs			
4			Jan	$521	
5			Feb	$352	
6			Mar	$456	
7					
8					
9					
10					
11			subtotal	$1,329	
12		Dipping Bowls			
13			Jan	$225	
14			Feb	$264	
15			subtotal	$489	
16		Mixing Bowls			
17			Jan	$385	

End

How-To Hints

Formulas Usually Self-Adjust

If you have written formulas that calculate across the table, the formulas adjust themselves automatically after you insert new rows or columns (unless you insert a row immediately above a subtotal—then you will need to adjust the formula).

Insert a Whole Row or Column

When you insert rows or columns, be sure you select the entire row or column before you click the **Insert** command. If you select only a few cells, Excel tries to insert more cells, which messes up the table completely.

TASK 9

How to Delete Columns and Rows

If you need to remove an entire row or column of data from a table, you could delete the data and then move the remaining data to close the empty space. It's faster, however, to delete the entire row or column because the table closes up the space for you.

If you have written formulas that calculate across the table, the formulas adjust themselves automatically after you delete rows or columns.

Begin

1 Select the Row

To delete a row, select the row you want to delete (click its row number to select it). Right-click the selection.

5	Baker	John & Mabel	PO Box 184
6	Balogh	William	5775 W. Mallory
7	Bedrosian	Dick & Annie	5980 E. Mallory
	Christensen	Jim	PO Box 150
9	Dandyn	Millard & Mary	5650 W. Kruger
10	eak	Gail A.	5730 W. Mallory
11	D mokos	Larry	5775 W. Mallory

2 Delete the Selected Row

Choose **Delete** on the shortcut menu.

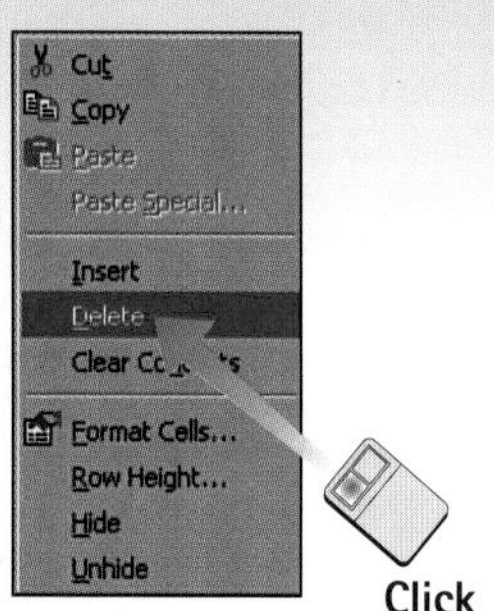

3 Select the Column

To delete a column, select the column you want to delete (click its column letter to select it). Right-click the selected column.

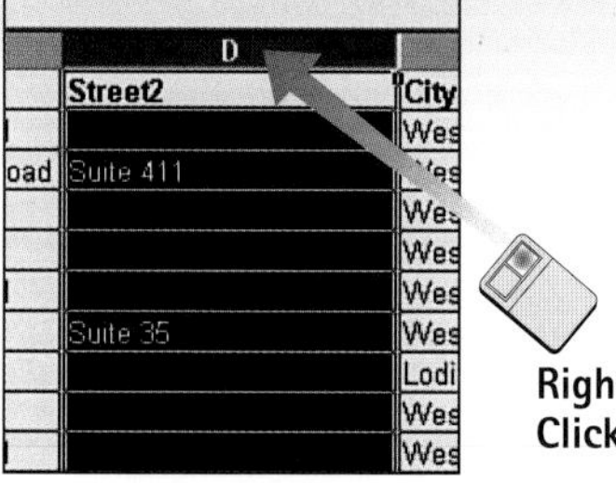

4 Delete the Selected Column

Choose **Delete** on the shortcut menu.

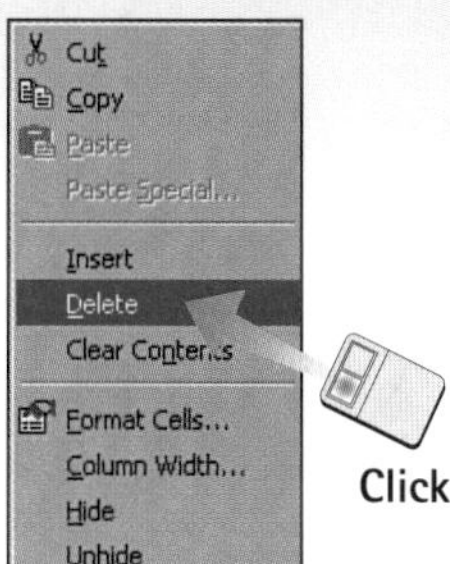

5 Delete Several Adjacent Rows

To delete several adjacent rows at one time, select the adjacent rows in the table, right-click the selection, and choose **Delete** from the shortcut menu.

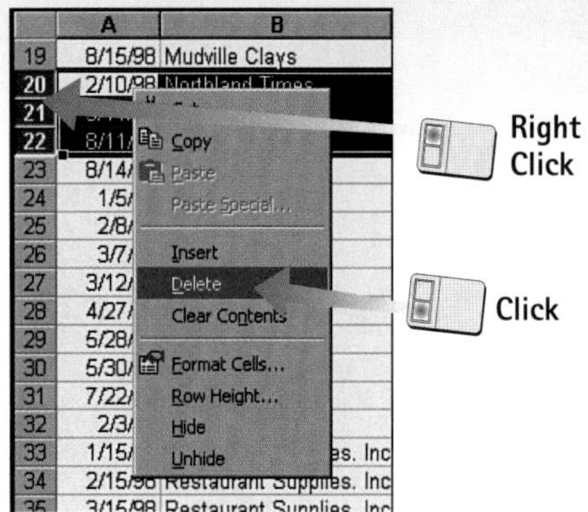

6 Delete Several Adjacent Columns

To delete several adjacent columns at one time, select the adjacent columns in the table, right-click the selection, and choose **Delete** from the shortcut menu.

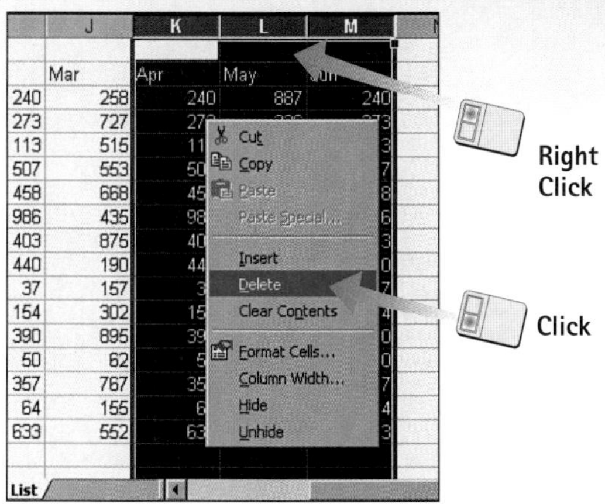

End

TASK 10

How to Delete Cells

It's easy to delete data from cells—you select the cells and press Delete. But sometimes you will want to remove the cells themselves. You might want to remove a row of data from a table, for example, but another table is next to it. If you delete the data by deleting the row from the worksheet, you will affect the second table because the row will be deleted all the way across the worksheet.

However, if you delete the cells in the one table, the table closes up the space where the cells were, but the table next to it is unaffected.

Begin

1 Select the Cells

Select the cells you want to delete. Right-click the selected cells.

	Item	Price	Item	Price
25				
26	Item	Price	Item	Price
27	HoneySuckle Soap	$3.50	Mixing Bowls	$20.00
28	Sea Soap	$3.50	Butter Crock	$5.00
29	Blueberry Soap	$3.50	Coffee Mug	$4.00
30	Christmas Spice Soap	$3.50	Soup Tureen	$25.00
31	Farmhand Soap	[illegible]	Lidded Casserole	$30.00
32	Skin Tonic Soap	$ 50	Dutch Oven	$40.00
33	Almond Loofah Soap	$ 50		
34				
35				
36				
37				

Right Click

2 Choose Delete

Choose **Delete** from the shortcut menu.

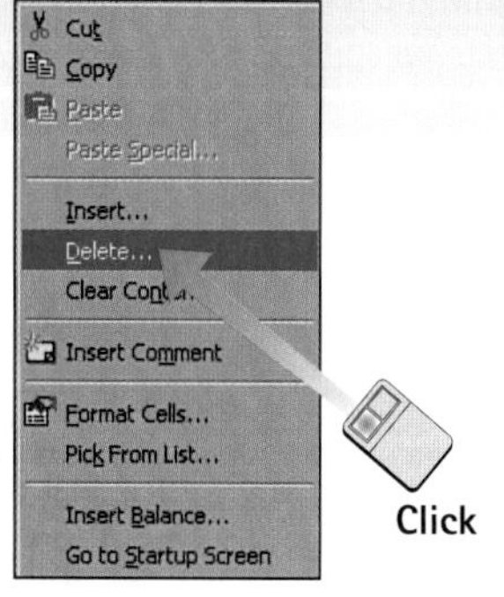

3 Shift Replacement Cells Up

In the Delete dialog box, click the **Shift cells up** option, and choose **OK**.

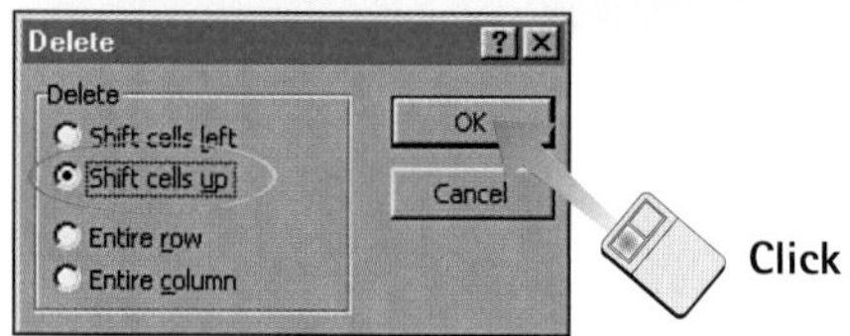

4 Cells Move to Fill in the Space

The cells are removed from the worksheet, and the cells below move up to fill in the empty space; the cells on either side of the deleted cells are unaffected.

	Item	Price	Item	Price
26	Item	Price	Item	Price
27	HoneySuckle Soap	$3.50	Mixing Bowls	$20.00
28	Sea Soap	$3.50	Butter Crock	$5.00
29	Blueberry Soap	$3.50	Coffee Mug	$4.00
30	Farmhand Soap	$3.50	Soup Tureen	$25.00
31	Skin Tonic Soap	$3.50	Lidded Casserole	$30.00
32	Almond Loofah Soap	$3.50	Dutch Oven	$40.00
33				
34				
35				

5 If You Shift Cells Left...

If you select the **Shift cells left** option in the Delete dialog box (in step 3), cells on the right side of the deleted cells move over, and cells above and below the deleted cells are unaffected.

	Item	Price		Item	Price
26	Item	Price		Item	Price
27	HoneySuckle Soap	$3.50		Mixing Bowls	$20.00
28	Sea Soap	$3.50		Butter Crock	$5.00
29	Blueberry Soap	$3.50		Coffee Mug	$4.00
30		Soup Tureen	$25.00		
31	Farmhand Soap	$3.50		Lidded Casserole	$30.00
32	Skin Tonic Soap	$3.50		Dutch Oven	$40.00
33	Almond Loofah Soap	$3.50			
34					
35					
36					

6 Clear Formatting, but Leave Data

If you don't want to delete the cells, but you want to remove their formatting (cell borders and colors) without affecting the data, select the cells and choose **Edit**, **Clear**, **Formats**.

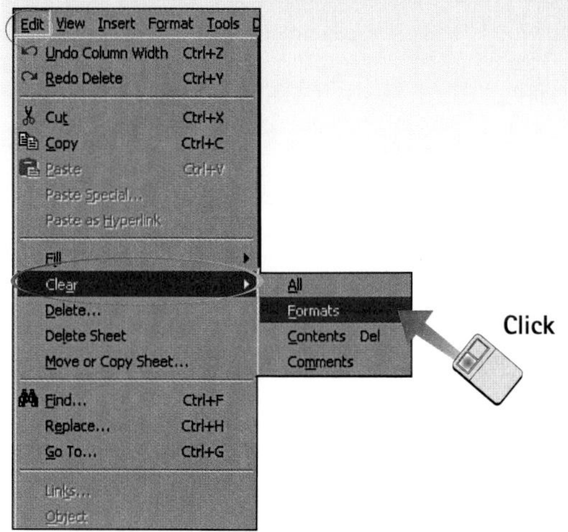

End

How-To Hints

What Happens to the Worksheet?

When you delete cells (or rows/columns) from a worksheet, you don't reduce the total size of the worksheet. New cells, rows, or columns are added to the bottom and right edges of the worksheet so that every worksheet still contains 256 columns and 65,536 rows.

TASK 11

How to Set the Column Width and Row Height

In a new worksheet, all the columns and rows are the same size. As you enter data, you will find that the default sizes aren't going to work for all your entries; it's quite common to exceed your column width when entering data. If it's a text entry, the text flows over into the cell to the right, until you enter data in the cell on the right; then the wide entry is cut off at the cell border (it's all there, but it's hidden). If it's a number entry, it won't flow over; instead it appears as **########** in the cell.

You can quickly adjust the column width or row height in your worksheets. You can drag a row or column to a new size, or you can specify an exact size.

Begin

1 Drag a New Column Width

To adjust the column width, point at the right border of the column letter for the column you want to widen. The mouse pointer becomes a two-headed arrow. Hold down the left mouse button and drag the border in either direction to adjust the column width. Release the mouse button when the column is the width you want.

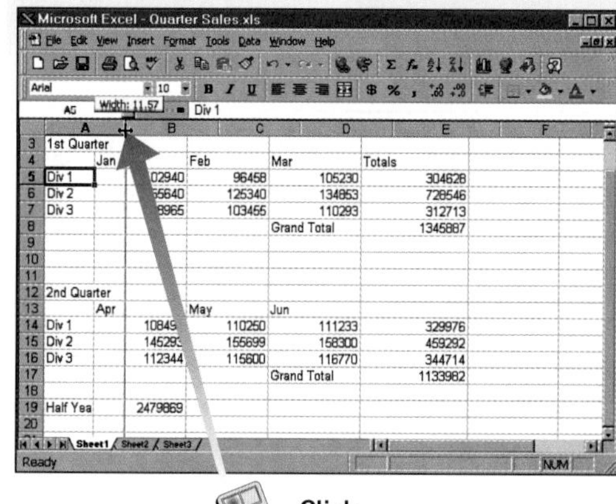

Click Hold & Drag

2 Resize Multiple Columns

To make several columns the same width, select all the columns by dragging over their column letters, and then adjust the width for any one of them while they're all selected. They will all adjust to the same width.

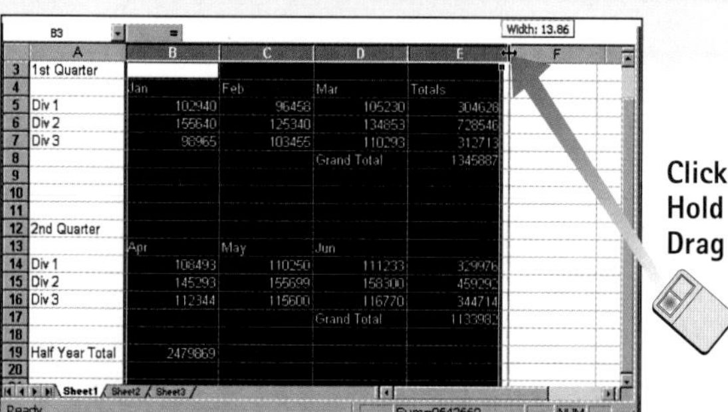

Click Hold & Drag

3 Open the Column Width Dialog

To enter an exact value for the column width, select the column, then open the **Format** menu and choose **Column, Width**.

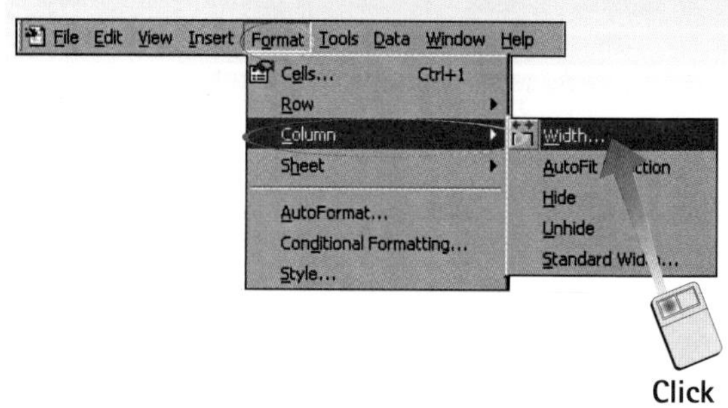

Click

4 Specify an Exact Size

Enter a measurement (in points) for the column width, then click **OK** to exit and apply the new setting.

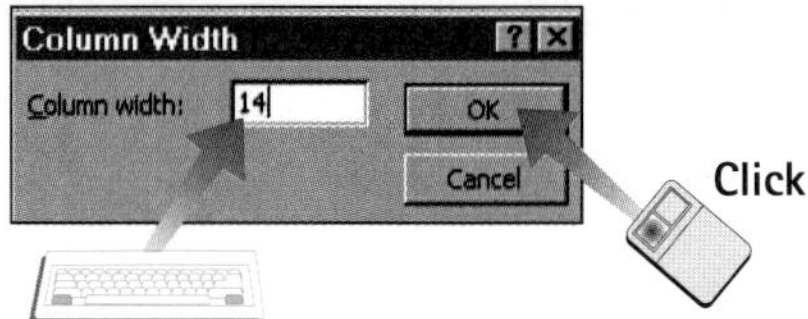

6 Open the Row Height Dialog Box

You can also specify an exact value for the row height. Select the row or rows to which you want to apply a new measurement, then open the **Format** menu and select **Row, Height**. Enter a new value (in points) and click **OK** to exit.

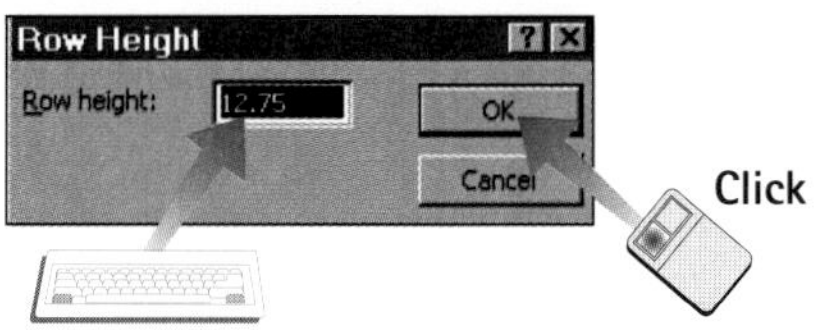

5 Drag a New Row Height

You can adjust row height the same way you adjust column width. Point at the bottom border of the row number for the row you want to deepen. The mouse pointer becomes a two-headed arrow. Hold down the left mouse button and drag the border in either direction to adjust the row height. Release the mouse button when the row is the height you want.

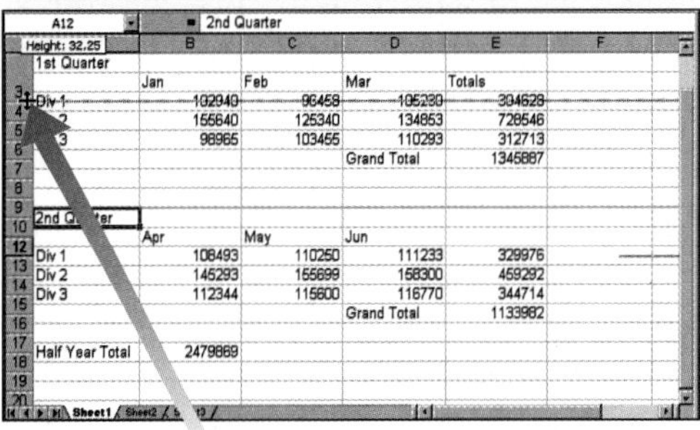

End

How-To Hints

Best Fit

To quickly make the column fit its widest entry exactly (even if you don't know which entry is widest because the list is really long), point at the right border of the column letter and double-click the two-headed arrow. This is called a best fit. You can do the same with a row; double-click the bottom border of the row heading.

Numbers Don't Print?

Occasionally, numbers that seem to fit the column onscreen don't fit on the printed page; if that happens, just widen the column a bit more.

Multiple Nonadjacent Columns

You can adjust nonadjacent columns to the same width the same way as adjacent columns (in step 2); to select nonadjacent columns, select the first column, then press and hold Ctrl while you select the others. Release Ctrl after you have selected all the columns you want to resize.

TASK 12

How to Define a Range Name

When you refer to cells in a formula, you can use a reference, but you risk a couple of potential problems: You occasionally have to work with relative versus absolute references; and a formula such as =B20+B21 is not very intuitive. However, you can name cells and ranges, and then refer to those names in formulas. Unlike =B20+B21, the formula =Subtotal+Tax is clear.

Names are always defined with absolute references, and they work the same as absolute references. The only difference is that when you move named cells, they take their names with them. Any formulas that refer to named cells can always find them.

Begin

1 Select Cell; Click in Name Box

To name a cell, click the cell to select it, and then click in the **Name** box. The cell address in the Name box is highlighted.

Click

	B	C	D	E	F
12	Coffee Mug	$4.00			
13	Soup Tureen	$25.00			
14	Lidded Casserole	$30.00			
15	Dutch Oven	$40.00			
16					
17		Subtotal			
18					
19					

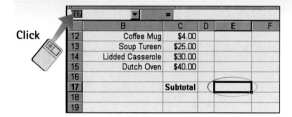

2 Type a Name and Press Enter

Type a name for the cell and press Enter. The name appears in place of the cell address when the cell is selected. Names can only be one word long and cannot be existing cell addresses (TotalSales is allowable, for example, but FY1998 isn't). Names must begin with a letter or an underscore (_); all other characters can be letters, numbers, periods, and underscores.

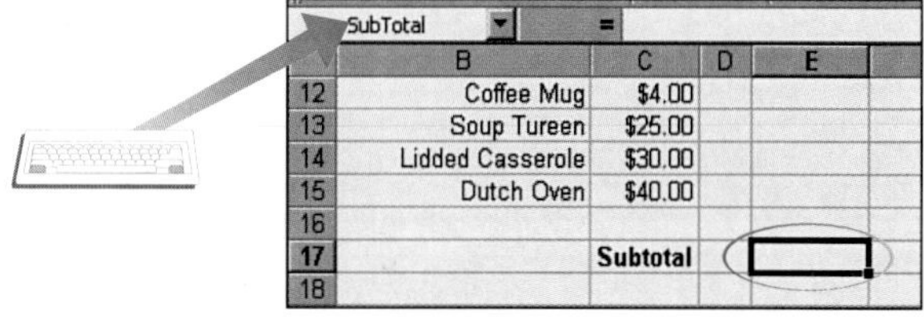
SubTotal

	B	C	D	E
12	Coffee Mug	$4.00		
13	Soup Tureen	$25.00		
14	Lidded Casserole	$30.00		
15	Dutch Oven	$40.00		
16				
17		Subtotal		
18				

3 Use Name Box to Go to the Cell

To jump to the cell from anywhere in the workbook, click the arrow next to the Name box and click the cell name on the list.

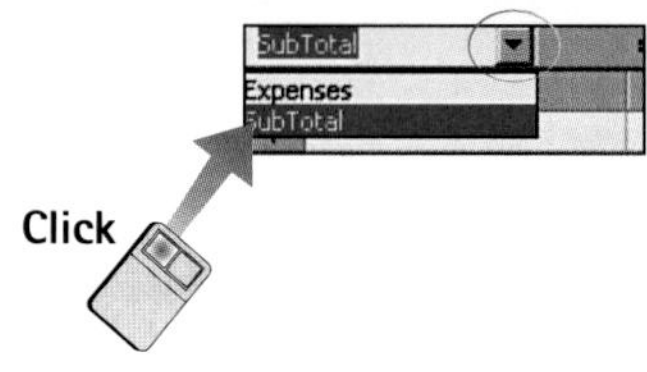

Click

4 Use the Cell Name in a Formula

To use the name in a formula, write the formula and click the cell to include it; the cell's name appears in the formula instead of the cell's reference.

=SubTotal+Tax

C	D	E	F
Subtotal		$49.00	
Tax		$3.92	
Total		$52.92	

5 Name a Range

To name a range, select the range. Click in the **Name** box, type a name, and press Enter.

Contacts = Last

	A	B	C	D
1	**Last**	**First**	**Street**	**City**
2	Abovian	Julia	5850 W. Mallory Road	Westwood
3	Andersen	George D.	17200 N. Trails End Road	Westwood
4	Bahir	Robin	5755 W. Kruger Road	Westwood
5	Baker	John & Mabel	PO Box 184	Westwood
6	Balogh	William	5775 W. Mallory Road	Westwood
7	Bedrosian	Dick & Annie	5980 E. Mallory Road	Westwood
8	Christensen	Jim	PO Box 150	Lodi
9	Dandyn	Millard & Mary	5650 W. Kruger Road	Westwood
10	Deak	Gail A.	5730 W. Mallory Road	Westwood
11	Domokos	Larry	5775 W. Mallory Road	Westwood
12	Dyhr	Richard & Tami	16750 N. Trails End Road	Westwood
13	Fabin	Leo & Gail	16980 N. Trails End Road	Westwood
14	Fairfax	Colleen	6195 W. Mallory Road	Westwood

6 Create Several Names at Once

If a worksheet contains labels, you can name the cells they refer to all at once. Select the label cells and the cells to which they refer. Choose **Insert**, **Name**, **Create**. In the Create Names dialog box, click the check boxes for the labels you want to use and choose **OK**. All the cells are named with their worksheet labels in one step.

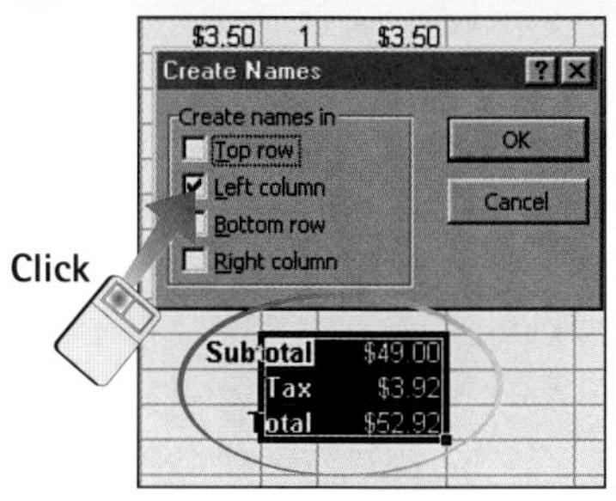

End

How-To Hints

Delete a Name

To delete a name, open the worksheet that contains the named cell or range. Choose **Insert**, **Name**, **Define**. In the Define Names dialog box, select the name and click **Delete**, and then choose **OK**.

Not Case Sensitive

Names are not case sensitive; if you create the name "TotalSales," Excel reads it and the names "TOTALSALES" and "totalsales" as the same name.

TASK 13

How to Find and Replace Data

As in Microsoft Word, you can search for and replace any character in a worksheet. You can find and/or replace text strings, such as a company or employee name, and you can find and/or replace numbers, either single digits or strings of numbers. You can also choose to search for characters in cell values, formulas, and worksheet comments.

If you have used Microsoft Word, you will discover that Find and Replace procedures are almost identical in the two programs. If you're new to the procedure, I will teach you how to use them in Excel, then you will know how to use them in Word.

Begin

1 Choose Edit, Find

To search for a word or number in a worksheet, choose **Edit**, **Find**.

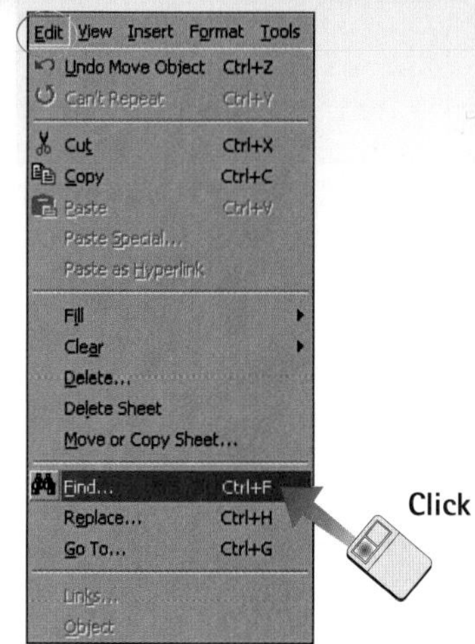

2 Search for Characters

In the Find dialog box, in the **Find what** box, type the characters (numbers, text, symbols) for which you want to search. In the **Look in** box, select what you want to search. Then click **Find Next** to find the first cell containing your search characters. Click **Find Next** repeatedly to find each occurrence of the character string.

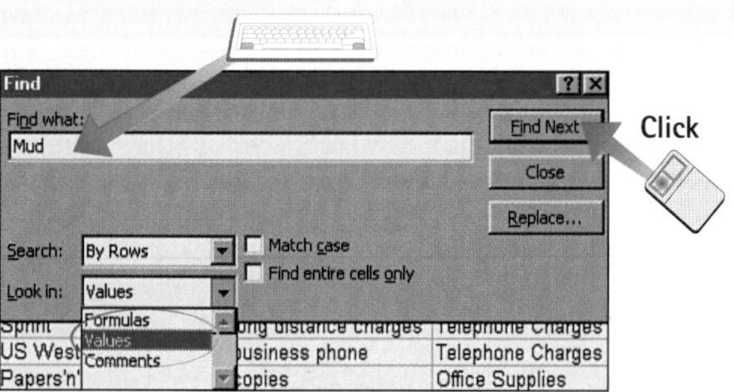

3 Search in Displayed Values

To search displayed values for number or text characters, select **Values** from the **Look in** box. Values searches both constant values and the results of formulas—anything displayed in a cell. Shown is the result of a search for the word "jar."

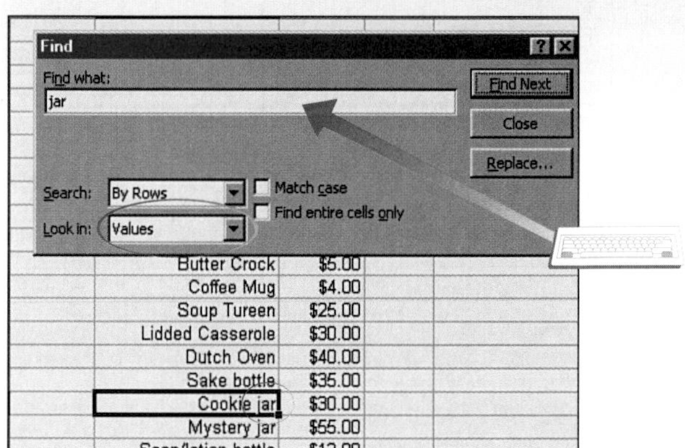

4 Search in Formulas

To search in formulas for numbers, cell names, function names, mathematical operators, or anything that's part of the formula, select **Formulas** in the **Look in** box, and then click **Find Next**. Shown is the result of a search for the cell name "products."

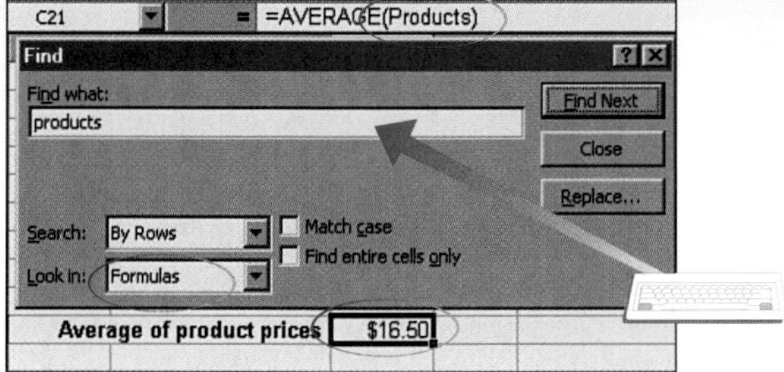

5 Search in Cell Comments

To search in cell comments for a text string, select **Comments** in the **Look in** box, and then click **Find Next**. Shown is the result of a search for the word "discontinued." (A *comment* is extra information added to a worksheet that doesn't appear in cells; a cell with a comment has a red triangle in its upper-right corner.)

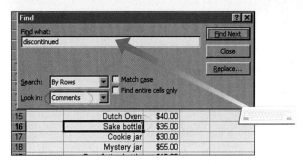

6 Replace Characters

To replace a character string, click **Replace** in the Find dialog box**.** In the Replace dialog box, type the old characters in the **Find what** box; type the replacement characters in the **Replace with** box. Click **Find Next** to find the first occurrence, then click **Replace**. Click **Replace** repeatedly to replace strings one at a time; click **Replace All** to replace all occurrences at once.

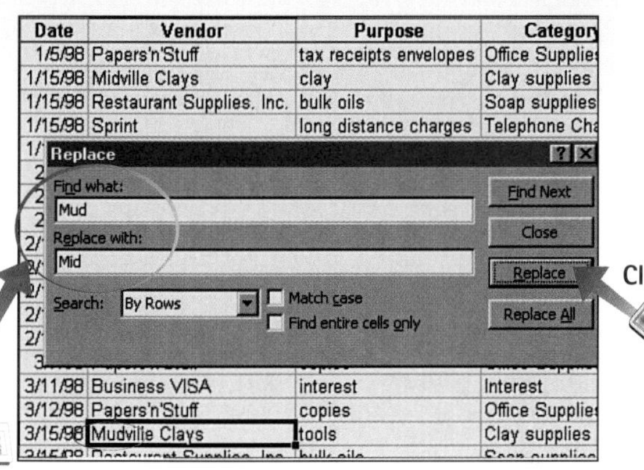

End

How-To Hints

Keyboard Shortcuts

The keyboard shortcut for Edit, Find is Ctrl+F; the shortcut for Edit, Replace is Ctrl+H. You can open the Replace dialog box without first opening the Find dialog box.

Narrow Your Search

To limit your search to text with specific capitalization, mark the **Match case** text box. To limit your search to complete entries instead of including partial entries (if you want to search for 100, for example, and not find 1,000 or 20,100), mark the **Find entire cells only** check box.

Speed Up the Search

In a large table, sometimes the search is faster if you select **By Rows** or **By Columns** in the **Search** box, especially if you start by selecting a cell in the specific row or column you want to search. In a small table, it makes no difference what's selected in the Search box.

TASK 14

How to Sort Data

Sorting data is the most basic procedure in organizing data. You can sort a list to see product names in alphabetical order, for example, then sort the list to see product prices from highest to lowest. When you add new products, type them at the end of the list, then sort the list to position the new products.

When you sort a list, the whole list is sorted and each record (row) in the list retains its integrity; other tables on the same worksheet are not affected by the sort.

Begin

1 Click in the Sort Key Column

To sort by a single *key*, or column, click any cell in that column.

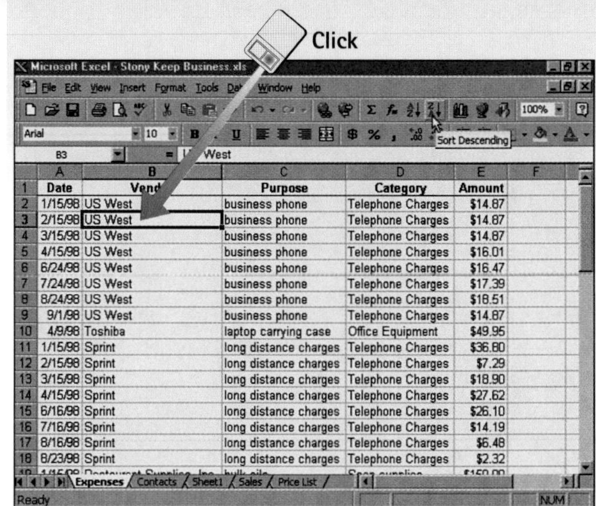

2 Sort in Ascending Order

To sort the list in alphabetical order (A-Z) or in lowest-to-highest numerical order, click the **Sort Ascending** button on the Standard toolbar. To sort the list in reverse alphabetical order (Z-A) or in highest-to-lowest numerical order, click the **Sort Descending** button on the Standard toolbar.

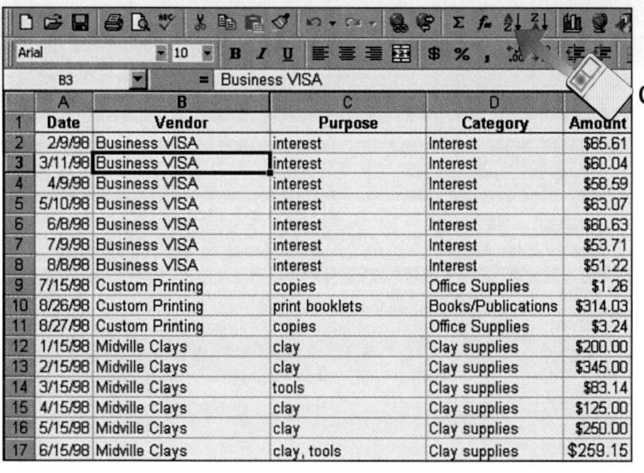

3 Set Up a Multikey Sort

To run a multikey sort, click anywhere in the list and then choose **Data**, **Sort**.

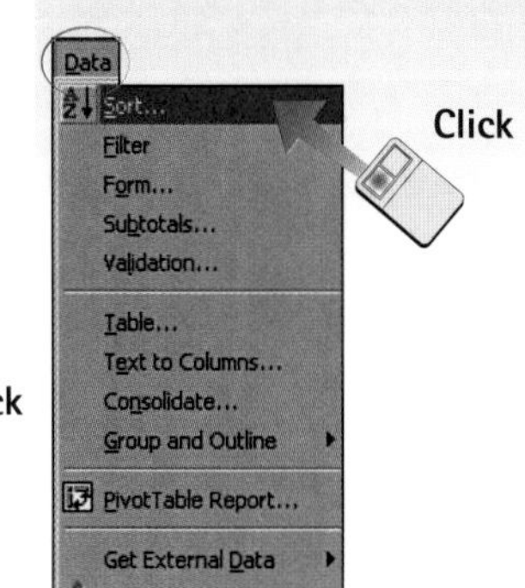

4 Set the First Key

In the Sort dialog box, in the **Sort by** box, select the column you want for your major sort (shown here, **Category** in a product list). Next to the column heading, click the sort order option you want (**Ascending** or **Descending**).

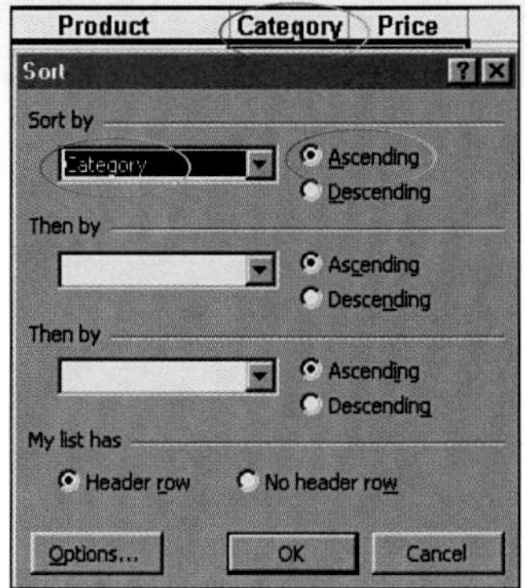

5 Set the Second Key

For the second key in the sort, select the column in the first **Then by** box (shown here, by **Product** within **Category**) and click a sort order option. To sort by a third key within the second key, use the second **Then by** box. Choose **OK** to run the sort.

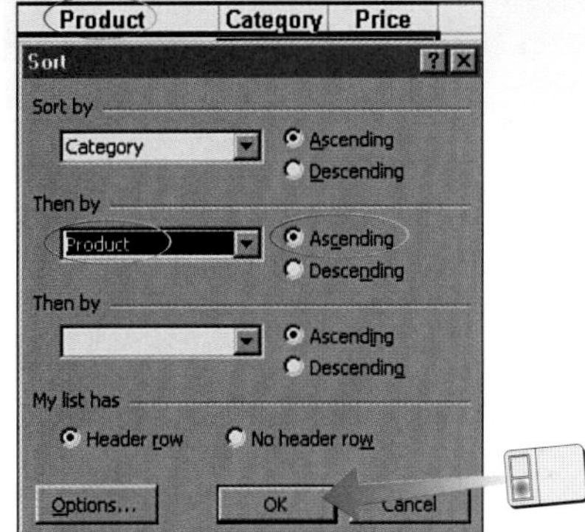

6 Results of a Multikey Sort

Shown here is the result of the two-key sort—by Category and then by Product.

Product	Category	Price
Butter Crock	Pottery	$5.00
Coffee Mug	Pottery	$4.00
Cookie jar	Pottery	$30.00
Dutch Oven	Pottery	$40.00
Lidded Casserole	Pottery	$30.00
Mixing Bowls	Pottery	$20.00
Mystery jar	Pottery	$55.00
Sake bottle	Pottery	$35.00
Soap/lotion bottle	Pottery	$12.00
Soup Tureen	Pottery	$25.00
Almond Loofah Soap	Soap	$3.50
Blueberry Soap	Soap	$3.50
Christmas Spice Soap	Soap	$3.50
Farmhand Soap	Soap	$3.50
HoneySuckle Soap	Soap	$3.50
Sea Soap	Soap	$3.50
Skin Tonic Soap	Soap	$3.50

How-To Hints

Sort One Column, Not the Whole List

If you want to sort a single column within a list but not sort the rest of the list with that column, select all the cells in the table column that you want to sort; only the cells in that column are sorted.

Lose Your Headings?

If your columns' headings are similar enough to the data in your list that Excel doesn't guess that they're headings, they may get sorted into the data. To fix that, click the **Undo** button to undo the sort. Choose **Data**, **Sort**. In the Sort dialog box, click the **Header row** option before you run the sort.

Sort Day or Month Names

If you sort day or month names, they will be sorted in alphabetical order, not calendar order; to sort them in calendar order, use the Sort dialog box. Click the **Options** button at the bottom. In the Sort Options dialog box, select the appropriate list from the list box and choose **OK**. Choose **OK** in the Sort dialog box to run the sort.

TASK 15

How to Filter Data

Filtering shows only the records you want to see and hides the rest. Records aren't removed; they're just temporarily hidden.

Filtering is based on *criteria*, data that's shared by all the records you want to see. If you filter a list of contacts to show only those whose city is Poughkeepsie, for example, your criteria is "Poughkeepsie" in the City column.

You don't have to sort a list before you filter, and you can have blank cells in the list; however, the top row should contain column headings or labels, and the list should contain no completely blank rows.

Begin

1 Click a Cell

Click any cell in the list or table.

Product	Category	Price
Lidded Casserole	Pottery	$30.00
Mystery jar	Pottery	$55.00
Blueberry Soap	Soap	$3.50
Dutch Oven	Pottery	$40.00
Sea Soap	Soap	$4.50
Skin Tonic Soap	Soap	$3.50
Sake bottle	Pottery	$35.00
Coffee Mug	Pottery	
Soap/lotion bottle	Pottery	$12
Farmhand Soap	Soap	$3.50
Cookie jar	Pottery	$30.00
Almond Loofah Soap	Soap	$4.50
Mixing Bowls	Pottery	$20.00
Butter Crock	Pottery	$5.00
Christmas Spice Soap	Soap	$3.50
HoneySuckle Soap	Soap	$4.50
Soup Tureen	Pottery	$25.00

Click

2 Click the Filter Command

Choose **Data, Filter, AutoFilter.**

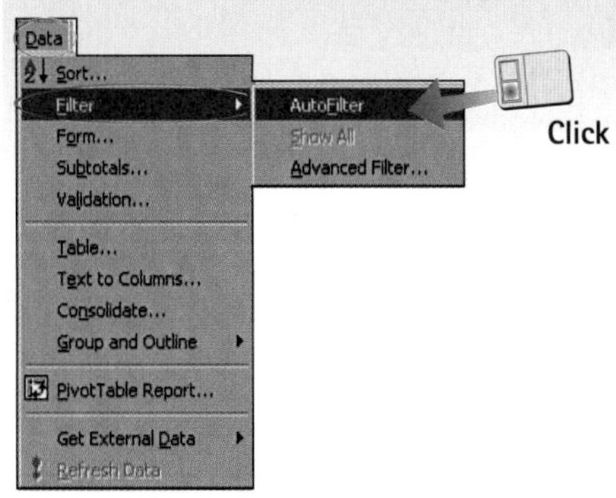

3 Click a Filter Arrow

Filter arrows appear in each column label cell. In the column that contains your criteria, click the filter arrow to drop a list of all the values in the column.

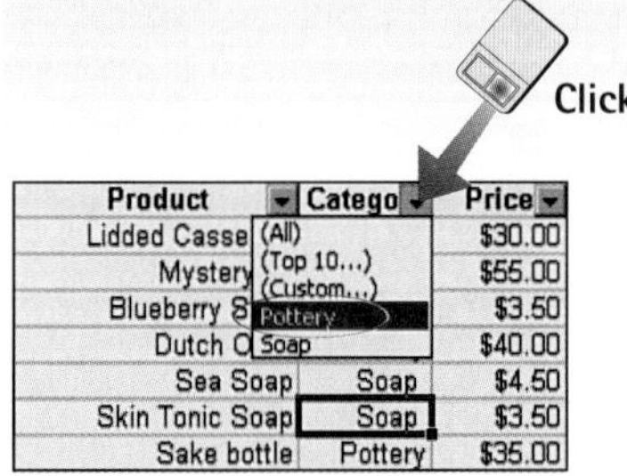

4 Click Filter Criteria

Click the criteria you want. All records that don't share that criteria are hidden. The filter arrow where you set the criteria turns blue, and the row numbers where records are hidden turn blue.

Product	Catego	Price
Lidded Casserole	Pottery	$30.00
Mystery jar	Pottery	$55.00
Dutch Oven	Pottery	$40.00
Sake bottle	Pottery	$35.00
Coffee Mug	Pottery	$4.00
Soap/lotion bottle	Pottery	$12.00
Cookie jar	Pottery	$30.00
Mixing Bowls	Pottery	$20.00
Butter Crock	Pottery	$5.00
Soup Tureen	Pottery	$25.00

5 Set Multiple Criteria

To set multiple criteria, set criteria in multiple columns (repeat steps 1–4). Shown is a list filtered to show all soaps that are priced at $4.50.

Product	Catego	Price
Sea Soap	Soap	$4.50
Almond Loofah Soap	Soap	$4.50
HoneySuckle Soap	Soap	$4.50

6 Remove the Filter

To remove the filter and show all the records in the list, either click the filter arrow where you set the criteria and click **(All)**, or choose **Data**, **Filter**, **AutoFilter** to turn AutoFilter off.

Product	Catego	Price
Blueberry S	(All)	$3.50
Sea S	(Top 10...)	$4.50
Skin Tonic S	(Custom...)	[illegible]
Farmhand S	Pottery / Soap	[illegible]
Almond Loofah Soap	Soap	$4.50
Christmas Spice Soap	Soap	$3.50
HoneySuckle Soap	Soap	$4.50

Click

End

How-To Hints

Field or Column?

The terms "column" and "field" are used interchangeably in Excel (and in Access, Word, and Outlook); *field* is a database term that refers to a column in a table.

Top 10

To filter the top (or bottom) 10 (or another number) of number items in a list, select the **Top 10** filter criteria. Select **Top** or **Bottom**, select a number, select **Items** or **Percent**, and choose **OK**.

Comparison Criteria

To set complex criteria such as "prices greater than $4," click the filter arrow in the column in which you want to set the criteria, and click **(Custom...)**. In the Custom AutoFilter dialog box, select comparison operators in the list box on the left, type or select criteria in the list box on the right, then choose **OK**.

TASK 16

Begin

How to Work with Worksheets

Multiple worksheets in a workbook act like extra pages in a binder; they're interactive and interrelated, and they always stay together in the same file. Their advantage is that you can keep several tables in the same file but not have to scroll to Timbuktu to find them. An efficient use for multiple worksheets might be monthly revenue and expenses—on separate month worksheets—all in the same file so they open together.

You can delete extra worksheets, add more worksheets, and move easily between them. You can also rename worksheets and reposition them in a workbook, or make copies.

1 Move Between Worksheets

To move from one sheet to another, click the sheet tab for the sheet to which you want to move. The selected sheet, the *active worksheet*, is the one with the bright white-and-black sheet tab; sheets that aren't selected have sheet tabs that are gray and black.

2 Rename a Worksheet

Double-click the sheet tab; the sheet name is highlighted. Type a new name and press Enter, or click a cell in the worksheet.

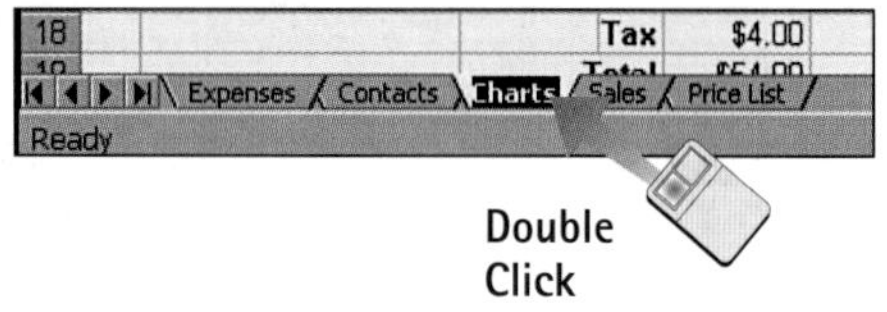

3 Delete a Worksheet

Right-click the sheet tab for the worksheet you want to delete and choose **Delete**.

4 Add Another Worksheet

Right-click a sheet tab and choose **Insert**. In the Insert dialog box, on the **General** tab, double-click the **Worksheet** icon. The new worksheet is inserted on the left side of the sheet tab you initially right-clicked.

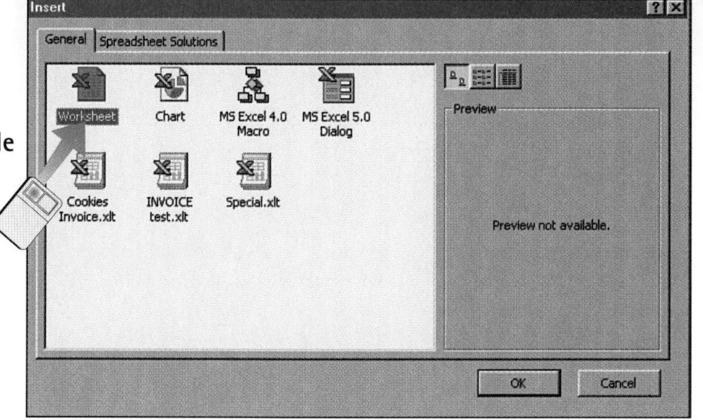

5 Move a Worksheet

To move a worksheet within a workbook, drag its sheet tab. While you drag, the mouse pointer acquires a sheet-of-paper symbol, and a small black triangle points to the position where the sheet will be moved.

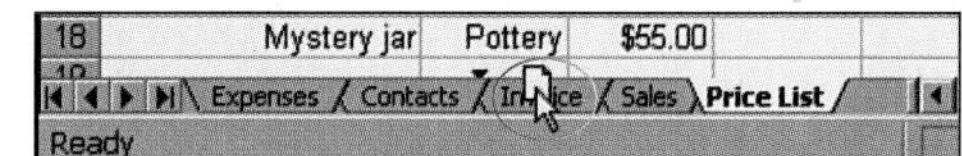

6 Copy a Worksheet

To make a copy of a worksheet within a workbook, drag its sheet tab. While you drag, the mouse pointer acquires a sheet-of-paper symbol, and a small black triangle points to the position where the sheet will be copied. Before you release the mouse button, press Ctrl (the pointer will show a small plus symbol on its sheet-of-paper symbol, which indicates a copy).

End

How-To Hints

Use the Shortcut Menu

Right-click over the worksheet tab to display a shortcut menu of commands you can apply to the worksheet. Be sure to position the mouse pointer directly over the sheet tab name or the wrong shortcut menu will appear.

Another Way to Move or Copy

Another way to move or copy a worksheet is to use the Move or Copy dialog box. Right-click over the sheet tab you want to move or copy and select **Move** or **Copy** from the shortcut menu. Select the workbook you want to move or copy the worksheet to, then choose where to place the sheet. Click **OK** to exit the dialog box and execute the move or copy.

Task

CHAPTER 7

How to Use Formulas and Functions

The real thrill of using a spreadsheet program such as *Excel* is the ability to perform calculations. From the simplest addition and subtraction to complex scientific exponential equations, Excel *worksheets* use *formulas* to perform all kinds of calculations on your data. Based on the *values* you have entered, for example, you can create formulas that calculate the average sales for your department, total the commissions each sales representative receives, and compare the figures to last year's numbers.

You don't have to worry that a calculation might be incorrect—Excel won't make a mistake. And whenever you change a value included in a formula, Excel updates the formula results automatically. In this chapter, you will learn the basic steps for creating and using Excel formulas.

In addition to formulas you create yourself, Excel comes with hundreds of built-in *functions*—calculation tools you can use to perform more complex financial, analytical, or statistical calculations. You will also learn how to apply these functions to your own worksheet situations.

Task 1

How to Use AutoSum

The most common mathematical calculation in Excel is the sum. You might sum the sales results for several months or the total items in an invoice. Summing is so common that a toolbar button enters a SUM formula for you. You can add the contents of cells by writing a formula such as =A1+B1, but using the SUM function in a formula is faster because Excel does the work for you. You will learn how to write a formula in Task 2, "How to Create Formulas," and you will learn more about functions (built-in equations) in Task 4, "How to Enter Functions;" in this task, you learn to enter a fast sum with the AutoSum button.

Begin

1 Enter the Numbers

Enter the numbers you want to sum in a column, row, or rectangular block of cells. The formula ignores any text entries in the *range* of cells (the collection of cells you will sum).

2 Select a Location for the Sum

Select the cell where you want the sum result to appear (usually at the end of the row or column of numbers).

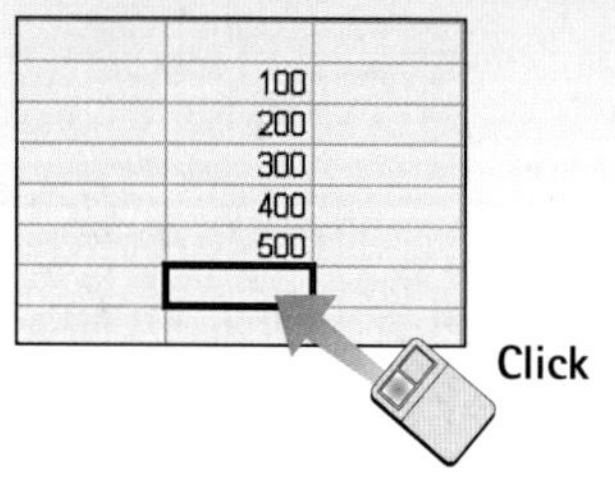

3 Click AutoSum

On the Standard toolbar, click the **AutoSum** button.

Click

4 The SUM Formula Is Entered

The **AutoSum** button inserts a formula that uses the SUM function, and surrounds the cells being summed with a temporary moving border.

=SUM(D12:D16)

C	D	E
	100	
	200	
	300	
	400	
	500	
	=SUM(D12:D16)	

5 Complete the Entry

If the moving border is surrounding all the cells you want to sum, press Enter to complete the formula; if the surrounded cells are wrong, drag to select the cells you want summed (the moving border surrounds the cells you drag), and press Enter. The result of the formula is displayed in the cell.

	100	
	200	
	300	
	400	
	500	
	1500	

6 Look at the Formula and Result

To see the formula and the result, click the cell where you entered the formula. The results appear in the cell, and the formula appears in the Formula bar.

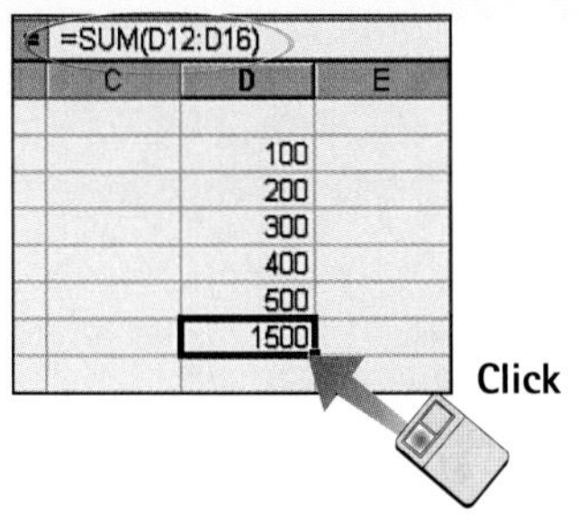

Click

End

How-To Hints

Sum a Whole Table at Once

To AutoSum all the columns in a table at once, select all the cells in the row below the table and click the **AutoSum** button; each column is summed in the cell below the column. To sum all the rows in a table at once, select all the cells in the column next to the table and click the **AutoSum** button. Each row is summed in the cell at the end of the row.

Put the AutoSum Anywhere

You can place an AutoSum formula anywhere on the worksheet, not just next to the range you're summing. To place the AutoSum formula away from the range of cells, click the cell where you want to display the result and click the **AutoSum** button. Drag to select the cells you want to sum, and then press Enter.

TASK 2

How to Create Formulas

On paper, formulas are written like this: 2+2=4. In Excel, a formula a slightly different form: type **=2+2**; the answer, 4, is displayed in the cell. All formulas in a worksheet begin with an equal sign (=).

In Excel, you're not limited to writing =2+2; you can type =(*a cell*)+(*another cell*), and the values entered in those cells are added together. If you change the values in those cells, the formula continues to add together their current values. You can also use *mathematical operators* to perform other calculations, such as subtraction (-), multiplication (*), or division (/).

Begin

1 Select a Cell

Click the cell in which you want to enter the formula.

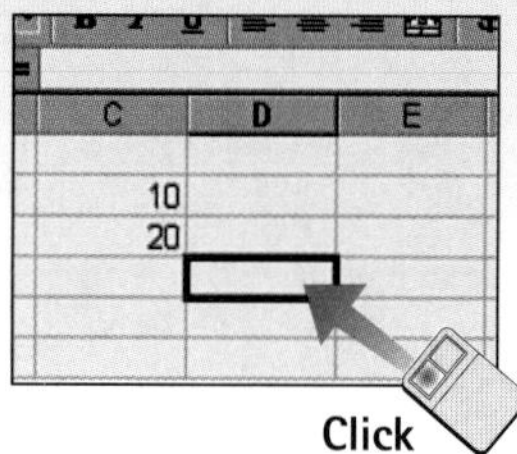

2 Type =

Type an equal sign (=).

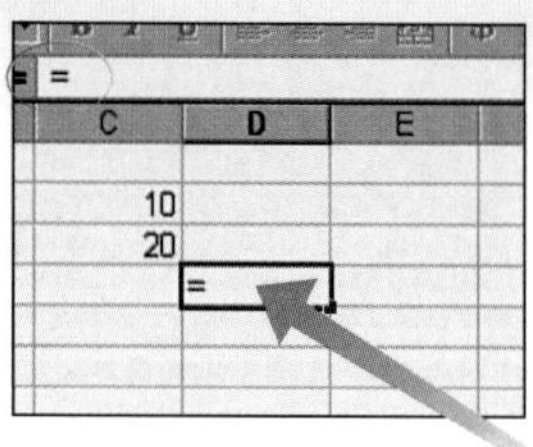

3 Build the Formula

Click the first of the cells you want to add, type a plus symbol (+), and then click the next cell you want to add. As you click each cell, its cell address, or *cell reference*, appears in the formula.

4 Complete the Formula

Press Enter to complete the formula. The formula is entered, and the result appears in the formula cell. (The formula is displayed in the Formula bar.)

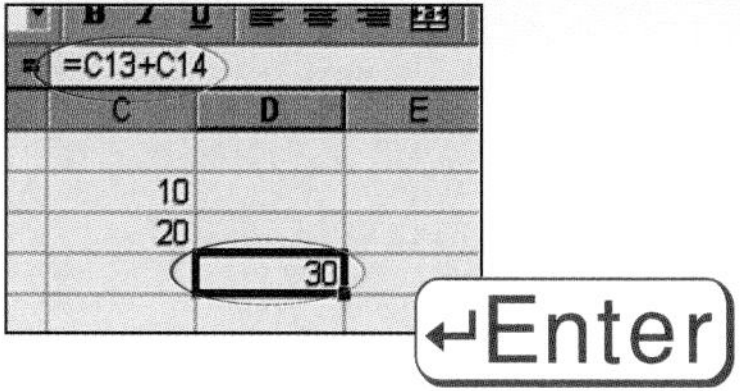

5 Test the Formula

Now change the values in the cells you referenced in the formula; the formula result changes automatically because the formula adds the values that are in the cells.

End

How-To Hints

Calculate a Large Range

To calculate a large range of cells on a worksheet without entering each cell into the formula separately, you can sum a *range* of cells by including the first and last cell; Excel includes all the cells in between. If you want to sum cells A1, A2, A3, A4, and A5 (the first five cells in column A), for example, a more convenient formula is =SUM(A1:A5). This formula tells Excel to sum all the cells between A1 and A5 (SUM is a specific Excel function; you will learn more about functions in Task 4).

What's Really in the Cell?

You can't tell by looking at a cell whether the value you see is a simple number or the result of a formula; to find out, select the cell and look at the Formula bar (what's actually entered in the cell is always displayed in the Formula bar).

Group Operators Within Parentheses

To use different operators in the same formula, use parentheses to divide the formula appropriately. If you want to add 4+6 and divide the result by 2, for example, the formula =4+6/2 gives the wrong answer (7); but the formula =(4+6)/2 gives the right answer (5). Operations within parentheses are performed first.

TASK 3

How to Work with Cell Addresses

Cell references are the worksheet addresses of cells. Three types exist: relative, absolute, and mixed. *Relative references* give a cell's location relative to the active cell, as in "two cells left and one cell up." *Absolute references* give an address that's unchanging, such as "the intersection of row 3 and column B." *Mixed references* return a mixture of the two—for example, "two cells below the active cell, in column D." Mostly you will want to use the default relative references.

The difference between types is that a relative reference looks like **A1**; an absolute reference looks like **$A$1**; and a mixed reference looks like **A$1** or **$A1**.

Begin

1 Enter a Formula

To demonstrate the difference between relative and absolute references, enter a formula that sums the two cells left of the formula. Shown here, the cells in columns C2 and D2 are summed.

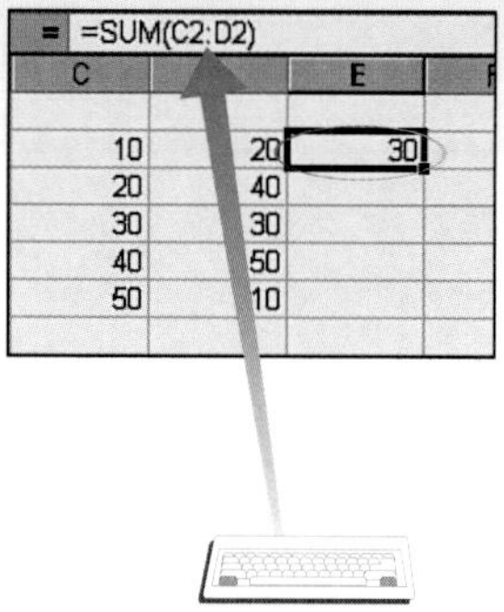

2 AutoFill the Formula

Copy the formula down the column using AutoFill. The formula for each cell adjusts to sum the two cells to its left. Usually, this is exactly what you want.

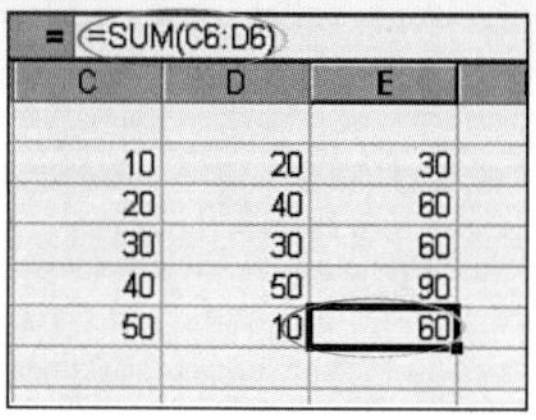

3 Rewrite the Formula

Now delete the formulas and rewrite the original so it multiplies the cell to its left by the value in cell F2.

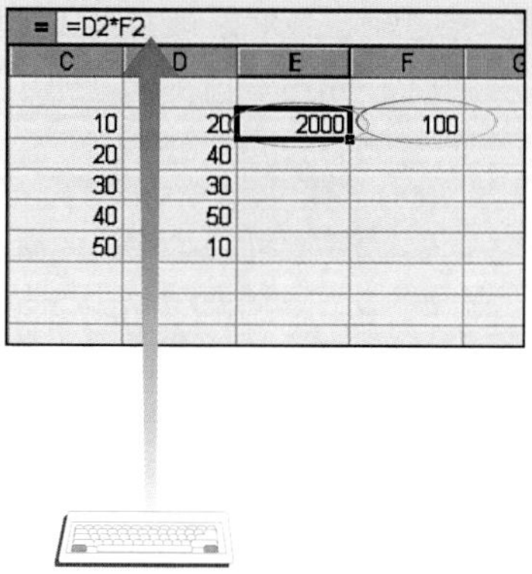

4 AutoFill the Formula

Use AutoFill to copy the formula down the column again—the results are wrong because relative references tell each formula to multiply the cell to its left by the cell on its right (instead of the value in F2). You need to change the F2 reference to an absolute reference so that each formula multiplies the cell on its left by the value in cell F2.

=D6*F6

C	D	E	F
10	20	2000	100
20	40	0	
30	30	0	
40	50	0	
50	10	0	

5 Change the Reference Type

To change the reference type, click the cell that contains the original formula. In the Formula bar, click the reference **F2**, and press F4. (Pressing F4 cycles the reference type repeatedly through all the reference types.) When the reference in the Formula bar reads $F$2, press Enter to complete the formula.

=D2*$F$2

C	D	E	F
10	20	=D2*$F$2	100
20	40		
30	30		
40	50		
50	10		

6 AutoFill the Formula

Use AutoFill to copy the formula down the column again. Now each formula multiplies the cell on its left by the value in cell F2.

=D6*$F$2

C	D	E	F	G
10	20	2000	100	
20	40	4000		
30	30	3000		
40	50	5000		
50	10	1000		

End

How-To Hints

Manual References

You can also enter absolute references by typing the appropriate symbol in the Formula bar. To make cell reference B4 absolute, for example, type **$B$4**.

Edit References

To edit a reference in a formula, click in the Formula bar where you want to edit and make your changes. Use the F4 command to change relative, absolute, or mixed references. Press Enter when finished editing.

Reference Other Sheets

You can also reference cells from other worksheets in your workbook. To do this, type the sheet name, an exclamation point, and the cell reference. For example, Sheet2!B4 would refer to cell B4 in worksheet 2.

TASK 4

How to Enter Functions

Task 2 showed you how to write formulas, and it briefly mentioned functions. A function is a built-in formula with a name that Excel recognizes; a function saves you time you would have spent setting up the math yourself.

To use a function, write a formula that includes the function name, the cells you want calculated, and any other information (called *arguments*) that the particular function needs. In Task 1, "How to Use AutoSum," you learned how to use AutoSum to automatically create a SUM formula; the formula consisted of an equal sign (=), the function name (SUM), and the cells you want summed (in parentheses).

Begin

1 Type =

Click the cell in which you want to write the formula and type an equal sign (=). On the Formula bar, click the down arrow next to the Name box. The Name box becomes a list of common function names.

2 Select a Function

Click a function name—I will demonstrate with the AVERAGE function. The AVERAGE function is better than a manual adding-and-dividing-cells formula because it ignores empty cells, which give an incorrect result.

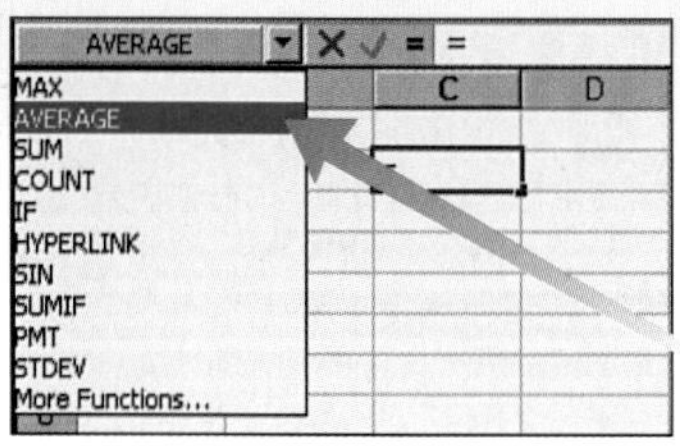

Click

3 Move the Formula Palette

The Formula palette appears (if the Office Assistant appears, click the **No, I don't need help now** option to make him go away). The palette may guess which cells you want to average, but you will replace those cells to be sure you're calculating what you want. Drag the Formula palette away if you need to uncover cells (click anywhere on the gray palette and drag).

4 Drag the Cells to Be Calculated

Be sure the **Number1** argument box is highlighted (if it isn't, drag over the cell references to highlight them), and drag across the cells you want to calculate. A moving border appears around the cells, and the cell references appear in the Formula palette's **Number1** argument box. Ignore the other argument boxes; they're for including other ranges in the calculation.

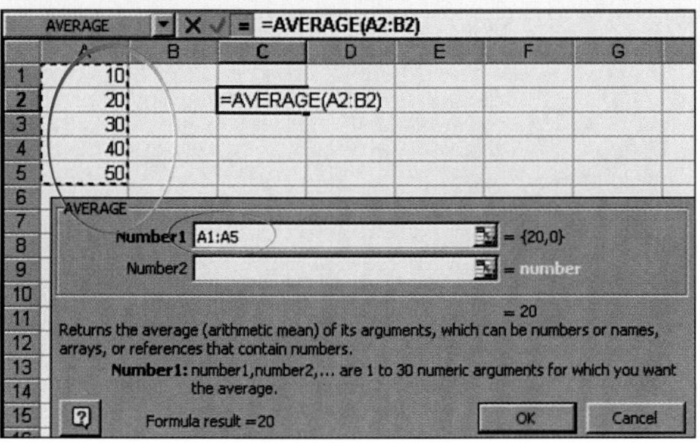

5 Complete the Formula

Choose **OK** to complete the formula. The palette disappears, and the formula result appears in the worksheet.

C2 =AVERAGE(A1:A5)

	A	B	C	D	E
1	10				
2	20		30		
3	30				
4	40				
5	50				
6					

6 Try the Other Functions

The MIN, MAX, and COUNT functions work the same way as the AVERAGE and SUM functions. Shown here are the results of each of these formulas for the same range of cells. If you don't see the function you want on the Functions list, click **More Functions** and find the function in the Paste Function dialog box.

C5 =SUM(A1:A5)

	A	B	C	D
1	10	**Average:**	30	
2	20	**Min:**	10	
3	30	**Max:**	50	
4	40	**Count:**	5	
5	50	**Sum:**	150	
6				

End

How-To Hints

Write Your Own Formulas

You can write formulas yourself by typing them. When you type a function name in a formula, it must be spelled correctly. Type the name in lowercase letters; Excel converts the name to uppercase letters if it's spelled correctly.

Change the Palette Size

If the Formula palette is so large that you can't drag it out of the way, minimize it temporarily by clicking the button on the right end of the argument box you want to fill (the small button looks like a busy grid with a little red arrow). After you drag the cells, click the button on the end of the minimized palette to return it to full size.

TASK 5

How to Use AutoCalculate

Sometimes you need an immediate calculation but you don't need the formula to be permanently entered in a worksheet cell. *AutoCalculate* is a feature that's always turned on, always out of your way, and available any time you need a quick answer to a simple calculation while you work. If you're entering a column of numbers and you want to know the total of what you have entered so far, for example, select the cells you want to sum and look at the AutoCalculate box. You can also get a quick average, a count of cells, or other calculations by changing the AutoCalculate function.

Begin

1 Select Cells

Select the cells you want to calculate.

	Telephone Charges	$26.10
	Telephone Charges	$14.19
	Telephone Charges	$6.48
	Telephone Charges	$2.32
	Telephone Charges	$14.87
	Telephone Charges	$14.87
	Telephone Charges	$14.87
	Telephone Charges	$16.01
	Telephone Charges	$16.47
	Telephone Charges	$17.39
	Telephone Charges	$18.51

2 Look at AutoCalculate

Look at the AutoCalculate box on the Status bar. The calculation result is displayed for the selected cells.

harges	$2.32
harges	$14.87
harges	$14.87
harges	$14.87
harges	$16.01
harges	$16.47
harges	$17.39
harges	$18.51

List / Sum=$112.99

3 See AutoCalculate Functions

To change the calculation function, right-click the AutoCalculate box.

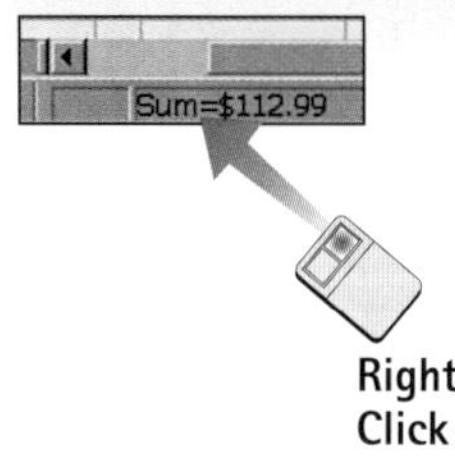

4 Select a Function

Click a different function, or click **None** to turn it off.

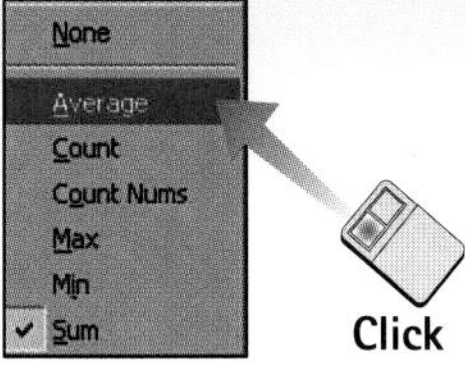

5 Look at the Results

AutoCalculate changes to show the results of your selected function.

End

How-To Hints

If AutoCalculate Isn't There

If AutoCalculate doesn't appear, make sure its calculation is set to a function (not to None) by right-clicking the **AutoCalculate** box, and make sure a range of cells that contain numbers is selected.

If Your Status Bar Isn't There

If your Status bar is missing, choose **Tools**, **Options**. On the **View** tab, mark the **Status bar** check box, and choose **OK**.

Task

CHAPTER 8

How to Use Excel's Formatting Tools

By their very nature, *Excel worksheets* aren't the most appealing, eye-catching way to present data. Granted, your data may be well organized, but with the plain presentation of *columns* and *rows*, your data can quickly become lost in a sea of never-ending cells. To help make your data more presentable, use Excel's many formatting features to create worksheets that are visually appealing.

You can easily change *fonts*, sizes, and formatting of your text and number entries to make the data easier to read. You can also apply borders and shading to your worksheet cells. If you're not too confident about choosing your own formatting options, let Excel do the work for you with AutoFormat.

In this chapter, you will learn five important formatting features that can help you format your worksheets quickly and painlessly. Just remember that it doesn't matter how powerful your *formulas* and *functions* are if you can't clearly see the results.

TASK 1

How to Change Number Formats

When you enter a number, it's displayed the way you type it. After you perform a few calculations, the results can have long strings of decimal places because of Excel's precision; if you're calculating money, for example, a half-dozen decimal places looks confusing. You can change the number display, without affecting the calculated value, by changing the cell's number format.

What you see in a cell is the displayed value, which, because of formatting, can be quite different from the actual value. To see the actual value that Excel is calculating, select the cell and look at the Formula bar.

Begin

1 Select the Cell or Range

Select the cell or range where you want to change the number format.

2 Click Currency

To change a format to accounting format (which adds a $, rounds the number to two decimal places, and spaces the $ so that all the dollar signs in the column are aligned), click the **Currency Style** button on the Formatting toolbar.

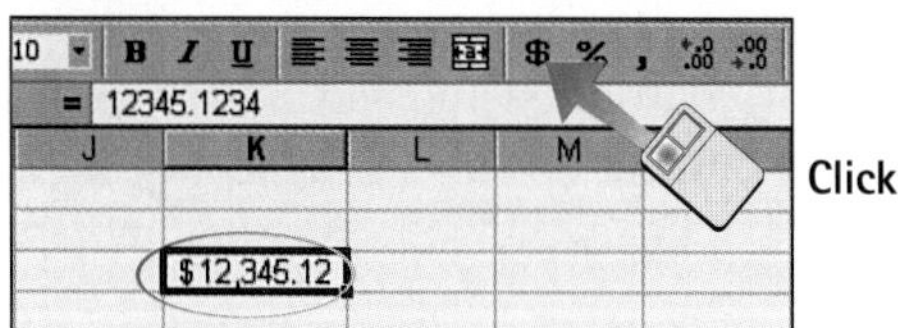

3 Click Percent

To change a format to percent format (which adds a % and changes the number from a fraction or integer to a percentage value), click the **Percent Style** button on the Formatting toolbar. (Remember, percent means hundredths, so 0.12 is displayed as 12%, but 12 is displayed as 1200%.)

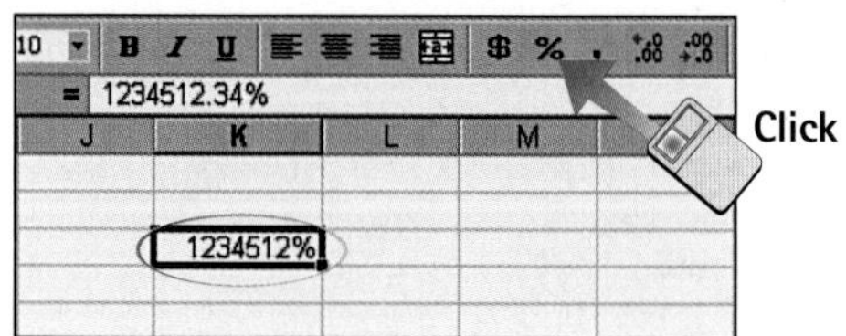

4 Click Comma

To apply comma format (which rounds the number to two decimal places and adds a comma at each thousands mark), click the **Comma Style** button on the Formatting toolbar.

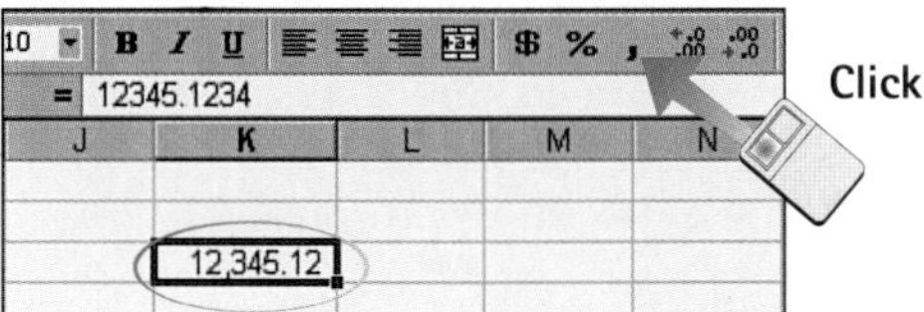

5 Use the Format Cells Dialog Box

To apply different formats that aren't on the Formatting toolbar, choose **Format**, **Cells**, and select a format from the list on the **Number** tab. When you click a format in the **Category** list, your selected number is displayed with that format in the **Sample** box. When you like what you see, choose **OK**.

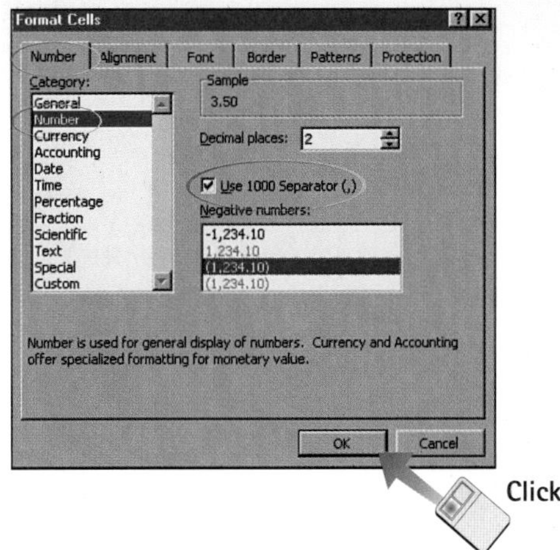

6 Set Format Options

Different formats in the Format Cells dialog box offer different options; select a **Category** and set the options for that format. A description of the selected category appears at the bottom of the dialog box.

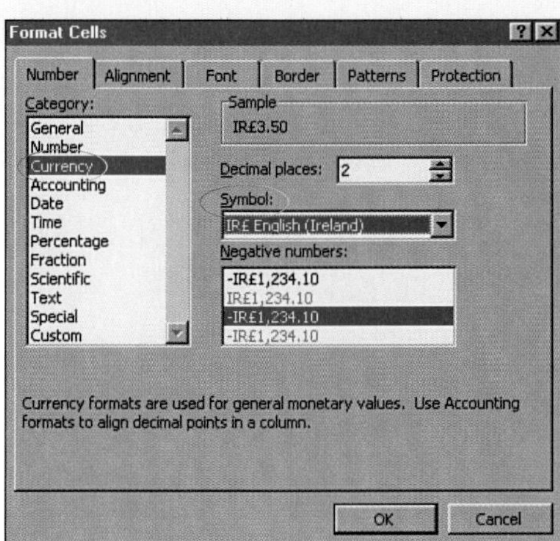

End

How-To Hints

Automatic Formatting

If you type a number with $ or %, the Currency or Percent formatting is applied automatically.

Currency Isn't Really Currency

Even though the toolbar button is named Currency Style, it doesn't apply Currency format; it applies Accounting format. In this format, your numbers, decimals, and dollar signs won't line up the same way.

You Can't Find a Formatting Problem

To remove number formatting, select the cell or range and use the Format Cells dialog box to apply the General format. If you have trouble with formatting somewhere on a worksheet, start over again by selecting the entire worksheet (press Ctrl+A) and applying the General format to the entire worksheet; then reapply your number formats.

TASK 2

How to Adjust the Cell Alignment

By default, Excel automatically aligns your entries based on their data type. Text entries always line up to the left of the cells. Number entries always align to the right. Both text and numbers align vertically at the bottom of the cells. However, you can change the alignment of any entry, both horizontally and vertically.

With Excel's alignment commands, you can also flip your text to read as if each letter is stacked on top of the next, or you can rotate the text to read sideways (top to bottom instead of left to right).

Begin

1 Quick Cell Alignment

For quick horizontal alignment changes, use the alignment buttons on the Formatting toolbar. Select the cell or range you want to align, and then click the appropriate button.

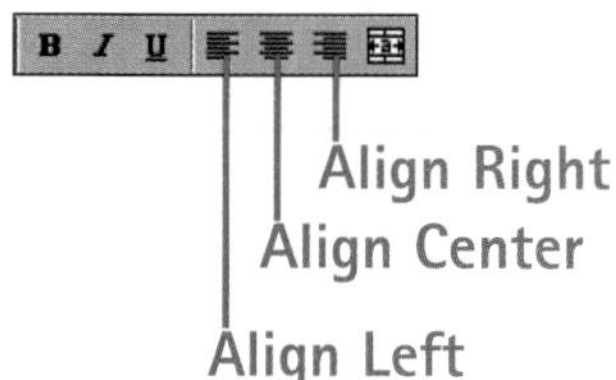

2 Center a Title Over a Range

If you want to center text over a range of cells, select the entire range of blank cells you want to center in, including the cell containing the text you want centered.

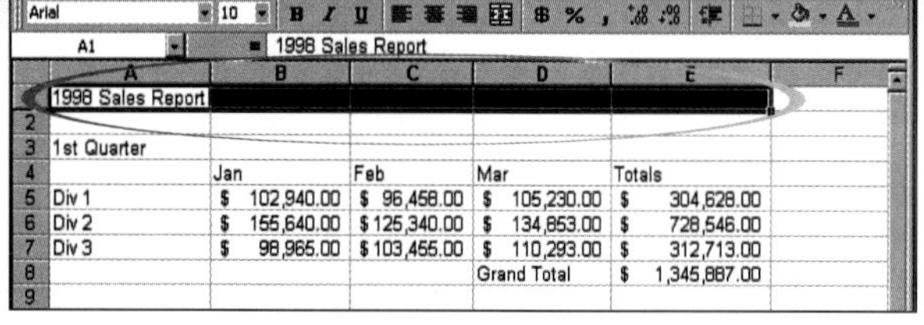

	A	B	C	D	E	F
1	1998 Sales Report					
2						
3	1st Quarter					
4		Jan	Feb	Mar	Totals	
5	Div 1	$ 102,940.00	$ 96,458.00	$ 105,230.00	$ 304,628.00	
6	Div 2	$ 155,640.00	$ 125,340.00	$ 134,853.00	$ 728,546.00	
7	Div 3	$ 98,965.00	$ 103,455.00	$ 110,293.00	$ 312,713.00	
8				Grand Total	$ 1,345,887.00	
9						

3 Click Merge and Center

Next, click the **Merge and Center** button on the Formatting toolbar.

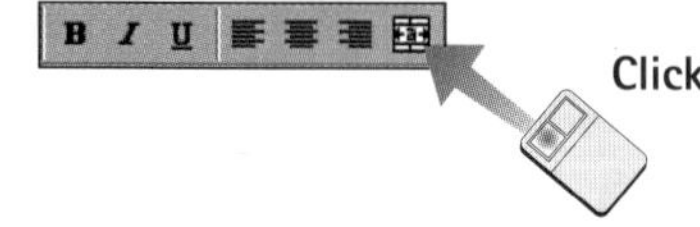

4 The Text Is Centered

Excel centers the title over the range.

	A	B	C	D	E
1			1998 Sales Report		
2					
3	1st Quarter				
4		Jan	Feb	Mar	Totals
5	Div 1	$ 102,940.00	$ 96,458.00	$ 105,230.00	$ 304,628.00
6	Div 2	$ 155,640.00	$ 125,340.00	$ 134,853.00	$ 728,546.00
7	Div 3	$ 98,965.00	$ 103,455.00	$ 110,293.00	$ 312,713.00
8				Grand Total	$ 1,345,887.00
9					

5 Change the Orientation

If you want to change the horizontal alignment, or flip or rotate your entry, use Excel's Format Cells dialog box. Open the **Format** menu and select **Cells**.

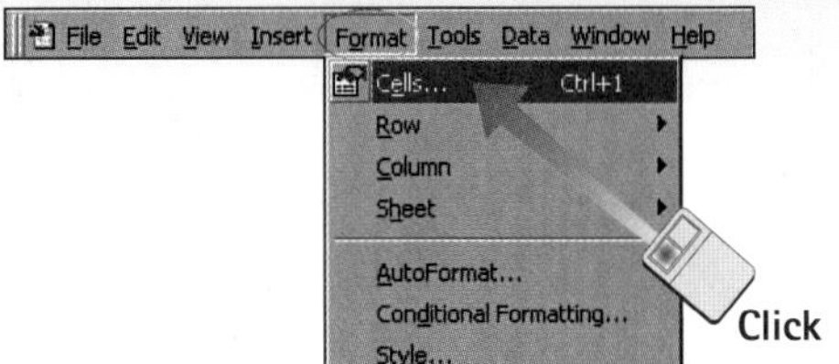

6 Select Alignment/Orientation

Click the **Alignment** tab. Use the **Vertical** alignment drop-down list to align your entry between the top and bottom cell borders. To change orientation, click the type of option you want to use from the **Orientation** settings. Click **OK** to exit the dialog box and apply the new settings.

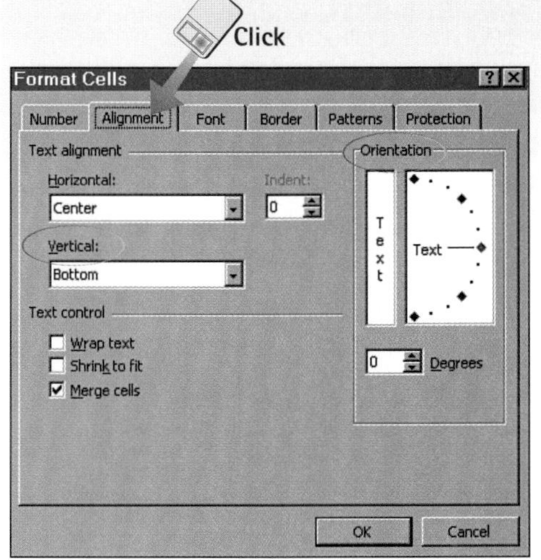

End

How-To Hints

What About Fonts and Sizes?

You can format Excel data the same as you format text in Word. You can use the Font and Size drop-down lists on the Formatting toolbar to change the font and size of your text. You can also apply bold, italic, or underline by clicking the appropriate toolbar buttons. To apply all these formatting options at once, open the **Format** menu, select **Cells**, and click the **Font** tab.

Format with Indents

You can indent text within a cell using Excel's **Increase Indent** button on the Formatting toolbar. Of course, this only works if the cell entry is left aligned.

TASK 3

How to Work with Borders and Patterns

The gridlines you see in your Excel worksheets are a little misleading. Normally, these lines do not print, and if you do print them, they may appear faint. To give your cells well-defined lines, use Excel's Border options. You can choose to add a border to a single cell or an entire range. You can specify a border on only one side, or border the entire cell.

If borders don't set your cells off, try adding a background pattern, such as color shading or a pattern effect. Keep in mind, however, that a background that's too busy will make it difficult for the reader to see your data.

Begin

1 Open the Format Cells Dialog Box

Select the cell or range to which you want to add a border or pattern, and then open the **Format** menu and select **Cells**.

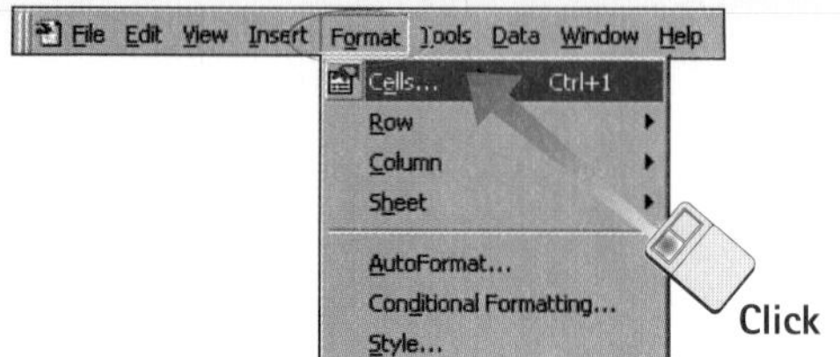

2 Use the Border Tab

Click the **Border** tab to see the various border options. To set a border around the outer edges of the cell or range, click the **Outline** preset. (To set gridlines within the range's inner cells, select **Inside**.)

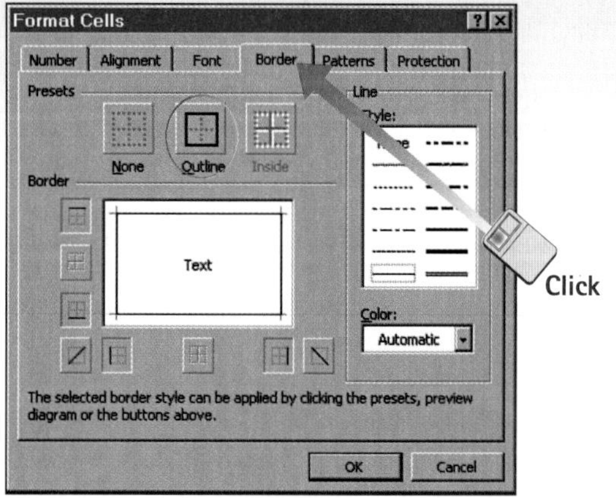

3 Set a Custom Border

If you're customizing your border, use the **Border** buttons to select which sides to border. Click a side to place it on the border position box. Continue adding sides as needed.

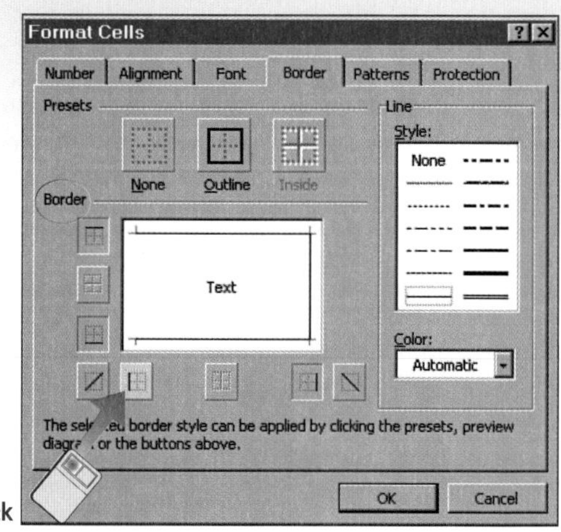

4 Set a Line Style

From the **Style** list, choose a border style. Use the **Color** drop-down list to select a border color. Click **OK** to exit and apply the new settings.

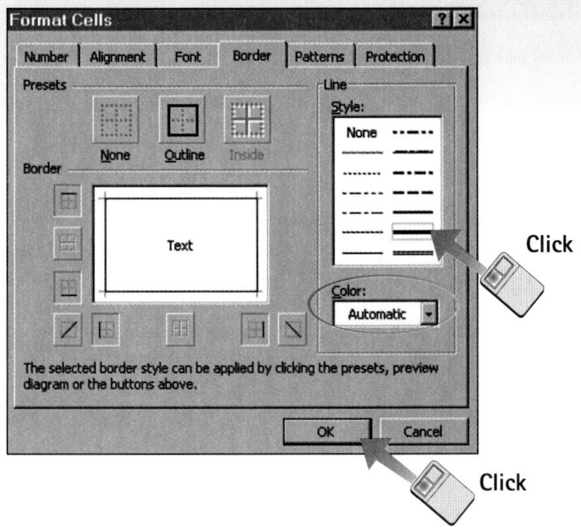

5 Use the Patterns Tab

To apply a pattern, click the **Patterns** tab. To select a color, click the Color effect you want to apply from the palette.

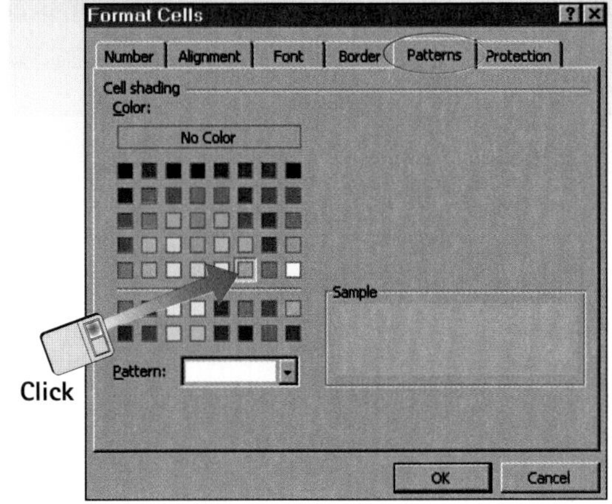

6 Exit the Dialog Box

Click the **Pattern** drop-down list to select a pattern to apply. Click **OK** to exit the dialog box and apply the pattern or shading.

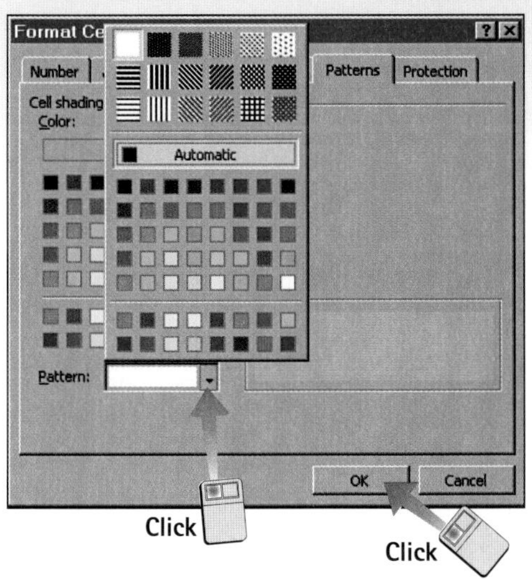

End

How-To Hints

Print Gridlines

By default, Excel's gridlines don't print, but to turn them on, open the **File** menu and select **Page Setup**. Click the **Sheet** tab, select **Gridlines**, and click **OK**. Now print the worksheet to see how the gridlines look.

Use the Formatting Buttons

To add a quick border to any cell or cells, click the **Borders** drop-down arrow on the Formatting toolbar, and then select a border style. To add color to your cell background, click the **Fill Color** drop-down arrow and choose a color from the palette. If it's font color you want to change, click the **Font Color** drop-down arrow and choose another color.

TASK 4

How to Copy Cell Formatting

If you have applied several formatting attributes (such as font, size, color, and borders) to a cell or range of cells, and then later decide you would like to apply the same formatting to another range, you don't have to apply those formats one by one to the new location. Instead, you can use Excel's Format Painter button to take all the formats from the original range and "paint" them across the new range.

Begin

1 Select the Range

Select the range that has the formatting you want to copy.

	A	B	C	D	E	F
1			1998 Sales Report			
2						
3	1st Quarter					
4		Jan	Feb	Mar	Totals	
5	Div 1	$ 102,940.00	$ 96,458.00	$ 105,230.00	$ 304,628.00	
6	Div 2	$ 155,640.00	$ 125,340.00	$ 134,853.00	$ 728,546.00	
7	Div 3	$ 98,965.00	$ 103,455.00	$ 110,293.00	$ 312,713.00	
8				Grand Total	$ 1,345,887.00	
9						
10						
11						
12	2nd Quarter					
13		Apr	May	Jun		
14	Div 1	$ 108,493.00	$ 110,250.00	$ 111,233.00	$ 329,976.00	
15	Div 2	$ 145,293.00	$ 155,699.00	$ 158,300.00	$ 459,292.00	
16	Div 3	$ 112,344.00	$ 115,600.00	$ 116,770.00	$ 344,714.00	
17				Grand Total	$ 1,133,902.00	
18						

Sheet1 / Sheet2 / Sheet3

2 Choose Format Painter

Click the **Format Painter** button in the Standard toolbar.

3 Mouse Pointer Changes

Your mouse pointer changes to a paint-brush pointer.

	A	B	C	D	E	F
1			1998 Sales Report			
2						
3	1st Quarter					
4		Jan	Feb	Mar	Totals	
5	Div 1	$ 102,940.00	$ 96,458.00	$ 105,230.00	$ 304,628.00	
6	Div 2	$ 155,640.00	$ 125,340.00	$ 134,853.00	$ 728,546.00	
7	Div 3	$ 98,965.00	$ 103,455.00	$ 110,293.00	$ 312,713.00	
8				Grand Total	$ 1,345,887.00	
9						
10						
11						
12	2nd Quarter					
13		Apr	May	Jun		
14	Div 1	$ 108,493.00	$ 110,250.00	$ 111,233.00	$ 329,976.00	
15	Div 2	$ 145,293.00	$ 155,699.00	$ 158,300.00	$ 459,292.00	
16	Div 3	$ 112,344.00	$ 115,600.00	$ 116,770.00	$ 344,714.00	
17				Grand Total	$ 1,133,982.00	
18						

Sheet1 / Sheet2 / Sheet3

4 Drag to Copy Formatting

Drag the paintbrush pointer across the range where you want to paint the format.

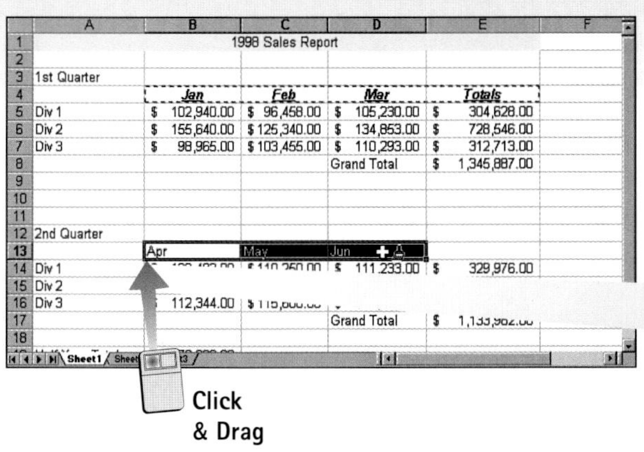

5 Formatting Is Applied

Release the mouse. The formatting is painted to the range of cells (click anywhere to deselect the range).

Release

End

How-To Hints

Keep Painting

To paint the same formatting to several ranges more quickly, double-click the **Format Painter** button. Format Painter remains turned on so you can paint the formatting repeatedly. For example, you could paint across all the headings in the worksheet. When you're finished painting the formatting, click the **Format Painter** button again to turn it off.

Use AutoFormat

Don't like the pressure of coming up with formatting yourself? Use Excel's AutoFormat feature to format your worksheets automatically, as explained in Task 5, "How to AutoFormat a Range."

TASK 5

How to AutoFormat a Range

If formatting worksheets isn't your cup of tea, you will be happy to learn that Excel comes with predesigned formats you can apply to your worksheet data. The AutoFormat features provide you with 16 table formats you can use to make your worksheet data look more presentable. Experiment with each one and see how it affects your data's presentation.

Begin

1 Select the Range

Select the range containing the data you want to format.

	A	B	C	D	E	F
1			1998 Sales Report			
2						
3	1st Quarter					
4		Jan	Feb	Mar	Totals	
5	Div 1	$ 102,940.00	$ 96,458.00	$ 105,230.00	$ 304,628.00	
6	Div 2	$ 155,640.00	$ 125,340.00	$ 134,853.00	$ 728,546.00	
7	Div 3	$ 98,965.00	$ 103,455.00	$ 110,293.00	$ 312,713.00	
8				Grand Total	$ 1,345,887.00	
9						
10						

2 Open the AutoFormat Dialog Box

Open the **Format** menu and select **AutoFormat**. This opens the AutoFormat dialog box.

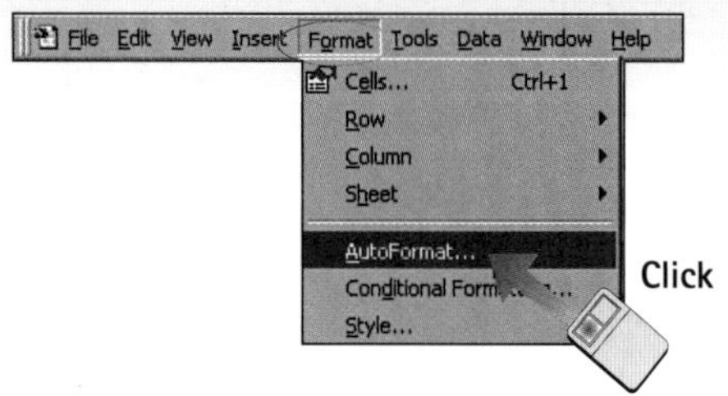

3 Choose a Table Format

From the **Table format** list box, choose a format style you want to view. The **Sample** area shows a preview of the table format.

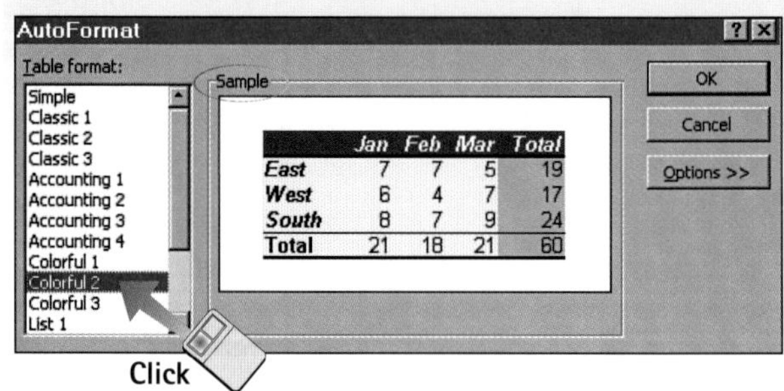

4 View Your Options

To exclude certain elements from the format set, click the **Options** button.

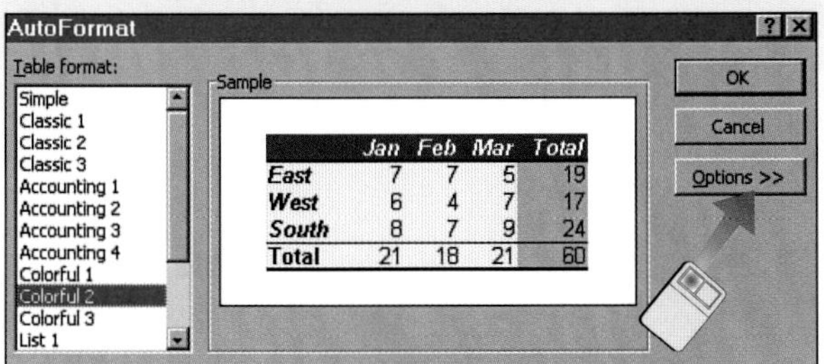

5 Turn Off Elements

Select or deselect the format options you want to turn on or off.

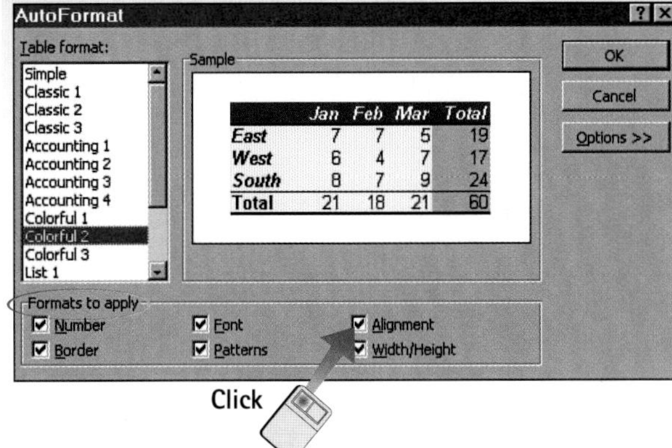

6 Exit the Dialog Box

Click **OK** to exit the dialog box and apply the new formatting.

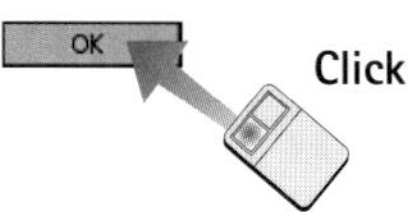

End

How-To Hints

Don't Like It?

If you decide you don't like the format you applied to your range with AutoFormat, select the range again and reopen the AutoFormat dialog box. From the **Table format** list box, select **None**, and then click **OK** to exit, or try another format.

Task

CHAPTER 9

How to Use Excel's Chart Tools

When you look at a *worksheet*, it may be difficult to see the relationship of the numbers. Even the most seasoned bean counter may have trouble spotting trends or patterns easily. To visually show trends, patterns, and relationships, turn your *Excel* data into a *chart*. Charts make it easy to see how your numbers relate.

A chart takes your data and represents it visually, much like a snapshot. You can create a pie chart of your household spending, for example, to easily see which area takes the biggest slice of the pie. Or you can create a bar chart that quickly tells you, or your audience, which division leads in sales. Not only can you see the relationship of numbers, but you can also see any trends and patterns, and quickly summarize the data.

With Excel, you can create charts as part of the worksheet or as a separate worksheet. To make it easy to create charts, use Excel's *Chart Wizard* feature. This feature leads you step-by-step through the process of turning your data into a chart. You can apply 14 chart types, as well as variations of each. Each type has a specific purpose. In this chapter, you will learn how to quickly turn your Excel data into a chart using Chart Wizard, and how to use Excel's chart tools to format and change the chart.

TASK 1

How to Create a Chart with Chart Wizard

A chart turns boring numbers into an instantly accessible, persuasive visual presentation. This task tells you how to create charts from your worksheet data.

The Chart Wizard builds the chart for you and asks for your input along the way. After the chart is built, you can resize it, rearrange it, recolor it, and personalize it so that it doesn't look like every other Excel chart in the computer world.

Begin

1 Select Data

Select the table or list of data you want to chart. Include headings and labels, but don't include subtotals or totals.

	Jan	Feb
HoneySuckle Soap	$125	$138
Sea Soap	$250	$275
Blueberry Soap	$225	$248
Christmas Spice Soap	$185	$204
Farmhand Soap	$120	$132
Skin Tonic Soap	$155	$171
Almond Loofah Soap	$190	$209
Total	$1,250	$1,377

2 Start the Chart Wizard

On the Standard toolbar, click the **Chart Wizard** button. The Chart Wizard starts (if the Office Assistant shows up, click **No, I don't need help now** to send him away). Click the **Chart type** you want on the left and the **Chart sub-type** you want on the right, and then click **Next**.

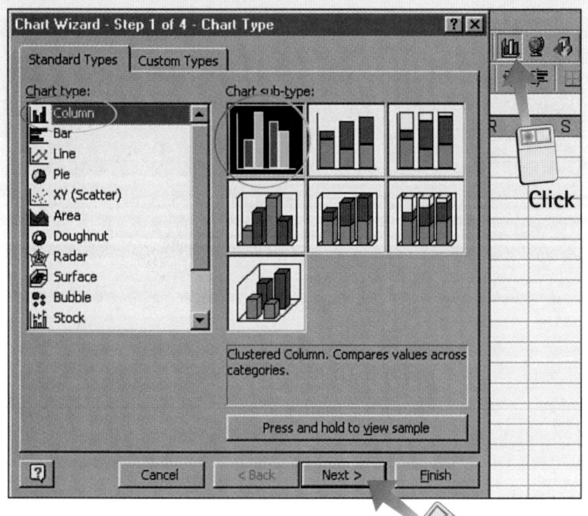

3 Check the Data Range

Check the **Data range** to be sure it's correct. Click the two **Series in** options (**Rows** and **Columns**) to see which layout is best, and then click **Next**.

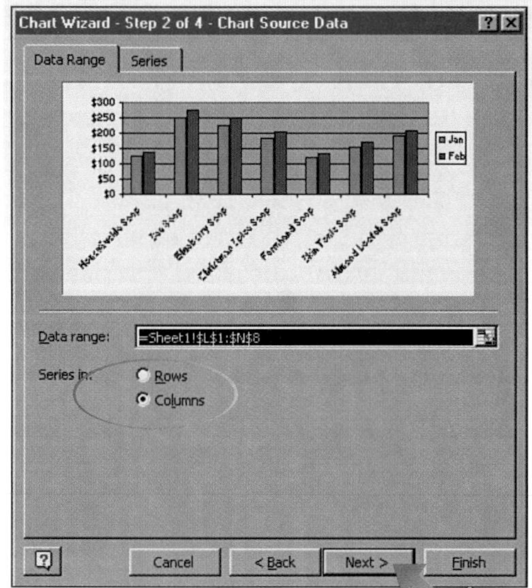

4 Set Chart Features

Type a **Chart title** and **axis** titles, if you want them, on the **Titles** tab. You can reposition or turn off the legend on the **Legend** tab, and append a data table to the bottom of the chart by clicking the **Show data table** check box on the **Data Table** tab. Click **Next**.

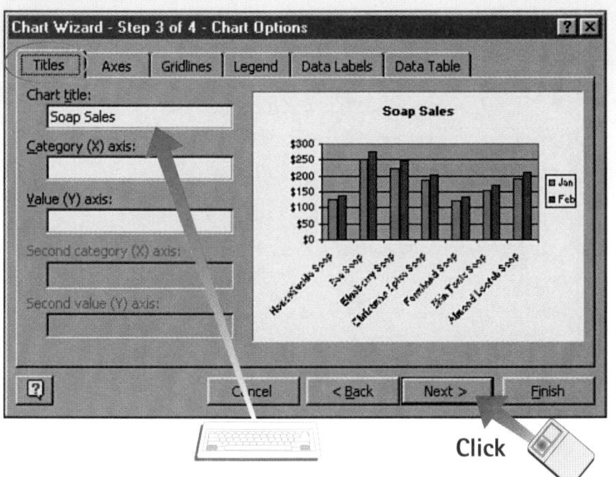

5 Finish the Chart

Choose a location for the chart; the **As object in** option creates an embedded chart object on the worksheet you select from the **As object in** drop-down list. The **As new sheet** option creates a separate *chart sheet* (this is similar to a worksheet, but it holds only a big chart) in the workbook. Then click **Finish**.

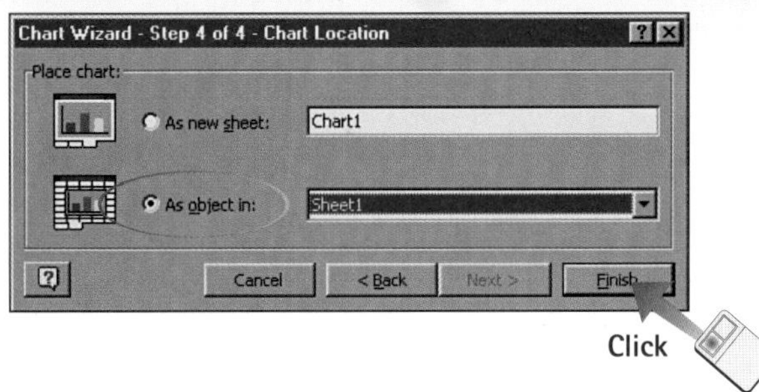

6 Resize and Move the Chart

To resize a chart object on a worksheet, click it and drag one of the handles that appears around its edges. To resize a chart without stretching it out of proportion, hold down Shift while you drag a corner handle. To move the chart, click anywhere near its edge and drag it. To deselect the chart and return to the worksheet, click in the worksheet.

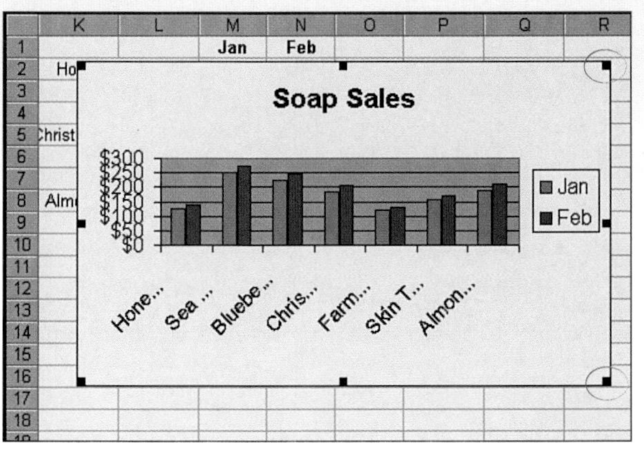

End

How-To Hints

Finish Fast

To create a chart quickly using all the default chart settings, click **Finish** in step 1 (step 2 in this task).

TASK 2

How to Change the Chart Type

When you create a chart, you have many options for the *chart type*. Standard chart types use columns or bars, lines and points, or a sliced-up pie. It's probably best to stick to standard chart types. If you use a chart type that your audience isn't used to seeing, they may have difficulty deciphering it, and the data may lose its impact.

After you have created a chart, you can easily change the chart type without having to re-create the chart, so you can try out different chart types to see which you like best.

Begin

1 Select the Chart

Click the chart to select it. If the chart is on a chart sheet, it is automatically selected when you click its sheet tab.

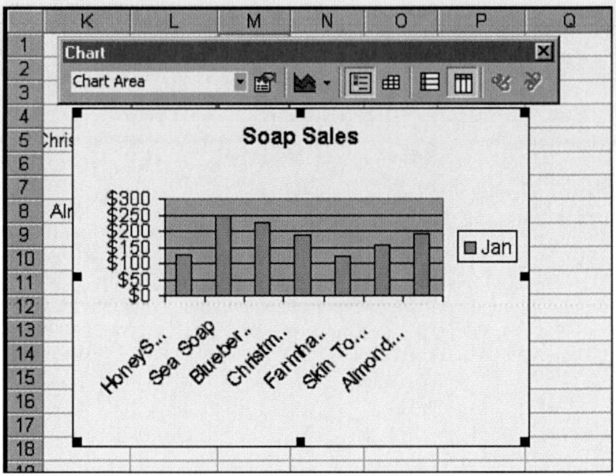

2 Click the Chart Type Button

On the Chart toolbar, click the down arrow on the **Chart Type** button. Click a chart type icon on the button's list.

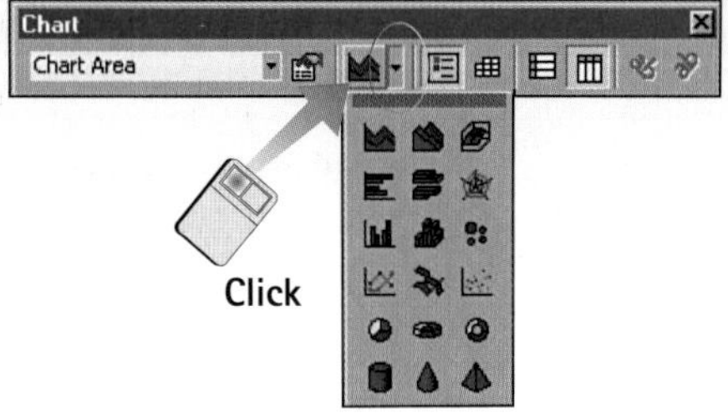

3 The New Chart Type Is Applied

The chart type changes to the type you select (shown is the same column chart changed to a pie chart).

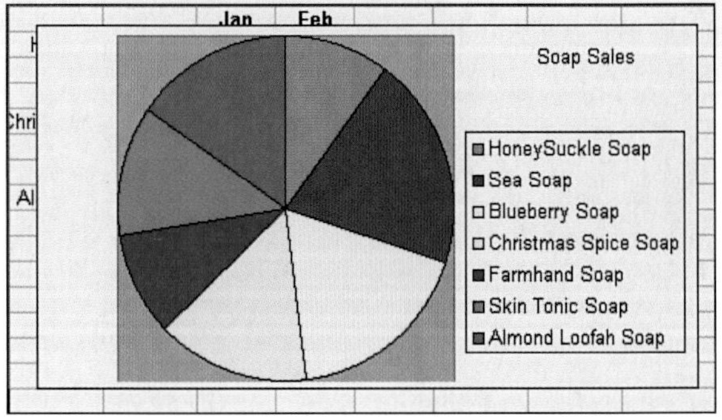

4 Use the Chart Type Command

With the chart selected, choose **Chart**, **Chart Type**. On the Chart Types dialog box, select a **Chart type** and **Chart sub-type**, and then choose **OK** (shown is the same chart changed to a 3D bar chart).

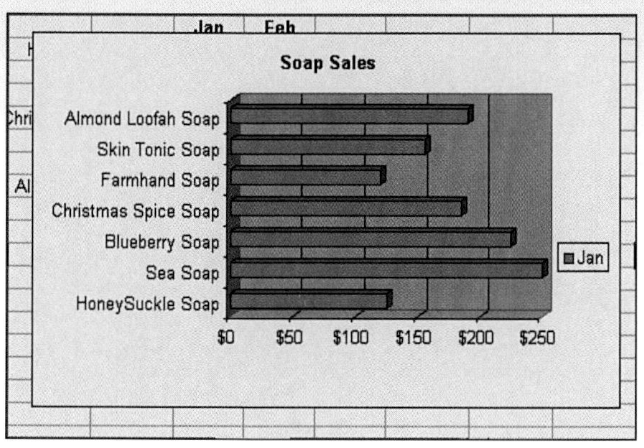

5 Change Markers for Single Series

To change the chart type for a single series in a multiseries chart, right-click one of the data markers in the series, and then choose **Chart Type**.

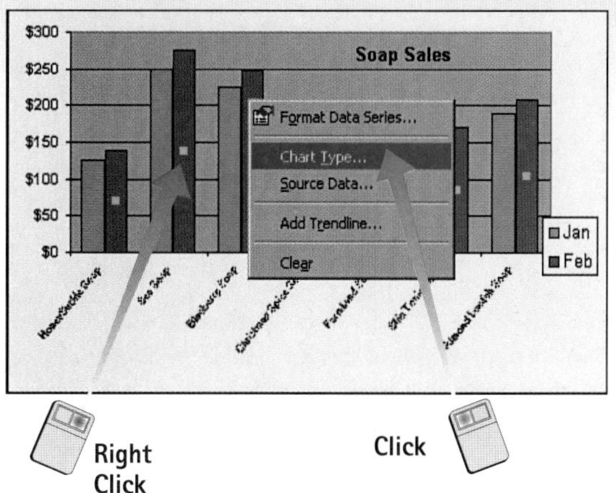

6 Select a Different Marker Type

On the Chart Types dialog box, select a new chart type for the selected series, and then choose **OK**. (Shown here, one series in a column chart is changed to a line chart type.)

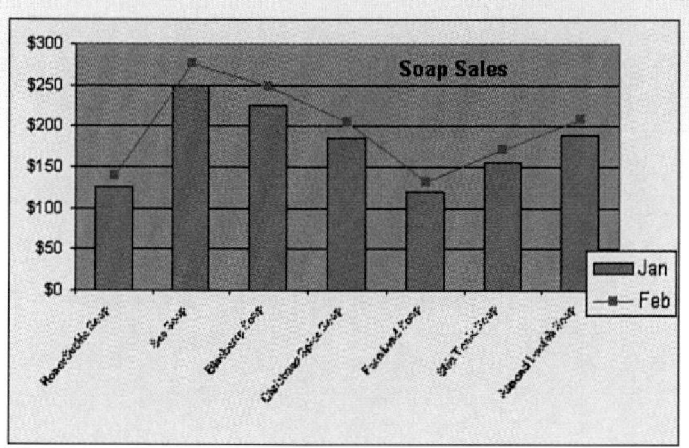

End

How-To Hints

Change Colors

To change the color of any element in the chart (data series, gridlines, axes, plot area, and so on), click the element to select it. Click the down arrow on the **Fill Color** button on the Formatting toolbar and click a different color.

Change Size for the Whole Chart

When you resize a chart, the axis and title characters may be too big or too small; to change the font size, click near the edge of the chart to select the **Chart Area**, and then select a new size in the **Font Size** box on the Formatting toolbar.

TASK 3

How to Work with Chart and Axis Titles

You don't need to spend a lot of time deciding on titles for your chart when you first create it because you can add, change, move, and delete titles at any time.

Begin

1 Move a Title

To move a title, click it to select it, and then drag its border.

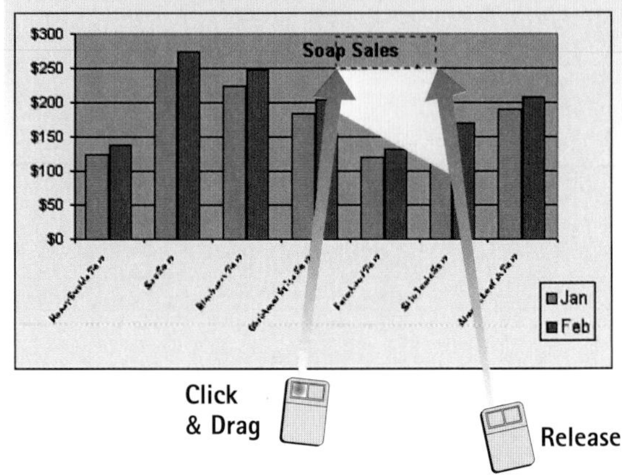

2 Change a Title's Text

Click the title to select it; when you point at the title text, the mouse pointer becomes a cursor. Drag to select the characters you want to change or delete, or click to place the insertion point within the title and type new characters (when you click or drag within the title text, the title's border disappears). Click anywhere outside the title to finish.

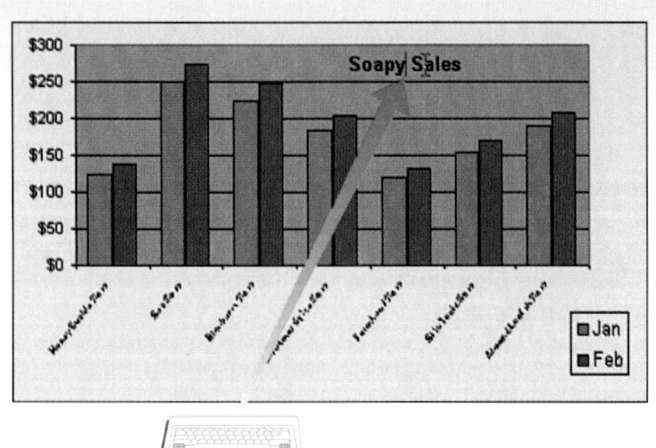

3 Delete a Title

To delete a title, click the title to select it, and then press Delete. You can also right-click the title and choose **Clear**.

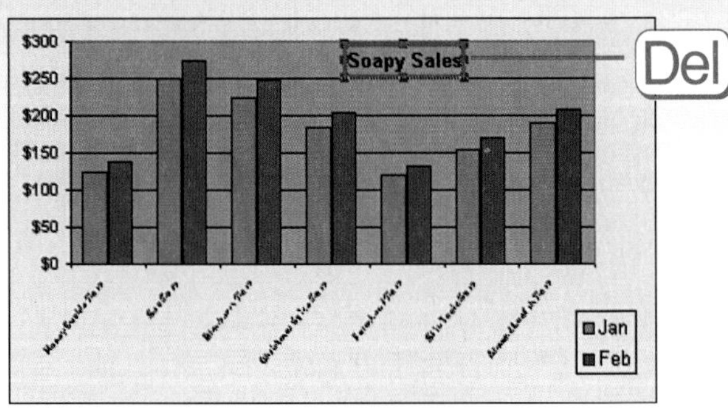

4 Add a Title

To add a new chart title, choose **Chart**, **Chart Options**. On the **Titles** tab of the Chart Options dialog box, type your title and choose **OK**.

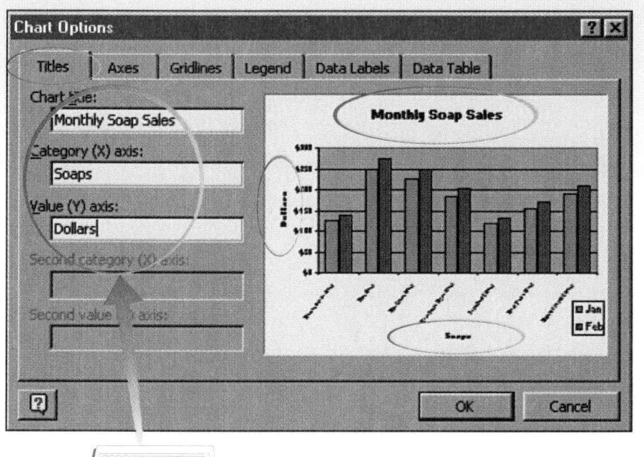

5 Use a Text Box

To add a text box as a title, select the chart, type your title text, and press Enter. When you type, the text appears in the Formula bar; after you press Enter, the text box appears on the chart. Move the text box by dragging its border. Text boxes are similar to titles, except you can resize a text box.

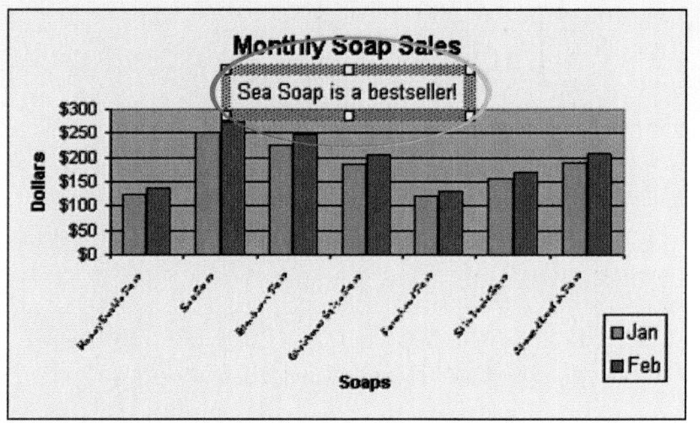

6 Change Colors

To format the colors in either a title or a text box, select the object and choose colors from the **Fill Color** and **Font Color** buttons on the Formatting toolbar; or right-click the object, choose **Format Chart Title** or **Format Text Box**, and set formatting details in the dialog boxes.

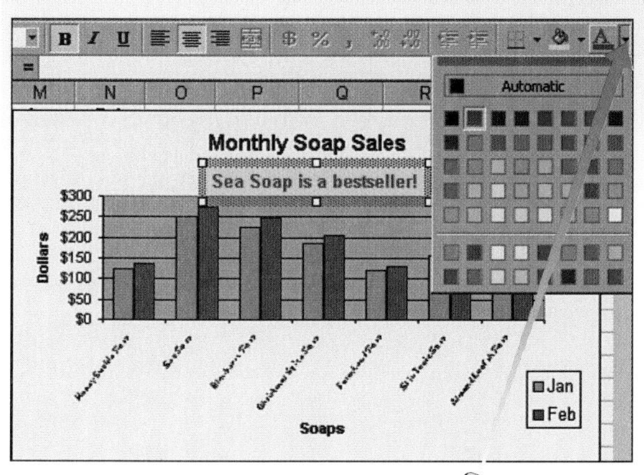

Click

7 Change the Font or Font Size

To change the font or font size in either a title or a text box, select the object and then drag to select the characters you want to change. Make changes in the **Font** and **Font Size** boxes on the Formatting toolbar; or right-click the object, click **Format Chart Title** or **Format Text Box**, and set formatting details in the dialog boxes.

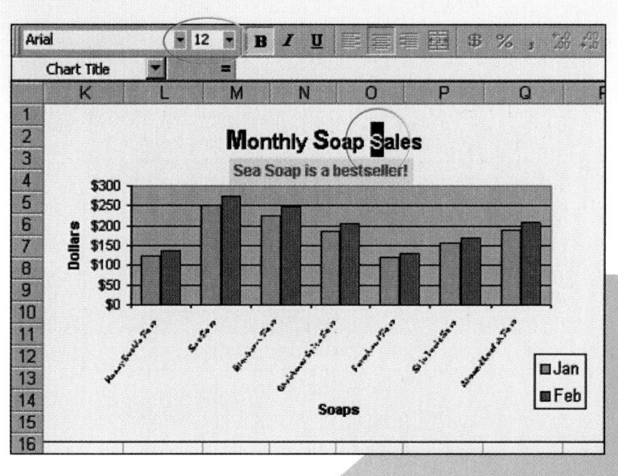

End

TASK 4

How to Change the Chart Data

If you delete a column or row of data from a chart's source data table, the chart adjusts automatically. But if you add data to the source table (for example, if you add another month's sales figures), you need to add the new data to the chart. You can add expanded data to a chart in several quick ways.

If you have already created a highly formatted chart and you want to use it to display a different source data table (instead of creating a new chart), you can change the chart's source data range in the Chart Wizard.

Begin

1 Drag the Source Range Border

Click the chart to select it. The source data is surrounded by a colored border; drag the corner handle of the colored border to expand (or reduce) the source data range.

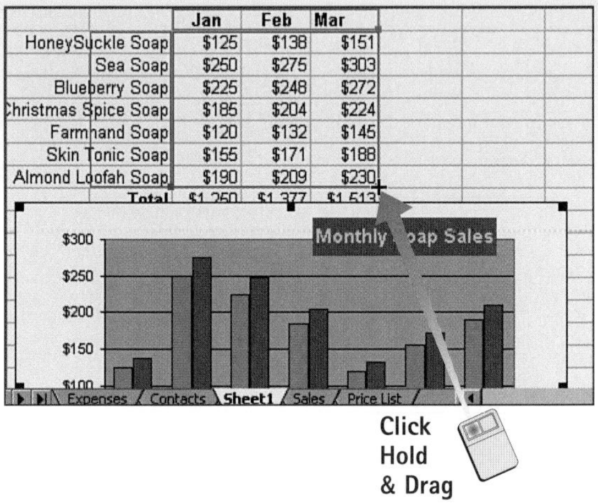

	Jan	Feb	Mar
HoneySuckle Soap	$125	$138	$151
Sea Soap	$250	$275	$303
Blueberry Soap	$225	$248	$272
hristmas Spice Soap	$185	$204	$224
Farmhand Soap	$120	$132	$145
Skin Tonic Soap	$155	$171	$188
Almond Loofah Soap	$190	$209	$230
Total	$1,250	$1,377	$1,513

2 Drag and Drop Data onto the Chart

Select the new data on the worksheet and drag the range border as if you were dragging and dropping to move it—but drag it onto the chart and drop it anywhere. When you drag the mouse pointer onto the chart, it acquires a small plus symbol; when you release the mouse pointer, the data is added to the chart.

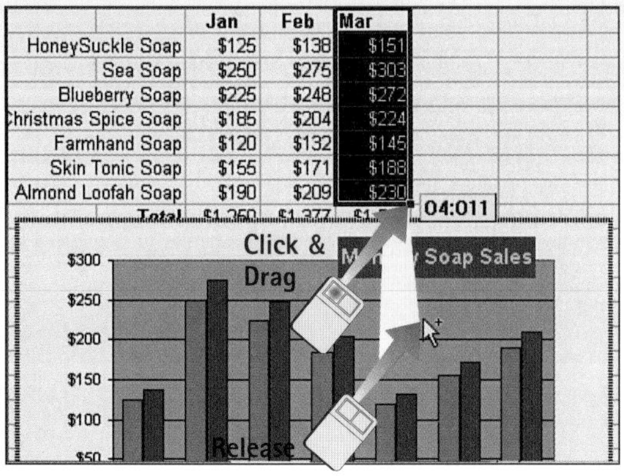

	Jan	Feb	Mar
HoneySuckle Soap	$125	$138	$151
Sea Soap	$250	$275	$303
Blueberry Soap	$225	$248	$272
hristmas Spice Soap	$185	$204	$224
Farmhand Soap	$120	$132	$145
Skin Tonic Soap	$155	$171	$188
Almond Loofah Soap	$190	$209	$230

3 Use the Add Data Command

Select the chart and choose **Chart, Add Data**. The Add Data dialog box appears.

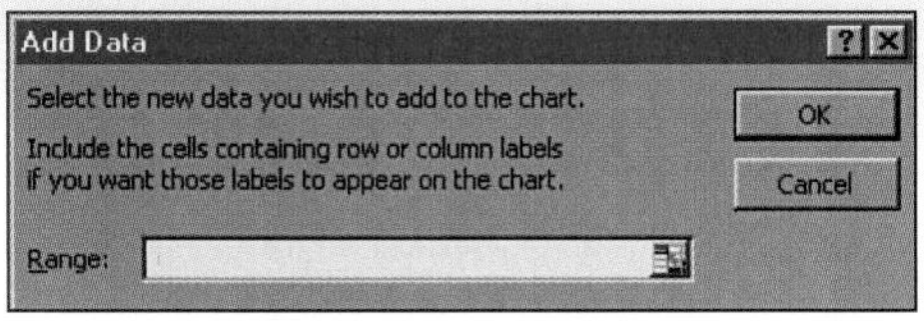

4 Drag the New Data

Drag to select the data on the worksheet you want to add (the added range appears in the Add Data dialog box), and choose **OK**.

		Jan	Feb	Mar
1		Jan	Feb	Mar
2	HoneySuckle Soap	$125	$138	$151
3	Sea Soap	$250	$275	$303
4	Blueberry Soap	$225	$248	$272
5	hristmas Spice Soap	$185	$204	$224
6	Farmhand Soap	$120	$132	$145
7	Skin Tonic Soap	$155	$171	$188
8	Almond Loofah Soap	$190	$209	$230

Add Data

Select the new data you wish to add to the chart.

Include the cells containing row or column labels if you want those labels to appear on the chart.

Range: =Sheet1!$O$1:$O$8

OK

Cancel

5 Use the Source Data Command

Use this method if you want to completely change the source range. Right-click in the chart area and choose **Source Data**.

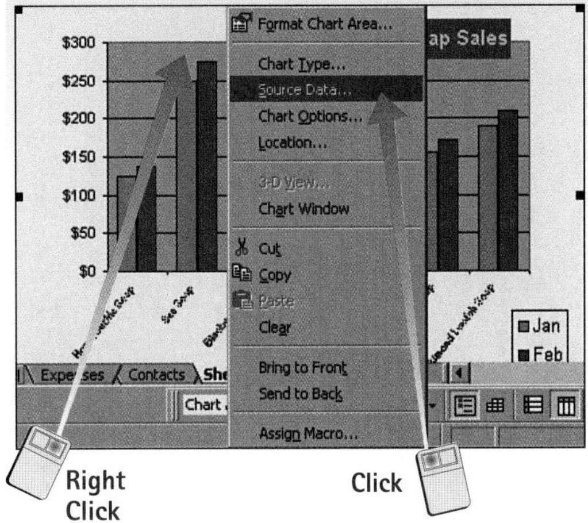

6 Drag the New Range

On the worksheet, drag to select the entire range you want the chart to display. The dragged range references appear in the **Data range** box in the Source Data dialog box. Choose **OK**.

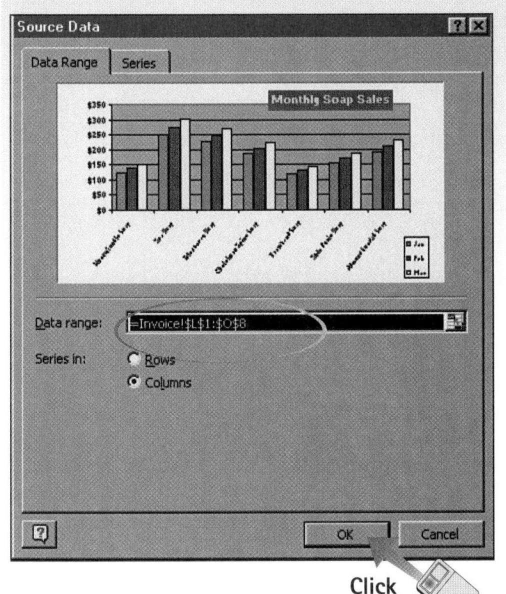

End

How-To Hints

Chart Help

For help with any chart, consult Excel's Help system. Open the **Help** menu and choose **Contents and Index** or click the **Help** button on the toolbar to summon Office Assistant for help. To learn more about using the help features, see Tasks 9, "How to Use the Office Assistant," and 10, "How to Use the Office Help System," in Chapter 2, "How to Use Common Office Features."

TASK 5

How to Change the Chart Background

Just about every part of an Excel chart can be formatted, including the background. You can add a background color or pattern to the chart to help it stand out on a worksheet, and choose a different border style to apply. Excel assigns a default border to your chart, but you can customize the border by changing a few formatting options.

Although Excel charts are colorful by nature, you can add complementary color backgrounds for a striking visual effect. You can choose from a variety of fill effects, including patterns, gradients, and textures; you can even turn a picture into a background.

Begin

1 Open the Shortcut Menu

Select the chart, and then right-click and select **Format Chart Area** from the shortcut menu.

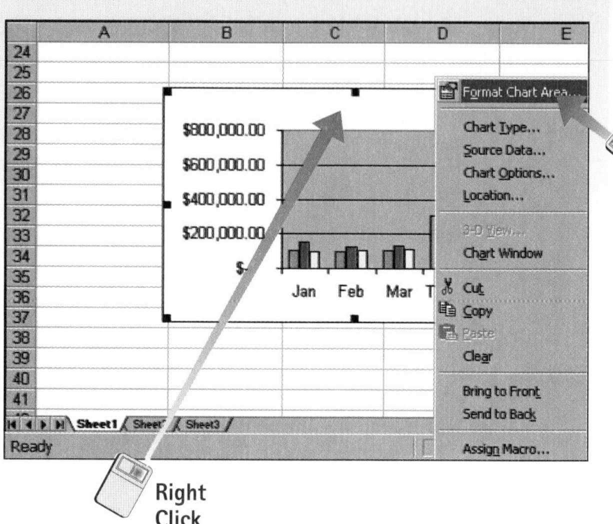

2 Display the Patterns Tab

Click the **Patterns** tab to bring it to the front of the dialog box. By default, Excel automatically adds a border to your chart. To specify any additional border formatting, use the **Style**, **Color**, and **Weight** drop-down arrows.

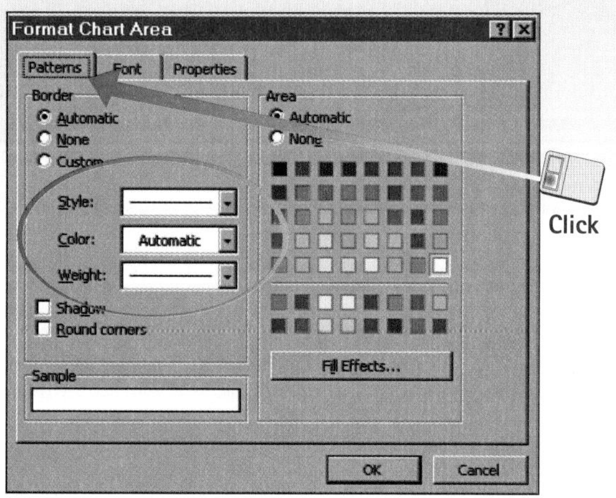

3 Add a Background Color

Under the **Area** options, choose a new background color from the palette. To select a background pattern, click the **Fill Effects** button to open the Fill Effects dialog box.

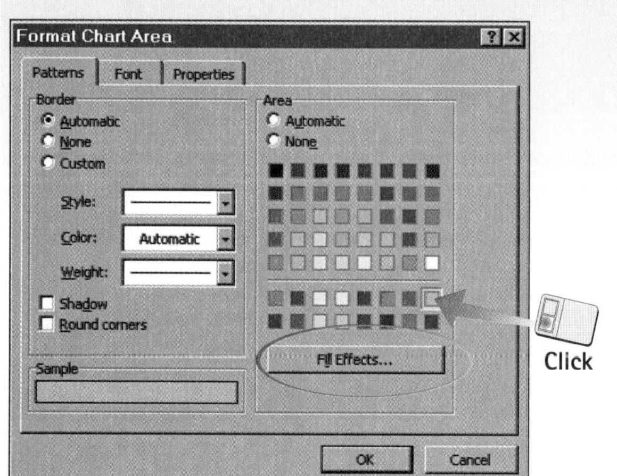

4 The Fill Effects Dialog Box

To set a pattern, click the **Pattern** tab and choose a pattern to use. You can also use the **Gradient** and **Texture** tabs to create other background fill effects. Click **OK** to exit the dialog box and return to the Format Chart Area dialog box.

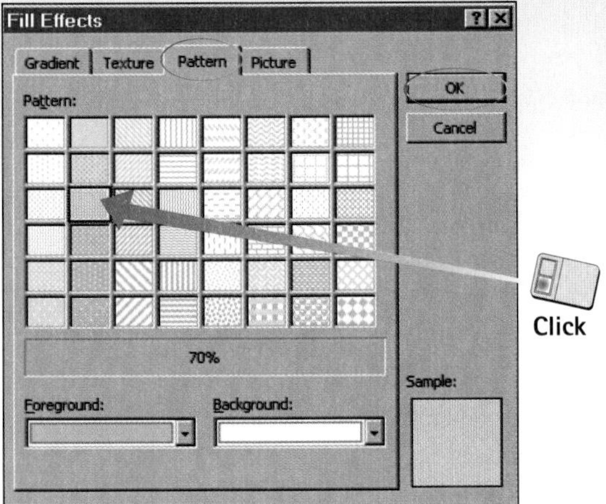

5 Apply the New Settings

Click **OK** to apply the new background color, border, or pattern to the chart.

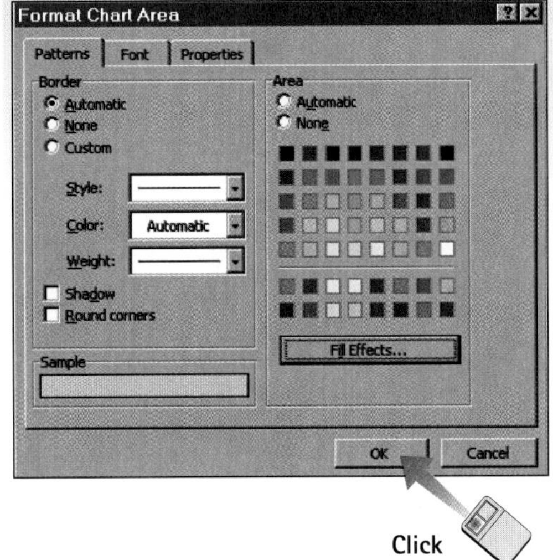

6 New Chart Background

Based on your selections in the previous steps, your Excel chart now exhibits a new background color, pattern, or border.

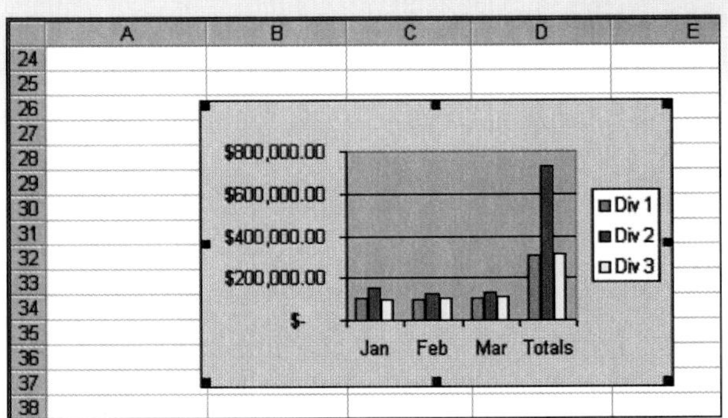

End

How-To Hints

Round Corners or Shadow?

To add a shadow effect to your chart border, click the **Shadow** check box in the **Border** options on the **Patterns** tab in step 2. To apply round corners to the border, click the **Round corners** check box.

Check Out the Textures

The **Texture** tab in the Fill Effects dialog box has some interesting texture backgrounds that you can apply to your chart.

How About a Picture Background?

If you have a picture that won't distract from the chart data, you can use it as a chart background. Display the **Picture** tab of the Fill Effects dialog box and use the **Select Picture** button to locate the picture file.

Task

CHAPTER 10

How to Use PowerPoint 97

PowerPoint is a presentation program designed to help you create visual presentations and *slide shows* for an audience, whether it's one person or a roomful of people. With PowerPoint, you can create and combine slides into a visual presentation that easily communicates your message with style and pizzazz.

You can create, for example, professional, self-running or interactive slide shows to give a training presentation. You can present the quarterly sales review as a slide show to the sales staff, or present a new budget to your local civic organization. With PowerPoint, not only can you create visual presentations for any purpose, but you can also create speaker notes and audience handouts to go along with it.

In this chapter, you will learn about PowerPoint's basic features, including how to get started creating your first slide show presentation and using PowerPoint's specialized tools for adding text and graphics.

TASK 1

How to Get Around the PowerPoint Window

When you first start PowerPoint, the opening dialog box presents you with several options for starting a presentation. You can use PowerPoint's AutoContent Wizard to create a slide show (see Task 2, "How to Use the AutoContent Wizard"), base the presentation on one of PowerPoint's many templates, build a show from scratch, or open an existing presentation file.

After you move beyond the opening dialog box, PowerPoint looks and feels the same as any other Office 97 program. You will find the typical title bar, menu bar, toolbars, scrollbars, and status bar. These features work the same as the other Office programs.

Begin

1 The Opening Dialog Box

From PowerPoint's opening dialog box, you can start a new presentation or open an existing one. Click the option you want to start. To close the dialog box without making a selection, click the **Cancel** button.

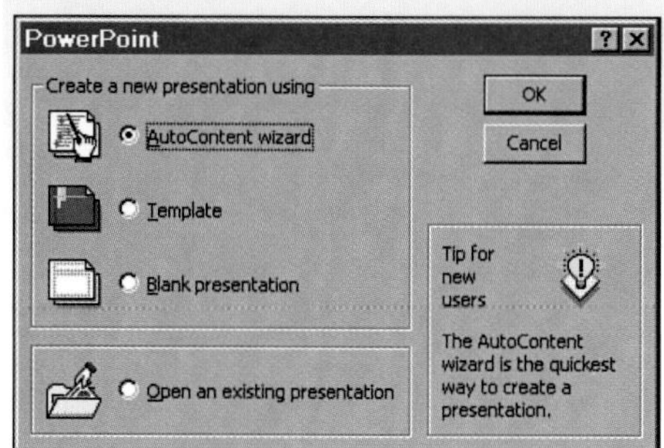

2 View the Title Bar

The title bar tells you what is in the window. When the presentation window is maximized, it has to share the title bar with the program window, so the title bar contains the names of both the program (Microsoft PowerPoint) and the file (such as Announcements.ppt).

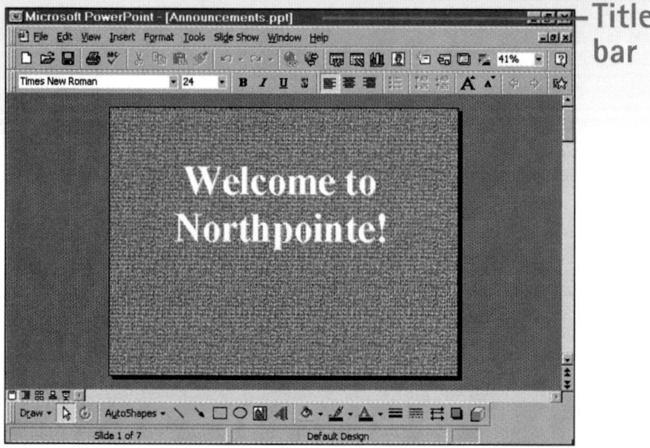

3 Use the Menu Bar

The PowerPoint menu bar contains menus that, in turn, contain all the available PowerPoint commands. All the tasks you need to perform are available through menu commands. To use the menu commands, click the menu name to display the commands, then click a command.

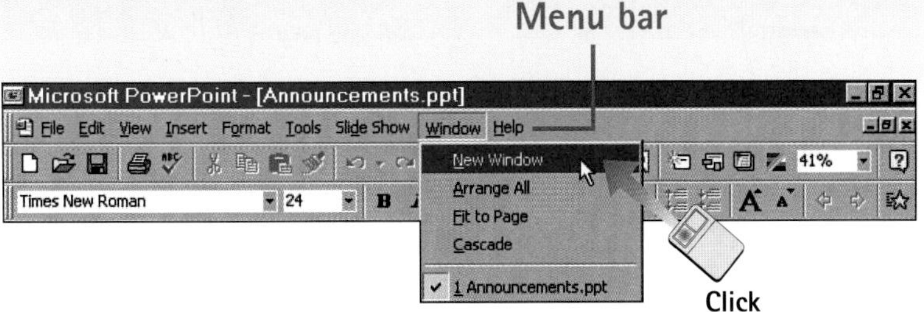

4 Use the Toolbars

The Standard toolbar contains shortcuts for frequently used commands, such as those to open, save, and print the presentation, and to undo mistakes. The Formatting toolbar (below the Standard toolbar) contains shortcuts for commands that change the appearance of the slide. To activate a toolbar button, click it. To see a button name, hover the mouse pointer over the button for a moment; a *ScreenTip* appears with the button name.

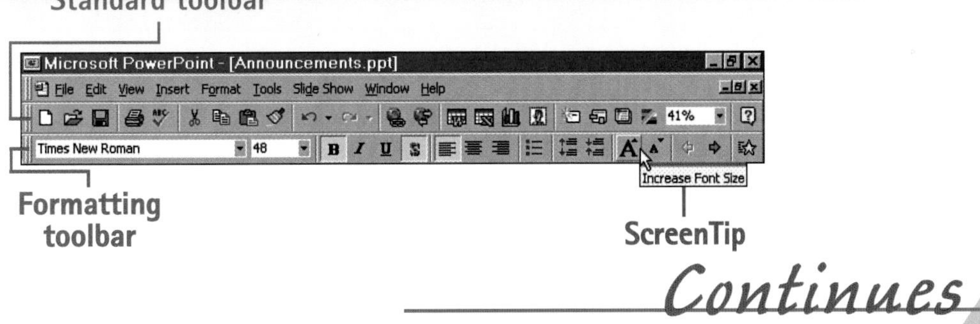

Continues

How to Get Around the PowerPoint Window Continued

5 The Drawing Toolbar

In addition to the Standard and Formatting toolbars, a Drawing toolbar at the bottom of the PowerPoint window contains commands for drawing and working with *graphics objects*.

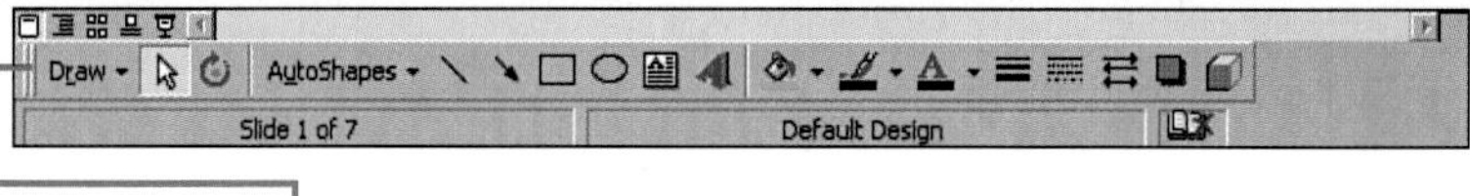

Drawing toolbar

6 Use the Presentation Window

Use the presentation window to create your slides and arrange them in the presentation.

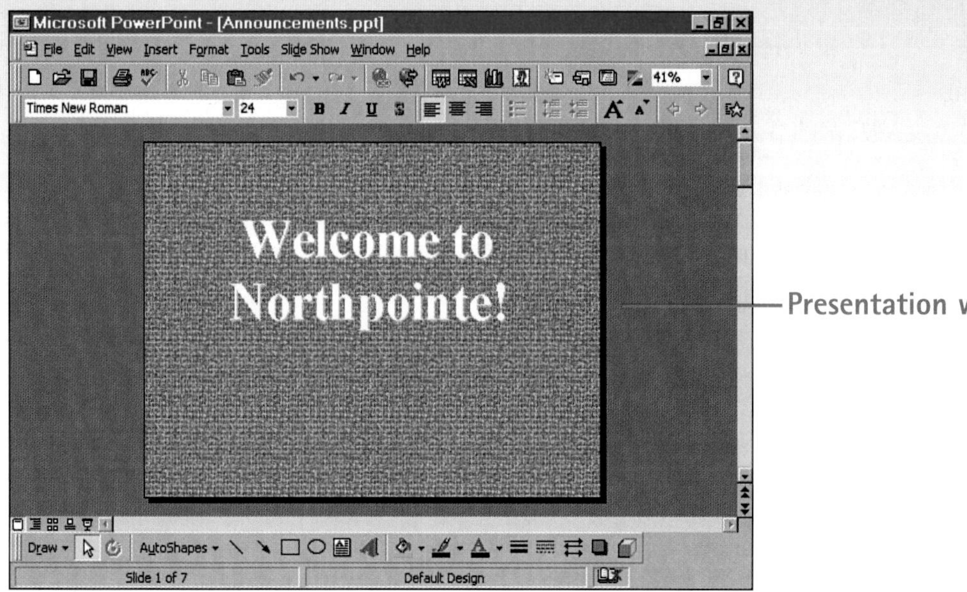

Presentation window

7 Use the Scrollbars

Use the vertical and horizontal scrollbars bordering the presentation window to navigate the presentation and view the current slide. To the left of the horizontal scrollbar are the View buttons that change the view of your presentation.

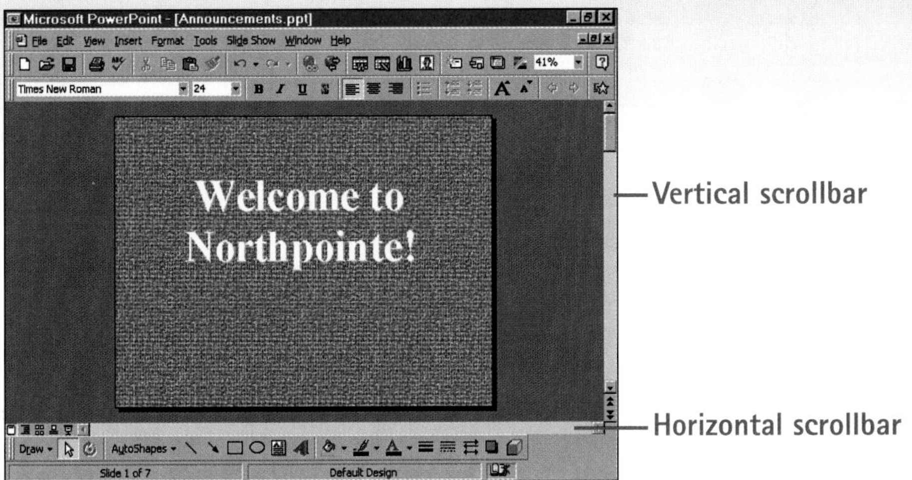

8 View the Status Bar

At the bottom of the screen, the status bar tells you which view you're currently using and displays the name of the PowerPoint design for the current presentation. The status bar indicates the current page, the total number of slides, and the name of the design.

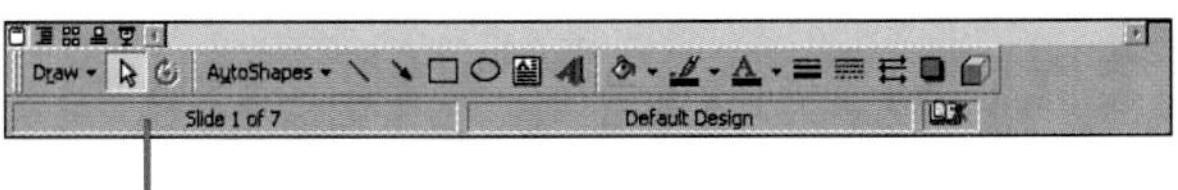

How-To Hints

Close the Opening Dialog Box

If you close the Opening dialog box using the Cancel button, you won't see the box again until you reopen PowerPoint. Don't worry, all the options in the dialog box are available through PowerPoint's File menu.

Other Toolbars

PowerPoint has different toolbars for different occasions. To add a toolbar to your window, right-click an existing toolbar and you can see a list of available toolbars. Toolbars that are already displayed have a check mark next to their names. You can click the toolbar name to select or deselect it for display.

Use the View Buttons

The PowerPoint View buttons, located to the left of the horizontal scrollbar, let you change how you look at your slides. To learn more about PowerPoint's Views, see Task 1, "How to Change the View," in Chapter 11, "How to Prepare a Slide Presentation."

TASK 2

How to Use the AutoContent Wizard

The easiest way to create a new presentation is to use the AutoContent Wizard. PowerPoint's AutoContent Wizard walks you through each step in designing and creating a slide presentation. You can select a type of presentation and PowerPoint builds an outline for it; it's up to you to fill in the text and choose graphics.

AutoContent Wizard taps into the many Presentation templates available. Presentation templates provide a color scheme, formatting, and a basic outline for the slide text.

Begin

1 Start the AutoContent Wizard

From the opening dialog box, click the **AutoContent wizard** option and click **OK**. If the dialog box no longer appears onscreen, open the **File** menu and select **New**. From the **Presentations** tab, double-click the **AutoContent wizard** icon.

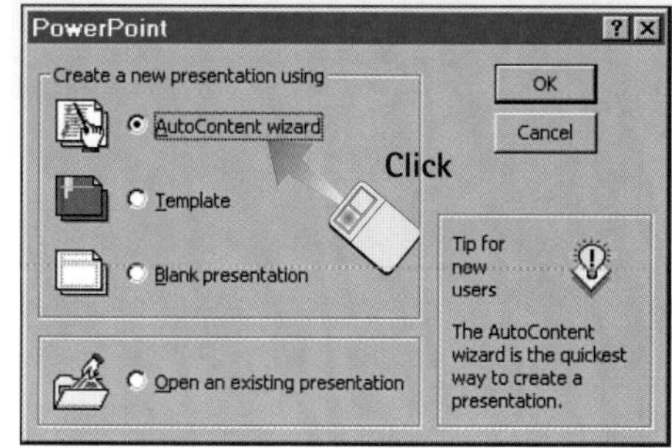

2 Click Next

When the first AutoContent Wizard dialog box appears, choose **Next** to get started.

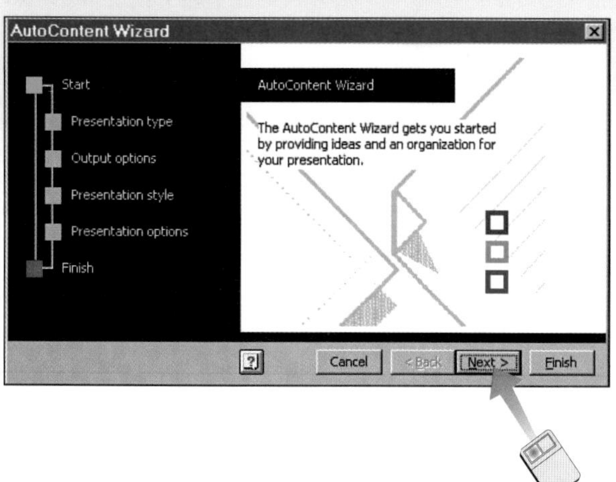

3 Choose a Presentation Type

From the next dialog box, click the button of the presentation that best represents the type of presentation you want to build. Select a presentation type, and then click **Next**. (To see all the available presentation types, click the **All** button.)

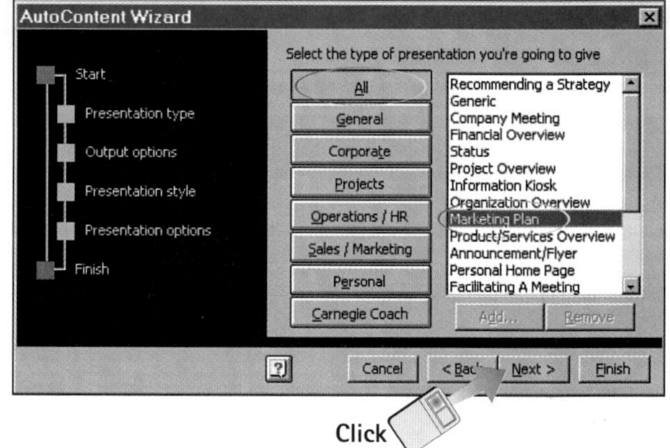

4 Choose a Method

Next, choose the method that best describes how you're going to give your presentation. Click **Next** to continue.

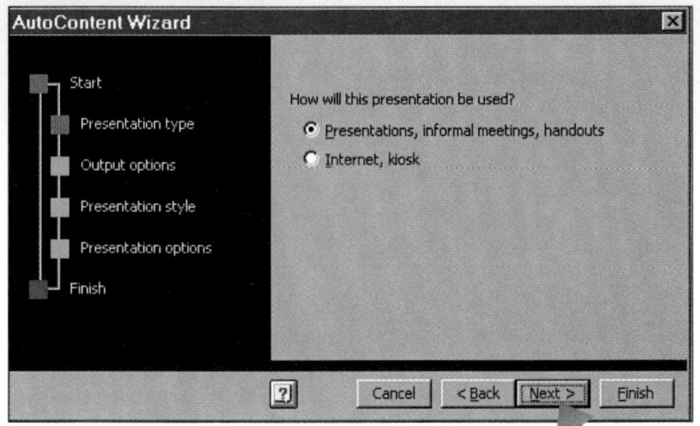

5 Choose an Output Type

Select the type of output you require and whether you need handouts. If you plan to run the presentation on a computer, select the **On-screen presentation** option. Use the other options to create overheads or actual 35mm slides. Click **Next** to continue.

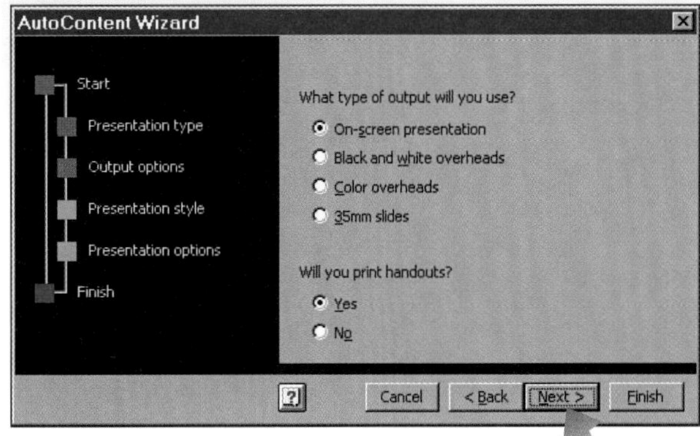

6 Enter a Title

Enter a title for the presentation and your name. Click **Next**.

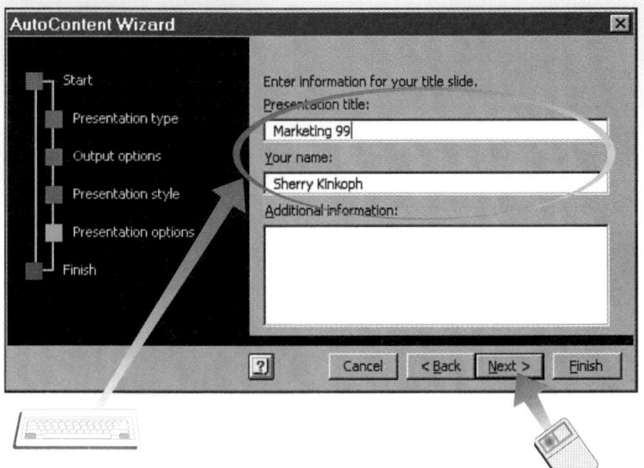

7 Finish

The last AutoContent Wizard dialog box appears. Click **Finish** to complete the procedure. PowerPoint opens the presentation in Outline view.

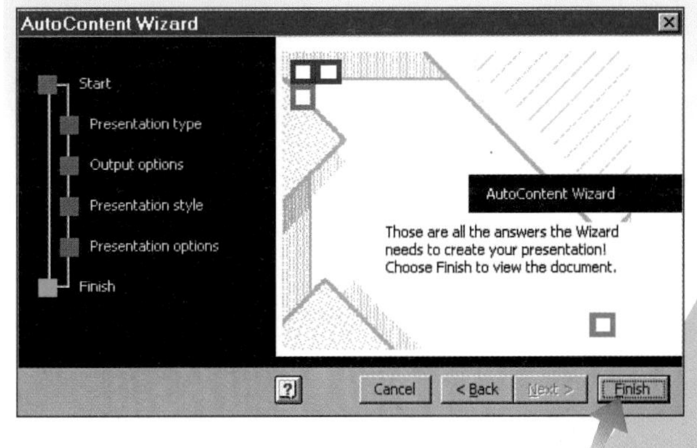

End

Task 3

How to Start a New Presentation Based on a Template

You can also create a slide show based on a PowerPoint template. Use the same templates offered by AutoContent Wizard, or use PowerPoint's Presentation Design templates.

The Presentation Design templates offer one color scheme for each slide, which gives the presentation a consistent look. You provide the slide content. Unlike AutoContent Wizard—which walks you through building a slide show—when you select a Design template, PowerPoint immediately opens a new slide based on your selection.

Begin

1 Select the Template Option

From PowerPoint's opening dialog box, click the **Template** option and click **OK**. If the dialog box is unavailable, select **File**, **New** to open the New dialog box.

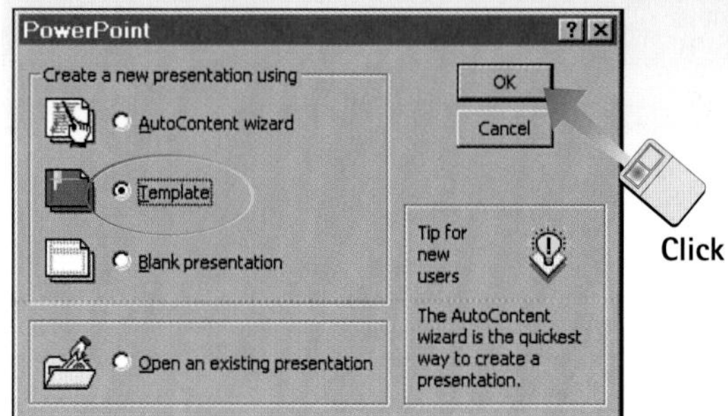

2 Preview a Template

Click the **Presentation Designs** tab to view the available templates. Select a template and the **Preview** area displays a sample of the design.

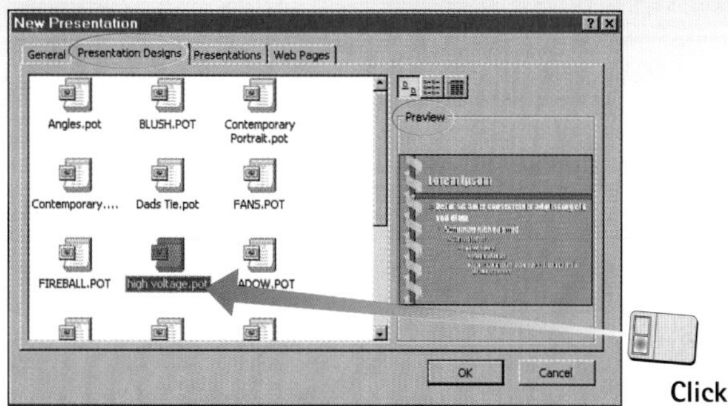

3 Select a Template

To choose a template, double-click its name or select it and click **OK**.

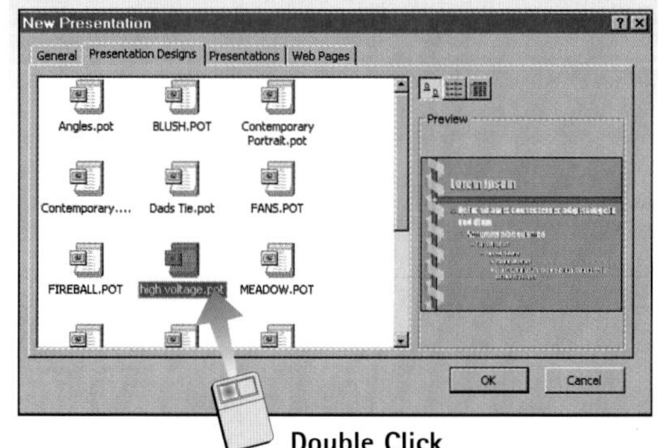

4 Choose a Layout

The New Slide dialog box appears for you to choose a layout for the slide. Click the AutoLayout you want to use and click **OK** (or double-click the layout example).

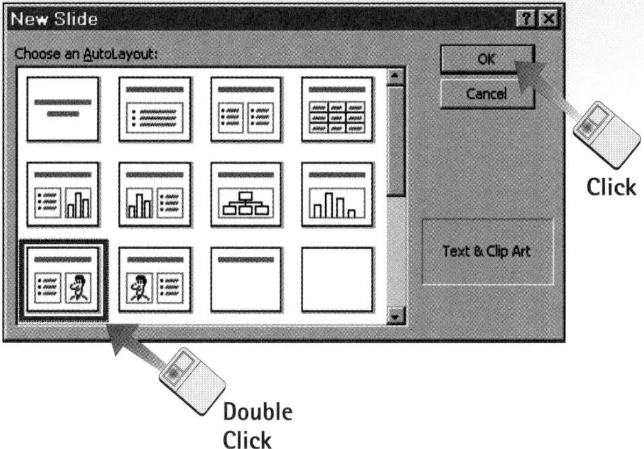

5 The Template Opens

PowerPoint opens the template and layout you selected. Notice the slide appears in Slide view in the presentation window. Now you're ready to start filling in text or graphics.

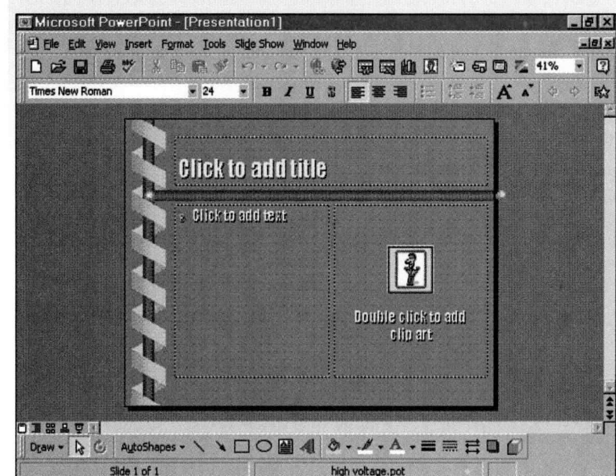

End

How-To Hints

Customize Templates

Create your own design template by making changes (color, font, and so on) to an existing template, and then saving the file as another template using the **File**, **Save As** command. In the Save As dialog box, name the new design and select **Presentation Templates** in the **Save as type** drop-down box.

Can't Find a Design You Like?

If you don't like any of the templates (including those used by the AutoContent Wizard), start with a blank slide and design your own presentation from scratch. Task 4, "How to Build a Presentation from Scratch," explains how to start a blank presentation.

TASK 4

How to Build a Presentation from Scratch

If you're the adventurous type, you may prefer creating your own presentations and designs. Rather than relying on a preset color scheme or format, build a blank presentation and add your own touches. After you start a blank presentation, you can add text boxes and graphics, and set backgrounds and colors as needed.

Begin

1 Start a Blank Presentation

From PowerPoint's opening dialog box, click the **Blank presentation** option and click **OK**; skip to step 4.

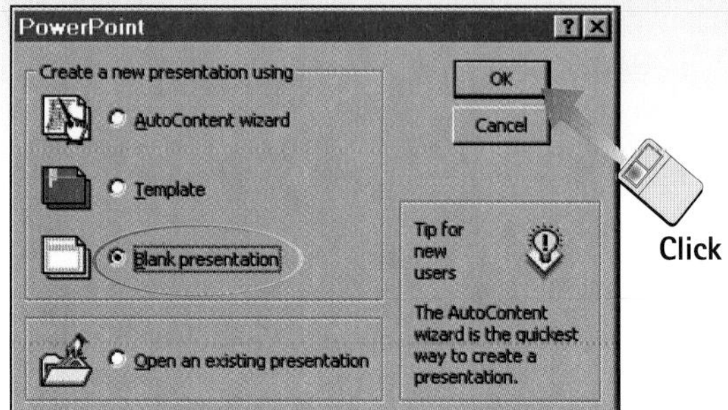

2 Or Use the New Dialog Box

If the dialog box is unavailable, select **File**, **New** to open the New dialog box.

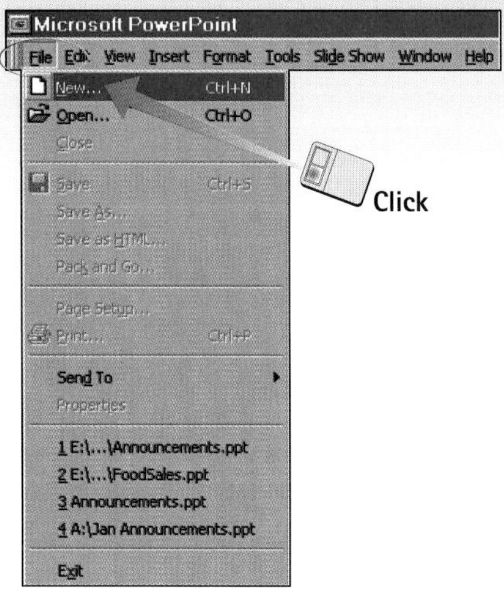

3 Display the General Tab

Click the **General** tab and double-click the **Blank Presentation** icon.

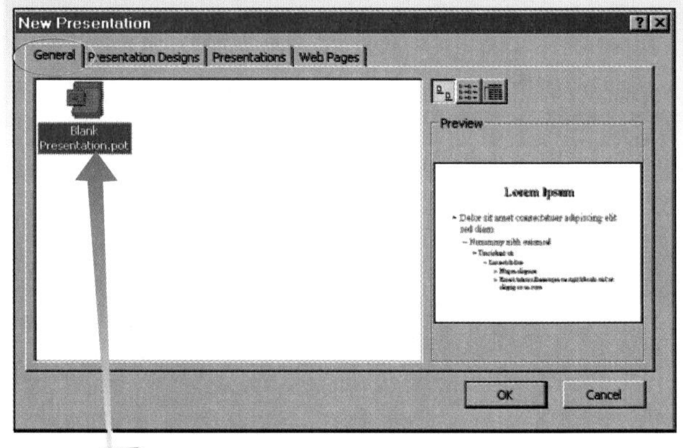

4 Choose a Layout

The New Slide dialog box appears for you to choose a layout for the slide. Click the AutoLayout you want to use and click **OK** (or double-click the layout example).

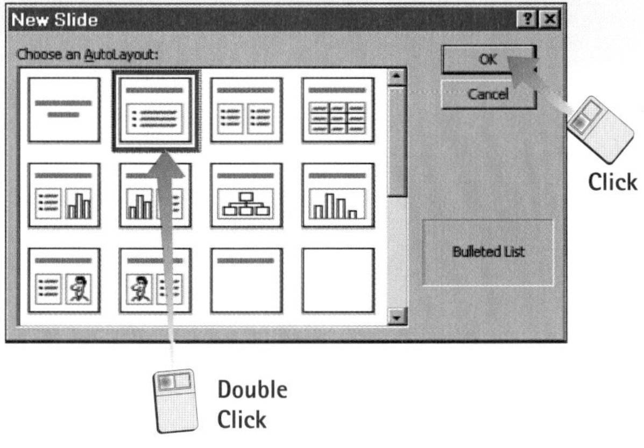

5 The Template Opens

PowerPoint opens the template and layout you selected in Slide view. Now you're ready to start filling in text or graphics (see Task 5, "How to Add and Edit Slide Text").

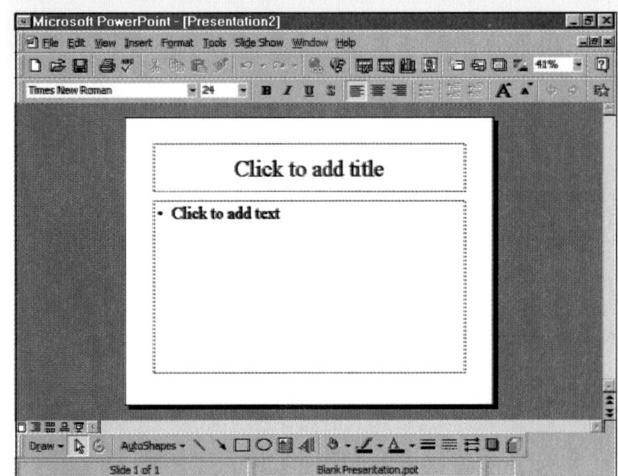

End

How-To Hints

Need Help?

For help adding text boxes to your blank slide, see Task 8, "How to Add New Text Boxes." For help adding graphics, see Task 9, "How to Add a Graphic to a Slide."

Choose a Color Scheme

To change the color scheme for your blank presentation, open the **Format** menu and select **Slide Color Scheme**. Click the **Standard** tab and choose a color scheme; then click **Apply**.

Customize the Background

To change the background of your blank presentation, open the **Format** menu and select **Background**. Click the **Background fill** drop-down list and select **Fill Effects**. The Fill Effects dialog box opens. Now you can set a gradient effect, add a pattern or texture background, or turn a picture into a background.

TASK 5

How to Add and Edit Slide Text

After you have started a presentation using one of the three methods described in the previous tasks, you're ready to start entering text. Your slides will have one or more text boxes, and some may include placeholder text. Placeholder text is simply default text included to give you some ideas about content and the overall appearance of the slide.

You can add and edit text in Outline view or Slide view (learn more about views in Chapter 11, Task 1). In Outline view, the presentation is organized in an outline format, with multilevels of text, based on the slide contents. In Slide view, you see one slide onscreen; text and graphic objects are represented as boxes you can click to select and edit. In this task, learn how to enter text in both views.

Begin

1 Select Text in Outline View

If you created a presentation using AutoContent Wizard, the presentation opens in Outline view. Select the placeholder text you want to replace. You can select text in PowerPoint just as you do in Word or Excel—click your mouse at the beginning of the text, hold down the left mouse button, and drag to select the text.

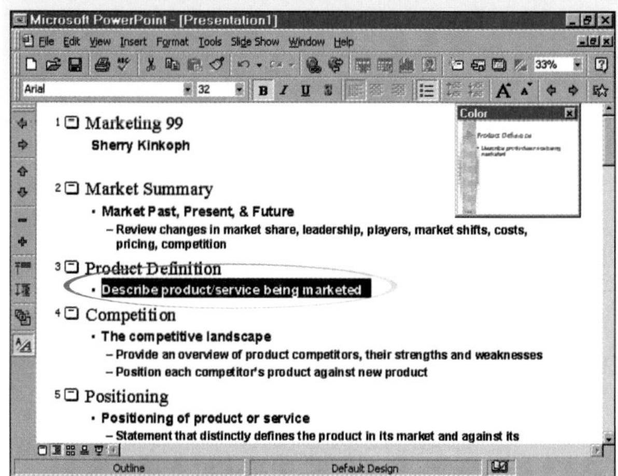

2 Enter Text in Outline View

Type your new text. Use the Delete key to delete characters to the right of the insertion point, or use the Backspace key to delete characters to the left.

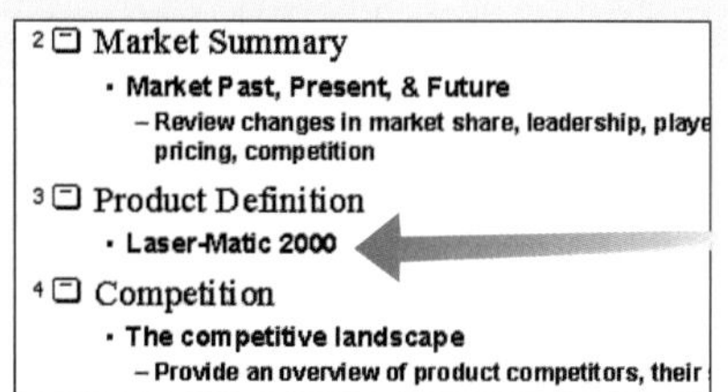

3 Work with Outline View

When in Outline view, your presentation is organized in an outline format. Each slide is represented by a numbered slide icon to the left of the slide title. Each slide's contents are subordinate to the slide title; some have multiple levels of subordination.

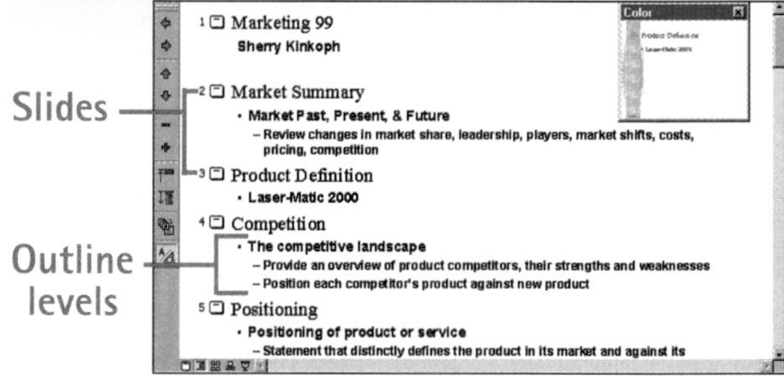

4 New Level Applied

To change the level at any time, select the text, and then press the **Demote** button on the Outlining toolbar to demote a level or the **Promote** button to promote a level. PowerPoint immediately changes the status of the text to the appropriate level. You can keep clicking the **Demote** or **Promote** buttons as needed to place the text in the level you want.

5 Select a Text Box in Slide View

If you create a slide show based on a Design template or a blank presentation, the presentation opens in Slide view. To enter text in Slide view, click the text box. After a text box is selected, you see selection handles surrounding the box.

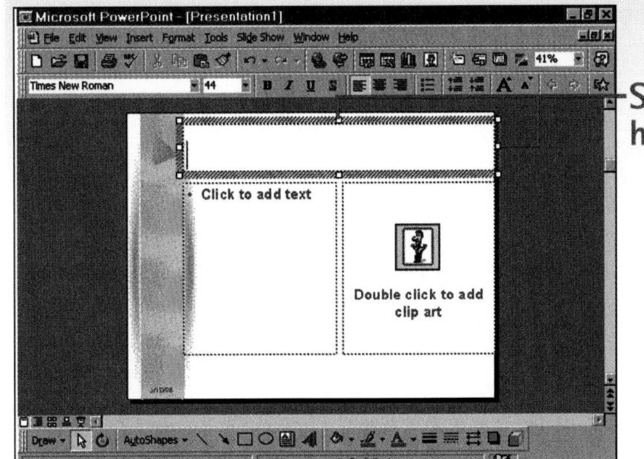

6 Enter New Text in Slide View

Select the placeholder text you want to replace, then type the new text. The placeholder text disappears. Use the Delete key to delete characters to the right of the insertion point, or use the Backspace key to delete characters to the left.

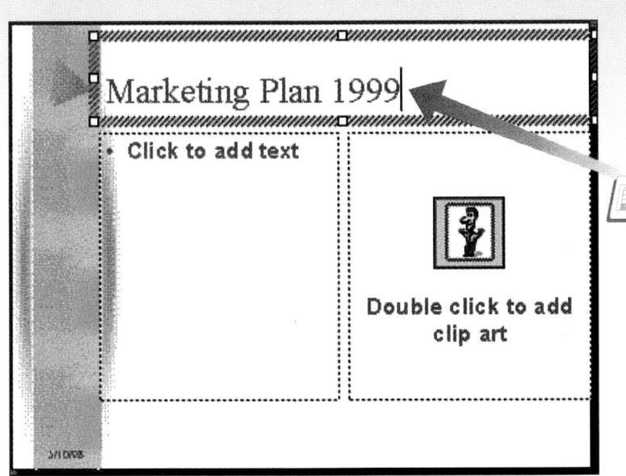

End

How-To Hints

Adding Lots of Text?

If you're going to add a lot of text, it's best to work directly on the slide in Slide view so you can have a better sense of when the slide is getting too cluttered to be effective. To switch your view, click the **Slide View** button to the left of the horizontal toolbar.

Move Slides in Outline View

To move a slide up or down in the outline and rearrange the presentation order, use the **Move Up** or **Move Down** buttons on the Outlining toolbar. Select the text to move, and then click the **Move Up** button to move up in order, or click **Move Down** to move down in order.

The Slide Miniature Window

When you're working in Outline view, PowerPoint displays a miniature color version of the slide where your cursor currently rests. The miniaturized window enables you to see how your slide actually appears. To turn the feature on or off, select **View, Slide Miniature**.

TASK 6

How to Format and Align Slide Text

You can quickly change the look of your slide text using PowerPoint's formatting commands. You can make text bold, italic, or underlined with a click of a button, or change the alignment to left, right, or center. You can even add a shadow effect to give text a three-dimensional look.

If you learned how to use formatting commands with Word, those same commands come into play with text in PowerPoint. The easiest way to format text in PowerPoint is to use the available buttons on the Formatting toolbar.

Begin

1 Select the Text

Start by opening the slide that contains the text you want to format and selecting the text. (It's easiest to format text in Slide view.)

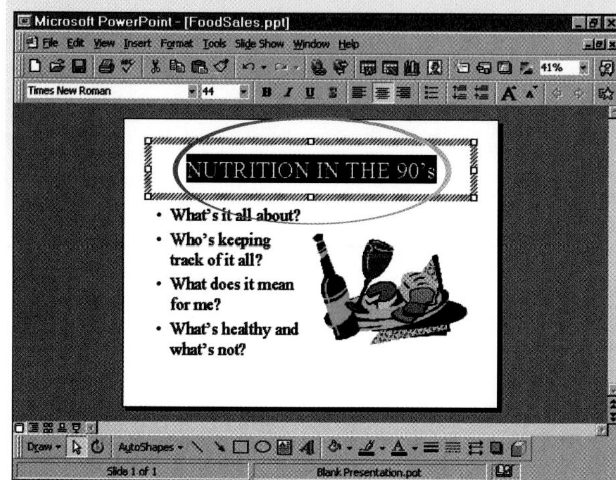

2 Bold, Italic, Underline

To bold text, click the **Bold** button on the Formatting toolbar. To italicize the text, click **Italic**. To add an underline to text, click the **Underline** button.

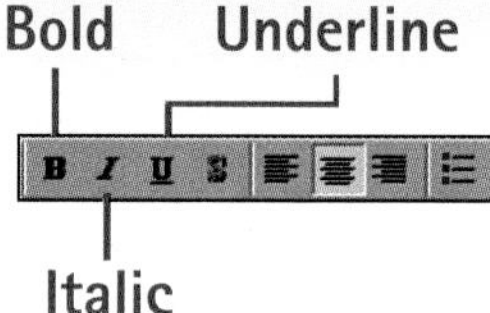

3 Create a Shadow Effect

To add a shadow effect to the text, click the **Shadow** button located next to the Bold, Italic, and Underline buttons.

4 Shadow Applied

PowerPoint adds a shadow effect to the text, as shown in this figure.

NUTRITION IN THE 90's

5 Change the Alignment

To align text to the left in the text box, click the **Left Alignment** button on the Formatting toolbar. To center text, click **Center Alignment**. To align text to the right, click **Right Alignment**.

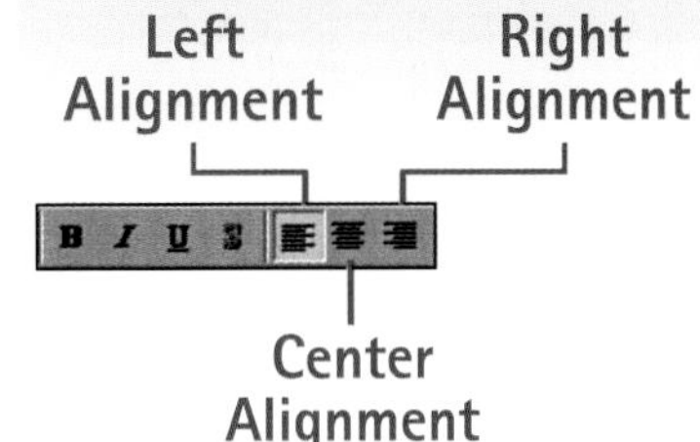

6 Alignment Applied

PowerPoint aligns your text in the text box as you specified. The figure below shows examples of each of the alignment options as applied to slide text.

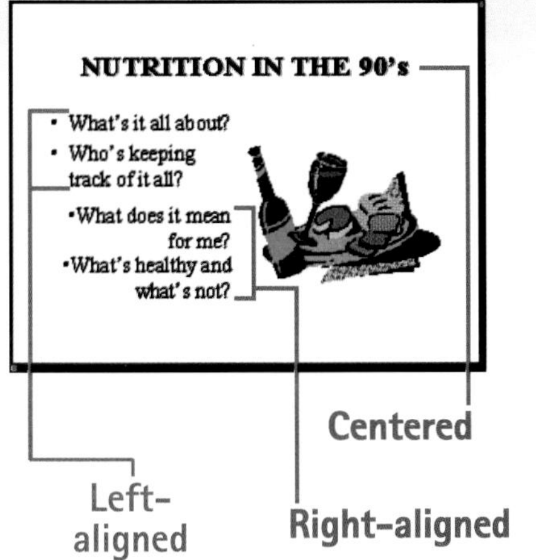

End

How-To Hints

Toggle On/Toggle Off

The Bold, Italic, Underline, and Shadow buttons toggle on or off. After you click the **Bold** button, for example, the bold formatting is on; click the button again to turn it off.

Switch to Slide View

To quickly switch to Slide view, click the **Slide View** button at the far-left end of the horizontal scrollbar.

TASK 7

How to Change Slide Fonts and Sizes

If you don't like the default font assigned to a slide by AutoContent Wizard or the template you chose, you can change it. You can use the Font button on the Formatting toolbar, or open the Font dialog box.

You can also adjust the font size as needed. Unlike Word or Excel, however, PowerPoint has an extra feature for adjusting font sizes. You can use the Increase Font Size or Decrease Font Size buttons on the Formatting toolbar to adjust the font size in increments. As you use these buttons, you can clearly see on the slide how the size affects the text.

Begin

1 Change the Font

Select the text you want to change, and then click the **Font** drop-down arrow on the Formatting toolbar and choose a new font from the list.

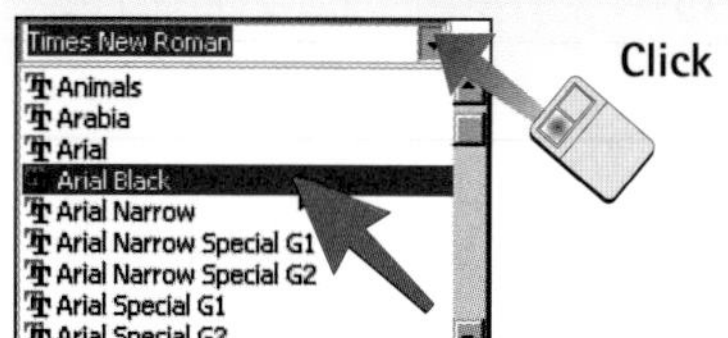

2 Change the Font Size

To choose a specific font size, click the **Font Size** drop-down arrow and select a size.

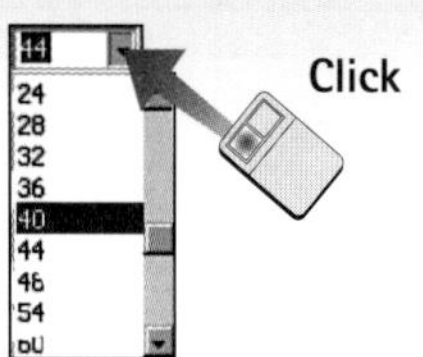

3 Use Increase and Decrease Buttons

If you would rather resize the text a little at a time until you reach the desired size, use the Increase and Decrease buttons. To nudge the selected text up a size, click the **Increase Font Size** button. To make the text smaller, click the **Decrease Font Size** button.

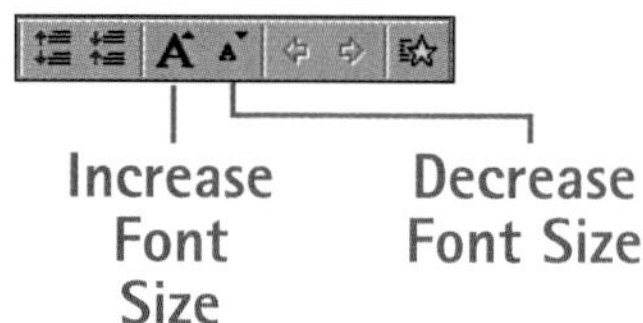

4 PowerPoint Nudges the Font Size

Depending on which direction you're going—enlarging the text or reducing its size—PowerPoint makes the necessary adjustments each time you click the Increase or Decrease buttons. The figure below shows one text box with the default size recommended by PowerPoint, and the text box below it shows the size increased with the **Increase Font Size** button.

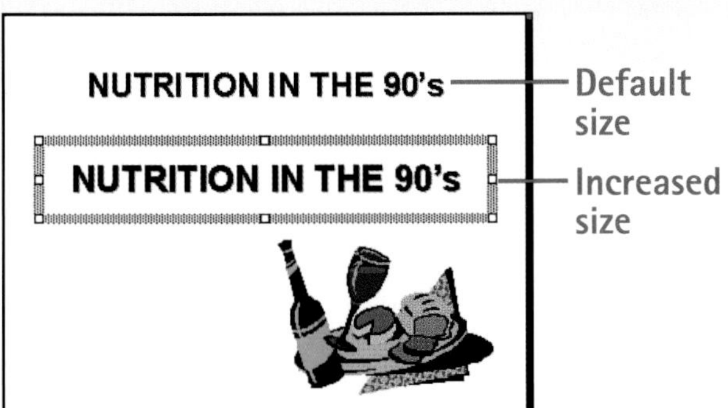

5 Open the Font Dialog Box

If you prefer handling all your formatting needs at once, open the Font dialog box and select new settings. Open the **Format** menu and choose **Font**.

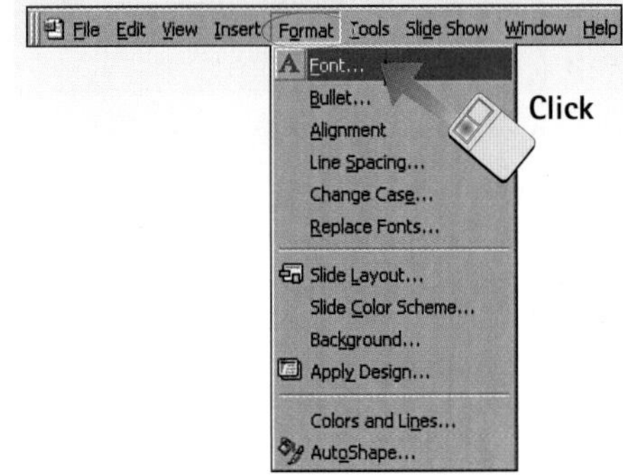

6 Change the Font Settings

In the Font dialog box, make any changes to the formatting settings, and then click **OK** to exit and apply the new settings to the text.

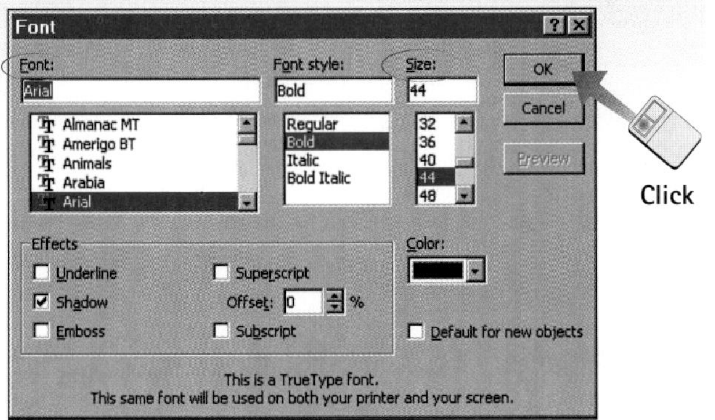

End

How-To Hints

Other Formatting Effects

Notice that the Font dialog box has other formatting effects you can apply to your PowerPoint text. You can add an Emboss effect, for example, or choose a color for the text. To preview your selections, click the Preview button. However, you will have to drag the Font dialog box out of the way to see how the settings look on your slide.

TASK 8

How to Add New Text Boxes

At times, you will need to add a new text box to a slide. You may need to add a box for your corporate slogan, for example, or add a caption text box for a graphic. When you add a new text box, you can decide how large to make the box or let PowerPoint create a default size.

In this task you learn how to use a tool from the Drawing toolbar. Make sure you're in Slide view. If the Drawing toolbar is not displayed, right-click over another toolbar and select **Drawing**.

Begin

1 Select the Text Box Tool

From the Drawing toolbar, click the **Text Box** button.

2 Click in Place

Move the mouse pointer to the area on the slide where you want the new text box inserted, and click the mouse button.

NUTRITION IN THE 90's

- What's it all about?
- Who's keeping track of it all?
- What does it mean for me?
- What's healthy and what's not?

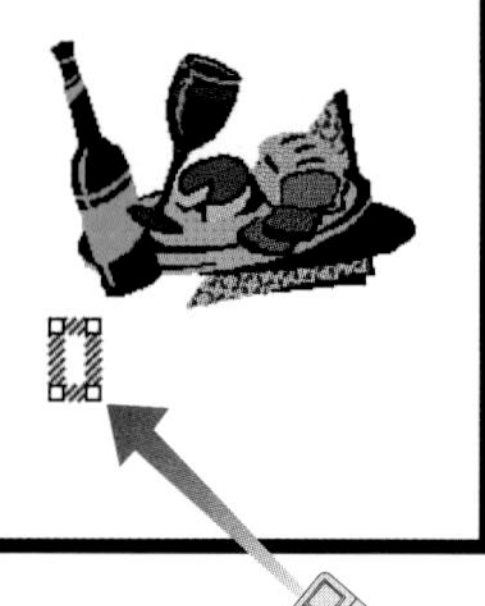

Click

3 Start Typing

A text box the size of one character appears. Start typing the text you want to add.

NUTRITION IN THE 90's

- What's it all about?
- Who's keeping track of it all?
- What does it mean for me?
- What's healthy and what's not?

Are you eating

4 The Box Expands

As you type, the size of the text box increases. To start a second line, press Enter.

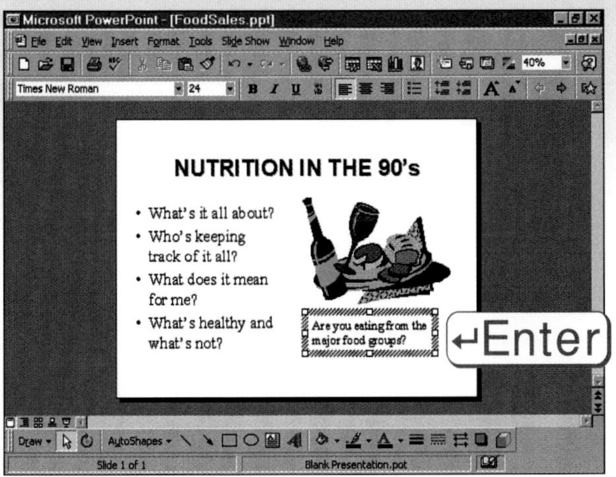

5 Drag the Text Box

Another way to insert a text box after clicking the Text Box tool is to drag the size of the box on the slide. Click in the upper-left corner where you want the text box to start, and then drag to the desired size and click again.

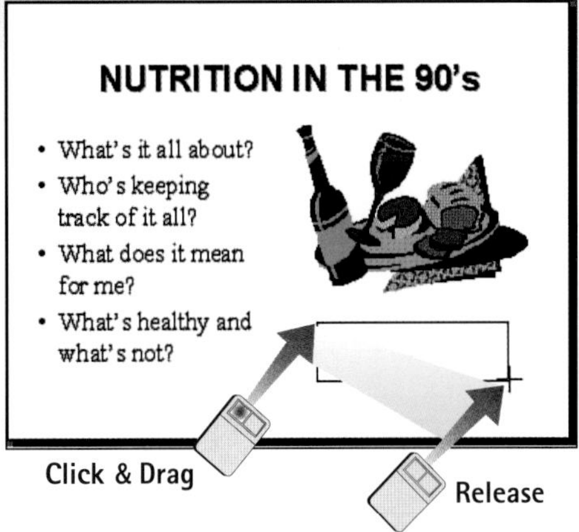

6 Enter the Text

Release the mouse button and the text box is set. To enter text, click inside the box and start typing.

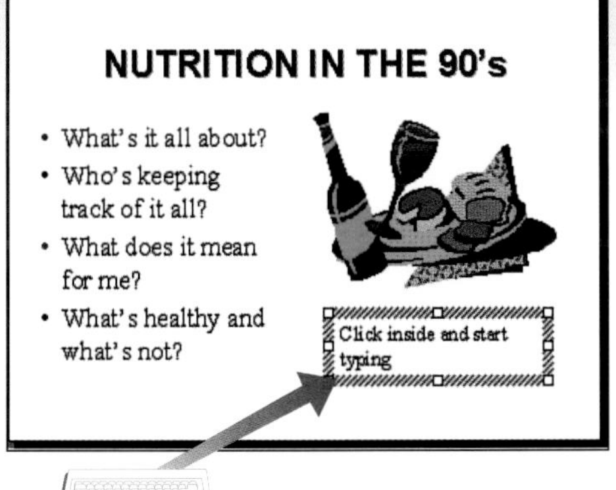

End

How-To Hints

Resize the Box

You can resize a text box by dragging any of its selection handles. Select the box, position the pointer over a selection handle, hold down the left mouse button, and drag the box to a new size.

Use Rulers

Sometimes it's helpful to display the PowerPoint rulers to assist in placing text boxes on the slide. To display the rulers, open the **View** menu and choose **Ruler**.

TASK 9

How to Add a Graphic to a Slide

Slide shows are meant to be visual, and part of their appeal is graphics—whether it's clip art, a picture you create from a drawing program, or a photo found on the Internet. Graphics can really spruce up your slides. For that reason, PowerPoint's templates and presentations created with AutoContent Wizard have areas on the slides already designated for graphics elements.

PowerPoint comes with a large collection of clip art you can use in your own slide shows, or you can easily use artwork from other files. After you insert a graphic, you can resize it, move it, rotate it, and more (see Task 11, "How to Move, Resize, and Rotate Slide Objects").

Begin

1 Filling a Graphic Placeholder

If your slide already has a placeholder for a graphic, double-click the placeholder to open the Clip Gallery (skip to step 3).

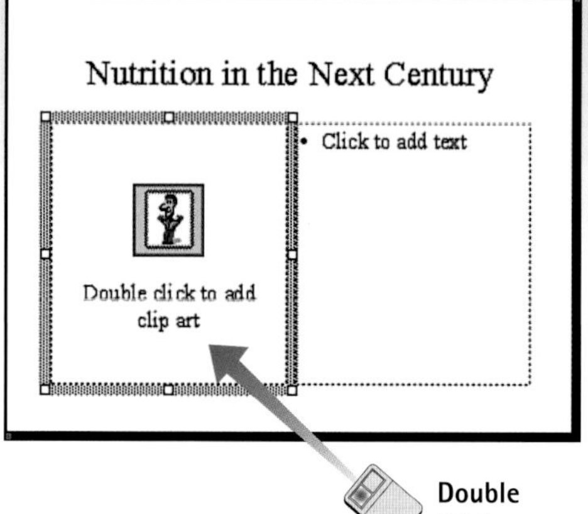

2 Adding a New Graphics Object

To add a new object box to hold a piece of clip art, click the **Insert Clip Art** button on the Standard toolbar.

3 Using the Clip Gallery Dialog Box

From the **Clip Art** tab, peruse the catalog of available clip art. To choose a category, click it, and the preview area shows the available graphics, or choose **All Categories** to see all the choices.

4 Select a Clip

When you find a clip art piece you want to use, double-click it to insert it into your slide.

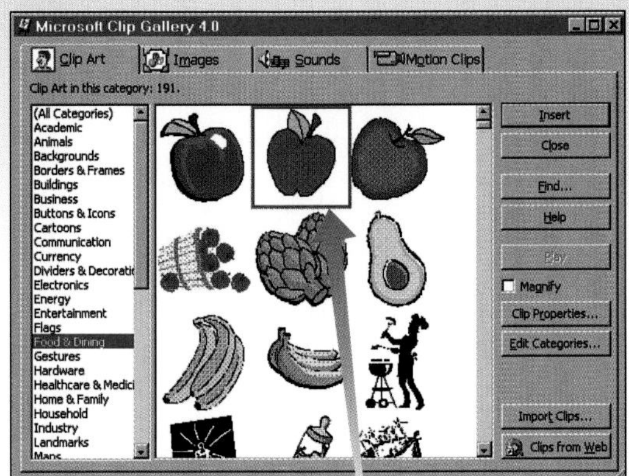

Double Click

5 Or Use an Image File

If you have a graphics image file stored elsewhere on your computer, you can insert it into a slide. Open the **Insert** menu and select **Picture**, **From File**. This opens the Insert Picture dialog box.

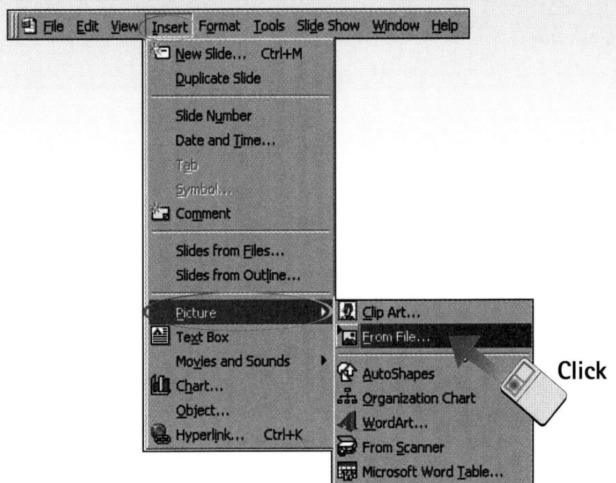

6 Locate the Image

Locate the image file you want to use. When you find the file, double-click it to quickly insert it into your slide.

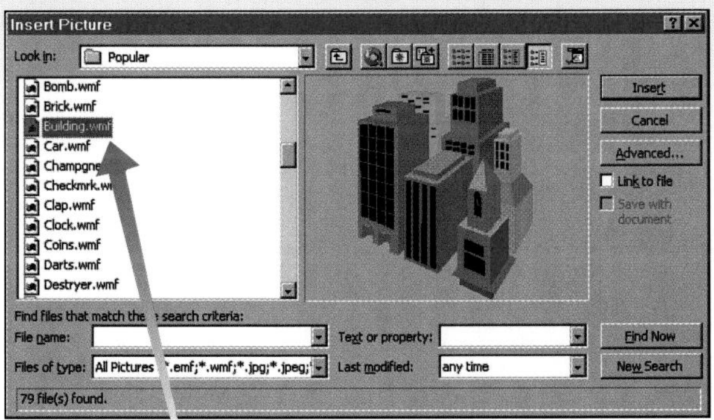

Double Click

End

How-To Hints

Use Photos, Sounds, and Videos

In addition to the vast collection of clip art, the Microsoft Clip Gallery also has photos, sound clips, and video clips you can add to your presentation. Be sure to check out the other tabs in the Clip Gallery dialog box and see what's available.

No Design Talent?

If you're not too confident about choosing a graphic to use in your presentation, why not let PowerPoint do it for you? Use the AutoClipArt feature to analyze your presentation and come up with clip art suggestions. Open the **Tools** menu and select **AutoClipArt**. After the feature examines your presentation, it opens the AutoClipArt dialog box where you can select important words from the drop-down list and see possible matches in clip art.

TASK 10

How to Add Shapes to a Slide

If you're having trouble finding just the right piece of art to add to a slide, consider using shapes instead. You can add a shape to draw attention to parts of your text, create a nice background effect, or use it simply as a design element.

It's easy to create shapes with the drawing tools available on PowerPoint's Drawing toolbar. If you're not comfortable drawing the shapes freehand, cheat a little and use the AutoShapes feature, which offers predrawn shapes.

Begin

1 Select a Tool

Click the shape tool you want to draw; choose from **Rectangle** or **Oval**. To draw a rectangle, for example, click the **Rectangle** tool on the Drawing toolbar. Your mouse pointer takes the shape of a crosshair.

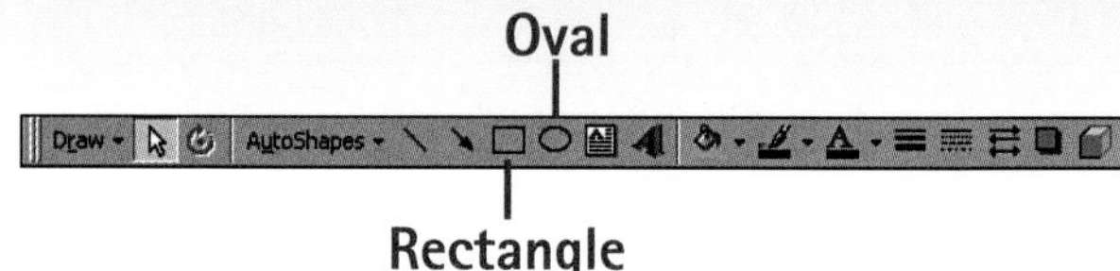

2 Drag the Shape

Move the mouse pointer to the location on the slide where you want the shape to appear. Click and drag the mouse to draw the shape. When the shape reaches the desired shape and size, click again. You can now resize, move, or format the shape object (see Task 12, "How to Use Colors, Line Styles, and Shadows," for more information).

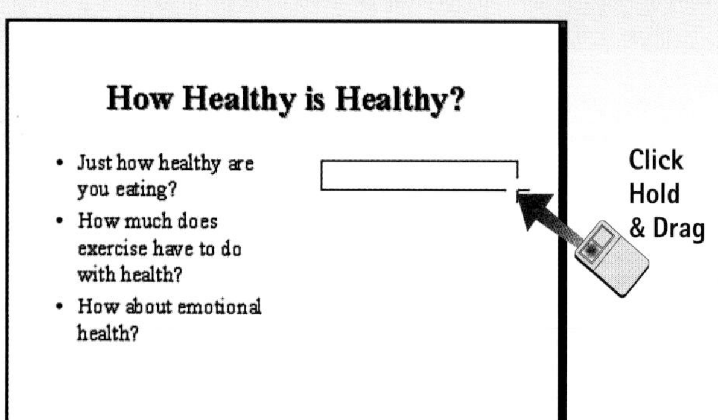

3 Use AutoShapes

Rather than spending time carefully drawing shapes on your slides, why not use PowerPoint's predrawn shapes? Click the **AutoShapes** tool on the Drawing toolbar to display a list of categories.

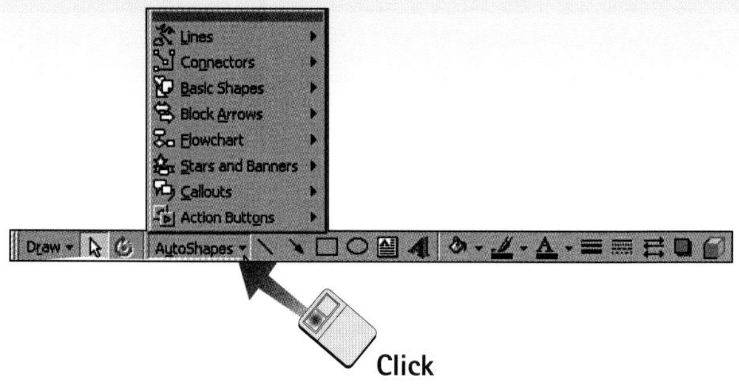

4 Choose a Shape

Click the category you want to use to display a palette of custom shapes. Click a shape. The mouse pointer becomes a crosshair icon.

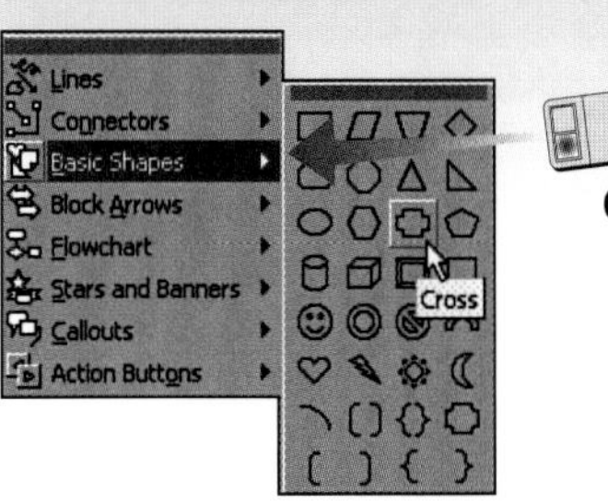
Lines
Connectors
Basic Shapes
Block Arrows
Flowchart
Stars and Banners
Callouts
Action Buttons
Cross
Click

5 Draw the Shape

Move the mouse pointer to the location on the slide where you want the shape to appear. Click and drag the mouse pointer until the shape reaches the size you want.

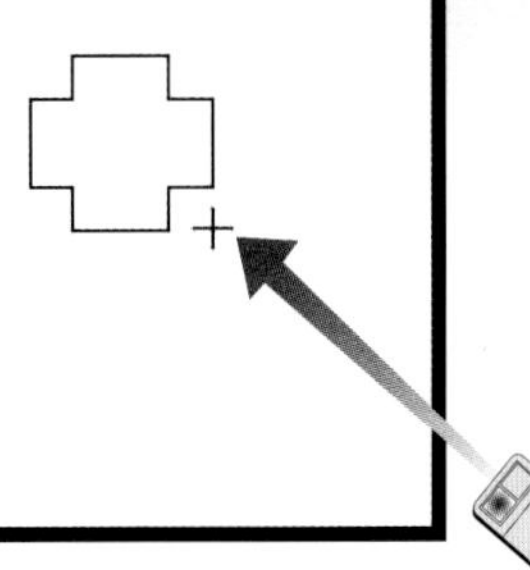
How Healthy is Healthy?
• Just how healthy are you eating?
• How much does exercise have to do with health?
• How about emotional health?
Click Hold & Drag

6 Click in Place

Click the mouse button again, and the complete shape appears on the slide, as shown in this figure. You can now resize, move, or format the shape as needed.

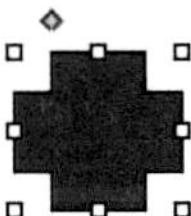
How Healthy is Healthy?
• Just how healthy are you eating?
• How much does exercise have to do with health?
• How about emotional health?

End

How-To Hints

Where's the Drawing Toolbar?

If your Drawing toolbar isn't displayed, right-click over any toolbar and choose **Drawing**.

More About the Drawing Tools

To learn more about using the Office 97 drawing tools, turn to Chapter 16, "How to Work with Office Graphics Tools." Here you will learn how to create WordArt images, draw lines and arrows, format images, add special effects, and more.

Draw Perfect Shapes

To draw a perfect shape every time, hold down the Shift key while you drag. This keeps the proportions intact as you drag.

TASK 11

How to Move, Resize, and Rotate Slide Objects

Any object you add to a slide can be resized and moved. After you select an object, selection handles surround it. These handles can be dragged in any direction to resize the object. You can also drag the object to a new location. In this task, you will learn how to move and resize any object. Objects you create with the Drawing tools can also be rotated or flipped, which you will also learn how to do.

Begin

1 Select the Object

Select the slide object you want to move. To move a text box, for example, first select the box; to move a shape, click it to display its selection handles.

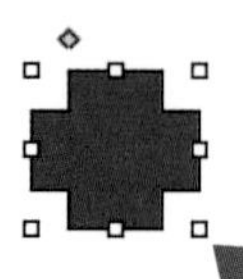
How Healthy is Healthy?
• Just how healthy are you eating?
• How much does exercise have to do with health?
• How about emotional health?

Click

2 Drag to Move

Hover your mouse pointer over any border of the selected object until the pointer takes the shape of a four-headed arrow. Drag the object to a new location on the slide, then click in place.

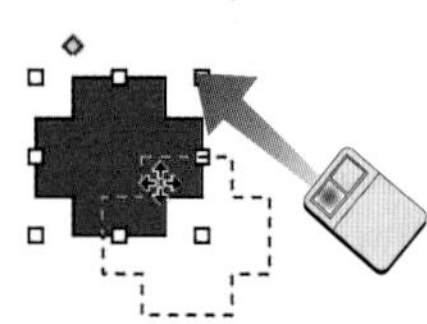
How Healthy is Healthy?
• Just how healthy are you eating?
• How much does exercise have to do with health?
• How about emotional health?
Click Hold & Drag

3 Drag to Resize

To resize a selected object, such as a graphic, hover your mouse pointer over any of the selection handles (tiny boxes) until the pointer takes the shape of a double-sided arrow icon. Now drag to resize the object. Drag the side or top handles to widen or deepen the object; use the corner handles to resize the height and width of the adjacent sides at the same time.

How Healthy is Healthy?
• Just how healthy are you eating?
• How much does exercise have to do with health?
• How about emotional health?
Click Hold & Drag

4 Rotate Shapes

Shapes you draw with the Drawing tools can be rotated or flipped. Select the object, click the **Draw** button on the Drawing toolbar, and then select **Rotate or Flip**, **Free Rotate**.

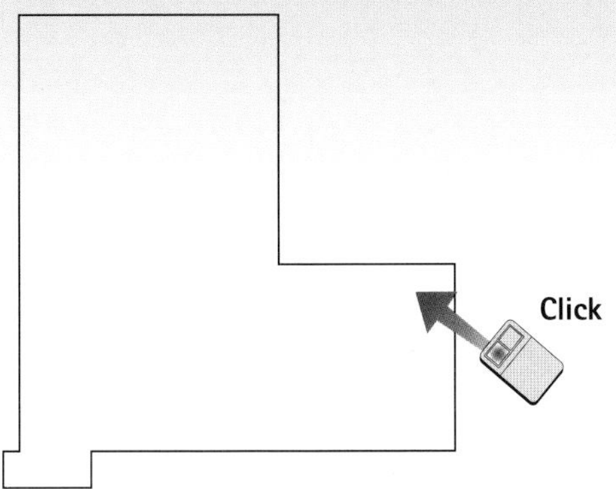

5 Drag to Rotate

The mouse pointer turns into a circular arrow icon. You can now rotate the object with any corner selection handle. Click and drag to rotate.

How Healthy is Healthy?

- Just how healthy are you eating?
- How much does exercise have to do with health?
- How about emotional health?

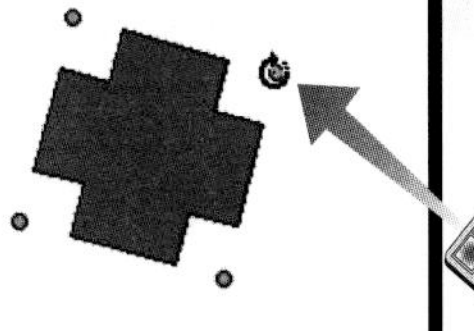

6 Flip Shapes

To flip an object you have drawn, select the object, click the **Draw** button, and then choose **Rotate or Flip**, **Flip Horizontal**, or **Flip Vertical**.

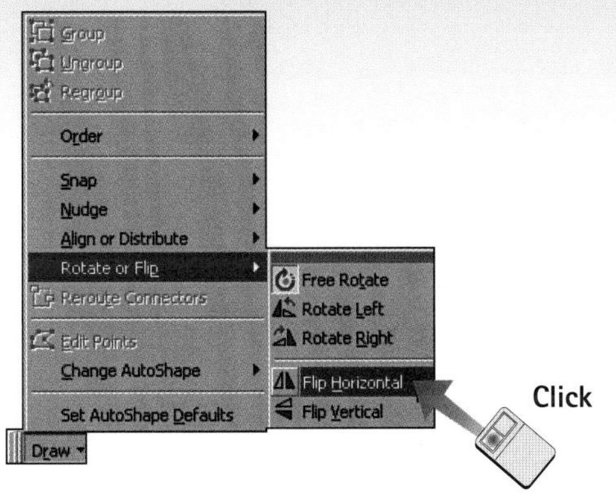

End

How-To Hints

Nudge Objects

Use the Nudge command to move objects by small increments in any direction on the slide. Select the object, click the **Draw** button on the Drawing menu, and select **Nudge**. In the submenu, specify which direction.

Or Use the Free Rotate Button

You can also use the Free Rotate tool on the Drawing toolbar to rotate objects.

Rotate Clip Art

If you select clip art and the rotation choices are inaccessible (grayed out), it means the clip art is a group of objects. Ungroup them, and then regroup them to rotate the clip art. Learn more about grouping and ungrouping in Task 13, "How to Layer and Group Objects."

But Not Text Boxes

You can't rotate or flip text boxes. However, you can use the WordArt feature to create text effects that can be rotated or flipped. Turn to Chapter 16 to learn how.

TASK 12

How to Use Colors, Line Styles, and Shadows

Use fill colors and line styles to change the appearance of objects on your slides. You can change the fill color (the color inside an object), the line color (the color of the outline or frame of an object), and the line style of any given object. In addition to fill colors, you can also create fill effects using shading and patterns. You can even add a shadow to an object to make it stand out on the slide.

Begin

1 Choose Format, Colors and Lines

Select the object, then open the **Format** menu and choose **Colors and Lines**. This opens the Format AutoShape dialog box.

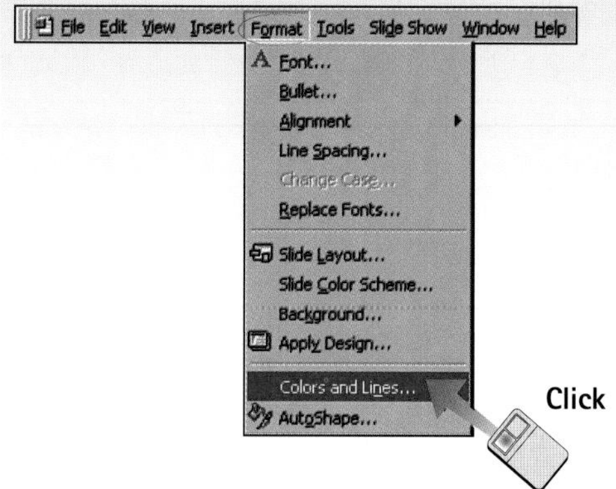

2 Choose a Fill Color

Click the **Colors and Lines** tab. To add a fill color, use the **Fill** area's **Color** drop-down list to choose a fill color.

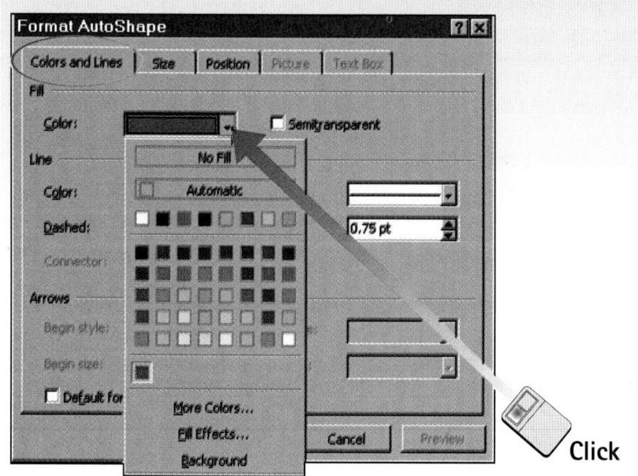

3 Open the Fill Effects Dialog Box

To add a gradient-shading effect or pattern to the object, click the **Fill** area's **Color** drop-down list and select **Fill Effects**. This opens the Fill Effects dialog box where you can choose a shading or pattern to add.

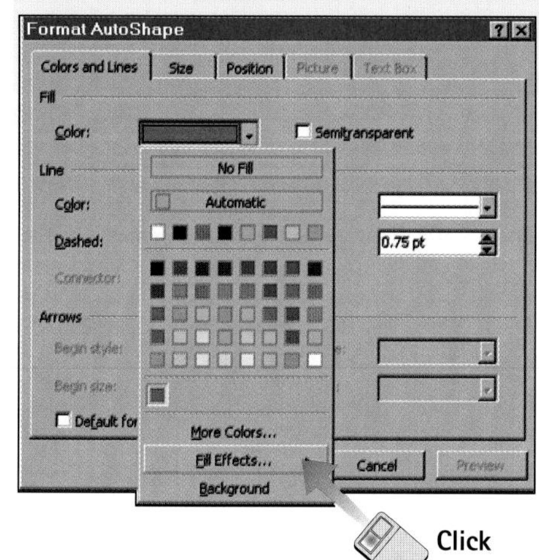

4 Choose a Gradient Effect

To add a gradient-shading effect to your object, click the **Gradient** tab and select a color option and a shading style. The **Sample** area shows you what the shading will look like.

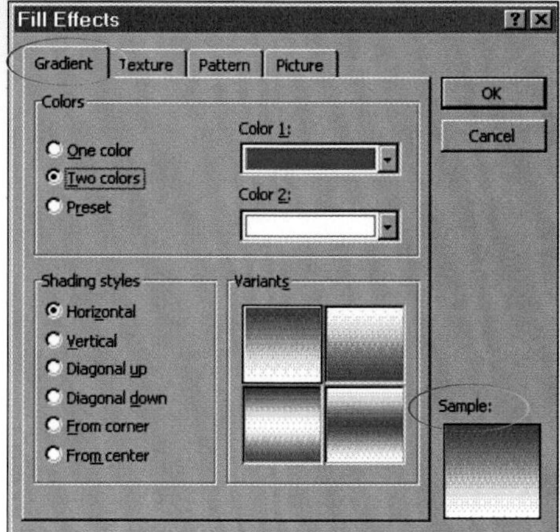

5 Choose a Pattern

To add a pattern to the object, click the **Pattern** tab in the Fill Effects dialog box and select a pattern to use. The **Sample** area shows what the selected pattern will look like.

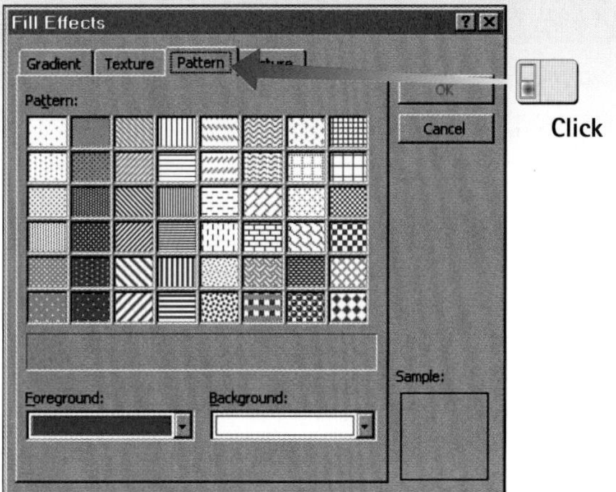

6 Add a Shadow

To apply a shadow effect to a selected object, you don't need the Format AutoShape dialog box. Instead, use the **Shadow** button on the Drawing toolbar. Click the button and choose a shadow effect for the object.

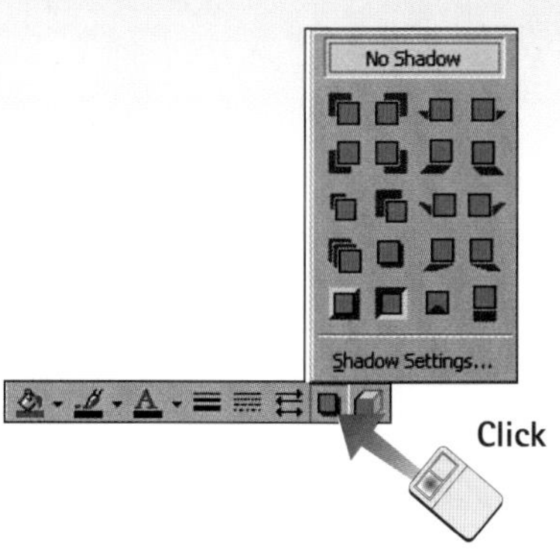

End

How-To Hints

How Do I Exit?

To close the Fill Effects dialog box after making a selection, click **OK**. This returns you to the Format AutoShape dialog box. Click **OK** again to exit this dialog box.

Try a Transparent Effect

Select the **Semitransparent** check box in the Colors and Lines tab to make the object appear transparent and show through to the background.

Format Objects

When it comes to formatting objects, experiment to find the look you want. Don't be afraid to try different selections and combinations of effects. If you decide you don't like your selections, use PowerPoint's Undo command to undo the effects.

TASK 13

How to Layer and Group Objects

As you move objects around on your slides, you may find you are able to create special design effects. For example, you can layer a text box on top of a shape you have drawn. PowerPoint lets you control the order in which the objects are stacked to create interesting effects.

You can also group objects together so you can treat them as a single object. Perhaps you have several objects stacked in place, but find you need to move them over a bit. Rather than move each object separately and relayer them, use the Grouping command. This enables you to move the entire group as one object. After you have moved the group, you can ungroup the objects again to edit them separately as needed.

Begin

1 Layer the Objects

To layer objects, start by moving them on top of each other to create an effect.

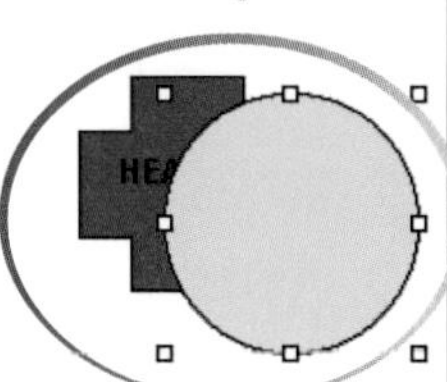

2 Bring an Object to the Front

To move an object to the top of the stack, select the object you want to reorder and right-click to display the shortcut menu. Select **Order, Bring to Front**.

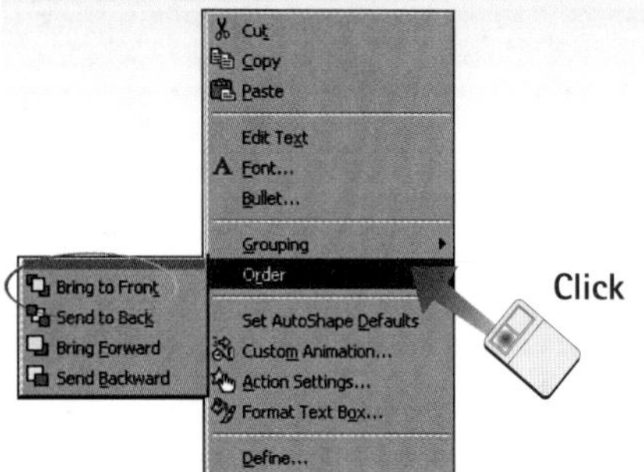

3 Move an Object to the Back

To move an object to the bottom of the stack, select the object, right-click to display the shortcut menu, and select **Order, Send to Back**.

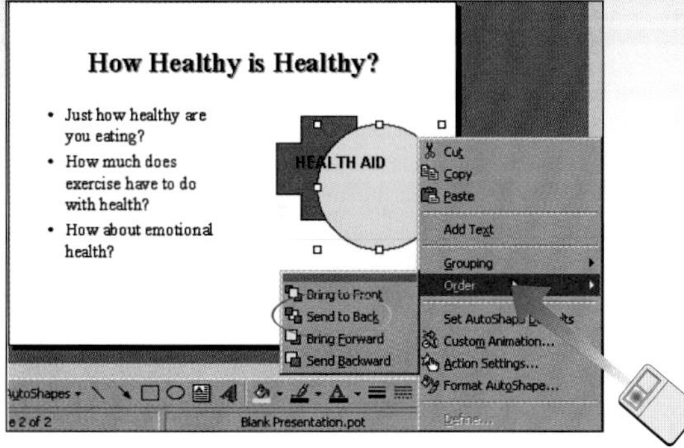

4 Select the Objects to Group

To group several objects together, select each object by clicking the object and holding down the Shift key. (Notice each object's selection handles are active.)

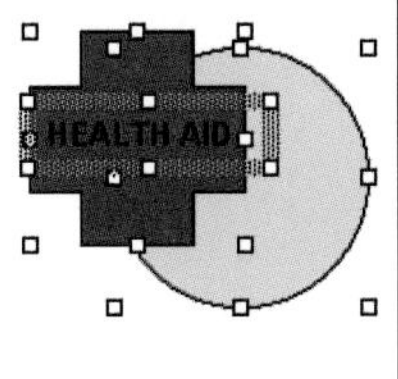

5 Use the Group Command

Right-click any of the selected objects and choose **Grouping**, **Group** from the shortcut menu.

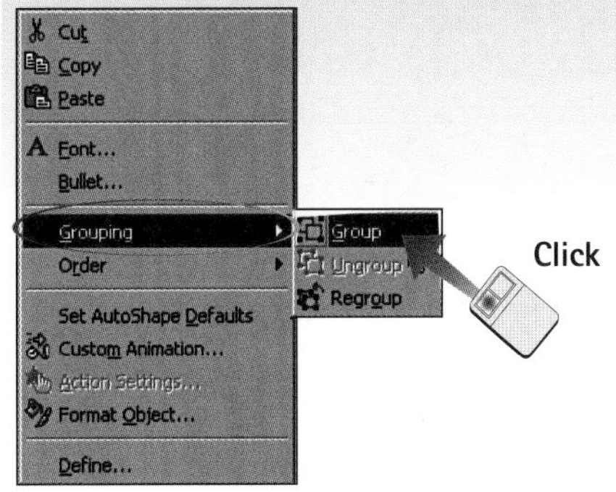

6 A Single Group

The objects are now grouped and surrounded by one set of selection handles.

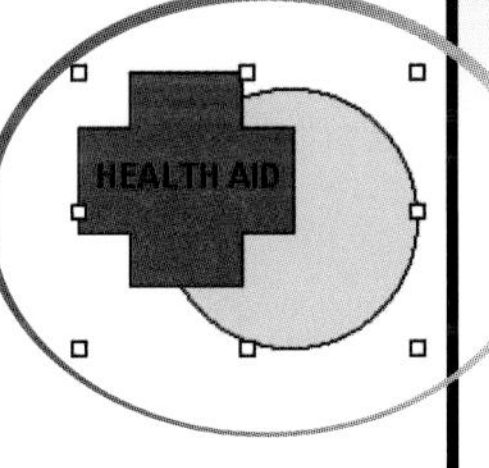

End

How-To Hints

Layer by Layer

To move layers backward or forward a layer at a time, use the **Bring Forward** or **Send Backward** commands.

Ungroup

To ungroup a group of objects, select the group, and then right-click and choose **Grouping**, **Ungroup**.

Group Shortcut

After you have a group of objects layered correctly, you may need to move them to another position on the slide. Drag your mouse in a rectangle that encloses all the objects and release your mouse to create a group. Drag the group to another part of the slide, and the layers will keep their places. Click anywhere outside the group to ungroup the objects.

Task

CHAPTER 11

How to Prepare a Slide Presentation

As you begin building your slide presentation, you will find that you need to add and delete slides, rearrange their order, and change layouts to fit your message. In this chapter, you will learn how to view and navigate your slides, and complete the necessary steps to assemble your slide show for viewing.

When you finally have every slide just the way you want it, you're ready to start assigning transition effects that control how each slide segues into the next. You will learn how to add animation effects, run the slide show, and create speaker notes to help you with the presentation. You can also create audience handouts based on your slide content.

TASK 1

How to Change the View

You can display your slide presentation in different views in PowerPoint to help you work with the slides. You can use the View buttons to the left of the horizontal scrollbar to quickly change your view, or you can open the View menu and select a view. In this task, you will learn about each view.

Begin

1 Use the View Buttons

To change your view, click the appropriate View button next to the horizontal scrollbar.

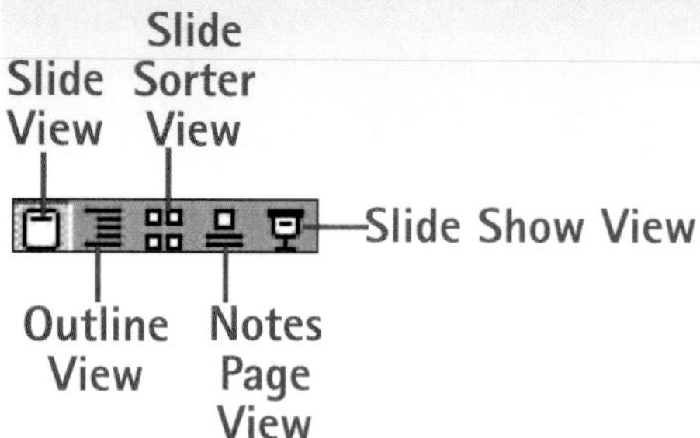

2 Or Use the View Menu

You can also switch views using the View menu. Simply click the **View** menu and make your selection.

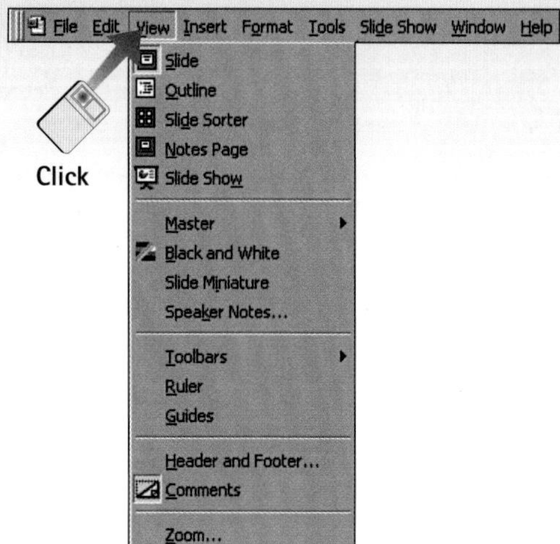

3 Slide View

In Slide view, you see a single slide, including its contents and background. You can work with the various slide elements, such as text boxes and graphics, and move them around the slide.

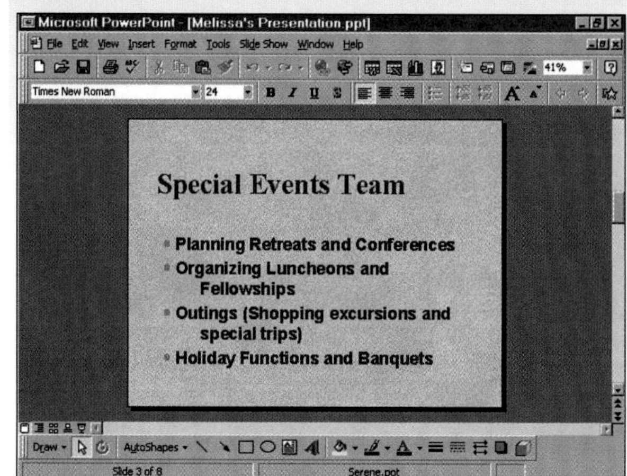

4 Outline View

In Outline view, your slide presentation is shown in outline form, which allows you to see the organization of your presentation's contents. (To learn more about entering text in Outline view, turn to Task 5, "How to Add and Edit Slide Text," in Chapter 10, "How to Use PowerPoint 97.")

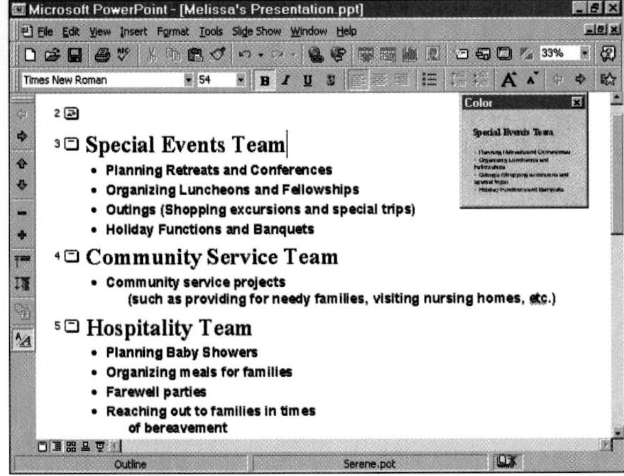

5 Slide Sorter View

In Slide Sorter view, you can see a thumbnail, or miniaturized version, of each slide in the presentation and the order in which the slides appear. You can easily rearrange the slide order and add or delete slides. (You can't select individual slide elements in Slide Sorter view; you will have to switch to Slide view to edit slide objects.)

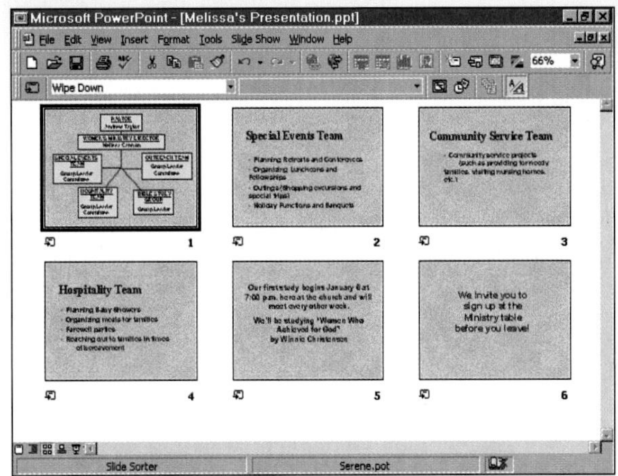

6 Notes Page View

Use PowerPoint's Notes Page feature to prepare special notes to help you as you make the presentation. Each notes page displays a smaller version of the slide, with room for typing your own notes about the slide. You can then print the notes to use when you make the presentation.

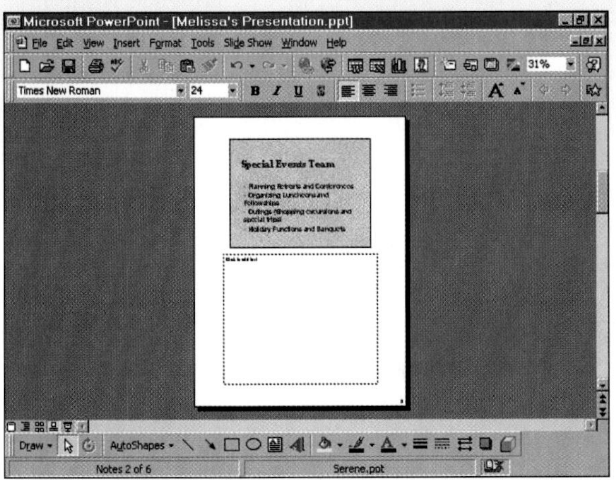

End

How-To Hints

What About Slide Show View?

PowerPoint has one more View button—Slide Show. It's used to actually run your slide show presentation. To learn more about this, see Task 8, "How to Run the Slide Show."

Zooming Your View

You can use PowerPoint's Zoom controls to change your perspective in any view. To get a closer look at a graphics object in Slide view, for example, click the **Zoom** drop-down list on the Standard toolbar and choose a zoom percentage.

Quick Switch

If you're in Outline view, you can quickly switch to Slide view by double-clicking the slide icon next to the outline text.

TASK 2

How to Navigate Slides

If your presentation has more than one slide, you can use PowerPoint's navigation tools to move from slide to slide. You will find navigation buttons at the bottom of the vertical scrollbar. If your slide show has a large number of slides, use the vertical scrollbar to view various slides.

Begin

1 Move Forward and Back

To advance to the next slide, click the **Next Slide** button on the vertical scrollbar. To display the previous slide, click the **Previous Slide** button.

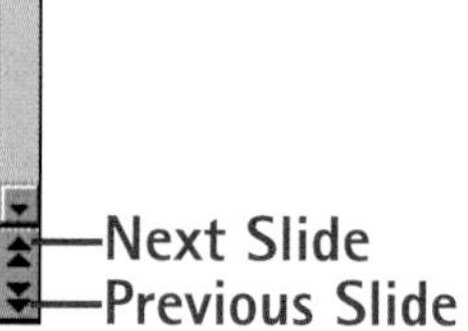

2 Use the Scrollbar

If your presentation has a lot of slides, clicking the **Next Slide** and **Previous Slide** buttons won't get you to the slide you want to view fast enough. Instead, use the vertical scrollbar. Move your mouse pointer over the scrollbox.

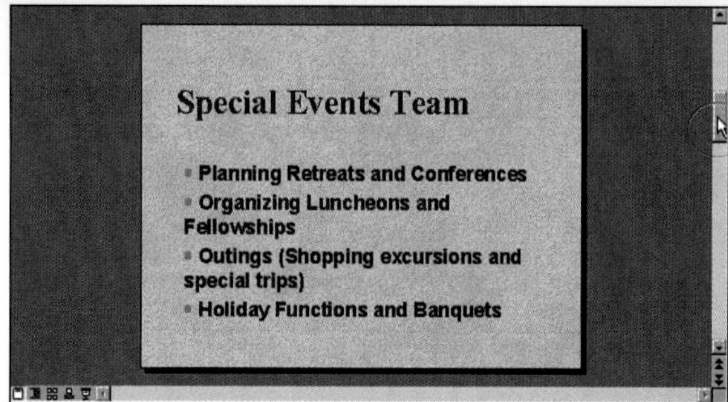

3 Drag the Scrollbox

Hold down the left mouse button and drag the scrollbox up or down, depending on which direction you want to go. As you drag, PowerPoint displays each slide number and the slide title text in a pop-up box. Use this feature to help you locate a specific slide.

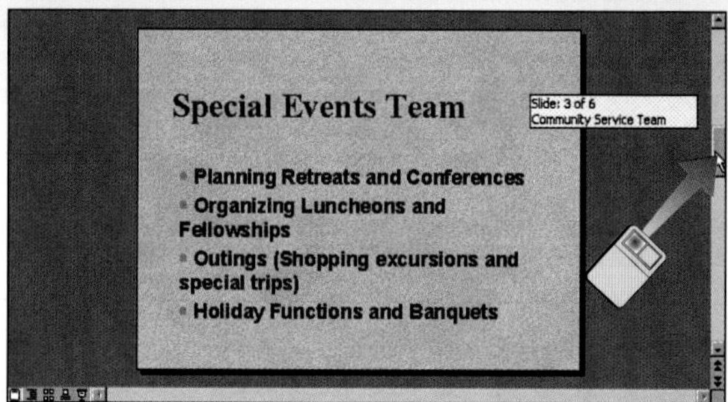

Click Hold & Drag

4 Release the Mouse Button

When you scroll to the slide you want to see, release the mouse button, and the slide appears in the presentation window.

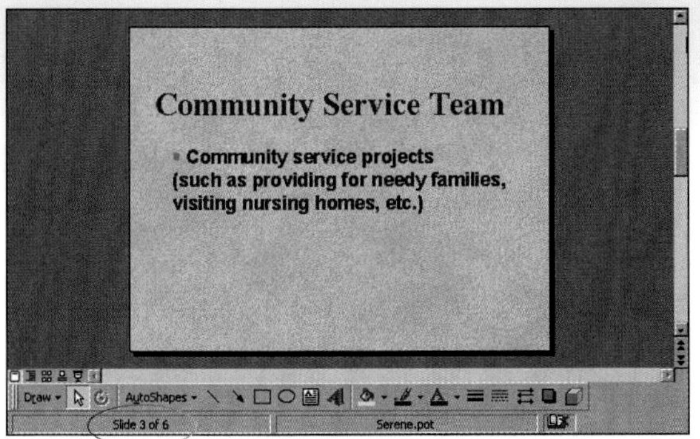

5 Keyboard Shortcut

If you prefer using the keyboard to navigate slides, use the Page Up and Page Down keys to move from slide to slide.

PgDn

PgUp

End

How-To Hints

Use Slide Sorter View to Navigate

You can also move from slide to slide using Slide Sorter view. Switch to Slide Sorter view, and then double-click the slide you want to view. This displays the slide in Slide view.

Running the Show

Another way to view slides is to actually run the slide show. To learn more about running a PowerPoint slide show, turn to Task 8 in this chapter. When you run the actual show, you won't see the menu bar, toolbar, or other screen elements. You will see only each slide, one at a time.

TASK 3

How to Insert and Delete Slides

Need to add a new slide to your presentation? Or perhaps you want to delete a slide you no longer need? PowerPoint makes it easy to add and delete slides. You can add or delete slides in Slide view or Slide Sorter view.

Begin

1 Insert a New Slide

Display the slide that precedes the place where you want to add a new slide, and then click the **Insert New Slide** button on the Standard toolbar.

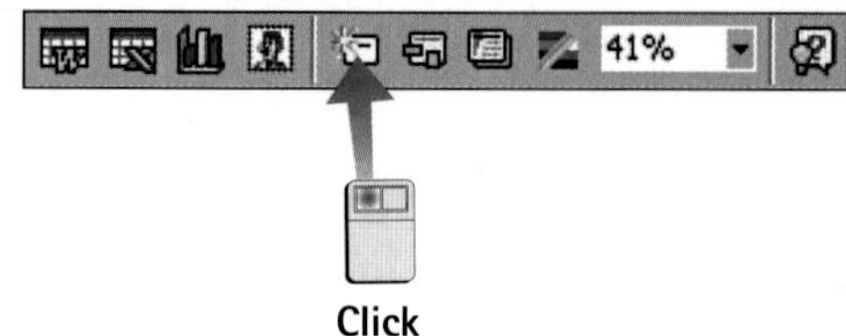

2 New Slide Dialog Box

From the New Slide dialog box, select the AutoLayout you want to use.

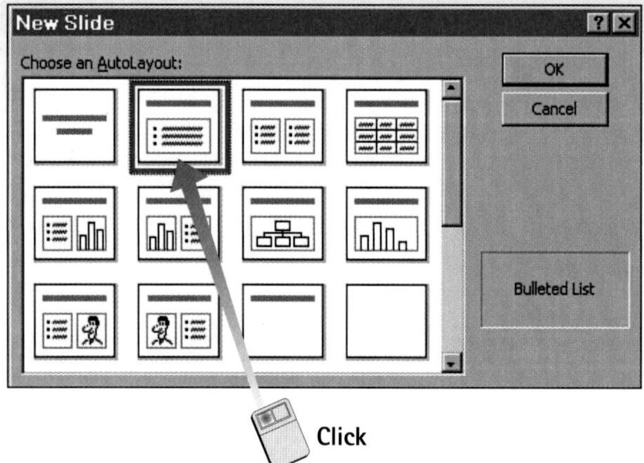

3 Click OK

Click **OK** and the slide is added. You can now fill it with text or graphics.

4 Delete a Slide

To delete a slide, display it and select **Edit, Delete Slide**.

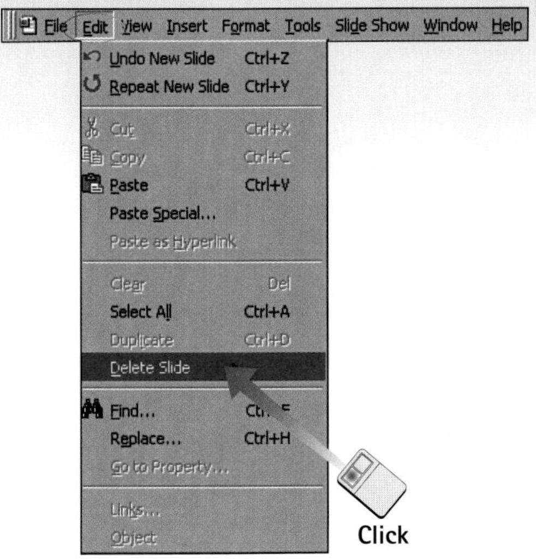

5 Insert Slides from Elsewhere

Use PowerPoint's Slide Finder feature to insert slides from other presentations into your current slide show. Open the **Insert** menu and select **Slides from Files**.

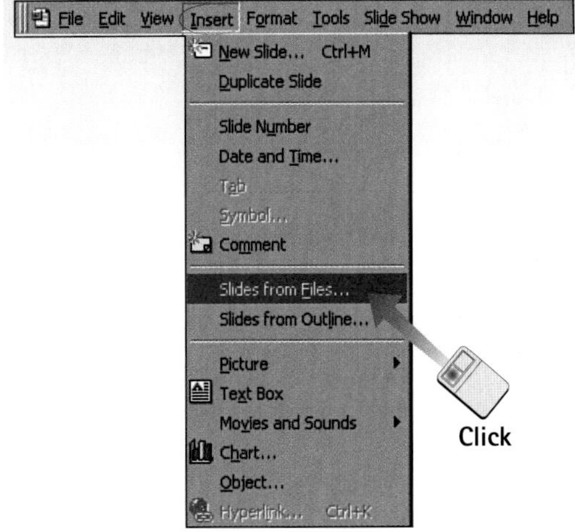

6 Use the Slide Finder Dialog Box

From the Slide Finder dialog box, locate the presentation you want to borrow slides from (use the **Browse** button, if needed); click the **Display** button to view the slides. Then select the slide or slides you want to insert and click the **Insert** button. (Click **Close** to exit the Slide Finder dialog box when you're finished.)

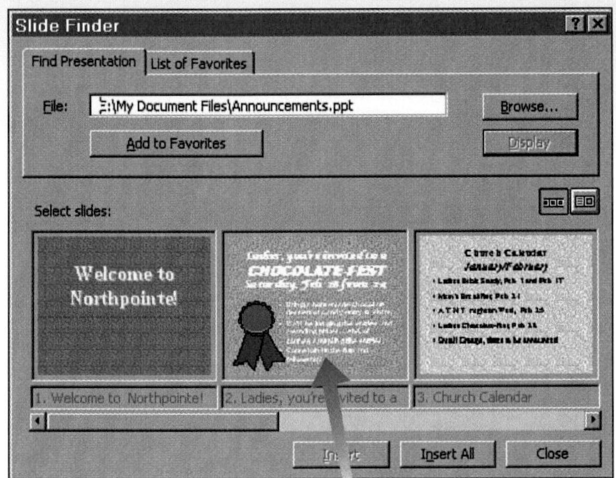

End

How-To Hints

Keyboard Shortcut

To insert a new slide using the keyboard, press Ctrl+M. This opens the New Slide dialog box where you can choose a layout.

Delete Slides in Slide Sorter View

To remove a slide in Slide Sorter view, click the slide, and then press Delete on the keyboard.

Oops!

If you accidentally delete the wrong slide, click the **Undo** button on the Standard toolbar.

TASK 4

How to Reorder Slides

Inevitably, you will need to rearrange the order of slides in your presentation. This is especially true after you have added new slides and deleted others. The easiest way to rearrange slides is in Slide Sorter view, where you can see all the slides at once. In Slide Sorter view, you can drag a slide from one location to another.

Begin

1 Switch to Slide Sorter View

Click the **Slide Sorter View** button at the left of the horizontal scrollbar to switch to Slide Sorter view.

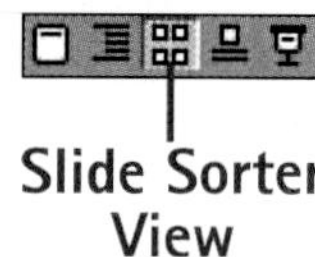

Slide Sorter View

2 Select the Slide to Move

Click the slide you want to move to a new location.

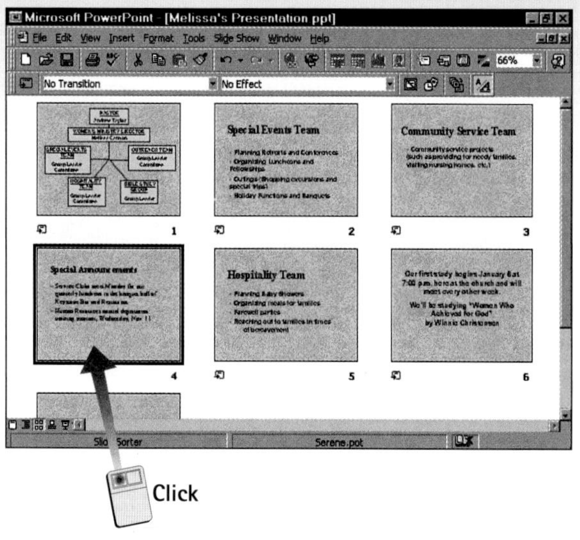

Click

3 Drag the Slide

Hold down the left mouse button and drag the slide to its new destination. As you drag, a line appears showing you where you're moving the slide.

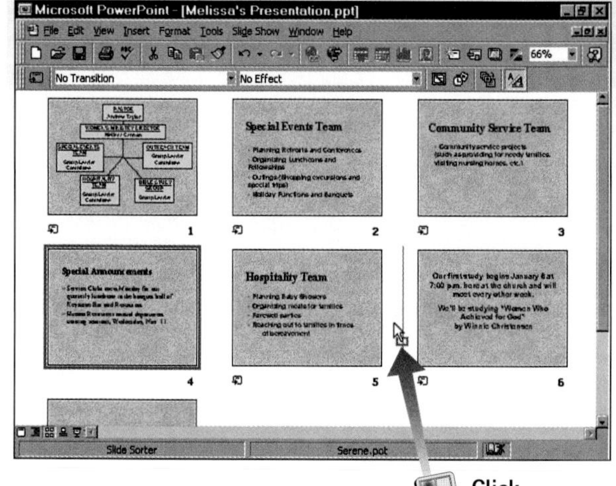

Click Hold & Drag

4 Release the Mouse Button

When the slide is positioned where you want it, release the mouse button; PowerPoint scoots the other slides over and places the moved slide in the new location.

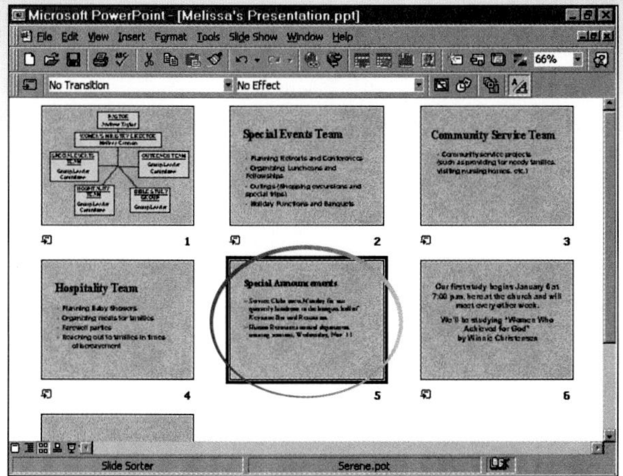

5 Scrolling and Dragging

Slide Sorter view only shows six slides at a time. If you want to move the selected slide beyond the slides in view, drag in the direction you want to go; the display will scroll in that direction.

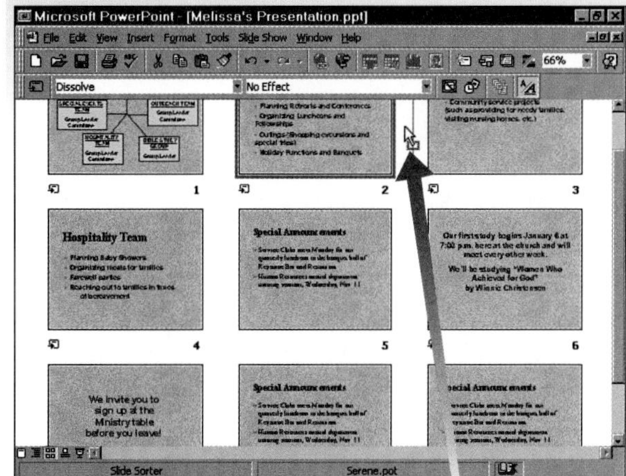

End

How-To Hints

Quick Switch

To quickly view any slide in Slide view, double-click the slide in Slide Sorter view.

Slide Sorter Toolbar

When you switch to Slide Sorter view, the Slide Sorter toolbar appears at the top of the presentation window. The toolbar has buttons for setting slide transitions, rehearsing timings, and controls for setting other special effects.

TASK 5

How to Change the Slide Layout

PowerPoint's AutoLayouts feature enables you to quickly establish a structure for a slide. When you add a new slide, the New Slide dialog box appears with a variety of layout options you can apply. You can also change the layout of an existing slide, using the same dialog box with a different name—the Slide Layout dialog box.

Applying a layout is much easier than adding your own text and graphics boxes. PowerPoint has layouts for just about any kind of slide you want. You will find layouts that offer a combination of title text, bulleted text, charts, and graphics. With AutoLayouts, these slide elements are already positioned in place and ready to go. All you have to do is add your own text or choose a graphic.

Begin

1 Switch to Slide View

Click the **Slide View** button at the left of the horizontal toolbar to switch to Slide view.

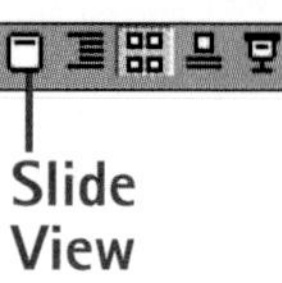

2 Display the Slide

Display the slide you want to change.

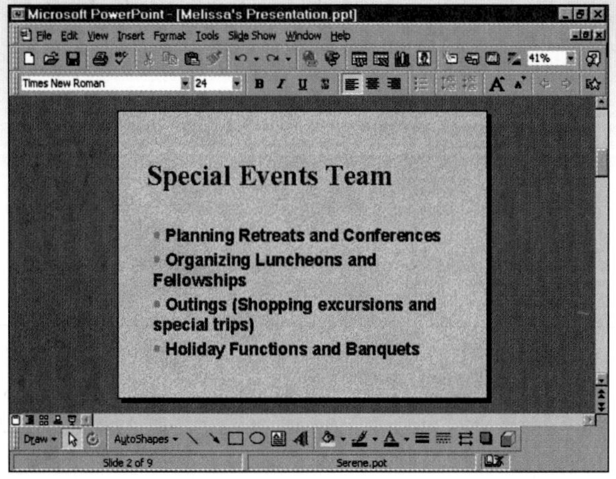

3 Open the Slide Layout Dialog Box

Click the **Slide Layout** button on the Standard toolbar to open the Slide Layout dialog box.

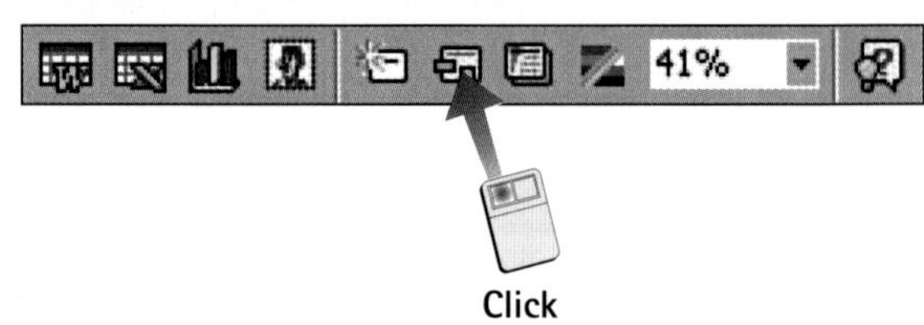

4 Choose a Layout

Click the new layout you want to use. When you select a layout, a description of the layout elements appears in the bottom-right corner of the dialog box.

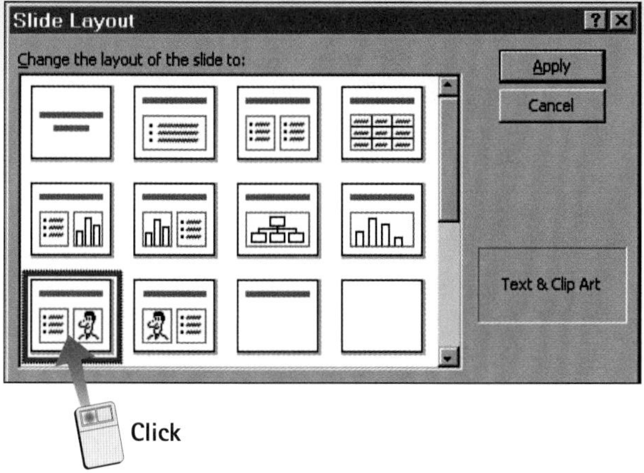

5 Apply the Layout

Click the **Apply** button.

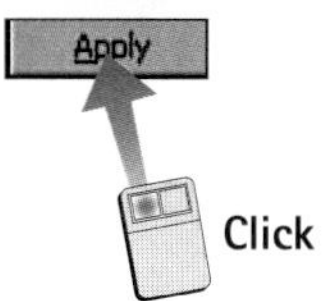

How-To Hints

Right-Click

You can also right-click the slide you want to change and choose **Slide Layout** from the shortcut menu to open the Slide Layout dialog box.

6 The New Layout Applied

PowerPoint applies the new layout. Depending on your slide's contents, you may have to resize or move some slide objects to fit the new layout.

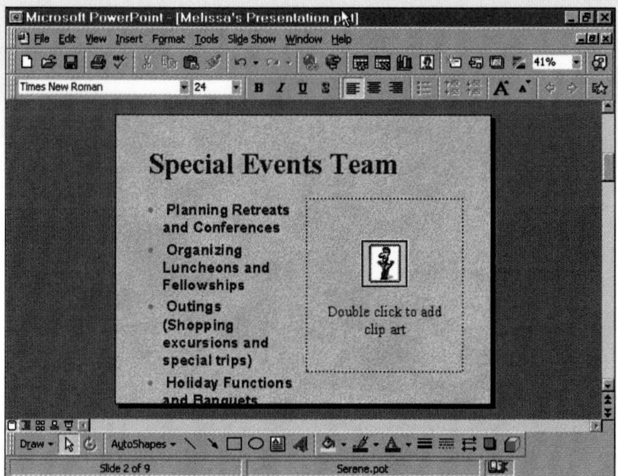

End

TASK 6

How to Define the Slide Transition

To make your slide show more professional, add slide transitions. Slide transitions determine how one slide advances to the next. PowerPoint has numerous transition effects you can use, such as dissolves, tiling effects, fades, split screens, and more. You can assign a different transition to each slide or the same transitions to the entire slide show.

Begin

1 Switch to Slide Sorter View

Click the **Slide Sorter View** button to switch to Slide Sorter view and choose the slide you want to set a transition for; if you want the same transition for all the slides, select the first slide.

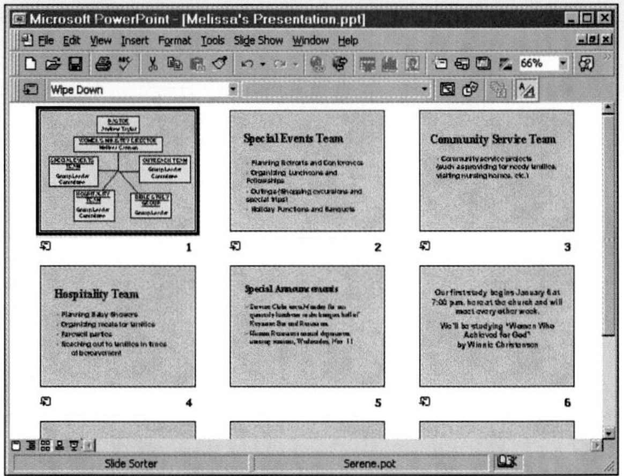

2 Click Slide Transition

From the Slide Sorter toolbar, click the **Slide Transition** button.

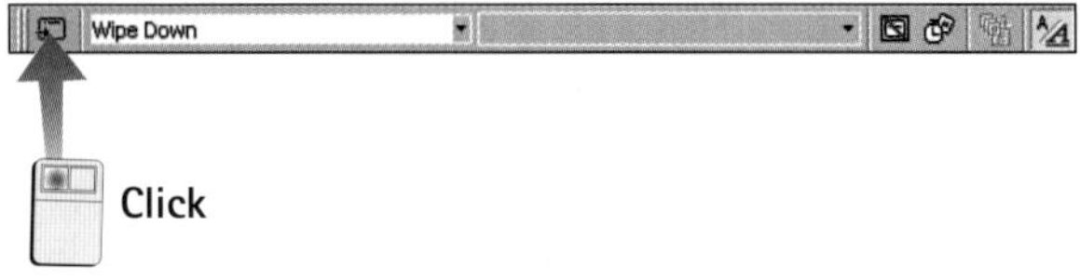

3 Choose an Effect

The Slide Transition dialog box opens. From the **Effect** drop-down list, choose a transition effect. When you make a selection, the transition effect is previewed in the picture area above the drop-down box.

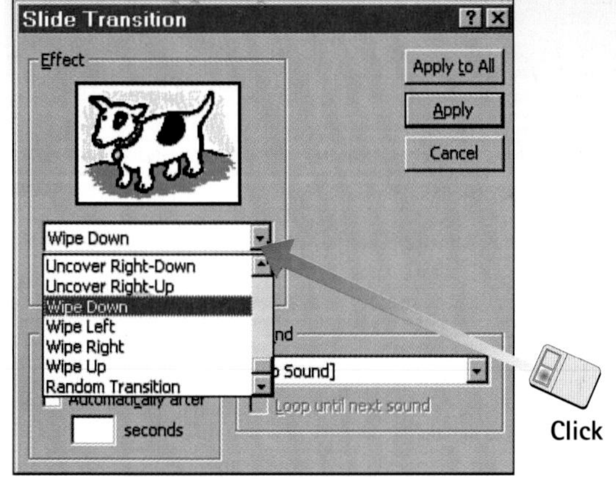

4 Choose a Speed

Beneath the Effect drop-down box, choose a speed option for the speed of the transition: **Slow**, **Medium**, or **Fast**.

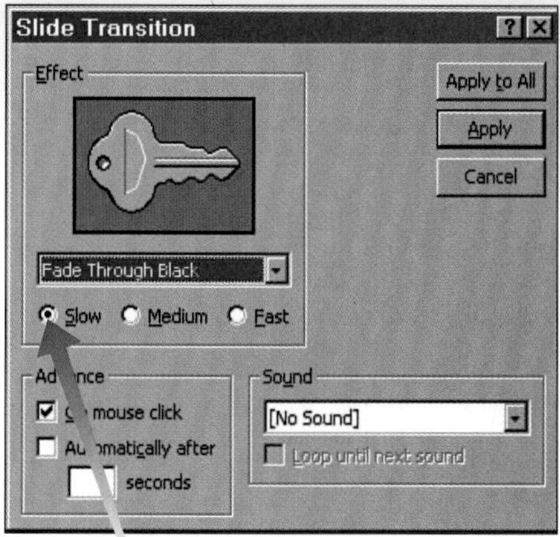

5 Choose How to Advance

Use the **Advance** options to control how the slides will advance—either by mouse click or automatic advance. If you select the **Automatically after** option, you must specify an amount of time, in seconds, for the advance. You can set the advance at 10 seconds, for example, and PowerPoint automatically advances the slide after 10 seconds.

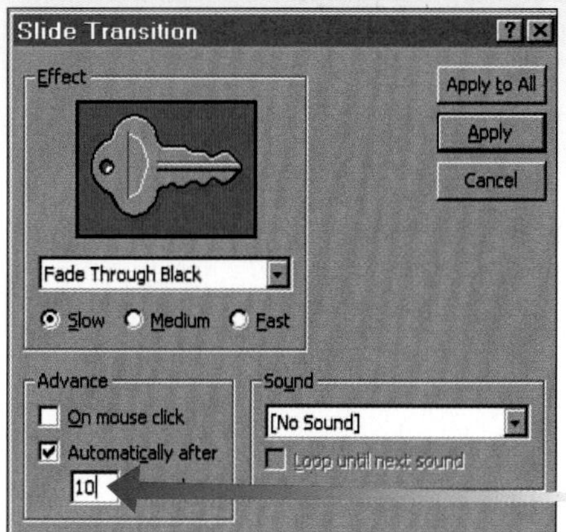

6 Apply the Transition

Click the **Apply** button to apply the transition effects to the slide. Click **Apply to All** to apply the transition to every slide in your presentation.

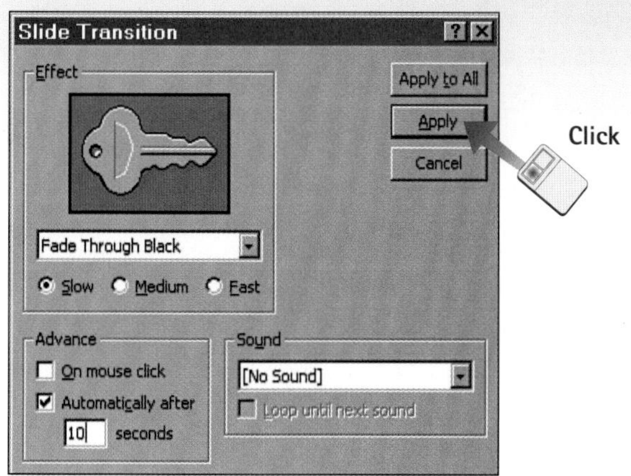

End

How-To Hints

View Transition Icons

When you return to Slide Sorter view after setting a transition, you will notice a transition icon under the slide (or slides). You can click any transition icon to see a demonstration of the transition effect.

Advance with Sounds

Use the Sound options in the Slide Transition dialog box to add sound effects to the slide transition. Click the **Sound** drop-down list and select a sound effect. The sound will play while the slide transition occurs.

Advancing Tips

When setting an advance time, make sure you practice viewing your slide show first to see how long it takes to read everything in the slide or read from your presentation notes. Learn how to run your slide show in Task 8.

TASK 7

How to Add Animation Effects

You can apply PowerPoint's build and animation effects to slide objects. You can make a bulleted list appear on the slide, for example, one bulleted item at a time during the presentation. You can control exactly when each item appears, which prevents your audience from reading ahead of you during the presentation. You can also make each list item fly in from the side of the screen, or fade in slowly.

Many effects are possible, so be sure to test each one to see what it does. You can apply animation effects to any slide object.

Begin

1 Display the Animation Effects

From Slide view, select the object you want to animate, and then click the **Animation Effects** button on the Formatting toolbar to display a palette of animation buttons. To find out what a button does, hover your mouse pointer over the button to display its ScreenTip name. Click a button to assign the effect to the object.

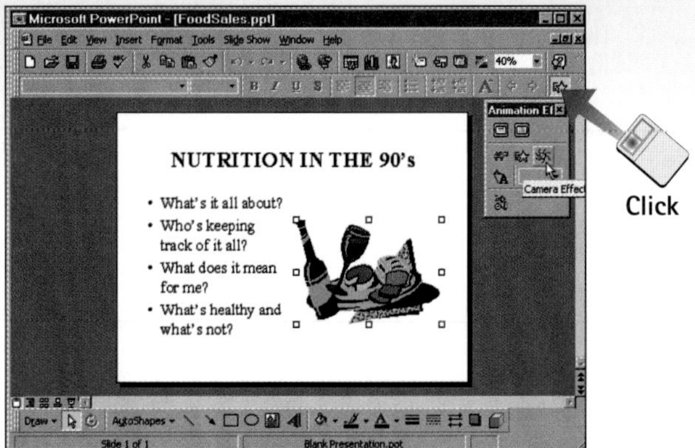

2 Open the Custom Animation

For more control over animation and build effects, open the Custom Animation dialog box. From the Animation Effects palette, click the **Custom Animation** button. (You can also open the dialog box by displaying the **Slide Show** menu and choosing **Custom Animation**.)

3 Assign a Build Effect

To assign a build effect to your slide text, click the **Timing** tab, select the slide object from the list box, and choose the **Animate** option. Now you can assign an effect, as described in the next step.

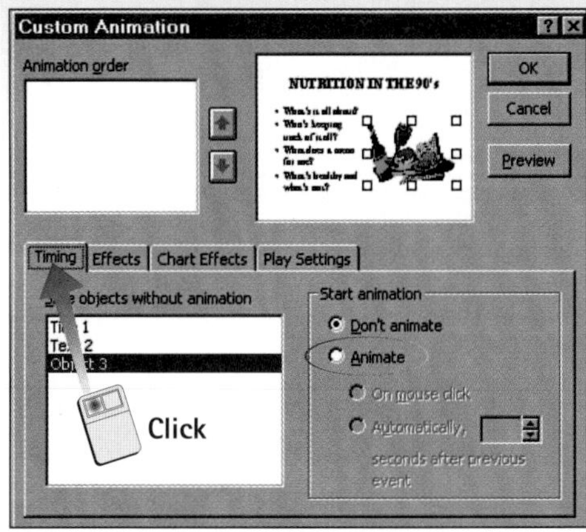

4 Assign an Animation Effect

Click the **Effects** tab to assign an animation effect. Use the first drop-down list to choose animation; use the second drop-down list to choose a sound effect (optional).

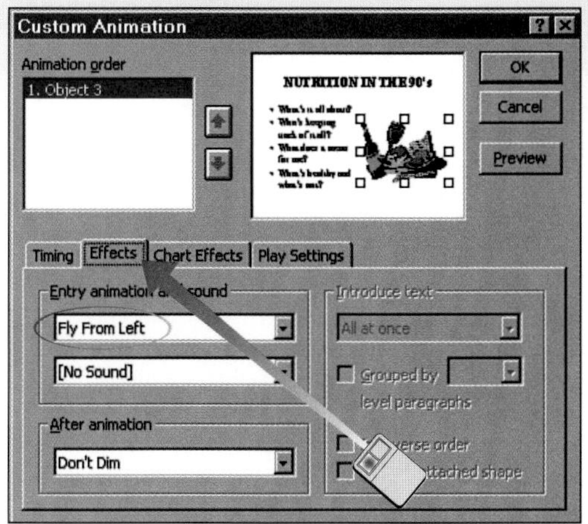

5 Preview the Effect

Click the **Preview** button to see a preview of the effects.

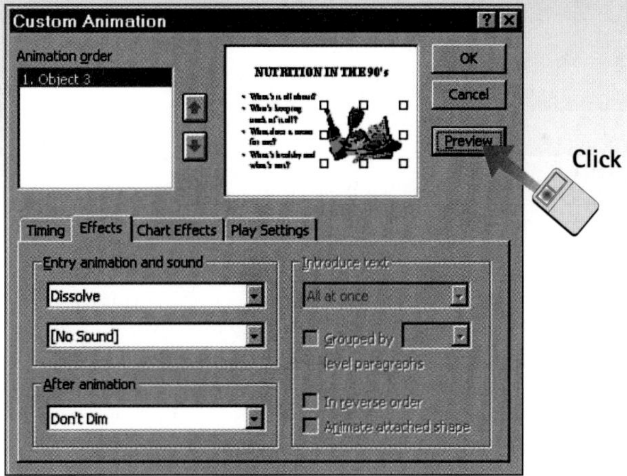

6 Exit the Dialog Box

Click **OK** to exit the dialog box and assign the animation or build effects you selected.

End

How-To Hints

Set Build Effects

When you assign an effect in the **Effects** tab for a build, the effect will occur for each item in your list. If you have a bulleted list, for example, each bulleted item will appear on the slide with the effect you select.

Set Advances

Use the **Timing** tab in the Custom Animation dialog box to set advance options. You can choose to advance each slide by mouse click, or you can have PowerPoint automatically advance each slide for you based on the timing you set. Click the **Automatically** option and specify the amount of seconds for the advance.

TASK 8

How to Run the Slide Show

After you complete your presentation, you're ready to run the show. It's a good idea to run the show several times while preparing your presentation so you have some idea of how the slides look, how long you want each slide displayed, and how transitions and animation effects are used.

You can set up a slide show to run manually, so that you click the mouse or press a keyboard key to advance each slide, or automatically, so that PowerPoint displays each slide for the amount of time you preset. You can even set the show to continuously loop.

Begin

1 Open the Set Up Show Dialog Box

Open the presentation you want to view, and then open the **Slide Show** menu and select **Set Up Show**. This displays the Set Up Show dialog box.

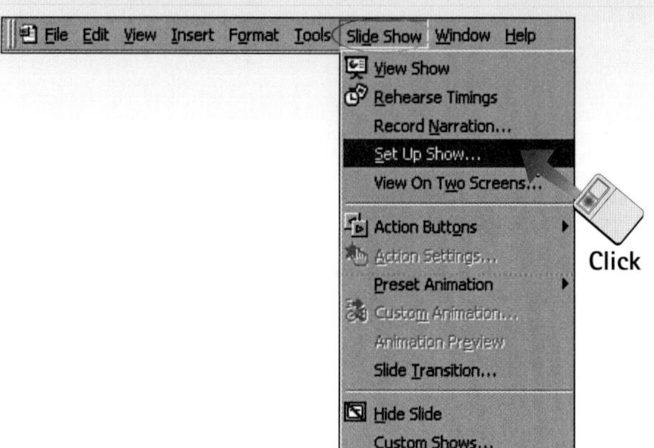

2 Choose Show Type Options

From the **Show type** options, select the option that best suits your situation.

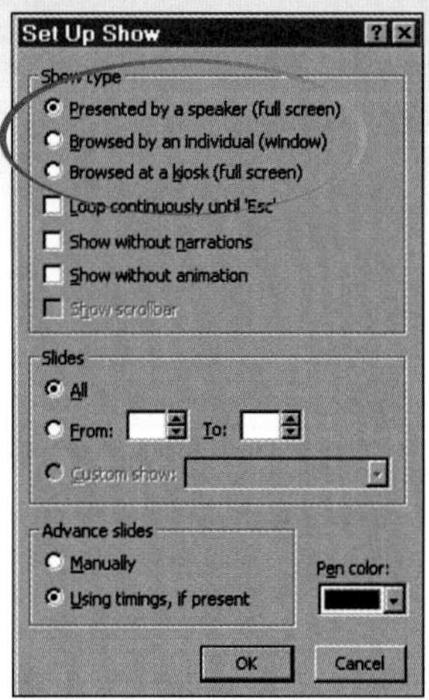

3 The Show Type Check Boxes

Use the **Show type** check boxes to indicate how the presentation should appear. You can choose to loop the show continuously, show without animation or narration, or display the scrollbar.

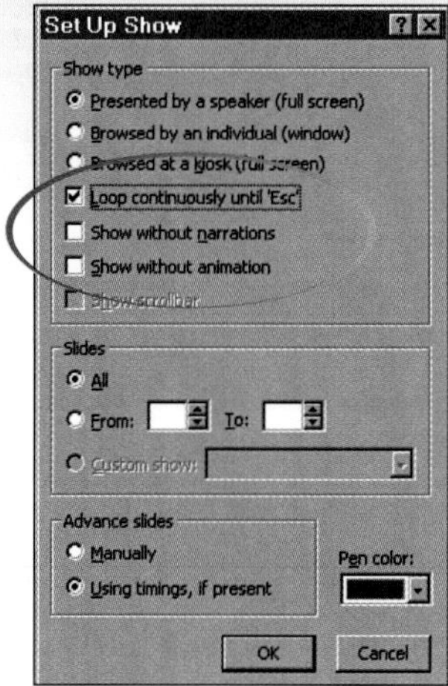

4 Choose Advance Options

From the **Advance slides** options, choose to advance your presentation manually or use preset timings. Click **OK** to exit the Set Up Show dialog box.

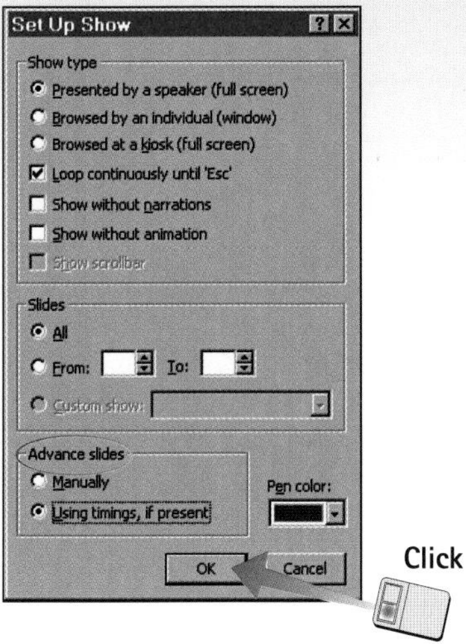

5 Run the Show

To start the slide show, display the first slide, and then click the **Slide Show View** button at the left of the horizontal scrollbar.

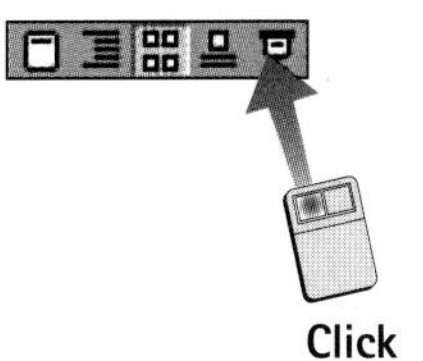

6 Stop the Show

PowerPoint starts your presentation. Each slide appears full screen, without toolbars or menu bars. To stop the show at any time, press Esc.

Special Events Team

- Planning Retreats and Conferences
- Organizing Luncheons and Fellowships
- Outings (Shopping excursions and special trips)
- Holiday Functions and Banquets

End

How-To Hints

Pack and Go

To take your show on the road, so to speak, you can package the presentation on disk to use at another computer. Open the **File** menu and select **Pack and Go**. Follow the Pack and Go Wizard steps to store the complete presentation, including a PowerPoint viewer, on disk. You can now view the presentation on another computer, even if it doesn't have PowerPoint installed.

Slide Show Controls

During the course of the slide show, you can use manual controls to advance slides, return to previous slides, or pause the show. Click the mouse or press the right arrow key on the keyboard to advance to the next slide. Press Backspace to return to the previous slide. Press the S key to pause or resume the show.

Rehearse Your Timings

You can automate your slide show to advance each slide based on slide timings you set. One way to set timings is with the Rehearse Timings feature. Open the **Slide Show** menu and select **Rehearse Timings**. You can then time each slide. At the end, PowerPoint tells you the total time for the presentation.

Task 9

How to Create Speaker Notes

To make your presentation professional, polished, and organized, you can make speaker notes to assist you with the slide show. Speaker notes can help you organize your thoughts, make sure you cover all the important points, and assure a cohesive presentation.

Speaker notes include a picture of the slide and an area for typing in your own notes. After you complete notes for the entire presentation, you can print them.

Begin

1 Switch to Notes Page View

Click the **Notes Page View** button to switch to Notes Page view and display the first slide in your presentation.

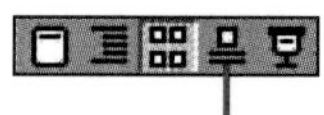

Notes Page View

2 Enter Note Text

Click inside the **Notes** text box in the lower half of the Notes Page and start typing your notes for that particular slide.

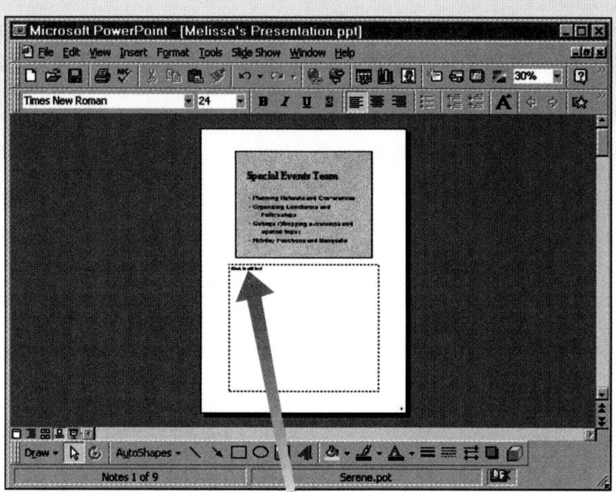

Click

3 Use the Zoom Tools

If you're having trouble seeing what you type, use the **Zoom** drop-down list on the Standard toolbar to zoom in closer—try 100%.

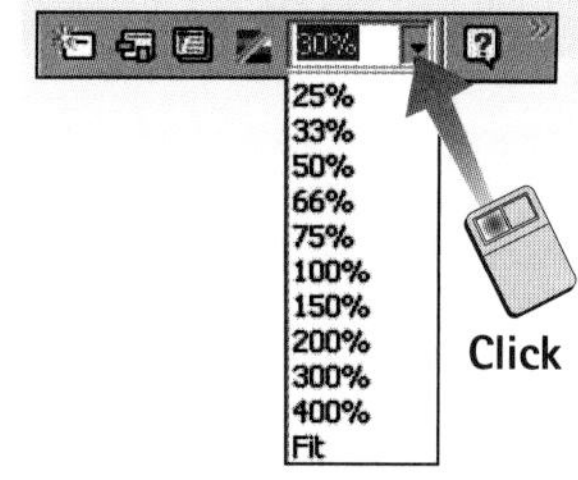

Click

4 Next Slide

When you finish your notes for the slide, click the **Next Slide** button to continue to the next slide in the presentation.

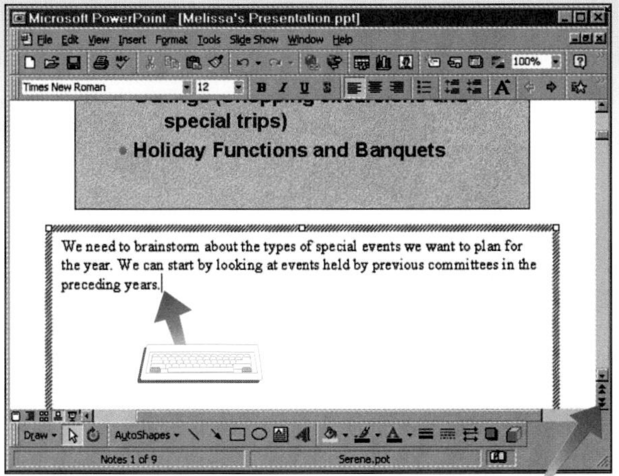

5 Prepare to Print

Continue entering notes for each slide in the presentation. When you're ready to print the notes, open the **File** menu and select **Print**.

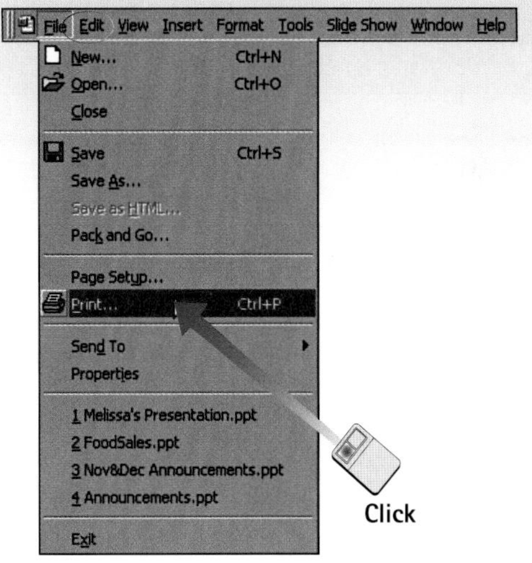

6 Select Notes Pages

In the Print dialog box, click the **Print what** drop-down list box and choose **Notes Pages**. Click **OK** to print.

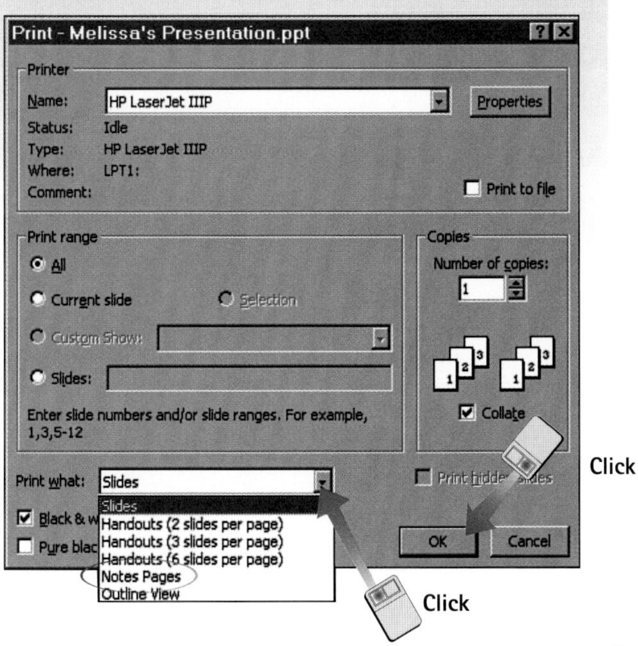

End

Task 10

How to Create Audience Handouts

To make your presentations more memorable, consider distributing handouts based on your slide show content to your audience. Handouts will help them recall the points you covered. PowerPoint makes it easy to create handouts; all you have to do is print them.

Begin

1 Open the Presentation

Start by opening the presentation for which you want to create handouts.

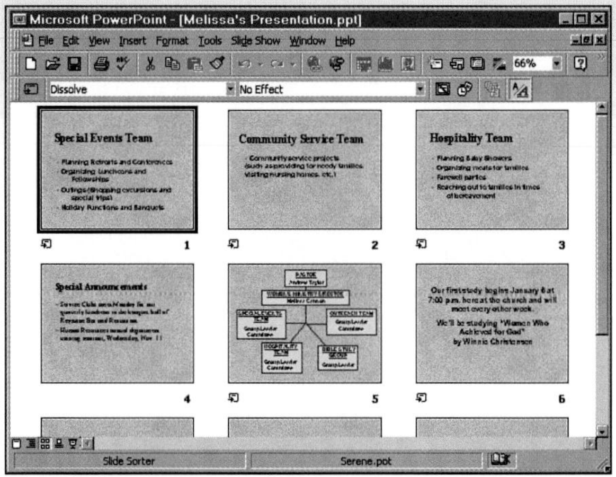

2 Open the Print Dialog Box

Display the **File** menu and select the **Print** command. This opens the Print dialog box.

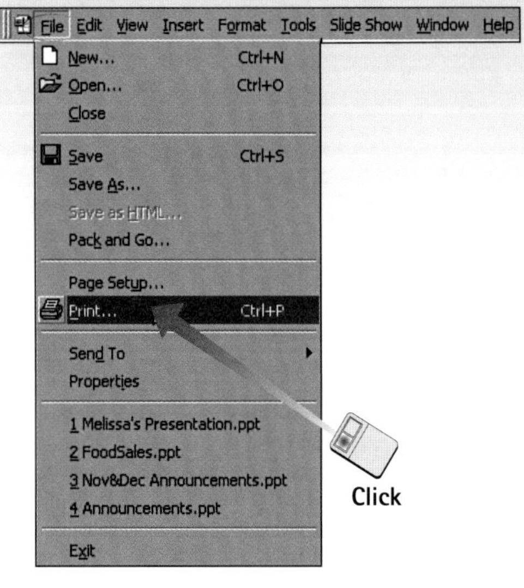

3 Set Up for Handouts

Click the **Print what** drop-down arrow to display a list of print options, and select **Handouts**. Notice the three layout styles: two, three, or six slides per page. Select the layout that best suits your presentation or paper needs.

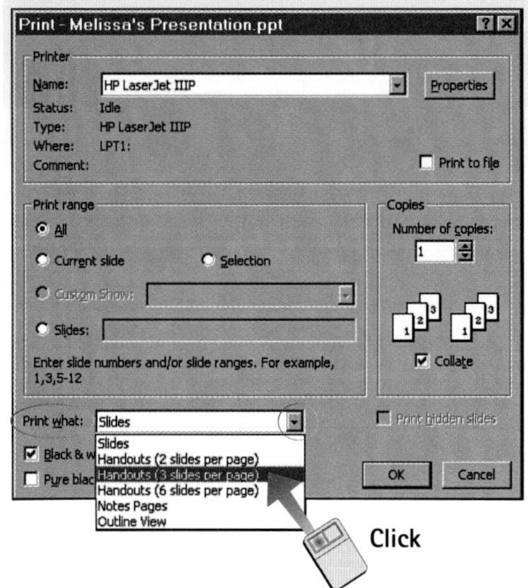

4 Change Other Print Options

Set any additional options in the Print dialog box before printing. Click the **Printer Name** drop-down box, for example, to choose which printer to use. Make sure the **Collate** check box is selected if you want to collate the pages.

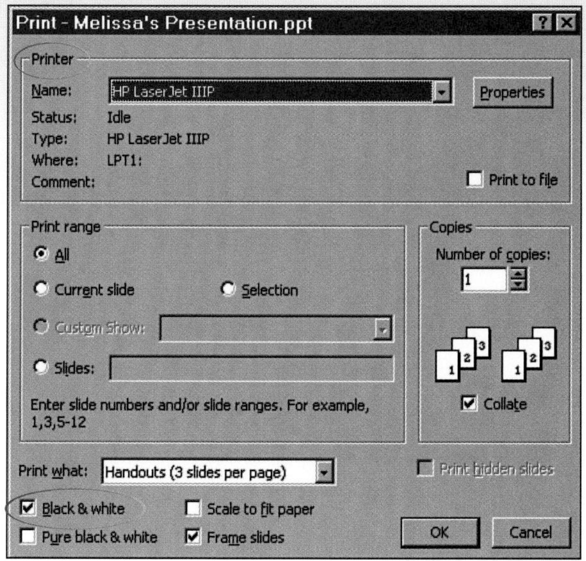

5 Print the Handouts

Click **OK** to print the handouts.

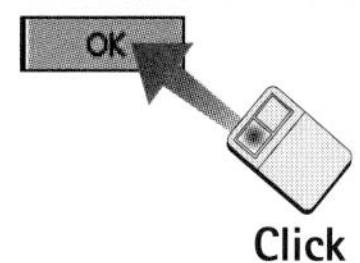

End

How-To Hints

Selective Printing

You can choose to print handouts for certain slides instead of every slide in the presentation. Under the **Print range** options in the Print dialog box, select the **Slides** option and enter the slide numbers you want to print, separated by commas, such as 2,3,5.

Task

CHAPTER 12

How to Use Access 97

Access is a computerized *database* program that enables you to store, manipulate, manage, and retrieve data. If you're new to the world of databases, this may sound a bit intimidating. However, you work with databases each day, so you probably know more about them than you think. Your local telephone directory, for example, is a database. Do you have a Rolodex file on your desk? That's a database, too. And so is the card catalog at your nearby library. In its strictest sense, a database is simply a collection of information.

An Access database can be used to store information, just as directories or Rolodex files do. In addition to storing the data, you can manipulate it in many ways. If you keep a database of your customers in Access, for example, you can sort them by zip code, print a list of all the customers who haven't ordered from you in the past six months, and create an order entry form your employees can use to process phone orders. That's only the tip of the iceberg—you can manage and manipulate your data for many purposes.

In this chapter, you will learn the basics for using Access 97. After you master these fundamental skills, you can tap into the power of Access to work with your own computerized databases.

TASK 1

How to Understand Database Basics

The basic components of a database are *tables*, *records*, *fields*, *forms*, *reports*, and *queries*. All these components make up an Access database file. Before you can begin building your own databases, you must first understand these basic elements and how they fit together.

Begin

1 Tables

The root of any database is tables. Access tables are a lot like Excel spreadsheets. Information is organized into columns and rows. You can have many tables in each database file. You might have one table listing customers and addresses, for example, and another table listing products you sell.

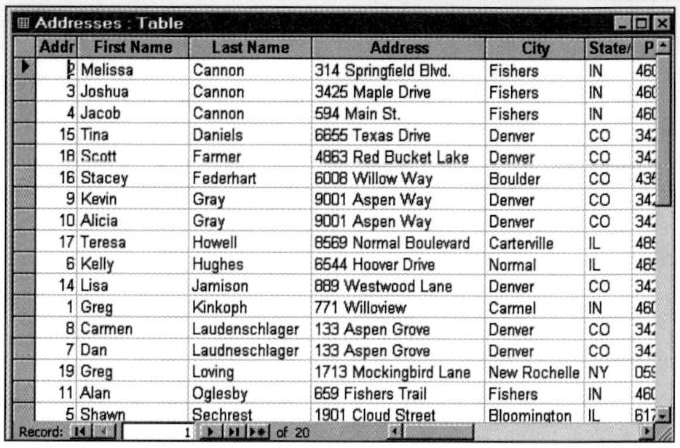

Addresses : Table

Addr	First Name	Last Name	Address	City	State/	P
2	Melissa	Cannon	314 Springfield Blvd.	Fishers	IN	46
3	Joshua	Cannon	3425 Maple Drive	Fishers	IN	46
4	Jacob	Cannon	594 Main St.	Fishers	IN	46
15	Tina	Daniels	6655 Texas Drive	Denver	CO	34
18	Scott	Farmer	4863 Red Bucket Lake	Denver	CO	34
16	Stacey	Federhart	6008 Willow Way	Boulder	CO	43
9	Kevin	Gray	9001 Aspen Way	Denver	CO	34
10	Alicia	Gray	9001 Aspen Way	Denver	CO	34
17	Teresa	Howell	8569 Normal Boulevard	Carterville	IL	48
6	Kelly	Hughes	6544 Hoover Drive	Normal	IL	46
14	Lisa	Jamison	889 Westwood Lane	Denver	CO	34
1	Greg	Kinkoph	771 Willoview	Carmel	IN	46
8	Carmen	Laudenschlager	133 Aspen Grove	Denver	CO	34
7	Dan	Laudneschlager	133 Aspen Grove	Denver	CO	34
19	Greg	Loving	1713 Mockingbird Lane	New Rochelle	NY	05
11	Alan	Oglesby	659 Fishers Trail	Fishers	IN	46
5	Shawn	Sechrest	1901 Cloud Street	Bloomington	IL	61

Record: 1 of 20

2 Records

Each entry in a database is called a record. Records appear as rows in a database table; each row represents one record.

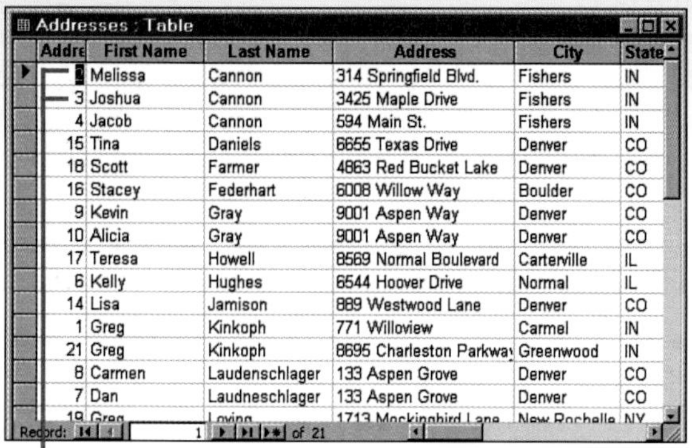

Addresses : Table

Addre	First Name	Last Name	Address	City	State
2	Melissa	Cannon	314 Springfield Blvd.	Fishers	IN
3	Joshua	Cannon	3425 Maple Drive	Fishers	IN
4	Jacob	Cannon	594 Main St.	Fishers	IN
15	Tina	Daniels	6655 Texas Drive	Denver	CO
18	Scott	Farmer	4863 Red Bucket Lake	Denver	CO
16	Stacey	Federhart	6008 Willow Way	Boulder	CO
9	Kevin	Gray	9001 Aspen Way	Denver	CO
10	Alicia	Gray	9001 Aspen Way	Denver	CO
17	Teresa	Howell	8569 Normal Boulevard	Carterville	IL
6	Kelly	Hughes	6544 Hoover Drive	Normal	IL
14	Lisa	Jamison	889 Westwood Lane	Denver	CO
1	Greg	Kinkoph	771 Willoview	Carmel	IN
21	Greg	Kinkoph	8695 Charleston Parkway	Greenwood	IN
8	Carmen	Laudenschlager	133 Aspen Grove	Denver	CO
7	Dan	Laudneschlager	133 Aspen Grove	Denver	CO
19	Greg	Loving	1713 Mockingbird Lane	New Rochelle	NY

Record: 1 of 21

Records

3 Fields

The detailed information that makes up a single record is broken into categories, called fields. When you're planning a database, think about what fields you need for each record. An address database, for example, needs fields for Name, Address, City, Zip code, and Phone number.

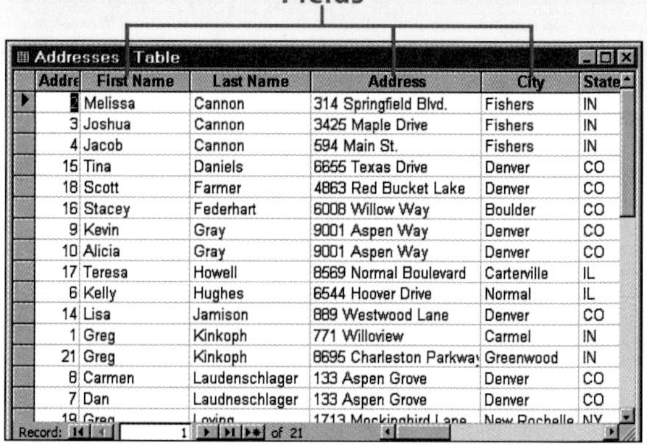

Fields

Addresses : Table

Addre	First Name	Last Name	Address	City	State
2	Melissa	Cannon	314 Springfield Blvd.	Fishers	IN
3	Joshua	Cannon	3425 Maple Drive	Fishers	IN
4	Jacob	Cannon	594 Main St.	Fishers	IN
15	Tina	Daniels	6655 Texas Drive	Denver	CO
18	Scott	Farmer	4863 Red Bucket Lake	Denver	CO
16	Stacey	Federhart	6008 Willow Way	Boulder	CO
9	Kevin	Gray	9001 Aspen Way	Denver	CO
10	Alicia	Gray	9001 Aspen Way	Denver	CO
17	Teresa	Howell	8569 Normal Boulevard	Carterville	IL
6	Kelly	Hughes	6544 Hoover Drive	Normal	IL
14	Lisa	Jamison	889 Westwood Lane	Denver	CO
1	Greg	Kinkoph	771 Willoview	Carmel	IN
21	Greg	Kinkoph	8695 Charleston Parkway	Greenwood	IN
8	Carmen	Laudenschlager	133 Aspen Grove	Denver	CO
7	Dan	Laudneschlager	133 Aspen Grove	Denver	CO
19	Greg	Loving	1713 Mockingbird Lane	New Rochelle	NY

Record: 1 of 21

4 Forms

Entering data into tables can be awkward as you try to keep track of which column represents which field. To make things easier, use a form. A form is an onscreen fill-in-the-blanks sheet for completing a record. The form is composed of each field needed to create a record. With forms, you enter data one record at a time.

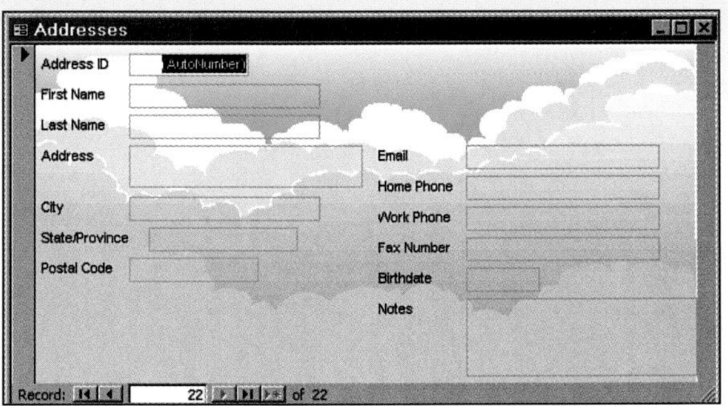

5 Reports

After you build a database, you will probably want to organize certain aspects of the information and create specialized reports. Reports summarize and organize the data; typically, they are printed out. You might generate a report, for example, listing your top 20 clients based on sales.

Addresses by Last Name

Addresses by Last Name

	Name	Address	City	State/Prov
C				
	Cannon, Jacob	594 Main St.	Fishers	IN
	Cannon, Joshua	3425 Maple Drive	Fishers	IN
	Cannon, Melissa	314 Springfield Blvd.	Fishers	IN
D				
	Daniels, Tina	6655 Texas Drive	Denver	CO
F				
	Farmer, Scott	4863 Red Bucket Lake	Denver	CO

Page: 1

6 Queries

Queries are a formal way of sorting and filtering your data to produce specific results. With queries, you can specify which fields you want to see, the order in which you want to view them, filter criteria for each field, and more.

Addresses Query : Select Query

Last Name	City	State/	Postal Code
Willard	Denver	CO	34439-
Laudneschlager	Denver	CO	34255-
Laudenschlager	Denver	CO	34255-
Gray	Denver	CO	34255-
Gray	Denver	CO	34255-
Jamison	Denver	CO	34255-
Daniels	Denver	CO	34255-
Federhart	Boulder	CO	43536-
Farmer	Denver	CO	34255-
Williams	Vandalia	IL	65456-
Howell	Carterville	IL	48593-
Willard	Kewanee	IL	64747-
Hughes	Normal	IL	46594-

Record: 1 of 21

End

How-To Hints

Planning Is Everything

Before you build a database, spend a few minutes planning it. What kind of data do you want to store, and how should it be organized? Each table should have a topic, such as Customer Transactions. Determine what actions you want to perform on the data to help you know what kind of forms to create. Think about what information you want to extract from the data to help you know what kind of reports to generate.

TASK 2

How to Use the Database Wizard

When you first open Access, you have the options of creating a blank database, using the Database Wizard, or opening an existing database. The easiest way to create a database is with the Database Wizard. The Database Wizard can help you create the tables, forms, and reports you will need. Choose the kind of database you want to build, and then follow each wizard step for completing the database structure.

To get started, click the **Database Wizard** option on the opening Access dialog box, and then click **OK** to begin. (If Access is already open, display the **File** menu and select **New**.)

Begin

1 Choose a Database

From the New dialog box, look through the wizards on the Databases tab to find the type of database you want to create, and then double-click the wizard name. To create an address book database, for example, double-click **Address Book**.

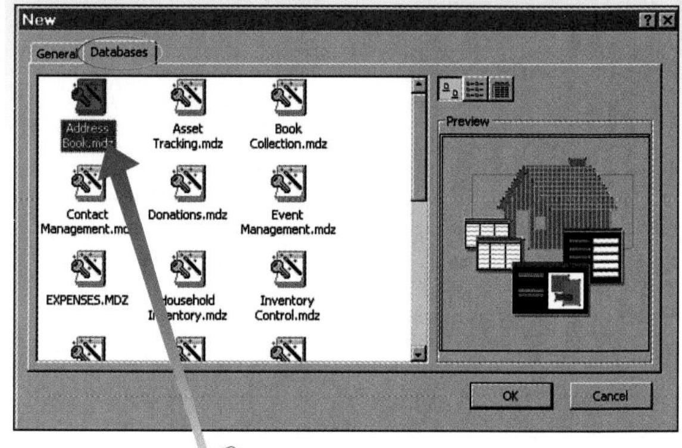

Double Click

2 Name the Database

First, name your new database file. Either accept the name supplied by Access or type your own in the **File name** text box. Make it something that will be easily identifiable the next time you want to use the database. Click **Create** to continue.

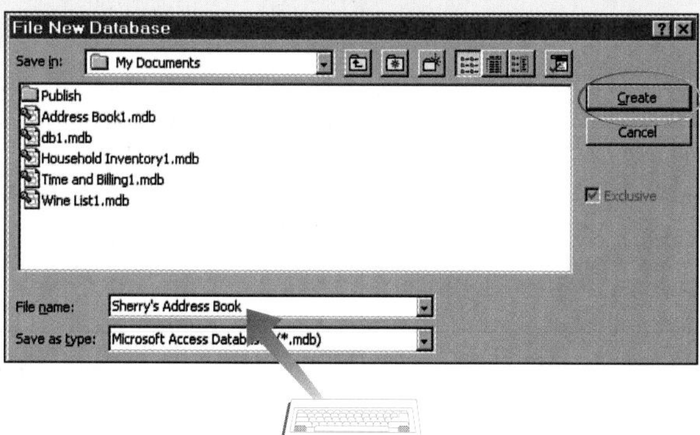

3 Determine the Structure

The next dialog box tells you that you are creating a database; click **Next**. The next box has options for the actual structure of your database, including the tables that will be created and the fields to be included. Choose the table from the left and select (or deselect) the fields to use in the right. Click **Next**.

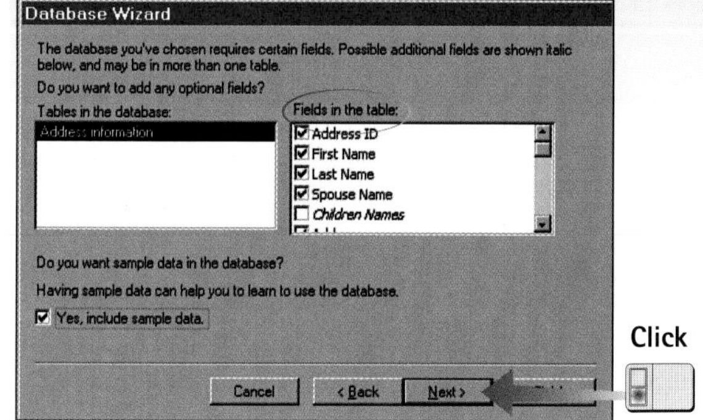

4 Choose a Screen Display

The next dialog box offers you several choices of backgrounds for screen displays and forms in the database. Click each name in the list to display the sample background. Choose a background and click **Next**.

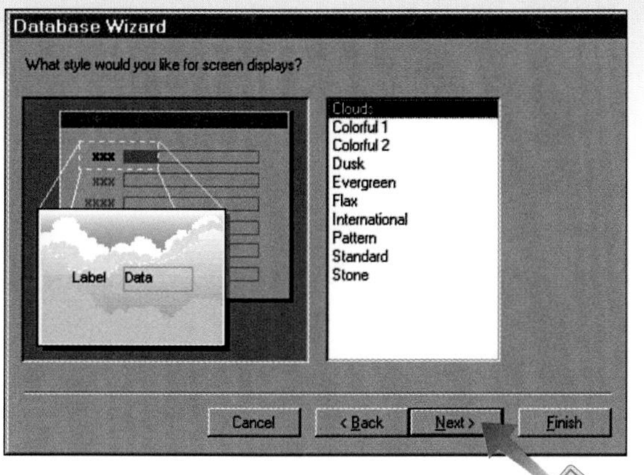

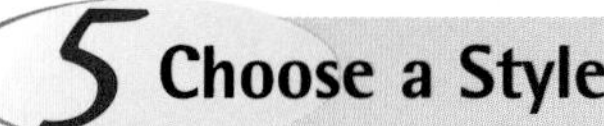

5 Choose a Style

From the next dialog box, choose the style for your printed reports, and then click **Next** to continue.

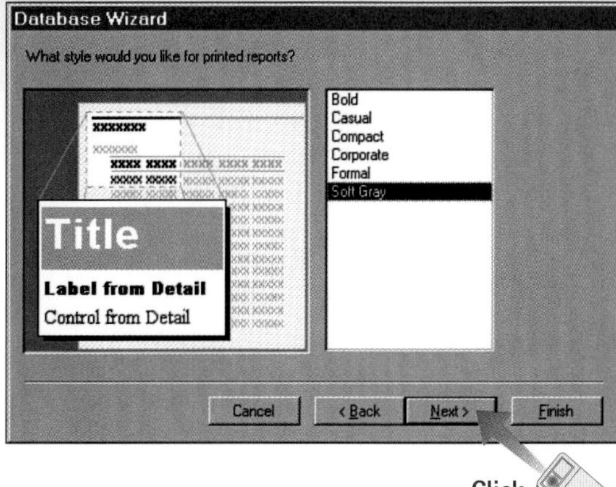

6 Choose a Title

Select a title for your database (it can be the same or different from the filename used in step 2). Indicate whether to include a picture on all reports. (If you choose to include a picture, you will have to locate the picture file you want to use by clicking the **Picture** button.) Click **Next**.

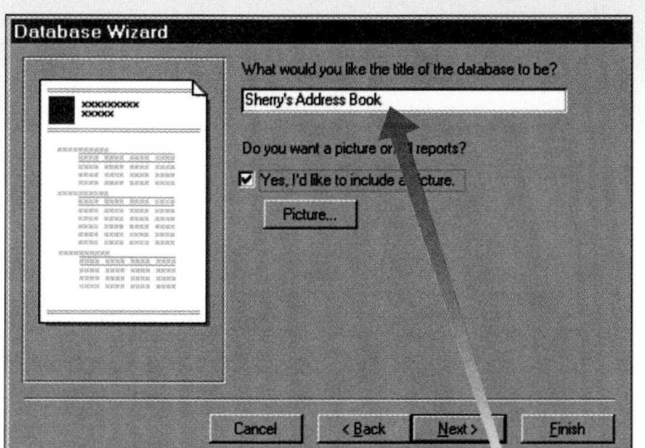

7 Last Dialog Box

In the final dialog box, you can choose to start the database immediately. Click **Finish** to create your new database.

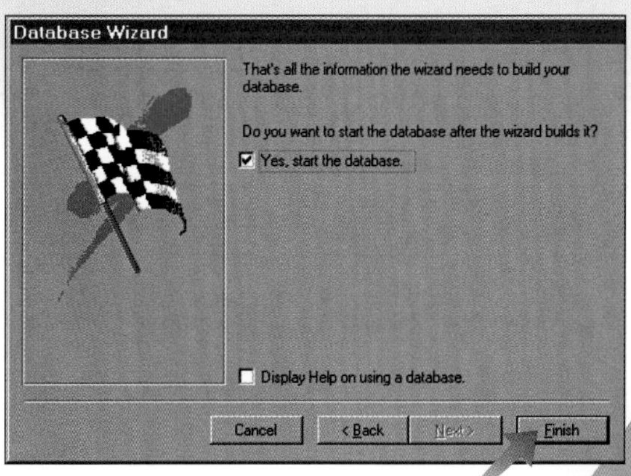

End

TASK 3

How to Use the Switchboard to Enter Data

When you construct a database using the Database Wizard, a Switchboard is created for you. The Switchboard is a handy menu system for entering, viewing, and modifying information in your database. If you create your own database, you can build a Switchboard of your own (see Task 10).

The Switchboard appears automatically after you create a database, and you can begin entering data. (If your database isn't open, click the **Open Database** button on the Database toolbar, then double-click the filename you assigned. From the **Forms** tab of the database dialog box, double-click **Switchboard**.)

Begin

1 Open the Form

Click the top option on the Main Switchboard to open the database form. If you created an Address Book database, for example, click **Enter/View Addresses**.

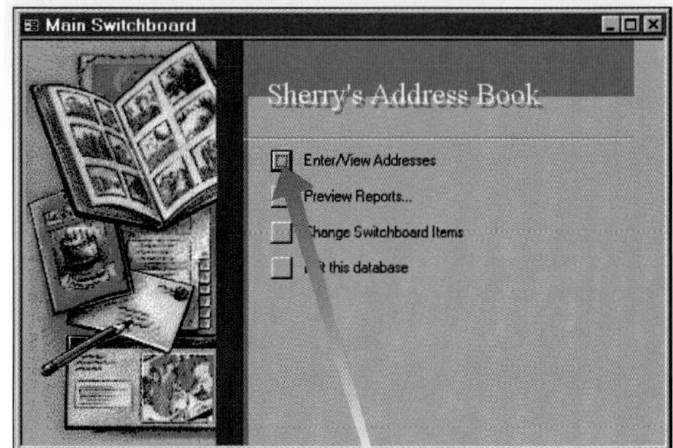

2 Fill Out the Form

A form opens for you to begin filling out. Depending on the type of database you're creating, your fields will vary. To enter data into a field, click inside the field and start typing. If you make a mistake, use the Backspace key to redo your typing. Press Tab to move from field to field.

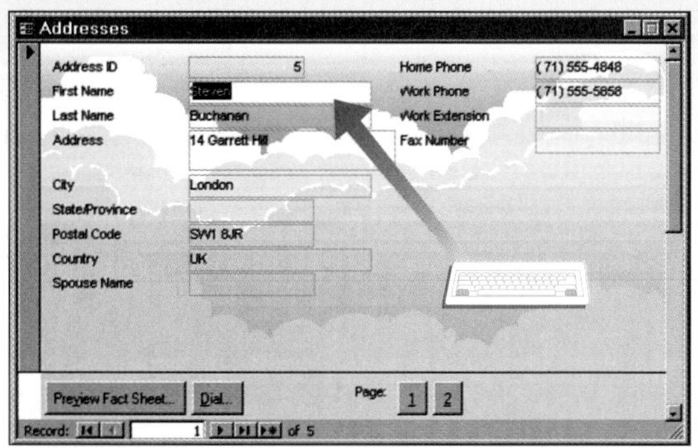

3 Use Drop-down Arrows

Depending on your database, some fields on your form may include a drop-down arrow to select a category. Click the arrow to display the drop-down list and make a selection.

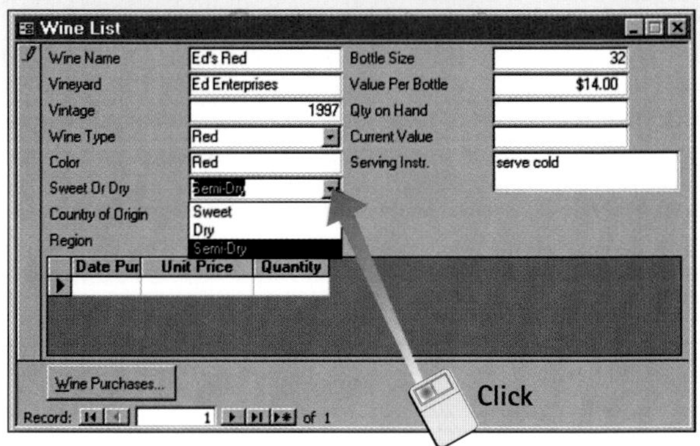

4 Page 2

Some forms include a second page of fields. Click the **Page 2** button at the bottom of the form to open page two, and then fill in the fields.

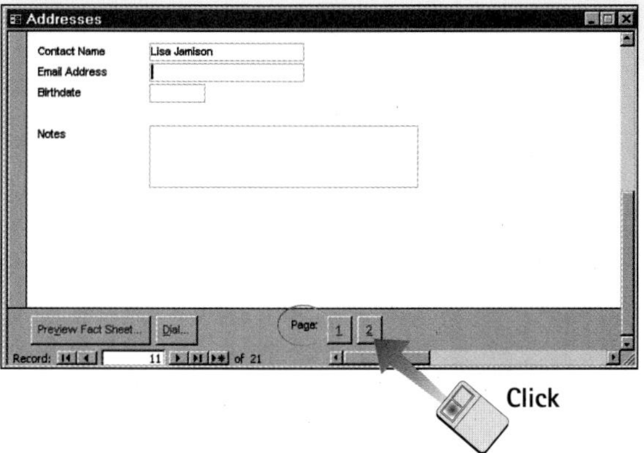

5 Enter a New Record

To enter another record, click the **New Record** button on the Database toolbar. Continue filling out the form for each new record you add.

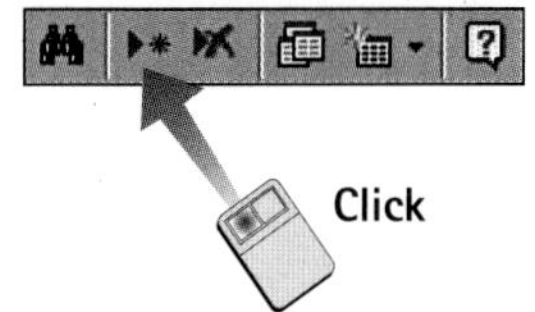

6 Close the Form

To close the form, click the **Close (X)** button in the upper-right corner of the form and return to the Main Switchboard.

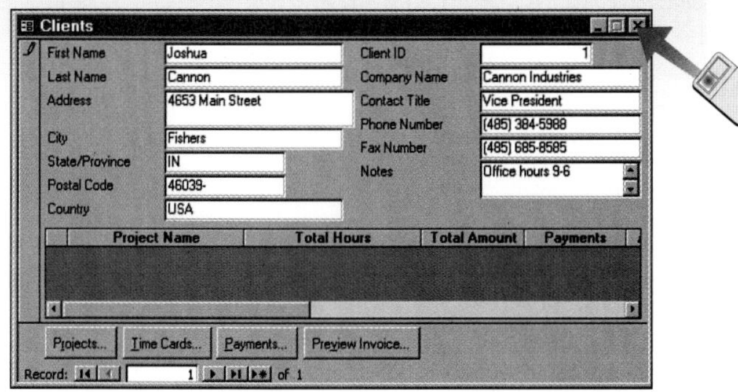

Click

End

How-To Hints

Empty Category List?

If you select a drop-down arrow on the form and the list is empty, you need to create categories. To do so, double-click the field to open the Categories form. Enter the necessary categories, and then click the **Close (X)** button to return to the form.

Navigate Forms

Use the **Record** arrow buttons at the bottom of the form to navigate back and forth to view your records. Click the **New Record** button (the right-pointing arrow with an asterisk) to start a new record.

Oops!

If you accidentally (or intentionally) close the Main Switchboard, you can reopen it by enlarging the database window (which is minimized upon opening a database containing a switchboard), clicking the **Forms** tab, and double-clicking **Switchboard**.

Task 4

How to Navigate the Access Window

Familiarize yourself with the elements of the Access program window before you start to use your database file. Most of the onscreen elements are the same as those in the other Office programs. You will also work with the Database window, the Switchboard window, and various other report and query windows.

After you create a new database with the Database Wizard, the Main Switchboard appears. The Switchboard is only one part of your database file. Your database includes tables, reports, and queries, too. Use the Database window to switch between the various elements of your database.

Begin

1 View the Access Window

The Access program window consists of a title bar, menu bar, Database toolbar, and status bar. Each of these elements works the same as they do in the other Office programs.

Title bar　Menu bar　Database toolbar

Microsoft Access

File Edit View Insert Format Records Tools Window Help

Addresses : Table

Addre	First Name	Last Name	Address	City	State/	F
2	Melissa	Cannon	314 Springfield Blvd.	Fishers	IN	46
3	Joshua	Cannon	3425 Maple Drive	Fishers	IN	46
4	Jacob	Cannon	594 Main St.	Fishers	IN	46
15	Tina	Daniels	6655 Texas Drive	Denver	CO	34
18	Scott	Farmer	4863 Red Bucket Lake	Denver	CO	34
16	Stacey	Federhart	6008 Willow Way	Boulder	CO	43
9	Kevin	Gray	9001 Aspen Way	Denver	CO	34
10	Alicia	Gray	9001 Aspen Way	Denver	CO	34
17	Teresa	Howell	8569 Normal Boulevard	Carterville	IL	48
6	Kelly	Hughes	6544 Hoover Drive	Normal	IL	46
14	Lisa	Jamison	889 Westwood Lane	Denver	CO	34
1	Greg	Kinkoph	771 Willoview	Carmel	IN	46
21	Greg	Kinkoph	8695 Charleston Parkway	Greenwood	IN	46
8	Carmen	Laudenschlager	133 Aspen Grove	Denver	CO	34
7	Dan	Laudneschlager	133 Aspen Grove	Denver	CO	34
19	Greg	Loving	1713 Mockingbird Lane	New Rochelle	NY	05
11	Alan	Oglesby	659 Fishers Trail	Fishers	IN	46

Record: 1 of 21

Datasheet View　NUM

Status bar

2 Use the Switchboard Window

When you create a database using the Database Wizard (see Task 2), the Main Switchboard window opens and the Database window is minimized onscreen. You can use the Switchboard to begin entering data into your database (see Task 3). To close the Switchboard window at any time, click its **Close** (**X**) button.

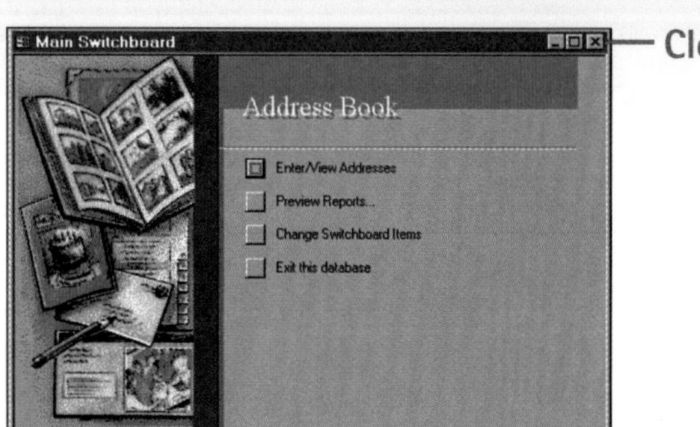

3 Resize the Database Window

As you're using different parts of your database, the Database window is often minimized onscreen. To restore the window to its default size, click the **Restore** button. To maximize the window, click its **Maximize** button. (To minimize the window again, click its **Minimize** button.) To close the database file completely, click the **Close** button.

Minimized Database window

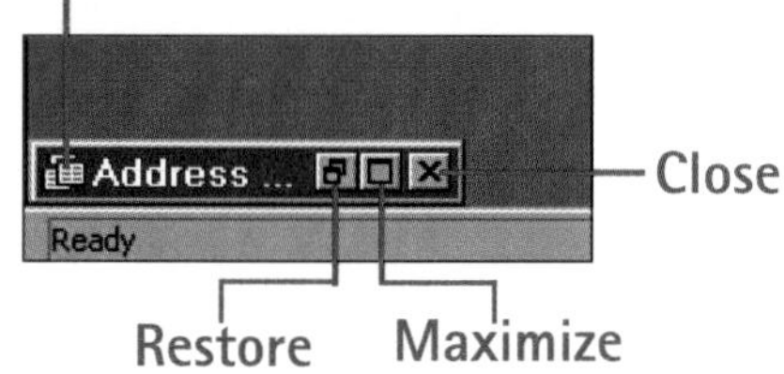

4 Use the Database Window

When the Database window is maximized or shown at its default size, you will notice it has several tabs that organize the elements of your database file. Click the tab to see its contents. To open any item in the Database window, double-click the item's name.

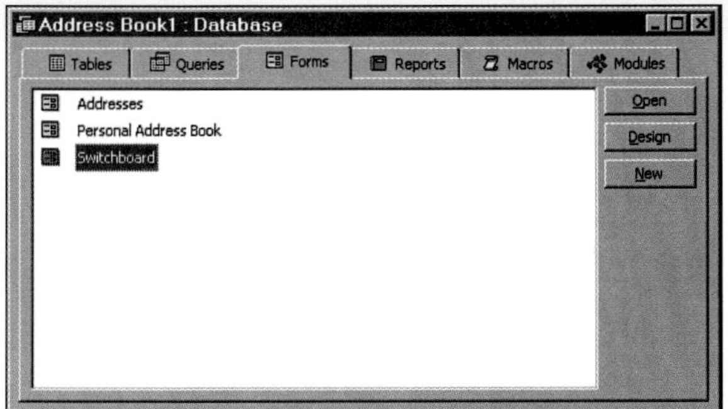

5 The Database Buttons

The Database window has three buttons. Click the **Open** button to open the selected item (or double-click the item's name). Click the **Design** button to open the selected item in Design view. Click the **New** button to start a new item in your database.

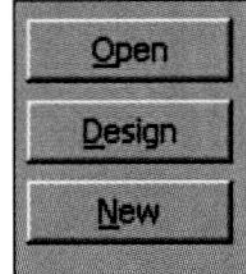

End

How-To Hints

Build Databases

When you first start Access, an opening dialog box appears with options for creating a blank database, using the Database Wizard to build a database, or opening an existing database you have already created and saved. If you're starting a new database, it's easiest to use the Database Wizard, as explained in Task 2.

Ever-changing Toolbar Buttons

As you use different features in Access, the toolbar buttons change to reflect the task you're trying to accomplish. In addition, with some tasks—such as changing items in Form view—a second toolbar is displayed. To learn about any toolbar button, hover your mouse pointer over the button to display the *ScreenTip* name.

TASK 5

How to Create a New Table Using the Table Wizard

After you have designed and refined your database, you can save time and energy by taking advantage of the Table Wizard. You can use the Table Wizard on an existing database or a new database.

The Table Wizard can help you create and format a table so it has all the correct fields. You can choose fields from a variety of sample tables to construct a table that's right for you. Even if you can't find the exact field you need, you can always go back and add it later.

Begin

1 Start a New Table

To create a new table in your database, open the **Insert** menu and select **Table**, or in the Database window, select the **Tables** tab and click **New**. The New Table dialog box opens.

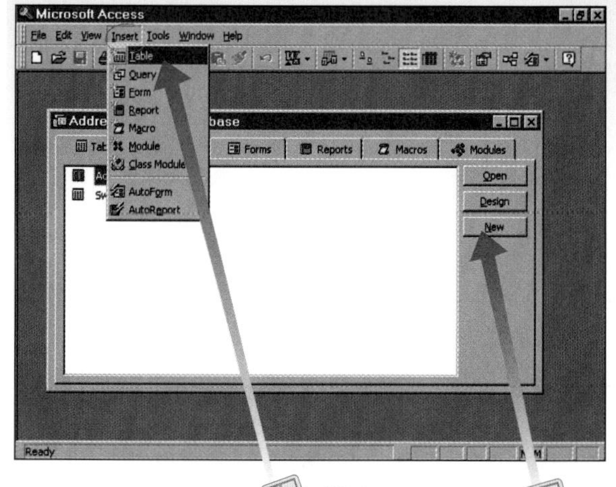

2 Choose Table Wizard

Select **Table Wizard** and click **OK** to open the Table Wizard.

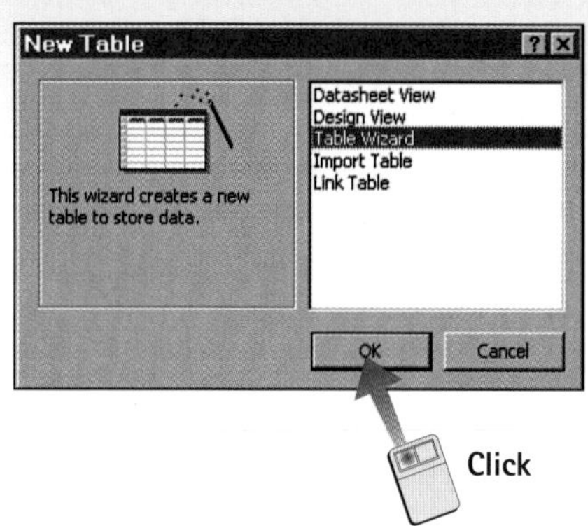

3 Choose a Table List

You can view two separate table lists, **Business** or **Personal**. Choose the appropriate option for the table you want to create.

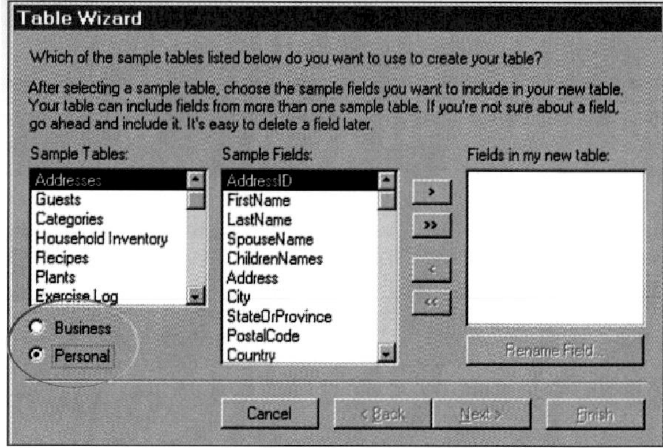

4 Choose Fields

You can build your table using fields from different sample tables; just mix and match what you need from the samples. Select a table and the **Sample Fields** list box displays the available fields. To add a field, select the field and click the > button. When you have finished, click **Next** to continue.

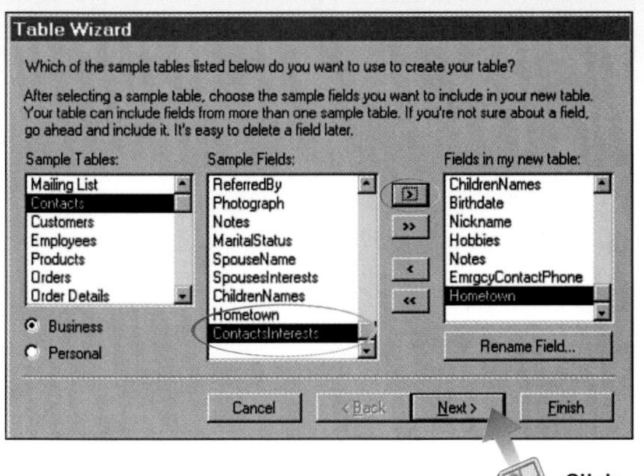

5 Assign a Name

In the next dialog box, enter a descriptive name for the table and let the wizard determine the primary key. Click **Next** to continue.

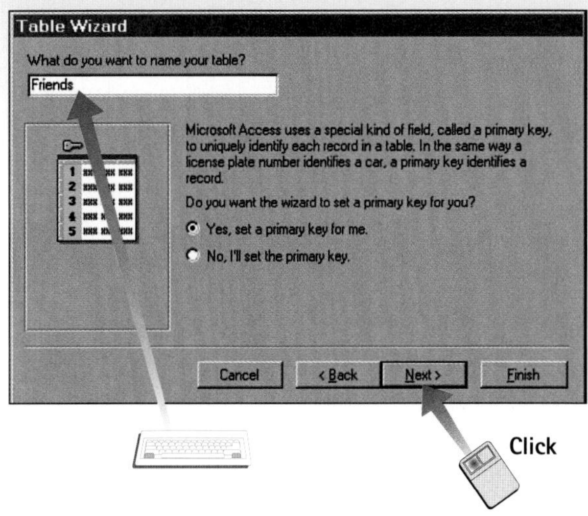

6 Create the Table

If your database already has at least one table, the next dialog box that appears asks about the relationship between tables. Click **Next**, for now, to open the final dialog box. Indicate whether you want to change the table design, enter data directly, or have the wizard create a data entry form for you. Click **Finish**.

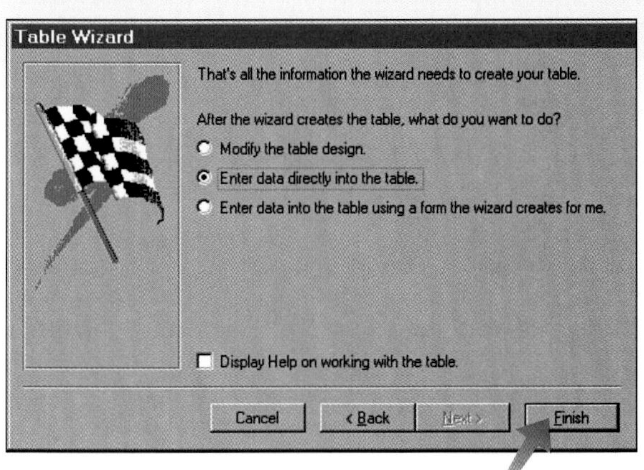

How-To Hints

Rename Your Fields

You can select fields that are similar to ones you need and then rename them using the **Rename Field** button in the Table Wizard.

Enter Table Data

After you create a table, you can start entering data into it at any time. Open the table, click in the first empty cell in the first empty column, and type the data for that field. Be sure to use the correct data type. If it's a text field, use text; but if it's a number field, use numbers. Press Tab to move to the next field, and continue filling out a complete record for the table. When you get to the last field, press Enter to start a new record.

End

TASK 6

How to Add, Delete, and Change Table Fields

Access databases are flexible in their design. You may find that you have a field that is almost always blank, for example, indicating that it is unnecessary and should be removed. Or you may want to enter information for a field that you forgot to create. In either case, you can open the appropriate table and make the necessary change.

Access makes it easy to change the various elements in your tables. You can change the look and design of any table, form, report, or query in Design view.

Begin

1 Open the Table

With your database open, click the **Tables** tab on the Database window and select the table you want to change. Click the **Design** button to open the table in Design view.

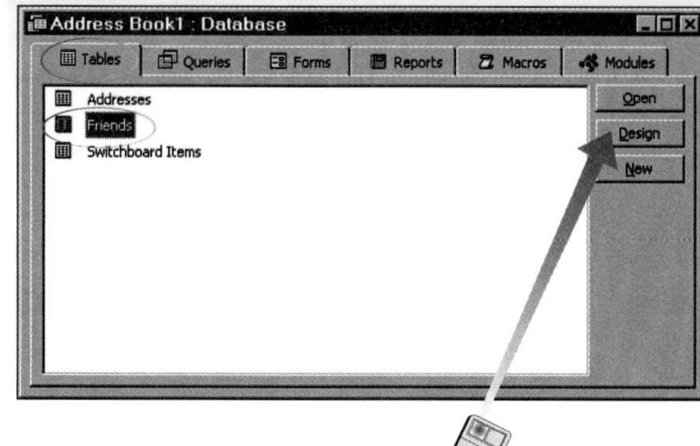

2 Add a Field

Click inside the first blank line of the **Field Name** column and enter the new field name.

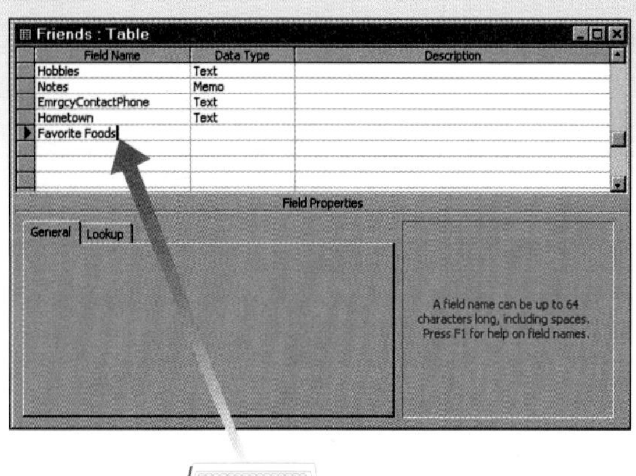

3 Select the Field Type

Tab to the **Data Type** column, click the down arrow to view the list of Data Type choices, and select a type. If the field will contain text entries, for example, select **Text**; if it requires number entries, select **Numbers**. (Note that the **Field Properties** sheet appears at the bottom of the window based on the data type.)

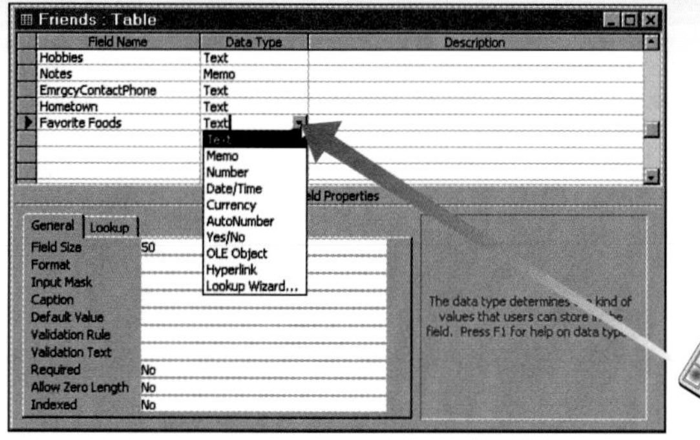

4 Remove a Field

To remove a field, click the row selector to the left of the field name to highlight the entire row.

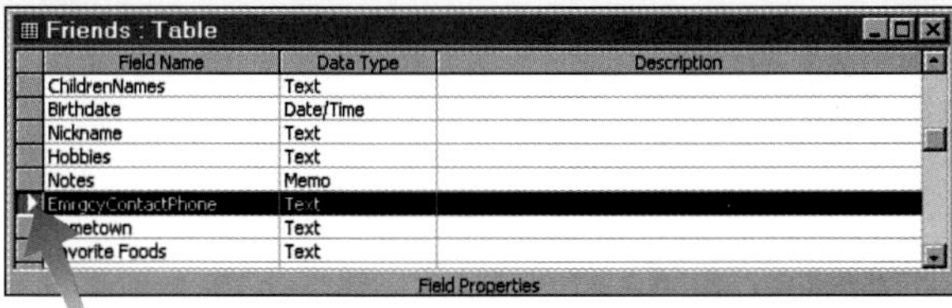

5 Use the Delete Rows Button

Click the **Delete Rows** button on the Database toolbar to remove the highlighted row. Click **Yes** when asked if you want to permanently delete the selected field.

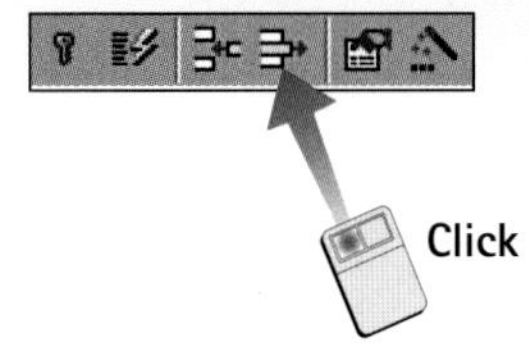

6 Close the Table

Click the **Close** button to close the table and return to the Database window. Click **Yes** in the dialog box that appears, asking if you want to save your changes.

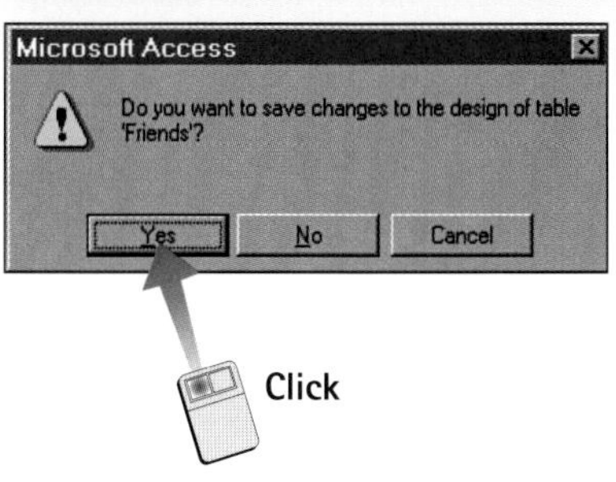

Click

End

How-To Hints

Use Field Properties

Use the Field Properties sheet in the Table Design view to change things such as the default size of the field, whether the field can be left blank when entering data, how many decimal places you want (number fields only), and more. To change a property, click its line and make the necessary changes.

Quick Delete

You can also delete rows by highlighting them, right-clicking, and selecting **Delete Rows** from the shortcut menu that appears.

TASK 7

How to Create a New Form with the Form Wizard

To make data entry easy, use a form. You can use three types of forms: data entry forms, switchboard forms, and dialog box forms. Data entry forms are self-explanatory. Switchboard forms enable you to create a switchboard menu system that makes using your database more intuitive. Dialog box forms enable you to provide a vehicle for user input and a follow-up action based on the input.

This task will focus on the data entry form, which can be produced using the Form Wizard. To begin, open the database you want to use.

Begin

1 Open the New Form Dialog Box

From the Database window, click the **Forms** tab. Click the **New** button to open the New Form dialog box.

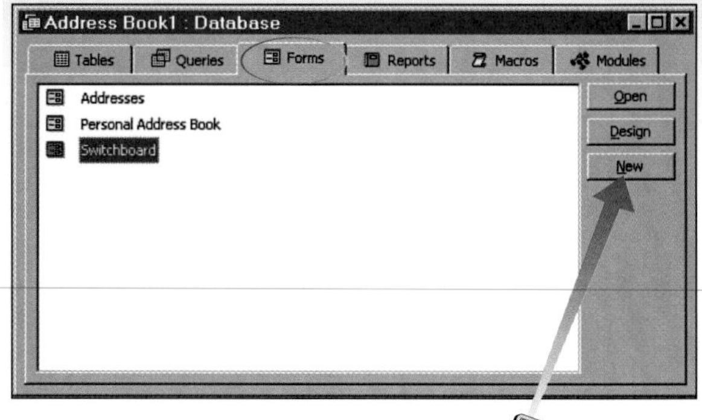

Click

2 Start the Form Wizard

From the New Form dialog box, select **Form Wizard** from the list of form options and click **OK** to start the wizard.

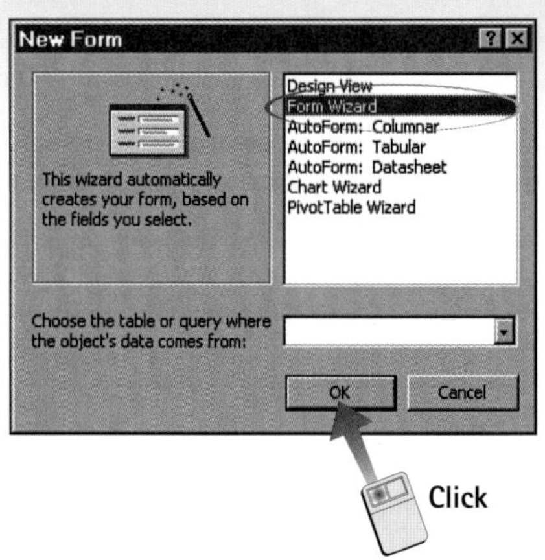

3 Choose a Table

From the **Tables/Queries** drop-down list, select the table that contains the fields you want to include on the form. Then select a field and click the > button to add the field to the new form. (To add all the fields at once, click the >> button.) When you're finished adding fields, click **Next**.

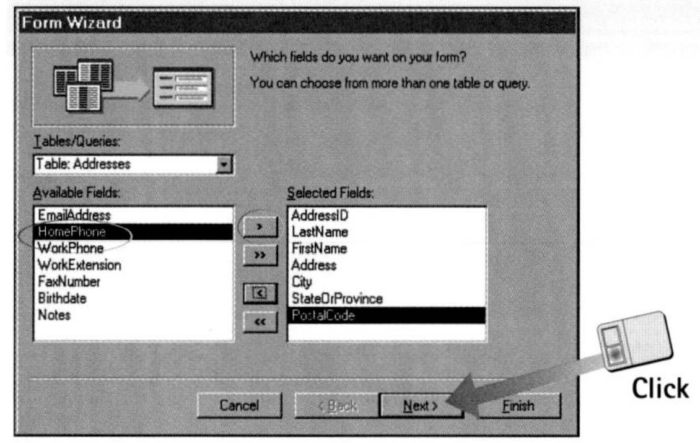

4 Choose a Layout

The next wizard dialog box asks you to choose a layout for the form. Click each option to see an example of the layouts. When you find the one you want, click **Next** to continue.

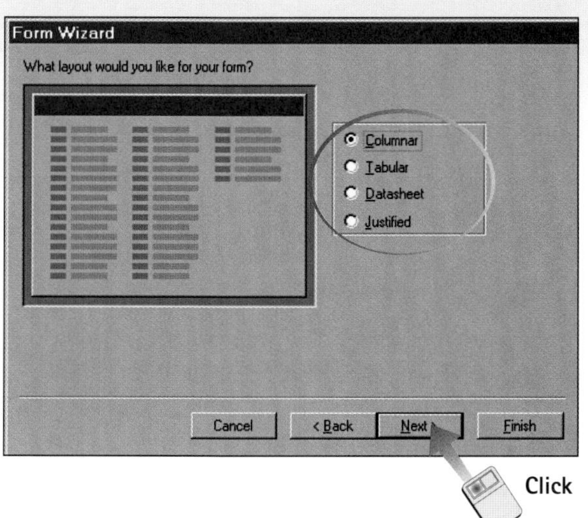

5 Select a Style

Choose a style to use for the form. As you click each style, its sample appears to the left. Select the one you want and click **Next** to continue.

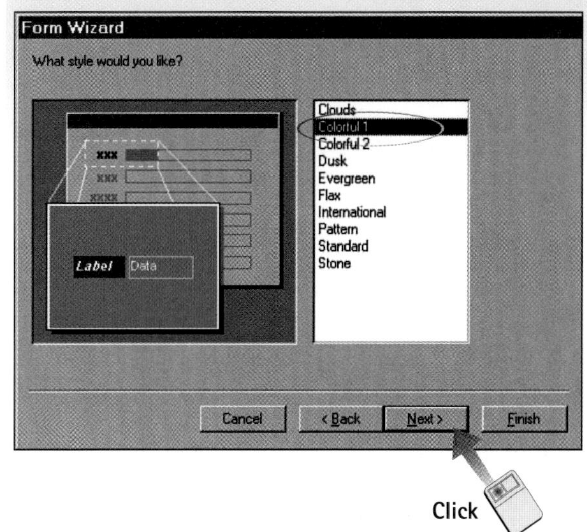

6 Name the Form

The final Form Wizard dialog opens and asks for a title for the form. Enter a descriptive name in the text box and click **Finish**.

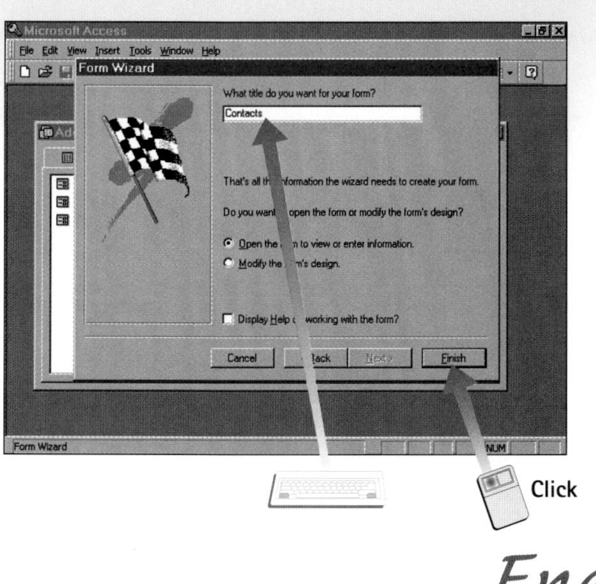

End

How-To Hints

Mix and Match Fields

If you have more than one table in your database, you can select fields from different tables to appear in a single form. In step 3, change the table that appears in the **Tables/Queries** drop-down list and add fields as needed.

Or Use AutoForm

If you want a generic form based on the fields in your table, use AutoForm. From the New Form dialog box, select **AutoForm: Columnar** to create a single column of fields in a form, select **AutoForm: Tabular** to create a form that looks like a table, or select **AutoForm: Datasheet** to make a form that looks like a datasheet. At the bottom of the New Form dialog box, use the drop-down arrow to select the table you want to associate with the form, and then click **OK**; a simple form is made.

TASK 8

How to Modify a Form in Design View

The Form Wizard is great for producing a quick form (refer to Task 7). However, you will frequently find that after you have your form, you want to change the layout or the fields. You can easily customize the form by using Design view.

After you open a form in Design view, you can move the form elements around, add new titles, or change the field size. Design view is rather like an electronic paste-up board that enables you to move items around until they're exactly where you want them.

Begin

1 Open the Form

Open the database you want to use if it's not already open. On the **Forms** tab of the Database window, select the form you want to modify and click **Design**. This opens the form in Design view along with the floating Form Design toolbox.

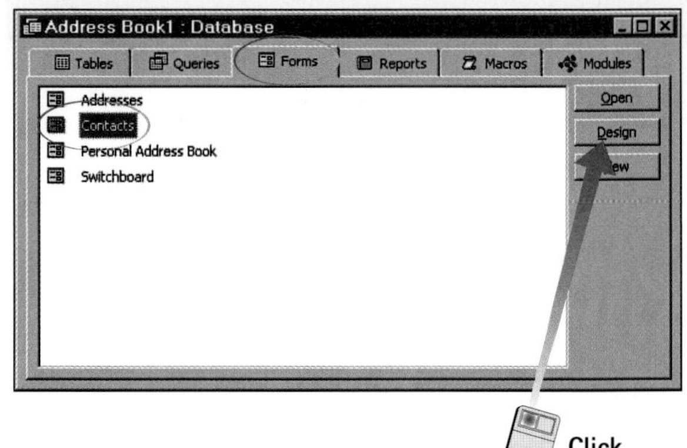

2 Use Form Design

In Design view, you can place various elements into the form and move them about. The form is divided into Form Header (holds title information), Detail (holds the form fields), and Form Footer (holds information placed at the bottom of each record). The Detail area is displayed by default.

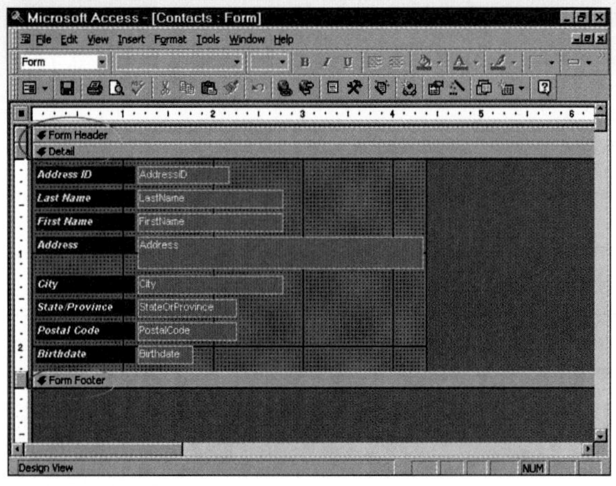

3 Delete a Field

To remove a field and its label, click the field and press Delete. Depending on the background design, it's not always easy to tell what's a field and what's a label. In most instances, fields appear larger than text labels; when you click a field, its label is also selected.

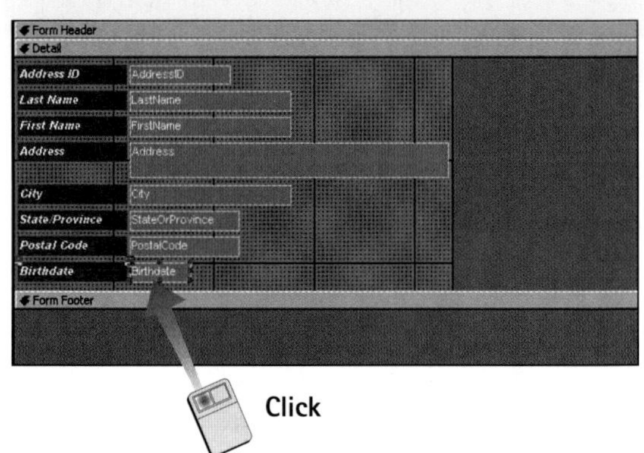

4 Add a Field

To add a field, first display the Field List; open the **View** menu and select **Field List**. Drag a field from the **Field List** box onto the **Detail** area where you want the new field. Release the mouse button and the field and its text label are added. Repeat this step to add as many fields as you like.

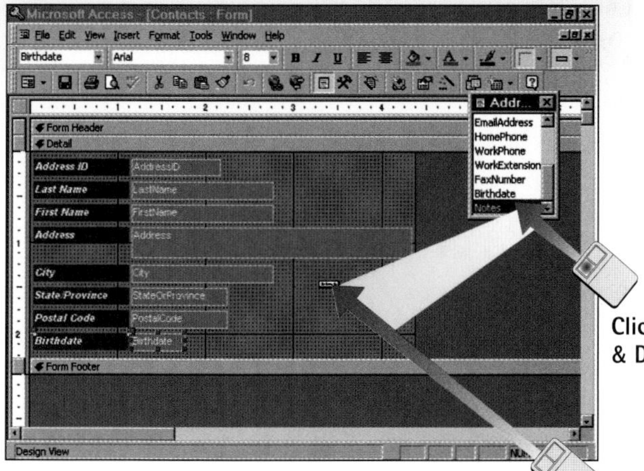

5 Move a Field

To move a field, click a field to select it; selection handles surround it. Position the mouse pointer over the field until it takes the shape of a hand icon. Hold down the left mouse button and drag the field to a new position. To resize a field, drag any of the field's selection handles.

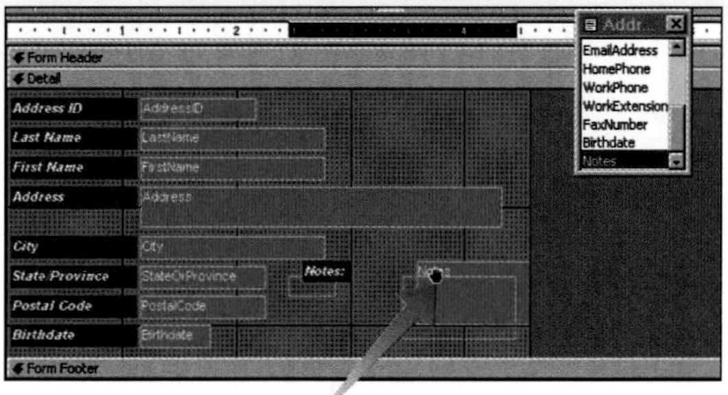

6 Add Text

You may want to add text to the form, such as subtitles or directions. Click the **Label** tool in the toolbox, click the form, and start typing the label text. Press Enter when you're finished. If you need to reposition the text, select it and drag it to a new location.

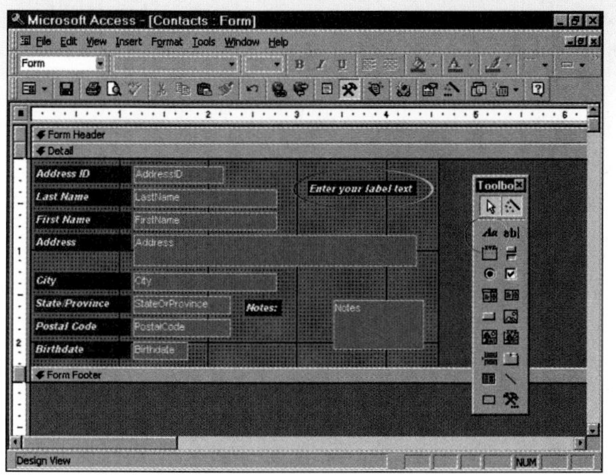

End

How-To Hints

No Toolbox?

If the floating toolbox isn't displayed, click the **Toolbox** button on the Form Design toolbar.

Save Your Changes

After moving around the form elements and adding or deleting fields and labels, click the form's **Close** button or press Ctrl+F4. In the prompt box that appears, click **Yes** to save your changes.

View Headers and Footers

To work with the header or footer area of your form, open the **View** menu and select **Form Header/Footer**. You can add text to a header or footer area the same as you add text to a form.

TASK 9

How to Enter Data in the Database

You can enter data in your database several ways. Although you can enter data directly into a table, it's much easier to use a form. Forms are more attractive and simpler to use. Form view shows fields as boxes with labels. If you prefer the plainness of the table format with endless columns and rows, you can also use Datasheet view. This task will illustrate both methods.

Begin

1 Open the Form

From the Database window, select the **Forms** tab and double-click the form you want to use.

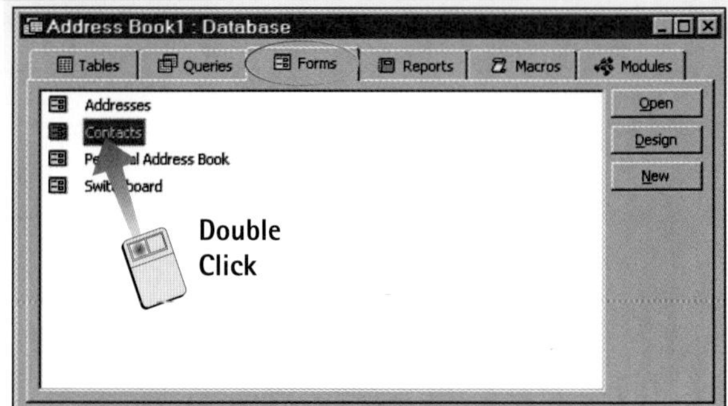

2 Enter the Data

By default, you start out in Form view. Begin filling out a record. Click inside a field and start entering text, or use the Tab key to move from field to field.

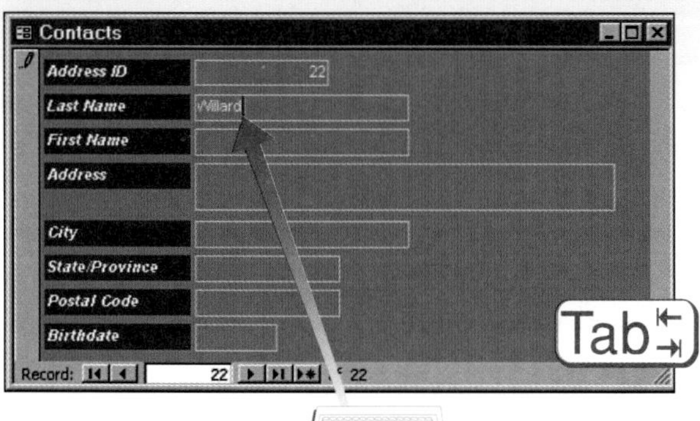

3 Start a New Record

After you complete a record, click the **New Record** button at the bottom of the form to open another record.

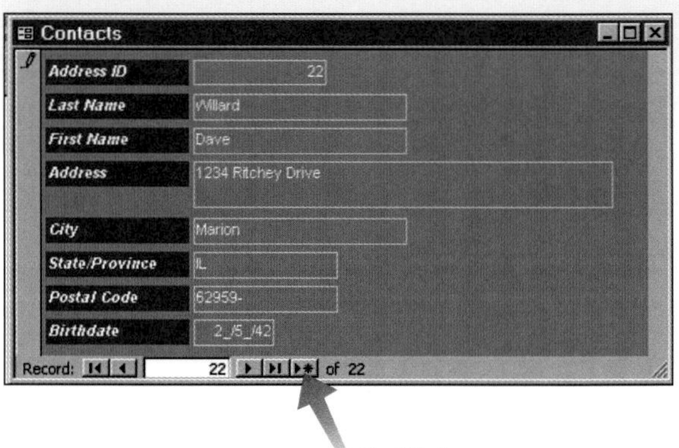

4 Switch to Datasheet View

To enter data using Datasheet view, open the **View** menu and select **Datasheet View**.

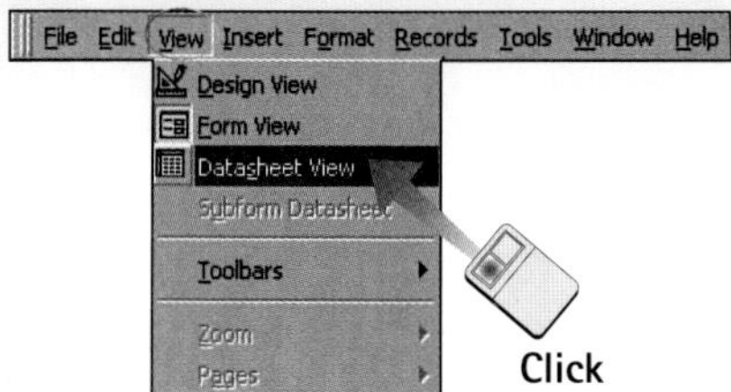

5 Enter the Data

Your form now appears as a table. Field names appear in the column headers, and each row represents a record. Click inside the first empty cell in the first column and enter data for that field. Press Tab to move from field to field. Press Enter to start a new record.

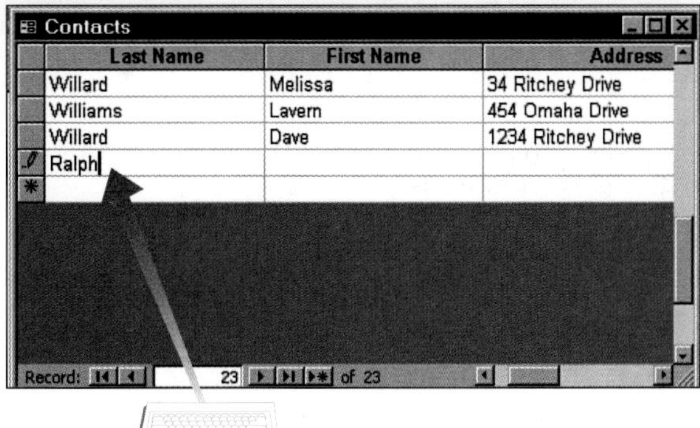

Last Name	First Name	Address
Willard	Melissa	34 Ritchey Drive
Williams	Lavern	454 Omaha Drive
Willard	Dave	1234 Ritchey Drive
Ralph		

6 Exit the Form

To exit the form in Form view or Datasheet view, click the window's **Close** button. (Don't confuse the form window's Close button with the program window's Close button or you will exit Access entirely.)

Contacts

City	State/Province	Postal Code	Birthdate
Kewanee	IL	64747-	
Vandalia	IL	65456-	
Marion	IL	62959-	2/5/4
Marion	IL	62955-	

Record: 23 of 23

Click

End

How-To Hints

Didn't I Enter Data Already?

If you created a database using the Database Wizard and opened the Switchboard form, as instructed in Tasks 2 and 3, you may have already begun the process of data entry. The Switchboard form is another way of entering data into your database.

Navigate Forms

Use the Record arrow buttons at the bottom of the form to navigate back and forth to view your records. Click the **New Record** button (the right-pointing arrow with an asterisk) to start a new record.

TASK 10

How to Create a Switchboard Form

If you choose to design a database from scratch, you may want to add a Switchboard menu to make it easier to use the database. Use the Switchboard Manager feature to whip one up. You can customize your Switchboard to include options for entering a blank form to start filling out, previewing reports, and exiting the database.

Start by opening the database for which you want to create a Switchboard, and then follow the instructions in this task. You can also follow these steps to edit your existing Switchboard.

Begin

1 Open Switchboard Manager

Open the **Tools** menu and select **Add-Ins**, **Switchboard Manager**. You will see a dialog box informing you that no switchboard exists for this database. Click **Yes** to indicate you wish to create one.

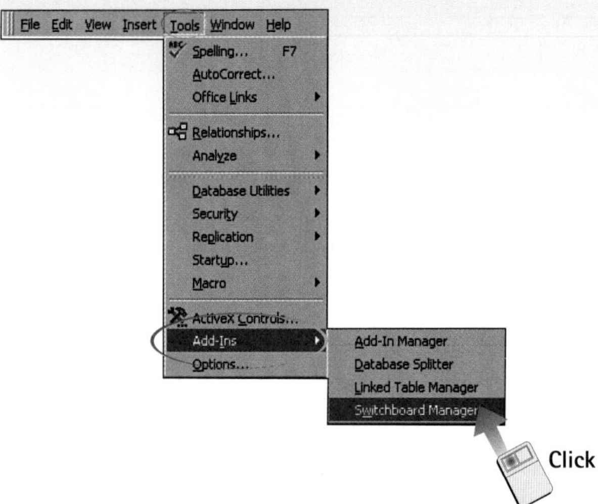

2 Open Edit Switchboard Dialog Box

The Switchboard Manager dialog box appears, with Main Switchboard (Default) listed. Click **Edit** to customize the Main Page. (If you're editing an existing Switchboard, select it from the list box, and then click **Edit**.)

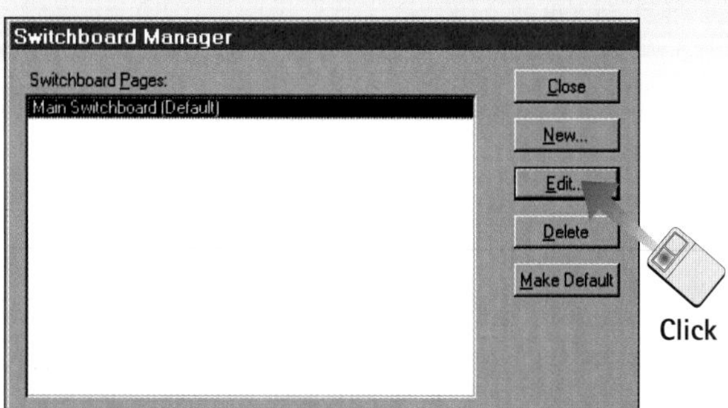

3 Add an Item

Click **New** in the Edit Switchboard Item dialog box to add your first item to the Main Switchboard. In the **Text** box, type **`Enter/View Name of Form`**, substituting the name of the form you want to use. From the **Command** drop-down list, select **Open Form in Add Mode**.

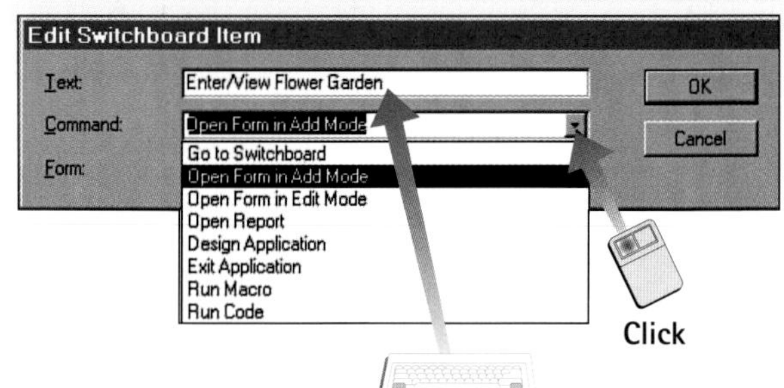

4 Choose a Form

From the **Form** drop-down list, choose the form you want to open. After this command is executed from the completed Switchboard, the form you specified will open, ready for you to enter data. Click **OK** to add the command to the Main Switchboard.

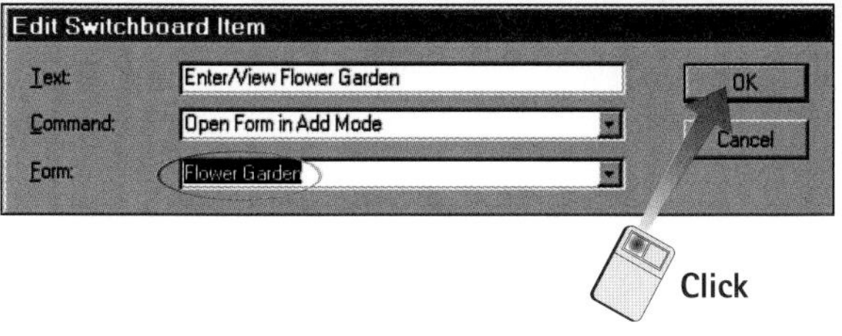

5 Add an Exit Button

Include an Exit button so that you can close the database from the Switchboard. Click **New** again, type **`Exit`** in the **Text** box, and select **Exit Application** from the **Command** drop-down list. Click **OK** to return to the Edit Switchboard dialog box.

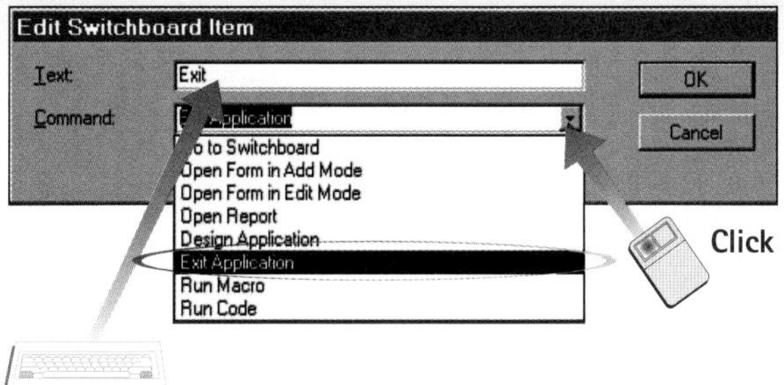

6 Exit Switchboard Manager

From the Edit Switchboard dialog box, you can continue adding elements to your Switchboard as needed; use the **Move Up**, **Move Down** buttons to change the order in which the items appear. To exit the Switchboard Manager now, click **Close**, and click **Close** again.

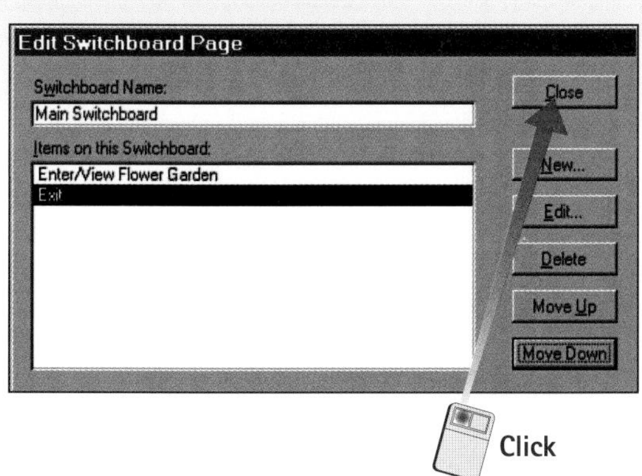

End

How-To Hints

Add an Edit Item

When you create a switchboard, it's a good idea to include a command that opens the Switchboard Manager if you want to make changes to the current setup. In the default Switchboard that's created when you use the Database Wizard, for example, the command is listed as *Change Switchboard Items*. Open the Switchboard Manager as directed in these steps, highlight **Main Switchboard** (default), and click **Edit**. Then click **New** and enter **`Edit Switchboard`** in the **Text** box. Choose **Design Application** from the **Command** drop-down list. Click **OK**, and **Close** out of the Switchboard Manager.

TASK 11

How to Format a Switchboard Form

In the previous task, you created a fully functional Switchboard. Although it works well, it is rather unattractive. You can easily change the font, add a picture, and make the Switchboard more attractive.

Open the database for the Switchboard you want to format. From the Database window, click the **Forms** tab, select **Switchboard**, and click **Open**. Open the **View** menu and select **Design View**.

Begin

1 Use the Property Sheet

To format or change an item on the form, such as the Switchboard label, double-click the item to open its property sheet (be sure to double-click the border of a selected item). The **All** tab has numerous properties you can edit for the item. Click a property to display a drop-down list or button for formatting the item.

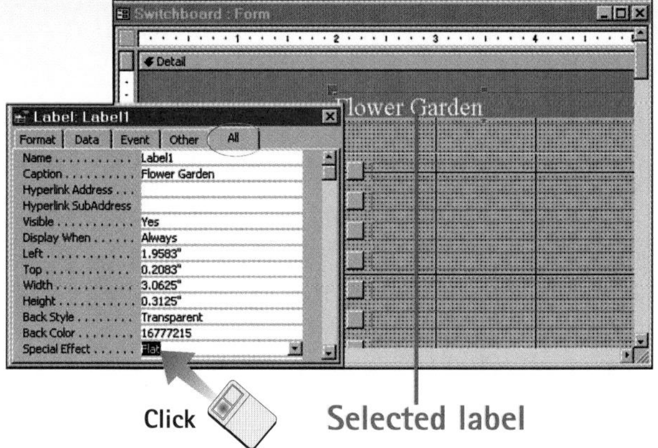

2 Change the Text

You can click in the **Caption** box and type a new caption, such as **`Robin's Address Book`** or **`My Household Inventory`**. To change the font, scroll down the list and click the **Font Name** property to display a drop-down list of fonts. Click the **Close** button to close the property sheet.

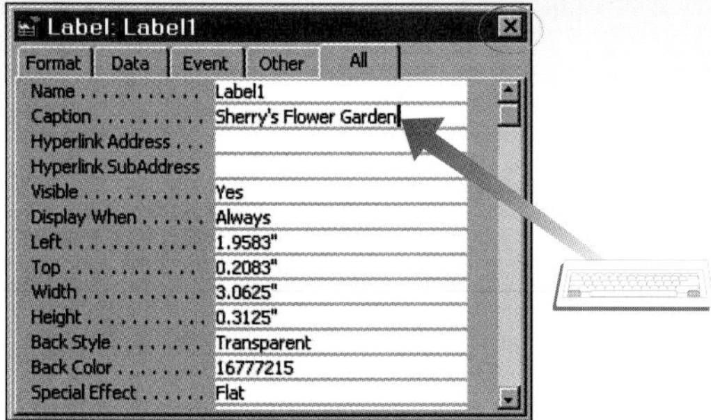

3 Move the Label

The new label text is now in place; to reposition the label, select it to display the selection handles. Position your mouse pointer at the edge of the label box until it turns into a black hand. Hold down the left mouse button and drag the label to a new location on the Switchboard.

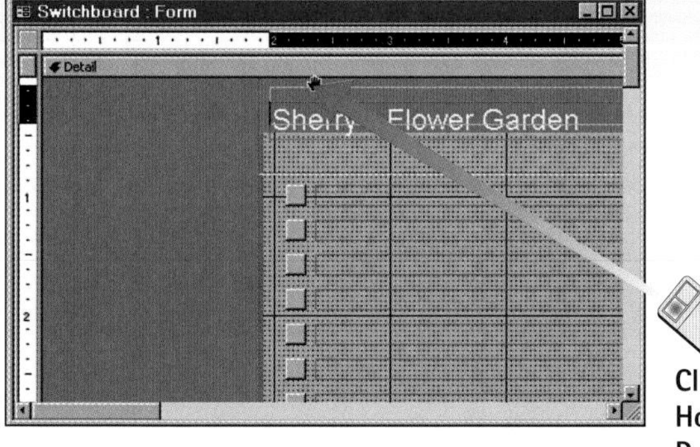

Click Hold & Drag

4 Change the Graphic

To change the graphic, double-click the **Image** box on the left side of the Switchboard form to open its property sheet. Click the **Picture** property line to access the Build button. Click the **Build** button to open the Insert Picture window.

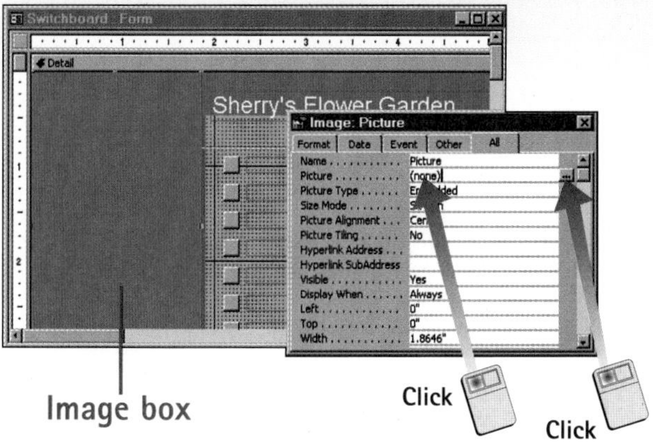

5 Choose a Graphic

Locate the graphics file you want to use and click **OK**. Close the property sheet to return to the form, and the new graphic is inserted.

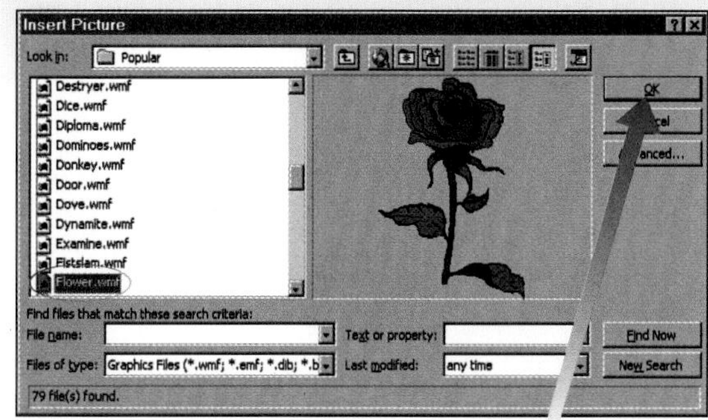

6 Check Your Changes

Open the **View** menu and select **Form View** to see how the spruced-up form actually appears. Close the form and click **Yes** to save your changes.

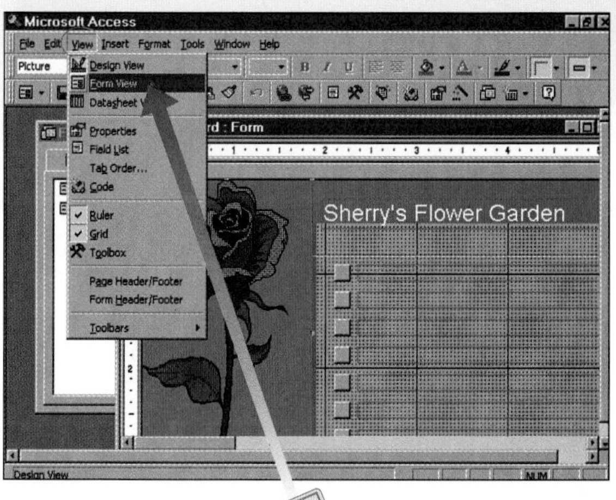

End

How-To Hints

Automatic Start

You can have the Switchboard automatically appear each time you open the database. With the database open, select **Tools, Startup** to open the Startup dialog box. Click the **Display Forms** drop-down list, choose **Switchboard**, and click **OK**. The next time you open the database, the Switchboard will appear on top of the Database window.

What About That Shadow?

If you're editing a Switchboard assigned by the Database Wizard, the shadow effect beneath the first label is a separate item box. To get rid of it, you must select it and press Delete.

TASK 12

How to Sort Records

After you have entered data into a database, you're ready to start manipulating it. One of the most important ways in which a database manipulates data is by *sorting* it—putting it in a logical order according to criteria you specify.

You may want to sort your address database, for example, by city, zip code, or last name. Access 97's Sort command is the tool to use. You can sort by ascending order (A to Z or 1 to 10) or descending order (Z to A or 10 to 1). To begin, open the database you want to sort.

Begin

1 Open the Table

From the Database window, click the **Tables** tab and open the table you want to sort (double-click the table name or select it and click **Open**).

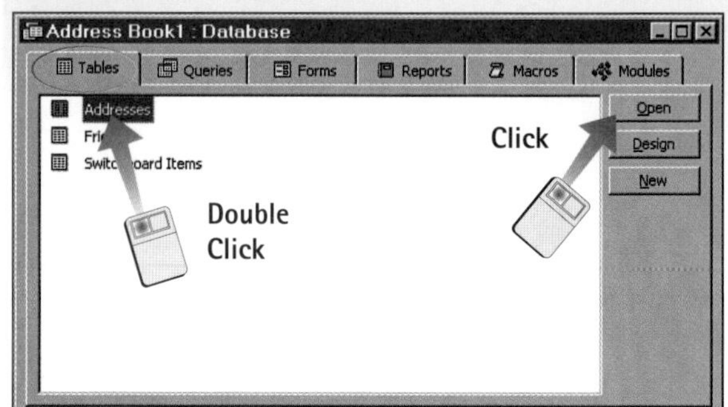

2 Choose the Sort Field

Click the column header for the field you wish to sort, or place your cursor anywhere in the column you want to use for the sort.

Addresses : Table

Addre	First Name	Last Name	Address	City	State/	F
2	Melissa	Cannon	314 Springfield Blvd.	Fishers	[illegible]	46
3	Joshua	Cannon	3425 Maple Drive	Fishers	[illegible]	46
4	Jacob	Cannon	594 Main St.	Fishers	[illegible]	46
15	Tina	Daniels	6655 Texas Drive	Denver	CO	34
18	Scott	Farmer	4863 Red Bucket Lake	Denver	CO	34
16	Stacey	Federhart	6008 Willow Way	Boulder	CO	43
9	Kevin	Gray	9001 Aspen Way	Denver	CO	34
10	Alicia	Gray	9001 Aspen Way	Denver	CO	34
17	Teresa	Howell	8569 Normal Boulevard	Carterville	IL	48
6	Kelly	Hughes	6544 Hoover Drive	Normal	IL	46
14	Lisa	Jamison	889 Westwood Lane	Denver	CO	34
1	Greg	Kinkoph	771 Willoview	Carmel	IN	46
21	Greg	Kinkoph	8695 Charleston Parkwa	Greenw[illegible]d	IN	46
8	Carmen	Laudenschlager	133 Aspen Grove	Denver	CO	34
7	Dan	Laudneschlager	133 Aspen Grove	Denver	CO	34
19	Greg	Loving	1713 Mockingbird Lane	New R[illegible]chelle	NY	05
11	Alan	Oglesby	659 Fishers Trail	Fishe[illegible]	IN	46

Record: 1 of 23

3 Use the Sort Buttons

To sort the table in ascending (A-Z) order, click the **Sort Ascending** button on the toolbar. To sort by descending order (Z-A), click the **Sort Descending** button.

4 The Data Is Sorted

The data is immediately sorted. Continue sorting the table fields as needed. When you exit the table after sorting, a prompt box asks you if you want to save the changes; click **Yes** if you do, or **No** if you don't want the sort to be permanent.

Addresses : Table

Addre	First Name	Last Name	Address	City	State/	F
12	Pat	Willard	714 Chestnut Street	Denver	CO	34
7	Dan	Laudneschlager	133 Aspen Grove	Denver	CO	34
8	Carmen	Laudenschlager	133 Aspen Grove	Denver	CO	34
18	Scott	Farmer	4863 Red Bucket Lake	Denver	CO	34
9	Kevin	Gray	9001 Aspen Way	Denver	CO	34
16	Stacey	Federhart	6008 Willow Way	Boulder	CO	43
15	Tina	Daniels	6655 Texas Drive	Denver	CO	34
14	Lisa	Jamison	889 Westwood Lane	Denver	CO	34
10	Alicia	Gray	9001 Aspen Way	Denver	CO	34
5	Shawn	Sechrest	1901 Cloud Street	Bloomington	IL	61
6	Kelly	Hughes	6544 Hoover Drive	Normal	IL	46
13	Lavern	Williams	454 Omaha Drive	Vandalia	IL	65
23	Ed	Ralph	65444 East Street	Marion	IL	62
17	Teresa	Howell	8569 Normal Boulevard	Carterville	IL	48
20	Melissa	Willard	34 Ritchey Drive	Kewanee	IL	64
22	Dave	Willard	1234 Ritchey Drive	Marion	IL	62
1	Greg	Kinkoph	771 Willoview	Carmel	IN	46

Record: 1 of 23

5 Sort by Form Fields

You can also sort your records using a form. From the Database window, select the **Forms** tab and open a form. Place your cursor in the field you want to sort by.

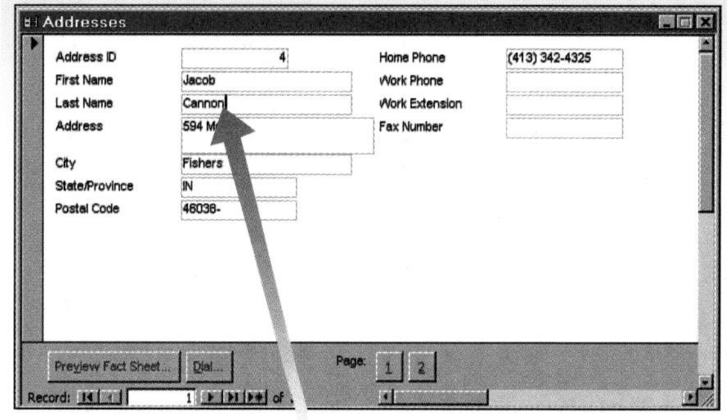

Click

6 Use the Shortcut Menu

This time, perform a sort using the shortcut menu. Right-click to display the menu, and then select **Sort Ascending** or **Sort Descending** to sort the form by the selected field. As you cycle through the records using the arrow buttons at the bottom of the form, the records appear in the new sort order.

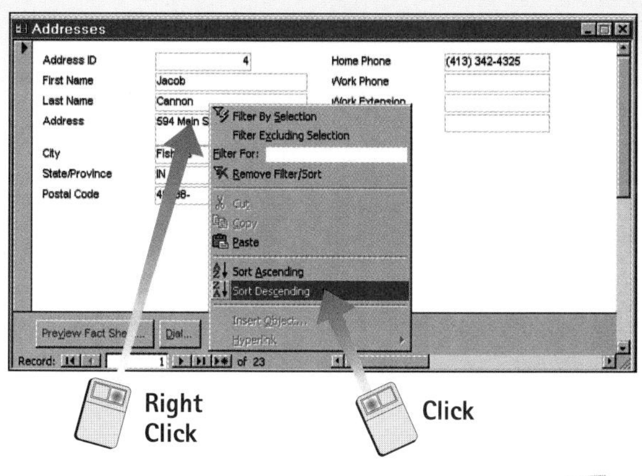

Right Click

Click

End

How-To Hints

What About Empty Records?

If you sort by a field that contains no information in some records, those records are automatically sorted first (ascending sort) or last (descending sort).

Sort Tip

Changing the sort order of a table does not cause a related sort order change in an existing form. However, if you create a form using a table with an established sort order, the form automatically takes on the sort order of the table.

Sort in Datasheet View

You can also sort a form in the Datasheet view. Open the **View** menu and choose **Datasheet View**. The Datasheet view of the form not only looks the same as the table in step 2, but it also sorts the same. After you select the column to sort by, you can use the **Sort Ascending** or **Sort Descending** button to perform the sort.

TASK 13

How to Filter Records

You can filter out specific records in your database. Perhaps you want to see information only on a certain vendor or group of vendors, or you may want to find everyone in your address book whose birthday is in the month of May. You can temporarily filter out all the records except those you need to see.

Access enables you to apply a filter in three ways: Filter by Selection, Filter by Form, and Advanced Filters. All the filters can be applied in a form, datasheet, or query. In this task, the first two methods will be demonstrated.

Begin

1 Filter by Selection

Open the form you want to use, and then click the field that contains the criteria you want to filter for—if you want to search for all the records using the same zip code, for example, first locate a record containing that zip code and click in the zip code field. To begin the filter, click the **Filter by Selection** button on the toolbar.

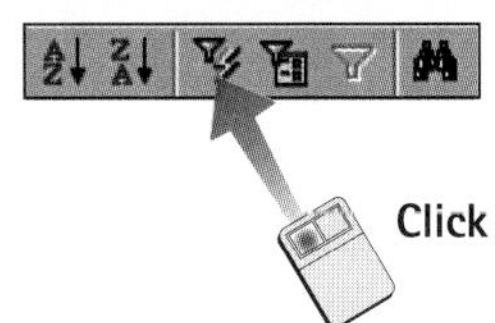

2 The Records Are Filtered

Any records that have matching information in the field selected have been retained, but all others have been hidden (filtered out). Use the form's arrow buttons to view the filtered records.

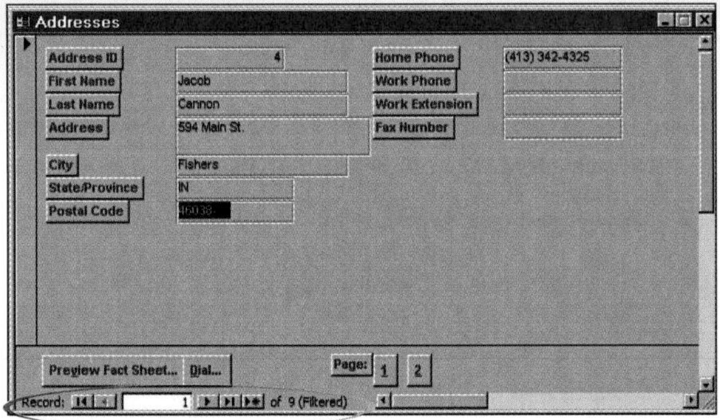

3 Remove a Filter

To remove the filter, click the **Remove Filter** button on the toolbar. (When no filter has been applied, the **Remove Filter** button does double duty as the **Apply Filter** button.)

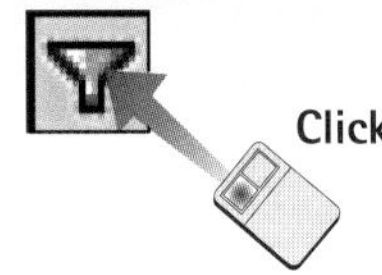

4 Filter by Form

Click the **Filter by Form** button to enter your own criteria for the filter. A blank form appears as a single record in a datasheet.

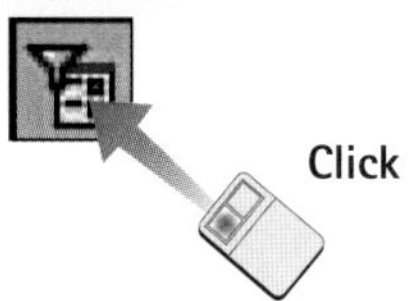

5 Enter Your Filter Criteria

Type your search criteria in the field of your choice or use the field's drop-down arrow to select a value. (To search for all contacts who live in Denver, for example, type **Denver** in the **City** field.) You can enter criteria in more than one field, but Access will find only records that match both entries.

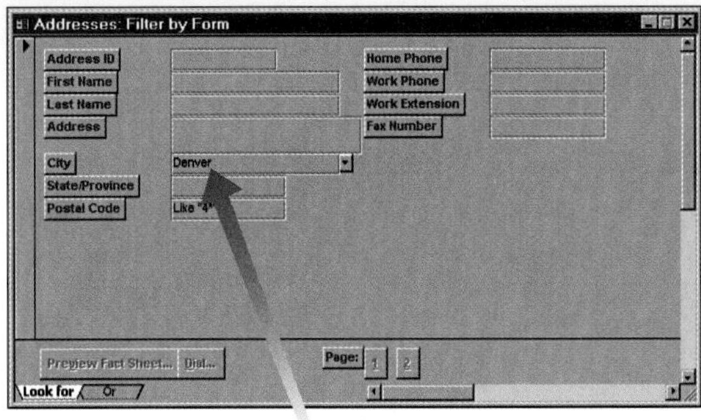

6 Filter the Records

To begin the filter, click the **Apply Filter** button on the toolbar. Access filters your database and displays any records matching your criteria. (Use the arrow buttons to scroll through each record.)

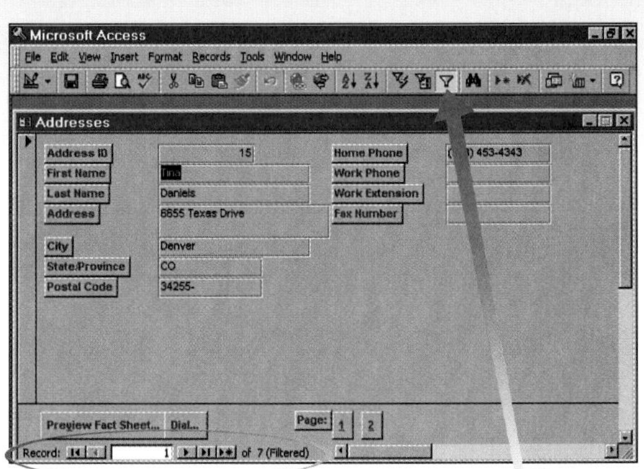

End

How-To Hints

Quick Filter

For a quick search based on input for a certain field, place your cursor in the desired field and right-click. Enter the search criteria in the **Filter For** text box on the shortcut menu and press Enter to apply the filter.

Filter by Exclusion

You can also filter out records that contain certain criteria. The regular filter finds records that contain the search criteria and filters out those that don't. The Filter by Excluding Selection returns all records that do *not* contain the search criteria you specify.

TASK 14

How to Use the Simple Query Wizard

Queries are similar to filters in that they extract information based on criteria that you specify. Queries can be used for editing and viewing your data, as well as furnishing the material for forms and reports.

The easiest way to create a query is to use the Simple Query Wizard. It enables you to select which fields you want to display; you can weed out fields you don't need and still see every record.

Begin

1 Open the New Query Dialog Box

From the Database window, select the **Queries** tab and click **New** to open the New Query dialog box.

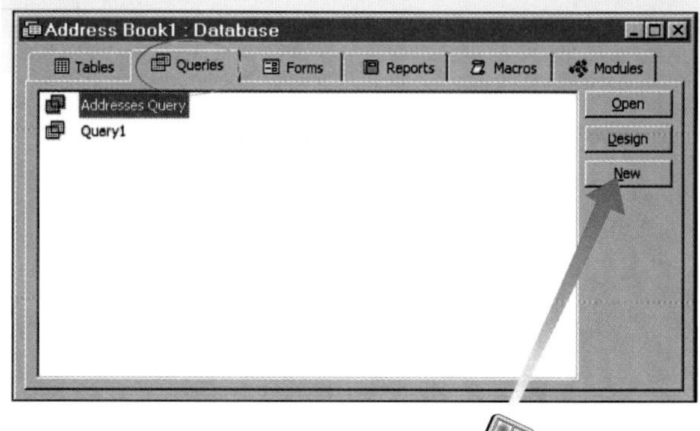

Click

2 Start the Simple Query Wizard

Choose **Simple Query Wizard** and click **OK** to open the first Simple Query Wizard dialog box.

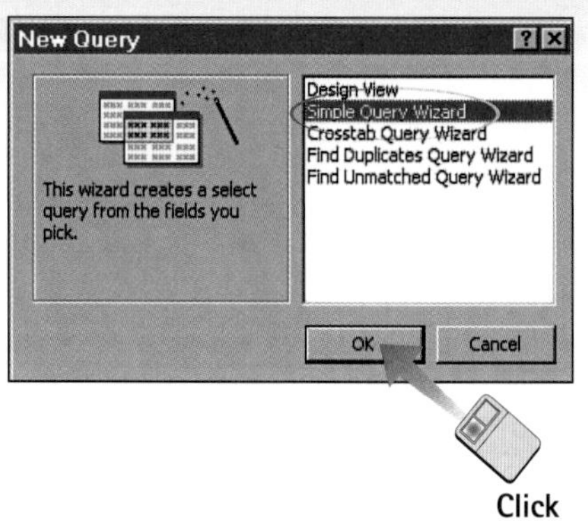

Click

3 Choose a Table

Open the **Tables/Queries** drop-down list and select the first table from which to choose a field.

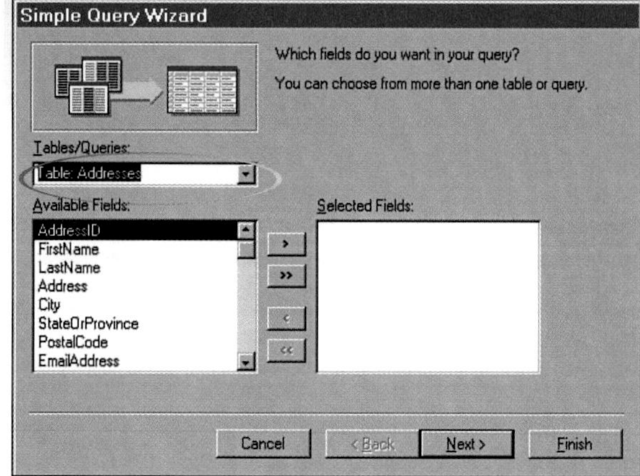

4 Choose a Query Type

Select a field and click the > button to add it to your query. Select as many fields from as many different tables as you wish and click **Next** when you're ready to continue.

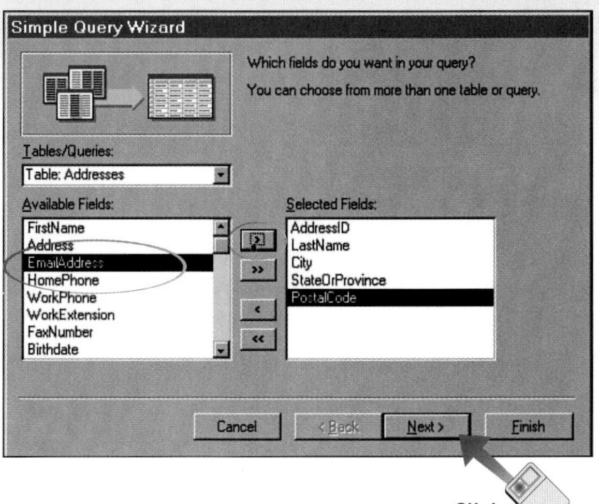

5 Give the Query a Name

The next dialog box asks you if you want a detail (shows every record) or summary (use for totaling values) query. Detail is the default, so click **Next** to continue. Then enter a name for the query and click **Finish** to create your query, which appears in table form.

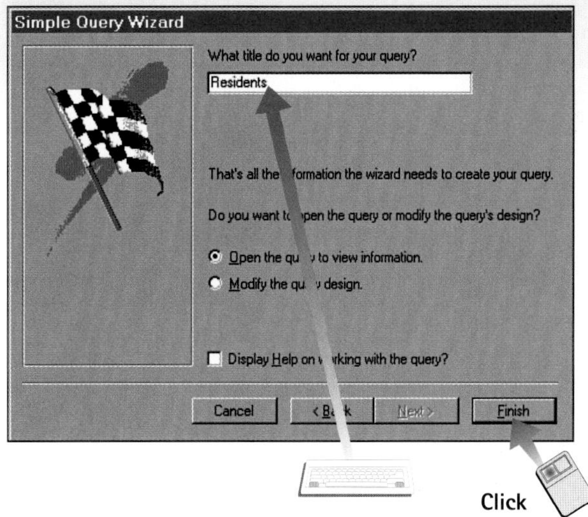

6 Query Results

Access produces the results of your query. To close the query, click its **Close** button.

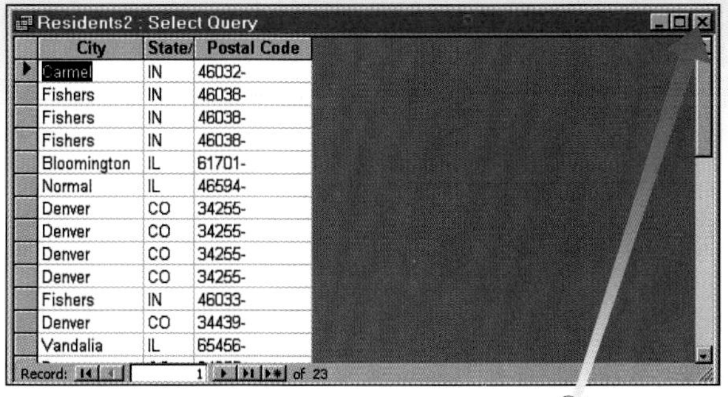

City	State/	Postal Code
Carmel	IN	46032-
Fishers	IN	46038-
Fishers	IN	46038-
Fishers	IN	46038-
Bloomington	IL	61701-
Normal	IL	46594-
Denver	CO	34255-
Denver	CO	34255-
Denver	CO	34255-
Denver	CO	34255-
Fishers	IN	46033-
Denver	CO	34439-
Vandalia	IL	65456-

Click

End

How-To Hints

Searching for Blanks

In addition to finding records that contain fields with information, you can also use a query to find records that contain blank fields. To search for blank numeric fields, use `is null` for the search criteria. For blank text fields, use double quotes (`""`).

TASK 15

How to Create a New Query Object

You can build a query from scratch using Design view. Design view enables you to build forms, tables, queries, and reports based on the fields you want to include, and it structures the items the way you want to see them. In the case of a query, Design view lets you create a query based on the tables you want to extract information from, and enter the criteria for each field you want to sort.

Open the database you want to use for this task, click the **Queries** tab, and click the **New** button to get started.

Begin

1 Open Design View

In the New Query dialog box, select **Design View** and click **OK**. This opens the Show Table dialog box.

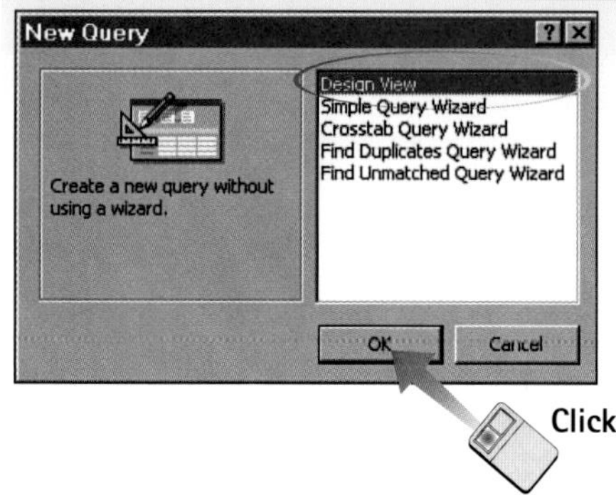

2 The Show Table Dialog Box

Choose a table you want to use and click **Add**. Repeat this step to add tables to the query. Click **Close** when you're finished.

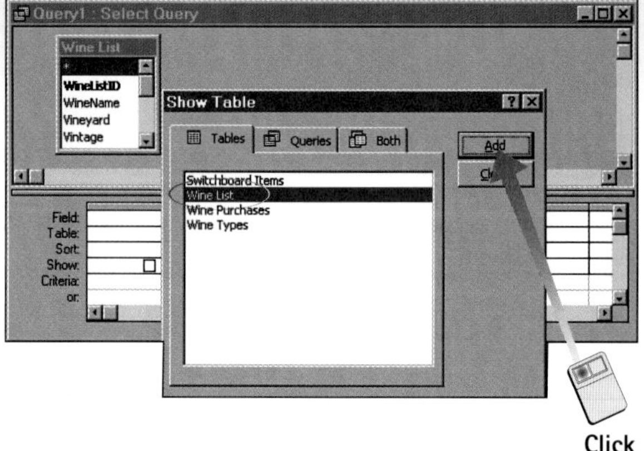

3 Specify Which Table

Access displays the query in Design view. Each column in the grid at the bottom of the window represents a field you can use in your query. You can start by designating a table; click in the **Table** row of the first blank column, and then use the drop-down arrow to open the list and select a table for your query.

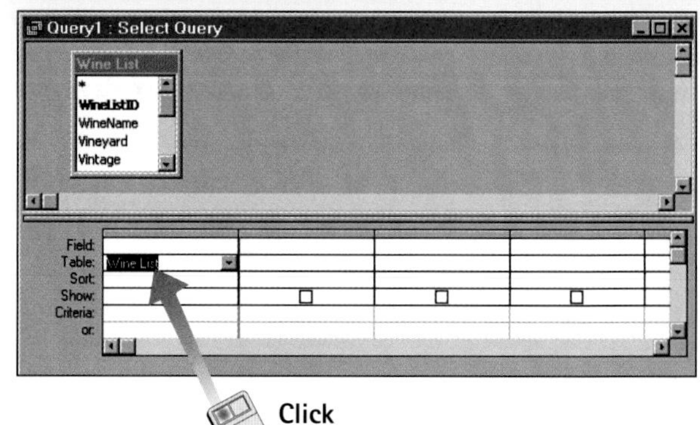

4 Specify a Field

Click the **Field** row, and then use the drop-down arrow to choose a field.

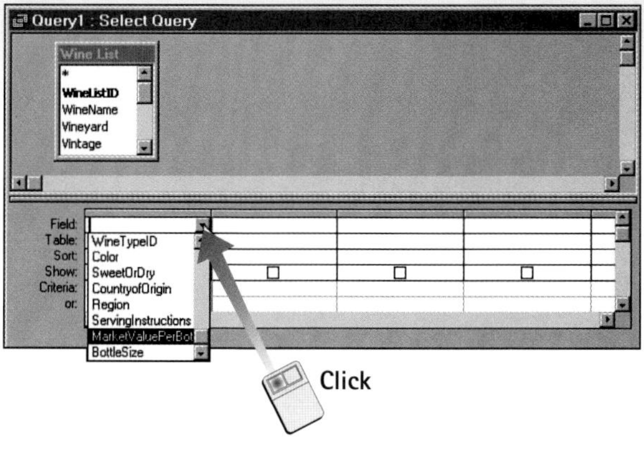

5 Enter the Criteria

The Criteria row lets you include only the records that match your specifications—your criteria. Click the **Criteria** row in the field you want to establish criteria for, and enter the criteria you want to use. You can use mathematical operators and comparison operators, such as greater than (>), less than (<), and equal to (=), in your criteria.

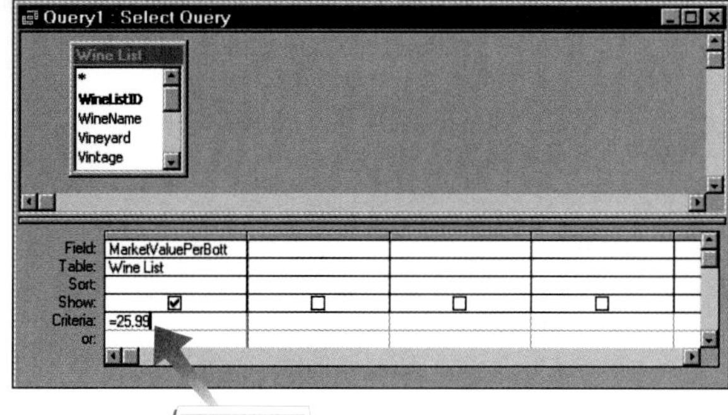

6 Run the Query

Continue entering additional columns containing query fields, tables, and criteria. When you're ready to run the query, click the **Run** button on the toolbar and the results appear in a separate datasheet.

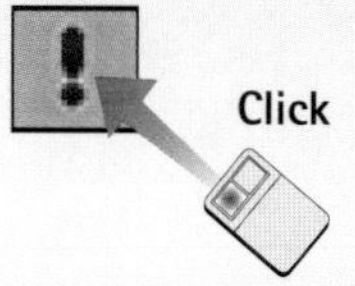

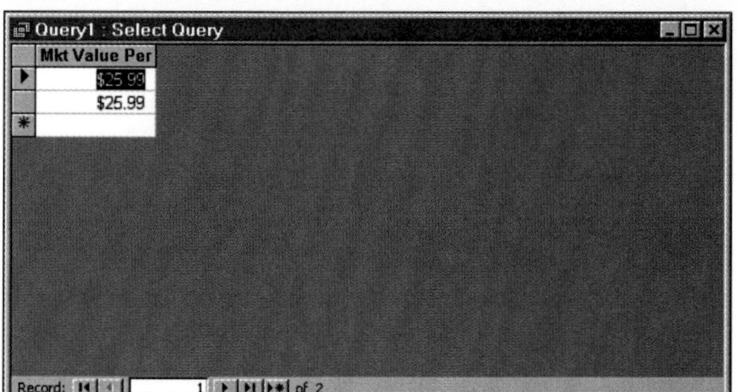

End

How-To Hints

Close the Query

To close your query and any results, click the **Close** button on each open window. You will be asked if you want to save the results; click **Yes** and give the query a name.

TASK 16

How to Create a Report with the Report Wizard

You can choose to print any table, form, or query at any time; however, using Access 97's Report tool can make the data appear more professional and polished. With the Report Wizard, the task of creating a meaningful report becomes simple and effortless.

Open the database you want to use and click the **Reports** tab of the Database window; then click **New** to open the New Report dialog box.

Begin

1 Open the Report Wizard

Select **Report Wizard** from the list of options, and then click **OK** to open the Report Wizard window.

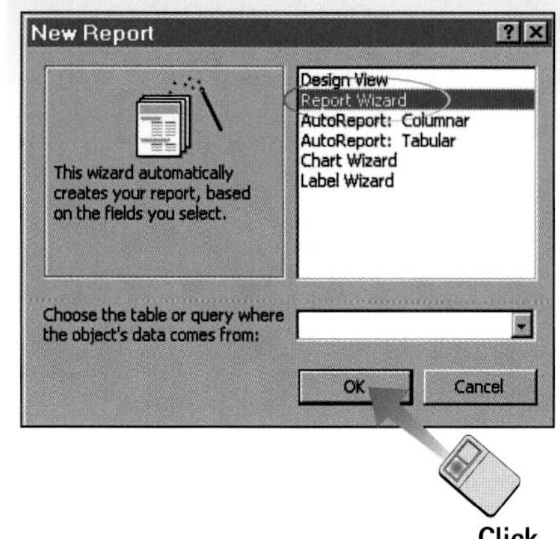

2 Choose a Table or Query

From the **Tables/Queries** drop-down list, select the table or query to use in your report. Select a field and click the > button to add it to your list. Select as many fields from as many different tables or queries as you wish and click **Next** when you're ready to continue.

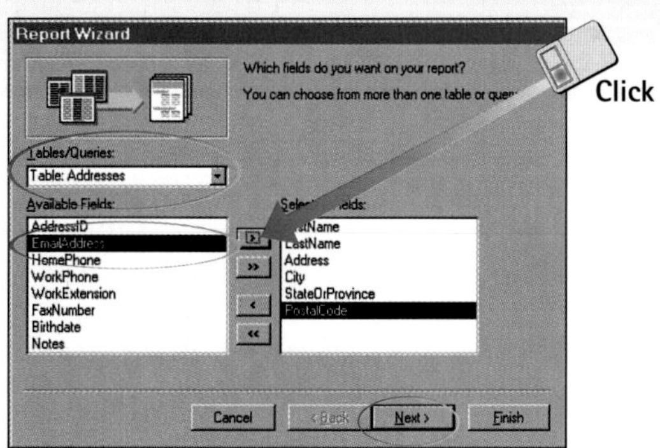

3 Choose a Grouping Category

A report that groups information by relevant categories is much more useful than one that simply lists information alphabetically. From the left display window, choose a field to use as a grouping category and click the > button. Click **Next** to continue.

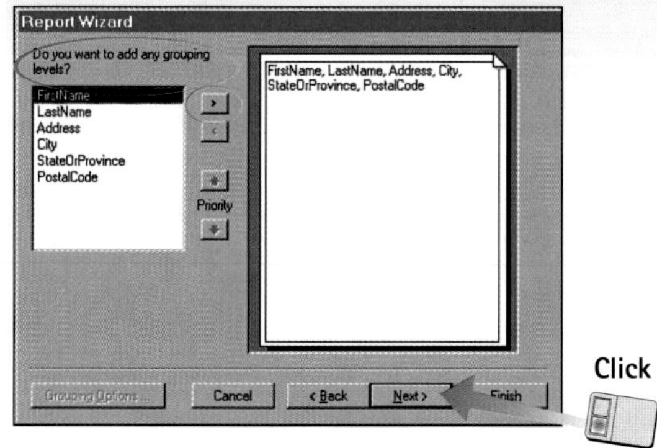

4 Choose a Sort

You can sort by as many as four fields, either in ascending or descending order. From the first drop-down list, select the field to use for the primary sort and continue until you have chosen as many sort fields as needed. Click **Next** to continue.

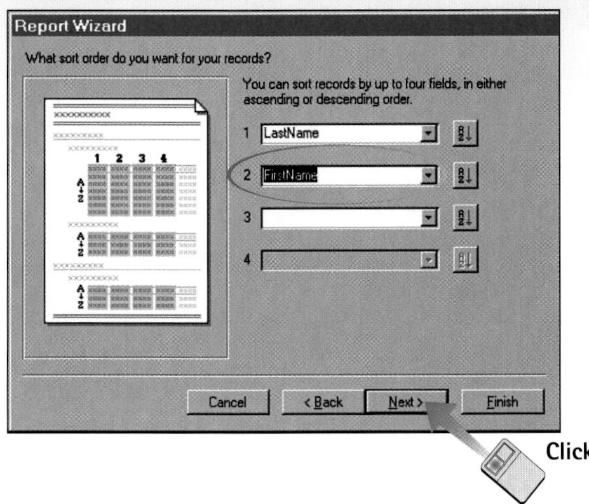

5 Select a Layout

Select a layout option to see an example of how it will look. When you have decided on the layout options, you're ready to move on. Click **Next**.

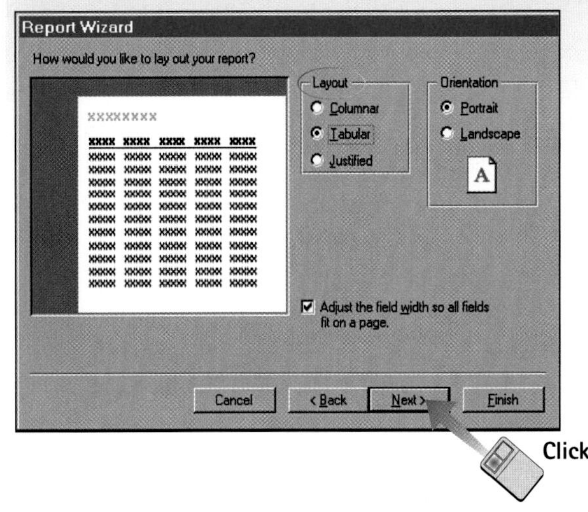

6 Select a Style

As with the layout options, you can see examples of the different styles by clicking the options. Choose a style for your report, and then click **Next**.

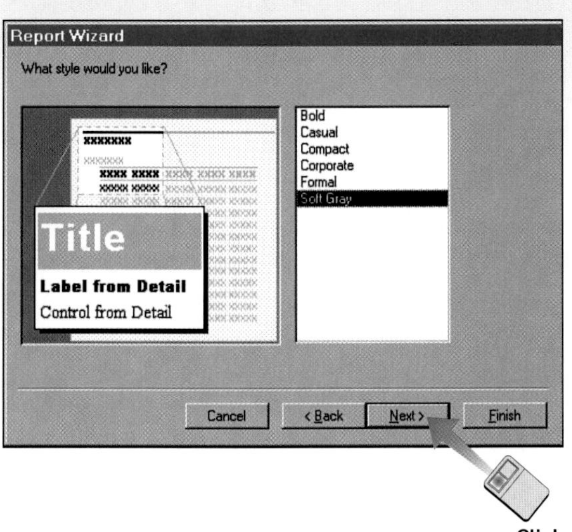

7 Assign a Title

Enter a report title and click **Finish** to create your new report.

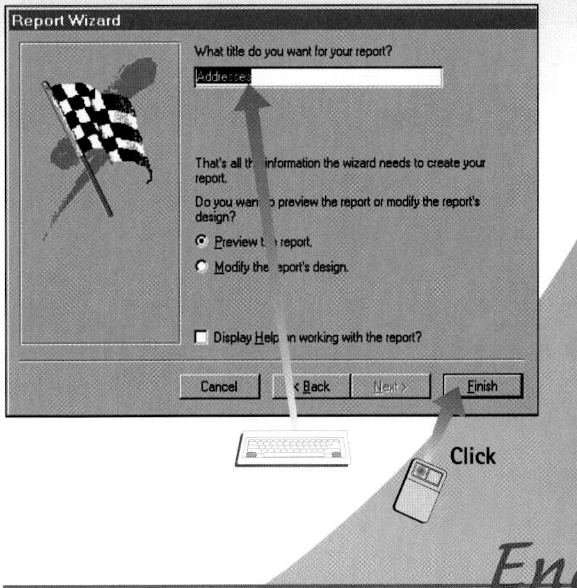

End

TASK 17

How to Modify a Report in Design View

To customize the report, open the report in Design view. The report is composed of six sections in Design view. The Report Header contains information that appears only at the very beginning of the report; the Page Header section contains information that appears at the top of each page; the CompanyName Header contains header information for each page, based on the grouping (CompanyName) selected during the report creation; Detail contains the actual report data; the Page Footer section contains information appearing at the bottom of each page; and Report Footer contains information that appears at the bottom of the last page.

Begin

1 Open the Report in Design View

To begin, open the Database window, click the **Reports** tab, select the report, and click the **Design** button.

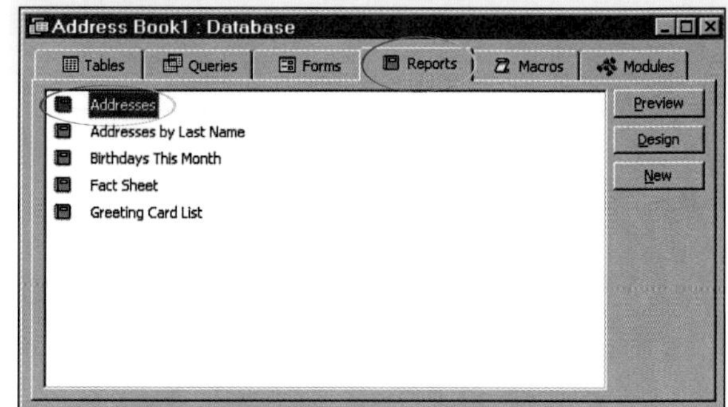

2 Add a Label

To add a text label to the report, click the **Label** tool on the toolbox. Move the mouse pointer to the section where you want to insert the text, click and hold down the left mouse button, and draw a label box. Type your text and press Enter.

3 Change the Font

To change the font size, double-click the label box (you may have to deselect it first) to open the property sheet, scroll down to **Font Size** and change the size. Close the property sheet to return to the Design view.

4 Add a Graphic

To add a graphic, click the **Image** tool on the Toolbox. Move the mouse pointer to the section where you want to add the graphic, hold down the left mouse button, and draw an image box.

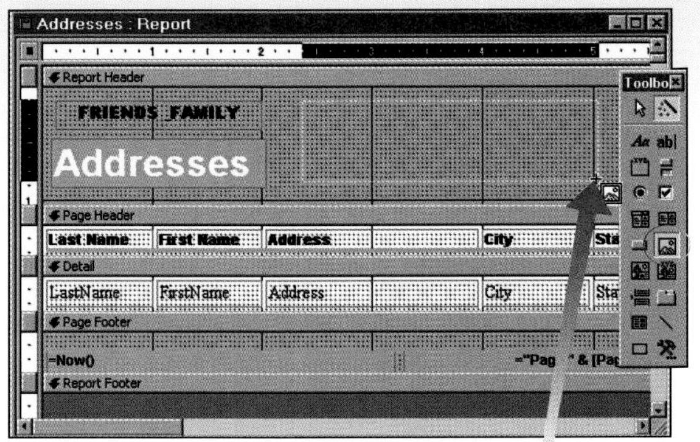

Click Hold & Drag

5 Select the Graphics File

From the Insert Picture dialog box, locate the graphics file you want to use. Double-click the graphics name and the graphic is inserted in your report (you may have to adjust the size of the image box).

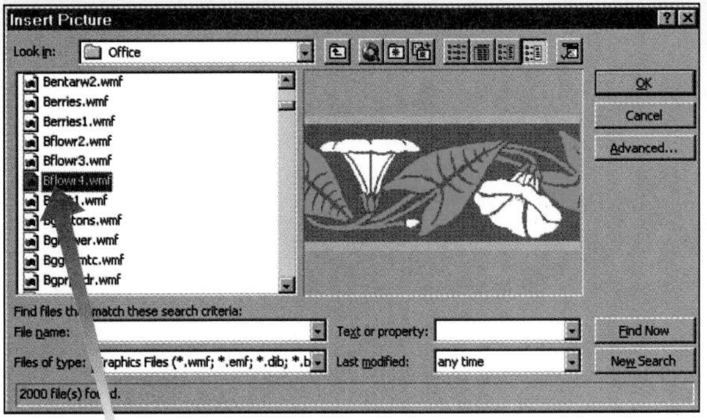

Double Click

6 Remove Objects

To remove any object from a report—including a label, field, or graphic—select it and press Delete.

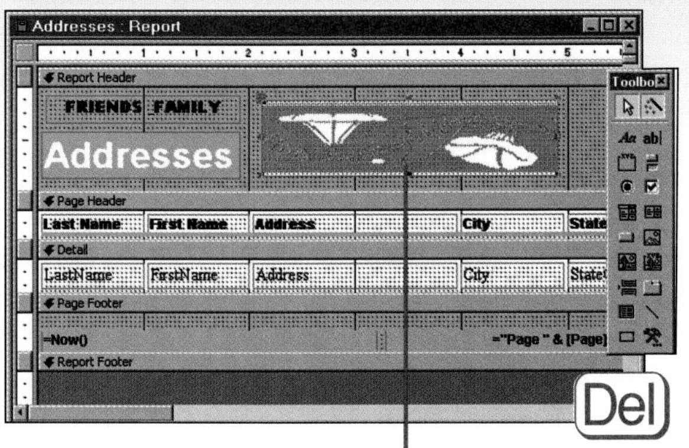

Selected object

End

How-To Hints

No Toolbox?

If the floating toolbox isn't displayed, click the **Toolbox** button on the Form Design toolbar to open it.

Open Properties

You can open an object's property sheet by right-clicking the object and selecting **Properties** from the shortcut menu.

Preview First

To preview your changes before saving the modified report, choose **View, Layout Preview** from the menu bar.

Task

CHAPTER 13

How to Use Outlook 98

Outlook is a desktop information manager you can use to organize and manage your daily activities at home or at the office. Outlook is extremely versatile; you can schedule and keep track of your daily appointments, build and maintain a *database* of people you contact the most, create "to do" lists for projects or events and track each item's status, jot down electronic notes, and more. In addition to helping you manage your daily commitments, you can also track and manage your *email* correspondence. You can send and receive email from the Outlook window, whether they're messages sent to Internet users or colleagues on your company LAN, WAN, or intranet.

Although Outlook 97 is part of the Office 97 suite of programs, Outlook 98 is now available. If you recently purchased a copy of Microsoft Office 97, you have a coupon for a free upgrade to Outlook 98. Outlook 98 is the latest improvement of the program, and you will definitely want to upgrade as soon as possible. If you have taken time to learn Outlook 97, you won't have trouble learning Outlook 98. Outlook 98 loads faster, performs more efficiently, and closes more quickly than Outlook 97. Microsoft has improved the command structure in the menus and dialog boxes to make Outlook even easier to use.

This chapter covers the basic features of using Outlook 98, including how to use the new Outlook Today view, and the basics for using each of Outlook's components, such as Calendar, Contacts, Tasks, and Notes.

TASK 1

How to Get Around the Outlook 98 Window

The Outlook window features the familiar title bar, menu bar, toolbar, and status bar used in other Office 97 programs. In addition, you see the Outlook Bar on the left side of the window. Use the Outlook Bar to access each Outlook component. Outlook's components are organized into folders, represented by icons on the Outlook Bar. When you click a component, such as Inbox, the appropriate folder opens in the work area.

Because the Outlook 98 window differs in appearance from the other Office program windows, take a few minutes to acclimate yourself to the window elements.

Begin

1 The Profile Box

When you start Outlook 98, a Choose Profile dialog box appears. For now, click **OK** to continue. You can always set up a personalized profile later. (To set a personalized profile, click the **New** button and set up a new profile.)

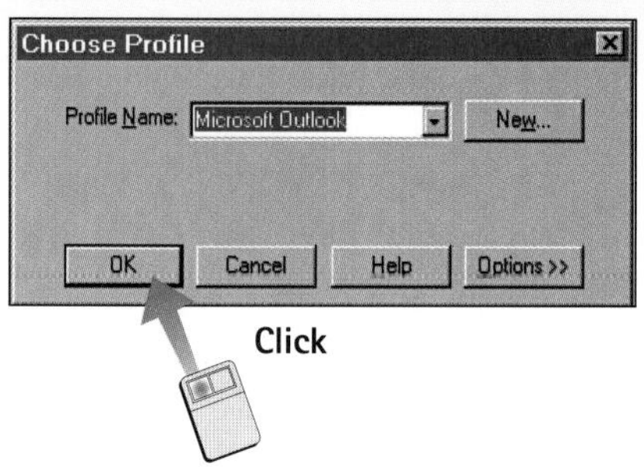

2 View the Outlook Window

The Outlook window contains many of the same program elements used in other Office 97 programs. Use the Minimize, Maximize, and Close buttons at the far right end of the title bar to manipulate the Outlook 98 window.

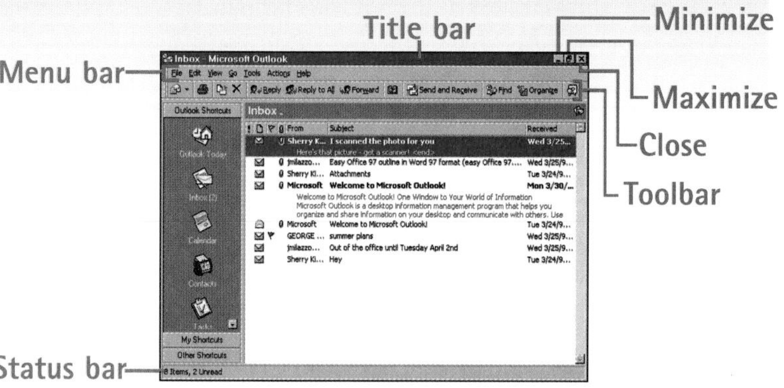

3 Use the Menu Bar

To display an Outlook menu, click the menu name. The menu drops down to reveal a list of commands. Select the command you want to use.

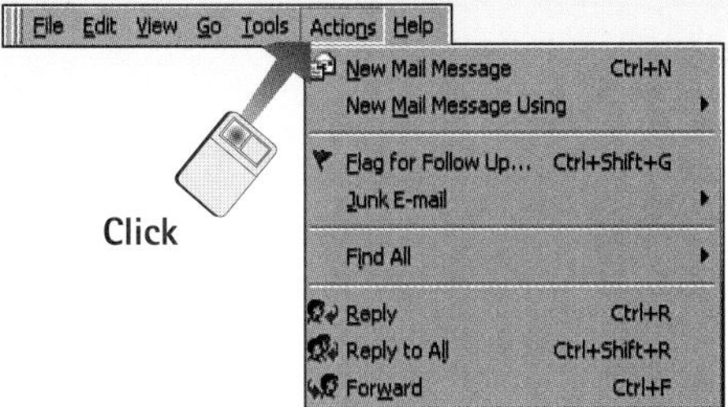

4 Use the Toolbar

Outlook's toolbar buttons change to reflect the component or task you're working on. To activate a toolbar button, just click it. To learn more about what a button does, hover your mouse pointer over the button to reveal a *ScreenTip*.

5 Use Group Buttons

The Outlook Bar has three group buttons that organize your folders and shortcuts: Outlook Shortcuts (which hold all the Outlook components), My Shortcuts (which hold various folders for sent messages, drafts, and more), and Other Shortcuts (lets you access My Computer, My Documents, and Favorites folders). To display a new folder group, click the appropriate group button.

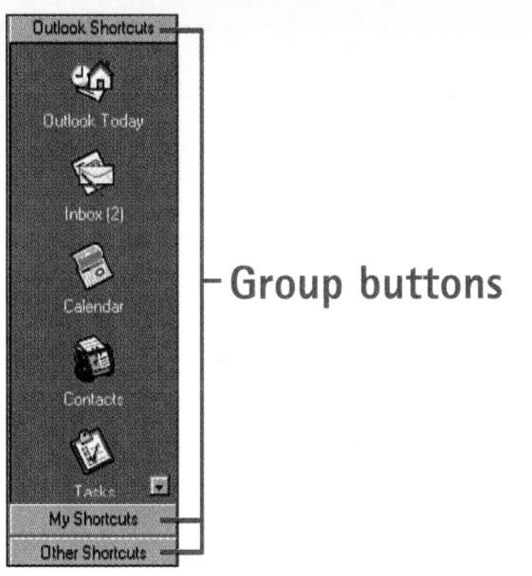

6 Change Folders

Each Outlook component has its own folder, represented by an icon on the Outlook Bar in the Outlook Shortcuts group. To open another Outlook component, click the appropriate icon in the Outlook Bar. To open the Calendar feature, for example, click the **Calendar** icon. Use the scroll button to view more icons on the Outlook Bar.

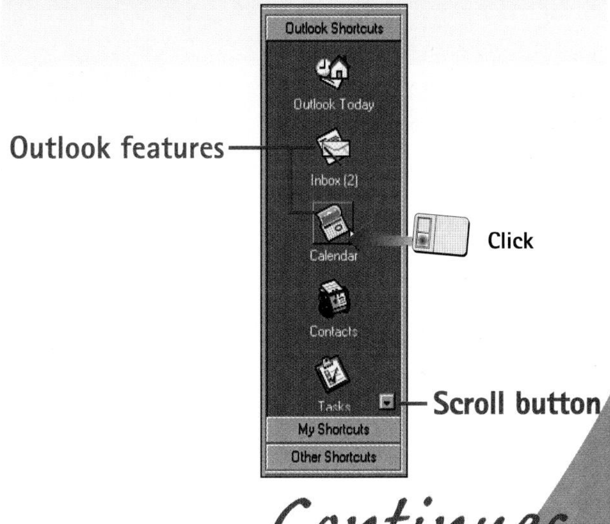

Continues

7 Display the Folder List

Another way to view Outlook's components is with the Folder List. Open the **View** menu and select **Folder List**, or click the **Folder** drop-down arrow in the work area. The Folder List displays each Outlook folder, including any you add to organize Outlook items you create. (Click the **Pushpin** icon to keep the Folder List open onscreen.)

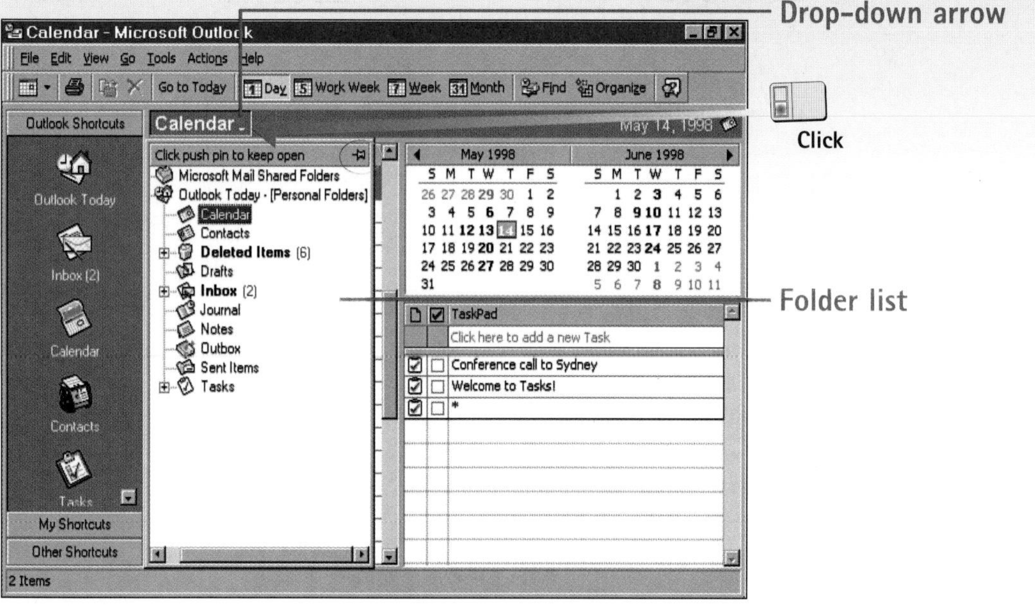

8 Change Views

Some of the Outlook components let you change your view of the information presented. Calendar, for example, lets you see your schedule by Day, Work Week, Week, and Month. To change a view, use the **View** menu or click the appropriate view button on the toolbar.

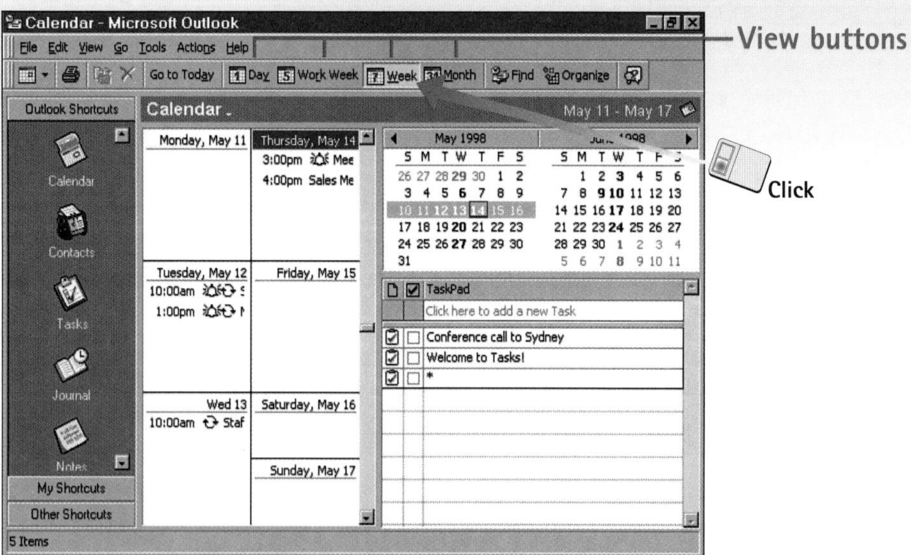

9 Use Outlook Today View

A new feature in Outlook 98 is the Outlook Today folder (click the **Outlook Today** icon on the Outlook Bar to open). This lets you see your day's schedule and projects at a glance. The items displayed are actually hyperlinks to other Outlook items. Click an appointment, for example, to open the Appointment window that has details about the appointment.

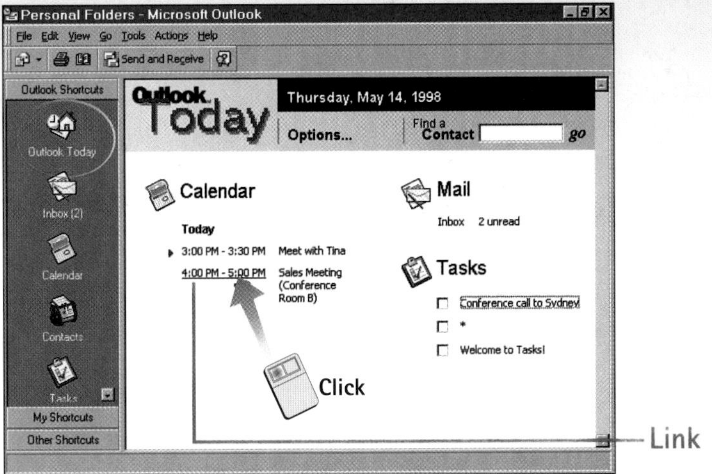

10 Find Outlook Contacts

Use the **Find a Contact** tool at the top of the Outlook Today display to quickly look up a name in your Contacts database (learn more about adding contacts in Task 9, "How to Phone a Contact"). Click inside the text box and type the person's name. Press Enter, and Outlook displays the Contact form with details about the person.

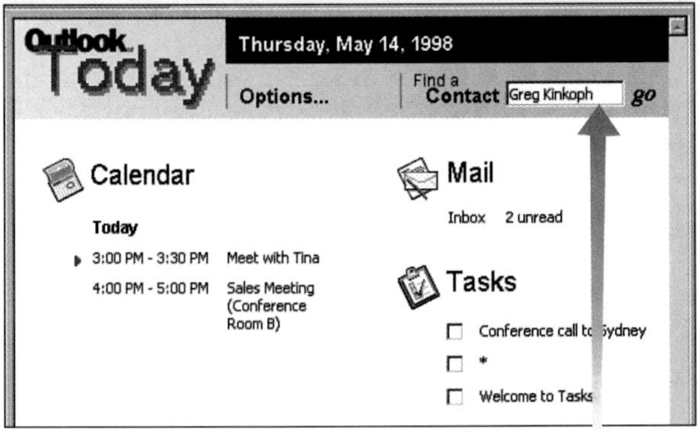

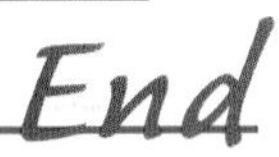

End

How-To Hints

Customize Outlook Today

By default, Outlook 98 opens with the Inbox displayed. However, you may want to customize Outlook to start with the Outlook Today feature displayed. That way, you can always see your day's events and tasks at a glance. To do this, click the **Options** link on the Outlook Today display. This opens another display page with several options. Click the **When starting, go directly to Outlook Today** check box. You can also customize how appointments and tasks appear. Click the **Back to Outlook Today** link to return to the previous display page.

TASK 2

How to Schedule an Appointment

Use Outlook's Calendar feature to keep track of appointments, events, and any other special engagements. When you open the Calendar folder, Outlook displays your daily schedule in the schedule pane, along with a monthly calendar pane and a miniaturized version of your TaskPad (learn more about creating Outlook tasks in Task 6, "How to Create a New Task").

You can easily add appointments to your calendar and set reminder alarms to let you know of imminent appointments. To open Calendar, click the **Calendar** icon on the Outlook Bar.

Begin

1 Choose a Date

In the monthly calendar pane, select the month and date for the appointment. Click the date and the schedule pane changes to reflect that date.

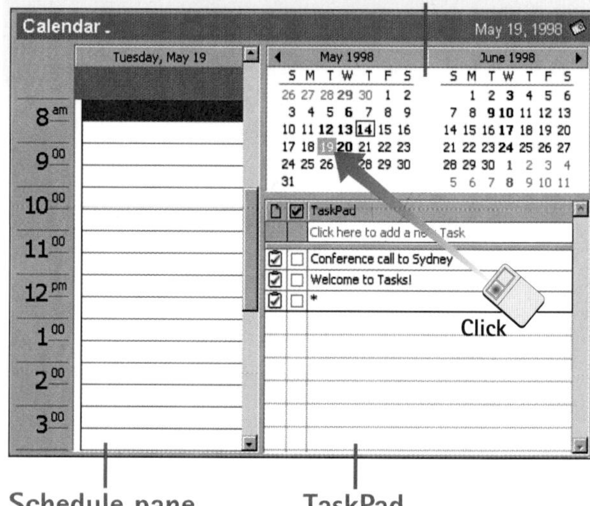

2 Choose a Time

On the schedule pane, double-click the time slot for which you want to schedule an appointment. This opens the Appointment window.

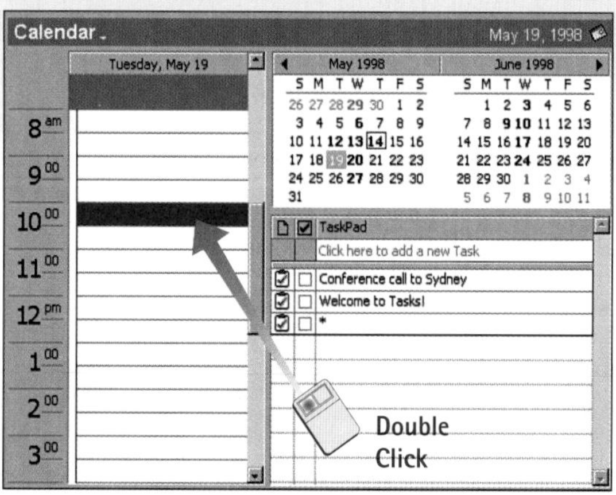

3 Fill Out the Form

The Appointment window lets you enter appointment details. Fill out the **Subject** and **Location** text boxes, the name of the person you're meeting with, and the place where you're meeting. Click inside the text boxes, or use the Tab key to move from field to field.

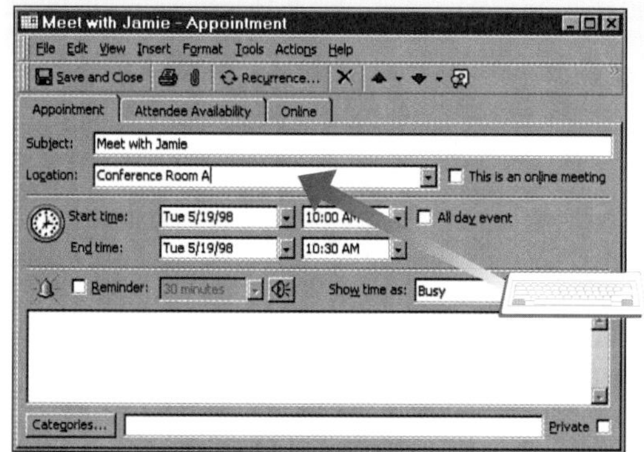

4 Enter Appointment Details

Use the **Start time** and **End time** drop-down arrows to set or change the date, time, and length of the appointment. By default, Outlook schedules your appointments in 30-minute increments, but you can easily set a longer time increment.

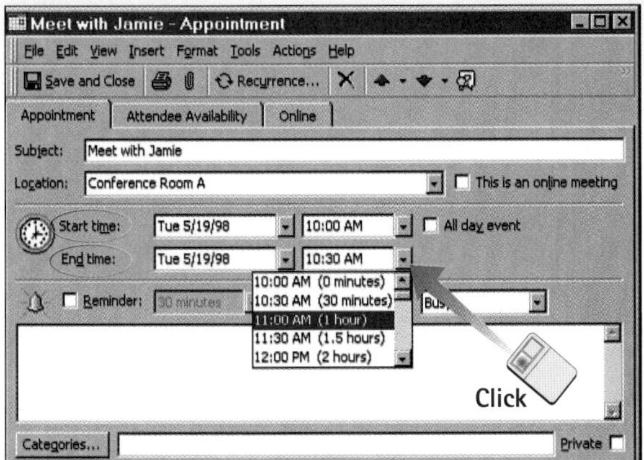

5 Need a Reminder?

Select the **Reminder** check box if you want Outlook to remind you about the appointment with a prompt box and an audible beep. Specify the amount of time before the appointment for which you want to be reminded.

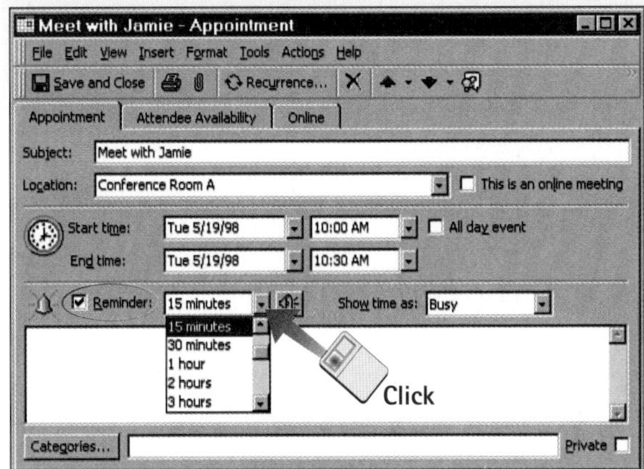

6 Save and Close

When you have finished filling in all the details you want to include with the appointment, click the **Save and Close** button on the Appointment window's toolbar to exit the form and return to Calendar.

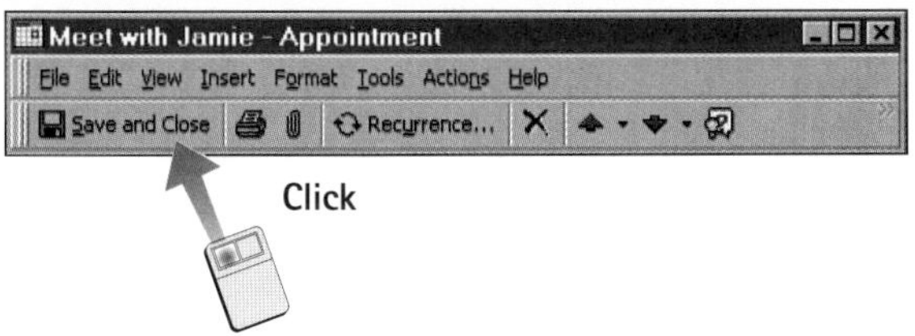

End

How-To Hints

Reminder Prompt

If you select the Reminder check box, Outlook reminds you about the appointment with a prompt box and a beep. However, this works only if Outlook is running at the time of the reminder prompt. You can minimize Outlook so it's a button on the Windows taskbar. This way, you can work with other programs, but Outlook can still remind you of imminent appointments.

Block Your Time

If you're using Outlook on a network, use the **Show time as** drop-down list on the Appointment form to determine how others see the appointment on your calendar.

TASK 3

How to Set a Recurring Appointment

If your schedule is prone to recurring appointments, Outlook's Recurring Appointment features can help. For example, perhaps you have a weekly staff meeting. Rather than schedule each meeting separately, set the meeting as a recurring appointment. Outlook will automatically add the meeting to each week's calendar for you.

With the Recurring Appointment feature, you can indicate the recurrence pattern to tell Outlook how often the meeting occurs (Daily, Weekly, Monthly, or Yearly), which day of the week it falls on, and other related options.

Begin

1 Schedule a Recurring Appointment

To schedule a recurring appointment from the Calendar folder, first open the Appointment Recurrence dialog box. Display the **Actions** menu and select **New Recurring Appointment**.

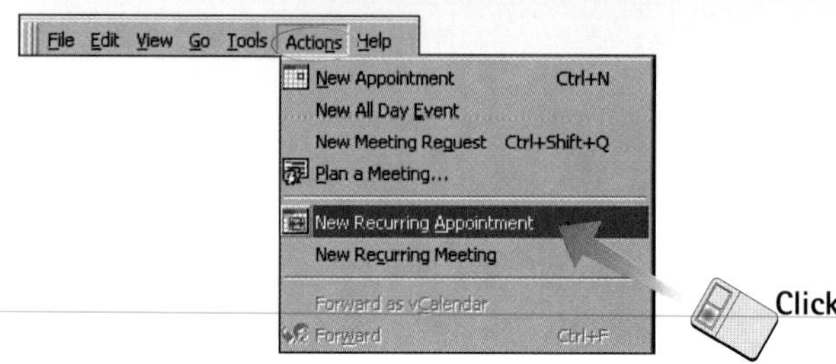

2 Enter a Time

Use the **Start**, **End**, and **Duration** drop-down lists to set the appointment start and end times and designate how long the appointment lasts.

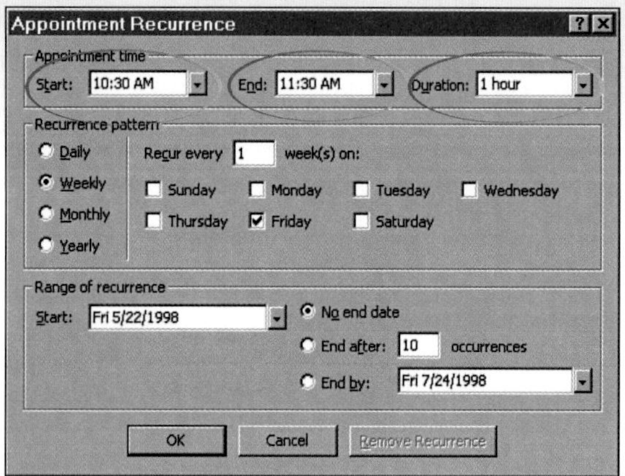

3 Enter a Recurrence Pattern

Under **Recurrence pattern**, select the frequency of the appointment and the day on which the appointment falls. Depending on your selection, the remaining recurrence options will vary. If you select **Weekly**, for example, you can specify every week or every other week.

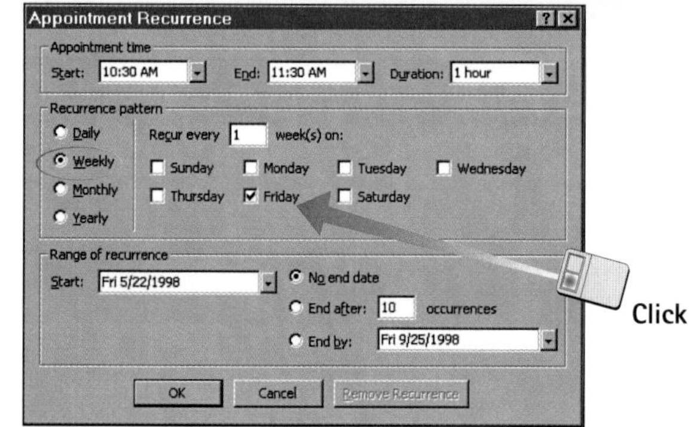

4 Range of Recurrence

Use the **Range of recurrence** options to enter any limits to the recurring appointment. You may need to schedule five dentist visits over the next five months, for example; after that, you no longer need the appointment. Use the **End after** option to set such a range.

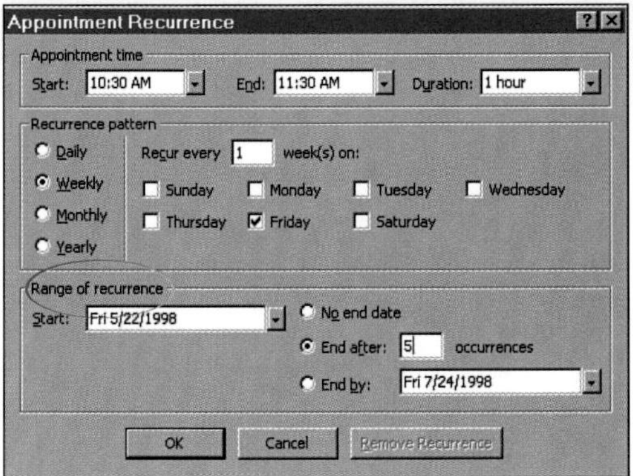

5 Fill In the Details

Click **OK** to close the Appointment Recurrence window and display the Appointment form. Now you can fill in any details about the appointment. Click the **Save and Close** button when you're finished.

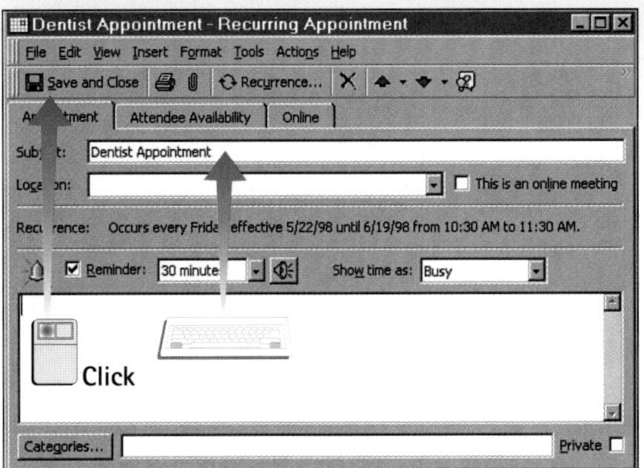

6 The Appointment Is Set

The recurring appointment now appears on your calendar with a double arrow icon to indicate it's a recurring appointment.

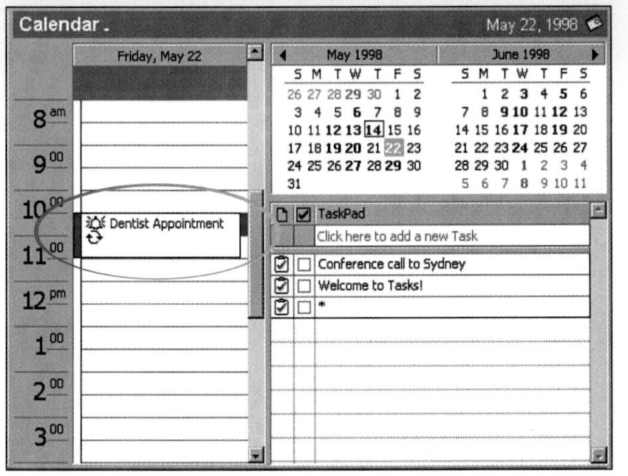

End

How-To Hints

Add a Reminder

Use the **Reminder** check box in the Appointment form to add a reminder alarm to your recurring appointment.

Edit Appointments

To edit a recurring appointment or any other appointment, double-click the appointment in your schedule. This opens the Appointment form where you can make any changes.

Other Recurring Ideas

You might also use recurring appointments to mark birthdays, anniversaries, and other special occasions on your calendar. This may keep you from forgetting them from year to year.

TASK 4

How to Schedule an Event

Not all items you add to your schedule are appointments. Some items are events. A calendar event is any activity that lasts the entire day, such as an anniversary, conference, trade show, or a birthday. Use events in your daily calendar to block off larger time slots than appointments. Events appear as banners at the top of the Daily schedule.

Begin

1 Open the Event Window

To schedule an event, open the **Actions** menu and choose **New All Day Event**. This opens the Event window.

2 Enter the Event Title

The Event window looks like the Appointment window. Fill in the details pertaining to the event. Start by filling in a title for the event in the **Subject** text box and entering a location in the **Location** text box.

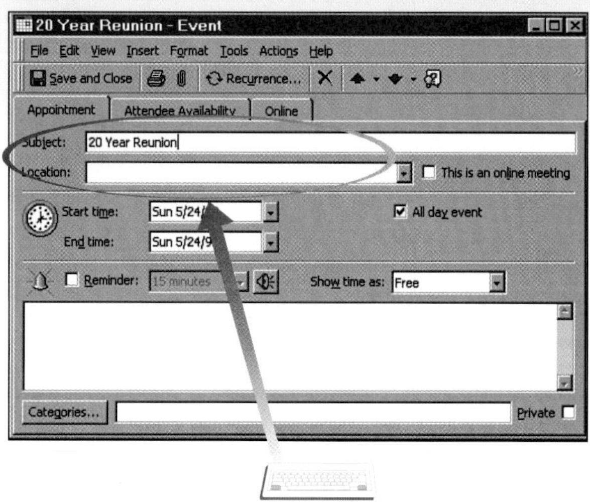

3 Enter Start and End Times

Use the **Start time** and **End time** drop-down lists to specify a time frame for the event.

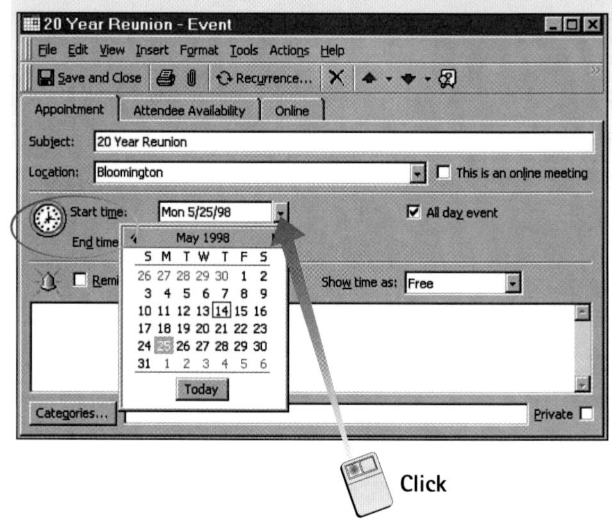

4 Set the All Day Event Option

Be sure to select the **All day event** check box (this option is what makes an event different from a regular appointment).

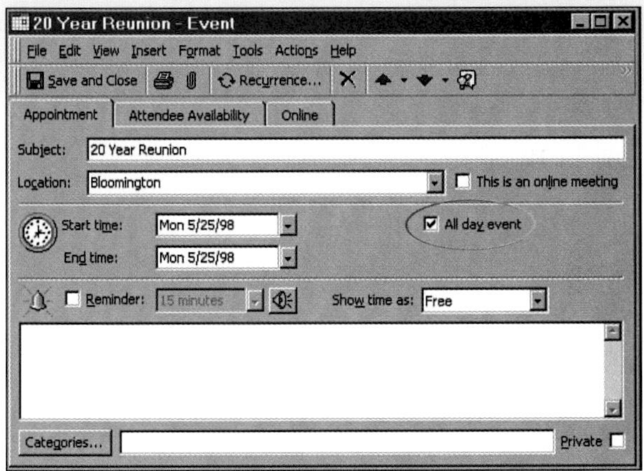

5 Save and Close

When you have finished filling in the Event details, click the **Save and Close** button to exit the Event window.

6 The Event Is Saved

The event now appears as a banner at the beginning of the day in the schedule pane (use Day view to see it).

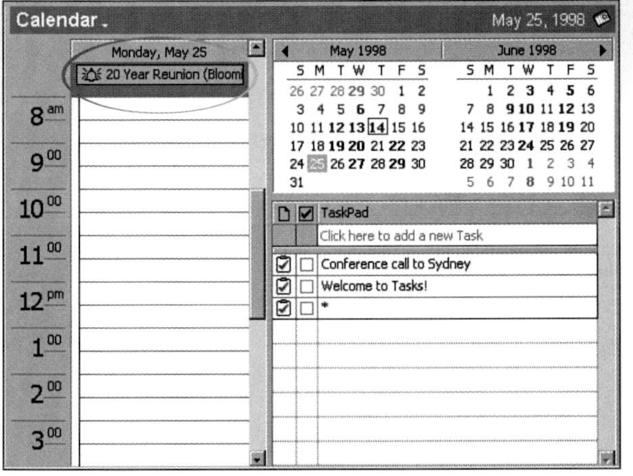

End

How-To Hints

Edit Events

To edit an event, double-click the event on your calendar. This reopens the Event form and you can make the necessary changes.

Event Reminder

Use the Reminder check box to assign a reminder alarm to alert you about the event.

Recurring Events

To schedule a recurring event on your calendar, click the **Recurrence** button on the Event window's toolbar.

TASK 5

How to Plan a Meeting

If you're using Outlook 98 on a network, you can utilize the Plan a Meeting feature to schedule meetings with others. The feature also lets you designate any resources needed for the meeting, such as a conference room or equipment.

The Plan a Meeting feature lets you invite attendees via email messages and track their responses. To get started, open the Calendar folder; click the **Calendar** icon on the Outlook Bar.

Begin

1 Open the Plan a Meeting Feature

From the Calendar folder, open the **Actions** menu and select **Plan a Meeting**. This opens the Plan a Meeting window.

2 Enter the Attendees

Enter the names of the attendees in the **All Attendees** list. Click **Type Attendee name Here** and enter the first person's name. Continue entering names on each line, as many attendees as you need.

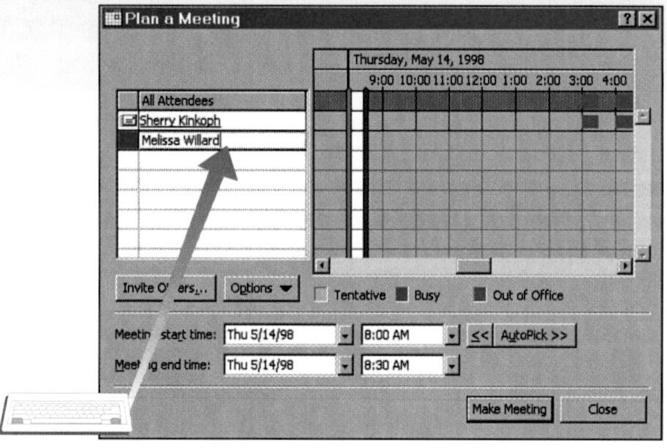

3 Set a Date

Click the **Meeting start time** drop-down arrows and choose a date and time for the meeting. Use the **Meeting end time** drop-down arrows to specify an end time for the meeting.

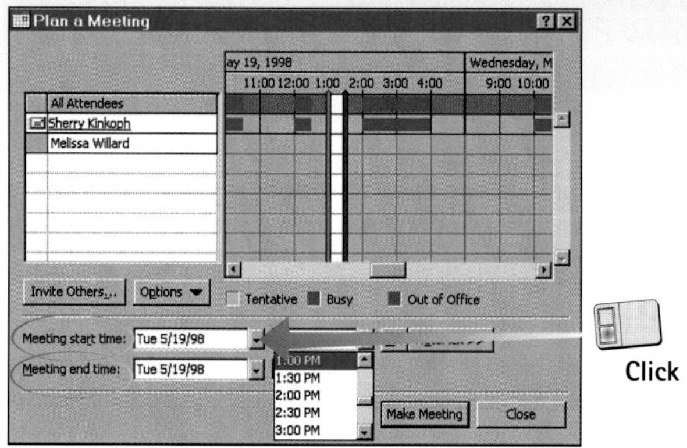

4 Or Drag a Time

Alternatively, you can drag the green bar in the schedule area to set a start time for the meeting, and drag the red bar to set an end time. (It's difficult to distinguish the colors on some monitors; just remember the bar to the left of the time increment starts the time and the right bar sets an end time.)

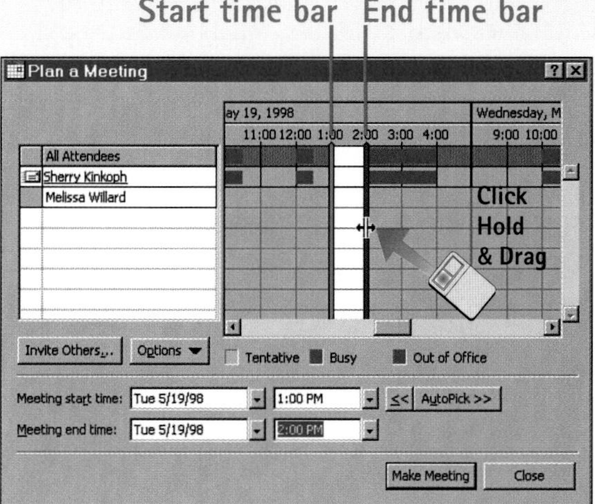

5 Fill In Meeting Details

When you have finished planning the meeting attendees and times, click the **Make Meeting** button. This opens the Meeting window, which resembles the Appointment form. Refine the meeting details as needed.

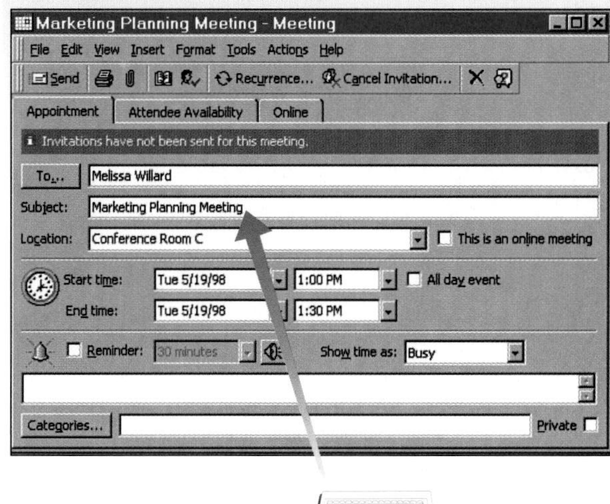

6 Send the Invitations

When you have finished filling out the meeting details, click **Send** to send email invitations to the attendees. Click the **Close** button to exit the Meeting window.

End

How-To Hints

Track Your Responses

To see how the attendees are responding to your meeting invitation, click the **Show attendee status** option in the **Attendee Availability** tab of the Meeting window.

TASK 6

How to Create a New Task

Use Outlook's Tasks folder to keep track of things you need to do, such as steps for completing a project or arranging an event. Tasks can be as complex as a year-long project or as simple as a shopping list you need to fill in on the way home. A task list can include things such as writing a letter, making a phone call, or distributing a memo.

After you create a task list, you can keep track of the tasks and check them off as you complete them. You can choose to view your task list in the Tasks folder or in the Calendar folder. To open the Tasks folder, click the **Tasks** icon in the Outlook Bar.

Begin

1 Open the Task Dialog Box

From the Tasks folder, open the **Actions** menu and select **New Task**, or click the **New Task** button on the toolbar.

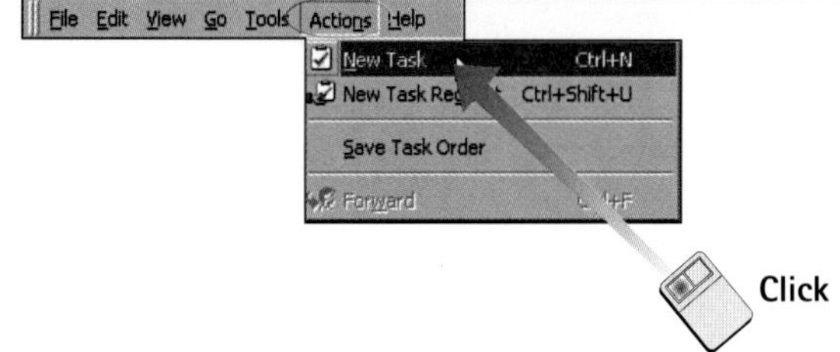

2 Enter a Title

The Task window, like the Appointment window, is a form you can fill out detailing the task. With the **Task** tab displayed, enter the subject or title of the task in the **Subject** text box.

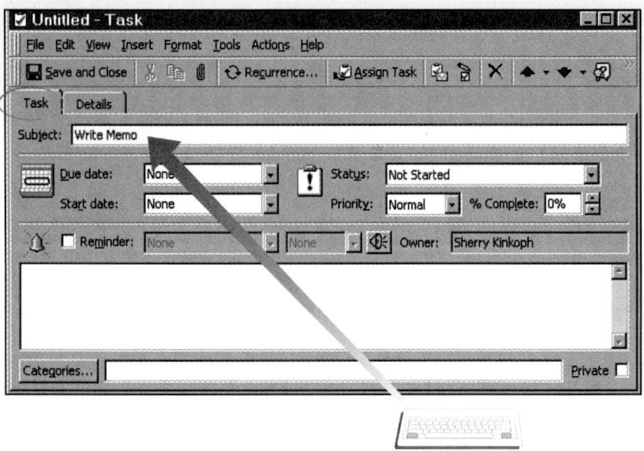

3 Enter a Due Date

If the task has a due date, click the **Due date** drop-down arrow and choose a due date from the calendar. (You can also enter a start date, if needed.)

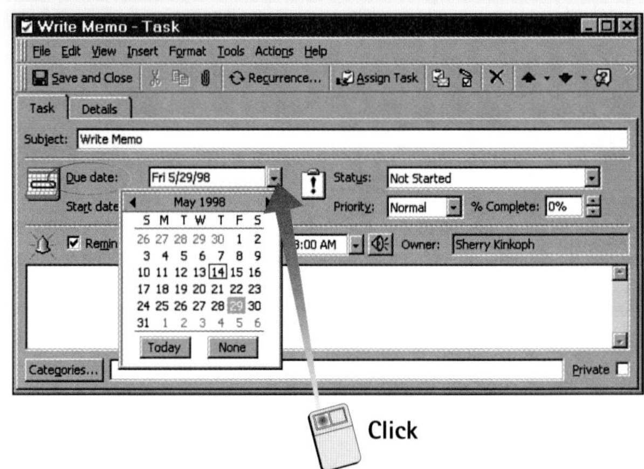

4 Select a Status Setting

Use the **Status** drop-down list to select a status setting for the project: **Not Started**, **In Progress**, **Completed**, **Waiting on someone else**, or **Deferred**. As you manage your task list, you can update the status as needed.

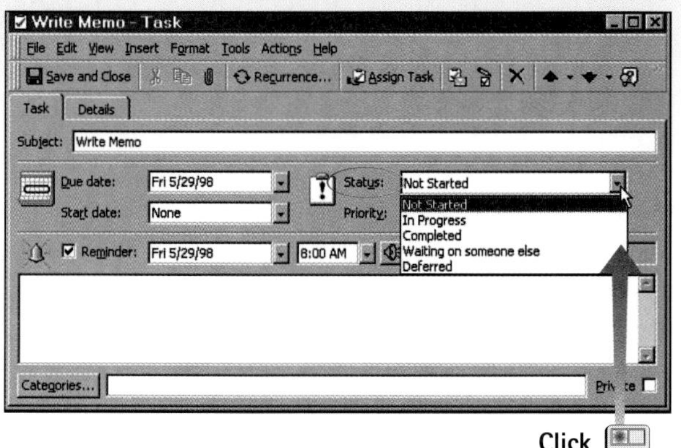

5 Set a Priority

Use the **Priority** drop-down list to give the task a priority level: **Normal**, **Low**, or **High**. Use the **% Complete** box to specify a percentage of completeness, if needed.

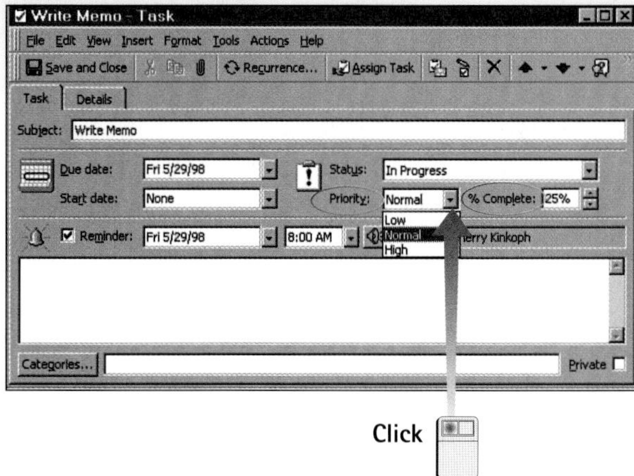

6 Enter Notes

Use the **Notes** box to enter any notes about the task. When you have finished filling out the Task form, click the **Save and Close** button. The task is now added to your Tasks folder's task list, as shown in this figure.

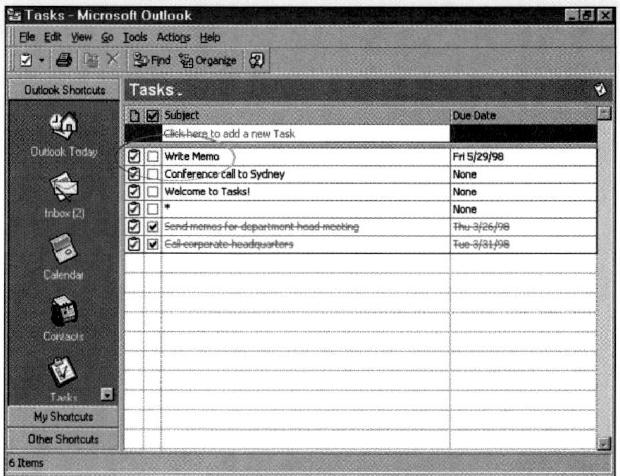

End

How-To Hints

Manage Tasks

To edit a task, double-click the task in the task list. To mark a task as complete, right-click the task and choose **Mark Complete**. To delete a task, right-click and choose **Delete**.

Record Statistics

To record statistics about a task, such as billable time, contacts, or mileage, double-click the task and display the **Details** tab of the Task form.

Work with the TaskPad

The TaskPad that appears in Calendar shows your current tasks. To quickly open a task from the TaskPad, double-click the task name.

TASK 7

How to Create a New Contact

Use Outlook's Contacts folder to build a database of people you contact the most. A contact can be any person you communicate with, such as a coworker, relative, vendor, or client. You can enter all kinds of information about a contact, including addresses, phone numbers, email addresses, birthdays, and Web pages.

After you enter a contact, you will always have access to information about that person. You can quickly fire off an email message, for example, or have your modem dial the phone number for you. To begin entering contacts, first open the Contacts folder; click the **Contacts** icon on the Outlook Bar.

Begin

1 Open the Contact Form

From the Contacts folder, open the **Actions** menu and select **New Contact**, or click the **New Contact** button on the toolbar. This opens the Contact window.

2 Use the General Tab

From the **General** tab in the Contact form, you can begin filling in information about the contact. Click inside each text box and fill in the appropriate information. To move from field to field, press Tab.

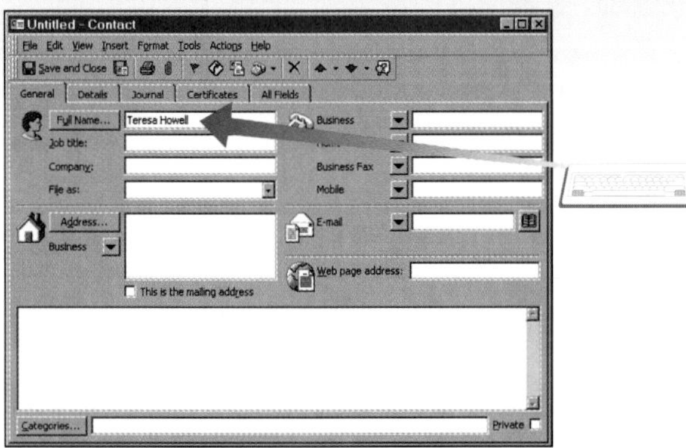

3 The File As List

Click the **File as** drop-down arrow and choose how you want to file your contact—by last name or first name. The default setting is to file the contacts by last name first.

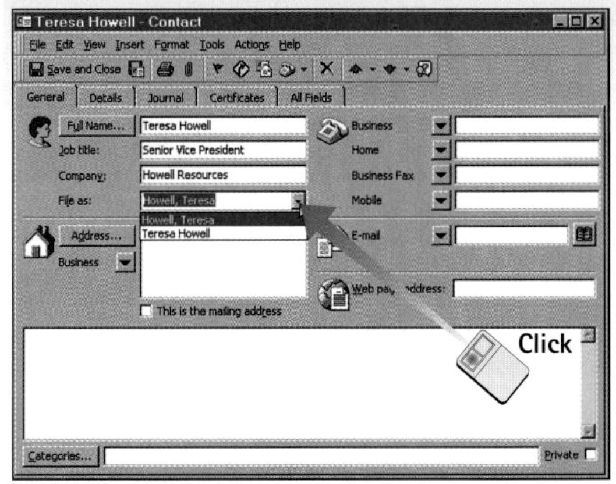

4 Enter Phone Numbers

Outlook gives you the option of entering numerous phone numbers for the contact, including business and home numbers, fax numbers, and cell phone numbers.

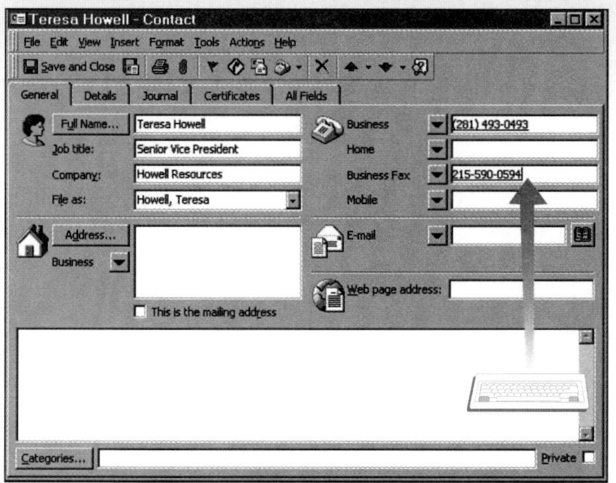

5 Enter an Address

Enter the contact's address in the **Address** box. Use the drop-down arrow to designate a **Business**, **Home**, or **Other** address. (Use the **Address** button to enter address information in separate fields.)

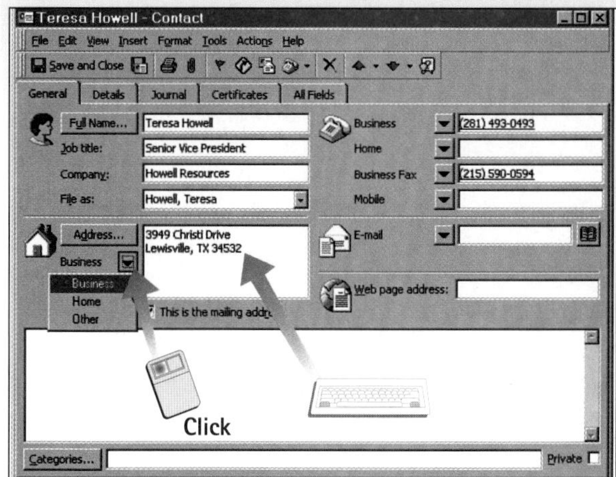

6 Save the Contact

After filling out all the pertinent information (don't forget to enter an email address), click the **Save and Close** button, and the contact is added to your database. To keep entering more contacts, click the **Save and New** button to open another Contact form.

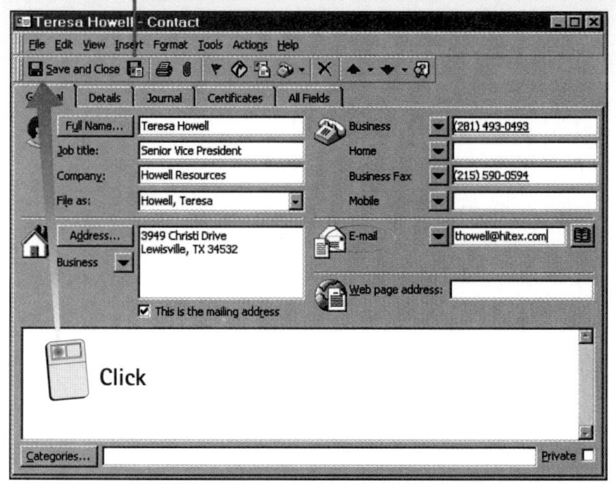

End

How-To Hints

More Details

Use the **Details** tab in the Contact form to enter information such as spouse name, birthdays, anniversary, and other details.

Edit Contacts

To edit a contact, double-click the contact's name in the Contacts folder. This reopens the Contact form where you can make changes to the data.

TASK 8

How to Import Contact Data

If you already have a contacts database in another program, whether it's an Office program such as Excel or Access, or a non-Microsoft program such as Lotus Organizer, you can import the database into Outlook. Use Outlook's Import and Export Wizard to walk you through the steps.

Begin

1 Open Import and Export Wizard

Open the **File** menu and select **Import and Export**.

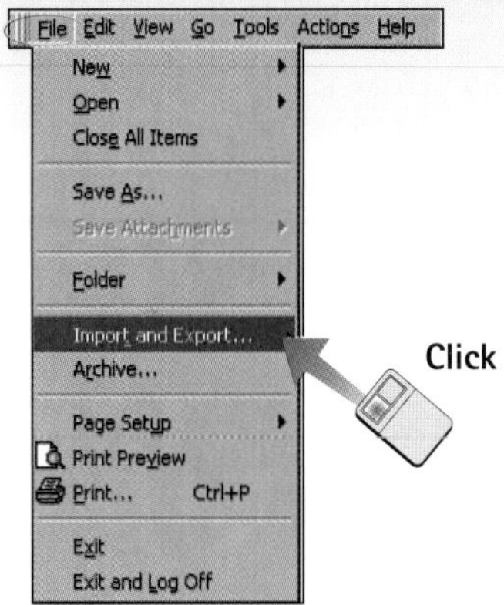

2 Choose an Action

In the first Wizard dialog box, choose an import or export action. Because you are importing addresses, choose **Import from another program or file**, and then click **Next** to continue.

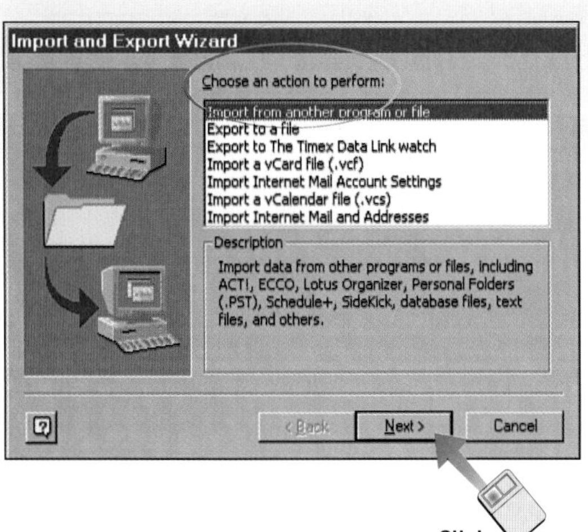

3 Choose a File Type

In the next Wizard dialog box, choose the type of address file you want to import. Scroll through the list and make your selection, and then click **Next**.

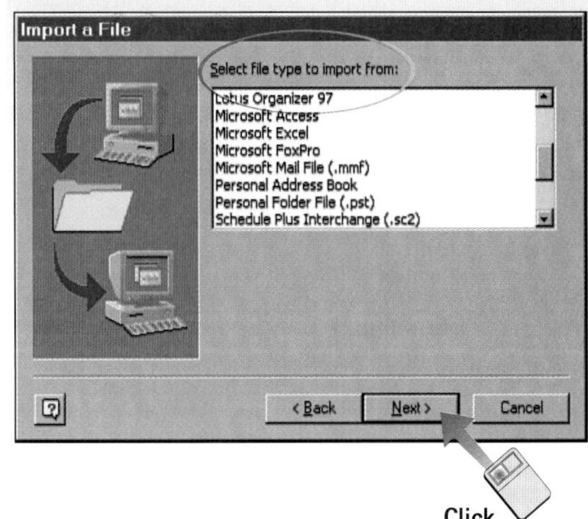

4 Locate the File

If you know the path of the file you want to import, type it into the text box. If you don't know for sure, use the **Browse** button to locate the exact file to import. Make your selection and click **Next**.

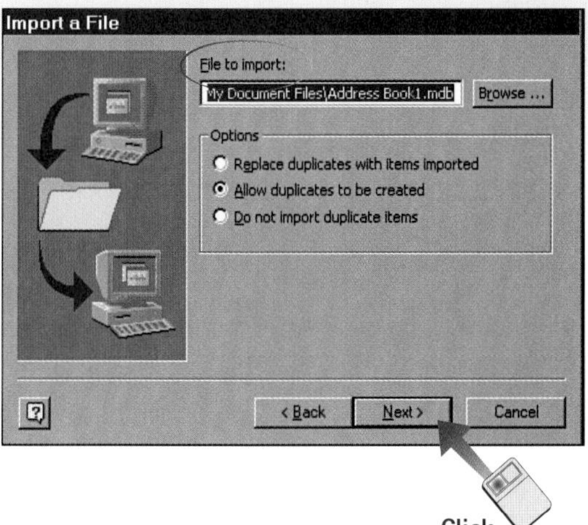

5 Choose a Destination Folder

Select a destination folder to hold the imported data. If you're importing addresses, consider placing them in the Contacts folder. Click **Next** to continue.

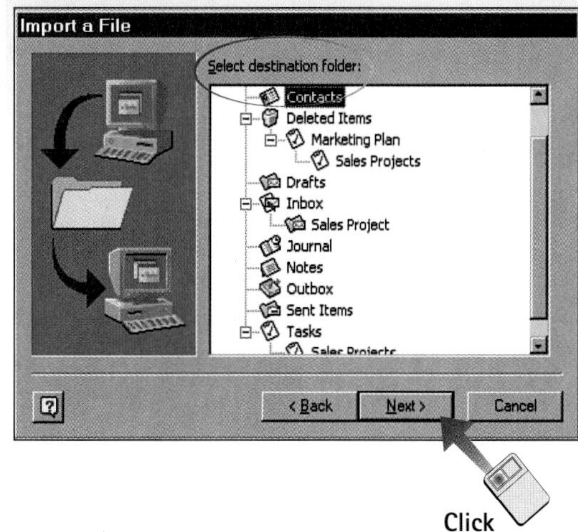

6 Select an Import Action

In the final Wizard box, select the import action to perform, and then click **Finish**. Outlook imports your address data as specified.

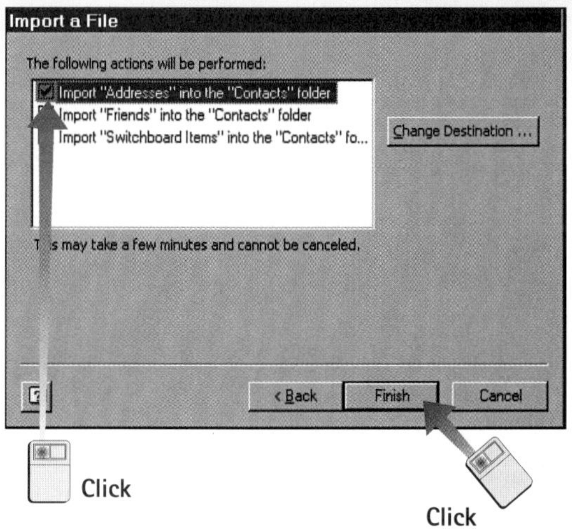

End

How-To Hints

Copy and Paste Outlook Items

Not only can you import and export with Outlook 98, you can also copy and paste Outlook items among the Office programs using the Copy and Paste commands. To learn more about sharing data among programs, see Chapter 17, "How to Integrate Office Applications."

TASK 9

How to Phone a Contact

If your computer has a modem, you can use it to dial the phone numbers of contacts in your Contacts list. Of course, after the number is dialed, you will have to pick up the receiver to start talking. However, rather than waste time trying to find a phone number or memorizing it yourself, let Outlook take care of it.

Begin

1 Select the Contact

From the Contacts folder, select the contact you want to call.

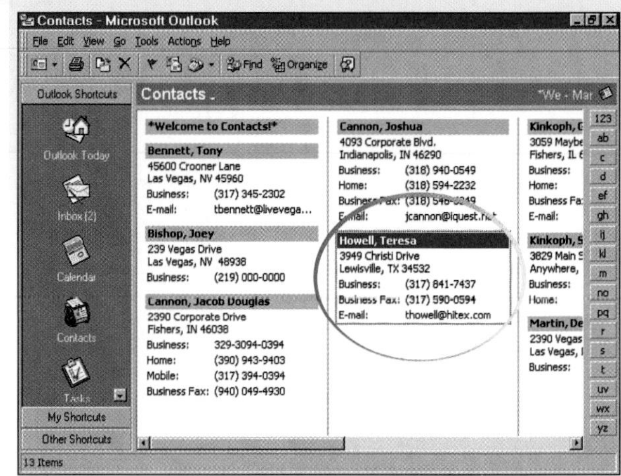

2 Use AutoDialer

Click the **AutoDialer** button on the Outlook toolbar to open the New Call dialog box.

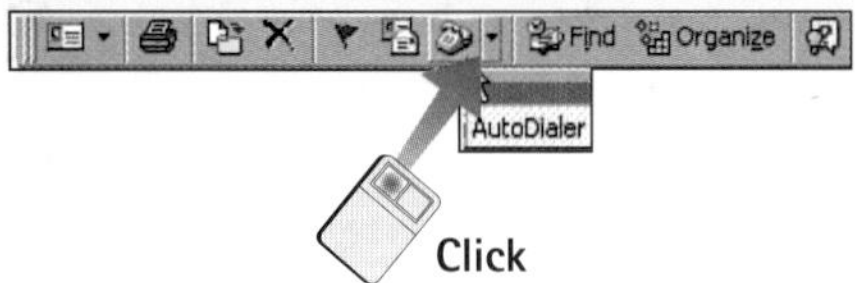

3 Choose the Number

Click the **Number** drop-down arrow and select which number you want to dial (such as business, home, or mobile).

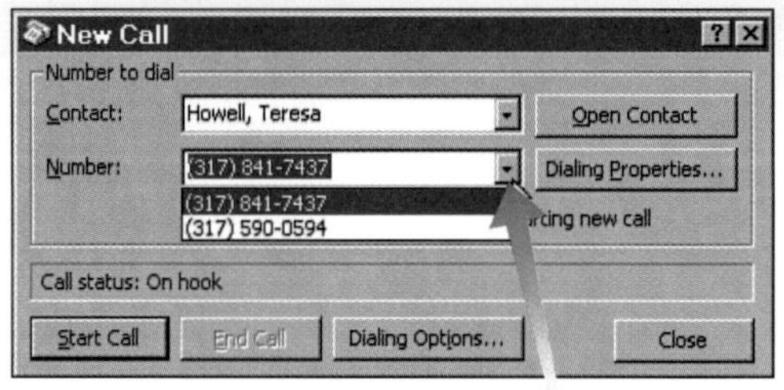

Click

4 Dial the Number

Click the **Start Call** button to have your modem dial the number.

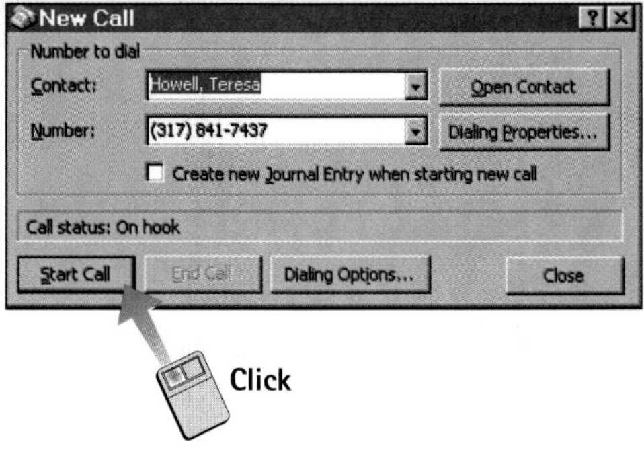

5 Pick Up Prompt

When prompted, pick up the receiver and click **Talk** to begin talking to the contact.

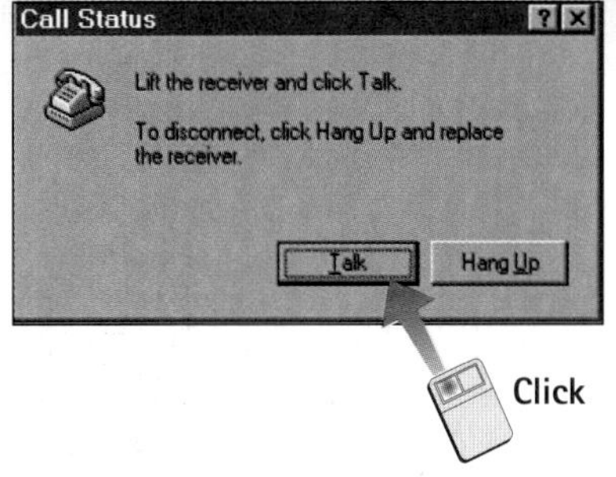

6 End the Call

When you're finished with the call, click **End Call**, and then click **Close** to close the dialog box.

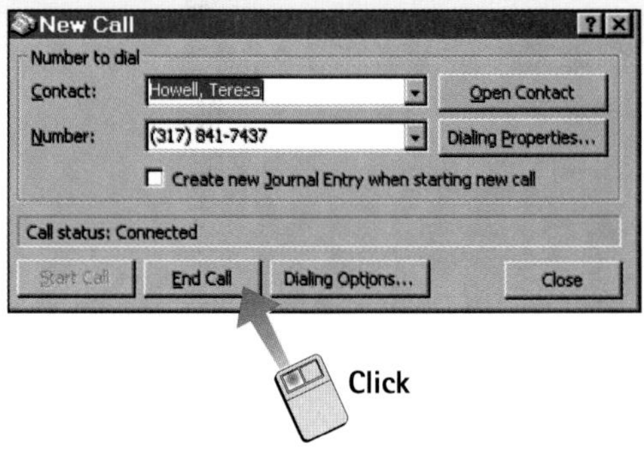

End

How-To Hints

Create a Journal Entry

To help you track your calls, use Outlook's Journal feature to create a journal entry that documents the call. Before dialing the number, click the **Create new Journal Entry when starting new call** check box.

TASK 10

How to Create a Journal Entry

Outlook's Journal feature can help you track chronological events, such as when you completed a job-related task or placed a call. Logging journal entries can help you track past happenings, but only if you're consistent in logging entries. Outlook can help by automatically logging entries for email messages, faxes, meeting requests, and tasks you assign to others. One of the most useful aspects of the Journal is to log phone calls you make, especially when you need to note details about conversations.

In this task, you will learn how to manually create a Journal entry. Open the Journal folder by clicking the **Journal** icon on the Outlook Bar.

Begin

1 Start a Journal Entry

To create a manual entry, open the **Actions** menu and choose **New Journal Entry** or click the **New Journal** button on the toolbar. This opens the Journal Entry window.

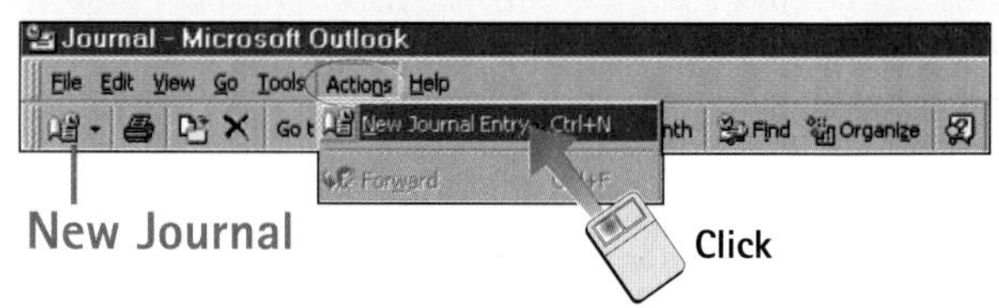

2 Fill In the Form

Like the other windows used in Outlook, the Journal Entry window acts like a form; it has fields you can to fill in with information about the entry. Start by clicking in the **Subject** text box and entering a title for the entry.

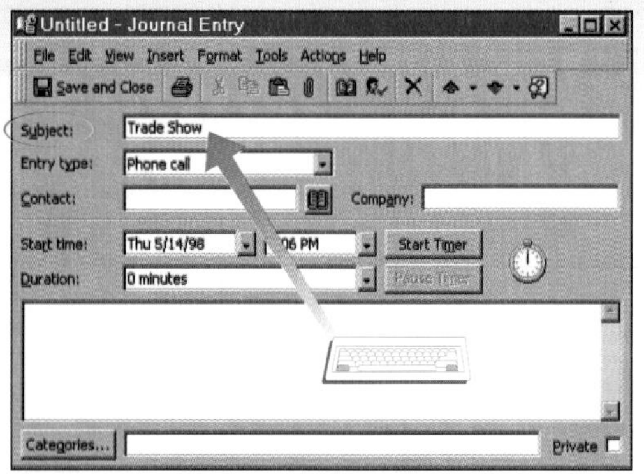

3 Select the Entry Type

Click the **Entry type** drop-down arrow and choose an entry type from the list, such as **Phone call**.

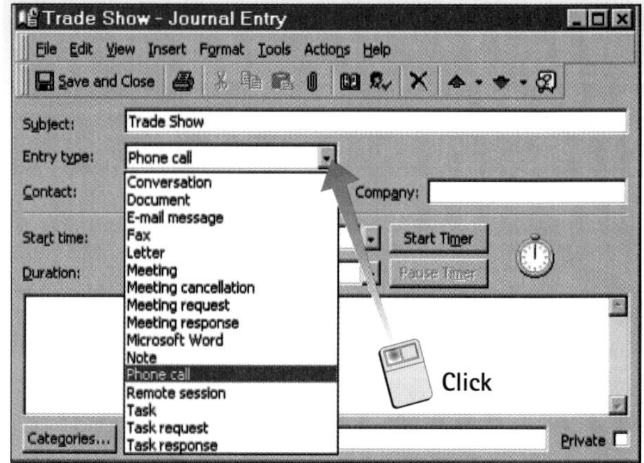

4 Enter the Contact

If the entry is about a particular contact or company, enter the names in the **Contact** and **Company** text boxes.

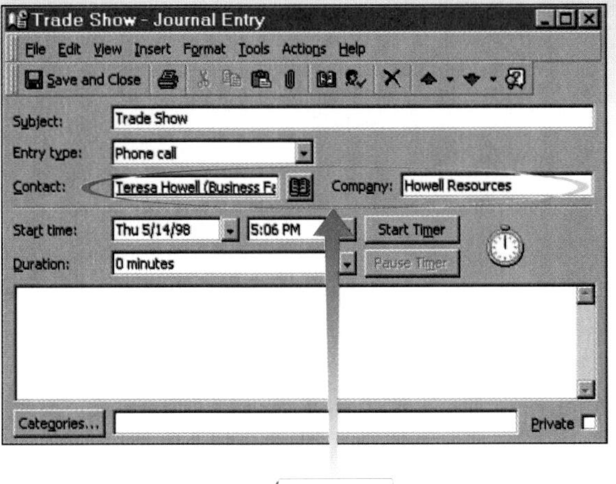

5 Record the Time

Use the **Duration** drop-down list to specify the amount of time spent on the journal activity. To let Outlook track the time (logging a phone call), click the **Start Timer** button.

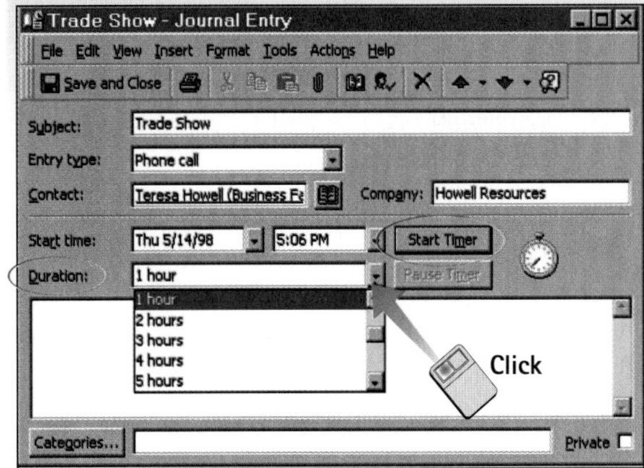

6 Finish Details and Exit

Use the bottom text box to enter notes about the activity (such as logging notes about a telephone conversation). Click **Save and Close** to exit the Journal form and add it to the Journal timeline, as shown in this figure.

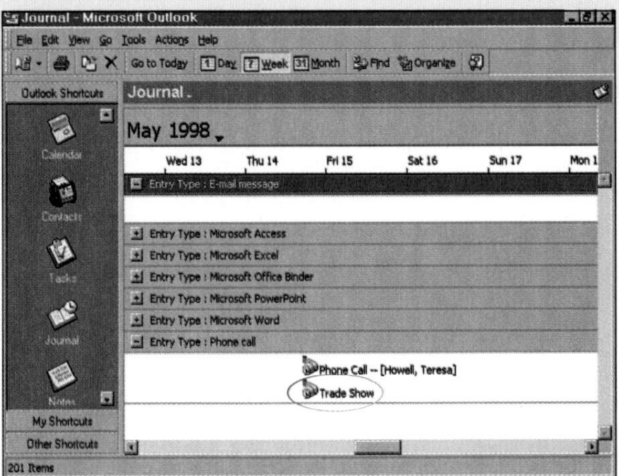

End

How-To Hints

Automatic Entries

To set Outlook to automatically log activities for you, open the **Tools** menu and select **Options**. Select the **Preferences** tab, click the **Journal Options** button, and select which types of items to record in your Journal. Click **OK** twice to exit.

Change Views

Be sure to check out the different view options for viewing journal entries. Click the **Day**, **Week**, or **Month** buttons on the toolbar and choose a different view of the Journal timeline.

TASK 11

How to Create a Note

Outlook's Notes feature is the electronic version of sticky notes, those yellow notes you stick onto your desk or computer to remind you of things. Use Outlook's Notes to do the same. You can attach a note to a contact to remind you to call him, or you can drag a note onto the Windows desktop to remind you of an important task. You can also drag notes into other Office 97 programs.

To work with Outlook notes, open the Notes folder and click the **Notes** icon on the Outlook Bar.

Begin

1 Start a New Note

To create a note, open the **Actions** menu and select **New Note**, or click the **New Note** button on the toolbar. This opens a small, yellow note box.

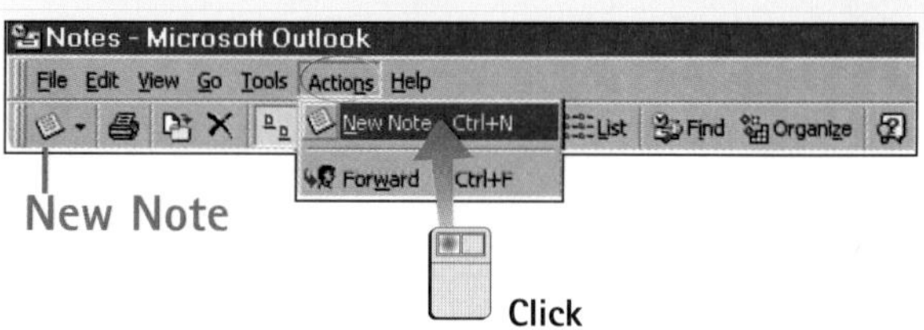

2 Enter Note Text

Notice the note already has the current date and time entered. Enter your note text.

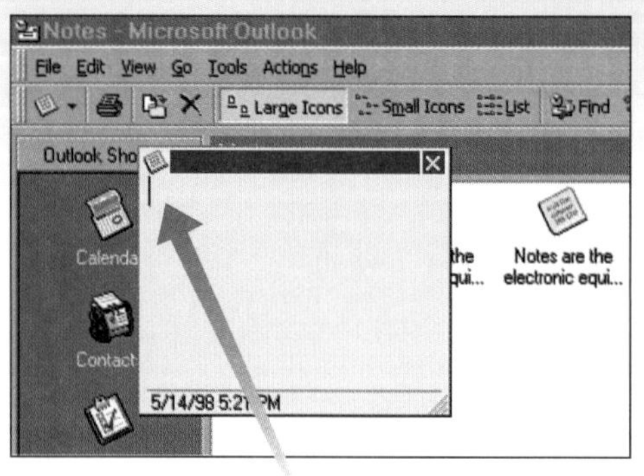

3 Resize the Note

Drag any edge of the note to resize it. When you hover your mouse pointer over an edge, it becomes a two-sided arrow. Click and drag the edge to resize the note box.

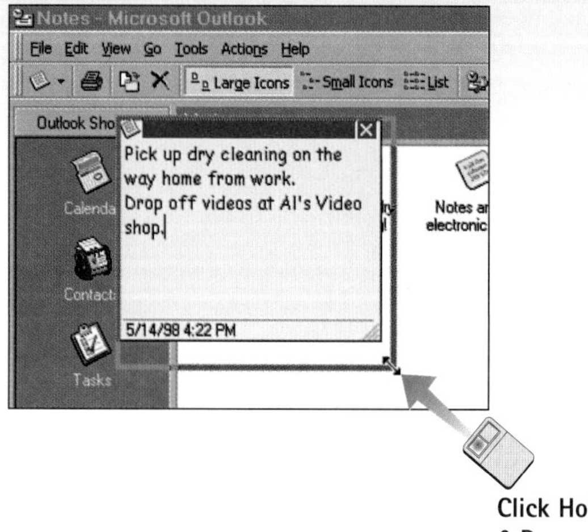

4 Change the Note Color

If you prefer a color other than the default yellow, click the upper-left icon in the note and select **Color**, then choose another color to use.

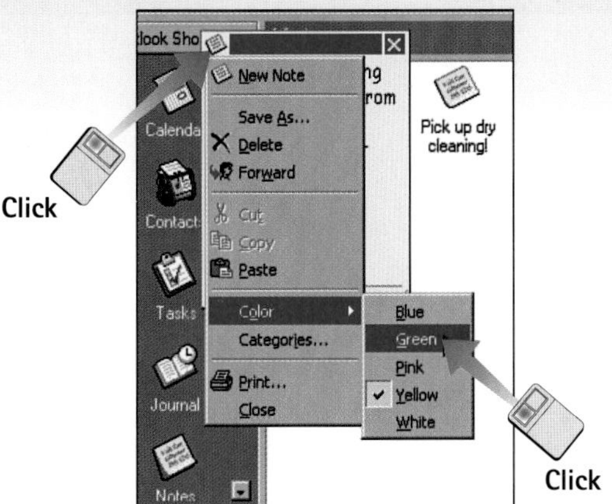

5 Close the Note

To close a note, click anywhere outside the note, or click the note's **Close** button. To drag a note elsewhere on the desktop, click and drag the note's blue bar (located at the top of the note box).

End

How-To Hints

Save as a File

You can save a note as a file. Click the icon in the upper-left corner of the note and select **Save As**. Assign a name to the note and designate which folder to save it in, and then click **Save**.

Print a Note

To print a note, first click the icon in the upper-left corner of the note and select **Print**. This opens the Print dialog box where you can change any print settings before printing.

TASK 12

How to Create a New Folder

Outlook saves items you create in folders and subfolders. Email messages are saved in the Inbox folder, notes are saved in the Notes folder, and so forth. When managing the many items you create, you may want to organize items into different folders. For example, you may want to store all the Outlook items related to a particular project in one folder. You can easily create new folders and move Outlook items into them as needed.

Begin

1 Open the Folder List

To see all the available folders that come with Outlook, open the Folder List. Click the **Folder name** drop-down arrow, and then click the **Pushpin** icon in the upper-right corner of the list to keep the list open onscreen.

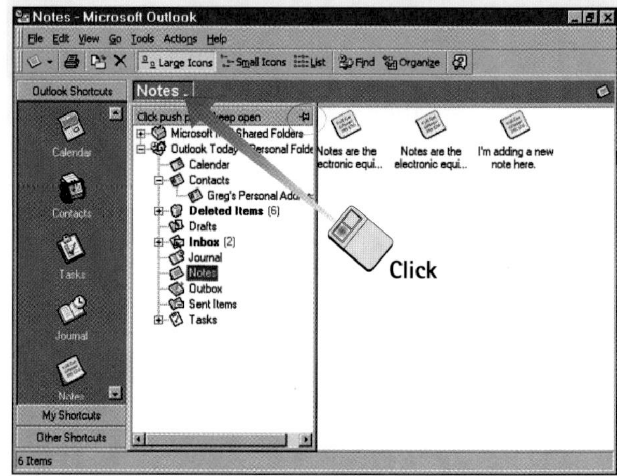

2 Choose a Parent Folder

To create a new subfolder, first select the parent folder (the folder to hold the subfolder). You may want a Sales Project folder, for example, to be stored in the Tasks folder. First, select the **Tasks** folder.

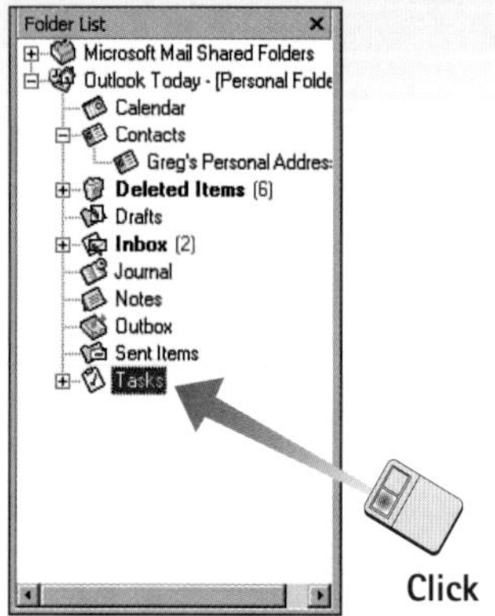

3 Open the Create New Folder Box

Right-click the folder to display a shortcut menu, and then select **New Folder**. This opens the Create New Folder dialog box.

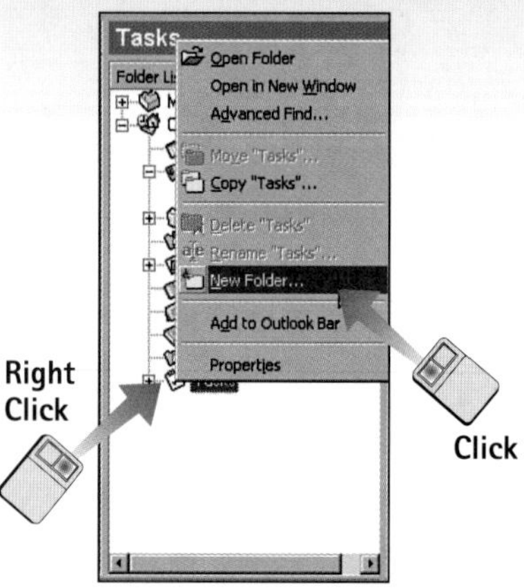

4 Enter a Folder Name

Enter a name for the new folder in the **Name** box.

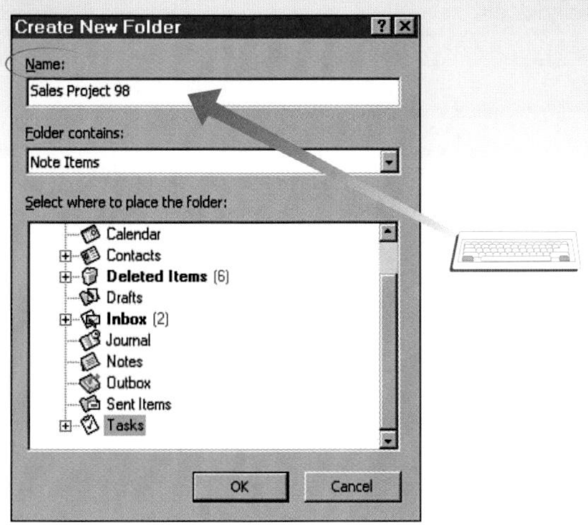

5 Select Items

Choose which items you want to store in the folder using the **Folder contains** drop-down list. Click **OK** to exit the dialog box and create the folder.

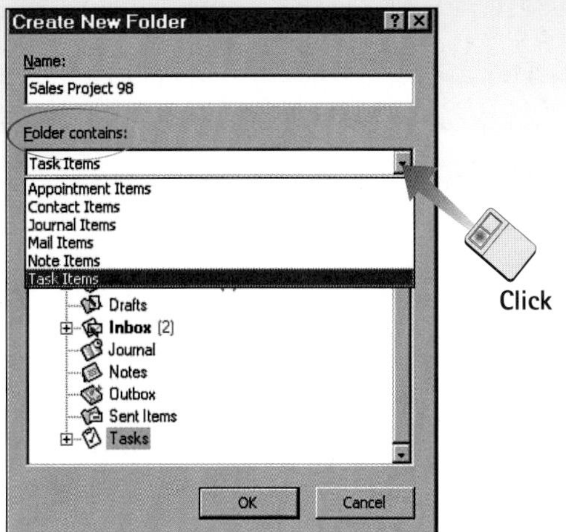

6 The Folder Is Saved

A prompt box asks if you want to save the folder as an icon on the Outlook Bar. Click **No**. The folder name is now added to the Folder List.

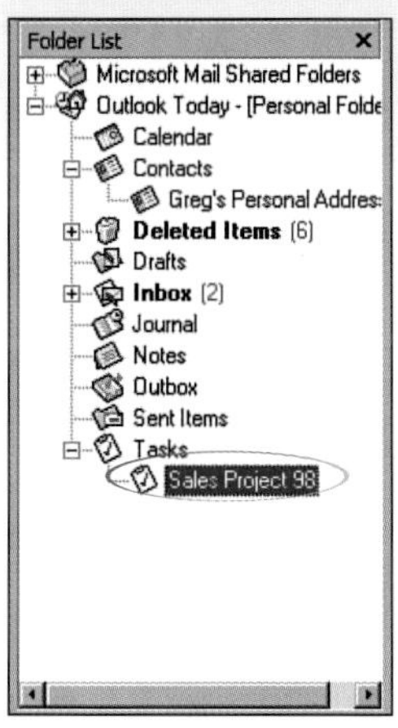

End

How-To Hints

How Do I Move Items to Folders?

Check out Task 13, "How to Move Items to Folders," to learn how to move items between folders.

Subfolders in Subfolders

You can create subfolders within subfolders. You might have a subfolder in the Inbox folder named **Vendor Mail**, for example, and additional folders within that folder named **Suppliers** and **Printers**.

TASK 13

How to Move Items to Folders

After you create your own folders, you will want to move Outlook items into the folders. You may want to keep all your email correspondence from a particular client in one folder, for example, so you can easily retrieve old messages. Or you might want to keep personal messages separate from business messages. Outlook makes it easy to move items from one folder to another.

Begin

1 Open the Folder List

To see your folders, open the Folder List. Click the **Folder name** drop-down arrow, or open the **View** menu and choose **Folder List**.

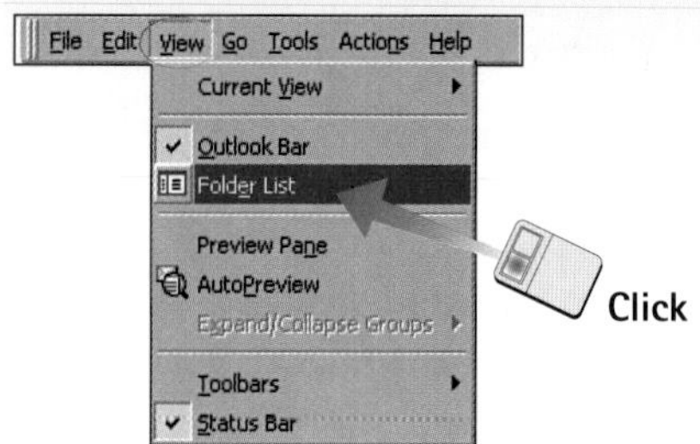

2 Select the Item

Open the folder containing the item you want to move and select the item.

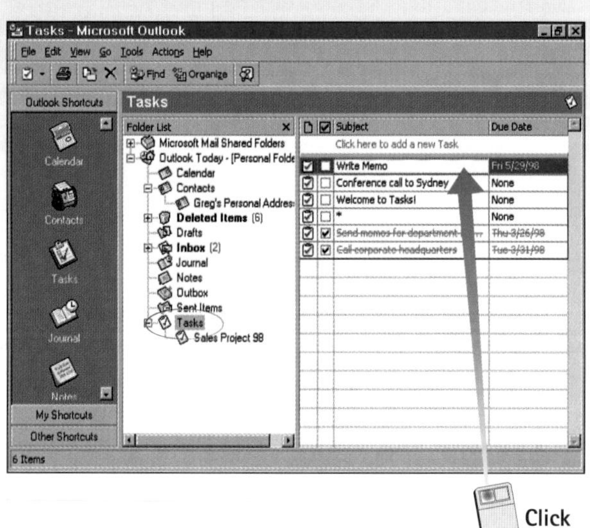

3 Use the Move Command

Open the **Edit** menu and select the **Move to Folder** command. This opens the Move Items dialog box.

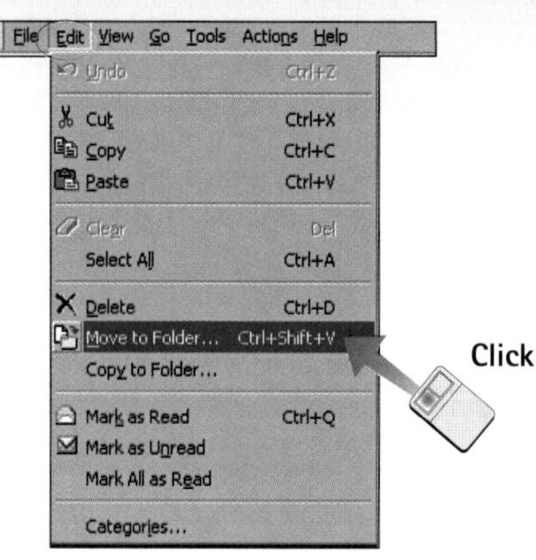

4 Choose a Folder

Choose the folder where you want to move the selected item and click **OK**.

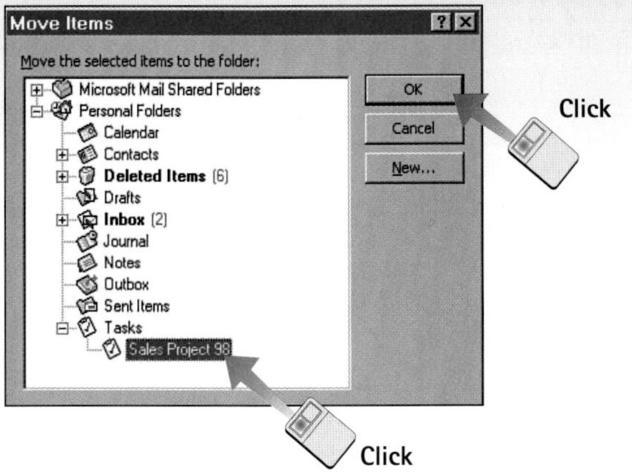

5 Or Use Click and Drag

Another method of moving items among folders is to click and drag them. Select the item you want to move, and then hold down the left mouse button and drag the item to the new folder name.

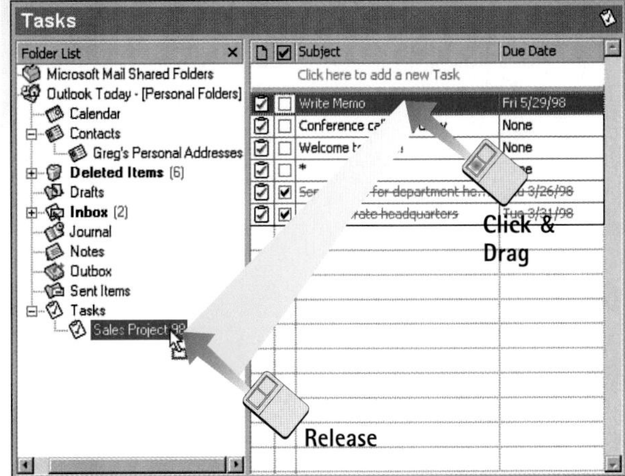

End

How-To Hints

Drag and Drop

You can also drag and drop items from open folders into any folder on the Outlook Bar. Select the item and drag and drop it into the appropriate folder.

TASK 14

How to Delete Items

Items you delete in Outlook don't disappear entirely. Instead, they're held in Outlook's Deleted Items folder. To truly delete them, you must empty the folder. This works the same as the Windows Recycle Bin. Items you delete from your Windows desktop are held in the Recycle Bin until you remove them.

It's a good idea to clear your Deleted Items folder before exiting Outlook. If you forget, the items tend to stack up and take up space on your hard drive.

Begin

1 Open the Deleted Items Folder

To empty your deleted items, first open the Deleted Items folder. Click its icon on the Outlook Bar. Use the Scroll arrow button to locate the icon.

2 Choose the Items to Delete

To permanently erase an Outlook item from your system, select the item from the Deleted Items folder. To select more than one item, hold down the Ctrl key while clicking items.

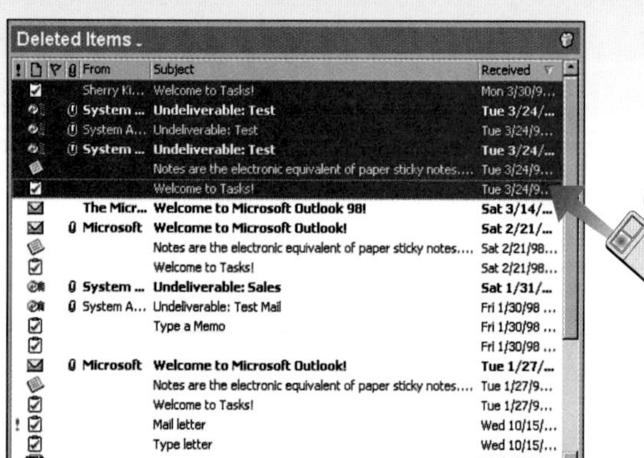

3 Click the Delete Button

Click the **Delete** button on the Outlook toolbar.

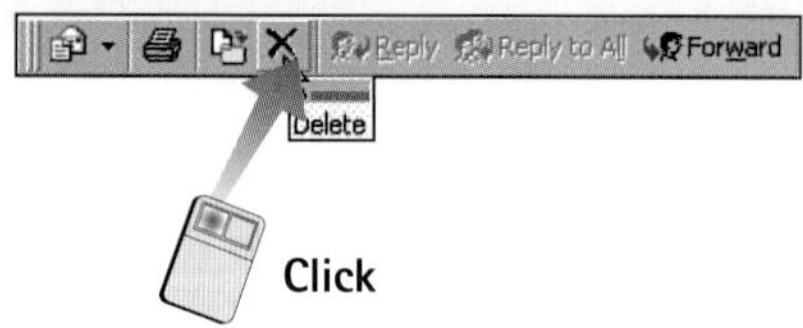

4 Confirm the Deletion

A confirmation box appears asking you if you really want to delete the item. Click **Yes**.

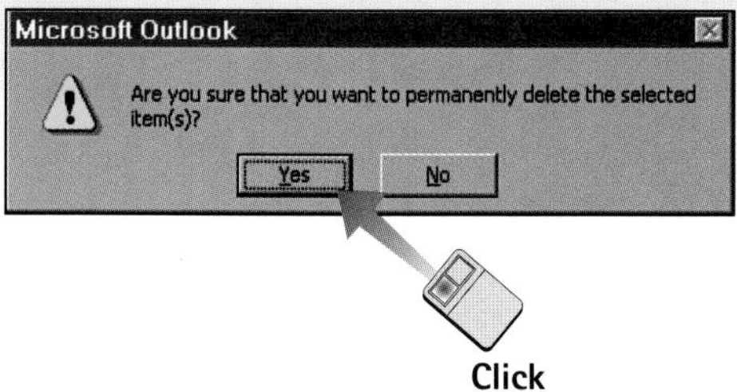

5 Undelete Items

If you have sent Outlook items to the Deleted Items folder but change your mind about deleting them, you can retrieve them. Select the item and drag it to any folder in the Outlook bar.

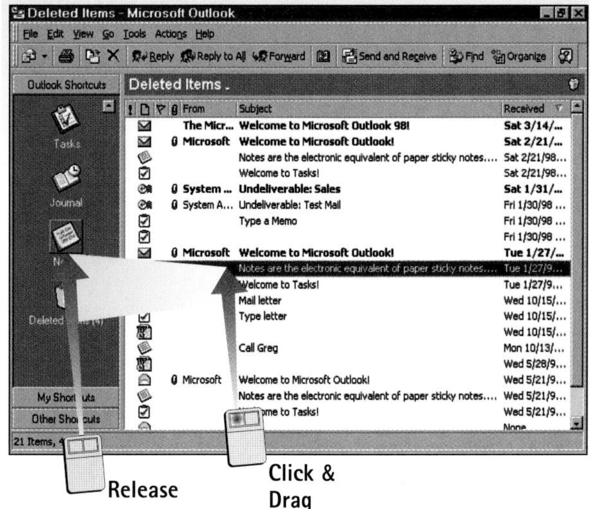

End

How-To Hints

Automatic Delete

You can set up Outlook so it automatically deletes items from the Deleted Items folder whenever you exit the program. Open the **Tools** menu and select **Options**. Display the **Other** tab and select the **Empty the Deleted Items Folder upon exiting** option and click **OK**.

Task

CHAPTER 14

How to Use Outlook's Email Features

Outlook's desktop management applications wouldn't be complete without messaging capabilities. Outlook is designed to be your personal message center, whether you're *emailing* colleagues on a corporate intranet or users on the global Internet. Outlook can monitor multiple mail sources and email accounts. You can collect email messages from commercial services, such as America Online, CompuServe, and your local *Internet service provider*, or internal post offices, such as Lotus Notes or Cc:Mail.

Outlook's email features include composing and sending messages, forwarding messages, and attaching files. Messages you send or receive are saved in folders, and you can easily organize email items into specific folders. You can keep all your business correspondence, for example, in a separate folder from your personal correspondence. The email features are also integrated with the other Outlook components. You can record your email messages, for instance, as Journal entries, or turn a message into a contact in your Contacts database.

In this chapter, you learn how to work with the basic email features.

TASK 1

How to Compose and Send a Message

Providing you have the correct email address, you can use Outlook to send a message to anyone with an email account. Like the other Outlook components, the email portion features a message form you can fill out. If you know the recipient uses Outlook, too, you can even add formatting to your message.

Before you can use Outlook's email options, however, you must have a modem and an email account, whether through a service provider, a network connection, or a commercial service. The easiest way to track and send messages is through the Inbox folder; click the **Inbox** icon on the Outlook Bar to open the folder.

Begin

1 Open a New Message Form

From the Outlook Inbox folder, open the **Actions** menu and select **New Mail Message**, or click the **New Mail Message** button on the *toolbar*. This opens the Message window.

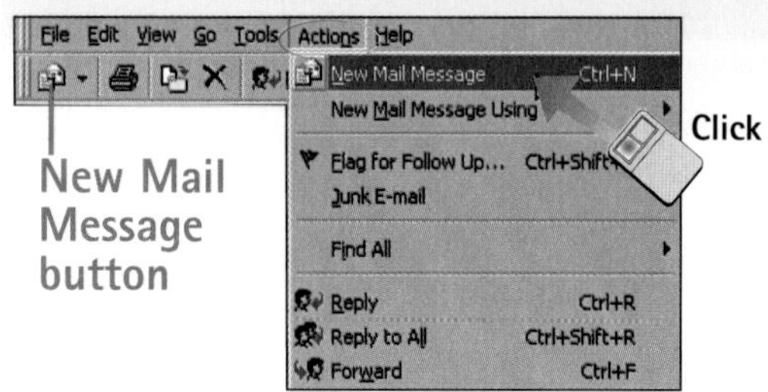

2 Enter a Recipient Address

The Message window resembles a form. Fill out the form, using the Tab key to move from field to field. To begin, click inside the **To** text box and type the name of the recipient.

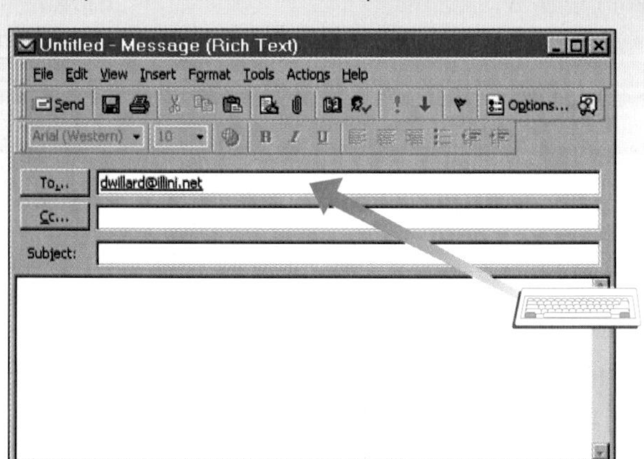

3 Carbon Copy

If you want to send the message to multiple recipients, enter the other recipients' addresses in the **Cc** text box.

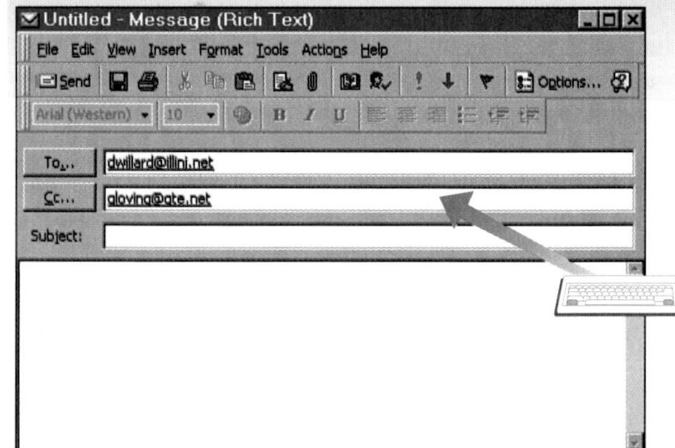

4 Enter the Subject

Click inside the **Subject** text box and enter a title or phrase to identify the content or purpose of your message.

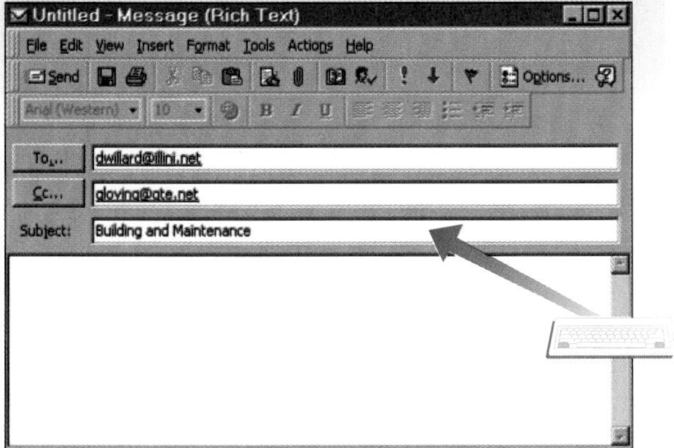

5 Type Your Message

Click inside the message box and type your message text. Outlook automatically wraps the text for you. Use the Delete and Backspace keys to fix mistakes, just as you would in a Word document.

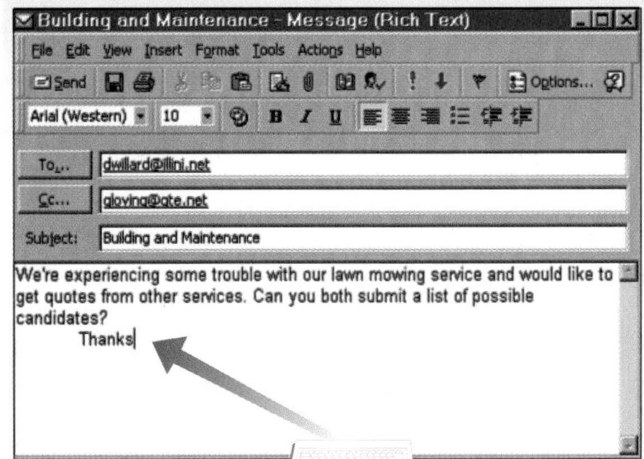

6 Send the Message

To send the message, click the **Send** button. If you're offline (not connected to the *Internet* or network) the message waits in the Outbox until the next time you go online to collect your mail.

End

How-To Hints

Spell Check

You can spell check your email messages before sending them. Open the **Tools** menu and select **Spelling**.

Message Options

Use Outlook's **Options** button on the Message form's toolbar to assign options such as priority levels or tracking options. Be sure to check out the variety of available options.

Use the Address Book

In addition to directly typing an email address, you can also click the **To** button in the message form and select the recipient from your list. Learn more about using the Address Book in Task 2, "How to Add an Address to Your Personal Address Book."

TASK 2

How to Add an Address to Your Personal Address Book

The Personal Address Book is one of two address sources you have in Outlook. The other address book is your Contacts list, which you can learn how to use in Chapter 13, "How to Use Outlook 98," Task 7, "How to Create a New Contact." Unlike the Contacts list, the Personal Address Book enables you to create Personal Distribution Lists, which are address groups that enable you to send a message to a large group of recipients without accidentally forgetting to include a name.

Begin

1 Open the Personal Address Book

From the Inbox folder, open the **Tools** menu and select **Address Book,** or click the **Address Book** button on the toolbar to open the Address Book window.

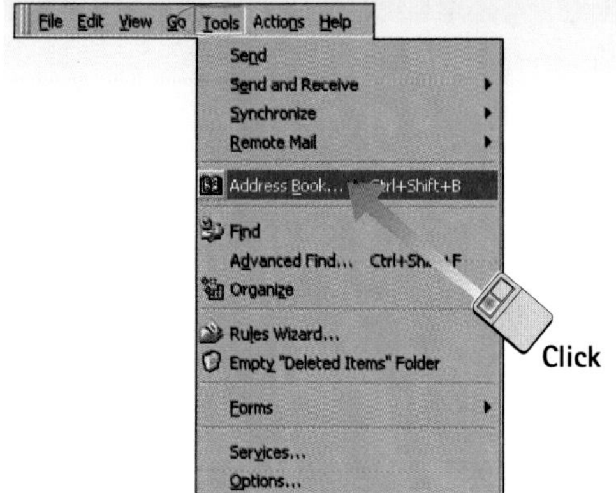

2 Click the New Entry Button

Click the **New Entry** button on the Address Book toolbar to open the New Entry window.

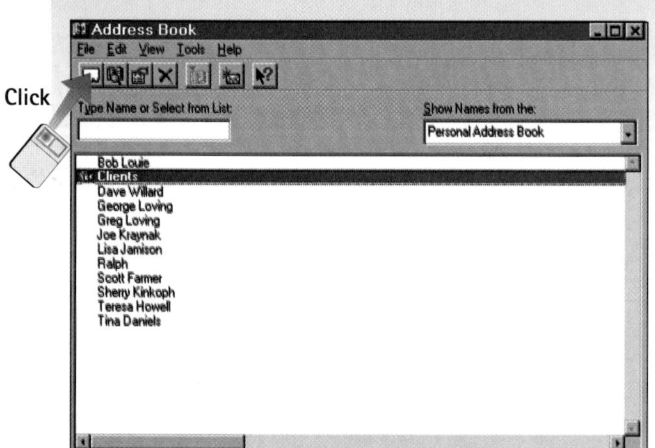

3 Choose an Email Type

From the **Select the entry type** list box, choose the type of email address you're adding and click **OK**. To add an Internet email address, for example, click **Other Address**.

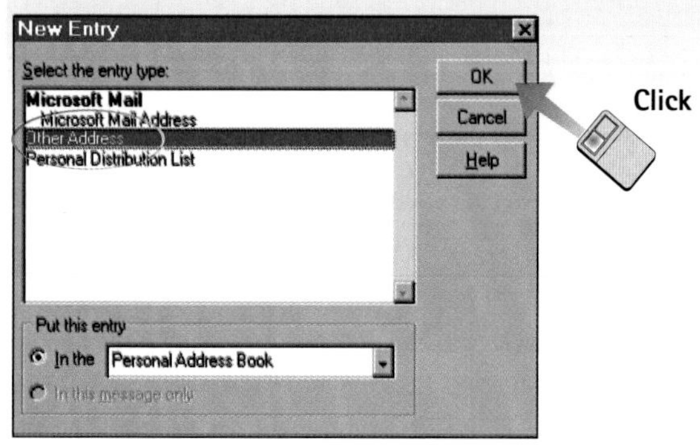

4 Fill In the Information

Use the various tabs to enter information about the email recipient. Enter the **Display name** (the name that appears on your messages), the **E-mail address** (the actual email address), and the **E-mail type** (usually **SMTP**). Choose **OK**.

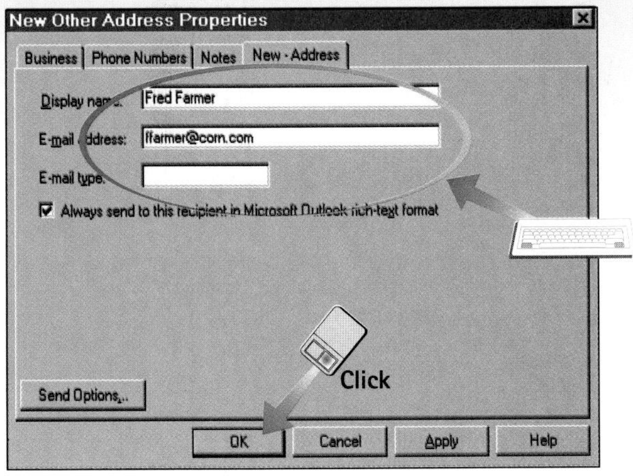

5 Exit

When you're finished adding new entries, exit the Address Book window. Click the **Close** button or select **File**, **Close**.

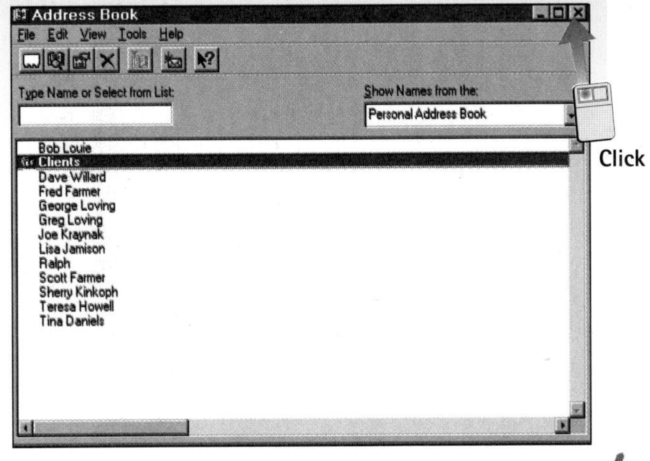

End

How-To Hints

Can't Find Personal Address Book?

If Outlook didn't pick up your Personal Address Book when it was installed, choose **Tools**, **Services**; in the Services dialog box, click **Add** (the Add Service to Profile dialog box appears). Click **Personal Address Book** and **Outlook Address Book**, and then choose **OK** to close both dialog boxes. Close Outlook and restart it.

Create a Personal Distribution List

In the Address Book window, choose **File**, **New Entry**. Double-click **Personal Distribution List**. Type a **Name** for the list, and then click **Add/Remove Members**. Double-click each name you want to add, choose **OK** twice, and then choose **File**, **Close** to exit.

Microsoft Exchange User?

If you've used Microsoft Exchange for email, all your addresses are stored in the Exchange Personal Address Book; Outlook and Exchange share the same Personal Address Book, so all those addresses are available in Outlook, too.

TASK 3

How to Read an Incoming Message

Use the Inbox to see messages you receive in Outlook. The Inbox displays each message as a single line with a From field that tells you who sent it, a Subject field that gives you a clue as to what's in the message, and a Received field that tells you when it was received. The symbol columns at the left of the Inbox provide important information about each message, such as priority level or whether it has a file attachment.

Use the AutoPreview feature to screen new messages by showing you the first three lines of a message before you open it. If AutoPreview isn't turned on, choose **View**, **AutoPreview** to turn it on.

Begin

1 Check for New Mail

To check for new messages from the Inbox folder, click the **Send and Receive** button on the Outlook toolbar to go online to pick up mail. Your new messages appear in your Inbox.

2 Open a Message

Double-click a message you want to open and read.

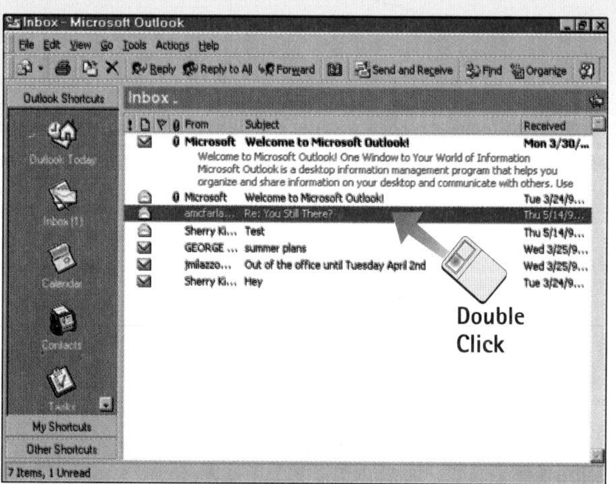

3 Read a Message

The message opens for you to read. If it's a long message, use the scrollbars to scroll through the message. If you want to print the message, click the **Print** button on the message toolbar.

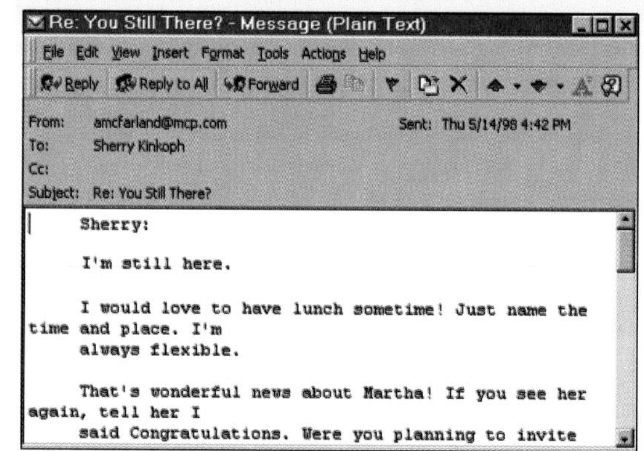

4 Read the Next Message

To continue reading new mail messages without returning to the Inbox, click the **Next Item** button on the message toolbar. To return to the previous message, click the **Previous Item** button.

Previous Item Next Item

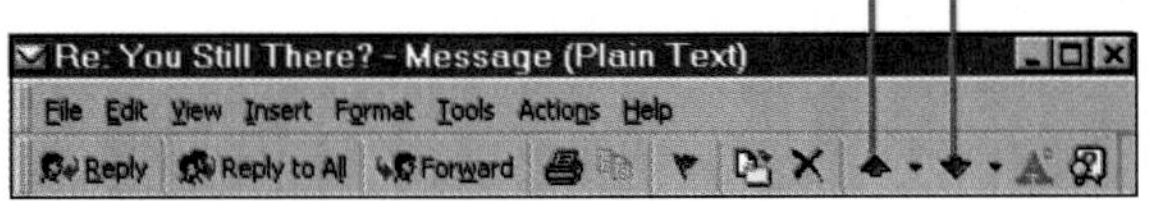

5 Delete a Message

If you don't need to keep a message, click the **Delete** button on the message toolbar.

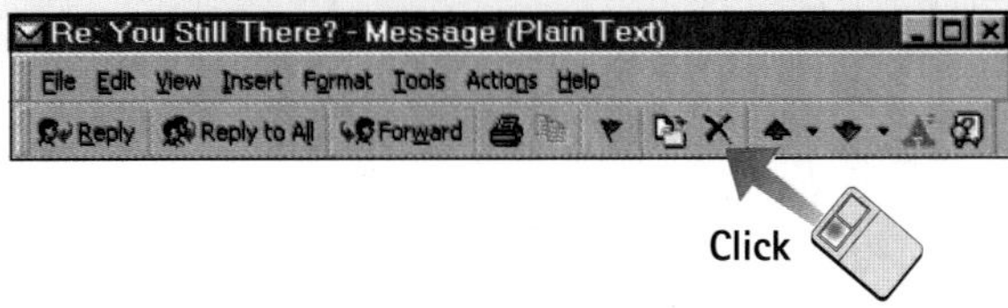

6 Close a Message

When you're finished reading a message, and you want to keep it, click the **Close** button in the upper-right corner of the message. If you want to reply to the message or forward it to someone else, see Task 4, "How to Reply To or Forward a Message" (don't close the message; replying and forwarding close it automatically).

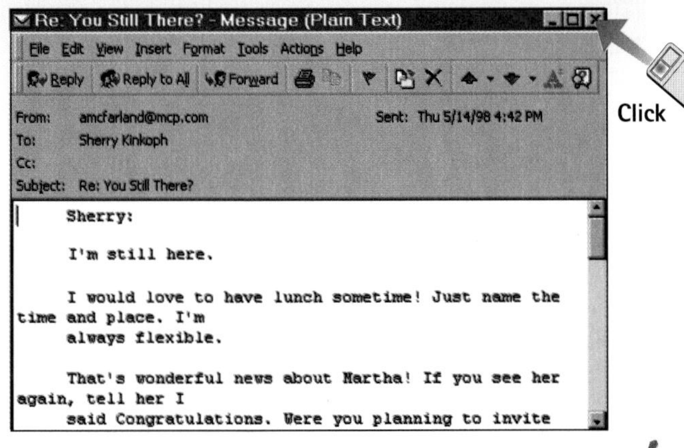

Click

End

How-To Hints

Read and Unread

You can mark messages in the Inbox as read or unread. By default, Outlook marks messages as read after you open them. If you want to remember to read the message again later, close it, and then right-click the message line in Inbox and click **Mark as Unread**. The message returns to unread-mail status.

Delete Messages

If you're cleaning out your Inbox, delete old messages by selecting the message, and then clicking the **Delete** button on the Outlook toolbar.

Transfer Info to Address Book

When you receive a message, the sender's name and address are always included is the **From** line of the message form. To transfer the name and address directly into your Personal Address Book, right-click the sender name, and then click **Add to Personal Address Book**.

TASK 4

How to Reply To or Forward a Message

You can quickly reply to or forward any message immediately after opening and reading it. A reply, of course, is an answer to a message sent to you, and a forward is a message you have received that you send on to others. Outlook creates a reply or forward message that includes all the original text. When you reply to or forward a message, the action and the date are recorded in the original message (and copies of your replies and forwards are kept in the Sent Items folder).

Begin

1 Click Reply

To reply to an open message, click the **Reply** button to open a Reply Message window. If the message you received has names in the **Cc** box, you can send your reply to all of the recipients by clicking **Reply to All** instead.

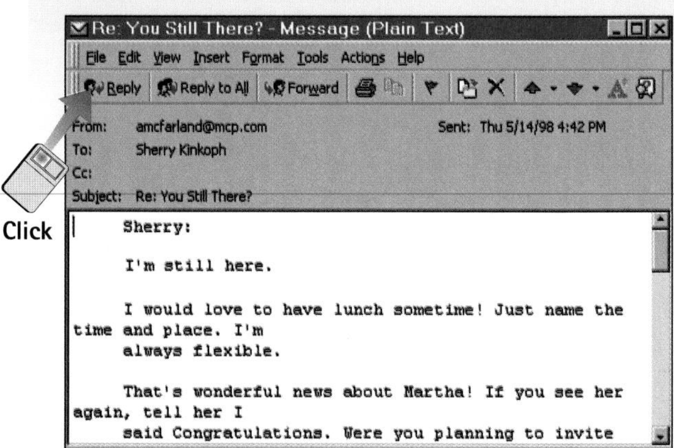

2 Enter Your Reply

The Reply Message window includes the original text with the sender's name in the **To** text box. Select and delete any text you don't need to include. Type your response to the message. (Text you type in the reply area is blue, and if your correspondent reads your message in Outlook or Windows Exchange, they will see your response in blue.)

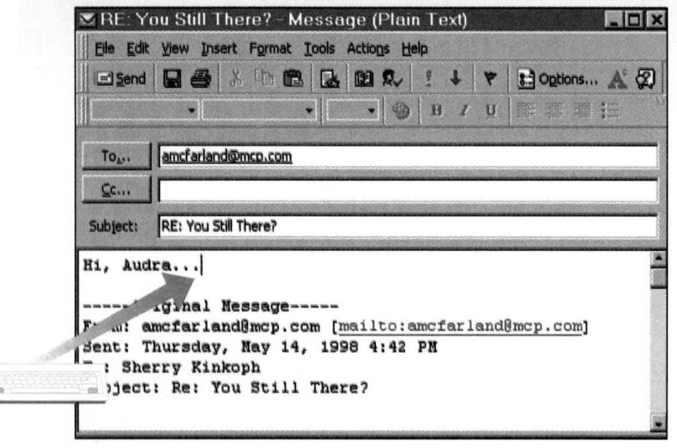

3 Send Your Reply

When your reply is ready, click the **Send** button on the message window's toolbar.

4 Or Forward the Message

To forward an open message to others, click **Forward** in the original message window. This opens a new copy of the message.

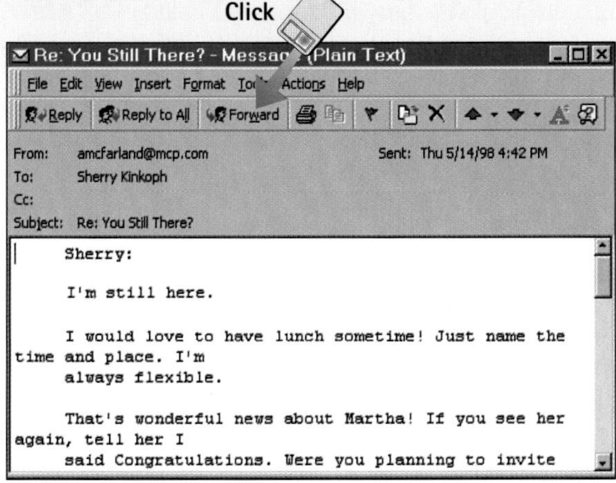

5 Enter the Forwardee's Address

Fill in the **To** box with the address of the person you're forwarding the message to. Add a note at the top of the message (it appears in blue to anyone reading it in Outlook or Windows Exchange), and select and delete any text you don't want to include in the forwarded message.

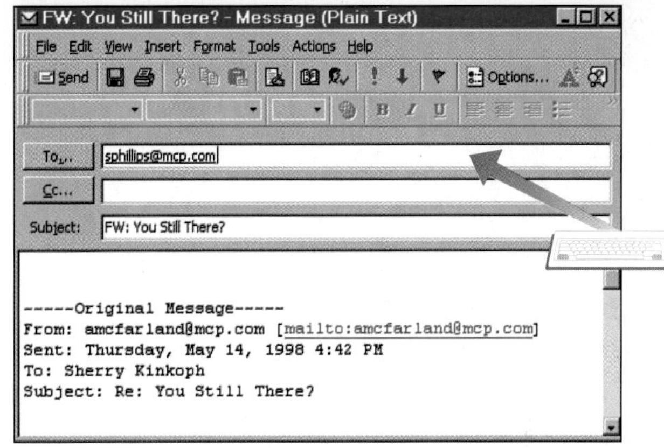

6 Send It Forward

When the message is ready to be forwarded, click the **Send** button on the message window's toolbar.

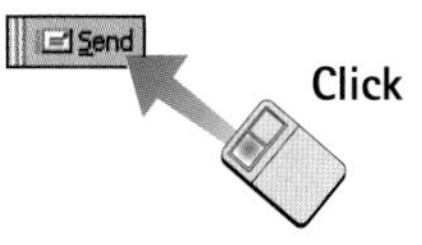

End

How-To Hints

What About Attachments?

When you forward a message, the attachments are also forwarded. If you want to delete the attachments, click each one and press **Delete**. When you reply to a message, the attachments automatically disappear. To keep the attachments in place, you must either forward the message instead of just replying to it, or you must reattach the attachment.

TASK 5

How to Attach a File to a Message

You can attach files of any type to Outlook messages. You can send your boss the latest sales figures from your Excel worksheet, for example, or pass along your Word report to your colleague on the Internet. You can also attach other Outlook items, such as a contact or note.

When you attach a file to a message, it appears as an icon on the message. The recipient can open the file from within the message or save the file to open later. Keep in mind, however, that the recipient *must* have the appropriate program to view the file. If you send a PowerPoint presentation to a coworker, for example, that person must have PowerPoint installed to view the file.

Begin

1 Click Insert File

After you compose the message, click the **Insert File** button on the message toolbar. This opens the Insert File dialog box.

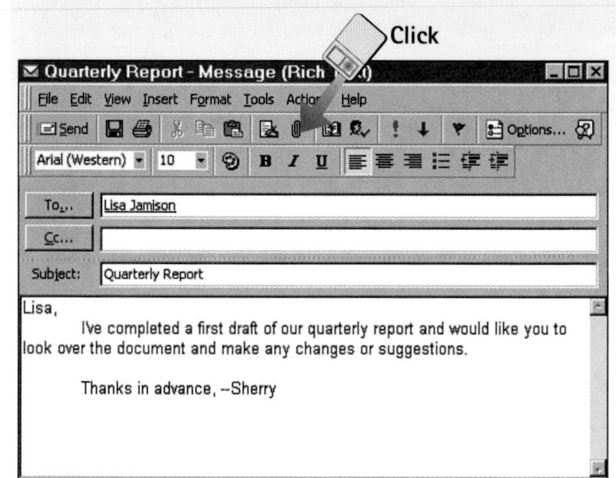

2 Locate the File

Use the **Look in** drop-down list to locate the folder or drive where the file is stored.

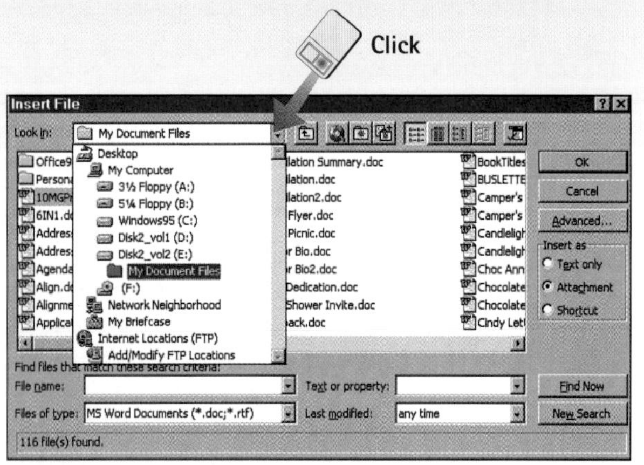

3 Select the File

From the list box, select the file you want to attach and click **OK**.

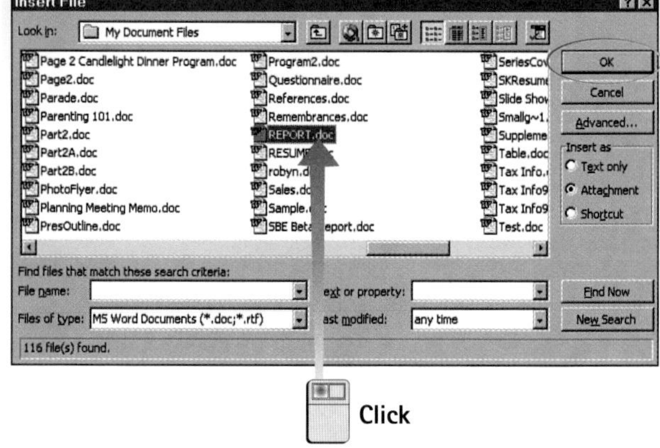

4 The File Is Attached

The file appears as an icon in your message text. You can now send the message.

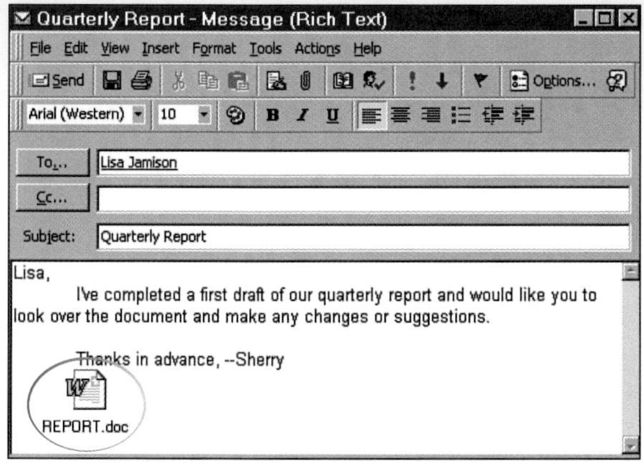

5 Attach Outlook Items

To attach an Outlook item to a message, open the **Insert** menu and select **Item**. This opens the Insert Item dialog box.

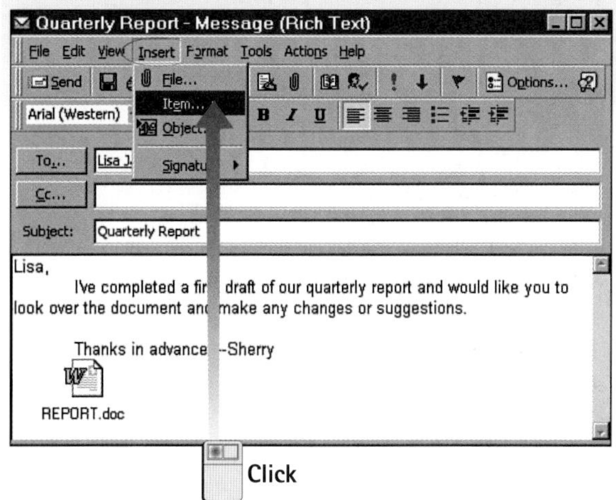

6 Locate the Item

Open the folder in which the item is stored, and then select the item. In the **Insert as** area, choose **Attachment**. Click **OK** and send the message.

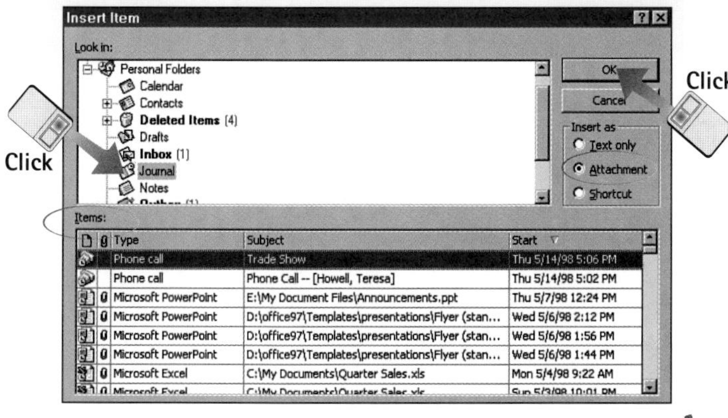

End

How-To Hints

Receive Attachments

If you receive a message that contains an attached file, you will notice a paper-clip symbol in the Attachments field in your Inbox. Open the message, and you will see an icon in it that represents the attached file. To view the file, double-click the attachment icon.

TASK 6

How to Archive an Email Message

Use Outlook's AutoArchive feature to automatically archive old email messages as well as other Outlook items. If unchecked, your Outlook Inbox will continue to grow as more and more email messages are added to the folder. To help remove clutter and restore disk space, archive items you no longer need to access.

You can archive old items manually or use AutoArchive to do it for you. When you archive items, they are removed from their current folder and copied to an archive file.

Begin

1 Open the Options Dialog Box

Open the **Tools** menu and select **Options**. This opens the Options dialog box.

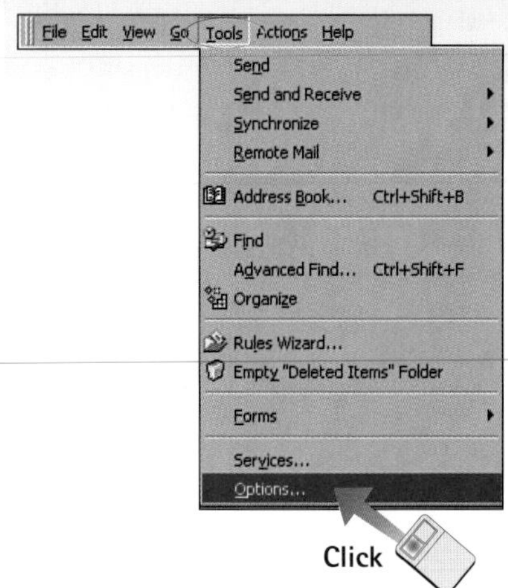

2 Display the Other Tab

Next, click the **Other** tab and click the **AutoArchive** button. This opens the AutoArchive dialog box.

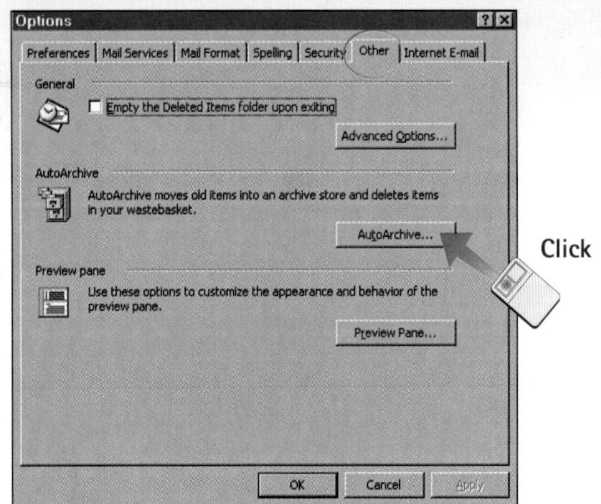

3 Turn AutoArchive On

Select the **AutoArchive every** check box. You can now specify the number of days between archives, or you can set up each folder's properties to archive differently (proceed to step 4 to learn how). Click **OK** twice to exit the dialog boxes.

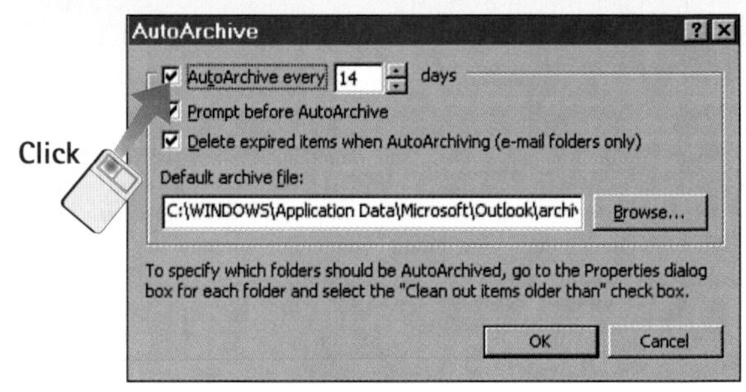

4 Open the Properties Dialog Box

You can set the AutoArchive properties for each Outlook 98 folder, including the Inbox. To display the Properties dialog box for a folder, right-click the folder in the Outlook Bar and select **Properties** from the shortcut menu.

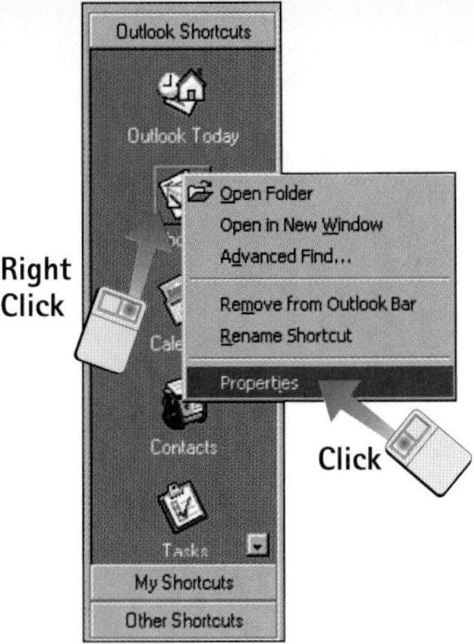

5 Set Archive Options

Click the **AutoArchive** tab and select the **Clean out items older than** check box. Designate the value in months when items are to be automatically archived.

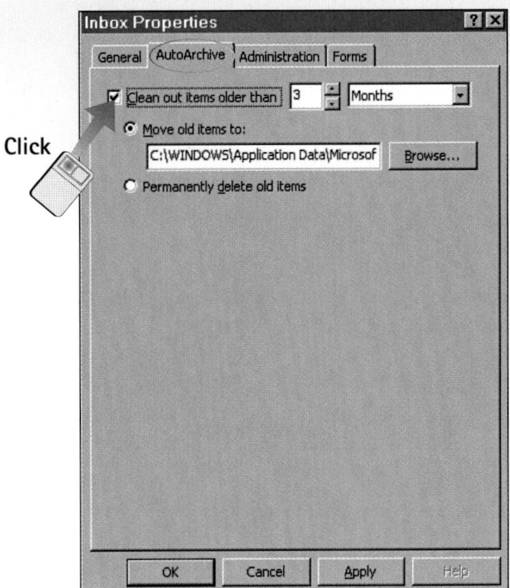

6 Set an Archive Folder

Outlook stores the archived items in a default archive folder, but you can choose another folder, if needed. Click the **Browse** button and select another archive folder. Click **OK** to exit the dialog box and the AutoArchive properties are set.

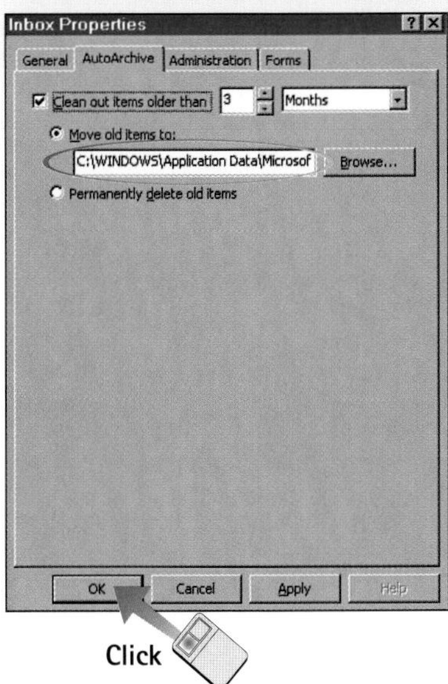

How-To Hints

Manual Archive

To manually archive an Outlook item, such as an email message, open the **File** menu and choose **Archive**. To archive all the folders, choose **Archive all folders according to their AutoArchive settings**. To archive one folder, choose **Archive this folder and all subfolders**, then select the folder. Use the **Archive items older than** option to set a limit to the archive items; items dated before the date specified will be automatically archived. Click **OK** to exit.

End

Task

CHAPTER 15

How to Use the Office 97 Internet Tools

Microsoft specifically designed the Office 97 suite of programs to utilize the *Internet* and the *World Wide Web*. You will find plenty of Web browsing features in each Office program. You can access information from the Web without leaving an application. You can also create Web documents using Web publishing features found in each Office program. Just about every file you create can be converted to an HTML file to publish on the Web or a corporate *intranet*.

In addition to Web-related features, you can also use Microsoft's Web *browser*, Internet Explorer, to view and access Web content. Internet Explorer 4.0 comes with Outlook 98, or you can download the latest copy of the program from Microsoft's Web site.

In this chapter, you will learn about Internet Explorer 4.0's basic features, and how to use the Office 97 program's Web tools.

TASK 1

How to Navigate the Web with Internet Explorer

Internet Explorer (IE) is a Web browser you can use to view Web pages on the Internet. Not only can you view Web content, but you can also search for information, download files, view multimedia clips, and more.

When you first install Internet Explorer 4.0, you can choose to use the new Active Desktop, which makes your desktop work like a Web page, or you can turn the active desktop off—right-click a blank spot on the desktop and click **Active Desktop**, **View As Web Page** to turn it on or off. This book's tasks will focus on the browser rather than the active desktop.

Begin

1 Log On

Internet Explorer starts the same as any other Office program. If the desktop has a shortcut icon, you can double-click it to open Internet Explorer. Before the program opens, however, you will be prompted to log on to your Internet connection (unless you have already done that).

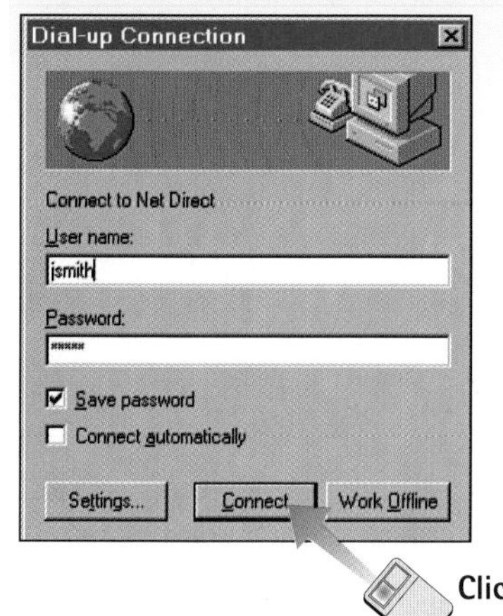

2 View the Onscreen Elements

When you open Internet Explorer, the browser window displays the default start page (the home page your browser is configured to load whenever you open the program). The program window consists of the familiar title bar, menu bar, and toolbar, along with scrollbars and a status bar. These features work the same way they do in the other Office programs.

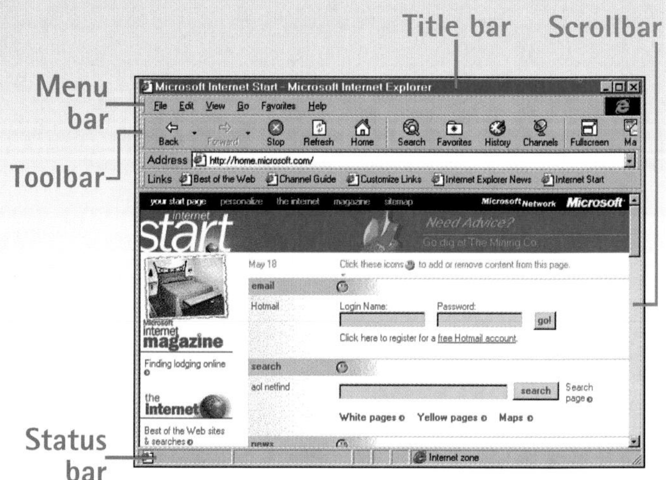

3 View Other Toolbars

Internet Explorer has two more toolbars: The Address toolbar enables you to enter Web page addresses, and the Links toolbar enables you to quickly access particular Web sites with a click of a button. Depending on your monitor's display mode, the Address and Links toolbars may share space in your program window. To make it easy to see the toolbars, I've displayed them as two separate bars. Your screen will differ.

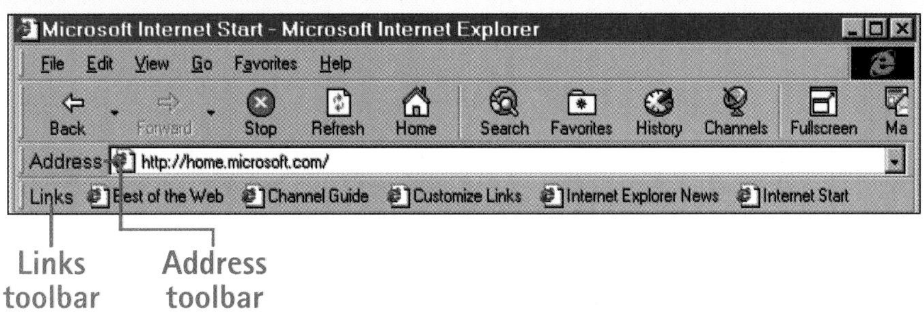

Links toolbar

Address toolbar

4 Visit a Web Page

Each page on the Web has a specific address, called an *URL* (Uniform Resource Locator). You can visit specific pages on the Web by typing their URLs. To practice, click inside the **Address** text box, type **`www.mcp.com`**, and press Enter. You don't need to enter the prefix **`http://`**—Internet Explorer inserts this prefix for you.

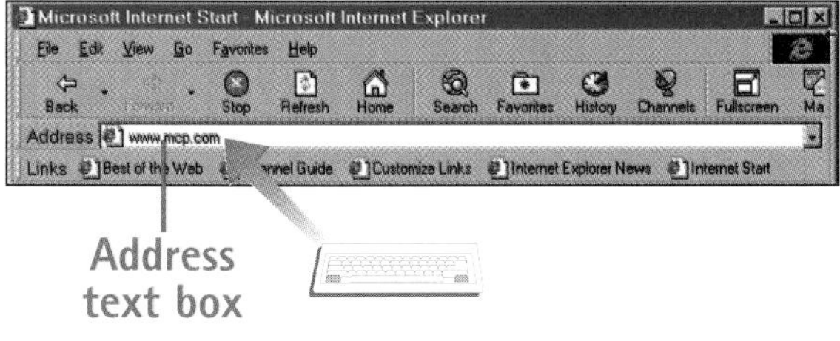

Address text box

5 The Page Loads

Internet Explorer displays the Web page. You can now read the information on the page. Depending on the size of the page, you can use the scrollbars to view different parts of the page.

Continues

6 Use Links

Another way to view Web pages is to follow links. Links take you to other Web pages, the same as entering URLs. Links commonly are underlined words on a Web page, but you will also find graphics images, buttons, or icons used as links on Web pages.

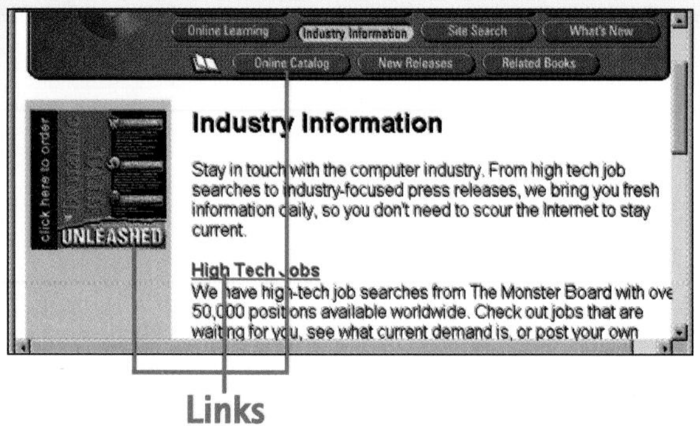

7 Follow a Link

When the mouse pointer hovers over a link, the pointer takes the shape of a hand. Click a link to display its Web page. As soon as you click a link, the corresponding Web page loads. Some pages take longer than others do to display; the status bar keeps you posted on the progress, both in contacting the Web site and when the page is fully loaded.

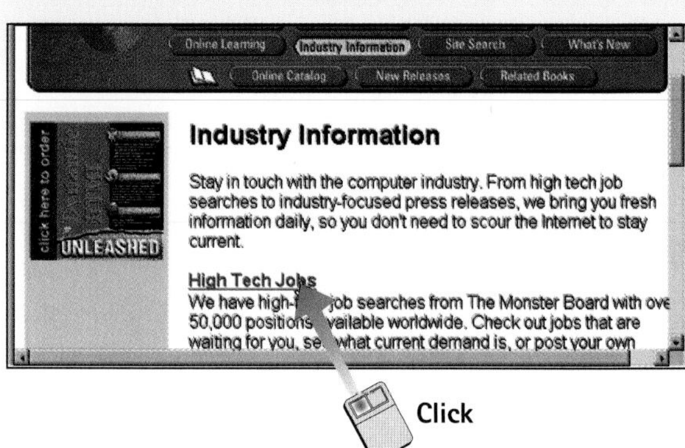

8 Use the Navigation Buttons

After you begin viewing pages, you may want to return to a previous page. Use the **Back** button on the Internet Explorer toolbar to return to the previous page. Use the **Forward** button to move to the page you were viewing before using the Back button.

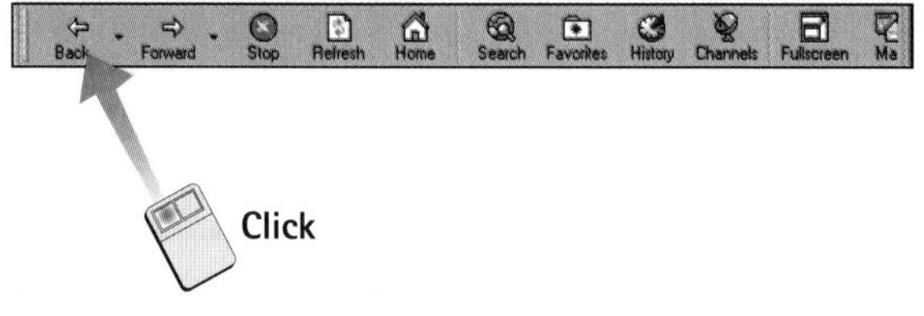

9 Use the Stop Button

If a page is taking a particularly long time to display, you can cease and desist by clicking the **Stop** button on the toolbar.

10 Use the Refresh Button

If for some reason a page doesn't display properly—perhaps it's missing some text or a graphic—try clicking the **Refresh** button to reload the page.

11 Return to Your Home Page

To return to your start page—the page that opens automatically whenever you open Internet Explorer—click the **Home** button.

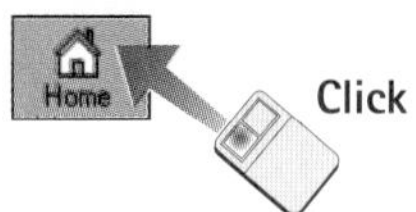

End

How-To Hints

Set Up an Account First

Before you can begin surfing the Web, you must first establish an Internet account with an *Internet service provider* (ISP); you will need a modem to make the connection. If you don't have an account, you can use the Internet Connection Wizard to walk you through the steps. Click the **Start** button on the Windows taskbar; then choose **Programs**, **Internet Explorer**, **Connection Wizard** and follow along with each wizard step.

Define a New Home Page

When you first install Internet Explorer, it uses a Microsoft Web page as the default home page. However, you can define another page as your home page. Open the **View** menu, select **Internet Options**, and then click the **General** tab. Under the **Home page** options, click inside the **Address** text box and enter the URL of the Web page you want to use as your home page. Click **OK**. The next time you start IE, the new home page appears automatically.

TASK 2

How to Mark Your Favorite Web Pages

As you come across Web pages you like and want to revisit, take time to mark them as favorites. When you save a Web page as a favorite, you can quickly access it again later. By default, favorite Web pages are stored in the Favorites folder, but you can easily create new folders and keep your favorite Web sites organized.

Begin

1 Add a Favorite

When you find a Web page you want to mark, open the **Favorites** menu and choose **Add to Favorites**. This opens the Add Favorite dialog box.

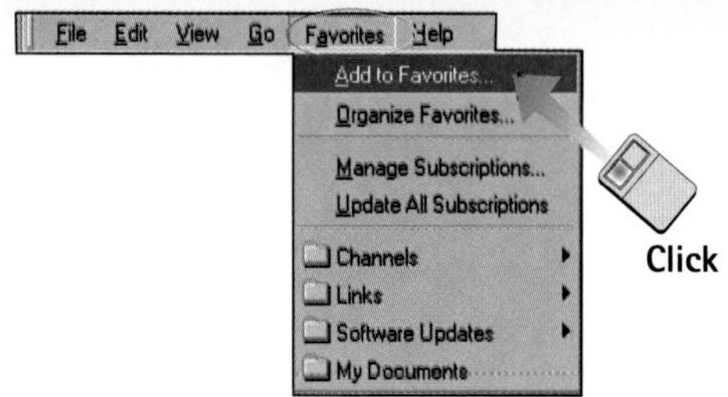

2 Give the Page a Name

Choose a subscription option if necessary; then click inside the **Name** text box and give the page a name you will recognize.

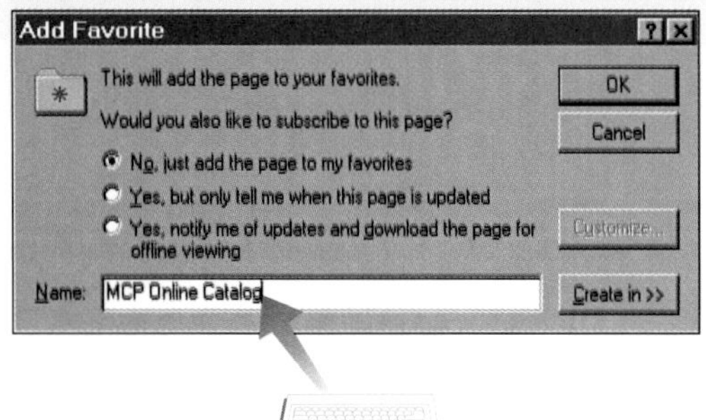

3 Exit the Dialog Box

Click **OK** and the page is added to your Favorites list.

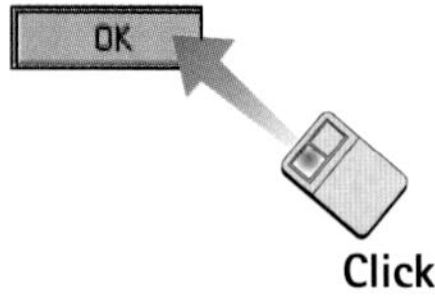

4 Open the Favorites List

To display the Favorites list, click the **Favorites** button. This opens the Favorites list as a separate pane in the Internet Explorer window.

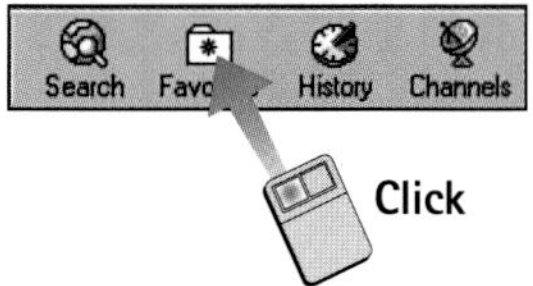

5 Select a Favorite

To revisit a favorite, click the page name. If you have organized the pages into other folders, open the folder with a double-click and then select the name.

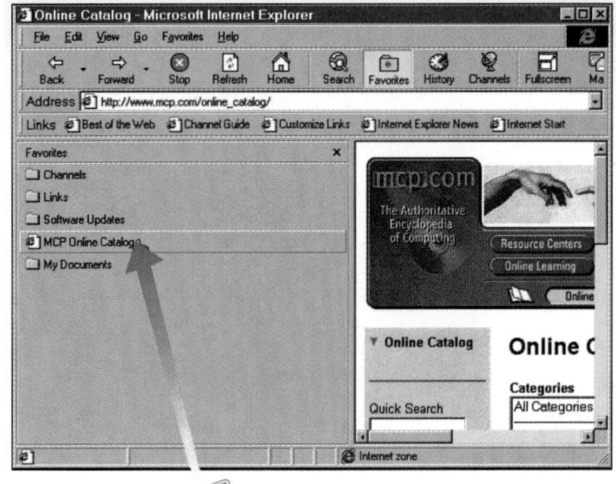

6 Close the List

To close the Favorites list pane, click the **Favorites** button again on the toolbar.

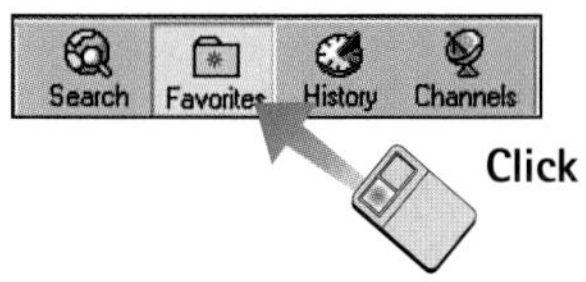

End

How-To Hints

Organize Favorites

Internet Explorer saves the pages you mark as favorites in folders. To create new folders or to organize the URLs into different folders, open the **Favorites** menu and select **Organize Favorites**. This opens the Organize Favorites dialog box where you can create new folders, move URLs between folders, or rename folders.

TASK 3

How to Perform a Web Search

One of the most frustrating aspects of using the Web is searching for information. Following links won't take you to the information you're looking for; you need to use a search engine to help narrow your search. Search engines are specially designed to frequently catalog and index World Wide Web pages. When you enter a key word or phrase, the search engine looks through its catalog and returns a list of related matches.

The following examples were created using the Excite search engine. Most search engines work in a similar fashion and provide many of the same features; however, because each search engine has its own design, the specifics may vary somewhat.

Begin

1 Begin at the Help Menu

To search the Web from within any Office 97 program, choose **Help, Microsoft on the Web, Search the Web.**

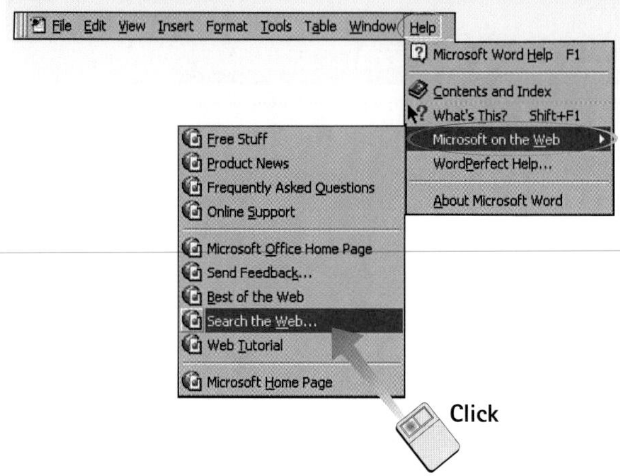

2 The Browser Opens

Internet Explorer 4.0 starts and opens to the Microsoft Find It Fast Web page. This page has links to several major Internet search engines as well as categories of Web sites. Click a search engine name to open its home page (this task uses Excite).

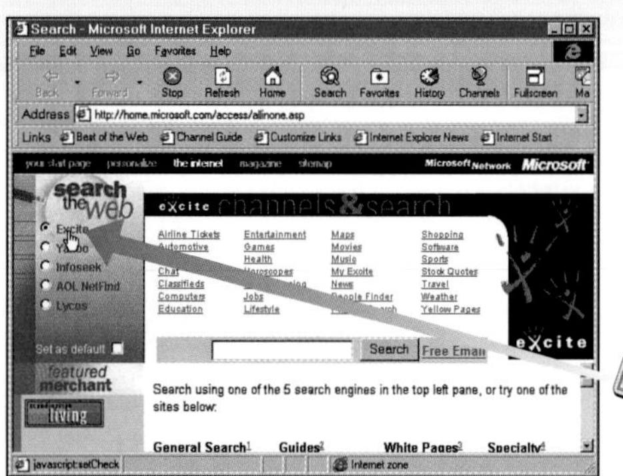

3 Enter Search Text

Enter a word or phrase in the text box and click **Search** to start the engine hunting (the button's name may be different in other search engines).

4 Click a Link in the Results List

The result of the search is a list of links to Web pages that contain your word or phrase; the list may be very long, or it may have no links at all. Repeat the search with other words or phrases to narrow or expand the search. In the results list, click a likely *hyperlink* to jump to that Web page.

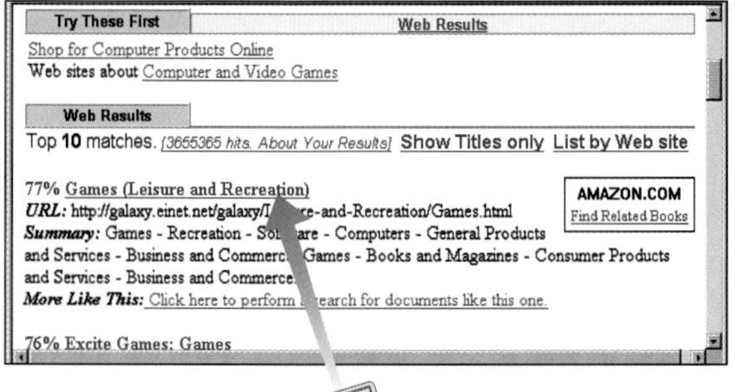

5 Get Search Help

If you have a problem finding what you want, get help with your search from the search engine. Most engines provide a **Search Tips** or **Help** link on their home page that can help you with your choice of search words or phrases.

6 Try Other Search Options

In addition to search tips, most search engines also provide search options to improve your chances of success. Depending on the search engine you're using, click the **Options** link to see the available options (for example, with Excite, click **the Power Search** link). Use the search option boxes to designate search criteria.

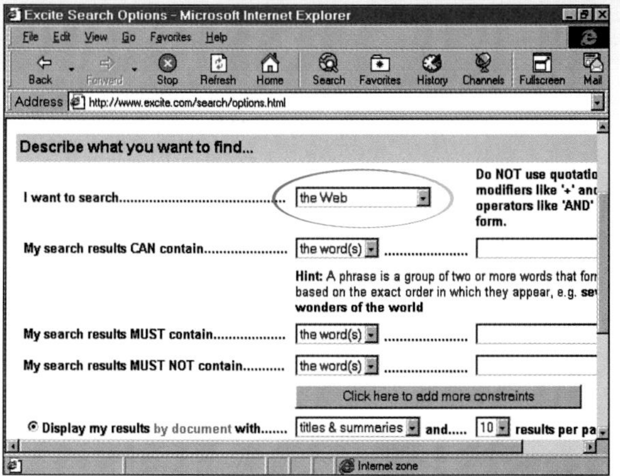

End

How-To Hints

Got Cookies?

Lots of Web sites send cookies that are stored on your computer without your knowledge. Although not harmful, they do contain information that allows a Web site to identify you and see where you have been. Unfortunately, avoiding cookies is practically impossible because you must either accept them blindly or reject them one at a time as they are sent (by turning on the Windows 95 Internet Cookies Alert option). But you can outsmart the marketing geniuses behind the "cookie conspiracy." Open the Cookies folder—c:\windows\cookies—and delete all the files except index.dat (you won't be allowed to delete index.dat). For more information about cookies, visit The Magic Cookie site at **`http://www.indranet.com/cookie.html`**.

TASK 4

How to Download Files from the Web

You will encounter all kinds of files on the Web: text files, graphics files, program files, multimedia files, and more. After you find a file you want, the next step is to transfer a copy of the file from the Internet site where it's stored to your computer. This is called *downloading*. (File transfer is called downloading when you receive the file, and uploading when you send the file.)

Before you download, be sure you have enough room on your hard drive to accommodate the file, and keep in mind that downloads of large files can keep your computer occupied for a considerable length of time (large files—5+ megabytes—can take hours).

Begin

1 Find a File

When you come across a file you want to download, select the file or follow its download link.

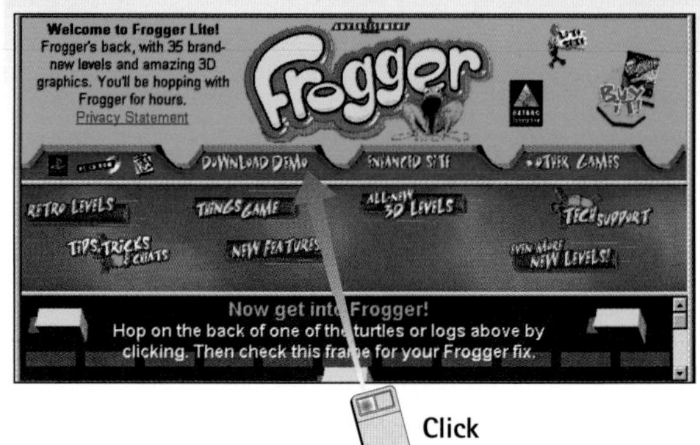

2 Start the Download

Click the file's download link to start the download process. If the file must be purchased, follow the directions given by the Web site.

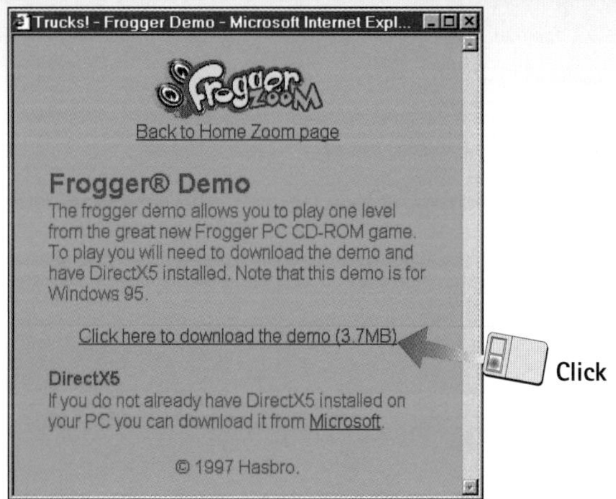

3 Save the File on Your Hard Drive

In the File Download dialog box, click the **Save this program to disk** option; then choose **OK**.

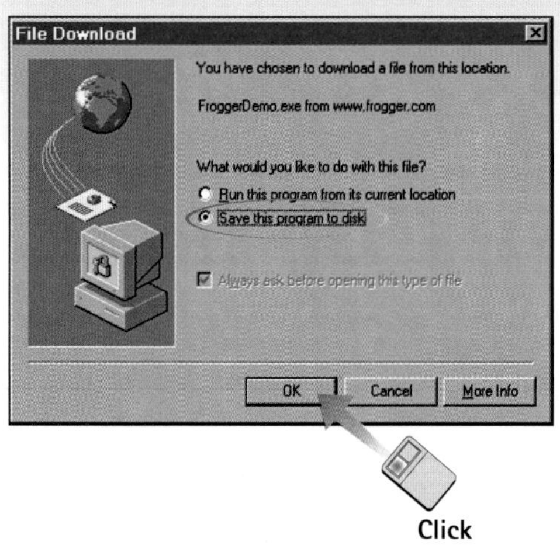

4 Choose a Hard Drive Location

When downloading is ready to begin, the Save As dialog box appears. Navigate to the folder in which you want to save the file, just as you would any document, and then click **Save**.

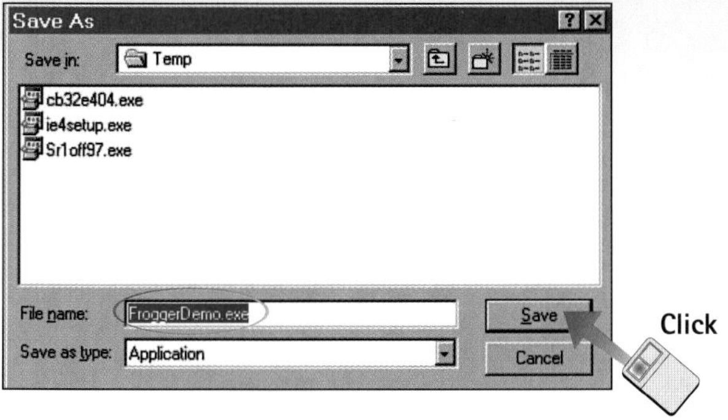

5 Wait for the Download

As the download begins, a dialog box appears that gives you as many details as Windows 95 can find out about the file size, time remaining, and so forth. If you decide you can't spend six hours waiting for the download, click **Cancel** to stop the download, and try it again later.

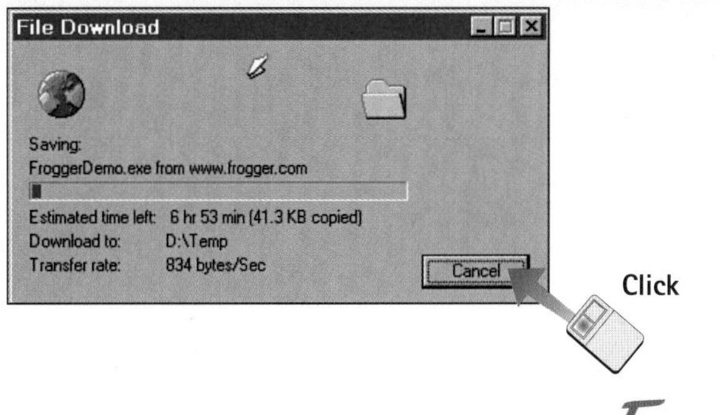

End

How-To Hints

Virus Alert

Be aware that any file you obtain from the Internet can contain a computer virus. To keep your computer protected against viruses, consider purchasing an anti-virus program. Programs such as McAfee VirusScan and Norton Anti-Virus can check for viruses while you are downloading the file, to ensure that a tainted file doesn't get into your hard drive.

Plan Your Download Times

If you have to download large files, try to do it during a time when most other users won't be using the Internet. If you're on the East Coast, download early in the morning before the rest of the country has had a chance to wake up; if you're on the West Coast, download late at night when everyone else is asleep.

TASK 5

How to Open a Web Document from an Office Program

If an Office 97 file has a link or URL, you can open the corresponding Web page without leaving your Office program window or opening your Web browser. Microsoft's programmers have designed each Office program to access the Web on its own. Using the Web toolbar, you can navigate pages, perform a search, and follow links. You can type the URLs for pages you want to view, or follow links from page to page.

Begin

1 Follow a Link

If you're currently viewing a document that has a link you want to follow, click the link.

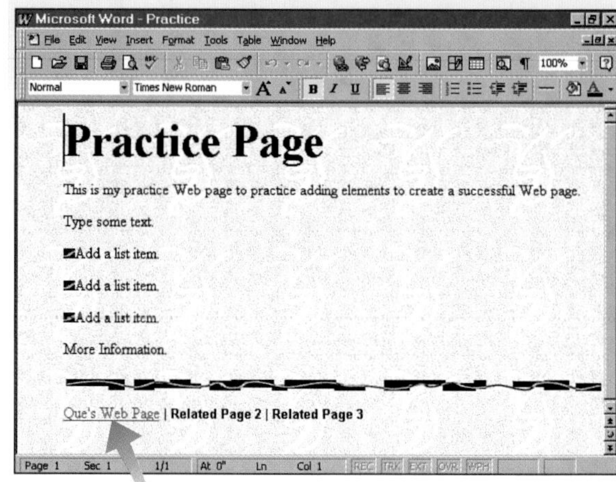

2 Log On

A Dial-up Connection dialog box appears for you to log on to your Internet account. Click **Connect**.

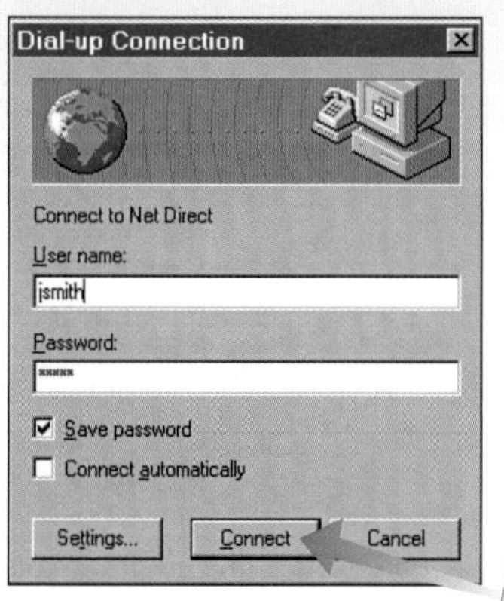

3 Document Displayed

After you have established your connection, your Office program window displays the Web page.

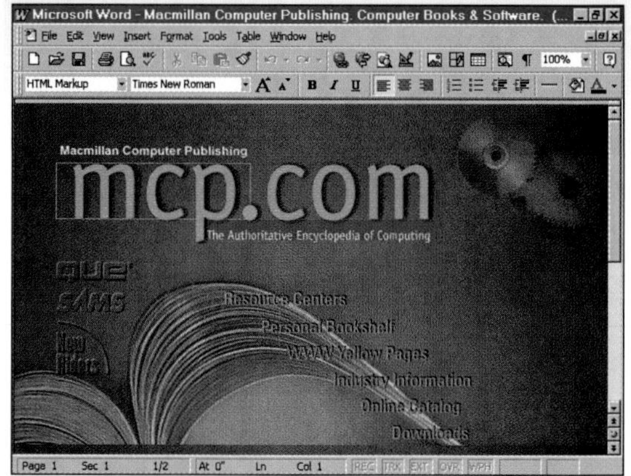

4 Display the Web Toolbar

Right-click a toolbar area and select **Web** (or open the **View** menu and choose **Toolbars, Web**).

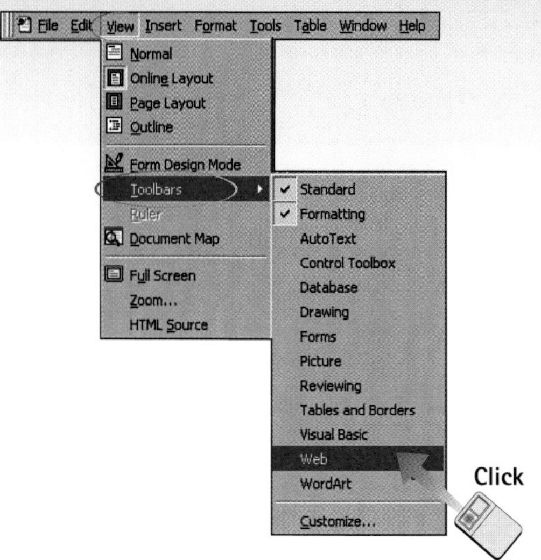

5 Navigate Pages

You can use the Web toolbar to navigate the Web from within the program window. Use the **Back** and **Forward** buttons to view pages you have loaded. You can enter new URLs or click links to see other pages.

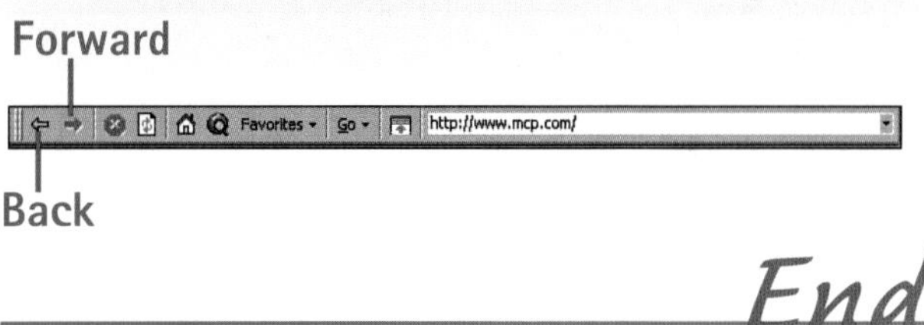

End

How-To Hints

Save Pages

You can save Web pages using the Save As dialog box. Open the **File** menu and select **Save As**. You can assign the page a name and choose to save it as an HTML document or another file type.

TASK 6

How to Convert Office Files to HTML

You can easily save any Office 97 file as an HTML document to be posted on the Web. If you have a Word document you would like to post on the Internet or add to your Web site, for example, save the file in HTML format. This converts the formatting into codes that can be interpreted by Web browsers.

Begin

1 Open the File

Open the file you want to save as an HTML document.

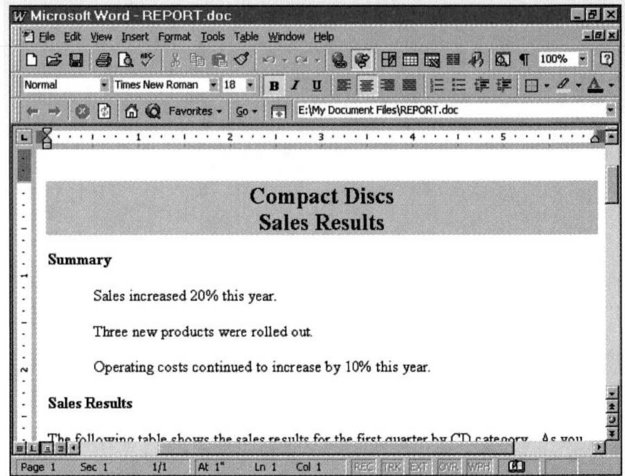

2 Open Save As HTML Dialog Box

Display the **File** menu and select **Save as HTML**. This opens the Save As HTML dialog box.

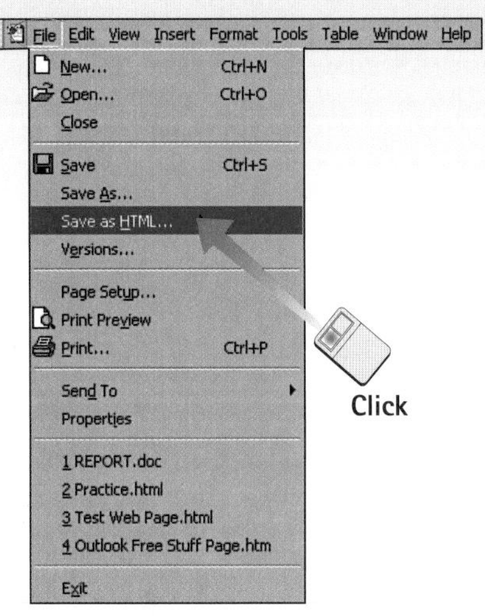

3 Enter a Filename

Designate a folder to save the file to, and assign a name to the file, if needed.

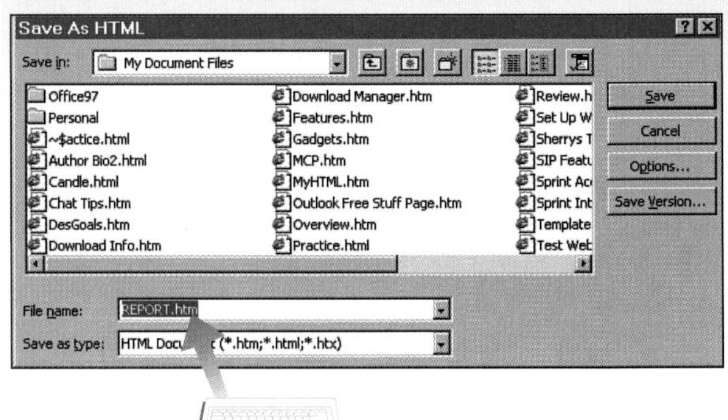

4 Click Save

Click the **Save** button.

5 File Is Converted

The file is converted to HTML format.

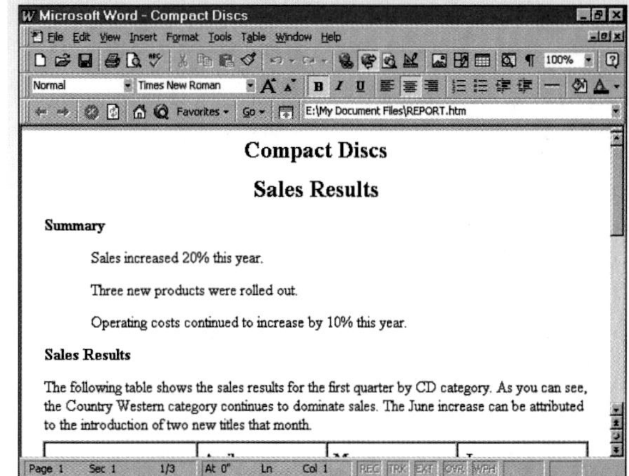

End

How-To Hints

Formatting Warning

Keep in mind that not all formatting you apply using Word's formatting features will translate to HTML code. When you save the file as an HTML document, some formatting may be lost. For that reason, it's best to keep your Web page formatting simple.

TASK 7

How to Use Word's Web Page Wizard

Word comes with an excellent wizard for helping you create professional-looking Web pages. Web pages are formatted in HTML code, which stands for Hypertext Markup Language—coding that Web browser programs can interpret. You can save any Word document you create as an HTML file, but the Web Page Wizard offers you preformatted layouts in a variety of styles. All you have to do is fill in your own text.

Begin

1 Open the New Dialog Box

From the Word program window, open the **File** menu and select **New**. This opens the New dialog box.

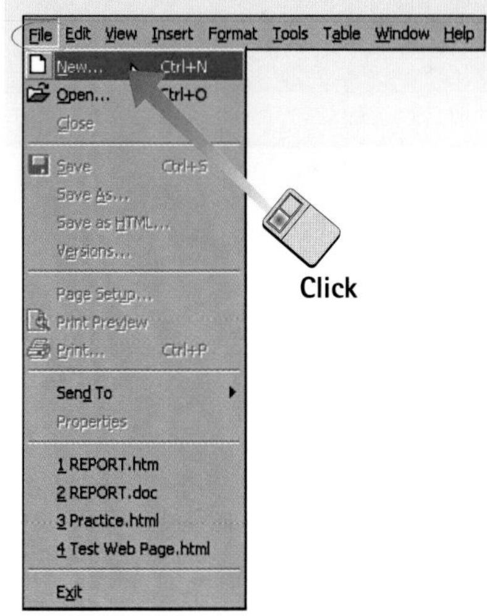

2 Choose the Web Page Wizard

From the Web Pages tab, double-click the **Web Page Wizard**. This opens the wizard and also displays a sample Web page in the background.

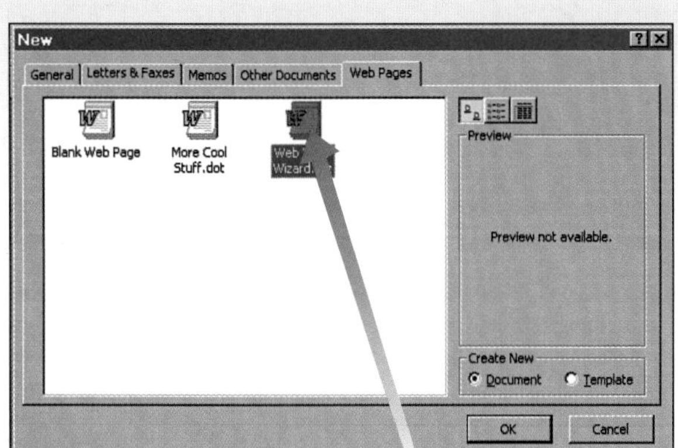

3 Select a Layout

Choose the layout you want to use for your Web page and click **Next**.

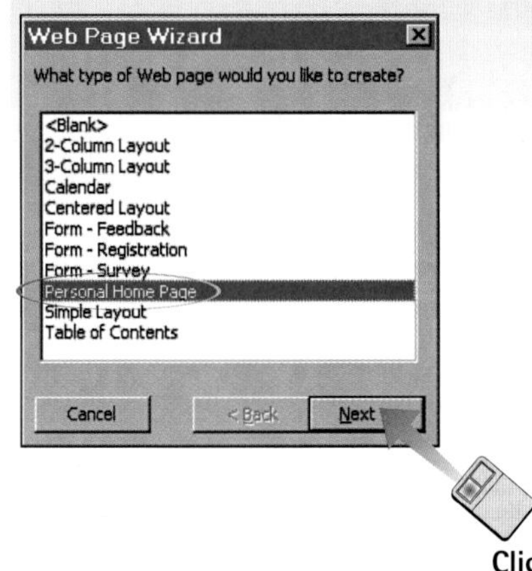

Click

4 Sample a Visual Style

In the next Wizard dialog box, choose a visual style to use. To sample the style, select it and wait a moment. The background page changes to the style.

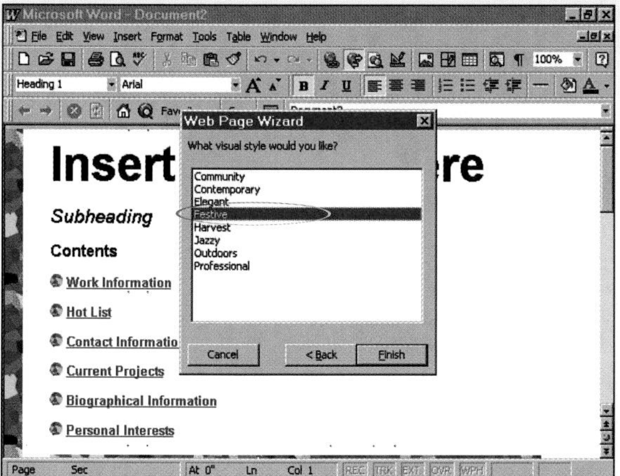

5 Select a Style

When you find a visual style you like, select it and click **Finish**.

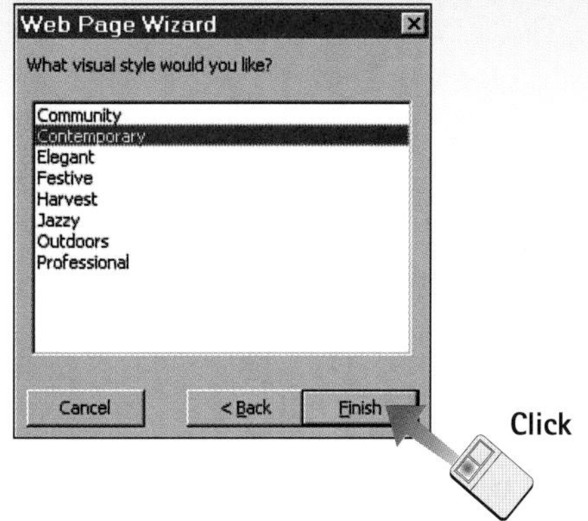

6 Insert Your Own Text

You can now fill in the Web page with your own text. Select the placeholder text and type your own. You can also enter your own hyperlinks.

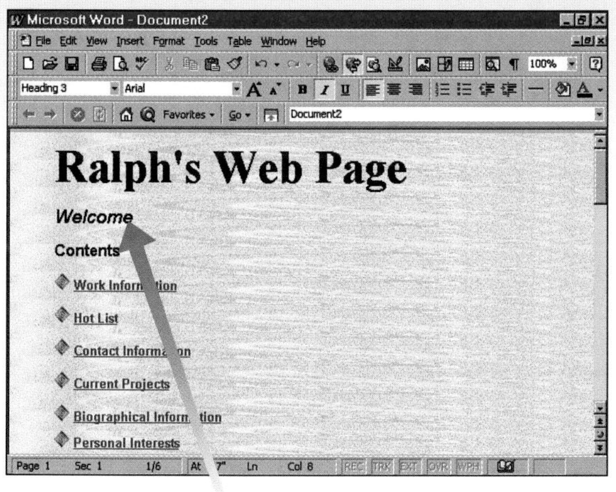

End

How-To Hints

Publish to the Web

Use Microsoft's Web Publishing Wizard to help you post your Web page to a server. If you're posting to a network server in your company, you will need to check with the system administrator for assistance. If you're posting the Web page to your Internet service provider's server, be sure to check the guidelines. When you're ready to post, click the **Start** menu and choose **Programs**, **Internet Explorer**, **Web Publishing Wizard**.

TASK 8

How to Create a Web Page in Word from Scratch

If you prefer to design your own Web page without help from Word's Web Page Wizard, you can use Word's formatting tools to assign styles and create headings and body text for your page. You can easily add lists and graphics (see Task 10, "How to Add Graphics to Your Web Page," to learn how). When you're finished, save your page to post on the Web.

Begin

1 Open the New Dialog Box

Display the **File** menu and select **New**. This opens the New dialog box.

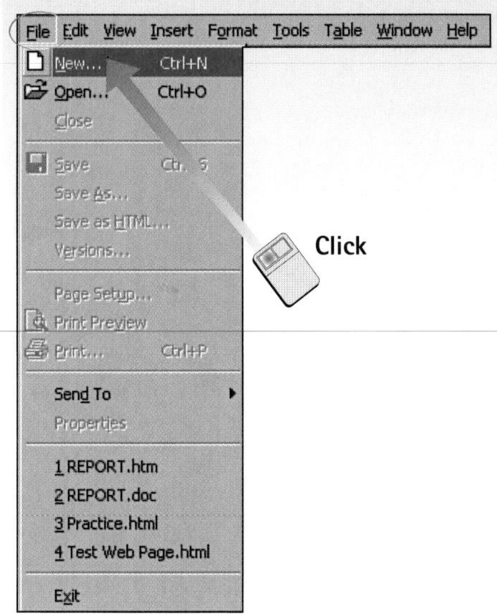

2 Select the Blank Web Page

From the **Web Pages** tab, double-click the **Blank Web Page** icon.

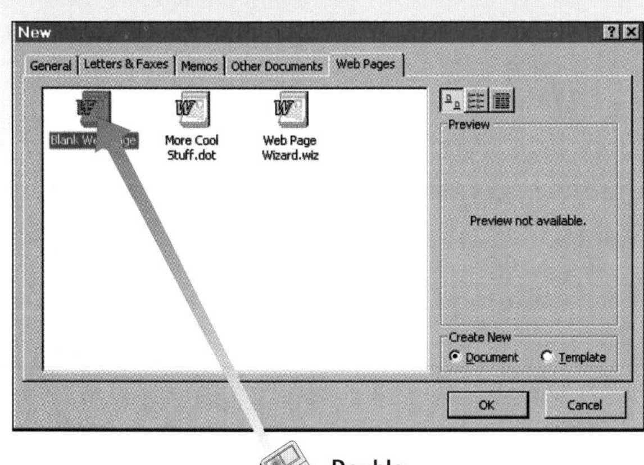

3 It's Blank

Word opens a very blank Web page in your program window.

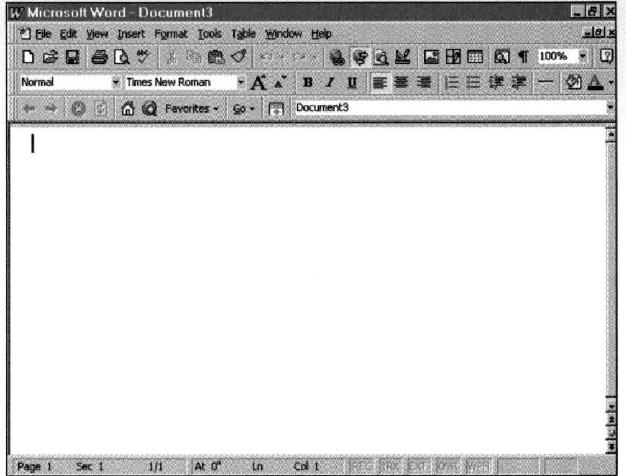

4 Select a Heading Style

To enter a heading for the Web page, click the **Style** drop-down list on the Formatting toolbar and choose a heading style, such as **Heading 1**. Heading styles range in size from large (Heading 1) to small (Heading 6).

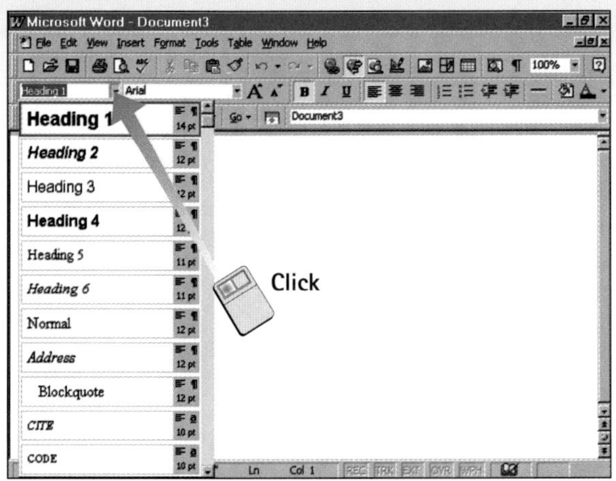

5 Type the Heading Text

Type the heading text. If you're creating a personal Web page, for example, you might type `Welcome to Ralph's Page`. If you're creating a company Web page, type the company name.

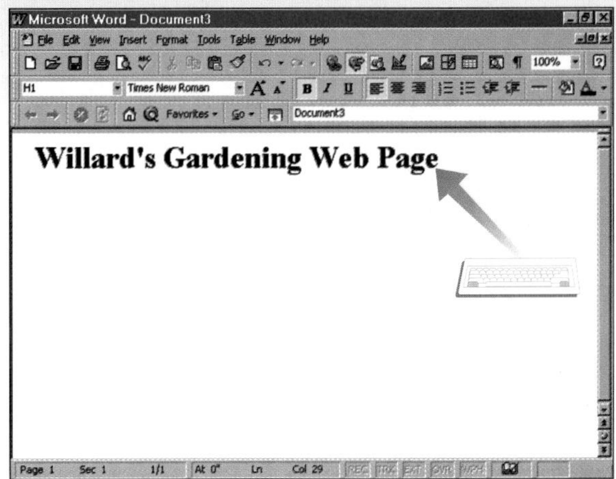

6 Keep Adding Text

Continue selecting styles to use and typing your own text. When you're finished, be sure to save your work. Check out Tasks 9, "How to Insert Hyperlinks," and 10, "How to Add Graphics to Your Web Page," to learn how to add links and graphics to your Web Page.

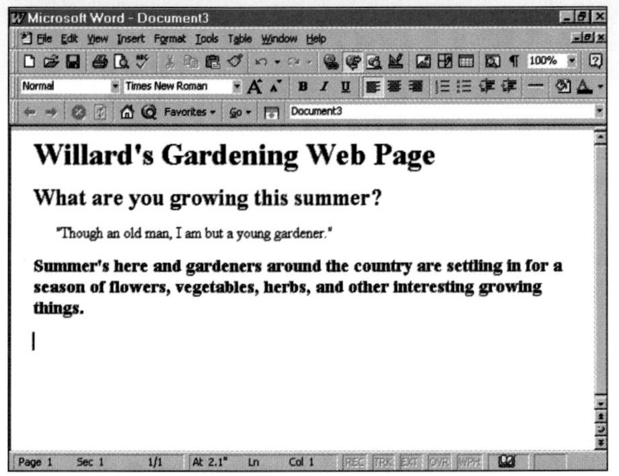

End

How-To Hints

Web Page Preview

You can preview how your Web page will look in a Web browser. Open the **File** menu and select **Web Page Preview**. This opens Internet Explorer and enables you to see how the page looks. Close the browser window to return to Word.

TASK 9

How to Insert Hyperlinks

You can quickly insert a hyperlink into your file, whether it's a Word document, an Excel worksheet, or any other Office file. The Office programs recognize URLs as links as soon as you type them. However, you must be careful about spelling the URL correctly.

When you're creating Web pages, you can turn any text into a link using the Insert Hyperlink dialog box. The dialog box enables you to create links to other Web pages or other Office files. If your Web page is exceptionally long, you can even link to other areas on the page.

Begin

1 Select the Text

Start by entering the text you want to use as a link. If you created a Web page using the Web Page Wizard, for example, you can select a pre-underlined link and type your own text. If you created a Web page from scratch, you can select any word or phrase to turn into a link.

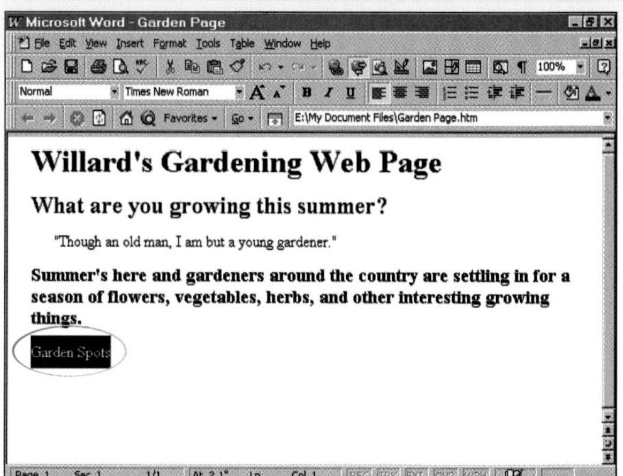

2 Open Insert Hyperlink Dialog Box

Click the **Create Hyperlink** button on the Standard toolbar. This opens the Insert Hyperlink dialog box.

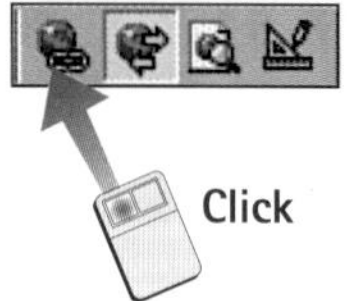

3 Enter the URL

Click inside the **Link to file or URL** text box and enter the URL of the Web page you want to link to.

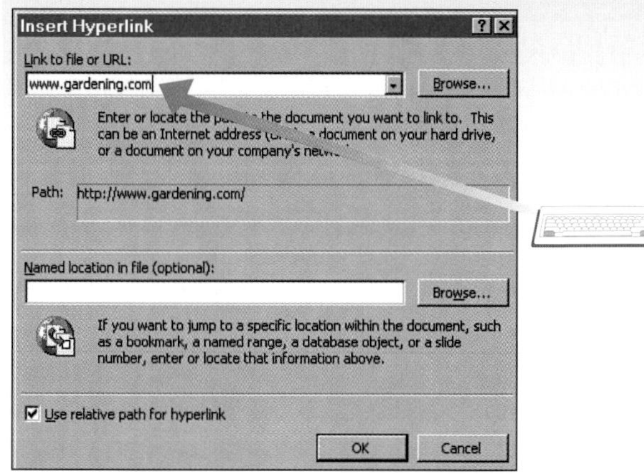

4 Exit the Dialog Box

Click **OK** to close the dialog box.

5 Examine the Link

The text you worked with appears in blue and has an underline to indicate it's a hyperlink. You can repeat these steps to add as many links as you like to the page.

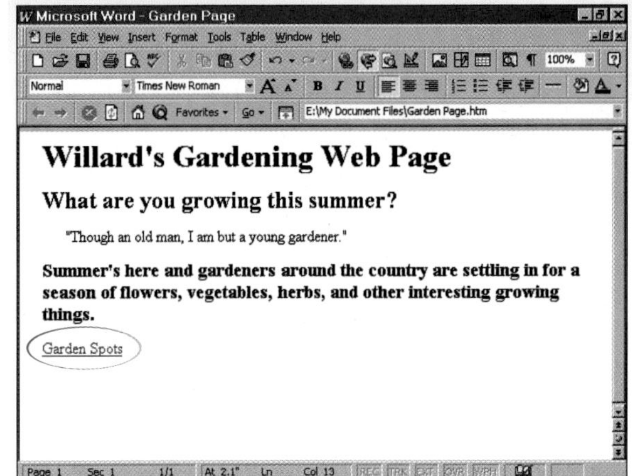

End

How-To Hints

Check Them Out

Be sure to check your URLs to make sure they're correct. It's frustrating to a Web surfer to encounter URLs that aren't up to date or that take the user to the wrong information.

Add Graphics

Learn how to add graphics to your Web page in Task 10. Graphics elements can add interest to your Web page.

TASK 10

How to Add Graphics to Your Web Page

Text isn't the only thing you can add to Web pages you create. You can also add graphics, ruled lines, tables, control buttons, multimedia clips, and more. This task will focus on adding images, which are easy to add to a page. Images can spruce up a drab Web page and add visual interest. You can use company logos, photos, and clip art, for example, or graphics objects you draw yourself.

Most Web browsers can only display GIF, JPEG, and XBM image files, so it's best to stick with these file types when inserting images into your own pages.

Begin

1 Click in Place

Click the insertion point where you want to insert the image. It's a good idea to put an image at the top of the Web page so the person viewing your page immediately sees your nice graphic.

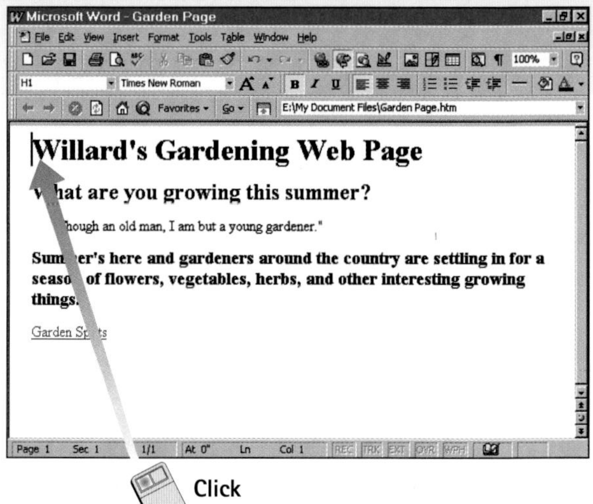

2 Click the Insert Picture Button

Click the **Insert Picture** button on the Standard toolbar. This opens the Insert Picture dialog box.

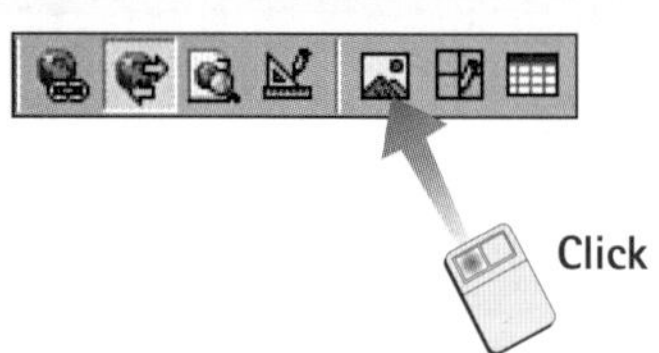

3 Locate the Image

Find and select the image file you want to use in your Web page and click the **Insert** button.

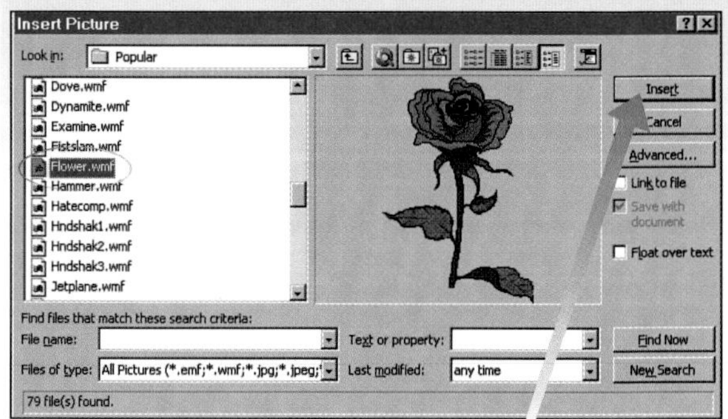

4 Resize the Image

The image is inserted into your page. You can resize it by selecting it and dragging any of the resizing handles.

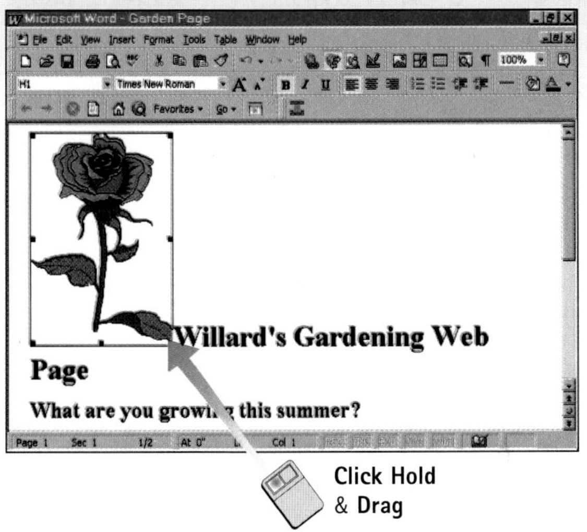

Click Hold & Drag

5 Position the Image

To better position the image next to text, right-click and select **Format Picture** from the shortcut menu. This opens the Picture dialog box, where you can fine-tune the wrapping and positioning controls for the image.

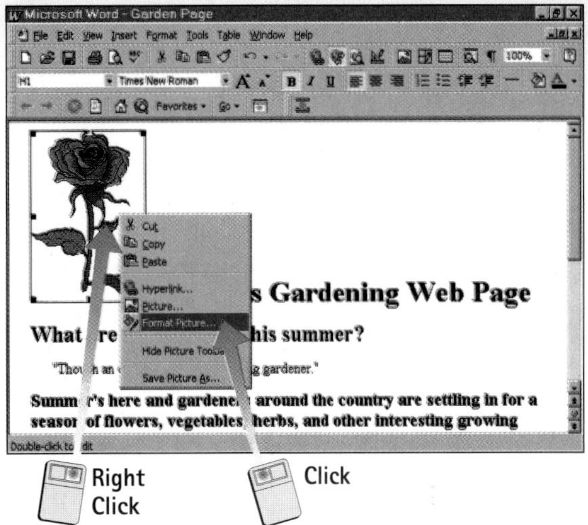

Right Click

Click

6 Change Position Settings

Click the **Position** tab and choose a **Text wrapping** option. You can also set the image a specific distance from the text using the **Vertical** and **Horizontal** distance controls. Enter the value in inches (such as .25 or 1).

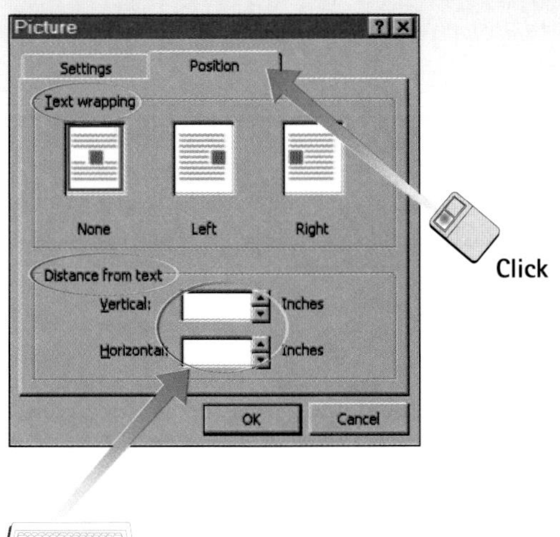

Click

7 Use the Settings Tab

Finally, click the **Settings** tab and enter a description of the image in the **Picture placeholder Text** box. This text will describe the image in case it doesn't display properly in the Web browser window. Some users choose to browse the Web without viewing graphics to speed up their downloading time. Click **OK** to save your new settings.

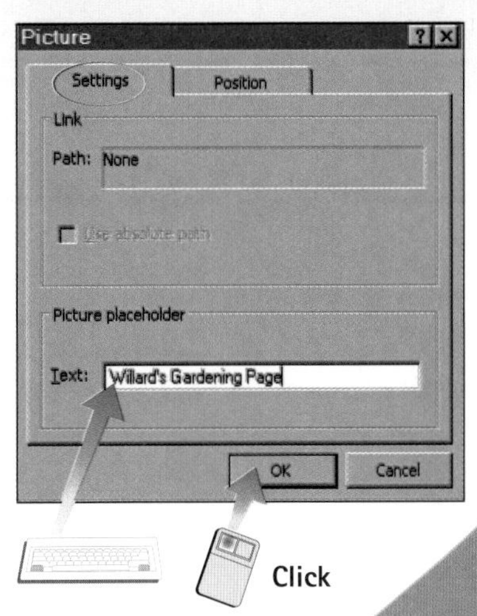

Click

End

Task

CHAPTER 16

How to Work with Office Graphics Tools

The Office programs share a lot of common features, but many users aren't aware of the common graphics tools available in each program. Each application enables you to add objects to your files, such as *clip art*, shapes, WordArt, and more. You can dress up a Word document with a piece of clip art from the Microsoft Clip Gallery, for example, or insert an image file from another program into your Outlook *email* message. You can draw your own shapes to include on *Excel charts* or *PowerPoint* slides.

In this chapter, you learn how to utilize the Office graphics tools to enhance your documents, *worksheets*, *database* tables and forms, slides, and more. Learn how to draw basic shapes, insert pictures and clip art, create a WordArt image, and manipulate and format graphics objects. Don't be intimidated by the thought of creating and adding visual objects to your files; the Office 97 graphics tools make it easy to illustrate any Office item you create.

TASK 1

How to Draw Basic Shapes

One of the easiest ways to add visual appeal to a document, worksheet, or slide is to add a shape, such as a rectangle or oval. A shape can draw attention to parts of your text, create a nice background effect, or function as a design element. You can also add lines, arcs, and freeform shapes using the drawing tools.

The Office 97 drawing tools are accessible in Word, Excel, and PowerPoint. To view them, open the Drawing toolbar; right-click over any toolbar and select **Drawing** or click the **Drawing** button (Word and Excel). By default, the Drawing toolbar appears automatically in PowerPoint.

Begin

1 Select a Tool

Click the shape tool you want to draw; choose from **Rectangle** or **Oval**. To draw a rectangle, for example, click the **Rectangle** tool on the Drawing toolbar. Your mouse pointer takes the shape of a crosshair.

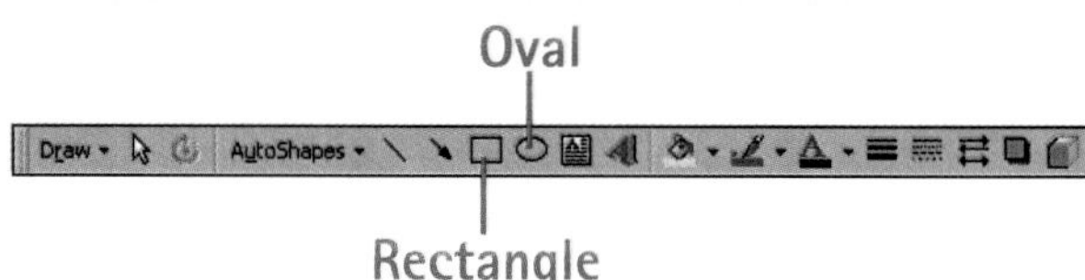
Oval
Draw
AutoShapes
Rectangle

2 Drag the Shape

Move the mouse pointer to the location on the document, worksheet, or slide where you want the shape to appear. Click and drag the mouse to draw the shape. When the shape reaches the desired shape and size, click the mouse button again. You can now resize, move, or format the shape object.

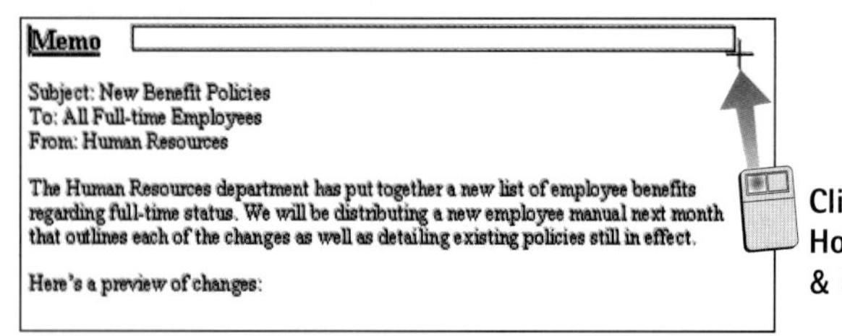
Memo
Subject: New Benefit Policies
To: All Full-time Employees
From: Human Resources
The Human Resources department has put together a new list of employee benefits regarding full-time status. We will be distributing a new employee manual next month that outlines each of the changes as well as detailing existing policies still in effect.
Here's a preview of changes:
Click
Hold
& Drag

3 Draw a Line

Drawing lines or arrows is a lot like drawing shapes. Click the tool you want to draw; choose from **Line** or **Arrow**. To draw a line, for example, click the **Line** tool on the Drawing toolbar. Your mouse pointer takes the shape of a crosshair.

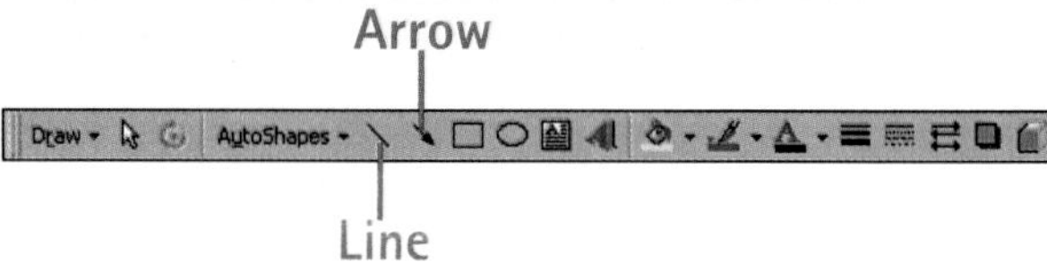
Arrow
Draw
AutoShapes
Line

4 Drag the Line

Move the mouse pointer to the location on the document, worksheet, or slide where you want the line to appear. Click and drag the mouse to draw the line. When the line is the size you want, click the mouse button again.

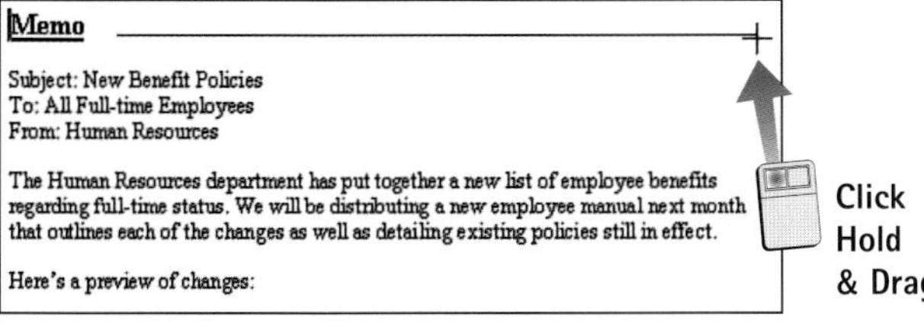
Memo
Subject: New Benefit Policies
To: All Full-time Employees
From: Human Resources
The Human Resources department has put together a new list of employee benefits regarding full-time status. We will be distributing a new employee manual next month that outlines each of the changes as well as detailing existing policies still in effect.
Here's a preview of changes:
Click
Hold
& Drag

5 Draw a Freeform Shape

Use the Freeform tool to draw a polygon or freeform shape. To open the Freeform tool, click the **AutoShapes** button on the Drawing toolbar, select the **Lines** category, and choose the **Freeform** tool.

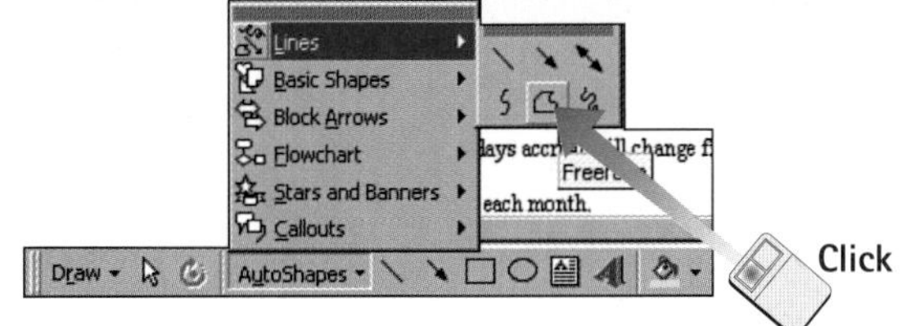
Lines
Basic Shapes
Block Arrows
Flowchart
Stars and Banners
Callouts
Draw
AutoShapes
Click

6 Drag or Anchor

To draw a polygon shape, click where you want the shape to start, and then keep clicking each anchor point (also called a vertex) in place until the shape is finished. To draw a freeform shape, drag the mouse instead of clicking (the mouse pointer takes the shape of a pencil icon), and then click in place when finished. The figure below shows the two types of techniques applied.

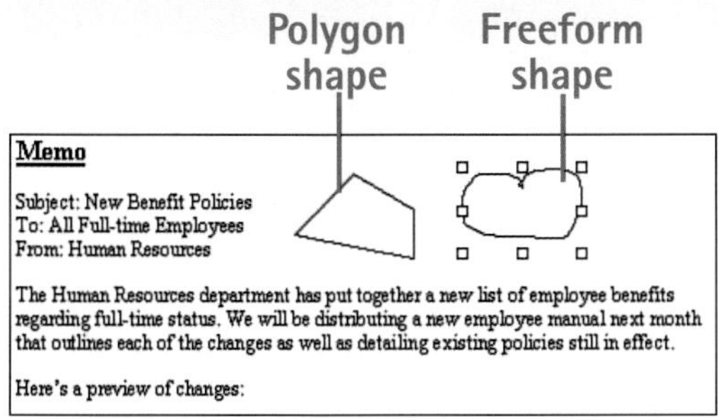
Polygon shape
Freeform shape
Memo
Subject: New Benefit Policies
To: All Full-time Employees
From: Human Resources
The Human Resources department has put together a new list of employee benefits regarding full-time status. We will be distributing a new employee manual next month that outlines each of the changes as well as detailing existing policies still in effect.
Here's a preview of changes:

End

How-To Hints

Use AutoShapes

If you're not too keen on drawing your own shapes, use the available predrawn shapes. Click the **AutoShapes** tool on the Drawing toolbar to display a list of categories. Click the category you want to use; a palette of custom shapes appears. Click a shape. You can now click and drag the mouse pointer on the document until the shape reaches the size you want. Release the mouse button, and the complete shape appears.

Draw Perfect Shapes

To draw a perfect shape every time, hold down the Shift key while you drag. This keeps the proportions intact as you drag.

Switch Views

When you draw a shape in Word, you're automatically switched to Page Layout view where you can see *graphics objects* onscreen.

TASK 2

How to Insert Clip Art

Another way to add visual impact to your Office files is to insert clip art. Clip art images are pre-made drawings covering a wide range of topics and categories. You can insert clip art into any Office item you create, such as a letter, a worksheet, a database form, an Outlook note, or a slide.

In the Microsoft Clip Gallery dialog box, you can choose from clip art and photographs, as well as sounds and videos. In addition to the clip art available in the Gallery, you can also find clip art on the Web.

Begin

1 Open the Clip Gallery Dialog Box

Click the mouse pointer where you want the clip art inserted, and then open the **Insert** menu and choose **Picture**, **Clip Art**. This opens the Microsoft Clip Gallery dialog box.

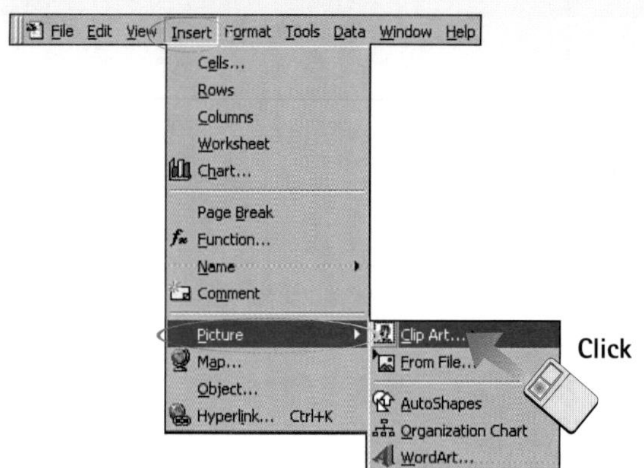

2 View Clip Art

From the **Clip Art** tab, peruse the catalog of clip art. To choose a category, click it, and the preview area shows the available graphics, or choose **All Categories** to see all the choices.

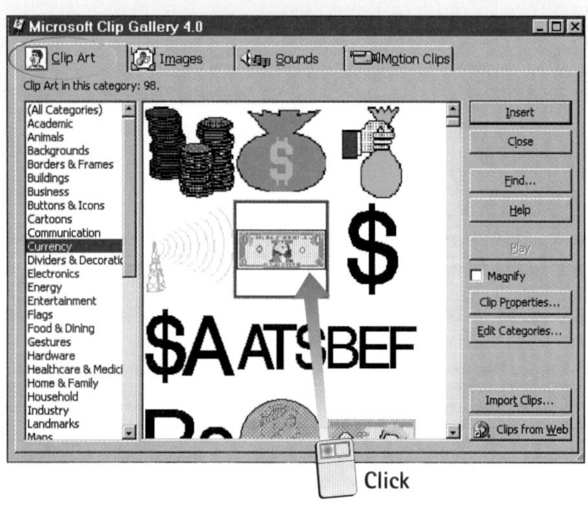

3 Magnify a Picture

To get a better look at any clip art picture, select the picture, and then select the **Magnify** check box.

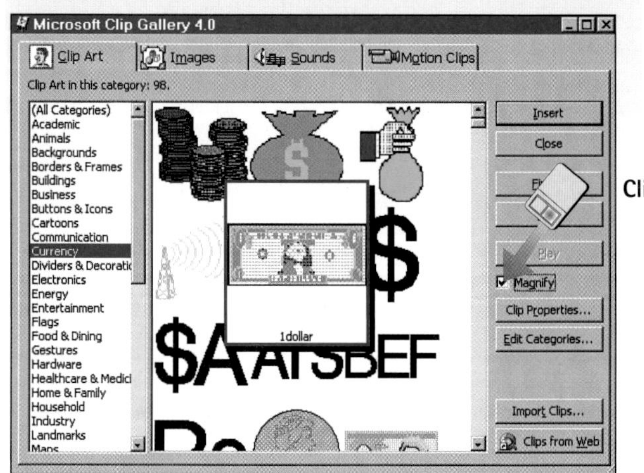

4 Select a Picture

When you find a clip art piece you want to use, double-click it to insert it into your file.

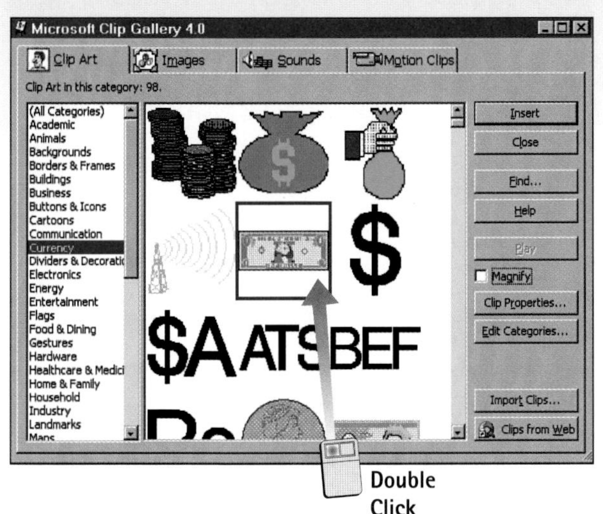

5 The Picture Appears

The Microsoft Clip Gallery dialog box closes and the clip art appears in your file. You can now resize or move the image.

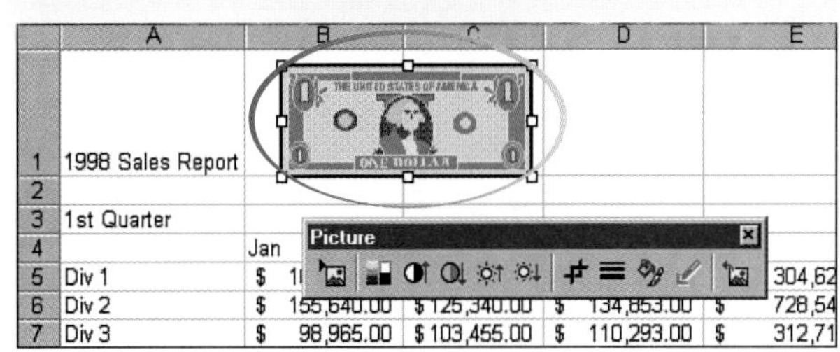

End

How-To Hints

Use Photos, Sounds, and Videos

In addition to the vast collection of clip art, the Microsoft Clip Gallery also has photos, sound clips, and video clips you can add to your presentation. Be sure to check out the other tabs in the Clip Gallery dialog box to see what's available.

Find Clip Art on the Web

You can import clip art images from Microsoft's Clip Gallery Live Web site. Click the **Clips from Web** button in the lower-right corner of the Clip Gallery dialog box. This opens your Web browser to the Microsoft site where you can choose more clip art.

Find More Clip Art

Microsoft's Web site isn't the only place to find clip art. Plenty of clip art is available on the Web; use Internet Explorer to conduct a Web search to look for more clip art. Turn to Task 3, "How to Perform a Web Search," in Chapter 15, "How to Use the Office 97 Internet Tools," to learn how.

Insert Other Graphics

You can also use graphics created in other programs. For example, you might have a picture file created with Microsoft Paint. You can use the picture file in your Office 97 documents. Task 3, "How to Insert an Object," explains how to insert other graphics objects.

TASK 3

How to Insert an Object

If you have a picture file from another program, you can insert it into your Office document, worksheet, database form, email message, or slide. You can also insert objects such as scanned images, Word tables, Excel worksheets, and other types of visual objects.

Visual objects can be inserted in different ways, depending on the program you're using. One way is to use the **Insert**, **Object** command. This opens the Object dialog box where you can access a variety of visual objects.

Begin

1 Open the Object Dialog Box

Display the **Insert** menu and select **Object**. This opens the Object dialog box.

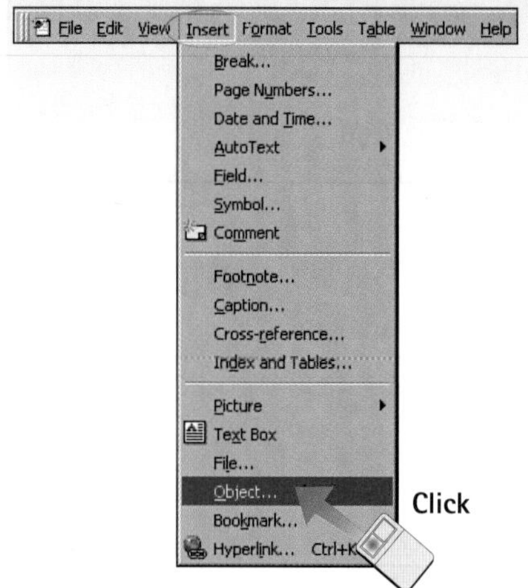

2 Display the Create from File Tab

To insert an existing object file, click the **Create from File** tab.

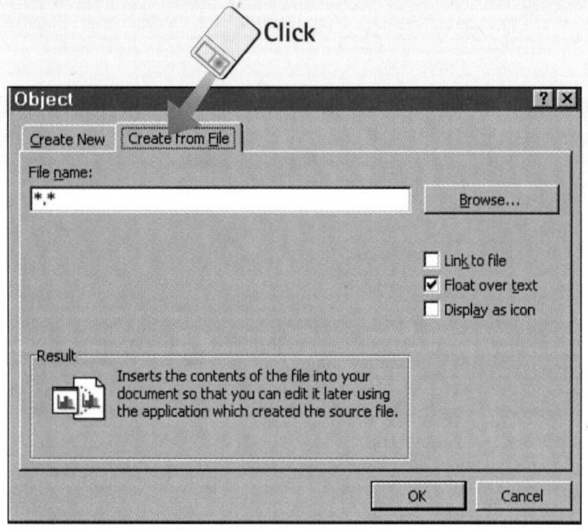

3 Open the Browse Dialog Box

To find the object file you want to insert, click the **Browse** button to open the Browse dialog box.

4 Locate the Object File

Locate the picture file or other visual object file you want to use. When you find the file, select it and click **OK** to return to the Object dialog box.

5 Click OK

When you're ready to insert the object file, click **OK**.

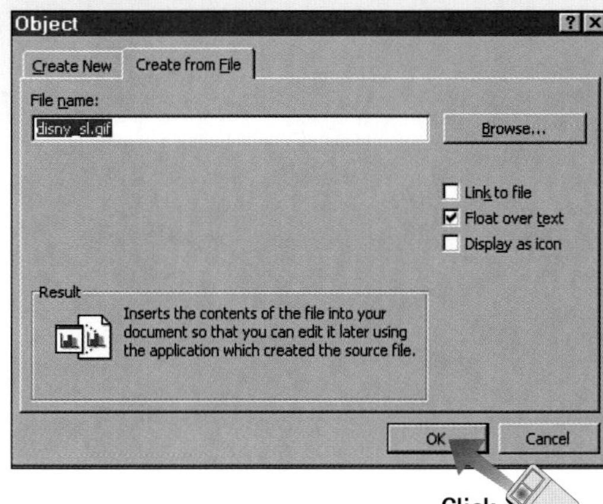

End

How-To Hints

Resize and Move

After you insert the picture, you can resize it or move it around. Learn how in Task 5, "How to Move and Size an Image," later in this chapter.

Insert Trick

If you find that you need to add the same picture file over and over to Word documents, add the picture file to Word's AutoCorrect collection. First, insert the picture file into a document and select the graphic. Open the **Tools** menu and choose **AutoCorrect**. In the AutoCorrect dialog box, enter the picture's filename in the **With** box and type a text entry for the picture in the **Replace** box. If it's a company logo, for example, you might type `mylogo`. Click **Add** to add the entry to the list and click **OK**. The next time you type `mylogo`, the text will be replaced with the picture.

TASK 4

How to Insert a WordArt Image

One of the more popular features of the Office graphics tools is the WordArt application. WordArt enables you to turn text into *graphics objects* that bend, twist, rotate, and assume a variety of special effects. You can turn ordinary words into works of art.

WordArt is especially helpful when you need to create a company logo, a banner for a newsletter or flyer, or draw attention to important words, such as SALE or URGENT. After you design a WordArt object, you can move and resize it as needed.

Begin

1 Open the WordArt Gallery

Open the **Insert** menu and select **Picture**, **WordArt**, or click the **WordArt** tool on the Drawing toolbar. This opens the WordArt Gallery dialog box.

2 Choose an Effect

Select a WordArt style that best suits your needs. The samples show the shape and effect of the style. Click **OK** to continue.

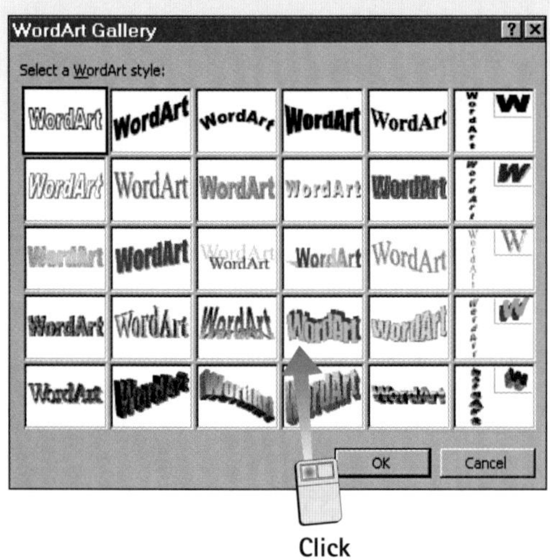

3 Enter Your Own Text

In the Edit WordArt Text dialog box, enter the text you want to use as your WordArt object.

4 Format the Text

Use the **Font** drop-down box to select another font style, if necessary. You can also change the formatting attributes for size, bold, or italic. When you have finished with your selections, click **OK**.

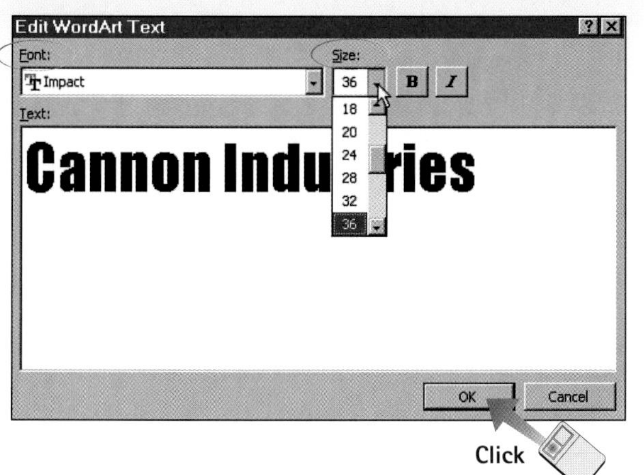

5 WordArt Is Created

The WordArt object appears in your Office file along with the WordArt toolbar. Use the toolbar buttons to fine-tune your WordArt object.

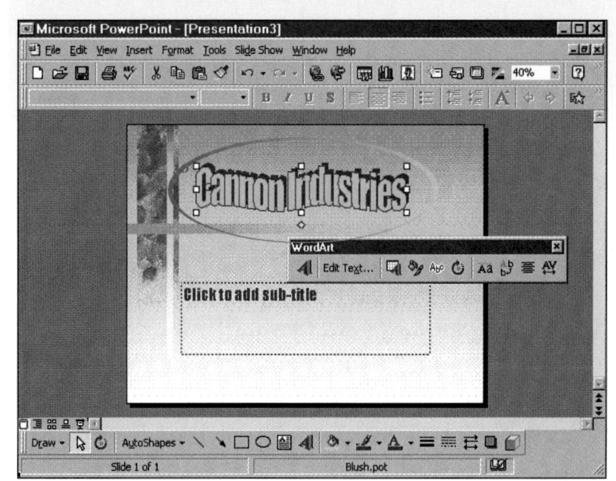

End

How-To Hints

Edit WordArt

Any time you need to edit your WordArt object, double-click it to reopen the text box where you can edit the text. You can use the tools on the WordArt toolbar to format the object.

Try Them All!

To change your WordArt's shape or style, select the WordArt object and click the **WordArt Gallery** button on the WordArt toolbar. This opens the WordArt Gallery dialog box again, and you can choose a new style to apply. You may need to experiment with several kinds before you find one you like.

Resize and Move

After you insert the WordArt object, you can resize it or move it around. Learn how in Task 5 later in this chapter.

I Changed My Mind!

If you open the WordArt Gallery and change your mind about using the feature, click **Cancel**. If you have already started creating an image, and then change your mind, click outside the picture. To remove a WordArt image you have already created, select it and press the Delete key.

Endless Selections

By changing the text effects, fonts, sizes, and formatting attributes, you can create different WordArt shapes and designs. To reverse any of the changes you make, click **Undo**.

TASK 5

How to Move and Size an Image

Any visual object you add to your Office file can be resized and moved. After you select an object, selection handles surround it. These handles can be dragged in any direction to resize the object. You can also drag the object to a new location. The tricky part is knowing exactly where to click to perform either action. In this task, you will learn how to move and resize any object.

Begin

1 Select the Object

Select the object you want to move or resize. Notice as soon as you select it, tiny boxes, called selection handles, surround it.

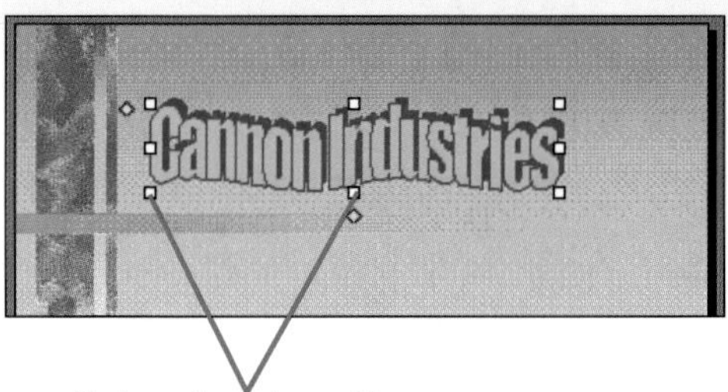

Selection handles

2 Drag to Move

Hover your mouse pointer over the selected object until you see a four-headed arrow. Drag the object to a new location.

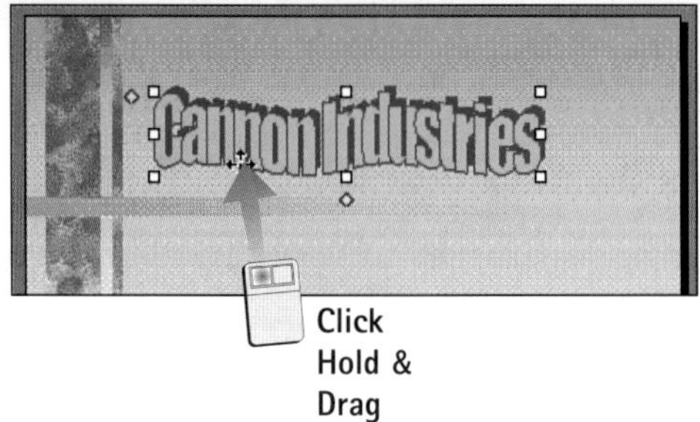

Click
Hold &
Drag

3 Resize in One Dimension

To resize a selected object in one dimension—that is, to stretch or shrink the object—use only the resizing handles along the sides of the object. To stretch the object, for example, hover your mouse pointer over the handle on the right side, then drag the handle. This stretches the object.

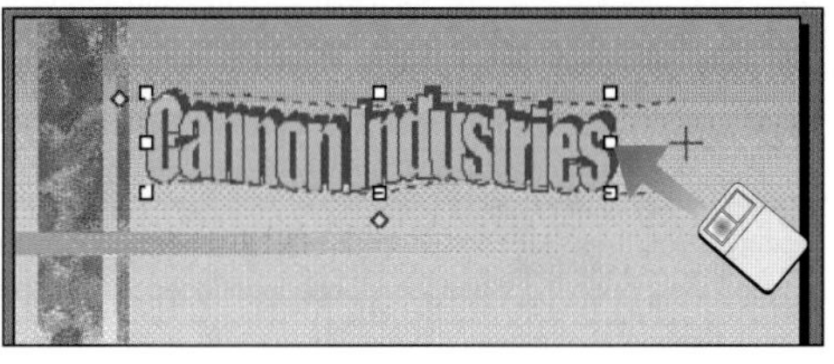

Click
Hold &
Drag

4 Resize in Two Dimensions

To resize the object in two dimensions, use any of the corner handles. This will enable you to resize both the object's height and width at the same time. Hover your mouse pointer over a corner handle and drag.

Click
Hold &
Drag

5 Use the Shift Key

To maintain the object's height-to-width ratio while resizing, hold down the Shift key while you drag a corner selection handle.

Click
Hold &
Drag

6 Use the Ctrl Key

To resize in two dimensions at once, from the center of the object outward, hold down the Ctrl key and drag any corner selection handle.

Control

Click
Hold &
Drag

End

How-To Hints

Copy and Paste

You can easily copy and paste objects you draw or insert with the Office graphics tools. Select the object, then use the **Cut**, **Copy**, and **Paste** commands to move the object to a new location; or copy the object and place it in a new location. Use the **Cut**, **Copy**, and **Paste** buttons on the toolbar, or use the **Edit** menu to move, copy, and paste.

TASK 6

How to Change Image Formatting

Many of the visual objects you add can be enhanced with formatting tools. You can format the shapes you draw, for example, by changing the fill color or line style. Adjusting your image's formatting can completely change the look of the object. You can tone down an object's loud primary colors by using pastel colors instead. Or change the importance of the line you have drawn by making its line weight thicker.

Begin

1 Select the Object

First select the object whose formatting you want to change.

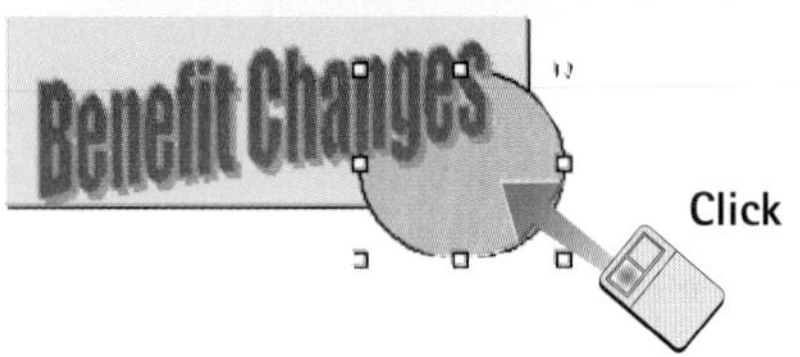

2 Choose the Format Command

Right-click the object to display the shortcut menu, and then select the **Format** command at the bottom of the menu. Depending on the type of visual object you select, the name of the command will vary. If you right-click a shape, for example, it appears as **Format AutoShape**. If you right-click a text box, it says **Format Text Box**.

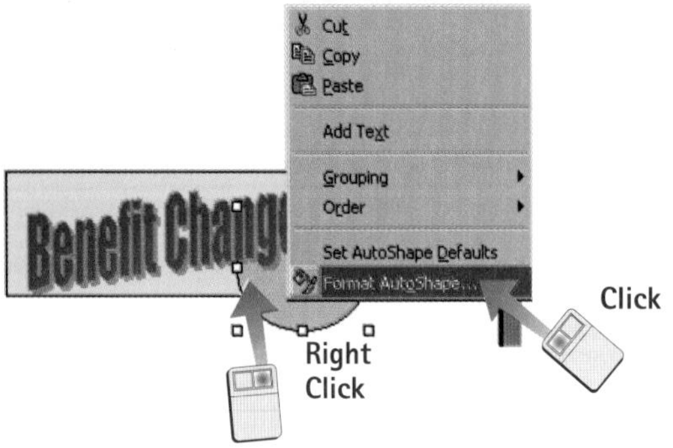

3 The Format Dialog Box

The Format dialog box appears, based on the type of visual object you selected. Click the **Colors and Lines** tab to find options for changing the color or line style of the object.

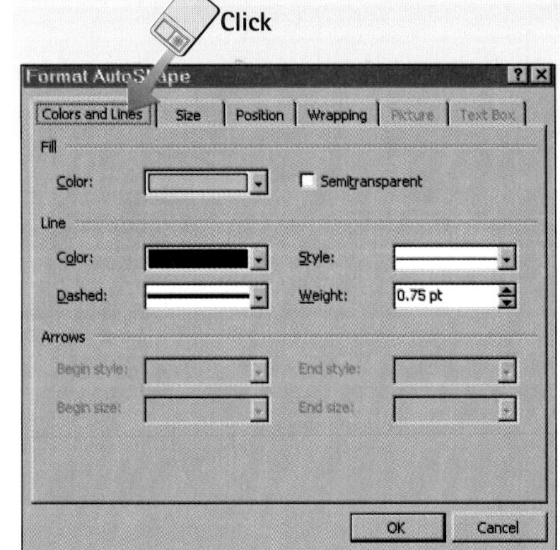

4 Change the Fill Color

To change the fill color, click the **Fill Color** drop-down list and choose another color from the palette.

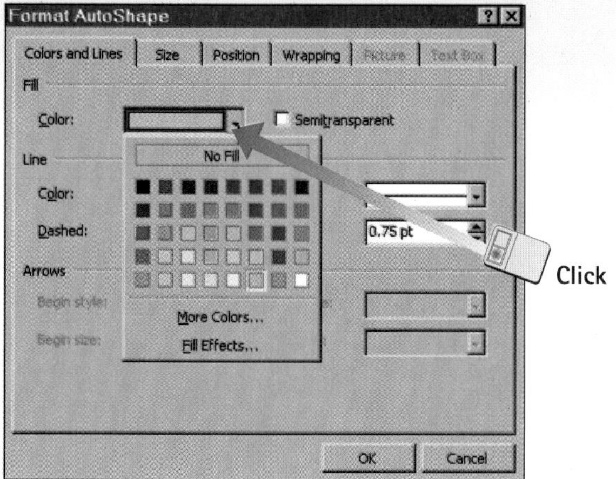

5 Change the Line Weight

If your object has an outline or border, or if it is a line or arc, use the **Line** options in the **Colors and Lines** tab to change the line's color, style, or weight (set an exact thickness). Click the **Style** drop-down arrow, for example, to display a list of line styles.

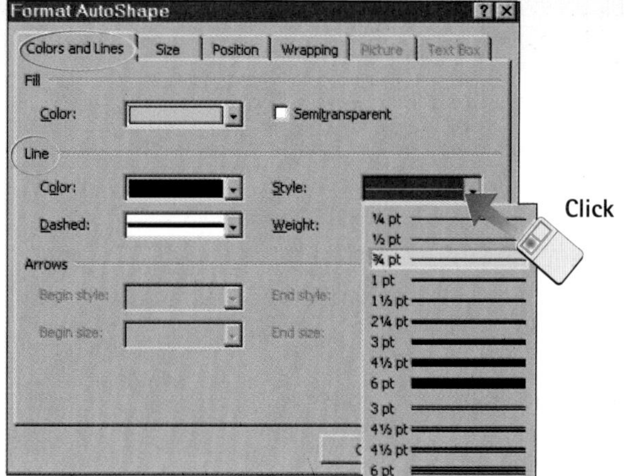

6 Wrap Text Around Objects

If you want the visual object to sit in the middle of text, you can apply wrapping commands to designate how the text flows around—or through—the object. Click the **Wrapping** tab and choose a wrapping style to apply. Click **OK** to exit the dialog box and apply any new formatting settings.

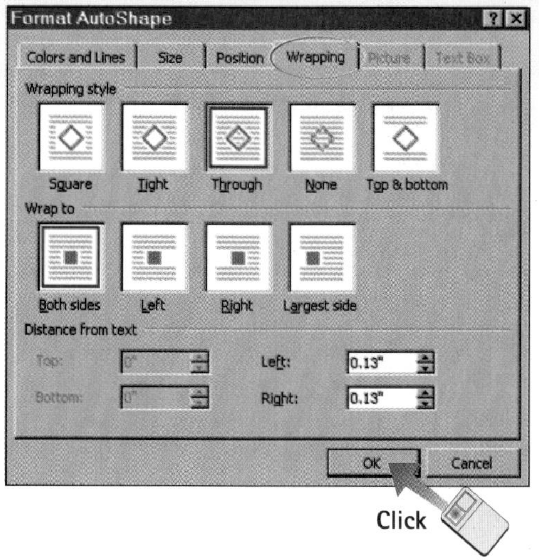

End

How-To Hints

Other Formatting Options

Be sure to check out the other tabs in the Format dialog box. You can apply numerous other options, depending on the visual object you selected.

Or Use the Drawing Toolbar

The Drawing toolbar has formatting tools you can apply directly to the objects you select. To quickly fill an object with a color, for example, click the **Fill Color** button. To choose another line style to use, click the **Line Style** button.

TASK 7

How to Add Shadow Effects

Another way to spruce up visual objects is to add shadow effects. A shadow can give a 3D effect to any text box, shape, clip art picture, line, WordArt design, or other visual object. With the drawing tool's Shadow Settings toolbar, you can control exactly where the shadow appears and its color, and you can turn the shadow off if you don't like it anymore.

Begin

1 Select the Object

To add a shadow effect to any object, first select the object.

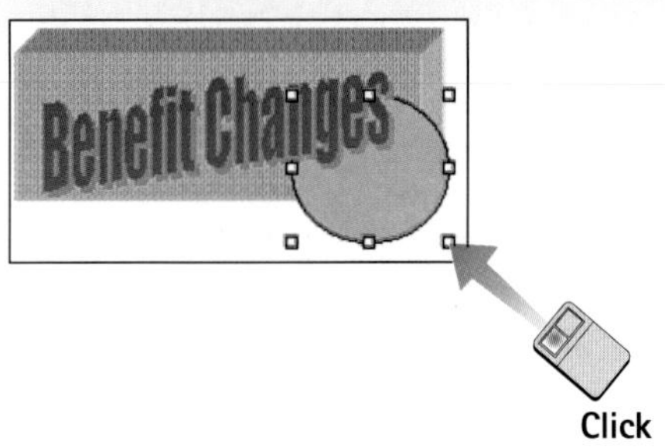

2 Click the Shadow Button

Click the **Shadow** button on the Drawing toolbar to display a palette of shadow effects. To apply an effect, click the one you want.

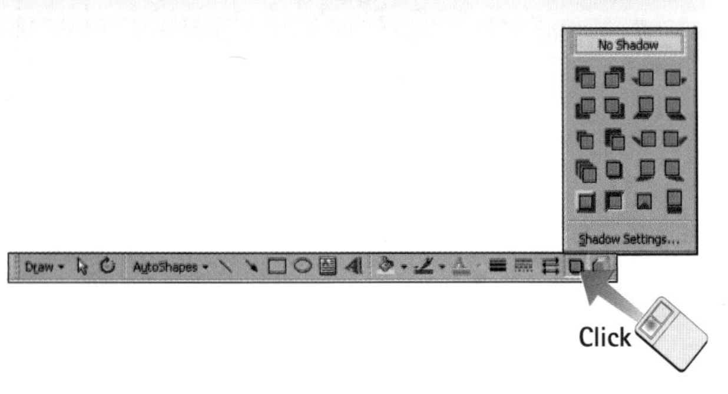

3 Shadow Applied

The shadow effect is immediately applied to the object.

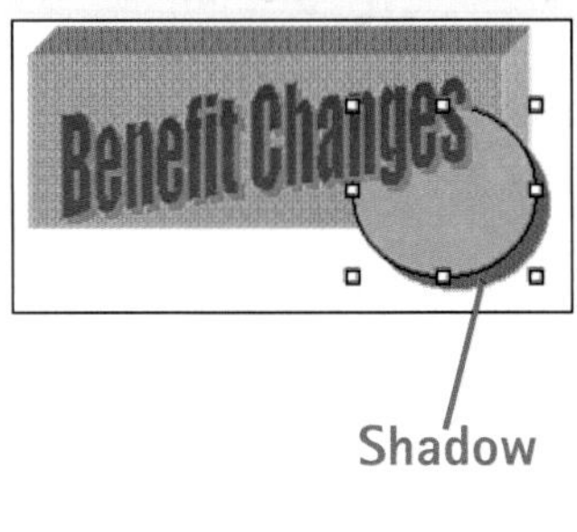

4 Open Shadow Settings Toolbar

For more control over the shadow, display the Shadow Settings toolbar. Click the **Shadow** button, and then select **Shadow Settings** from the palette.

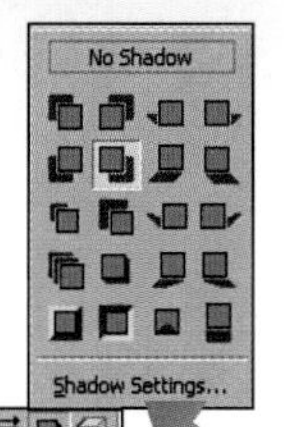

5 Nudge the Shadow

Use the Shadow Settings toolbar buttons to nudge your shadow and position it exactly where you want it to fall. Use the **Nudge** buttons to nudge the shadow effect in the direction you want it to go.

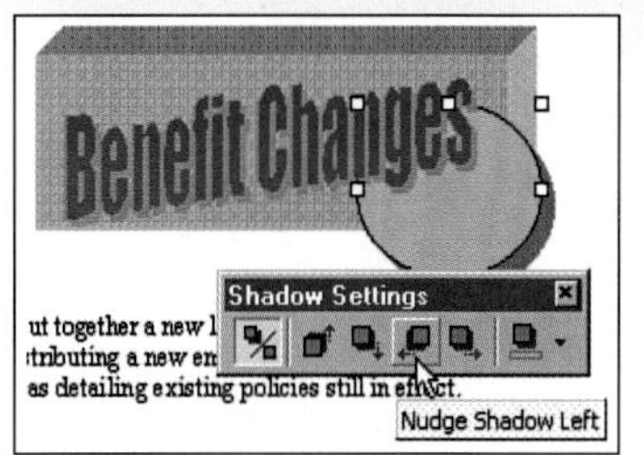

6 Choose a Shadow Color

To change the shadow's color, click the **Shadow Color** drop-down box and click a new color to use. As soon as you select a new color, it's applied to the visual object. To close the Shadow Settings toolbar, click its **Close** button.

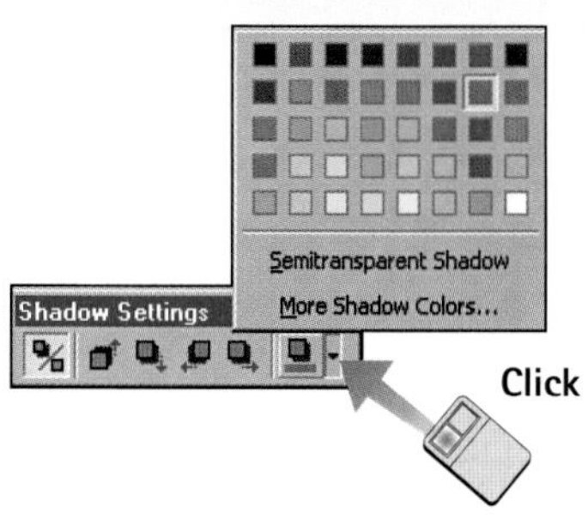

End

How-To Hints

Instant 3D Effects

You can give your visual objects instant 3D effects with the **3-D** button on the Drawing toolbar. Click the button to display a palette of 3D effects you can apply. To open the 3D Settings floating toolbar, click **3-D Settings** on the palette. Now you can fine-tune the effects until you find just the right effect for your object.

TASK 8

How to Group and Ungroup Objects

Use layering and grouping commands to change the way the objects appear on the document. You can stack objects on top of each other to create interesting effects, for example, such as positioning a WordArt effect over a shape object to create a logo.

You can also group objects together so you can treat them as a single object. Perhaps you have several objects stacked in place, for example, but find you need to move them over a bit. Rather than moving each object separately and relayering them, use the Grouping command to move the entire group as one object. After you have moved the group, you can ungroup the objects again to edit them separately.

Begin

1 Layer the Objects

To layer objects, start by moving them on top of each other to create an effect. You might place a WordArt object on top of a shape you have drawn, for example, or stack a clip art object onto a larger shape to act as a background.

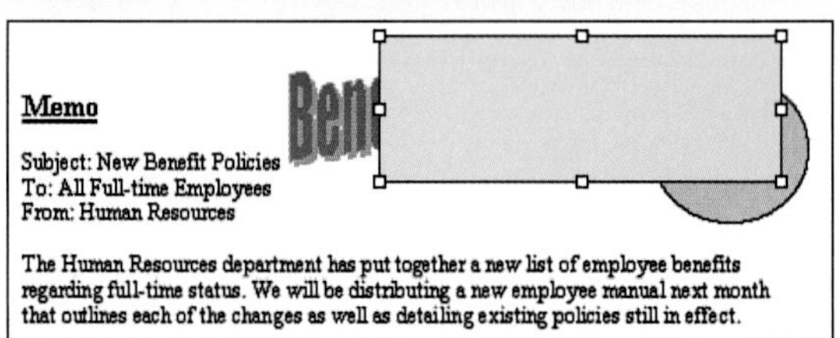

2 Bring an Object to the Front

To move an object to the top of the stack, select the object you want to reorder, and then right-click to display the shortcut menu. Select **Order, Bring to Front.**

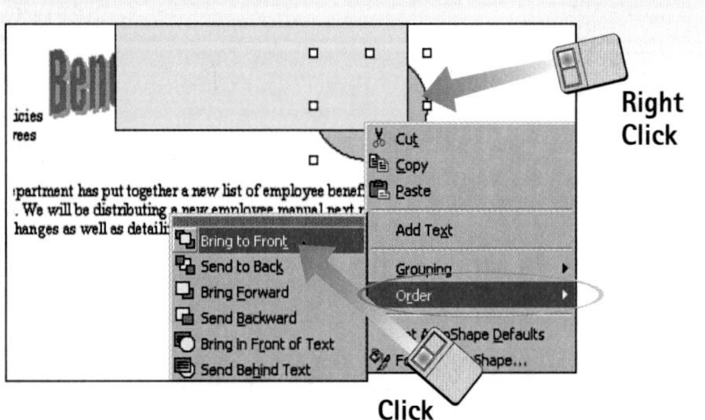

3 Move an Object to the Back

To move an object to the bottom of the stack, select the object, right-click to display the shortcut menu, and select **Order, Send to Back.**

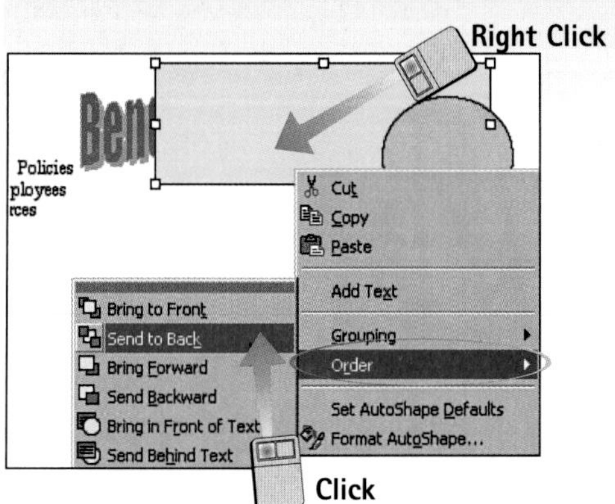

4 Select the Objects to Group

To group several objects together, select each object by clicking the object and holding down the Shift key. (Notice each object's selection handles are active.)

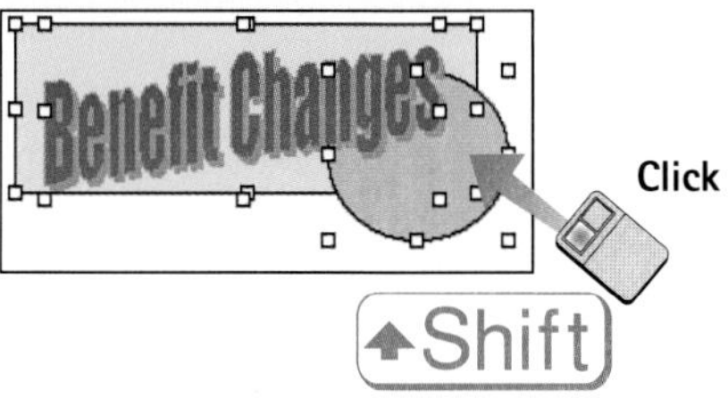

5 Use the Group Command

Right-click any of the selected objects and choose **Grouping**, **Group** from the shortcut menu.

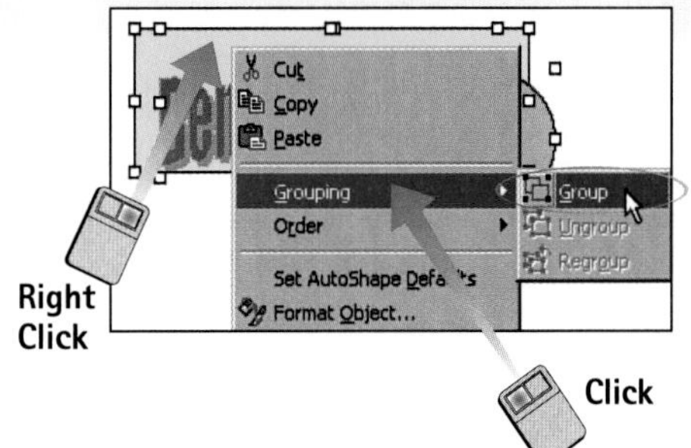

6 A Single Group

The objects are now grouped and surrounded by one set of selection handles. To ungroup the objects again, right-click and select **Grouping**, **Ungroup**.

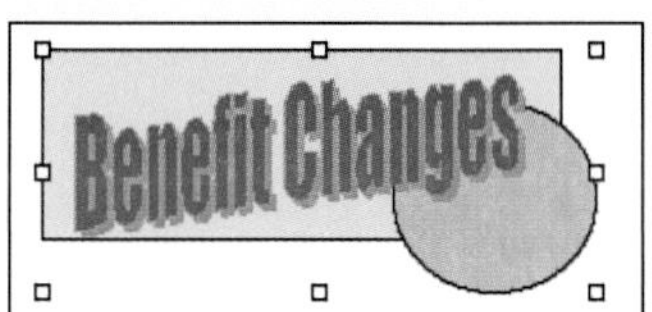

End

How-To Hints

Layer by Layer

To move layers forward or backward, one layer at a time, use the **Bring Forward** or **Send Backward** commands.

Group Shortcut

After you have a group of objects layered correctly, you may need to move them to another position. Drag your mouse in a rectangle that encloses all the objects; when you release your mouse, you have created a group. Drag the group to another part of the slide, and the layers keep their places. Click anywhere outside the group to ungroup the objects.

Task

CHAPTER 17

How to Integrate Office Applications

Although each Office 97 application is a powerful tool in itself, the combined programs offer even more versatility. Integrating the Office programs expands the type of tasks you can perform, and sharing data among programs can save you valuable time.

You can share data among programs in several ways. You can use the standard Cut, Copy, and Paste commands to quickly move or copy data from one program to the next, by way of the Windows Clipboard (a temporary storage area). However, the cut or copied data does not retain a relationship with the original program. Use linking and embedding, or *OLE* (stands for object linking and embedding), to retain a connection to the data's source of origin. For example, you can link an Excel range to a Word report. Any time the information changes in the Excel range, the linked data in the Word report reflects the changes, too. You can link entire files or specific data. You can embed objects you have already created, or embed new objects you create from scratch.

In this chapter, you will learn how to use the various methods for sharing data across programs, and learn how to integrate information from one Office program into another.

TASK 1

How to Cut, Copy, and Paste Data Among Programs

The easiest way to share data among programs is to use the Cut, Copy, and Paste commands. Use the Cut command to move data from one program to the next. Use the Copy command to duplicate the data in one program and place it in another. When you cut or copy data, it's placed in the Windows Clipboard, a temporary storage area, until it's pasted into a new location.

You can use the Cut, Copy, and Paste commands to move or duplicate text, pictures, formulas, or any type of data you place in a file. You can also use these commands to share data among non-Microsoft programs, too.

Begin

1 Select the Data

First, select the data you want to cut or copy.

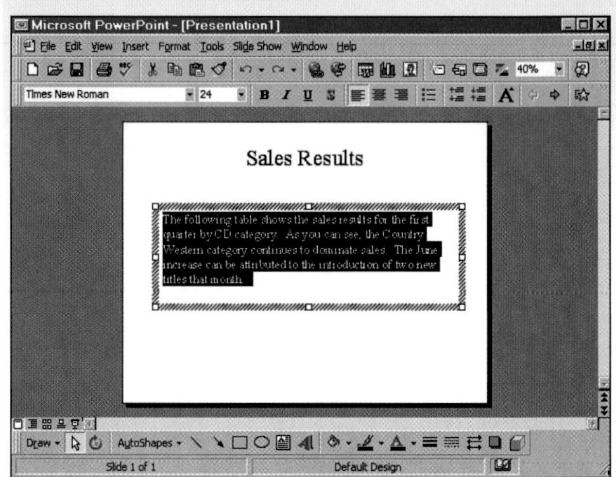

2 Move the Data

To move the data from one file to another, click the **Cut** button on the toolbar, or open the **Edit** menu and select **Cut**. This removes the data from the file and places it in the Windows Clipboard.

3 Copy the Data

To copy the data from one file to another, click the **Copy** button on the toolbar, or open the **Edit** menu and choose **Copy**. This places a duplicate of the data in the Windows Clipboard.

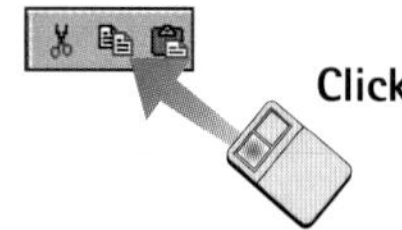

4 Open the File to Cut or Copy To

Next, open the file in which you want to place the cut or copied data. Click the cursor where you want to insert the data.

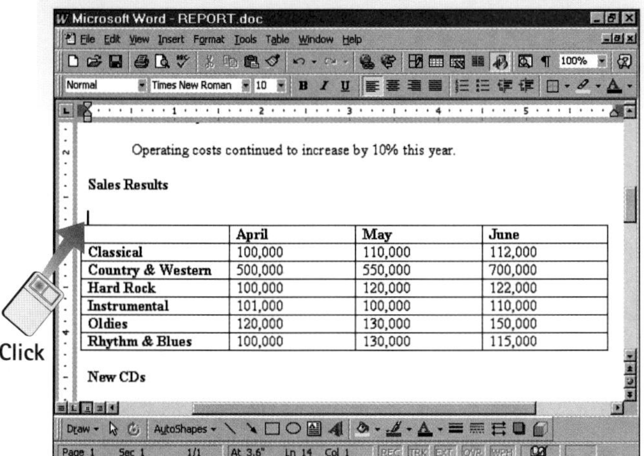

5 Paste the Data

Click the **Paste** button on the toolbar or open the **Edit** menu and select **Paste**.

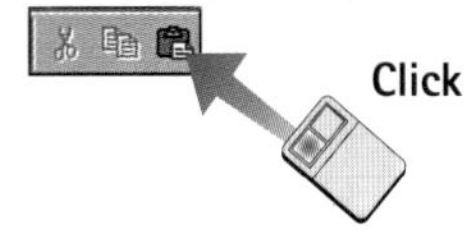

6 The Transfer Is Complete

The cut or copied data now appears in the new file.

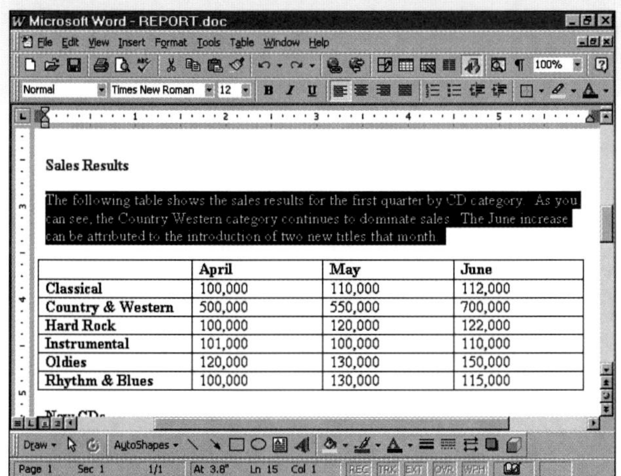

End

How-To Hints

Shortcut Menu

You can also right-click the data to find the Cut, Copy, and Paste commands on the shortcut menu.

Work with Multiple Files

To learn more about working with two or more open program files, turn to Task 7, "How to Work with Multiple Files," in Chapter 2, "How to Use Common Office Features."

Drag and Drop

You can also drag and drop data among programs. If both the *source* and *destination documents* are open, use the Windows taskbar to switch between open program windows, or resize the windows so you can view both onscreen at the same time. Then you can drag the data from one program window to another and drop it in place. To copy data with the drag-and-drop method, hold down the Ctrl key while you drag.

TASK 2

How to Link and Embed Data

Object linking and embedding, called *OLE* for short, enables Windows programs to share data transparently. The data maintains a relationship with the original program. When you link data, any changes made to the data in the source program (the program you originally used to create the data) are reflected in the destination file (the program receiving the shared data).

When you embed data, the data, when changed, isn't updated in the destination file, but it does retain a relationship with the source file. Any time you want to edit the data in the destination file, double-click it to reopen the source file where you can make your changes.

Begin

1 Copy to the Clipboard

The first step in linking or embedding is to copy the data to the Windows Clipboard. Open the source file containing the data you want to link or embed, select the data, and then choose **Edit**, **Copy** or click the **Copy** button.

2 Open the Destination File

Next, open the file you want to link or embed the data to, and click where you want the data to appear.

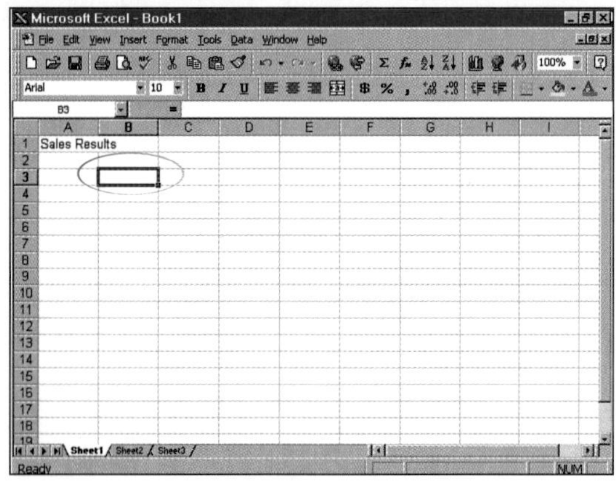

3 Open the Paste Special Dialog Box

Display the **Edit** menu and select **Paste Special**. This opens the Paste Special dialog box where you can link or embed data.

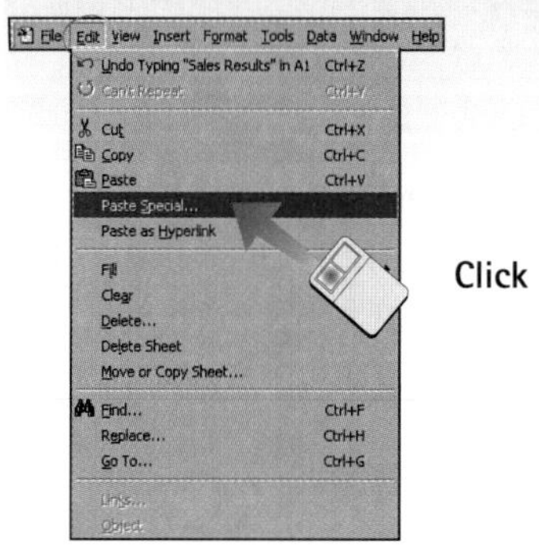

4 Link the Data

To link the data, choose the **Paste link** option and select a format to use from the **As** list box. The formats listed will vary depending on the type of data you select to link. When you select a format, the **Result** area at the bottom of the dialog box displays notes about what will happen.

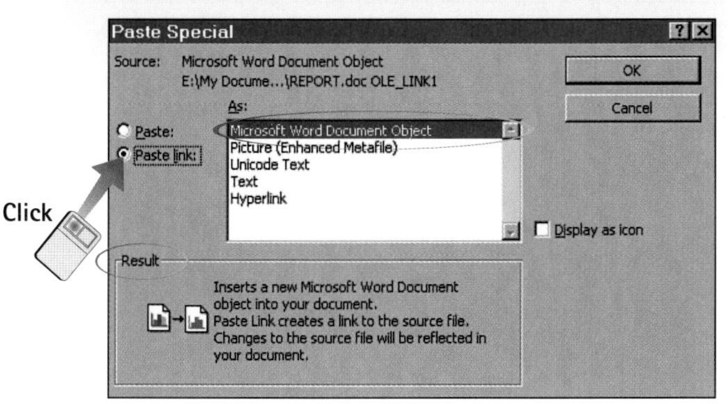

5 Embed the Data

To embed the data, choose the **Paste** option, and then select a format from the **As** list box. (Notice the **Result** area describes what will happen.) Then click **OK**.

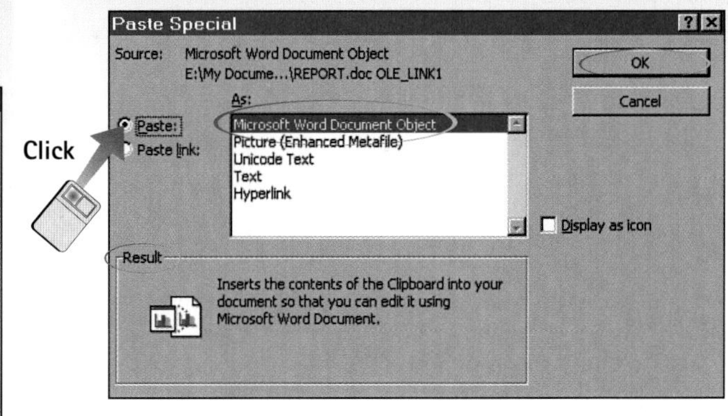

End

How-To Hints

Link Options

Use the **Display as icon** check box in the Paste Special dialog box to display the pasted object as an icon instead of the data. If you're linking sound clips to an Office file, for example, display the link as an icon. To play the sound clip, double-click the icon.

Edit Links

If you rename, delete, or move the source file, the link between the source and the destination files is broken and you will see an error message in the destination file. To edit your links, use the **Edit, Links** command. This opens the Links dialog box where you can break the link, change the link's source, or apply other options.

Edit an Embedded Object

With embedding, you can access the source file directly and bypass opening the source program and file, making the changes, and copying and pasting data into the destination file. To edit data you have embedded, double-click the data to open the original program in which the data was created. Make your changes, and then choose **File, Exit** or click anywhere outside the selected object.

TASK 3

How to Manage Links

After you link data to a file, you must maintain the source file's name and keep the file in the same location. If you move or rename the file, the link is broken, and an error message appears in the destination file. Microsoft Office makes it easy to manage links and make changes using the Links dialog box, as explained in this task.

Begin

1 Open the Links Dialog Box

To change a link, open the **Edit** menu and select **Links**. This opens the Links dialog box.

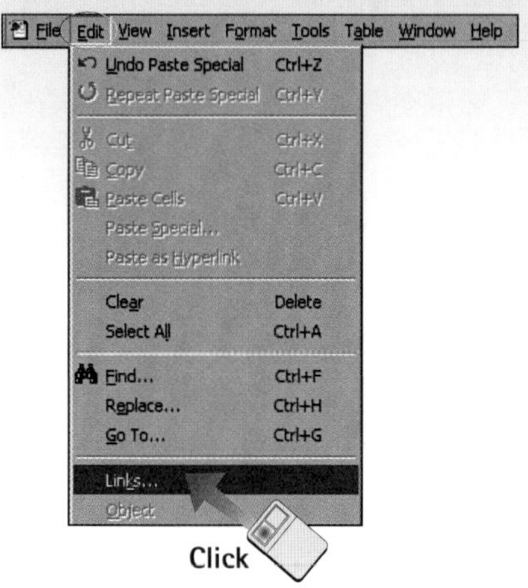

2 Select the File

From the Links dialog box, select the file containing the link you want to change in the **Source file** list box.

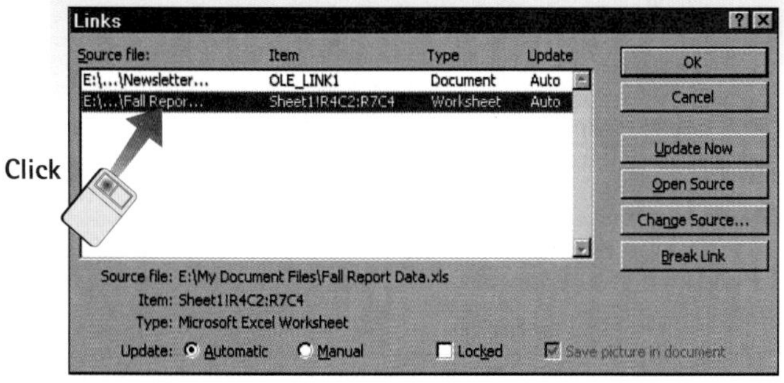

3 Automatically Update the Link

If you want the link updated automatically any time the data changes, choose the **Automatic** option.

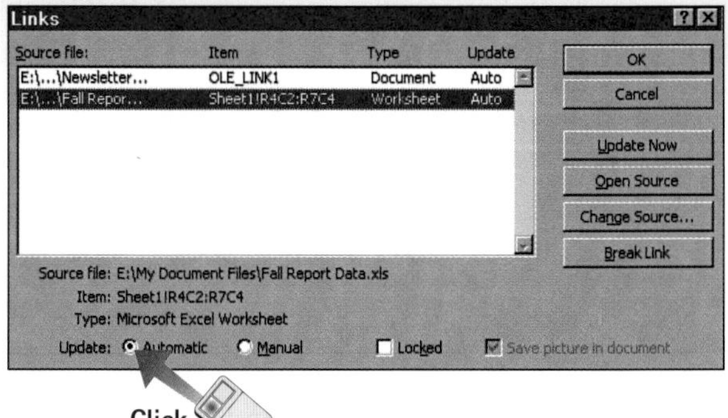

4 Manually Update the Link

If you prefer to update the link only when you want it updated, thus avoiding minor changes in data, for example, select the **Manual** option. The next time you need to update the link, open the Links dialog box, choose the link, and click the **Update Now** button.

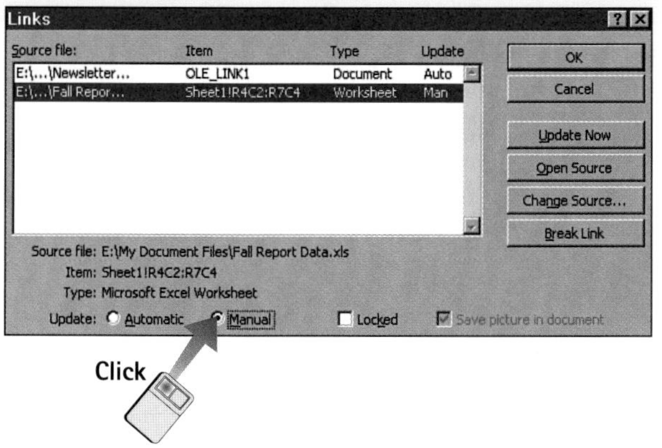

5 Change the Source

If you need to change the source file the link uses, click the **Change Source** button. This opens the Change Source dialog box where you can enter the new filename or location.

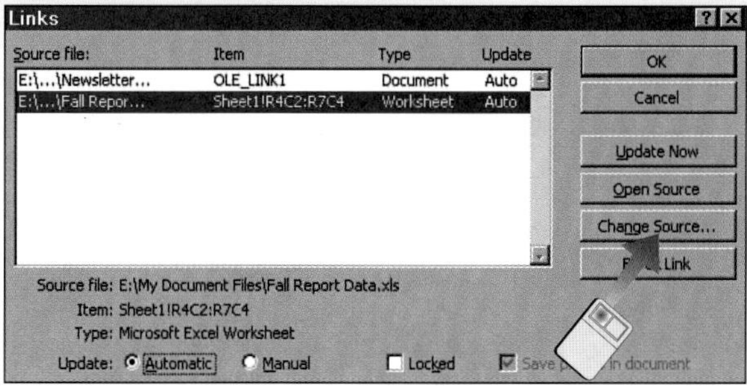

6 Break the Link

To discontinue an associated link, click the **Break Link** button. A message box asks you to confirm the break. Click **OK** and the link is broken, meaning the data is no longer associated with the source file.

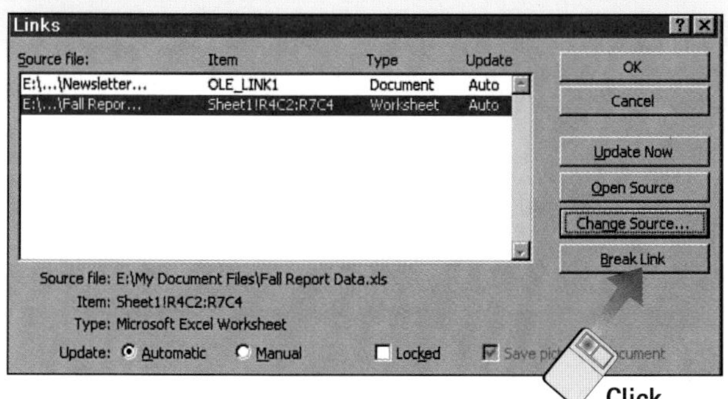

End

How-To Hints

Lock Links

To prevent additional updates to a link, use the **Locked** check box in the Links dialog box. Select this option to lock out any changes made at the source file. To unlock a link, select the link data and press Ctrl+Shift+F11, or reopen the Links dialog box and deselect the locking option.

Exit

To close the Links dialog box after editing your links, click **Close** or **Cancel** to exit the dialog box and return to the program window.

Open the Source Program

Use the **Open Source** button in the Links dialog box to open the source program. You can then check the source data and make changes to the data in the source program.

TASK 4

How to Insert Entire Files

Another way to share data is to use the Insert, File command. This command enables you to insert an entire file into another. Unlike the Paste Special command, the Insert, File command doesn't require you to open the source file. You can insert the data from within the destination file. You can insert an Excel worksheet into your Word document, for example, as demonstrated in this task.

Begin

1 Click to Indicate Insertion

To insert an Excel worksheet into your Word document, first click the cursor in the place where you want the data inserted.

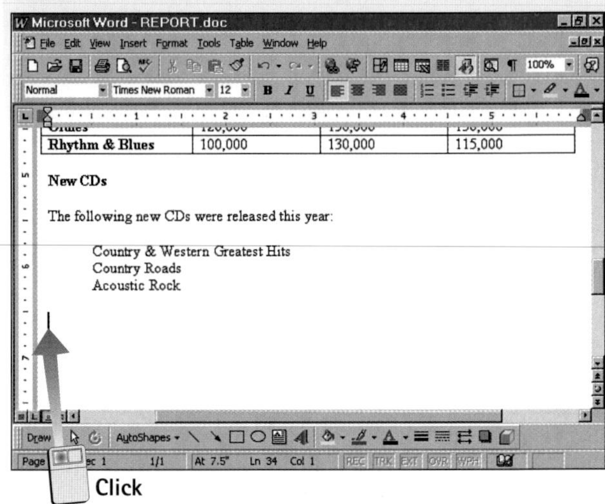

2 Open the Insert File Dialog Box

Open the **Insert** menu and select **File**. This opens the Insert File dialog box.

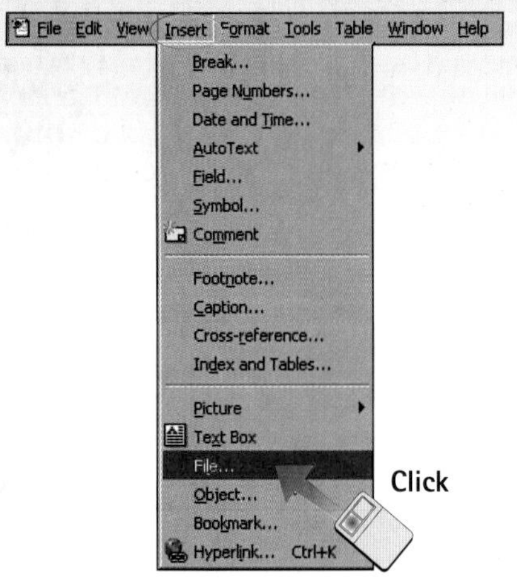

3 Locate the File

Locate the Excel worksheet you want to insert. Use the **Look in** drop-down list to locate the folder or drive where the file is stored, and then select the filename from the list box. To display all file types, click the **Files of type** drop-down list and select **All Files**.

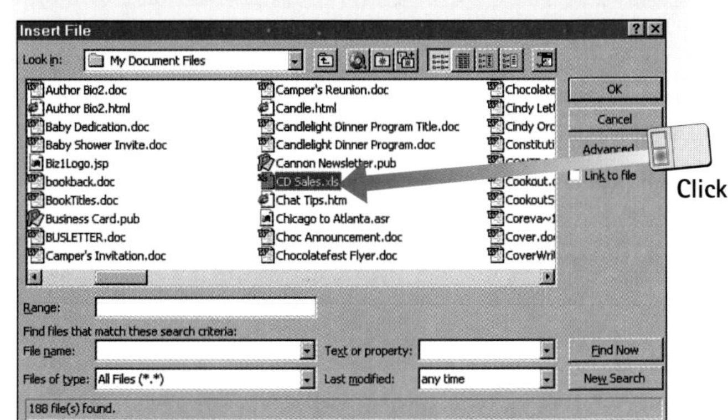

4 Link the File

Click the **Link to file** check box to link the Excel data to the Word document.

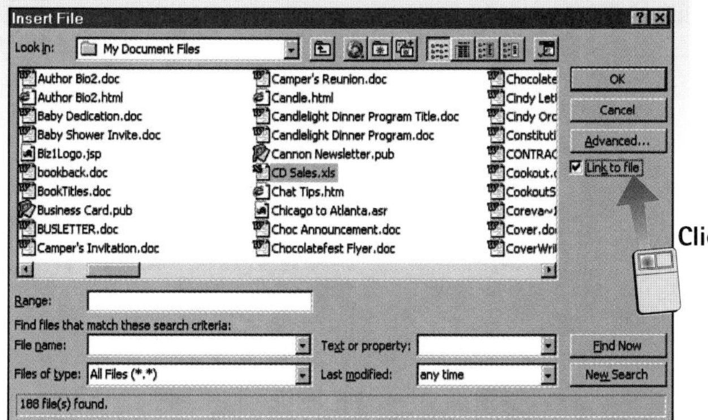

5 Exit the Dialog Box

Click **OK** to exit the dialog box.

6 Open Worksheet

An Open Worksheet dialog box appears. Use the **Open document in Workbook** drop-down list to designate whether you want the entire workbook or a single worksheet inserted. Click **OK**, and the data is inserted into your document.

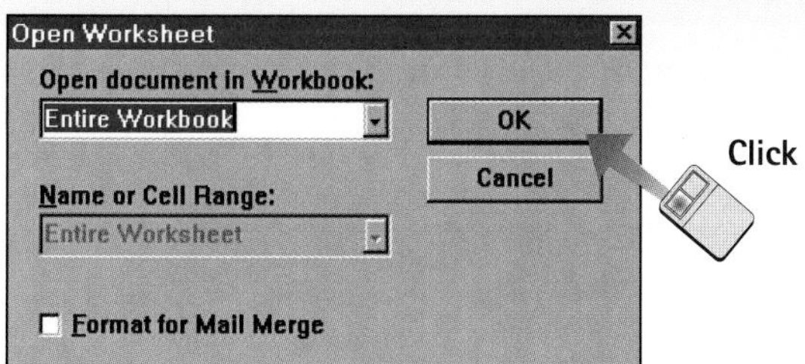

End

How-To Hints

Link a Range

Rather than inserting an entire worksheet into Word, you can choose to link a range. Copy the range data to the Clipboard, and then in Word, select **Edit**, **Paste Special**. Choose the **Paste Link** option and choose a format for the range. To insert the data as an object, choose **Microsoft Excel Worksheet Object**. To insert the range as a table, choose **Formatted Text**. To insert the range with tabs separating the data, choose **Unformatted Text**. Then click **OK** to link the data.

TASK 5

How to Embed a New Object

Use the Insert, Object command when you know you want to link or embed something, but you have not yet created the object in the source program. With the Insert, Object command, you don't have to leave the program window to open the source program and create the object. You can create a new object from within the program window you're using.

Begin

1 Open the Object Dialog Box

From the file in which you want to embed an object, open the **Insert** menu and select **Object**. This opens the Object dialog box.

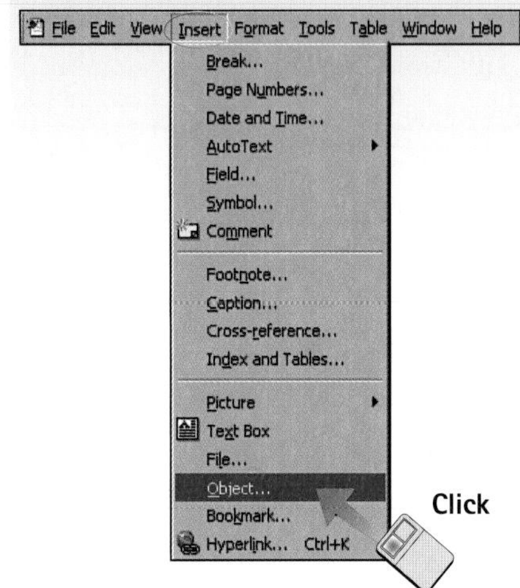

2 Select the Program Object

Click the **Create New** tab and select the program you want to use to create the new object. To create a range of cells, for example, select **Microsoft Excel Worksheet**; to create a PowerPoint slide, select **Microsoft PowerPoint Slide**.

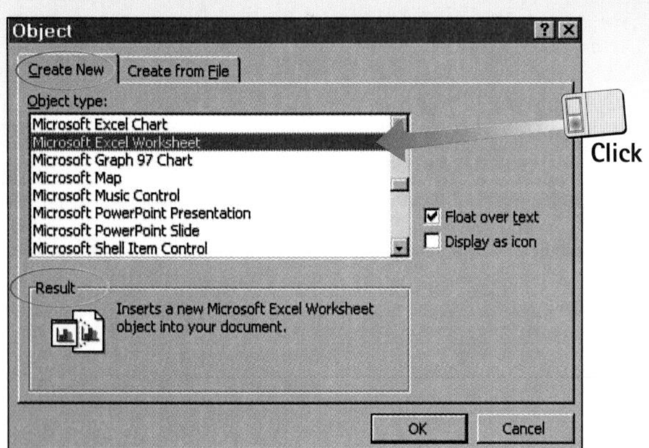

3 Check the Notes

Look in the **Result** area to see notes about the object that you're about to create. When you're ready, click **OK**.

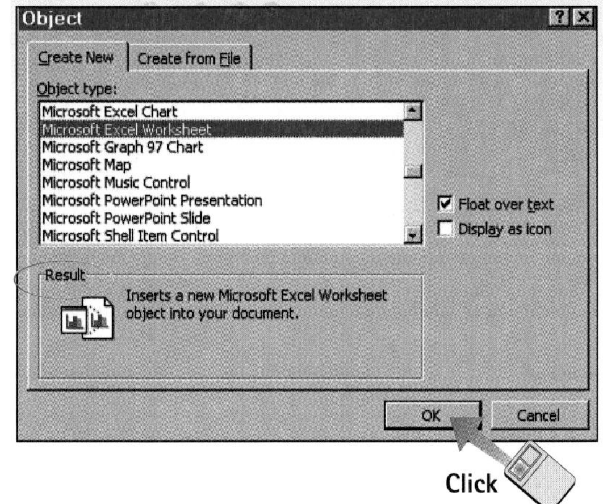

4 Create the New Object

Your program window changes to reflect the object type you selected. Sometimes the change is subtle, depending on the program you selected; at other times, it's quite obvious. If you examine the menus and toolbars, you will notice that the commands and tools are now related to the object application you chose in step 2. You're ready to use the object program's features to create the new object.

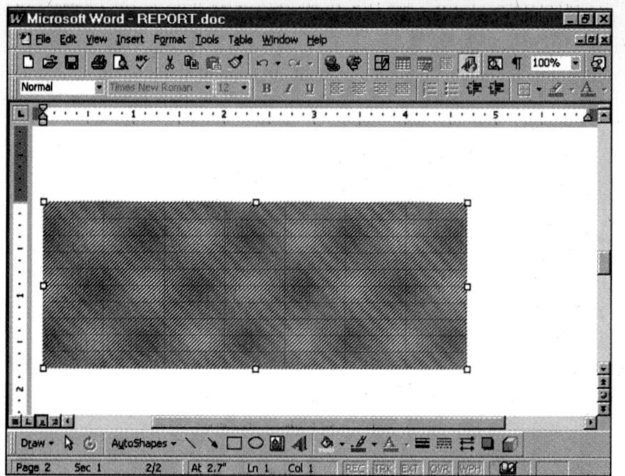

5 Exit the Object

When you finish creating the new object, click anywhere outside the object to return to your original program window. The object is treated like any other object you add to your file. When selected, selection handles surround it. To edit the object, double-click the object.

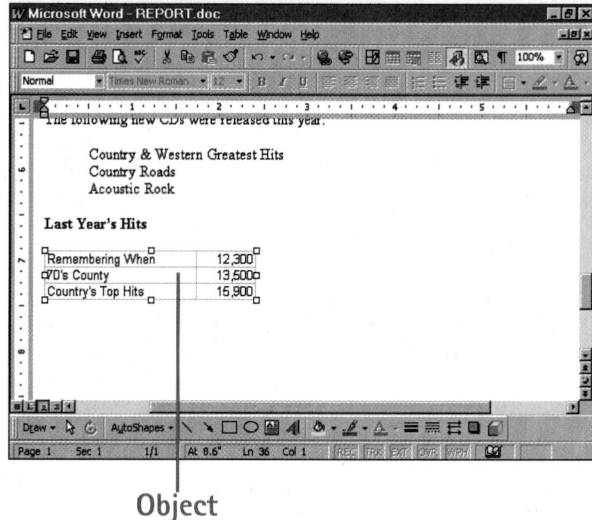

Object

End

How-To Hints

Move and Resize

The object you create can be resized or moved the same as any other object. To learn more about working with objects, see Task 5, "How to Move and Size an Image," in Chapter 16, "How to Work with Office Graphics Tools."

TASK 6

How to Integrate Access Data

Although Access is a perfect tool for organizing data, it's not always the best tool for performing calculations, and its formatting capabilities are limited. You can easily integrate the Access data to Excel or Word. You can then use Excel to analyze the data, or tap into Word's numerous formatting tools.

Begin

1 Choose an Access Item to Analyze

Open Access and select the table, form, query, or report you want to send to Excel.

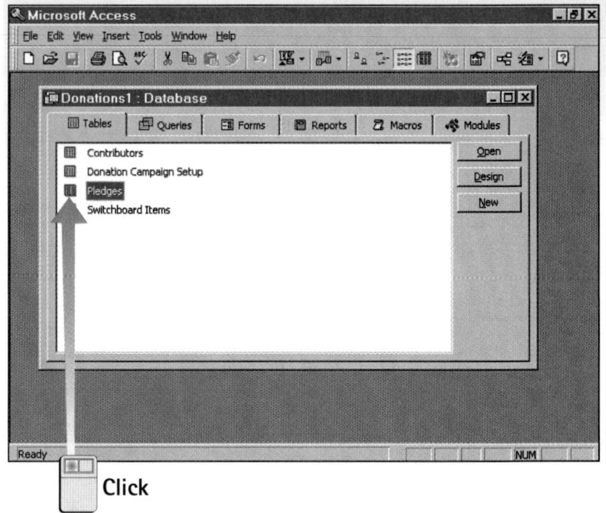

2 Use the Office Links Feature

Open the **Tools** menu and choose **Office Links, Analyze It with MS Excel**.

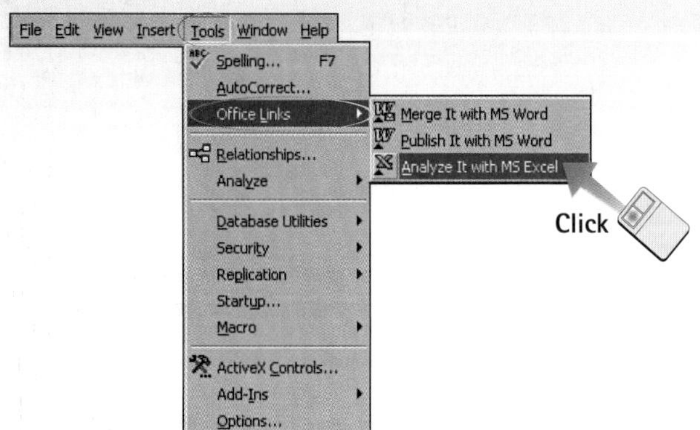

3 Excel Opens

Access immediately sends the data to Excel and opens a new worksheet for the data. You can now manipulate the data using Excel's features and tools.

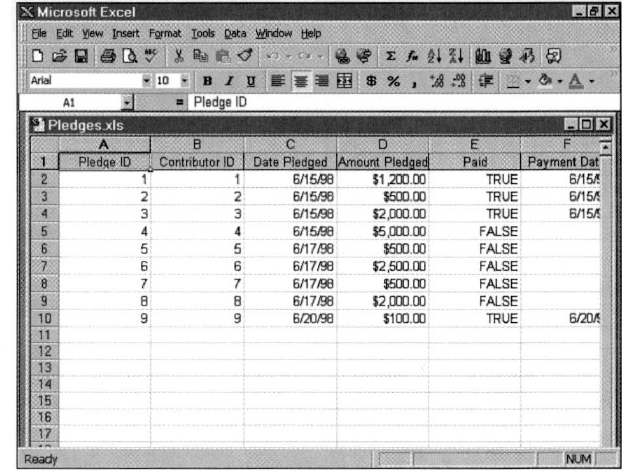

4 Convert an Access Report

To convert an Access report to Word format, first select the report you want to use.

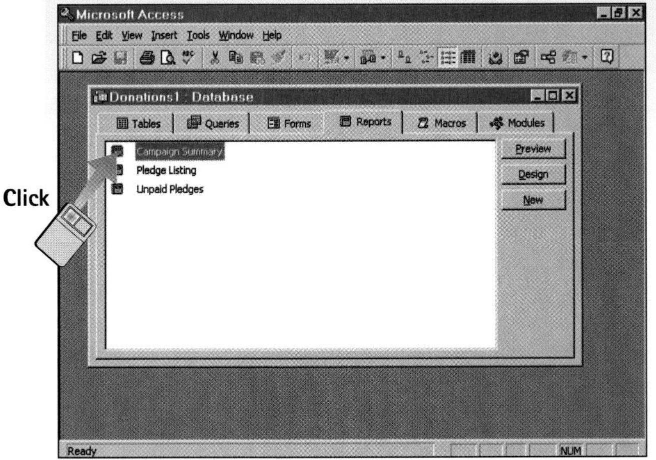

5 Use the Office Links Feature

Open the **Tools** menu and choose **Office Links, Publish It with MS Word**.

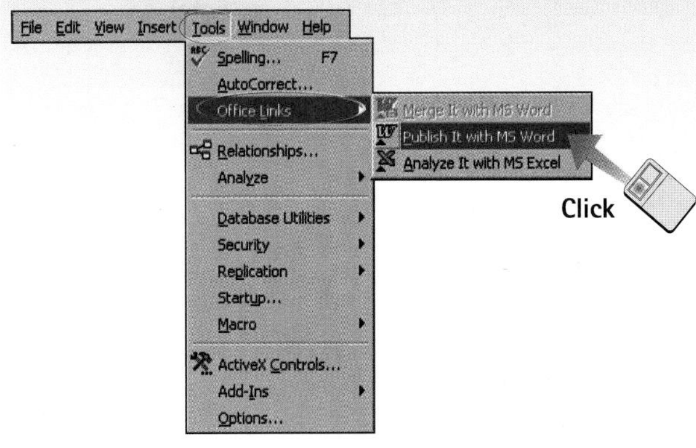

6 Word Opens

Access immediately sends the data to Word and opens a new document for the data. You can now format the data using Word's formatting tools.

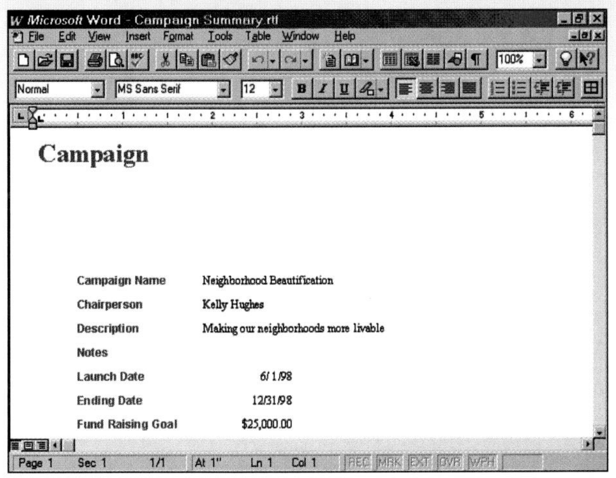

End

How-To Hints

Why Analyze in Excel?

If you create a database that works with lots of number data, you may want to analyze the data in Excel rather than Access. In addition, by moving the data into Excel, you can play with Excel's scenarios features to see how changes to the numbers affect your data overall.

Why Convert a Report?

You may also want to convert an Access report to Word so you can format the information and make it more presentable for distribution. The Access formatting tools are limited, but by bringing the information into Word, you can use Word's more advanced formatting commands to make a readable report.

TASK 7

How to Use the Binder

Many projects you create using Microsoft Office 97 will probably contain multiple files, possibly of different types. One project may require several files; for example, you may use Word to generate proposals and memos, Excel to calculate and analyze the financial information, and PowerPoint to prepare the presentation.

Use the Office Binder to organize the files in one location as a single document. By adding the various files to the Microsoft Office Binder, not only do you have an archive of the project, but also the capability to print it as a single document.

Begin

1 Open the Binder

Select **Start**, **Programs**, **Microsoft Binder** from the Windows 95 taskbar to open the Microsoft Office Binder and create a new binder.

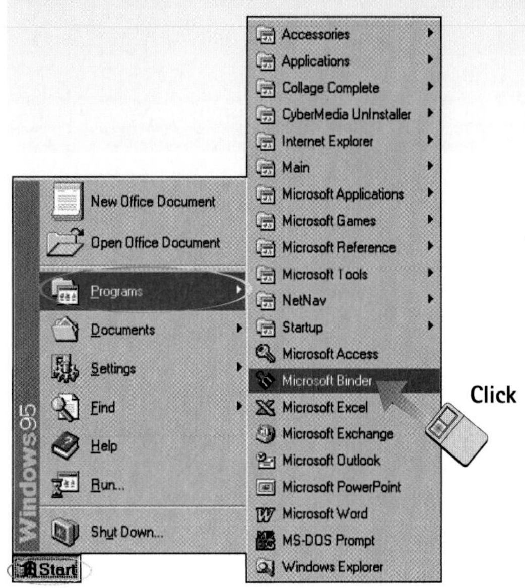

2 Add Existing Documents

Every time you open Office Binder, it begins with a blank binder. Microsoft Office Binder refers to each document in your binder as a section. To add an existing document to a binder, select **Section**, **Add from File** from the menu bar.

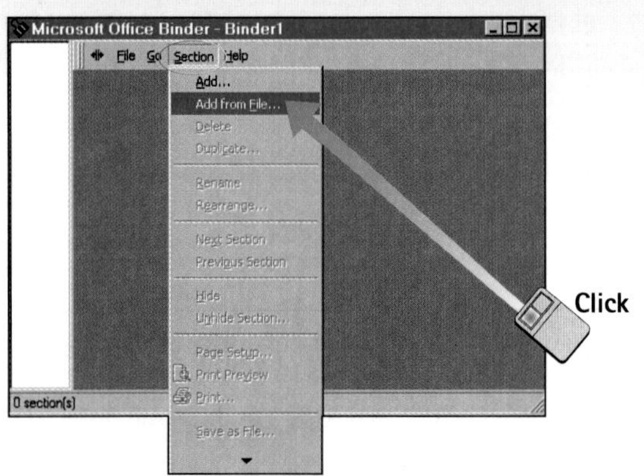

3 Choose Project Files

Use the Add from File dialog box to locate and choose the existing file you want to include in your binder. To select more than one file, hold down the **Ctrl** key while you click the filenames you want to include.

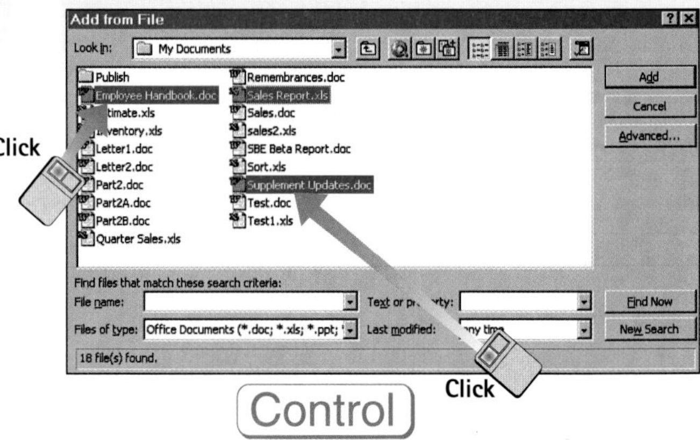

4 Add the Files to the Binder

After you have highlighted the desired file(s), click **Add** to attach the file(s) and return to the binder.

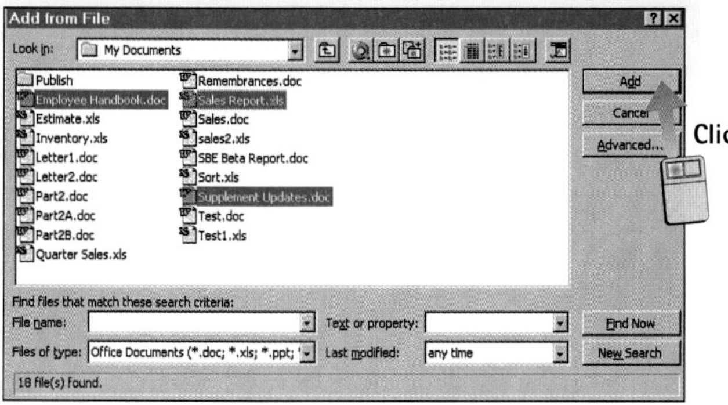

5 Prepare to Print

Because printing a multidocument project as a single print job is a primary reason for creating a binder, you should familiarize yourself with the print settings. From the menu bar select **File, Binder Page Setup**.

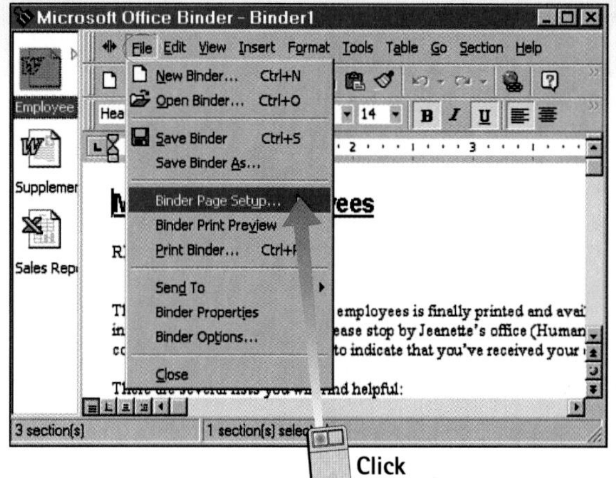

6 Print the Project

Click the **Print Settings** tab in the Binder Page Setup dialog box to access the print settings. You have the option to print all sections or selected sections, and you can choose how to handle page numbering. When you're finished, click **Print**.

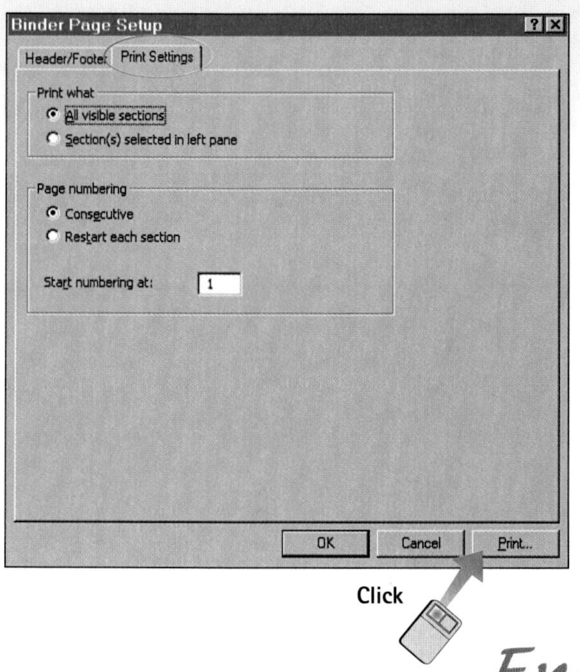

End

How-To Hints

Close the Binder

To close the binder, click the **Close (X)** button in the corner, or select **File, Close**.

Change Binder Options

Select **File, Binder Options** from the menu bar to change the Office Binder's settings. From the Binder Options dialog box that appears, you can choose to print the binder as a single print job, change the default location of the binder file, and make changes to the appearance of the binder window.

Edit Sections

Because documents added to the binder are embedded, and therefore no longer connected to the original document, you cannot make revisions to a section and reflect the changes in the original document. If you want to make changes that appear in both the binder section and the original document, you must delete the section, open the original document, make the changes, save the document, and again add it to the binder.

Project

One of the most common projects that utilizes the Office programs is performing a mail merge to create mass mailings—duplicate letters you want to send to different people. You can merge your address book from Outlook or an address database created in Access with a form letter document you create in Word. Before you can perform this project, you must have an address database created in Access that contains the mass mailing information you want to use, a Personal Address Book, or a contacts list created in Outlook 98.

When you build a form letter, you use fields wherever you want to insert data from the address database (referred to as the *data source*). When the mail merge is complete, you will have a letter for each person in the address database. You can print them immediately or save them to print later.

1 Type the Form Letter

To begin, open Word and create the form letter you want to use. Omit information that can be inserted from the data source (such as name and address). Leave the form letter open (you can save it if you like).

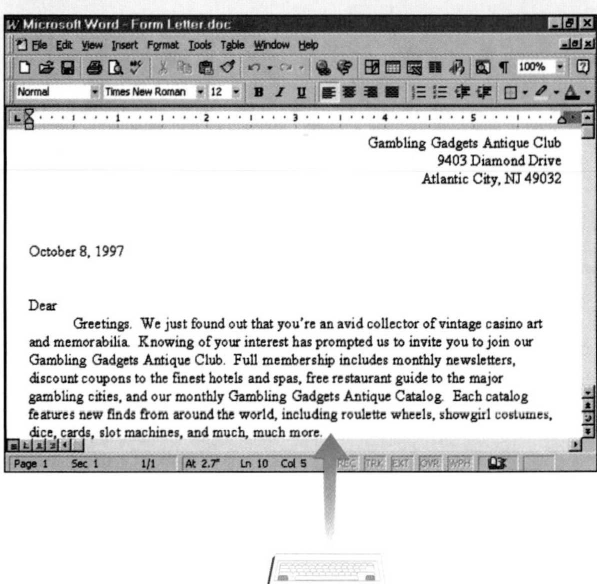

2 Open Mail Merge Helper

Open the **Tools** menu and select **Mail Merge**. This opens the Mail Merge Helper dialog box.

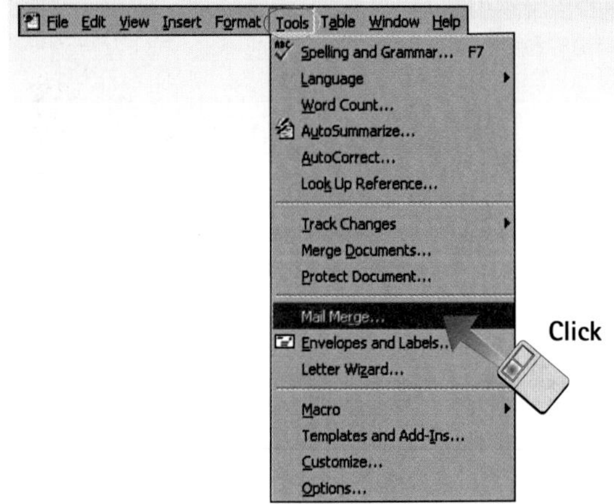

3 Designate the Main Document

Under the **Main document** heading, click the **Create** button, and then choose **Form Letters**.

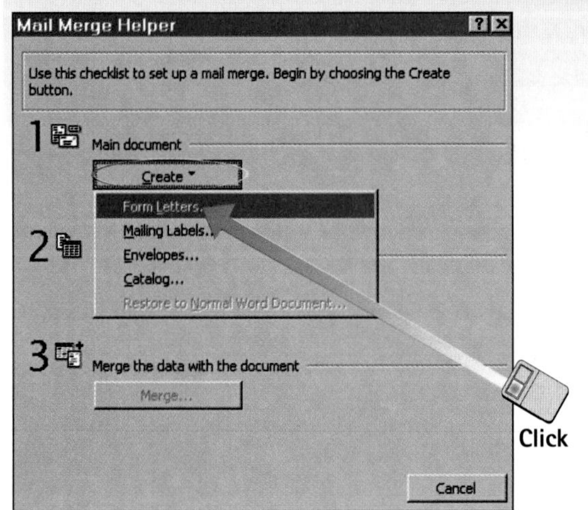

4 Active Window Prompt

A prompt box appears, asking whether you want to use the active window as the main document or create a new main document. Click **Active Window**. This tells Word to use the open document you created in step 1 as your main document for the mail merge.

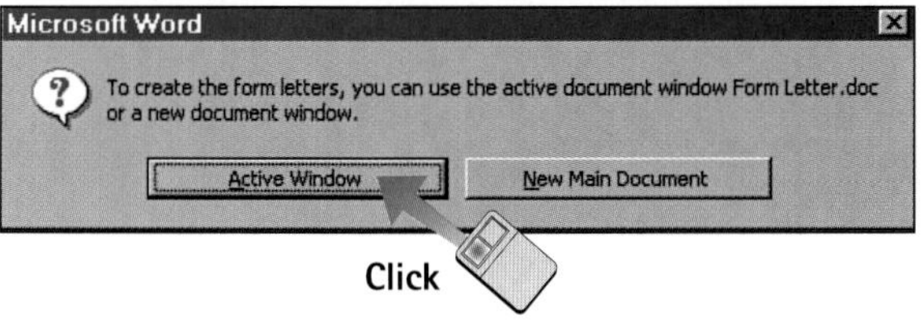

5 Specify the Data Source

Under the **Data source** heading, click the **Get Data** button and choose a data source option. If you're using Outlook's address book, choose **Use Address Book**. If you're using an Access database, choose **Open Data Source**.

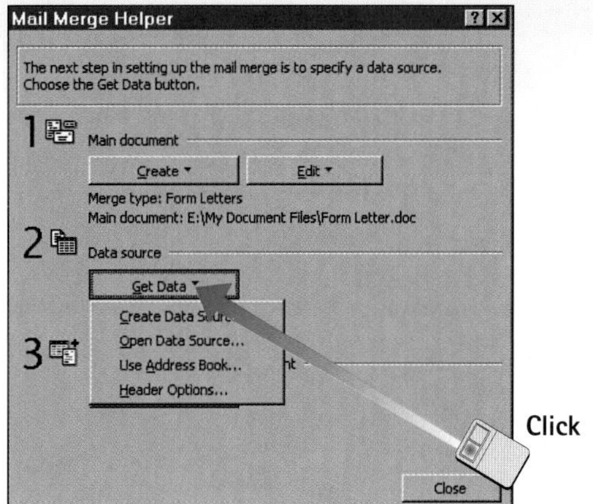

6 Choose an Address Book

If you selected Use Address Book in step 5, you will be prompted to select the Outlook address book you want to use. After making your selection, click **OK**. You will also be prompted to choose a profile; select a profile and skip to step 8.

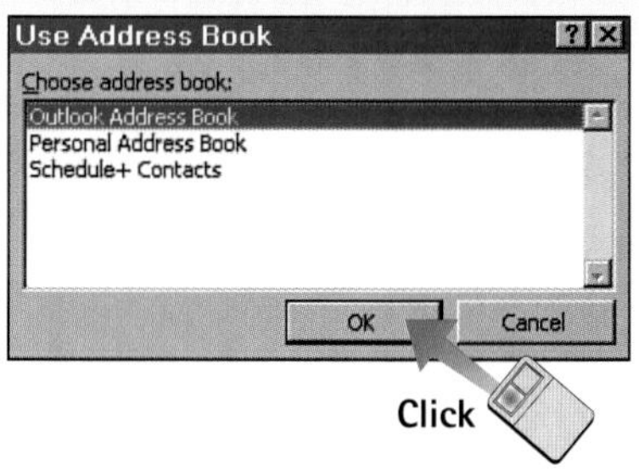

7 Choose a Database File

If you selected Open Data Source in step 5, you must locate the Access database file you want to use. Locate and select the file and click **Open**. (Use the **Files of type** drop-down list to display Access database files.)

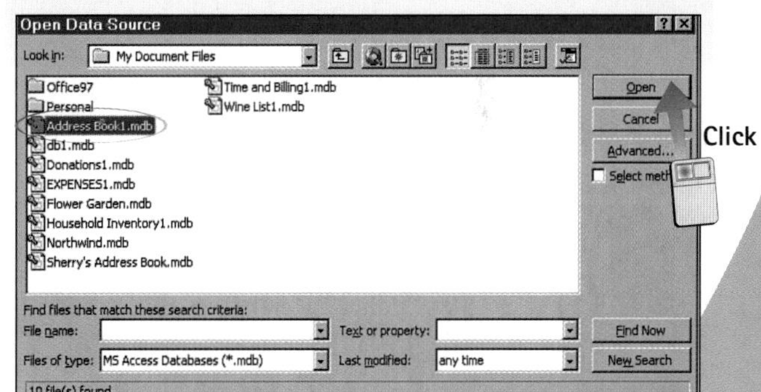

Continues

8 Another Message Prompt

Another prompt box appears, telling you that your form letter has no merge fields. Click **Edit Main Document**.

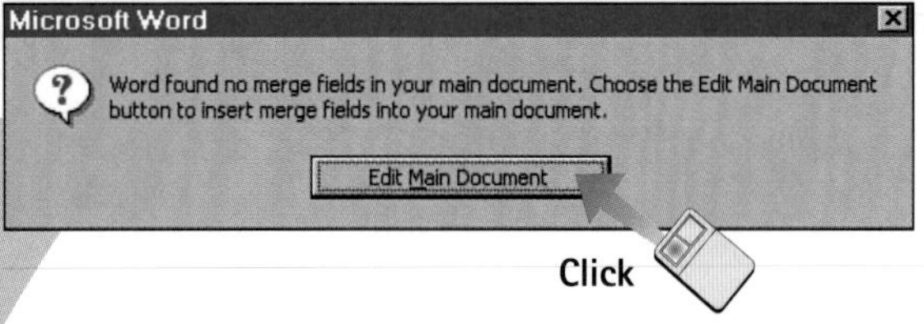

9 Insert Data Fields

Begin inserting data fields into your form letter where you want to place data from the address book or database. Click where you want a field inserted, and then click the **Insert Merge Field** drop-down list on the Mail Merge toolbar and choose a field. To insert a name, such as Bob, for example, select the **First_Name** field, as shown in this figure.

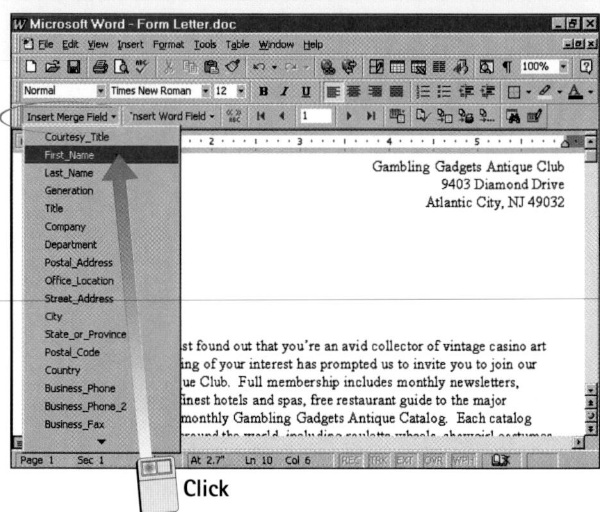

10 View Field Codes

When you insert a field into your form, it appears as a field code surrounded by brackets. This field code will pull specific data from your address book or database to insert into the letter.

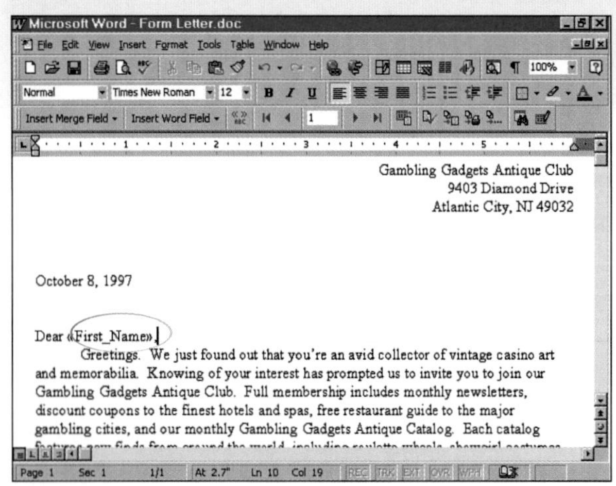

11 Add Punctuation

Continue entering as many field codes as needed in your form letter using the **Insert Merge Field** drop-down list. Be sure to add punctuation or spacing between codes where needed.

October 8, 1997
«First_Name» «Last_Name»
«Postal_Address»
«City», «State_or_Province» «Postal_Code»

Dear «First_Name»,
Greetings. We just found out that you're an avid

12 Merge the Data

When you're ready to merge the data from your data source with the form letter, click the **Mail Merge** button on the Mail Merge toolbar.

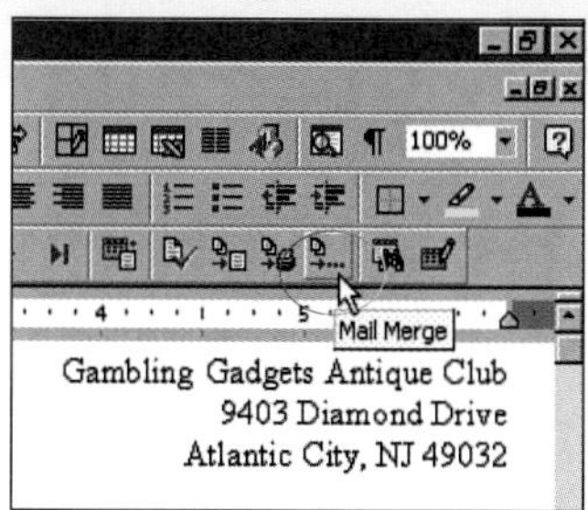

13 Use the Merge Dialog Box

When the Merge dialog box appears, select how you want the merge to occur. You can choose to merge to a new document, printer, or email program. Click the **Merge to** drop-down arrow and choose an option.

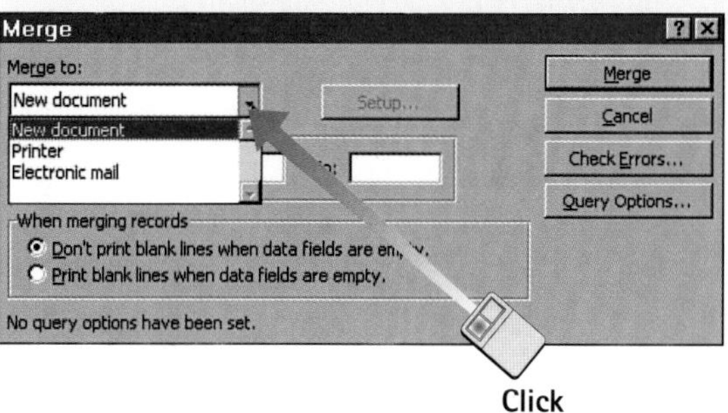

14 Select Which Records

Use the **Records to be merged** options to choose exactly which records you want to use with the mail merge. You can choose a range of records, for example, or choose to merge all the records. To use all the records in your database, click **All**.

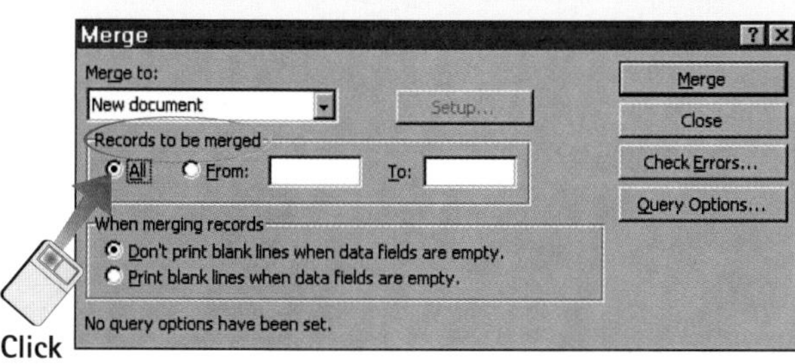

15 What About Blanks?

You can also designate how the mail merge should handle blank fields in your records. Select the options you want to use, and then click **Merge**.

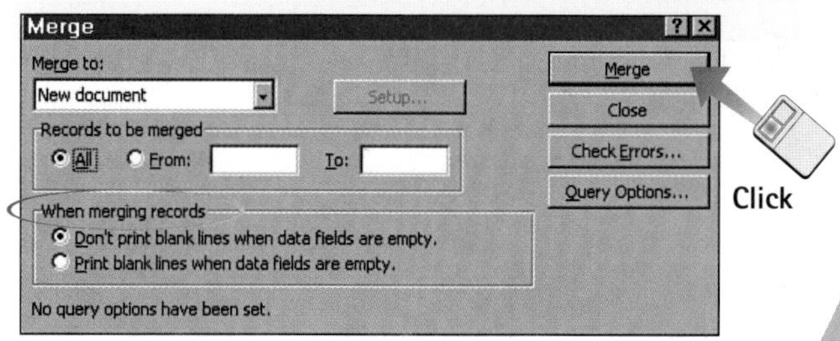

Continues

16 Word Merges the Data

Word merges your form letter with the fields you specified from the database and creates an individual letter for each record in your database. Scroll through the pages to see the results.

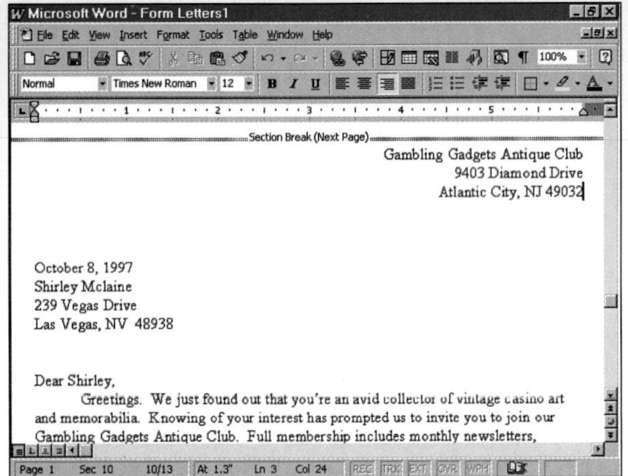

17 Save It

You can print the letters now or save them to print later. To save the merge, open the **File** menu and select **Save As**.

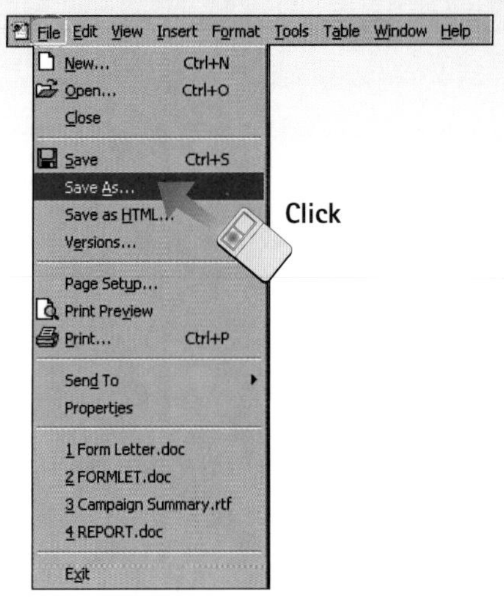

18 Assign a Filename

From the Save As dialog box, enter a filename for the form letters and click **Save**.

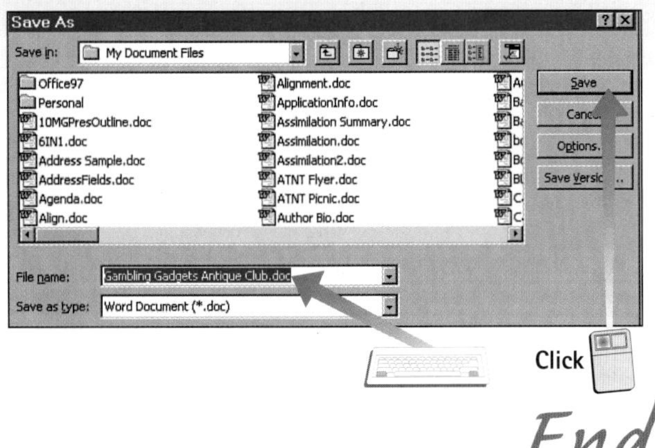

End

How-To Hints

Create Mailing Labels

You can also make address labels to go along with the form letters you created with the mail merge. Use the same Mail Merge Helper dialog box, this time choosing **Mailing Labels** instead of **Form Letters**.

Glossary

absolute reference A *cell reference* that specifies the exact address of a cell. An absolute reference takes the form $A$1, $B$3, and so on.

Access A *database* program designed to organize and sort large quantities of *data*.

active cell The selected *cell* (it's surrounded by a dark border). You can enter or edit data in the active cell.

active document The *document* that is currently selected in your software window.

active window In a multiple-window environment, the window that you are currently using, or that is currently selected. Only one window can be active at a time, and keystrokes and commands affect the active window.

active worksheet The *Excel worksheet* or *chart sheet* on which you are currently working. When a sheet is active, the name on the sheet tab is bold.

add-in A small program that can be installed to add *commands* and *functions* to a main program.

alignment The way text lines up against the margins of a page, within the width of a *column*, against tab stops, or in a *worksheet cell*.

applet An Outlook mini-program, such as Tasks or Calendar.

archiving The process of moving Outlook items out of Outlook and into storage files, where they are saved for future reference.

argument Information you supply to a *function* for calculation. An argument can be a *value*, a *reference*, a name, a *formula*, or another function.

attachment A complete file or item that is sent with an *email* message or stored with an Outlook item, such as a task or journal entry.

AutoCalculate An *Excel* feature that automatically calculates any selected *cells*.

AutoCorrect An *Excel* feature that corrects text or changes a string of characters to a word or phrase automatically.

AutoFill An *Excel* feature that enables you to create a series of incremental or fixed *values* on a *worksheet* by dragging the *fill handle* with the mouse.

AutoText A formatted block of boilerplate text that you can insert wherever you need it.

axes Borders on the *chart plot area* that provide a frame of reference for measurement or comparison. On *column* charts, data values are plotted along the Y axis and categories are plotted along the X axis.

Bcc Blind copy. A copy of an *email* message that you send without the primary recipient's knowledge.

browser A program for surfing the *Internet* (such as Netscape or Internet Explorer).

build A special effect in a *PowerPoint* slide show that presents one slide item at a time.

Cc Copy; when you send an *email* message, you can send Cc (copies) to other recipients.

cell The intersection of a *column* and a *row*.

cell address The location of a *cell* on a sheet; this consists of a *row* address and a *column* address, such as F12, which indicates the intersection of column F and row 12. Also referred to as *cell reference*.

cell reference The set of *row* and *column* coordinates that identifies a *cell* location on a *worksheet*. Also referred to as the *cell address*.

chart A graphical representation of *worksheet* data. Charts are linked to the data from which they were created and are automatically updated when the *source* data changes.

chart area The entire region surrounding the *chart*, just outside the *plot area*. When the chart area is selected, uniform *font* characteristics can be applied to all text in the chart.

chart sheet A sheet in a *workbook* that's designed to contain only a *chart*.

chart type The way *chart* data is displayed; column, bar, and pie are common chart types.

Chart Wizard A *wizard* that guides you through the steps required to create a new *chart* or to modify settings for an existing chart.

client A program that receives data that is linked, copied, or embedded from another program. (Also called a destination program or *document*.)

clip art A predrawn illustration or *graphics object* you can insert into an Office file. Microsoft Office comes with a collection of clip art files you can use to illustrate your documents.

Clipboard See *Windows Clipboard*.

close box A small box with an X in it that's located in the upper-right corner of every Windows 95 window; click it to close the program or file or item in the window.

column A vertical range of *cells*. Each column is identified by a unique letter or letter combination (such as A, Z, CF).

column heading The label at the top of a *column* in a *table* view (also called the *field name*).

command An instruction that tells the computer to carry out a task or perform an action.

comment Extra information provided for an *Excel cell* or *Word* text. The comment remains hidden until you point to the Comment indicator symbol.

constant A *cell* value that does not start with an equal sign. For example, the date, the value 345, and text are all constants.

criteria Information in a specific *field* that identifies items you want to find, such as a last name of Smith or the category Business; criteria are used to filter a view to find only those items containing the criteria.

cursor The flashing vertical line that shows where text is entered (for example, in a *cell* during in-cell editing). Also referred to as the *insertion point*.

data marker A bar, area, dot, slice, or other symbol in a *chart* that represents a single data point or value originating from a *worksheet cell*. Related data markers in a chart comprise a *data series*.

data point An individual value, plotted in a *chart*, that originates from a single *cell* in a *worksheet*. Data points are represented by bars, columns, lines, pie or doughnut slices, dots, and various other shapes, called *data markers*.

data series A group of related data points in a *chart* that originates from a single *worksheet row* or *column*. Each data series in a chart is distinguished by a unique color or pattern.

data source The underlying *worksheet* data that's displayed in a *chart* or *PivotTable*.

database A computer program that specializes in organizing, storing, and retrieving data. The term also describes a collection of data.

delimiter A character (such as a tab, space, or comma) that separates *fields* of data in a text file.

destination document The *document* or file containing the data you *link* or *embed* from the *source* document.

document Any independent unit of information (such as a text file, *worksheet*, or *graphics object*) that is created with a program. A document can be saved with a unique filename by which it can be retrieved.

Document Map A vertical display of the headings in a Word *document*. For easy document navigation, click an entry to move quickly to that part of the document.

document window A rectangular portion of the screen in which you view and edit a *document*. A document window is typically located inside a program window.

download To transfer a file from the *Internet* to your computer through telephone lines and a modem.

drag and drop A technique for moving or copying data from one location to another. Select the item to move or copy, hold down the left mouse button, drag the item to a new location, and release the mouse button to drop it in place.

email Electronic mail; a system that uses the *Internet* to send messages electronically over telephone wires instead of on paper.

embed To insert an object from a *source* program into a *destination document*. When you double-click the object in the destination document, the source program opens and you can edit the object. See also *link*.

embedded chart A *chart* that's located on a *worksheet* instead of on a separate *chart sheet*.

Excel A popular spreadsheet program designed for organizing and working with numbers, performing calculations, and other mathematical operations.

export The process of converting and saving a file to be used in a another program. See also *import*.

field In a list or *database*, a *column* of data that contains a particular type of information, such as Last Name or Phone Number or Quantity.

field name The name of the *field*, also commonly called a *column heading*.

fill handle The small black square in the lower-right corner of the selected *cell* or *range*. When you position the mouse pointer over the fill handle, the pointer changes to a black cross and the contents can be *AutoFilled*.

filter A set of *criteria* you can apply to show specific items and hide all others.

flag A visual symbol indicating that some sort of follow-up to an *email* message is requested; flags appear in the Flag Status *column* in table views.

floating palette A *palette* that can be dragged away from its *toolbar*.

floating toolbar A *toolbar* that is not docked at the edges of the application window. A floating toolbar stays on top of other windows within the application window.

font A typeface, such as Arial or Tahoma.

font formatting Characteristics you can apply to text to change the way it looks; these include bold, italic, color, and *font* size.

footer Text that appears at the bottom of every printed page. See also *header*.

form An onscreen, fill-in-the-blanks sheet used to enter data into an *Access database*.

formula A sequence of *values*, *cell references*, names, *functions*, or *mathematical operators* that produces a new value from existing values. A formula always begins with an equal sign (=).

Formula bar A bar near the top of the *Excel* window that you use to enter or edit *values* and *formulas* in *cells* or *charts*. This bar displays the formula or constant value from the active cell or object.

function A built-in *formula* that uses a series of values (*arguments*) to perform an operation and then returns the result of the operation. You can use the Function Wizard to select a function and enter it in a *cell*.

graphics object A line or shape (button, text box, ellipse, rectangle, arc, picture) you draw using the tools on the *toolbar*, or a picture you paste into a file.

gridlines Lines that visually separate *columns* and *rows*.

gridlines (chart) Lines you can add to your chart that extend from the tickmarks on an axis across the *plot area*. Gridlines come in various forms: horizontal, vertical, major, minor, and various combinations. They make it easier to view and evaluate data in a *chart*.

handles Small black squares located around the perimeter of selected *graphics objects*, *chart* items, or chart text. By dragging the handles, you can move, copy, or size the selected object, chart item, or chart text.

header Text that appears at the top of every printed page. See also *footer*.

hyperlink Colored, underlined text that you can click to open another file or go to a *Web* address.

import The process of converting and opening a file that was stored or created in another program. See also *export*.

insertion point A flashing vertical line that shows the text entry point. Also referred to as the *cursor*.

Internet The worldwide network of networks, in which everyone is connected to everyone else.

Internet service provider (ISP) A private enterprise that provides a *server* through which you can connect to the Internet (also called *Local service provider* and *mail service*).

intranet A miniature Internet that operates within a company or organization.

key The *criteria* by which a list is sorted.

label Text you provide to identify data, such as *column headings*.

Landscape The horizontal orientation of a page; opposite of *Portrait*, or vertical, orientation.

link To copy an *object*, such as a graphic or text, from one file or program to another so that a dependent relationship exists between the object and its *source* file. The dependent object is updated whenever the data changes in the source object.

list A *range* of cells containing data that is related to a particular subject or purpose. In *Excel*, the terms *list* and *database* are used interchangeably.

Local service provider See *Internet service provider*.

mail merge The process of creating several identical *documents* (such as form letters or mailing labels) that each pull a different set of information (such as addresses) out of a *database*.

mail service See *Internet service provider*.

mathematical operators Characters that tell *Excel* which calculations to perform, such as * (multiply), + (add), - (subtract), and / (divide).

merge fields The placeholder text in a *mail merge document* where *database* information is inserted in each finished, or merged, copy of the document.

message An *email* message, or any text typed into the large message box in an item dialog box.

mixed reference A combination of a *relative reference* and an *absolute reference*. A mixed reference takes the form $A1 or A$1, where A is the *column cell address* and 1 is the row cell address. The $ indicates the fixed, or absolute, part of the reference.

name A unique identifier you create to refer to one or more cells. When you use names in a *formula*, the formula is easier to read and maintain than a formula containing *cell references*.

object A *table*, *chart*, graphic, equation, or other form of information you create and edit. An object can be inserted, pasted, or copied into any file.

Office Assistant Animated Office help system that provides interactive help, tips, and other online assistance.

OLE Short for object linking and embedding, the technology that allows different programs to share data.

Outlook Bar The vertical bar on the left side of the Outlook window; the Outlook Bar contains icons for Outlook applets and folders.

Outlook Bar group A group of icons displayed in the *Outlook Bar*, such as the Mail group, the Outlook group, and the Other group; display a group by clicking the button for that group.

palette A dialog box containing choices for color and other special effects that you use when designing a form, *report*, or other object. A palette appears when you click a *toolbar* button, such as Border or Fill Color. See also *floating palette*.

Personal Address Book An address book that is separate from Contacts, although it stores similar information (name, address, phone numbers, *email* address, and so on). In a Personal Address Book you can create *Personal Distribution Lists* (which cannot be created in Contacts).

Personal Distribution List A group of names and *email* addresses; when you send mail to a personal distribution list, the email goes to everyone on the list.

PivotTable A special *Excel* table that analyzes data from other lists and tables.

plot area The area of a *chart* in which data is plotted. In 2D charts, it is bounded by the *axes* and encompasses the *data markers* and *gridlines*. In 3D charts, the plot area includes the chart's walls, axes, and tick-mark labels.

Portrait The vertical orientation of a page; opposite of *Landscape*, or horizontal, orientation.

PowerPoint A presentation program designed to create and view *slide show* programs and other types of visual presentations.

precision The number of digits *Excel* uses when calculating *values*. By default, Excel calculates with a maximum of 15 digits of a value (full precision).

Preview A view that displays your document as it will appear when you print it. Items such as text and graphics appear in their actual positions.

primary key A field in an *Access* table that supplies entries to a corresponding *field* in another Access *table*. For example, a table containing information about customers might supply customer names to a table containing order information.

print area An area of a *worksheet* that is specified to be printed.

query A set of criteria that tells Access to extract data from a database, sort the data, and arrange it for a report.

range Two or more *cells* on a sheet. Ranges can be contiguous or discontiguous.

record A single row in a *database* or list. The first *row* of a database usually contains *field names*, and each additional row in the database is a record.

reference The location of a *cell* or *range* of cells on a *worksheet*, indicated by *column* letter and *row* number.

reference type The type of reference: *absolute*, *relative*, or *mixed*.

relative reference Specifies the location of a referenced *cell* in relation to the cell containing the reference. A relative reference takes the form A4, C12, and so on.

report A tool in *Access* that lets you extract data and create a report you can print and view.

row A horizontal set of *cells*. Each row is identified by a unique number.

scenario A named set of input *values* that you can substitute in a worksheet model to perform what-if analysis.

ScreenTips Helpful notes that appear on your screen to explain a function or feature.

server A computer used on the *Internet* or a network environment that stores *email* messages, *Web* pages, and other data.

shareware Software programs, created by individuals or smaller software firms, that are usually available for a reasonable cost after you try them out.

sheet tab The name tab at the bottom of a *worksheet* that identifies the worksheet.

slide show A visual presentation you can create with *PowerPoint* which uses text, graphics, and other effects. Use slide shows for business presentations, training presentations, and other tasks that require visual presentations.

sort A method of organizing items so that you can find the items you want easily.

sort key The *field name* or *criteria* by which you want to *sort* data.

source The *document* or program in which the data was originally created.

split bar The horizontal or vertical line dividing a split *worksheet* or *document*. You can change the position of the split bar by dragging it, or you can remove the split bar by double-clicking it.

style A collection of formatting settings you can apply to text.

Switchboard A main menu in *Access* you can use to quickly perform tasks on a *database*. The Switchboard acts as your main starting point for viewing or working on a database.

tab, sheet The name at the bottom of a *worksheet* that identifies and selects the worksheet.

table Data about a specific topic that is stored in *records* (rows) and *fields* (columns).

taskbar The horizontal bar across the bottom of the Windows 95 desktop; it includes the Start button and buttons for any programs, documents, or items that are open.

template Available in *Word*, *Excel*, and Publisher, templates provide predesigned patterns on which Office documents can be based.

toolbar A collection of frequently used *commands* that appear as icon buttons you can click to activate.

URL (Uniform Resource Locator) A *Web* site address.

value A numeric entry in a spreadsheet or *database* program.

Web See *World Wide Web*.

Windows Clipboard A temporary holding area in computer memory that stores the last set of information that was cut or copied (such as text or graphics). You transfer data from the Clipboard by using the Paste *command*.

wizards A set of dialog boxes that ask you questions to walk you through processes such as creating a file or an *object* based on your answers.

Word A popular word processing program used to create text-based *documents*.

workbook An *Excel document* that contains one or more *worksheets* or *chart sheets*.

worksheet A set of *rows*, *columns*, and *cells* in which you store and manipulate data. Several worksheets can appear in one *workbook*, and you can switch among them easily by clicking their tabs with the mouse.

World Wide Web (WWW) The part of the *Internet* where *Web* sites are posted and available to Web *browsers*.

X axis On most *charts*, categories are plotted along the X axis. On a typical *column* chart, the X axis is the horizontal axis.

Y axis On most *charts*, data *values* are plotted along the Y axis. On a typical column chart, the Y axis is the vertical axis. When a secondary axis is added, it is a secondary Y axis.

Index

Symbols

A

B

C

E

F

G

H

I

J-K

L

M

N

O

P

Q-R

T

W

X-Z